International security management and the United Nations

International security management and the United Nations

Edited by Muthiah Alagappa and Takashi Inoguchi

**United Nations
University Press**

TOKYO · NEW YORK · PARIS

© The United Nations University, 1999

The views expressed in this publication are those of the authors and
do not necessarily reflect the views of the United Nations University.

United Nations University Press
The United Nations University, 53-70, Jingumae 5-chome,
Shibuya-ku, Tokyo, 150-8925, Japan
Tel: +81-3-3599-2811   Fax: +81-3-3406-7345
E-mail: sales@hq.unu.edu
http://www.unu.edu

United Nations University Office in North America
2 United Nations Plaza, Room DC2-1462-70, New York, NY 10017, USA
Tel: +1-212-963-6387   Fax: +1-212-371-9454
E-mail: unuona@igc.apc.org

United Nations University Press is the publishing division of the United Nations
University.

Cover design by Jean-Marie Antenen

Printed in the United States of America

UNUP-1001
ISBN 92-808-1001-4

Library of Congress Cataloging-in-Publication Data

International security management and the United Nations / edited by
Muthiah Alagappa and Takashi Inoguchi.
    p.   cm.
  Includes bibliographical references and index.
  ISBN 92-808-1001-4 (pbk.)
  1. Security, International Congresses.   2. United Nations Congresses.
  I. Alagappa, Muthiah.   II. Inoguchi, Takashi.
  JZ5588.I58   1999
  341.5'23—dc21
                                                    99-6178
                                                    CIP

Contents

Introduction

The United Nations' role in global security: Peace builder or peace enforcer?

Takashi Inoguchi

Organization and background of the "UN21" project

The papers in this volume were presented at a symposium hosted by the United Nations University in Tokyo on 8 and 9 November 1996. They represent an instalment of a multi-year project launched by the United Nations University in 1995, the purpose of which is to stimulate thinking about the United Nations in the twenty-first century. In 1996 we addressed the theme of "Peace and Security" for discussion and analysis. The assignment was to consider some of the following questions.

In the twenty-first century, what conditions will be necessary to build and maintain peace? Can the United Nations act as an effective mediator? Why do some peace-keeping operations succeed, and others fail? Should the United Nations adopt a traditional approach to peace-making, or a more comprehensive strategy incorporating conflict management, peace-keeping, and conflict prevention?

Our presumption is that the international system is in a state of flux, and that the United Nations must adapt both institutionally and philosophically to a new, as yet amorphous global order.

The current structure, roles, and functions of the United Nations reflect the international system that emerged at the end of the Second World War. This system initially gave great prominence to the United Nations. One power, the United States, was dominant in the immediate post-war period, and it used the United Nations as its proxy to uphold economic

1

development and freedom from aggression as the twin rights of states. The United Nations was seen as a bulwark against fascism and protector of an ever-growing number of weak, post-colonial states.

With the rise of Soviet power, however, initial hopes for the United Nations as an institution of global governance gave way to the schisms and ideological confrontation of the Cold War. The strategic interests of the superpowers superseded the altruism of the original mandate. Development assistance became a tool of ideological propaganda, while the defence of territorial rights became a pretext for proxy wars and elaborate balancing games.

The end of the Cold War in 1989–1990 was greeted with euphoria around the world, not least by the United Nations Organization. In theory at least, it presents the United Nations with an opportunity to return to its original mandates to deliver economic growth and security, both universally acknowledged as public goods. But how to get from here to there? There are no road maps.

The organizing principle behind this multi-year "UN21" project is to view the international system from the perspective of five major "actors" in world affairs. We formed core research groups to look at global issues from each of these perspectives – nation states, non-governmental organizations (NGOs), market forces, regional institutions, and international organizations.

Our choice of "actors" is necessarily a loose one, and reflects a free reading of Immanuel Kant's 1795 masterpiece, *On Perpetual Peace*. Kant argued that representative democracy, economic interdependence, and international law were forces that underpinned peace among nations, by eliminating reasons for conflict. In Kant's day as in our own, states are the dominant actors in the international system. But new types of institutions have developed global presence. They range from 24-hour computer-driven financial markets to NGOs which provide basic human services on the battlefronts of collapsing states. Their impact on the international system is of growing importance. Our five "actors" are merely the most prominent of the institutions whose global role has been reinforced by the end of the Cold War.

Each year of the project, the core groups are taking up a different theme. In 1995, the first year of the project, we tackled overarching themes relating to each of the major actors and how they might evolve in the twenty-first century. In 1996, the core groups concentrated on issues of peace and security.

As part of our task in 1996, we had to sort through an emerging new vocabulary in the realm of peace and security. The 1990s have provided a huge new body of experience. We now have to distinguish between a spectrum of military and quasi-military activities on the part of the

United Nations and other international or transnational organizations whose primary mission is preserving peace and stability. At one end of the spectrum is the 1991 Gulf War, sanctioned by the UN Security Council and fought by a multinational alliance assembled by the United States of America. At the other end are measures that fall under the category of preventive diplomacy – peace-keeping, peace-making, peace building.

Somewhere in between are the roles of active mediation in a crisis. As with our choice of actors, our use of these terms is necessarily loose. Many of the attempted mediations, preventive efforts, and applications of force are unprecedented, and may be difficult to repeat for a variety of reasons – the Gulf War is an example. We view the present exercise as more descriptive than normative or prescriptive, although our ultimate goal is to arrive at recommendations for reforming the United Nations.

The UN21 project was conceived as a tribute to the fiftieth anniversary of the establishment of the United Nations on 26 June 1945. Our idea was to put together academics, practitioners, and experts from within the United Nations system. We wanted to combine theoretical and empirical approaches to problems. By associating the five core research groups with five international "actors," we hoped to look at issues through different prisms, and to capture aspects of issues that are ordinarily invisible when seen from a single perspective. In a sense, each of our core research teams became advocates for their entities within the international system, seeking ways in which each "actor" could more effectively shape events to our desired outcomes – global development and peace.

Reaffirming the UN's central role in global conflict management

No other issue on the UN's reform agenda has received so much attention as the need to play new roles in peace and security. No other issue brings the United Nations so much back to its roots.

Global peace and security are among the UN's core missions. At its founding in 1945, hopes were high that the United Nations could serve as a global high command to keep the peace in a post-colonial, post-fascist world. The end of the Cold War has similarly lifted expectations. With the closing of the ideological gap between East and West many look to the peace-keeping apparatus of the United Nations as the best tool to deal with the lesser crises that emerged after the collapse of the Soviet Union.

Implicit to the arguments in this volume is a belief that the United Nations has a pre-eminent role to play in global peace and security. The end of the Cold War has made the United Nations an ever more impor-

tant partner and player in the varied tasks of conflict resolution and conflict avoidance. Yet, much as within the United Nations community itself,
there is little agreement on other basics – among them, how the United
Nations can best perform its peace-keeping and peace-making roles.

Everybody involved in the UN21 project agreed that the United
Nations should not serve as a tool, or proxy, for national interests. We
agreed as well that the UN's role as an actor in security matters would
increase while its value as a political arena might decline. It was also clear
that few thought the United Nations should step back from active
involvement in global security, in the manner of a "global council" of
wise men and women providing advice from the sidelines.

Our disputes were over issues relating to the management of global
peace and security, not the mission. The arguments were about the specific job description of the United Nations as a service provider in the
field of security. Who are its clients? What services should it delegate?
What services fall squarely within the UN mandate? And, most importantly, what services might cross the line between intervention in the
name of humanity and intervention for the sake of power projection?

This volume offers critiques from a variety of perspectives of the way
the United Nations has managed its security roles in the immediate post-
Cold War period. Some see threatening trends in the strengthening of the
powers of the UN Security Council since the Gulf War; most agree that
the Security Council has limits to its effectiveness as a global policeman.

Others are highly optimistic about the possibilities for the United
Nations to play an ever-larger role in conflict prevention – an exceedingly
broad concept which spans development assistance, counselling on the
processes of democratization, political risk analysis to provide "early
warning" of hot spots, and other forms of institutional support. This view
of the United Nations as peacemaker, however, assumes that the mass of
NGOs, regional councils, and member country governments can cope
with internal and external conflict in a selfless, objective and coherent
manner. Such an assumption runs counter to much of human history.

Thus, if there is a pattern to the differences among the UN21
researchers, it centres on two formal constructs of the United Nations as
security provider: one as peace enforcer, one as peacemaker. In terms of
the real world, it is highly unlikely that the United Nations will play
either role in a pure form. Reality must lie somewhere in between. Yet,
for the sake of clarifying ideas, it is useful to imagine these two poles as
book-ends, as the outer parameters of two potential lines of evolution.

Both models, or both extremes, assume a change in the nature of states
and national sovereignty. The United Nations as peace enforcer would
have authority to intervene directly in certain types of conflict without the
consent of the warring states or factions. As peace builder, the United
Nations would play a supporting role, perhaps providing legitimacy to the

conflict mediation and enforcement activities of a myriad of regional organizations, NGOs, and humanitarian relief bodies.

Should the United Nations be seen as global policeman or global peace consultant? The first image became familiar after Iraq's invasion of Kuwait in August 1990, when the United Nations became the vehicle for sanctions and finally a full-scale military campaign against Iraq. During the heady period from the victorious end of the Gulf War in March 1991 to the collapse of the UN mission in Somalia in October 1993, the United Nations launched 14 peace-keeping missions – almost as many as in the previous 46 years. In the aftermath of the Gulf War, the United Nations and other organizations broke new ground in dispensing with the rights of national sovereignty in the name of arms control. According to Brahma Chellaney of the Centre for Policy Research, the UN Special Commission on Disarmament of Iraq was intrusive "to a degree unprecedented in the history of arms control."

The notion of the United Nations as peace consultant stems from former Secretary-General Boutros Boutros-Ghali's 1992 "Agenda for Peace." The Agenda argues that the UN mission in security encompasses a range of services beyond military intervention – preventive diplomacy, peace-making, peace enforcement, and post-conflict peace building. Under this concept, organizations which were once at the fringe of the peace business will move to the centre. The United Nations becomes a provider of services on demand. Its "clients" range from NGOs specializing in development and humanitarian relief to regional entities that may in turn promote economic development, monitor elections, or send military forces into conflict zones in the name of regional stability.

One of the least predictable outcomes of the end of the Cold War has been a deepening of schisms within the UN membership between developing countries of the "South" and advanced industrial nations of the "North." This may be due in part to the release of pent-up passions suppressed during the period of East–West confrontation.

With the end of the Cold War, developing countries feared that funds for economic assistance would shrink along with the strategic motivations behind aid. In this anxiety, the countries of the South have largely been correct. Less comprehensible is their reaction to the thinking behind Boutros-Ghali's Agenda for Peace. Connie Peck, of the UN Institute for Training and Research, writes that the Agenda for Peace – which essentially has gone nowhere – was caught in the crossfire between UN hawks and UN doves. UN hawks were highly sceptical of the concept of preventive diplomacy, which they felt would blunt and dissipate the energies of the Security Council.

UN doves, on the other hand, were critical of the Boutros-Ghali proposals for the opposite reason. According to Peck, the doves, mainly countries of the South, saw "preventive diplomacy" as yet another excuse for great power domination and intervention. Peck writes, "Concern grew that preventive diplomacy could become the thin end of another neo-colonialist wedge."

The end of the Cold War was a time of inflated expectations. The American political scientist Francis Fukuyama predicted the "end of history." The world was to unite under the twin banners of capitalism and democracy. The "borderless" global economy would eliminate most reasons for conflict. The state would take second place to a host of new transnational organizations, large and small – multinational corporations, regional economic associations, and citizens groups to oversee new standards of environmental conduct, human rights, and other global "public goods."

Perhaps the least surprising of our findings on peace and security is that the historical nation-state is by no means ready to give up the ghost. Any future roles of the United Nations, as policeman, consultant, or bystander, will have to deal with the fact that statehood remains a given condition of the international order. Strong states, such as the United States, will seek to use the United Nations as a tool and limit its autonomy as an actor. Weak states may be unable to prevent infractions of their sovereignty in conflict situations.

It goes without saying that intervention, if it is to succeed, must be timely and effective. Intervention after states have failed – as in the case of Somalia and Rwanda – is far less desirable than mediation in advance of a collapse. Painful and frustrating though the UN intervention in Bosnia and Herzegovina has been, it has at least been successful in preserving the shell of Bosnia and Herzegovina left over after the aggressions. The most durable future role of the United Nations as a security organization is likely to be that of an arena – a focus of efforts to negotiate differences between nations, mediate conflicts, and arrive at agreed-upon strategies to bring conflicts to an end. But it also has a significant, if disputed, role as a tool to enforce international regimes of weapons control and environmental protection, among others. And it has a significant role as a direct actor, particularly in second-generation peace-keeping operations, as in Cambodia or El Salvador, and the ongoing campaigns in Guatemala, Slovenia, and Angola.

Perspectives on the UN's role in peace and security

On states and sovereignty

Has the end of the Cold War brought about the end of the nation-state? Has it kindled new types of conflict? These two questions occupied the research group on states and sovereignty.

We habitually define international conflicts as conflicts between states. Conflicts between or among states frequently involve an infringement of sovereignty, in terms that are universally understood.

When Saddam Hussein invaded Kuwait in August 1990, there was no question that the situation was one nation-state invading, and thus violating the territorial rights of, another. Over the ensuing months the United States was able to develop a moral consensus against Iraq, culminating in the launching of the Gulf War in January 1991. Most nations agreed that Iraq's invasion of Kuwait was not a good thing. In the end, there was little opposition to the US-led campaign or the way the United States conducted itself over the three weeks of war.

But what happens when ethnic rivalries, or competition over resources, or differences of religion, erupt in conflicts that spill across borders? Such conflicts create "international" problems of a different order. And what happens when a civil war or ethnic feud leads to humanitarian tragedies on a scale to provoke international concern? When refugees escaping a conflict become a problem for their neighbours? If the objective is to mediate conflict, with whom does one mediate? Who's in charge? The state? Tribal leaders?

The security environment of the 1990s has begun to challenge some of our basic premises about states and sovereignty. On the one hand, there are more and more weak or failed states which are increasingly a source of global instability. The end of the Cold War has seen a sharp rise in domestic tumult. The list of collapsed states includes Somalia and Liberia; according to Charles Aiodun Alao of King's College, London, there are at least 20 more states that could collapse soon.

Another risk to the international system comes from the lopsided power imbalance in favour of the United States – which is the uncontested strongest of the strong states. According to Sherle Schwenniger, the United States has shown an inclination to block the "emergence of other arrangements for order-keeping that are less dependent on American military power." This has resulted in an ad hoc approach to conflict management, writes Schwenninger. The international system has charged some states huge penalties for their sins, such as Iraq, while leaving others in the lurch, such as Somalia, Bosnia and Herzegovina, and Rwanda.

Much of the instability in the international system since the Gulf War has come from fragile states newly bereft of their Cold War patrons. At the same time the United States, self-acknowledged to be the last remaining global superpower, has shown a strong tendency to retreat into its traditional isolationist shell. Thus, weak states have come to dominate the foreground of international events. Our four researchers offer varying perspectives on this disturbing shift, together with several policy recommendations.

Two of our analysts, Georg Sørensen and Charles Abiodun Alao, concentrate on the problems of weak states. Sørenson argues that the West-phalian concept of the state is in the process of breaking down, and in the process exposing the irrationality of borders drawn around post-colonial states with little or no sense of national identity. He blames the international donor agencies for perpetuating a sense of "secure insecurity" among these states, and their leadership élites for an exaggerated attachment to juridical borders.

Sørenson recommends that policy makers seek to engage civil society more deeply in their activities because of the erosion of the state's authority.

Africa is the subject of Charles Abiodun Alao's analysis of the "failed state." Alao disagrees with Sørenson on most points, including the factors that have traditionally been cited as the causes of African instability – the shallow historical bonds of states forged in recent independence movements, the structural problems of inherited colonial economies, and the recent rise of "ethno-nationalism."

Instead, Alao argues that contemporary policy decisions by the advanced industrial countries were directly responsible for the "wave" of failed states in Africa in the 1980s and 1990s. In particular, he blames the new regime of "accountability" that replaced Cold War patronage and the structural adjustment programmes of the World Bank and International Monetary Fund. These created political and economic stresses that have driven fragile states to the brink of destruction – 20 states, to be precise. In Alao's book, "ethno-nationalism" gets off easy; it is a symptom, not a cause, of the pressure these nations face.

Alao has little good to say about the UN's efforts in Africa, recalling United Nations officials in Liberia who became known for their fondness for "driving expensive vehicles around the capital." If there is one policy thread in common between Alao and Sørenson, it is that the solution to Africa's problems must be a local one. Alao's policy recommendations are explicit. He states also that the international system should favour a three-part strategy of reducing or cancelling African debt burdens; supporting democratic movements in Africa and ostracizing authoritarian regimes; and establishing an African mediation committee consisting of elder statesmen to tackle "brewing conflicts." This last is an approach that has been tried with some success, as Margaret Vogt points out in her paper for the research group on regional organizations.

Sherle Schwenninger and Amin Saikal tackle the future of strong states in the international system. Both argue, from different perspectives, that strong states will continue to be a dominating feature of the international system, blocking the trend in the direction of "post-modern" states, to use Sørenson's term for countries with advanced networks of economic, social and political connections linking them to regional and international systems.

In Saikal's interesting analysis of five emerging "strong" states, such states show little inclination to abandon their "statist myths" in favour of either the Kantian model or the sort of world envisioned by Samuel Huntington, in which states are less meaningful than "civilizations." In terms of the security theme, Saikal's analysis leads to the conclusion that strong states get stronger because they employ self-correcting mechanisms to avoid conflict, a characteristic which also strengthens the international system. He writes: "It is clear that the nation-state is set to underwrite the structure and define the operation of the international system beyond this century." As to policy makers, Saikal implies that they, too, will have to settle for a world in which the United Nations serves neither as manager nor counsellor, but as something in between.

Schwenninger's point is almost the opposite. He argues that the post-Cold War dominance of the United States is wrecking a system that would otherwise converge along Kantian lines. In fact, he paints the United States as a major source of global instability. This is firstly because of its opposition to multilateral security arrangements which might dilute US military authority. This opposition, Schwenninger writes, has led to a pattern of ad hoc conflict response, and reinforced a long-term trend towards regional fragmentation of the international system along Huntingtonian lines.

Secondly, Schwenninger blames the United States for setting a "bad example" by withholding funds for "international public goods." The retrenchment of US bilateral aid, and cutbacks and arrears on its payments to international organizations (especially the United Nations) have all undermined regimes of conflict prevention which underpin a Kantian approach to international security.

What can be done? Obviously, as far as Schwenninger is concerned, the United States must grow up, by accepting its responsibilities as a partner among equals in multilateral security organizations, and it must make good on its financial obligations to the international community. Schwenninger argues that part of a maturation process on the part of the United States will be meeting its financial obligations to the United Nations and other international organizations. In effect, Schwenninger envisages a system in which the United States remains the principal donor to international organizations, yet relinquishes its instinct to dominate and acquiesces to a benign multilateralism.

Clearly, the central question for UN reform in the area of states and sovereignty will be how to deal with fragile and failed states; the underlying message of all the analysts in this research group is that strong states can take care of themselves. How are we to nurture links between the international system and civil society in weak states, without arousing fear, resentment, and perhaps retaliation against the very groups we seek to support? How do we cope with self-absorbed yet fragile regimes committed to survival through military means? We must give more thought to what Saikal calls the persistence of the "statist myth." Any wide-ranging UN reform will have to reflect the fact that weak states, rather than strong ones, pose the greatest risk of conflict.

On global citizenship

One of the least predictable outcomes of the end of the Cold War has been to strengthen enormously the role of civil society in conflict management. The Gulf War was, from this as from so many other perspectives, a watershed event. In 1991 the UN Security Council passed a resolution authorizing humanitarian relief organizations to cross into northern Iraq without the consent of the government. This meant that, for the first time, the United Nations upheld the rights of victims over the rights of their governments. But it also underscored the new and important role civil society has acquired in conflict management and peace building.

Not even the International Committee of the Red Cross had been able to disregard national borders in its long operational history. The end of the Cold War may have marked the beginning of an era in which global civil society generates its own mechanisms for crisis response, conflict reconstruction, and conflict prevention, without waiting for decisions at the level of states and international organizations.

Nice idea – but how will it work? Our second core research group, on civil society, examined the ever-growing role of "transnational civil society actors" from four perspectives. How effectively have transnational social movement organizations influenced global public policy on peace and security? Can NGOs move beyond conflict response to the more complex business of peace building? Can transnational civil society actors build a sense of common purpose by establishing networks of international peace-keeping organizations and training institutes? Finally, are the same forces behind the growing importance of civil society "actors" and the rapid expansion of global criminal organizations?

In an overview of the team's work, Volker Rittberger of the University of Tubingen wryly notes that the features most NGOs – including criminal societies – have in common are ones which sharply limit their efficacy. They are constantly preoccupied with a competition for funds; any impulse towards cooperation is undercut by differences on strategies and fears of domination; and their normal operating platform is states in conditions of war or civil collapse. The first two characteristics are shared by practically all movements and service organizations; the last is unique to the subset of organizations which operate in war zones and fragile or failed states.

Paradoxically, these shortcomings of NGOs are all too evident even in the two areas of global conflict management where they have had the most profound influence: in the anti-nuclear movement, and in post-Cold War humanitarian relief work.

The anti-nuclear movement, as chronicled by Jackie Smith of the University of Notre Dame, inspired some of the best and brightest minds of the post-war period. Launched just three months after the bombings of Nagasaki and Hiroshima, over a 40-year period the movement most certainly created a highly visible lobby in favour of nuclear disarmament.

Smith writes that the movement profoundly changed the cost-benefit calculations of the nuclear superpowers – they had to take into account the numbers of influential scientists who demanded total disarmament. It also forced a certain level of transparency and accountability upon nuclear arms negotiations, because an informed public demanded information. Finally, the scientists did everything they could to channel information on the horrific consequences of nuclear war to both the public and the negotiators.

Yet in essence the anti-nuclear movement, represented by such groups as the Parliamentarians for Global Action, the Pugwash Conference on Science and World Affairs, and the Soviet-controlled World Peace Council, never managed to reach a consensus on goals, and thus never had a decisive influence on multilateral disarmament talks. Their influence was at the fringes, in the public atmosphere in which talks were conducted by the superpowers, and in nuances of the debate rather than in its substance. The clear implication is that transnational civil society must learn more about goal formulation, consensus building, and strategic management of issues before it can be an effective influence on international security policy.

Service organizations have a different problem – graduating from conflict reaction to conflict prevention. Roland Koch, of the Technical University of Munich, offers a close analysis of the increasing autonomy of humanitarian relief organizations. Until the early 1990s, NGOs were on their own as far as the international community was concerned. They had to negotiate their way into conflict situations, and often continue negotiations with hostile parties in order to stay. They were frequently accused of partisan leanings. If they got in the line of fire, there was no way out.

The orphan status of humanitarian relief NGOs changed with the end of the Cold War for a simple reason: conflicts themselves became too widespread, complex, and muddled for governments and the larger international institutions to handle all the problems. At the same time, Koch argues, governments began to cut back on development assistance and step up funding for humanitarian relief. The result was an expanded role for NGOs, and a greater recognition of the services they performed.

Chronologically, the shift began in 1990, with the granting of observer status in the UN General Assembly to the International Committee of the Red Cross. It culminated with the 1994 Oslo Declaration on Partnership in Action, which sanctioned cross-border relief operations without the consent of governments. In between, in northern Iraq, Bosnia and Herzegovina, and Somalia, NGOs were increasingly thrust to the front lines of conflicts, pursuing a newly activist agenda.

Koch describes this phenomenon as part of a "complex international governance" that has emerged since the end of the Cold War. Nonetheless, both Koch and Rittberger point to a central weakness of NGOs in conflict management. As Rittberger writes, they are "not yet capable of taking effective action to prevent humanitarian emergencies." Koch notes that many of these organizations have an institutional aversion to establishing or accepting leadership structures, which naturally weakens their impact on policy.

What are some of the potential roles of civil society in conflict management? Alex Morrison and Stephanie Blair, of the recently established Lester B. Pearson International Peacekeeping Training Centre, present the concept of "peace-keeping by proxy," in which informal networks of peace-keepers may assume some of the functions traditionally managed by governments and the United Nations. Such networks might be composed of peace-keeping training centres in different countries, together with individuals or organizations focusing on some aspect of conflict management or prevention.

Finally, Phil Williams of the University of Pittsburgh speculates that global criminal organizations have been given a boost by the end of the Cold War, for some of the same reasons that NGOs have become more prominent in international affairs. The breakdown of states has meant that existing organizations cannot cope with the myriad situations that arise; this has created an opening for criminal networks that Williams describes as only very loosely organized. The Cold War also served as an incubator for some of these organizations, he argues. Western governments were supportive of anti-communist political parties with criminal links, particularly in Italy and Japan. But the real story is the rise of the Russian mafia, which has taken advantage of economic and military reforms to amass enormous power.

The core group's analysis leaves us with a number of questions for further study. Should the United Nations create a special registry for NGOs specializing in conflict management? Such a registry was set up for development NGOs at the Rio Earth Conference in 1992. Clearly, the United Nations should be working more closely with civil society actors on a range of issues. But how much cooperation is feasible, given the enormous diversity of NGO agendas and leadership, or anti-leadership

styles? Where should NGOs concentrate their efforts in conflict management – on prevention or response? How can the United Nations support
the work of NGOs in conflict situations without losing control of its own
conflict management agenda?

On regional arrangements

One of the striking outcomes of the end of the Cold War is the growing
prominence of regional organizations in mediating disputes and peace-
keeping. Even more striking is the increasing importance of subregional
organizations, which have been increasingly assertive and effective in
conflicts in Africa and Latin America over the last decade. It is clear
that the United Nations will be delegating more rather than less peace-
keeping work to such organizations.

Unlike NGOs, regional organizations have specific mandates in the
field of security. They have the recognition and cooperation of their
member states, and usually that of the international community. Their
track records are well known, and if there are severe differences between
member countries they generally do not survive. Nonetheless, these
organizations have their limits, and our third core research group set out
to explore them.

What do we mean by "regional organizations"? Muthiah Alagappa of
the East-West Center supplies a definition that is both unconventional
and precise. A regional organization, or "regionalism," consists of cooperation among three or more governments or NGOs (with the emphasis
on governments); the members must be in geographical proximity, and
focus on one or more issues that represent common concerns; and they
must have some motive for cooperation. In his overview paper synthe-
sizing the work of the group, he argues that there are two main limitations faced by regional organizations.

First, the principle of non-intervention prevents members of a regional
organization from active intervention in the domestic affairs of any other
member. Regional organizations generally play a role in organizing dialogue; they can constrain but not actually restrain combatants from the
use of force.

Second, Alagappa argues, regional organizations seem to have no
ability to mobilize effectively against an external threat. There is "no
sense of community at this level," he writes, and a hostile outside state
may react with even greater hostility when faced with the perceived
threat of a regional bloc. Even if the reaction is not hostile, it may yet be
distant; Alagappa cites the examples of US opposition to nuclear-free
zone proposals by the Association of South-East Asian Nations and the
South Pacific Forum. "It viewed the proposals ... as undermining its

global strategy while working to the advantage of its rival, the Soviet Union."

How can such deficiencies be addressed in the context of UN reform? Alagappa's policy recommendations are, again, simple and practical. He urges against replacing the existing loose arrangements between the United Nations and regional organizations with any precise set of guidelines. Instead, he argues that there should be a clear division of labour between the Security Council and regional institutions; he defines this as a system whereby the Security Council should retain "control" and delegate "everything else." At the same time, regional organizations must remain "accountable" to the Security Council, but this must not lead to "micro-management" on the part of the Council.

The difficulty of generalizing about regional organizations is shown by three empirical studies of regional security organizations in Africa, Asia, and Latin America. Each case represents many of the same elements, in terms of an increasing interest in peace-keeping and some highly successful instances of mediation. Even so, the reasons for involvement in peace-keeping, as well as the success of interventions, are quite different.

The African study, by Margaret Vogt of the International Peace Academy, is perhaps the clearest example of the inhibiting effect of the non-intervention principle. Although the Organization of African Unity (OAU) has established a peace-keeping operations fund and begun to hold meetings of defence officials, there is still no consensus among member states about the propriety of intervention by the organization; many member states prefer UN peace-keeping because they see it as more impartial than the OAU.

Largely because of such contradictions, the OAU's track record in peace-keeping is anything but even. There is as yet no command structure for peace-keeping. In the Rwanda conflict in 1994, when the United Nations refused to intervene, the OAU decided to go in – but arrived five months late with its troops. In the aftermath of the Rwanda debacle, the United Nations learned enough to encourage the OAU and other regional organizations to develop programmes for the selection, preparation, and training of peace-keeping forces.

Vogt argues that the OAU's most effective interventions have been when it has assigned elder statesmen to mediate disputes in the Democratic People's Republic of the Congo and Burundi, while efforts at more comprehensive peace-keeping have stumbled. She recommends that the OAU concentrate on coordinating subregional efforts at peace-keeping, while the larger regional organization handle doctrine and training.

Asia's security organizations illustrate Muthiah Alagappa's second point remarkably well – the difficulty that regional organizations have in dealing with an outside threat. Shiro Harada and Akihiko Tanaka, of the University of Tokyo, present a cogent history and analysis of security organizations in Asia, particularly the Association of South-East Asian Nations (ASEAN). ASEAN has two great problems – China and the United States. Any aggressive intervention by ASEAN in regional conflicts would be likely to raise concerns in both Washington and Beijing.

As a result, ASEAN and the related ASEAN Regional Forum have never engaged in peace-keeping or any other form of domestic or international interventions. However, ASEAN has played a highly effective role as mediator in resolving the Cambodian conflict in the late 1980s and early 1990s. Harada and Tanaka point out that confidence building and preventive diplomacy are all well and good, but the true test will come if the region experiences a serious instance of conflict or domestic violence beyond the regular suppression of political dissidents that characterizes some ASEAN member countries.

ASEAN's greatest contribution, according to Alagappa, is that it has altered the normative context of South-East Aisa. This change has considerably enhanced the chances for political survival of some member states, he argues. ASEAN has also increased the collective diplomatic weight of South-East Asian states.

Latin America represents yet another variation on the theme. Cristina Eguizábal of the Ford Foundation argues that regional organizations in Latin America have become effective precisely because Latin Americans were united in wanting an alternative to US solutions and overwhelming US influence. They started with strategies of using informal mechanisms to reduce conflict; after the Cold War, these informal mechanisms flowered into a "very dense web" of regional organizations.

As in Africa, Eguizábal finds that subregional groupings have been more effective than larger and more highly politicized organizations such as the Organization of American States. The Contadora process was less effective than the Equipulas grouping in ending the Nicaraguan quagmire because Equipulas was more "local" to the conflict, Eguizábal argues.

Where does this leave us in terms of UN reform? Questions for further study might include some or all of the following. As Alagappa observes, no single set of guidelines fits all cases. Nonetheless, can the United Nations do more to prepare regional organizations, or subregional organizations, for peace-keeping roles? Should regional organizations maintain their own standing forces of peacekeepers trained in UN methods? Would it be useful to develop international networks of regional organizations for peace-keeping? International training standards? Conventions on humanitarian intervention to which all regional organizations might agree?

On international organizations

In the euphoric period immediately after the end of the Cold War, the UN Security Council and other international security organizations seemed to experience a great rush of confidence.

The Security Council, free of internal bickering among members of the Permanent Five for practically the first time in its history, launched 14 peace-keeping operations between 1991 and 1993, compared to 17 in the previous 46 years. The International Atomic Energy Agency (IAEA) introduced "challenge inspections" in 1992, which basically ignored the sovereignty of states suspected of harbouring nuclear weapons production. When the IAEA tried out its first "challenge inspection" in the Democratic People's Republic of Korea, the ensuing confrontation nearly led to war on the Korean Peninsula. The UN Special Commission on Disarmament of Iraq, established in 1991, amounted to a virtal occupying force in Baghdad.

Logically, such expansion of the powers of international organizations would be a necessary stage in the evolution of global governance. Yet not a single member of our research group on international organizations found anything particularly positive in these developments. Rather, the central question for the team on international organizations became how best to limit and define these powers. It appears that none of our analysts believes that the United Nations, or other international organizations, should attempt the role of peace enforcer – instead, the analysts emphasized such roles as training, coordinating, and delegation of peace-keeping tasks to regional organizations.

Thomas Weiss, of Brown University, urges that the United Nations should attend to "seven lessons" in peace-keeping in order to gain public consent. First, he says, in order to be effective there should be "no compromise on security" in peace-keeping operations. Second, the United Nations should emphasize prevention. Third, it should use regional organizations. Fourth, it should control the humanitarian impulse. Fifth, it should avoid enforcement. Sixth, it should provide "multifunctional services." Finally, it should make better use of NGOs.

The three empirical studies are no less adamant about restraining the powers of the United Nations and other international security organizations. Of the three, Brahma Chellaney is the most indignant about the increasingly autonomous behaviour of some international organizations, particularly the IAEA. He claims that arms control is being used to support the global status quo, and urges that the IAEA should rediscover its mandate for technical cooperation and moderate its campaign to strengthen nuclear safeguards.

Frustration is a running theme of Connie Peck's essay on the lack of progress within the United Nations on setting up an apparatus for conflict prevention or early warning, despite the blessing of the 1992 Agenda for Peace. The reason why so little has happened is a curious study in post-Cold War politics within the UN membership. We have already noted Peck's analysis of the politics of "preventive diplomacy." A related effort to set up an early warning office to detect conflicts before they happen has foundered administratively; so tight is the budget that some political officers have never even visited the countries they are supposed to cover.

David Malone's essay on the post-Cold War evolution of the UN Security Council contains some of this volume's most sensible suggestions on UN peace-keeping. He reminds us that political will and resources must be present before the decision is made to use force, and that objectives and strategy must be clearly related before launching peace-keeping operations. Malone believes that, after the sobering experiences of the mid-1990s, the Security Council is far more likely to work through member countries rather than using peace-keeping to enforce its will.

"The Security Council today is a cautious body, heavily weighed down by financial constraints," Malone writes. But, he adds, "We should not turn our backs on the United Nations because it has stumbled on occasion, sometimes spectacularly."

This last comment sums up the mood of the research group on international organizations. Contrary to expectations in the late 1980s, nobody wants the United Nations as global policeman. Yet nobody thinks it should sit on the sidelines of conflict, either. Further study is necessary to define a more effective way for the United Nations to involve itself in peace-keeping. Rather than policeman or consultant, a better metaphor might be that of orchestra conductor or air traffic controller, managing a complex system without actually playing the instruments or flying the planes. The United Nations succeeds best in peace-keeping where it delegates, as in Haiti. But there are exceptions to this rule, when the United Nations has succeeded in "playing the instruments" itself, with the full consent of the states and populations involved, as in Cambodia, El Salvador, and Mozambique.

Conclusion

As we have seen, the role of the United Nations in peace and security is among its most important missions. That role has evolved substantially since the end of the Cold War, and will continue to change and grow, most likely in ways that we cannot predict at present. The title of this introduction posed a question – should the United Nations focus on building peace, or enforcing it? Based on our research, we argue that the United Nations should be delegating both roles as much as possible – to regional organizations, subregional organizations, and in some cases NGOs.

This is not just a matter of finances. Obviously, in its current financial straits, the United Nations does not have the resources to maintain a global standing army for peace-keeping. It relies on US and European powers to launch major peace-keeping initiatives, and is frequently made a mockery of.

However, our analysts have demonstrated that money problems are not the only reason for the United Nations to look at formulas for broader delegation of peace-keeping roles and tasks. Organizations closer to the scene of conflict have a vested interest in restoring stability; they also are frequently more sensitive to local cultural nuances than international organizations, including the United Nations.

Since the 1992 Agenda for Peace, the UN membership and bureaucracy has paid more attention to the variety of tasks associated with stabilizing fragile countries to prevent conflict, and reconstructing countries torn apart by conflict. Yet "preventive diplomacy" and "conflict reconstruction" are also tasks that take enormous time, patience, and local knowledge. Local organizations, NGOs, and international development and humanitarian organizations are far more likely to be effective than the United Nations.

There are many more questions for study and research. Perhaps new understandings need to be reached on the circumstances and conditions that justify certain limited infringements of national sovereignty. Perhaps we need an international code on the rights of victims. We definitely need to study more carefully ways and means of working with NGOs, while clearly recognizing their limits.

One of the most promising areas for delegation of authority is between the United Nations and regional organizations. We should be looking for new ways to prepare regional organizations for peace-keeping and other conflict management roles. We need to pay more attention to the destabilizing impact of market forces upon certain weak countries, and seek the means to strengthen their financial and market institutions prior to imposing the harsher forms of conditionality and structural adjustment.

Changing states and the security problematique

1

Introduction

Atul Kohli and Georg Sørensen

The design of the current United Nations system is premissed mainly on a world organized as a system of states. As we move into the next century, however, sovereign states are under pressure from both "above" and "below." Global forces from "above" – economic, technological, and cultural – are forcing states, even powerful states, to reorganize and reconceptualize conventional notions of sovereignty. The room for weaker states to manoeuvre is severely constrained, both by their internal limitations and by the preferences of powerful states. Moreover, many states are being challenged from "below," as groups within them redefine themselves as a "people," or even a "nation," and demand greater rights of self-determination; a number of existing states are bound to become failed states of the future. None of these developments spells an end to a world of states; states remain, and are likely to remain, powerful global actors well into the twenty-first century. Nevertheless, these emerging trends do focus attention on the changing nature of states and the state system.

Two broad questions guide the papers that follow. How are new challenges altering states and the state system on the one hand, and on the other hand, what type of a United Nations – global counsel or global manager[1] – will facilitate peace, prosperity, and human dignity within this changing state system? The focus of collective research efforts is less on the reform of specific institutions of the United Nations and more on an analysis of the changing parameters within which a future United Nations may function. States and the state system are clearly one such parameter.

Since this is a rather large research agenda, these papers focus on peace and security issues.[2] The central concern of the papers is to analyze what implications the changing nature of states and the state system have for global peace and security. Is the post-Cold War world radically different as far as global peace and security issues are concerned? Has the usefulness of military power undergone any serious change? Are major future conflicts likely to resemble conventional conflicts of the past (for example, inter-state warfare) or will newer types of conflicts, such as civil wars in failed states, be more likely to dominate the peace and security agenda? Irrespective of the type of conflict, what type of peace and security role is the major global actor, the United States, most likely to play in this changed world? And finally, what role can a future United Nations play in facilitating global peace and security?

The four papers that follow provide some answers to these questions. The first paper, by Georg Sørensen, sets forth a typology of states that constitute the "state system" at the end of the twentieth century. In addition to the modern "Westphalian" state – often perceived as the standard type of state in the modern international system – there is the weak, unsubstantial state in parts of the South; and the post-modern state in parts of the North (especially Western Europe) – a complex, transnationally interpenetrated entity immersed in globalization and multi-level governance.

Sørensen argues that the different types of statehood are tied in with different patterns of conflict and cooperation. The modern Westphalian state is given to balance-of-power play and rivalry with other states in the system, according to the conventional realist view of inter-state conflict. Yet modern Westphalian states can also cooperate in various ways, as analyzed by liberals. Unsubstantial states, by contrast, are plagued mainly by internal conflict, because weak statehood presents a perennial problem of domestic security. The problem is at its worst in sub-Saharan Africa: violent conflicts in unsubstantial states are responsible for the largest number of casualties by far over recent decades. Finally, post-modern states in the European Union cooperate intensely in new ways which rule out violent conflict. They constitute a security community amongst themselves. In sum, we are facing an increasingly complex world with different types of states, each with specific consequences for patterns of conflict and cooperation.

Sherle Schwenninger provides a rather disconcerting but illuminating view of the United States as the lone but "reluctant" superpower in the post-Cold War world. He underlines the persistent and growing tension between the desire of the United States to "remain the world's premier power" and its refusal to "bear the costs of this position."

The short-term result of US reluctance to help develop effective collective security arrangements around the world is the continuation of a host of problems. The United States is in basic respects torn between the traditional role of a modern Westphalian global power player, and the new role of a post-modern state intensively cooperating and bargaining with other states in international institutions and elsewhere. Because of the dominant position of the United States in the post-Cold War world, the consequences of that predicament are felt in many parts of the world.

Amin Saikal draws attention to the role of a number of emerging Asian powers that continue to behave very much like conventional, West-phalian, security-conscious states. That is because the states analyzed in Saikal's paper are those that aspire to be, and in many respects already are, modern Westphalian states. Israel, China, and India are the countries which have moved furthest in that direction. It is thus in that part of the world that we have on current display a typical modern, Westphalian balance-of-power game with very high levels of armament in a context of rapid modernization. That balance-of-power game is characterized by a further complication which increases the dangers of conflict: neither China, India, nor Israel are satisfied states. That is, the question of their permanent borders and territory under their control is not settled. This is a dangerous additional fuel to inter-state conflict in an already somewhat unstable environment.

Finally, Charles Abiodun Alao analyzes the forces that continue to undermine the "stateness" of a number of unsubstantial states in sub-Saharan Africa. This analysis reminds us that states with formal, juridical sovereignty are not necessarily substantially effective states, and that the types of conflicts that characterize regions composed of such states are likely to be rather unconventional. In the Conclusion we will draw some general implications from these four papers for the question at hand; namely, the implications of the changing nature of states for issues of peace and security in the next century.

Notes

1. These concepts are elaborated in the UNU document, *The United Nations System in the Twenty-first Century*, Revised Proposal, January 1996, especially p. 3.
2. Research efforts in future years will focus on the implications of changing states and sovereignty in such other areas as economic development, management of the environment, problems of governability, and ensuring human dignity.

2

A state is not a state: Types of statehood and patterns of conflict after the Cold War

Georg Sørensen

The basic unit in the UN system is the sovereign state.[1] The United Nations is a community of states based on the sovereign equality of each member, as stressed in Article 2 of the UN Charter. The United Nations therefore stresses the equality as well as the similarity of its constituent units: each is a sovereign state on a par with every other sovereign state, enjoying equal status under the terms of the Charter.

The emphasis on similarity and sovereign equality of states which we find in the UN context is duplicated in most theories of international relations. It is commonplace in these theories to treat states as fixed, "like units."[2] They are not, of course, and the difference between states amounts to much more than the variation in power capabilities noted by realists or the absence of liberal democracy as analyzed by liberals.

In order to appreciate current and future patterns of cooperation and conflict we need a conceptual handle on different main types of state. I have already rejected the notion of treating states as standard, uniform, "like units." The opposite extreme, to treat every single state as *sui generis*, is not helpful either. It would lead to an ultra-complex view of the world, where every state and every type of relation between states was unique.

In other words, we need to aim for the intermediate level, where different main types of state are identified in order to achieve some general overview without totally sacrificing empirical complexity. Some conceptualizations of different states types are available. Perhaps the best known is "developed" versus "developing" countries (DCs and LDCs);

24

this is similar to the distinction between North and South. Another often-used distinction is between geographical regions (Latin America, South Asia, East Asia, sub-Saharan Africa, etc.). In the field of international relations, the most frequently used distinction is between states in terms of their military-economic strength: small powers, medium, great, and superpowers.

These concepts may be well suited for a number of different purposes, but they are less useful for our present task: the identification of main types of state in relation to specific patterns of conflict and cooperation. In other words, there are qualitatively different types of state in the present international system, and an identification of them is necessary to appreciate current and future patterns of cooperation and conflict. I identify three main types of state in the present international system. Before proceeding, however, it is helpful to summarize the main theoretical views on conflict and cooperation after the Cold War.[3]

International relations theory about conflict and cooperation after the Cold War

What are the theoretical expectations as regards conflict and cooperation now that the Cold War has ended? According to the dominant tradition in the discipline of international relations, namely neorealism, the changes we have seen are of a limited nature. After all, anarchy prevails, and the international system remains a system of sovereign states with no system-wide authority, no world government. Therefore, states will have to fend for themselves in the age-old game of balance-of-power.

What we have now, according to neorealists, is "bipolarity in an altered state."[4] Bipolarity continues because militarily Russia can take care of itself and because no other great powers have yet emerged. "With the waning of Soviet power, the United States is no longer held in check by any other country or combination of countries... Balance-of-power theory leads one to predict that other countries, alone or in concert, will try to bring American power into balance."[5]

The presence of nuclear weapons modifies the balance-of-power game, according to neorealists. Nuclear weapons reduce the scope of military competition between the nuclear powers (including their allies), and dramatically decrease the probability of war between them. The emphasis moves to economic and technological competition.[6] Yet this neorealist view of the world faithfully continues a very long tradition of realist analysis; since Thucydides, realists have stressed how imbalances of power produce fear, and fear can lead to war in a system of sovereign states.

Liberalist analysis supports a more optimistic view of the post-Cold War world. Democracies do not go to war against each other;[7] moreover, democracy creates domestic institutions aimed at cooperation which help pave the way for international institutions. Economic interdependence promotes transnational relations in general and creates an incentive for developing international cooperation.[8] Overall, there is a "Zone of Peace,"[9] comprising consolidated liberal democracies in the West (including Japan), gradually expanding to include new democracies. And there is a "Zone of Conflict," where liberal democracy, international institutions, and cooperative interdependence remain in short supply.

We thus have two main views of the world after the Cold War. A pessimistic realist view, and a rather more optimistic liberal view. Who is right? I argue that both the pessimistic and the optimistic positions have problems, because they fail to analyze substantial changes in statehood as well as changes in the institution of sovereignty and the consequences of such changes for relationships of conflict and cooperation.

Analyzing change and variation in contemporary statehood will help us get away from the misleading realist picture of the state as a given, fixed entity. And it will provide us with some hints, direly needed in liberal analysis, about what we can expect in terms of more democracy and interdependence in coming years. In what follows I set forth a typology of three main types of state in the present international system. They are (a) the unsubstantial state, that is, the weak and unconsolidated state in the periphery, often in an ongoing state of entropy; (b) the modern, "Westphalian" state, a consolidated nation-state with its own structural dynamic and relative autonomy; and (c) the "post-modern" state, a complex, transnationally interpenetrated entity immersed in globalization and multi-level governance.

I begin with a characterization of the Westphalian state. That is the traditional realist notion of a modern state, most often implicitly accepted as the analytical point of departure in international relations. I question the claimed universal relevance as well as the theoretical adequacy of this modern, Westphalian notion of state. Against that background, two additional types of state are identified.

The Westphalian state: Standard international relations state concept

In broader historical terms the modern "Westphalian"[10] state is the result of a long process of development which includes empires, city states, barbarian tribes, feudal systems, and absolutist states.[11] Several interrelated factors were at work in this process. In the economic sphere, the development of capitalism and industrialization helped provide the necessary resource basis for modern Westphalian statehood. At the same time, the separation of economic institutions (in a private sector) and political institutions (in the public sector) is a feature of modern Westphalian statehood; there is no such separation in earlier forms of state.[12]

Another important factor in the development of the Westphalian state was the industrialization of warfare. The emerging states in Europe took shape in a long series of battles and wars. "It was war, and the preparations for war, that provided the most potent energizing stimulus for the concentration of administrative resources and fiscal reorganization that characterized the rise of absolutism."[13] A final element helping the emergence of the modern state was the growth of administrative power, both in terms of increasing capacities for communication and storage of information, and in terms of effective organization.[14]

In modern Westphalian states, sovereignty is more than a formal, juridical label. It is substantial, in the sense that the state possesses a capacity for self-government, an economic resource base, and an ability to defend itself militarily. The modern economies are thus national economies in the basic sense that economic development took place in a national space, regulated and nurtured by the state. This does not exclude a high level of exchange with other economies, of course, but the national economy is normally self-sustained in the sense that it comprises the main sectors (means of production and distribution, and means of consumption) needed for its reproduction. The economy is also homogeneous, so different sectors are at similar levels of development and there is a very high degree of cross- and inter-sectoral exchange.

The state has a monopoly on the means of violence, but the military capacity of the modern state is turned outward, in defence against external enemies, not inward. Westphalian states are internally pacified; there is a police force, but rulers do not sustain their position by access to the use of force. Domestic law and order is based primarily on popular support for rules and norms defining deviant behaviour.[15] In broader terms, the vastly expanded powers of the Westphalian state as regards domestic surveillance and control of the population tend to be accompanied by the expansion of civil and political rights of citizenship. Anthony Giddens even takes the argument a bit further and suggests that there "are inherent connections between the nation-state and democracy (understood as polyarchy),"[16] because of the high level of reciprocity between rulers and subjects in the modern Westphalian state. In other words, internal pacification without means of violence depends instead on reciprocity between those who are governed and those who govern, and that is only possible with some measure of political democracy.

Finally, the Westphalian state is a nation-state. The development of substantial aspects of the modern state came together with the development of nationhood, a "we-ness" most often based on a common cultural and ethnic heritage, but also possible without such a basis. There is not necessarily anything romantic about the process: appeals to "the nation" in the course of modern state development have often had ulterior motives. But the end result, in the context of a developed national polity and economy, is the nation-state, the modern Westphalian state.

In summary, the modern Westphalian state has substantial statehood in the sense of a viable national economy, a national polity with efficient and capable political and administrative institutions, and nationhood – a sense of national community which also bestows legitimacy on the political and administrative institutions. Finally, Westphalian states also have formal, juridical sovereignty, as members of the community of sovereign states.

Modern Westphalian states grew out of the Peace of Westphalia in Europe in 1648. They are emerging elsewhere, for example in Latin America and Asia. Their relations with each other are the games of conflict and cooperation depicted by realist and liberals. I will have more to say about those relations later.

The Westphalian state is not an empirically precise account of modern statehood, although it is often assumed to be. History since Westphalia demonstrates that in many cases a state never enjoyed the high degree of external or even internal autonomy implied by this concept of state. Demonstrating such empirical variation is, however, not sufficient reason to reject the theoretical adequacy of the concept.[17] We have to demonstrate that there are a number of "big and important things"[18] that remain poorly understood and explained without additional concepts of state which reflect changes in statehood. It is the burden of what follows to demonstrate that such additional concepts are necessary, and that they do help explain big and important things concerning patterns of conflict and cooperation in the present international system.

The unsubstantial state

Sovereign states are actually "like units" in certain respects: there is a defined territory, a population, and a government. The state is member of a society of states which recognize each other's independence and juridical equality. In that basic sense, it is true that "a state is a state is a state." But not all states exhibit the elements connected with substantial statehood; therefore, not all states are modern Westphalian states.

Unsubstantial states are deficient in several respects. The first problem is economic: there is a lack of a coherent national economy, capable of sustaining a basic level of welfare for the population. These are the Less Developed Countries and the Least Less Developed Countries (LDCs and LLDCs). Another possible measure of the socio-economic aspect is the Human Development Index.[19]

The poorest, least developed countries are in Africa south of the Sahara, but there are also considerable pockets of poverty in Central America and Asia (Myanmar, Nepal, and Bhutan). It should be added that a relatively large number of the world's poor are in India, a country of enormous internal economic variation. Other large countries in the third world (China, Brazil, and Indonesia) also have many poor.

The second problem in unsubstantial states is political, concerning the institutions of the state and their legitimacy in the population. Focus is on the state in the narrow sense, as a set of institutions and their relationship to the population. Whereas we use the terms "LDCs" or "LLDCs" about countries with economic deficiencies, we may use the term "weak states" about countries with political-institutional deficiencies.

States that function well sustain a number of activities which are more or less taken for granted by their citizens: security against external and internal threat; order and justice in the sense of an operational rule of law; and personal freedom including basic civil and political rights. Weak states sustain such functions only to a limited extent, or not at all.

On the one hand, the institutions of the state are weak: lacking capacity, competence, and resources. Weak states lack what Michael Mann calls "infrastructural power," defined as "the capacity of the state actually to penetrate civil society, and to implement logistically political decisions throughout the realm."[20]

On the other hand, power is frequently concentrated in the hands of state élites who exploit their positions for personal gain. The system is known in sub-Saharan Africa as "personal rule" or "the strongman."[21] The most important positions in the state apparatus, whether they be in the bureaucracy, military, police, or politicians, are filled with the loyal supporters of the strongman. Loyalty is strengthed through the (unequal) sharing of the spoils of office. That is, the strongman commands a complex network of patron-client relationships.

The functions of the state are concerned with procuring public or collective goods only in a very limited sense. The state apparatus is a source of income for those fortunate or clever enough to control it.[22] Such a state is by no means a source of security, order, and justice for its citizens; it is more of a threat, an apparatus against which citizens must seek protection.

Against that background there has to be a lack of legitimacy. Vertical legitimacy is low, because large parts of the population have no reason to support the government; and the government has no authority in the sense that people support or follow its rules and regulations. Horizontal legitimacy – people's sense of belonging together in a nation-state – is also low because the state is appropriated by specific groups; it is not the state of the whole people. Christopher Clapham has emphasized that such systems comprehensively lack "the capacity to create any sense of moral community amongst those who participate in them, let alone among those who are excluded."[23]

There is a partial overlap between lack of economic substance (LDCs) and lack of political-institutional substance (weak states). But not all LDCs are weak states; Uruguay, Chile, and Costa Rica are LDCs, but not weak states (although they may feature some elements of weak statehood).

The reverse also holds; not all weak states are LDCs. Yugoslavia earlier and Bosnia and Herzegovina today may be the clearest examples of states that are in many respects weak without being LDCs. Yet in most cases there will be an overlap, so that weak states are also LDCs. It is in this overlapping category that we find those states that are in danger of becoming "failed states."

The notion of unsubstantial states is an ideal type. Real-world states approximate to that type in varying degrees. Most of the unsubstantial states are in sub-Saharan Africa. But the least developed Central American states and the least developed Asian states, and the Central Asian states coming out of the former Soviet Union, share many of the traits of unsubstantial states as outlined above.

Unsubstantial states are characterized by high levels of domestic conflict. Before adressing that situation, however, it is helpful to introduce a third type of state.

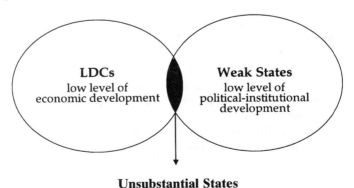

Unsubstantial States

Figure 2.1 Unsubstantial states, weak states, and LDCs

The post-modern state

After the Second World War new forms of political organization have emerged, especially in Western Europe. These new forms are post-modern in the sense that they comprise political space organized either on a non-state territorial basis (such as the European Union), or on a functional basis (such as international regimes in specific issue areas). For the post-modern label to apply, the new organizations must be more than mere cases of inter-state cooperation; they must have autonomous power which has consequences for the sovereignty of the participating states. The most obvious example is the European Union (EU). In some low politics areas, especially those related to realization of the single market, the EU is able to make binding rules for its members.[24]

The EU thus interferes in the domestic affairs of member states. At the same time, states continue to have a large degree of influence on the EU and on the implementation of EU measures at home; how then, should the consequences for state sovereignty be described? Robert Keohane has suggested the term "operational sovereignty,"[25] indicating a situation where states choose to limit their substantial, operational sovereignty through international agreements. According to Keohane, this points to a situation where sovereignty "is less a territorially defined barrier than a bargaining resource for a politics characterized by complex transnational networks."[26]

States engaging in such procedures are called post-modern in the present context. Why do some states choose to do this? There is hardly a single determining factor. In Western Europe security considerations were paramount in the early advances of cooperation between Germany and France. In recent years, economic globalization has increasingly restricted the national autonomy of many states.[27] Increased supra-national cooperation is thus partly an attempt to regain some of the influence lost in the national political space due to the very success of the modern state in organizing transnational economic development during the post-Second World War era. Processes of globalization – meaning the intensification of economic, political and cultural relations across borders – have made states much more dependent on each other. While some elements in globalization are merely the intensification of economic intercourse between national economies, there are also qualitatively new elements in globalization, pointing to a transnational economic system no longer based on autonomous national economies.[28]

This is the background for identifying a post-modern ideal type of state. Sovereignty is used as a bargaining chip, meaning that the sharp distinction between domestic and foreign affairs which characterizes modern states is less valid. Post-modern states allow a large degree of mutual interference in what were traditionally domestic affairs.[29] Their economies are different from merely interdependent national economies; at least some important sectors or areas are deeply integrated in a transnational economic system.[30]

These changes lead to a different role for the state in terms of governance. Member states remain central actors in the EU, especially as regards the "big bangs" of decision-making involved in setting up the basic framework of treaties (although even here the bargains made by state élites are subject to processes of ratification). Yet in day-to-day decision-making, the EU is more aptly described as a system of multi-level governance between various groups of actors at three interconnected political arenas: supranational, national, and subnational.[31] The diagnosis set forth by Philip Cerny, about an increasing diffusion and decentralization of power both upwards to the supranational and downwards to the subnational level, appears an adequate description of the post-modern, "plurilateralist" realm.[32] It is important to emphasize, however, that this need not be a zero-sum game with the state in the role of the loser; international cooperation can also strengthen states.[33] The accent is on change of the state – including change of the policy networks conventionally organized along national lines – not on the state "winning" or "losing."

The notion of post-modern states also indicates a change in the identity and loyalty of citizens away from "we-ness" singularly based on nationhood toward a more mixed palette of identities. This does not mean a transfer of identity and loyalty from one level to another. In the context of the EU, for example, there is no indication that the populations of member states are switching loyalties to the supranational level; a strong EU-European popular identity is not in the making.[34] But that does not mean that there is no change at all. James Rosenau's notion of "sovereignty-free" individuals squares well with the picture drawn here of a post-modern world marked by the forces of globalization.[35] It could lead to what Seyom Brown has called "a *polyarchy* in which nation-states, subnational groups, and transnational special interests and communities are all vying for the support and loyalty of individuals."[36]

It is the members of the EU that play the post-modern sovereignty game described in this section. This does not mean that other states are untouched by the features of post-modernity depicted here. The modern states that are developed market economies take part in the process of economic globalization, albeit to a lesser extent than in Western Europe. They are also engaged in some of the plurilaterlist networks, and they are exposed to the other changes of the conditions for traditional modern statehood. Yet multi-level governance is more developed in Western

Europe than elsewhere, and it is only in Western Europe that a new sovereignty mode has developed. Both the United States and Japan appear to response to post-modern challenges with more conventional forms of regional cooperation.

In sum, post-modern statehood is comprised basically of (a) a globalized economy; (b) multi-level governance and a loosening of identity ties to the nation-state; and (c) a new sovereignty game of intense cooperation. It is EU-Europe that has developed these elements most; the United States and Japan are touched by them to a much lesser degree.

Types of statehood and patterns of cooperation and conflict

The core argument in this section is that different types of statehood are tied in with different patterns of conflict and cooperation. Let us begin with the best-known entity, the modern Westphalian state. The realist idea about dangers of violent conflict between states in an anarchic world, and the continued balance-of-power game among states, is based on the notion of the modern Westphalian state. The liberal idea about possibilities for cooperation towards mutual gain and a peaceful world of liberal democracies is also based on the notion of the modern Westphalian state. In other words, the modern Westphalian state plays the game of inter-state conflict and cooperation depicted by realists and liberals.

The states analyzed in Amin Saikal's paper are states which aspire to be, and in many respects already are, modern Westphalian states. Israel, China, and India are the countries which have moved farthest in that direction. Other states in East Asia, including Malaysia, Thailand, and Indonesia, are moving in the same direction. It is thus in that part of the world that we have on current display a typical modern, Westphalian balance-of-power game with very high levels of armament in a context of rapid modernization. That balance-of-power game is characterized by a further complication which increases the dangers of conflict: neither China, nor India, nor Israel is a satisfied state. That is, the question of their permanent borders and territory under their control is not settled. This forms a dangerous additional fuel to inter-state conflict in an already somewhat unstable environment.

The security problem in unsubstantial states is qualitatively different from the security problem in Westphalian states. The most significant difference is that the serious threat to security in terms of large-scale violent conflict is internal, not external. Lack of developed statehood presents many unsubstantial states with a perennial problem of domestic security. Such states are not internally pacified. I have only space for an outline of the problems. Further analysis is offered in the paper by Charles Abiodun Alao.

Violent conflicts in unsubstantial states are responsible for by far the largest number of casualties in the last decade. Three domestic conflicts alone have each cost the lives of 500,000 to one million people; they were in Sudan, Ethiopia, and Mozambique. Each of the conflicts in Angola, Uganda, and Somalia had casualties of between 100,000 and 500,000 people.[37]

At the same time, unsubstantial states' participation in inter-state conflict is more an outgrowth of domestic conflict in these states than it is an effect of international structure. Copson's recent analysis of Africa's wars supports such a view in suggesting that "the causes of every war were, at their root, internal."[38]

The frail processes of democratization under way in many unsubstantial states tend to increase, not decrease, the level of domestic conflict.[39] This is not a refutation of republican liberalism's argument about peace between consolidated liberal democracies. But Kant's argument is clearly aimed at the consolidated liberal democracies where a democratic culture of peaceful conflict resolution has become ingrained. Unsubstantial states seldom reach this level of democratization; they tend to become stuck in the early phases of transition where liberalization fuels conflict between ethnic as well as other groups.[40]

African state leaders in the OAU (Organization of African Unity) have joined forces with the society of states in one basic respect: support for the persistence of post-colonial borders. This has created an element of stability but it has also fuelled conflict in maintaining the artificial divisions of many ethnic groups. The end of the Cold War has changed nothing in this respect. "The states system is wedded, for better or for worse, to the practice of recognizing and respecting inherited juridical borders."[41]

The external relations of unsubstantial states also differ qualitatively from those of the Westphalian states. Decolonization involved the creation of a set of norms which gave unsubstantial states a right to existence even though they possessed very little in terms of substantial statehood. In earlier days such weak states would have gone under; Westphalian state-making in Europe thus involved a substantial decrease in the number of states on the continent. A similar process is not at work when it comes to unsubstantial states. Their legal existence is secure;[42] in that sense, the international environment facing unsubstantial states is not one of unregulated anarchy, but one of regulated order and secure legal persistence.

This peculiar external situation for unsubstantial states does not give them a privileged position in the international system, of course. On the contrary: as substantially weak entities, they are often forced to take what they can get from richer and stronger countries in the North. Unsubstantial states are thus frequently incapable of participating in the *quid pro quo* reciprocal relationships which typically characterize links between Westphalian states.[43]

Cooperation becomes a non-reciprocal relationship between highly unequal entities: a donor at one end, formulating economic and political conditionalities as a precondition for any relationship; and a recipient at the other end, taking in what's possible while attempting to retain maximum autonomy in terms of freedom of manoeuvre.[44] This situation of secure insecurity is a unique feature of unsubstantial statehood.

Finally, we have the post-modern states in the EU. With multi-level governance characterizing the internal relations between EU members, the resulting political space is no longer adequately described in terms of the neorealist dichotomy between an international realm which is anarchic and a domestic realm which is hierarchic. Both rule-making (the European Commission, the European Council, and the European Parliament) and rule adjudication (the European Court of Justice) take place at a supranational level. These significant elements of transnational political authority in the context of larger networks of political and economic cooperation comprise the substantial basis for identifying the EU as a security community; that is, a realm where participant states do not prepare for, expect, or fear the use of military force in their relations with each other.[45]

Cooperation in the EU in low politics areas involves a significant number of political networks which qualitatively transcend the traditional Westphalian standards of cooperation between states. For example, the Committee of Regions gathers representatives from regional and local authorities. The Committee interacts directly with the European Commission on regional and local development issues. The Economic and Social Committee is advising the Commission and the Council in vocational matters. "Euregio" is a vehicle for regional cross-border cooperation between Germany and the Netherlands; the Council is active in a wide range of policy areas, including technology, education, tourism, and agriculture.[46]

In external affairs the EU also exhibits some distinctive features. The EU is represented in some fora which are normally reserved for sovereign states; they include a number of UN organizations including some specialized agencies. The highest external profile, however, is in the GATT where the Commission negotiates on members' behalf. The EU has also developed a high profile in Eastern Europe policies since 1989. Intensified cooperation in foreign affairs is foreseen as a part of the

Maastricht Treaty; yet there is already a high degree of coordination between member states at the informal level.[47]

It should be stressed that the features of the new types of relations set forth here concern relations within the group of post-modern states. When it comes to dealing with other states in the system, EU countries continue to act, collectively and individually, in conventional Westphalian ways, promoting whatever interests they may have. For example, we see this in their dealing with "rogue" states such as Iraq, or on issues such as debt rescheduling *vis-à-vis* the South as a whole, or in the EU promoting their trade interests in GATT/WTO (the General Agreement on Tariffs and Trade, and the World Trade Organization).[48]

The above remarks on post-modern statehood have focused on the EU. It was noted earlier that the United States also features some of the characteristics of post-modern statehood, but to a much lesser degree than the EU. The United States is presently torn between the traditional role of a modern, Westphalian global power-player, and the new role of a post-modern state intensively cooperating and bargaining with other states in international institutions and elsewhere. The dilemmas of that role are analyzed in detail in Sherle Schwenninger's paper.

Statehood, conflict, and cooperation

The significant patterns of conflict and cooperation in world politics after the Cold War remain insufficiently explored. Existing contributions to the debate fail to investigate adequately substantial changes in statehood and their consequences for conflict and cooperation. The international relations discipline is burdened with a "taken for granted" understanding of states as fixed, "like units" which vary only in a very few respects, the main one being relative capabilities.

I have argued that this view is misleading, and that there are two other main types of state in the present international system in addition to the Westphalian state; they are the unsubstantial and the post-modern state. Each of these types contains distinctive features which separate them from Westphalian states and which entail specific consequences for patterns of cooperation and conflict.

A thorough investigation of conflict and cooperation requires the analysis of different types of contemporary statehood. Specific types of statehood set the stage for distinct forms of conflict and cooperation. The high level of domestic conflict and the secure insecurity in external relations are tied in with the specific type of unsubstantial statehood. And the unique kind of security community which characterizes relations between EU members is tied in with the specific type of post-modern statehood.

What about future developments of these different types of state? There is no uniform path of state development; the three types of state constitute a hierarchy only in the sense that the unsubstantial and the post-modern states deviate from the modern, Westphalian type in different directions. The unsubstantial state has weak and unconsolidated statehood, whereas the post-modern state is a recent phenomenon moving towards more complex forms of governance, partly in response to economic globalization.

The direction of development of contemporary statehood is not given beforehand. States do not move in an identical pattern from unsubstantial, through modern, to post-modern. For example, some states were never post-colonial; others may never be able to become anything else. The conventional claim by realists, that states would be pressed to become "like units" – that is, they would develop the characteristics of modern Westphalian statehood – has not held up. Yet given the stage set by the three types of state identified above, some future patterns of state development are at least more likely than others.

First, as for modern Westphalian states, they will increasingly be exposed to the challenges of post-modernity. At present this is most strongly felt in the economic sphere due to the forces of globalization. It will be increasingly difficult to uphold the primarily national economy upon which the Westphalian state is based. Groups favouring economic integration will prevail over groups favouring protectionism.[49] At present this appears to lead in the direction of a "regionalization" of the world. But on the one hand there is no determinate link between economic globalization and specific forms of cooperation; on the other hand the leading regional states, the United States and Japan, are also global economic players.

In any case, such developments must increase the relative importance of cooperation based on the soft power resources required in complex, plurilateralist networks, and decrease the relative importance of conflict based on more traditional forms of power, especially military power. The latter form of power is less relevant for the creation of multi-level governance regulating increasingly globalized economies and societies.[50]

The standard expectation for unsubstantial states is that they will gradually develop the features of modern Westphalian statehood; this is the process called development. Yet we only have to go back to the 1930s to find a completely different form of standard wisdom: namely that many of the colonies and dependencies would never be able to stand on their own feet.[51] Ironically, the colonial legacy continues to present obstacles to development, especially in sub-Saharan Africa.

At the same time, the advantages accruing to unsubstantial states today in terms of aid and access to modern technologies must be considered against some serious drawbacks. The main instruments used by modern states to achieve statehood – the change of borders and the disappearance of weaker state entities altogether through warfare – are not available options for the unsubstantial states. Meanwhile, a number of states in Asia and Latin America are graduating toward modern statehood. But a large number of unsubstantial states are, ironically, secured continued misery and violent domestic conflict through the guarantee of the international society of states that they cannot go under, no matter what; "the price of failure is no longer absolute."[52]

Finally, post-modern states in the EU appear to be heading towards increased differentiation, in two ways. First, with the expansion of membership the tendency for a "variable geometry" mode of integration will increase. That is, countries will participate in the various structures of cooperation in different ways and degrees, probably around a "hard core" of mostly integrated countries with Germany, France, and the Benelux nations. Second, differentiation will increase inside each country, where some areas are winners and some losers in the larger process of cooperation. That is, integration will go hand in hand with fragmentation. Together with the problem of "democratic deficit" in the supranational institutions, these are the greatest challenges to the EU, in addition to the paramount challenge of keeping the integration process on the move.[53]

Yet the smooth creation of a federal state is by no means on the cards. If more intense cooperation succeeds it will most probably be accompanied by more, not less, conflict between areas and groups in the Community. At the present time, however, there is little indication that such conflict will be violent.

In sum, the post-Cold War world is made up of three distinct types of state: the unsubstantial state in some parts of the South, where domestic conflict is the main problem; the Westphalian state in other parts of the South and in parts of the North, where there is a mix of a realist balance of power and liberal forms of cooperation (South and South-East Asia are characterized by this pattern); finally, we have the post-modern states in the North, with high levels of economic and political integration, where any violent conflict between these states is not likely.

Conclusion: Change of statehood – consequences for the United Nations

The idea that the state is in the process of withering away is misleading; the state is changing, but not becoming less important; and there are different main types of state in the present international system. More intensive cooperation between post-modern states in the North will mean decreasing risk of violent conflict in that part of the world; yet at the same time, post-modern states will tend to face the South more as a unified group/bloc of countries with less room for the South to play on different national interests in the North.

The weakest unsubstantial states with their high levels of domestic conflict will present an increasing dilemma for the United Nations, because large-scale domestic conflict presents an awkward problem for a collective security system based on sovereign states.

In overall conclusion, we are not entering a world where states are unimportant. But we are entering a world of different types of state, with more complex relationships between states and societies. The tension between the rights of states and the rights of people will increase. So will the tension between the different problems of different types of state.

Notes

1. I am grateful for comments on an earlier draft of this paper from Robert Jackson, Asbjørn Sonne Nørgaard, James Rosenau, Michael Zürn, and Hans-Henrik Holm, as well as from Atul Kohli.
2. This is the well-known formulation by Kenneth Waltz: "so long as anarchy endures, states remain like units." "To call states 'like units' is to say that each state is like all other states in being an autonomous political unit." "We abstract from every attribute of states except their capabilities." Kenneth N. Waltz, *Theory of International Politics* (Reading, Mass., 1979) pp. 93, 95, 99.
3. The argument developed here draws on a previous paper of mine, "An Analysis of Contemporary Statehood: Consequences for Conflict and Cooperation" (Aarhus: Dept. of Political Science, 1996).
4. Kenneth N. Waltz, "The Emerging Structure of International Politics," *International Security*, vol. 18, 2 (1993), p. 52.
5. Ibid. pp. 52–3.
6. Ibid. p. 74.
7. Georg Sørensen, "Kant and Processes of Democratization: Consequences for Neorealist Thought," *Journal of Peace Research*, vol. 29, 2 (1992), pp. 397–414; Bruce Russett, *Grasping the Democratic Peace: Principles for a Post-Cold War World* (Princeton, New Jersey, 1993).
8. Robert O. Keohane, "Hobbes's Dilemma and Institutional Change in World Politics: Sovereignty in International Society," in H-H. Holm and G. Sørensen (eds.), *Whose New World Order? Uneven Globalization and the End of the Cold War* (Boulder, 1995), pp. 165–87.
9. Max Singer and Aaron Wildawsky, *The Real World Order: Zones of Peace/Zones of Turmoil* (Chatham, 1993).
10. The emergence of states with sovereign authority over a given territory is normally tied in with the Settlement of Westphalia in 1648. The concept of the modern Westphalian state as employed here, however, is the product of a longer development which also includes industrialization, political modernization, and the establishment of nationhood. In the present context, the Westphalian state is the same as the modern state.
11. See Anthony Giddens, *The Nation-State and Violence* (Cambridge, UK, 1985).

12. See Spybey, *Social Change, Development, and Dependency* (Polity Press, 1993), pp. 93–4. See also Giddens, *The Nation-State and Violence*, p. 150, who emphasizes that "'the economic sphere' should not be seen as a residual one, merely left outside the constitutional form of the modern state, as an unincorporated 'civil society.' *Rather, it derives from the very same sources as the sphere of sovereignty so elemental to the nature of the modern state.*" Emphasis in original.

13. Giddens, *The Nation-State and Violence*, p. 112. See also Bruce D. Porter, *War and the Rise of the State. The Military Foundations of Modern Politics* (New York, 1994), p. 298: "By breaking down class, ethnic, gender and ideological barriers, the wars of the modern era – some of them, at least – contributed to the emergence of such positive fruits of modernity as egalitarianism and a more meritocratic and mobile social structure." Ulf Hedetoft has explored the importance of what he calls "the mentality of war" for national identity-building; see Ulf Hedetoft, "National Identity and Mentalities of War in Three EC Countries," *Journal of Peace Research*, vol. 30, 3 (1993), pp. 281–300.

14. The importance of this factor is stressed in Giddens's analysis, *The Nation-State and Violence*, pp. 172–81.

15. This and the following paragraph draw heavily on Giddens, *The Nation-State and Violence*, pp. 181–209.

16. Ibid., p. 201.

17. Waltz confronts the issue in discussing the dichotomy between international realms, which he defines as anarchic, and domestic realms, which are defined as hierarchic: "Increasing the number of categories would bring the classification closer to reality. But that would be to move away from a theory claiming explanatory power to a less theoretical system promising greater descriptive accuracy." *Theory of International Politics*, p. 115.

18. Cf. the remark in Kenneth N. Waltz, "Reflections on *Theory of International Politics*: A Response to My Critics," in Robert O. Keohane (ed.), *Neorealism and its Critics* (New York, 1986), p. 329.

19. UNDP (annual). *Human Development Report* (New York: Oxford University Press).

20. Michael Mann, "The Autonomous Power of the State: Its Origins, Mechanisms, and Results," in John Hall (ed.), *States in History* (New York: Basil Blackwell, 1986), p. 113.

21. Robert H. Jackson and Carl G. Rosberg, *Personal Rule in Black Africa. Prince, Autocrat, Prophet, Tyrant* (Berkeley, California, 1982); Richard Sandbrook, *The Politics of Africa's Economic Stagnation* (Cambridge, UK, 1985); David E. Apter and Carl G. Rosberg (eds.), *Political Development and the New Realism in Sub-Saharan Africa* (Charlottesville, 1994).

22. Robert H. Jackson and Carl G. Rosberg, "The Political Economy of African Personal Rule," in *Political Development and the New Realism in Sub-Saharan Africa*, p. 300.

23. Christopher Clapham, *Africa and the International System* (Cambridge, UK, 1996), p. 59.

24. This paragraph is indebted to the penetrating analysis by Asbjørn Sonne Nørgaard, "Institutions and Post-Modernity in IR. The 'New' EC," *Cooperation and Conflict*, vol. 29, 3 (1994), pp. 245–87.

25. Robert O. Keohane, "Hobbes's Dilemma," p. 177.

26. Loc. cit.

27. Cf. for example Michael Zürn, "The Challenge of Globalization and Individualization. A View from Europe," in Holm and Sørensen, *Whose New World Order?*, pp. 137–65.

28. These aspects of globalization are analyzed in Holm and Sørensen, "Introduction," in Holm and Sørensen, *Whose New World Order?*, pp. 1–19. Note that forces of globalization and forces of supranational institution-building affect each other: the latter may push the former, not just vice versa; this has clearly been the case in the EU.

29. For a similar view, see Robert Cooper, "Is There a New World Order?" in Sato Seizaburo and Trevor Taylor (eds.), *Prospects for Global Order*, vol. 2 (London, 1993), p. 18.

30. Some sectors of the economy will be more globalized or transnationalized than others. The financial sector is an obvious candidate for such a role. See Philip G. Cerny, "Patterns of Financial Globalization. Financial Market Structures and the Problem of Governance," paper for the International Studies Association Annual Meeting, Washington, DC, 28 March – 1 April 1994. Cerny claims that "'Free Banking' is in free fall. Institutions and markets will continue to be drawn into more complex *transnational* structures of interaction – in other words, structures which cut across and link elements once seen as distinctly domestic with those once seen as distinctly international. This distinction now makes little difference to the markets... Without a much denser transnational regulatory order with the capacity to impose systematic controls on the financial markets – a system with not only a stabilizing but also a Keynesian, pro-production rationale – narrowly financial criteria will continue to play an even larger role in the allocation of capital across the world." p. 52.

31. Gary Marks, Liesbet Hooghe, Kermit Blank, "European Integration Since the 1980s. State-Centric Versus Multi-Level Governance," paper presented at American Political Science Association Annual Meeting, Chicago, 31 August – 3 September 1995.

32. Philip G. Cerny, "Plurilateralism: Structural Differentiation and Functional Conflict in the Post-Cold War World Order," *Millennium: Journal of International Studies*, vol. 22, 1 (1993), p. 27.

33. See for example Alan Milward, *The European Rescue of the Nation-State* (Berkeley, 1992); and Andrew Moravcsik, "Why the European Community Strengthens the State: Domestic Politics and International Cooperation," paper presented at the American Political Science Association Annual Meeting, New York, 1–4 September 1994.

34. For a similar view, see Nørgaard, "Institutions and Post-Modernity in IR," p. 275. Yet at the formal level the first elements of overlapping citizenship are in place: EU citizens living in EU countries other than their own have voting rights in local elections, right of work, and certain social and economic rights.

35. James N. Rosenau, "Citizenship in a Changing Global Order," in J. N. Rosenau and E-O. Czempiel (eds.), *Governance without Government: Order and Change in World Politics* (New York, 1992), pp. 272–94.

36. Seyom Brown, *New Forces, Old Forces, and the Future of World Politics* (Glenview, Illinois: Scott Foresman, 1988), p. 245 (italics in the original).

37. Estimates from Raymond W. Copson, *Africa's Wars and Prospects for Peace* (Armonk, New York: M. E. Sharpe, 1994), p. 29. Copson also emphasizes that "the roots of Africa's wars lie in what many scholars now acknowledge to be a 'problem with the African state,'" p. 74. He quotes Martin Doornbos, "The African State in Academic Debate: Retrospect and Prospect," *Journal of Modern African Studies*, vol. 28 (June 1990), p. 179.

38. Copson, *Africa's Wars and Prospects for Peace*, p. 103. See also Muhammed Ayoob, *The Third World Security Predicament* (Boulder, 1995).

39. Edward D. Mansfield and Jack Snyder, "Democratization and the Danger of War," *International Security*, vol. 20, 1 (1995), pp. 5–39.

40. See Georg Sørensen, *Democracy and Democratization. Processes and Prospects in a Changing World* (Boulder, 1993).

41. Robert H. Jackson, "International Boundaries in Theory and Practice," unpublished paper, University of British Columbia, Canada, p. 9.

42. See Jackson, "International Boundaries in Theory and Practice"; and Ayoob, *The Third World Security Predicament*.

43. On reciprocity in international relations, see Robert H. Jackson, *Quasi States: Sovereignty, International Relations, and the Third World* (Cambridge Studies in International Relations, vol. 12: Cambridge University Press, 1993), pp. 34–47, 109–64, and Robert O. Keohane, "Reciprocity in International Relations," *International Organization*, vol. 40, 1 (1986), pp. 1–27.

44. On political conditionality, see Georg Sørensen (ed.), *Political Conditionality* (London, 1993); see also Jackson, *Quasi-States*, and Ayoob, *The Third World Security Predicament*.

45. The notion of security community was developed by Karl Deutsch et al., *Political Community and the North Atlantic Area: International Organization in the Light of Historical Experience* (Princeton, 1957), pp. 5–9.

46. See for example Desmond Dinan, *Ever Closer Union? An Introduction to the European Community* (Boulder, 1994); Thomas Christiansen and Knud-Erik Jørgensen, "Towards the 'Third Category' of Space: Conceptualizing the Changing Nature of Borders in Western Europe," paper for Second Pan-European Conference of the ECPR Standing Group on International Relations, Paris, 13–16 September 1995.

47. See Knud-Erik Jørgensen, "European Governance in the Field of Foreign Policy-Making: The Informality/Formality Issue," paper for International Studies Association Annual Meeting, Chicago, 21–25 February 1995.

48. I am grateful to Atul Kohli for emphasizing this point.

49. Cf. Helen V. Milner, *Resisting Protectionism: Global Industries and the Politics of International Trade* (Princeton, 1988).

50. On the distinction between types of power and the importance of soft power, see Joseph S. Nye Jr., *Bound to Lead: The Changing Nature of American Power* (New York, 1990); see also David A. Baldwin, "Neoliberalism, Neorealism, and World Politics," in Baldwin (ed.), *Neorealism and Neoliberalism* (Columbia University Press, 1993), pp. 20–22. For a careful discussion of the choices facing the United States' foreign policy in this situation, see Robert O. Keohane, "International Multiple Advocacy in US Foreign Policy," in Dan Caldwell and Timothy J. McKeown (eds.), *Diplomacy, Force, and Leadership: Essays in Honor of Alexander L. George* (Boulder, 1993), pp. 285–305.

51. Cf. Jackson, *Quasi-States*, pp. 13–14.

52. Gabriel Ben-Dor, quoted from Ayoob, *The Third World Security Predicament*, p. 83.

53. See Michael Zürn, "The Challenge of Globalization and Individualization: A View from Europe," in Holm and Sørensen, *Whose New World Order?*, pp. 137–65.

3

The United States as a great power

Sherle R. Schwenninger

Introduction

The United States has shown itself to be a reluctant superpower in the post-Cold War world, seeking on the one hand to continue to enjoy the privileges of that status, while on the other displaying an increasing unwillingness to assume its obligations. This contradiction – between Washington's desire to remain the world's premier power and its deepening aversion to bearing the costs of this position – is in turn the product of another tension, namely, that between its role as a traditional great-power hegemon and its uneven evolution as a post-modern state incapable of commanding the sacrifices required on the part of its citizens to project power globally.

In the post-Cold War world, the assertion of global leadership remains a central feature of America's larger national identity. And in a number of ways the United States can still lay claim to being the world's only superpower. Only Washington, for example, could have convinced Russia to disarm most of its nuclear arsenal, and it alone has had the military muscle to police Saddam Hussein. Indeed, no other power can match America's global military reach, which spans all three geo-economic regions and encompasses the critical oil-producing region of the Persian Gulf. Yet, as is revealed by its hesitancy to intervene in conflicts like Bosnia and Herzegovina and Rwanda, there is a growing reluctance to undertake the responsibilities of this position. Many of the same leaders who declare the US leadership central to world order also shy away from committing American forces in any prolonged military mission that might entail the risk of American casualties, especially in areas where the vital interests of the United States are not at stake. And they rankle at the thought of maintaining previous levels of foreign assistance – even though, in doing so, they deny the international institutions they continue to insist on presiding over the money they need to function properly.

That the American public wants to shoulder less of the world's burdens after the Cold War is understandable given the ones it bore during the Cold War and the social problems that now afflict American society. What is worrying is not that the United States might want a more modest global engagement in the period ahead, but that its increasingly unilateralist tendencies and its growing disdain for multilateralism work to block the emergence of other arrangements for order-keeping that are less dependent on American military power.

Thus the question is not whether the United States will remain the world's leading power, but whether in continuing to aspire to that position it can play a constructive role in dealing with security problems which will trouble the world in the decade ahead. Those challenges require more than ever an internationalist leadership; a leadership that is steadily engaged, that can build and sustain broad coalitions of states, that can put aside immediate domestic advantage for the sake of international consensus, and that is willing to pool sovereignty in institutions of collective security and collective economic management, whether at the global or regional level. Indeed, the successful management of security problems in the early twenty-first century depends more than ever on an internationalist America. Yet what we see in the United States is not the appreciation of the internationalist demands of this new era, but the hollowing out of the internationalist ethos and the political structures that supported that ethos. In this sense, America's evolution as a post-modern state is incomplete, for it has not yet acquired an understanding of the need for multilateral cooperation and the complex bargaining normally associated with post-modern states.

World order and the decline of US internationalism

The United States has always had a weak internationalist tradition. As diplomatic historian Robert W. Tucker has pointed out, in moving from a position of relative isolation to global engagement, the United States "did not go from unilateralism to multilateralism but from the unilateralism of a position of isolation to the unilateralism of a position of undisputed leadership over a global alliance." To be sure, there were some multilateral features to America's leadership role – for example, its alliance relations in Europe and in its participation in the United Nations and the Bretton Woods institutions – but these features were inextricably linked to and thus were given legitimacy by its global crusade against communism and its overwhelming economic dominance. Thus analysts have been correct to question whether American engagement can be sustained, particularly the more internationalist features of that engagement, in the absence of such an overriding international cause and in a multipolar economic world where globalization creates painful dislocations and insecurities for many Americans. Indeed, there are worrying signs to suggest that it cannot be sustained.

American military power and world order

To begin with, any system of world order depends upon reliable peace enforcement and peace-keeping, especially in an era when the greatest threat to order may be the collapse of states and the development of rogue elements within them. In a world where the United States maintains a large margin of military dominance, spending more than all the other major powers combined, and holds itself out to be the keeper of the democratic peace, as both the Bush and Clinton Administrations have done, then it is only natural for the world to look for the United States to deal with problems like Bosnia and Herzegovina and Rwanda.

Yet the US military doctrine that has emerged over the last decade, along with the American public's sensitivity to the risk of American casualties, makes the United States an unreliable keeper of the peace. The "Powell doctrine," as it is known in the United States, calls for overwhelming and decisive force with quick results and minimal casualties. But as critics of American policy toward Bosnia and Herzegovina have pointed out, this doctrine is inappropriate to an American peace enforcement and peace-keeping role, for many of the world's most serious conflicts demand more selective use of force and entail greater risk of casualties than this doctrine allows.

The Clinton Administration has modified the Powell doctrine in some potentially key ways, with its more incremental use of force in Bosnia and Herzegovina and against Iraq, and with its peace-keeping efforts in Haiti and Bosnia and Herzegovina. Yet the prospect of casualties remains a key political constraint on the deployment of American forces in most world crisis situations. This extreme sensitivity towards casualties – a prominent feature of a post-modern state – renders American action, except in response to the most dire threats, all but impossible. This is true even though the United States has a professional armed force, and within that force special élite units for more risky operations. Indeed, the very social contract this country has with its military has changed fundamentally since the Vietnam War. This is most evident in the way military service is presented to prospective recruits. As political analyst David Rieff notes, "the most cursory look at the recruitment ads of today's volunteer army, with the possible exception of the Marine Corps, shows that everything is being done to avoid any unpleasant talk of, well, war. These ads do not warn of sacrifice, or even of the prospective dangers of military life, but rather treat it like a gadget-filling outing and an occasion for enhancing self-esteem, of 'being all you can be.'"

In order to get around this constraint of the public's resistance to putting American soldiers in harm's way, the Pentagon is relying more and more on sophisticated high-tech weapons systems, such as cruise missiles, as it has done in its operations against Iraq. Indeed, a new military doctrine seems to be emerging whereby US military planners increasingly emphasize the importance of defeating an enemy with minimal combat and brief, intense electronic warfare and precision-guided weapons. This approach downgrades the traditional emphasis on ground troops, and tries to capitalize on America's technological advantages.

In theory this approach, along with the new weapons programmes developed pursuant to it, would seem to resolve the dilemma the American commander-in-chief now faces when considering whether to commit US military power. They would appear to make it possible for Washington to be able to conduct military operations globally (and, in this sense, have an internationalist strategy), but without the risk of major casualties and without the political complications of having to consult unwanted allies (and, in this sense, be as unilateralist as it wants). In practice, however, these weapons systems may have little practical utility in many of the world's conflicts. They may make it somewhat easier to strike Iraq and police the international sea-lanes. But would they have made any real difference in Bosnia and Herzegovina, or in the streets of Mogadishu? Not likely. Thus the dilemma for the United States and world order will remain.

The United States has made the dilemma more serious than it needs to be, in part because it has systematically opposed any realistic alternatives to American military power. For example, the sensible alternative to the deployment of American troops in conflicts like Bosnia and Herzegovina is a well-trained and adequately funded United Nations standing army made up of volunteers or national contingents from other countries. There is no shortage of willing fighting men and women in the world – just the organization, resources, and training to make an effective force. But Washington has vigorously opposed this alternative. If there were a United Nations standing army under Security Council political control, then the United States could concentrate on providing sea and air-lift capabilities and intelligence as it did during the evacuation of UN forces from Somalia, and as it seems to prefer in other conflict situations. But it seems the United States would prefer the risk of greater disorder to the creation of an institutional arrangement that would make the world less dependent on American power. In fact, it now even opposes more modest proposals, such as that of earmarking some US forces for UN-related peace-keeping purposes.

Granted, there are reasons to doubt the effectiveness of a UN-based peace-keeping and peace enforcement system. But American behaviour has been disturbingly similar toward European efforts to develop a greater defence capacity. For years Washington has urged Europe to share more of the alliance's security burden, but has repeatedly tried to snuff out any European initiative that would do just that in a way that was too independent from current NATO (North Atlantic Treaty Organization) military command, which it controls. As with a United Nations standing army, the United States seems to fear a Europe that is too independent of Washington in its order-keeping capabilities. Similarly, in Asia it has looked askance at suggestions for a multilateral security forum that would institutionalize discussion of confidence-building measures and arms control. It is this tendency – to oppose institutional arrangements that would make the world less dependent on the United States – rather than its reluctance to engage its military forces in global peace enforcement actions which may pose the most serious obstacle to world order in the next decade or two.

The United States and the fiscal crisis of internationalism

Another worrying trend in American policy is the growing resistance to pay its share of the financial burdens of internationalism. While the US military continues to enjoy more than ample funding, Washington has cut its foreign economic assistance and is ever more resistant to come up with its support for international institutions, including the IMF (International Monetary Fund) and the World Bank. The United States is the world's largest deadbeat among nations in arrears with UN dues: Washington owes the United Nations more than US$1.5 billion in dues and assessments. Even in the best of times, of course, American support for international development assistance and other internationalist concerns was stingy. American non-military assistance, for example, always ranked near the bottom of that of the OECD (Organization for Economic Cooperation and Development) countries.

But US support for foreign assistance and world order institutions has fallen to an all-time low. The sad fact is that the United States devotes just a little more than 0.10 per cent of its gross domestic product to foreign economic aid, placing it proportionately last in foreign assistance among OECD countries. Its record would be even worse if one excluded the largest recipients of US aid – Israel, Egypt, Ukraine, Turkey, the Russian Federation, and Greece – and assistance for these countries owes as much to strong ethnic lobbies and strategic considerations as it does to concern for the world's welfare.

Moreover, as the experience last year with the Mexico rescue package illustrates, the United States is increasingly unwilling to bear the costs and burdens of international leadership even when core American interests are at stake. Indeed, no programme is more unpopular with Capitol Hill than is foreign aid. It was only by skirting congressional approval that the Clinton Administration was able to put together the American portion of the international bail-out package for Mexico.

What is worse, the United States has sought to make up for its lack of financial support by opportunistically using the resources of the international financial institutions – the IMF and the World Bank – to pursue specific American foreign policy goals. Although the United States remains the largest contributor to these institutions, its share has declined with the growing weight of Germany and Japan. Yet America's call on IMF and World Bank resources for specific US foreign policy objectives has increased at the expense of poorer and more needy countries. The 1989 Brady debt-relief plan for Mexico and other Latin American debtors (the Brady Plan also included the Philippines) would not have been possible without World Bank and IMF participation. Similarly, the US$50 billion financial rescue package for Mexico, the largest international aid package since the Marshall Plan, was made possible only by a major commitment of US$17.6 billion in IMF funds.

Washington's "commandeering" of IMF funds for US foreign policy purposes, as it has been referred to in Europe, has at times provoked bitter reactions from Germany and other European members of the Fund, who believe IMF and World Bank resources could be used more wisely. The geo-economic rivalry that is developing over limited IMF and World Bank resources is one product of a larger fiscal crisis of internationalism that promises to become particularly severe in the late 1990s. At its simplest, the fiscal crisis of internationalism is the result of the fact that the demand for international public goods – whether for development assistance, international peace-keeping, humanitarian relief, environmental clean-up, or to assist in the dismantling of nuclear weapons – has greatly outstripped the political will of the major economic powers (particularly the United States) to provide funding on the scale required.

As a defence against Washington's poor foreign assistance record, American officials claim that the United States bears a disproportionate burden of the bill for international institutions; that in the case of the

United Nations its share should be cut from 25 per cent of all levies to a more appropriate 20 per cent, with more of the burden shifted to other wealthy nations like Germany and Japan. They also point out that the United States does at least as much if not more by keeping its markets open and by providing military defence. All this is true. But the irony of the US position is that over the past two decades Washington has blocked various proposals that would have reallocated the costs among the major Western nations and put these institutions on a sounder financial footing. It did so because the measures threatened America's pre-eminent position – and in the case of the IMF and the World Bank, its de facto veto, since increasing Japan's and Germany's allocations would have increased their weighted vote.

Washington preferred cash-strapped international agencies it could easily control. Now that it has changed its tune somewhat, alternative donors are themselves feeling financially challenged, and are thus reluctant to increase their contributions significantly. This means that the world has in recent years been investing less in development assistance in real terms than it did in the 1960s, and a lot less than it should have if it wanted to avoid the spectre of failing states that we are witnessing across the globe. Starved for funds, international lending agencies have resorted to ever-tougher conditionality terms and shorter repayment periods when extending aid. Without the funds needed to invest in human capital and public infrastructure, and to soften some of the pain of wrenching economic changes, many recipient countries have not had enough political and social cohesion to sustain the painful economic adjustments required to root out corruption, increase savings and investment, and implement economically rational policies. And with fewer success stories, public support for international development assistance has collapsed, creating something of a vicious circle: more collapsing states, bigger emergency bills, and more need for troops.

This is not likely to change in the near future, for there is virtually no organized constituency for development assistance in the United States, except from parts of the American investment community at times like the Mexico bail-out. American investors would prefer to pick the ripe cherries of the big emerging markets rather than to chip in to help poorer developing countries. For the larger emerging markets, private capital flows now suffice, they believe – at least until a bail-out Mexican style is needed, and then they can count on Washington to raid IMF funds for this purpose.

American unilateralism, great-power diplomacy, and world order

The third and most worrying trend is the growing unilateralist tendencies in American great-power diplomacy, which in turn is a reflection of increasing neo-isolationist and unilateralist propensities in US leadership circles. The growth of unilateralism is perhaps best illustrated by the Clinton Administration's retreat from its early multilateral commitments. This Administration came into office talking up the virtues of multilateralism, but has since discovered the convenience of acting unilaterally on a range of issues – from its campaign against rogue states to its diplomacy toward China.

Americans, of course, have always been wary and fickle internationalists – internationalists when things go their way, but unilateralists when they turn sour. And Americans have always had a healthy scepticism of international institutions – wary of ceding American privileges as well as national sovereignty – especially when those institutions pursued what seemed to be anti-American courses. It is therefore especially worrying that these unilateralist tendencies are emerging at a point when everything is going relatively well for the United States and when Washington is having its way in the United Nations.

The growing intensity of American unilateralism is most obvious in its resistance to foreign assistance and in its disdainful treatment of the United Nations. But these unilateralist tendencies have surfaced in other more subtle ways that are as equally detrimental to world order. At the heart of American unilateralism is not just a distrust of multilateral cooperation, but a deep-rooted tendency for the United States to arrogate itself to be sole judge and jury of other nations' behaviour. As a result, Washington tends to ignore the legitimate interests of other major powers, including its closest allies. Moreover, rather than accepting other countries' views and seeking to find a compromise position that incorporates consideration of their interests, the United States has increasingly displayed a disturbing tendency to seek to impose its policy views on others. The American actions in trying to isolate and economically strangulate Cuba, Libya, and Iran are an illustration of this tendency. In attempting to impose its policy choice of economic isolation on its allies, it has resorted to extraterritorial legislation – the Helms-Burton Act and the Iran-Libya Sanctions Act – that seeks to establish what are known as "secondary embargoes" by punishing foreign companies for doing business with Cuba, Iran, and Libya. This is not only a violation of international law but corrosive of building the structures of world order, for collective action is needed to deal effectively with outlaw states, especially when it comes to applying economic and political pressure.

It is true that in some cases, such as in its early handling of Iraq following the Gulf War, the United States has pursued a more consciously multilateral route. Washington created a UN Security Council-based consensus to act to deny Iraq weapons of mass destruction and to contain Iraqi actions against its neighbours; moreover, it set up a structure of intrusive UN inspections to do so. But even in these cases, Washington has had a tendency to pursue its own agenda – interpreting UN resolutions to justify attacks on Iraq which clearly exceeded its UN mandate and which were openly opposed by other powers. These same unilateral tendencies have also been evident in its human rights and trade diplomacy toward China. The United States may indeed have been correct to press Beijing on both human rights and trade issues, given China's deplorable record in each of these areas. But Washington's lone sheriff approach – in particular, in its failure to involve Europe, Japan, and other Asian countries in its effort – undercut the legitimacy of its actions and allowed China to deflect American efforts as a product of Washington's efforts to contain China.

America's unilateral tendencies – particularly its insistence on being the principal judge and jury – tend to lead to blatant double standards which undercut the legitimacy of the world order it is seeking to establish. For example, Washington punishes Iraq for Hussein's intervention against the Kurds, but turns a blind eye to Turkey's campaign against the Kurds. It singles out Iran and Libya for their support of international terrorism, but ignores the equally strong links of terrorists to Pakistan and Saudi Arabia, two American friends. It squeezes Cuba economically for its suppression of internal dissent, but pursues a policy of economic engagement with a China that is equally brutal toward political dissidents.

This propensity for American unilateralism to result in double standards takes another form as well. As political columnist Jessica Mathews has noted, "Washington pushes a widening set of rules of international behaviour and simultaneously claims a growing number of exemptions." It opposes secondary boycotts when they affect American interests (such as the Arab countries' boycott of Israel), but seeks to impose its own in the cases of Cuba, Iran, and Libya. It complains of Europe and Japan putting commercial interests above human rights considerations when dealing with China and Iran, but then ends up doing the same with regard to Saudi Arabia as well as China. It pushes for financial and management reforms in the United Nations as a price for its payment of its dues, then moves the goalposts when those reforms are adopted as an excuse for not meeting its own commitment. This behaviour inevitably raises suspicions not only of American bad faith but also that what Washington wants is to run things its own way.

A system of world order can tolerate some inconsistencies, but double standards as blatant as these are bound to call into question its legitimacy at some point. The United States seems currently incapable of understanding this basic point – in part because it has become so self-absorbed in believing in its own wisdom, and in part because other powers have so readily acquiesced in American behaviour.

US domestic constraints on internationalism

Many of the characteristics of Washington's international behaviour described in the previous section have long been part of the American
character and political culture – the propensity for unilateralism; the
tendency to demonize its "enemies"; the faith in technology at the
expense of politics and political compromise; and the suspicion of international institutions and the jealous guarding of American sovereignty.
Yet these negative tendencies have been held in check or balanced by
many appropriately internationalist traits – a sense of duty and global
responsibility; a pragmatic ability to build bridges, as evidenced by the
embrace of Yassir Arafat after many years of demonization; its capability
for initiative, both as an architect and as a facilitator; and a commitment
to human decency expressed by its support of human rights, however
uneven. It is these other positive traits which have allowed the American
system to self-correct – to veer away from its more destructive tendencies. In short, the United States is a complex polity with contradictory
tendencies. Which of these tendencies dominates in any one particular
period depends not only on the leadership at the time (who is at the
helm) but also on deeper structural and cultural changes, and there are a
number of changes that help explain the current erosion of internationalism in America's political life.

First, the new industrial revolution – to a globally integrated,
information-based economy – that the United States is now experiencing
is creating serious strains in America's post-war social contract, upon
which internationalism rested. Indeed, the public distemper that has
given rise to "isolationism" and unilateralism is in part a product of
global integration itself. Although the country as a whole has no doubt
benefited from the global market, large segments of the American population clearly have not – as evidenced by falling wages and widening
income inequalities. As a result, radical nationalists, like Senator Jesse
Helms, have found fertile ground for their anti-internationalist and
America-first appeals. Why, after all, should struggling working-class
taxpayers bail out wealthy Americans in Mexico when free trade has only
made their own jobs less secure? Or support United Nations or World
Bank development assistance when their own neighbourhoods are falling
apart around them? In the absence of programmes to help the losers
from free trade or to rebuild communities devastated by job flight, there
is no good answer to these questions. In failing to provide an answer,
however, America's more internationalist-inclined leaders have allowed
the radical right to channel the public's fears and anxieties over economic
change into a revolt against America's internationalist obligations – in
particular, the United Nations and international assistance – as well as
against government in general.

Anti-internationalist voices represent only a minority of the American population, but in the United States one does not need to hold power or even be in the majority to have a decisive effect on American policy. For example, according to public opinion surveys the United Nations continues to enjoy widespread public support among the American people (although that support may be shallow and the beliefs upon which it is based may be less strongly held than those held by anti-internationalists). Yet the views of an organized and vocal minority have intimidated a multilaterally inclined Administration to retreat on the United Nations and a number of other key internationalist issues. In contrast to the well-organized efforts of the radical right to bash and discredit the United Nations, there is no comparable pressure group or even organized constituency for the United Nations, just as there is no organized constituency for foreign assistance. Thus it is not surprising that foreign aid programmes as well as the United Nations have become easy targets of the unilaterally inclined right in the United States, especially given the widespread misunderstanding that exists among the American public about these programmes (the public believes the United States spends 10 times the amount it actually does on foreign aid).

That, unfortunately, is not likely to change in the near future. In the face of the relentless pressures of the new economy and the anxieties they create in a majority of Americans, the foundation for internationalism – a healthy and workable social contract – may even be eroded further. The danger is not greater protectionism, as so many internationalists worried about in the early 1990s, for "protectionist" forces in the United States have largely been defeated as import-sensitive sectors have been downsized and organized labour's power reduced. Rather, the real risk is a continued revolt more generally against America's internationalist responsibilities. This does not mean an American retreat from the world, but instead a generally more prickly and less cooperative approach to the world.

Second, with this new industrial revolution has come a realignment of American business élites, and this realignment is beginning to have a major effect on America's international posture. The old Atlanticist and internationalist élites so often associated with America's older blue-chip multinationals, law firms, and investment banks are being replaced by new, rising, Sun-belt and Silicon Valley digital entrepreneurs and a new generation of lawyers and investment bankers, as well as by executives from entertainment and multimedia giants. This new rising élite is more committed to global commerce than even the old élite were – indeed, globalization has been central to their world view and business strategy. Yet they largely take for granted the world order infrastructure and alliance relations, which took decades of American power and diplomacy to build. In general, this new, rising élite is more suspicious of government and, not surprisingly, of great-power diplomacy and world order institutions. They look to government to help open markets in particular sectors or product areas, and to protect their interests related to copyright and patents. But they oppose any sustained role of the government in economic diplomacy, and they fail to appreciate the more subtle aspects of the relationship between military power and international commerce, or how diplomacy and alliance-building work together to create a stable order upon which liberal rules of international commerce depend.

This élite realignment has in turn been accompanied by a larger political alignment – toward the south and the Sun-belt, regions that are more libertarian in their economic outlook and more conservative in their social views. This expanding group of voters favours a smaller government, a strong military, but more limited diplomatic engagement. This realignment has produced a new generation of "cheap hawks," as Speaker of the House Newt Gingrich once described himself. Indeed, it is the prevalence of this group in the baby-boom generation which is now coming to power in large numbers that explains the paradox of America's heightened global activity in the commercial and cultural spheres but without the previous generation's commitment to alliance relations and world order institutions.

Another dimension of this political realignment, as political commentator David Rieff has noted, is the end of the dominance of mainline Protestantism and its replacement by a variety of evangelical creeds represented by the Christian coalition. This development, too, has significance for America's role in the world, since it means that the ideal of service has been supplanted by the belief that people get the fate ordained for them. We can see the effect of this change in the callous disregard for the world's poor which has reinforced prejudices against development assistance and humanitarian intervention. We also see it in America's moralistic crusade to bring American-style democracy and free markets – salvation – to the world.

A third development that helps explain America's changing international role is the proliferation of interest groups and civil society groups, each with its own agenda in the international policy arena. This development may represent an advance for democracy in one sense, but it has also added to the unilateralist tendencies as the government rushes to please one group or another – Cuban-Americans on Cuba, Afro-Americans on Haiti, Jewish-Americans on Israel, human rights groups on Tibet, environmentalists on tuna nets, fundamentalist Christian groups on population control, Hollywood on copyrights. Indeed, American policy is "hostage" to a steadily expanding range of domestic interest groups, and is increasingly formulated with those interests in mind. Pandering to specific groups – like the Cuban-American community in Florida and

New Jersey – as successive Administrations have done, has given these groups a de facto veto over American policy on the issue concerned – no matter the national interest and the concerns of other countries. This used to be only an election-year phenomenon, but now it has become a regular feature of the American political landscape.

The proliferation of civil society groups has also reinforced, and given greater legitimacy to, the process of the privatization of American foreign policy, leading to the belief that the US government can step aside in its world order responsibilities. There are, of course, many good things that civil society organizations bring to the international community – from their moral concern for human rights and the environment to their more efficient delivery of some forms of technical assistance and humanitarian relief. But they have also had the short-term effect of delegitimizing government and international diplomacy generally, when both are still very much needed in the international arena. There is, for example, in some circles a mistaken sense that non-governmental organizations are a substitute for state power or international cooperation. This has been evident in the way the United States has seen humanitarian relief groups as an alternative to American intervention in the humanitarian crises of the 1990s. Just as charities cannot create an adequate social safety net domestically, voluntary organizations alone cannot deal effectively with global poverty and the world's order-keeping needs.

Finally, there is a trend toward the further popularization of American culture, at the expense of some traditional values that are critical to internationalism. Over the last decade we have seen in the United States the triumph of a culture of celebrity, sentimentality, and technological fantasy over that of reason and duty. In this hyper-popularized culture, words substitute for deeds, feelings of victimization for responsibility, greed and "spin" for a sense of common good. Inevitably, this culture, as powerful and seductive as it is, has begun to influence American foreign policy. For one thing, this culture has created a short attention span and a demand for quick results that are incompatible with the painstakingly difficult process of creating international consensus and building workable institutions. For another, it contributes to the mistaken belief that everything can be made right in one fell swoop with the use of the latest technology and with overwhelming force – anything that can't is not worth worrying about, or more accurately too boring to concern oneself with. American military doctrine is a reflection of these pop-culture tendencies and symbols – whether power rangers, star wars, or the other technological wizardry offered up in the standard Hollywood action fare. It has also reinforced the propensity for crisis management – America is there (sometimes) to put out a fire, but almost never there to prevent it or to repair the damage once the fire is extinguished.

Lastly, this popularization of culture has led to a collective narcissism, a country preoccupied with itself and its vainglorious ways – a nation that needs to think of itself as world leader even as it shuns the obligations that position entails, a nation that is easy to take offence and quick to overreact to anyone who seeks to defy its will. It is also a culture that increasingly abhors sacrifice and seeks instant gratification – and then makes excuses for itself if it fails. These, of course, are not the traits needed to deal with the problems of the late twentieth century.

Conclusion: America's international role

From these structural and cultural changes in the American polity, and from the tendencies we have seen develop in US foreign policy in the post-Cold War world, we can draw some tentative conclusions about America's role as a great power over the next decade and its implications for world order. To begin with, America's resistance to more institutionalized forms of collective security under the United Nations and regional organizations, along with the constraints on deployment of American forces already discussed, mean that responses to the breakdown of order and aggression within countries and even between some countries will be ad hoc and unreliable. The United States may tolerate some efforts to improve the speed and efficiency of UN responses to humanitarian problems, but it will continue to refuse to commit American troops to UN command and oppose the development of a standing UN army. Moreover, it will continue to hamstring European efforts to develop an independent peace enforcement capacity. Similarly, it will continue to be ambivalent about putting forward arms control initiatives in Asia, and wary of Asian countries developing defence alliance relations among themselves that would exclude the United States.

At the same time, the use of American military forces will continue to be seen as discretionary, not imperative, in most of the world's conflicts, as it has in Bosnia and Herzegovina, Haiti, and Somalia. There will be three exceptions to this general rule: 1) cases involving vital national security interests, particularly a serious threat to America's position in the Persian Gulf; 2) the protection of the international sea-lanes, the oldest of American commitments and a mission in which the United States can bring its new high-tech military strategy and naval and air dominance to bear without risk to American lives; and 3) in the case of relatively weak rogue states – Iraq, Libya, Cuba, and Iran – in which the United States can be expected to act firmly. In the latter instance, the danger is not American inaction but overreaction, which would prevent the development of a common international strategy to counter specific troubling behaviour.

In the short term, the consequences of a policy of ad hoc intervention and a refusal consciously to develop legitimate collective security arrangements, whether through the United Nations or regionally, will be a continuation of disorder in many parts of the world. Over the longer term, this policy is likely to lead to the emergence of regional powers – the Russian Federation, China, India, Indonesia, Iran, and possibly Japan – willing to fill the vacuums left by the absence of American power or international institutional arrangements. In these areas, regional powers will be increasingly tempted to project power, and not always in benign ways. And in some cases, the danger of regional competition will increase, as it has in Central Asia (among the Russian Federation, China, Iran, Pakistan, and Turkey) and as it could in South-East Asia (among China, Japan, Indonesia, Australia, Malaysia, and to some extent India). In such cases the United States will be faced with the choice of either backing its regional favourite, or seeking to serve as a balancer among regional rivals, or withdrawing entirely. In either case, this development portends greater instability and more militarization for those regions of the world.

Second, in part because of America's bad example, the world will continue to underfund many international public goods – development assistance, environmental protection, and economic reconstruction, to name just a few – that constitute the basis for conflict prevention. The aversion to taxes, especially for international assistance purposes, runs so deep in the United States that we cannot expect much improvement in Washington's international assistance efforts. Worse still, based on past behaviour Washington can be expected to stand in the way of the growth of international agencies and the United Nations, partly out of ideological convictions and partly to prevent the further dilution of American power and influence in those institutions. Even if other powers are willing to ante up, the United States can be expected to use its influence to block any significant expansion of their activities.

In brief, the United States will continue to short-change investment in conflict prevention, and will look to other powers to fund American initiatives and US-sponsored peace settlements. At some point, Washington's commandeering of "other people's money" will provoke greater protest from Europe and Japan, introducing further geo-economic rivalry over the use of international funds. This in turn could lead to the further weakening of these global institutions and a greater resort to geo-economic regional groupings as Europe and Japan seek to shield themselves from America's tin-cup economic diplomacy.

Finally, there is the question of the important reassurance role the United States has played in Europe and East Asia that has helped prevent the re-emergence of traditional great-power rivalries in those regions. In Europe, the worry of great-power rivalry has been diminished not only by the success of the European Union and NATO, but by the web of arms-control arrangements and confidence-building measures that were initiated under the umbrella of the Conference on Security and Cooperation in Europe, now the Organization for Security and Cooperation in Europe, and more recently by Western efforts to support the transition to democracy and a market economy in the Russian Federation. In short, the foundations of a system of cooperative security are in place in Europe. Although this system failed to deal effectively with the disintegration of the former Yugoslavia, it is sufficiently strong to avoid the kind of great-power tensions that afflicted the continent earlier this century. The biggest threat to that cooperative security order would be a too-hasty enlargement of NATO, which would unsettle the countries left out of the initial expansion and create a new sense of isolation for Moscow at a time of continuing economic pain. A lesser concern is whether the United States and Europe can work out a *modus vivendi* for reforming NATO to give Europe more of a say in its future.

The situation in East Asia is more complicated, in part because the regional power aspirations of China may be more difficult to accommodate, and because of the uncertainty regarding Japan's regional role. It is also more difficult because of an absence of an agreed-upon framework for managing political security problems. Asia, unlike Europe, has no collective security institutions, only a series of bilateral treaties between the United States and individual Asian countries. The region has no history of arms-control or confidence-building measures – none of the tools of either collective or cooperative security – in spite of the existence of deep-seated territorial conflicts and a worrying, albeit quiet, arms race.

The biggest threat to reassurance in Asia is not a withdrawal of American forces, as some analysts contend, but the American mismanagement of China's regional ambitions. If the United States is too vigorous in opposing China's more menacing actions – such as its gunboat diplomacy towards Taiwan – then it will only reinforce China's sense that Washington is out to deny China its rightful place as a great power. On the other hand, if the United States is too lax this will provoke worry on the part of other countries that China is an unchecked security threat which must be either appeased or militarily deterred. The latter could accelerate the pace of the arms build-up in the region and set the stage for a dramatic shift in Japan's military posture, which would in turn reinforce China's determination to establish itself as the dominant regional power.

China is an especially difficult case for the United States because it is both a potential geopolitical rival, challenging American interests not only in Asia but also in the Persian Gulf, and a geo-economic challenge, in so far as its rising trade surplus with the United States may at some point become unsustainable politically if not economically. It is also still an authoritarian state with an unflattering human rights record. This dual challenge makes it difficult for the United States to pursue an unqualified strategy of economic and political engagement that could relieve some of the tensions occasioned by the geopolitical rivalry. For these reasons, dealing with China will be the biggest test of America's internationalist credentials as a great power. Successfully accommodating China in the emerging order of the post-Cold War world, while helping Japan to evolve into a more normal power, will require a dexterity of mixing principle and power and a commitment to the multilateral process in Asia that will severely test Washington's internationalist abilities.

In both Europe and Asia – indeed, globally – the United States faces the question of whether to continue to try to impede the emergence of potentially competing powers (China, Germany, India, Japan, and the Russian Federation) or to welcome the prospect of a genuinely multi-polar world, one that would be based not on classical balance-of-power notions, but on cooperative concert security principles. In most of its actions, US policy leans towards the former. Washington, of course, denies that the maintenance of unipolarity is official American policy, but it does reflect the mind-set of many of those in and out of government who shape US policy.

Unipolarists argue that the policy of pursuing American dominance has been a success because other powers have not banded together against American power, as they would be expected to do under classical balance-of-power theory. This is true, but that does not make the policy a success, for among other things it ignores the extent to which other powers have withdrawn from the global political arena to shield themselves from American power and American demands. Indeed, the European Union is in large part an exercise by France and Germany to counter American power by in effect creating a domain that the United States can't control; Japan has pursued a somewhat different strategy to accomplish the same end by saying "yes," but on many issues following its own interests without regard to American power and wishes. Only China and occasionally France and India have openly confronted the United States. But the withdrawal of major potential powers like Germany and Japan from the global arena into more comfortable regional orders of their own making is not necessarily conducive to a stable and secure world order in the future. And by discouraging their full partnership in international institutions as well as in alliance relations, the United States bears some of the responsibility for this unfortunate outcome.

In sum, unipolarist advocates in the United States may have their unipolar world for a while longer, especially in the security and military realm – but it may be a unipolar world that gives birth to a more unstable multipolar world than if the United States worked more consciously to create a multipolar world now that in the future would benefit from workable multilateral institutions and a concert of similarly-minded great powers.

4

Emerging powers: The cases of China, India, Iran, Iraq, and Israel

Amin Saikal

Introduction

As we move towards the twenty-first century, debate about the role of states as political and territorial actors, and about their viability as the building blocks of a stable post-Cold War international system, has gained potency. We are often warned of the increasing inability of states to cope with growth in social and economic disparities, scarcity and mal-distribution of resources, and ethno-nationalist demands and conflicts at both subnational and national levels (as examples of factors pressuring states from "below"); and of internationalization of forces of the market, finance, mass communications, technological innovation, cross-border migration, and environmental problems (as examples of variables challenging states from "above"). Some scholars have strongly argued that this has not only eroded state sovereignty, with some states fragmenting and losing their sovereignty so that in general the "end of state sovereignty" may be in sight,[1] but also rendered the statist international system somewhat obsolete and ineffective.

Yet some others have suggested that while anti-statist forces in the international system have increased and, in some cases, reached the point of being "out of control"[2] so that weak states have become a main source of instability, this is more a manifestation of adjustments necessary in the transition from Cold War to post-Cold War politics than anything else. They maintain that statism is still the most dominant functional factor in

61

world politics, and that this may remain so for the foreseeable future. They argue that most of the statist power élites have skilfully managed these forces of globalization and manipulate them in pursuit of their statist goals.

This discourse has engendered a range of prescriptive formulations, reflecting differing methodological and ideological perspectives. They have been advanced as ways to understand and explain the changes in the role of states, and address their consequences. In general, the formulations are premissed on an understanding that there is now a definite need either to reorientate or, if possible, to restructure drastically the statist international system in order to promote a more viable one in its place, or to retain the statist system but contain the current changes and their consequences in such a way as to make the statist system work more effectively. The most salient of these formulations can be divided into three clusters.

The first, whose origins can be traced to Kantian views, emphasizes a reassessment of the ideas of "global society" and "global federalism."[3] These ideas gained scholarly salience in the 1960s and 1970s, to underscore the need for a new and more humane international system. However, they lost much of their gloss in the context of an upsurge in the competitive geopolitics of the later Cold War era, when wider scholarly stress was given to the Hobbesian view of international relations which characterized the international realm as one of power politics among sovereign states.[4]

Nonetheless, a variant of those earlier ideas has lately emerged, theorized by Richard Falk. While emphasizing that the "world is moving rapidly toward a more integrated economic, cultural and political reality" or "set of circumstances" identified as "geo-governance," this variant seeks the creation of such conditions as to give rise to what it projects as "humane governance." By the latter Falk means "a set of social, political, economic and cultural arrangements that is committed to rapid" growth of "transnational democracy," "the extension of the primary democratic practices," and "global civil society."[5] Falk recognizes the limitations and difficulties in achieving this goal, but argues: "To the extent that global civil society becomes a reality in the imagination and lives of its adherents, the reality of territorial states will often recede in significance even though it may never entirely disappear. In some settings, states under inspired leadership might engender strong loyalties precisely because the outlook is compassionate and globalized."[6] Furthermore, he stresses that while it may ultimately be desirable to move towards creating a "world government," nonetheless "humane governance" can be achieved without such a government, and he proffers this as the most likely course of development. Falk considers this to be the best way to create a new, viable international order, in which states may not disappear altogether but alter to the point that they will be able to cope with challenges facing them and live in more peaceful zones of common interests and security.

The second cluster relates to a belief that, parallel to the absence of a better alternative to statism, the conditions are growing for civilizational clashes in world politics.[7] It contends that it is imperative to manage forces which have emerged to undermine the statist system in such a way as to accelerate democratization across the globe, on the one hand, and provide for modifying world political and security systems in ways which would be based on regionalization of world order[8] within the frame of a regime of checks and balances (derived from theories of balance of power, concert of powers, deterrence, and containment) on the other.[9] This formulation upholds the position of the United States as the only post-Soviet superpower capable of playing a central role in the creation of such a system, in order to ensure its pivotal global status and prevent the rise of any other comparable power. It claims that in this way the United States will not only pre-empt any serious challenge to its own interests, but also prevent any further destabilization in world politics without overstretching itself or incurring too many costs.

The third group of formulations arises from a consideration that, for better or worse, statism is most likely to be dominant in the next century and that, on the whole, the assertion that there is "post-Cold War chaos" in world politics is more of a myth than reality. It intimates that the efforts of world powers, most importantly the United States, should be not to create a new world order, but essentially to reclaim what was created during the Cold War and what emerged in the wake of the break-up of the Soviet Union.[10] Some scholars proffer constructive engagement, diplomacy, and regional confidence-building as the means to enhance security within and between states, and deal with challenges facing states and the international system from subnational sources and the forces of globalization.[11]

It is within the parameters of these formulations that various proposals have also emerged about the role of the United Nations. Whereas the proponents of the first formulation wish to see a wider managerial role for the world body in the direction of global governance, the second one stresses the need for the United Nations to assume a counselling role. On the other hand, the third tends to favour a role for the United Nations somewhere between management and counselling as the most practical way to enable the organization to survive the challenges confronting it, and yet at the same time achieve a position whereby it would be able to have substantial input in shaping a more peaceful and stable world.

Whatever the pros and cons of the formulations, no one argues that states and their associated sovereignties have uniformly weakened. One thing that is certain about the current statist international system is that it is a mixture of "strong" and "weak" states. In this paper, "strong state" means the modern "Westphalian" state, which is, as Georg Sørensen puts it, a consolidated nation-state with its own structural dynamic and relative autonomy (whose relative strength can be measured by the degree to which it features the rule of law, tolerant pluralism, and vigorous civil society), and where the strength of the state is a normative reflection of the strength of society. On the other hand, a "weak state" means what Sørensen refers to as "the post-colonial state," that is the weak and unconsolidated state in the periphery, often in an ongoing state of entropy[12] (whose level of weakness can be further measured by an assessment of such variables as personalization of politics, and attempts at arbitrary imposition of ideologically-driven values and practices), and where the state reflects little of the complexity of society. In this sense the sovereignty of a state is always relative to the location of the state in the various global "systems" – economic, political, military, and cultural.

What we can observe is that while one category of state may have been seriously impaired by pressures from below and above, with some even losing their sovereignty and territorial integrity in various forms and to different degrees (such as former Yugoslavia, Afghanistan, and Somalia), another cluster of states has emerged with greater strength and claims to sovereignty. Thus even if the declining position of weak states, which have become a major source of conflicts in the post-Cold War and post-Soviet era, calls for a new international system, the interests of the strong states in the maintenance of a statist system may continue to militate against this for a long time to come.

The broad objective of this paper is to look at examples of both strong and weak states in the zone stretching from East Asia to the Middle East, focusing primarily on China, India, Iran, Iraq, and Israel; and to do so with a view to investigating which direction these states are likely to take into the next century, especially in the context of the changes which have come to beset states and the present statist international system. The aim is not to provide a detailed account of the internal and external dynamics affecting each of these states, but to focus on the question of how nationalist/aggressive/expansionist, or for that matter, inward-looking and contractionist, each might be in the coming decades. This will of course be done against the backdrop of the paper's introductory remarks, which form the frame within which the relevant issues about each country, but in regional and global contexts, will be raised and evaluated.

Common features

While the countries under consideration are marked more by their differences than commonalities, they share certain features which have in some ways influenced them to develop similar outlooks and which can also facilitate their study as a cluster of strong and weak states, both in relation to one another and within the international system. Ostensibly, the governing regimes of all of these countries are statist, where the maintenance and strengthening of the state as a sovereign political and territorial actor are the professed goals and important, if not overriding, functions of the national government. Within this frame, power and authority are exercised in the name of the state to regulate domestic order and conduct foreign relations; premissed on a given principle that the state has the right to engage in political and social engineering, exercise dominance over resource distribution, and uphold and defend national territoriality against forces which may seek, either advertently or inadvertently, to undermine its integrity and sovereignty, although this is pursued differently from country to country. The difference in pursuance depends on a number of interrelated variables, including a state's national make-up; ideological disposition; mode of political operation and approach to territorial organizations; resources capability; cultural, social and economic persuasion; external disputes and conflicts; security postures; foreign policy goals and priorities; and its perception of its place in a changing world system and assessment of intentions and capabilities of other actors and threats from them at regional and international levels, as well as how it is perceived and treated by those actors.

Concurrently, it is important to remember that all these states feature various degrees of sociocultural diversity, giving rise to a variety of internal and cross-border ethno-nationalist and sectarian challenges and conflicts, and as a consequence also obliging the central authority to be watchful of any links between internal dissatisfied groups and outside hostile forces. In this respect, none is more diverse than India in its ethnic, cultural, linguistic and religious constitution. With a population of about 900 million, it has some 15 major languages and hundreds of minor ones, as well as a major ethnic cleavage between the north and south, and many smaller ones within those regions. While Hindus make up 83 per cent of its population, India has about 120 million Muslims, not to mention members of smaller minority religions such as Sikhs, Christians, Jains, and Parsis. At the same time, Hindu society is itself highly fragmented, in terms of both regional tradition and caste.

China's position is also of concern in this respect. Although an overwhelming majority of China's population of over a billion is ethnic Chinese, there are some 50 minority groups with their own distinct ethnic, cultural and linguistic affinities. Even among the Chinese there are 57 Chinese dialects, with many of these dialects unintelligible to the speakers of other dialects. Some of the minorities, such as Tibetans and Uighurs, have waged struggle for secession and independence, resulting at times in bloody encounters and massive Chinese violations of human rights.

In the same vein, Iran is quite heterogeneous. While ethnic Persians form some 80 per cent of its population of over 60 million, it has substantial non-Persian Kurdish, Azeri, Arab and Baluch minorities, amongst whom many are followers of Sunni Islam who have not willingly accepted Persian Shi'ite domination, and have periodically posed challenges to Persian dominance. Among them, perhaps the most restless have been the Kurds, who have on numerous occasions revolted for wider autonomy or independence, inviting bloody Persian responses.

The Iraqi case is even more striking than the Iranian. Of the country's 20 million population, 80 per cent are Arabs, while the rest are Kurds. The situation is further complicated not only by the fact that the Kurds, as a distinct people in their own right, have never willingly accepted Arab rule and have pursued a bloody struggle for independence, but also by the divisions within each of the two communities. Whereas political and tribal rivalries have marred the Kurds, who also have millions of their restless kindred in Turkey as well as Iran, the Iraqi Arabs have historically suffered from their sectarian division between the Sunnis, who form the minority (but with one of its families ruling Iraq), and the Shi'ites, who form the majority and have sectarian affiliation with Iranians, but who have been deprived of political power.

Similarly, Israel has a more heterogeneous population than is often appreciated. Of its 5 million population, Jews make up 80 per cent, Arabs 15 per cent, and the Christians and Druze the remaining 5 per cent. Although Judaism provides the foundation for the identity and legitimacy of the state, the Jewish citizens come from various ethnic and cultural backgrounds, with a clear divide between Ashkenazy (European) Jews, who have historically dominated state power, and Sephardi and Oriental (mostly non-European) Jews, who have often scorned such dominance, as well as Soviet Jews, whose numbers have dramatically increased in recent years. Complicating the situation has been the further division between orthodox and non-orthodox Jews, on the one hand, and the Jews and Arabs, who have found themselves consigned to "second-class citizen" status in a Jewish-dominated and Jewish-run state. This, in the context of the Arab–Israeli conflict, has been a factor causing tension between state and society in Israel, and complicating Israel's relations with its Arab neighbours.

Another important shared factor, impacting upon these states' out-looks in a similar fashion, is that they have all been disposed (though to different extents and at various times) to use force, in both defensive and offensive capacities, as a means of either promoting certain national objectives or addressing certain foreign policy problems. Located in some of the world's most volatile regions and subregions, plagued by per-ceived security risks, and subjected to sustained outside power involve-ment and competition, they have been locked in numerous external dis-putes and conflicts: in some cases acting directly against one another and in others against their neighbours, with three of them (namely Israel, Iraq, and Iran) going as far as to operate, either directly or through proxies, against targets well beyond what may be considered to be their zones of security. Irrespective of the nature of their domestic set-ups, each one of them has been a highly security-conscious state, according higher priority to defence expenditures – above the average when com-pared with a majority of other states with similar national incomes[13] – and often at the cost of their national development.

Associated with this is the fact that each one of these states has exhib-ited, in one form or another, signs of what could be termed expansionist tendencies, motivated by a variety of considerations: ideological, terri-torial, political, nationalistic, security, or a combination of these. To illus-trate, one could point to a number of examples, including most impor-tantly China's disputes over the Spratly Islands and islands in the East China Sea; India's resolve to maintain a determining influence in Bhutan, and to ensure that Nepal is not in a position to act at variance with India's interests – something it clearly demonstrated when it imposed an eco-nomic blockade of Nepal in 1988; Iran's take-over of the strategic islands of Greater and Smaller Tumbs and Abu Mussa, which has given rise to potentially dangerous disputes with some of Iran's Arab neighbours in the Gulf; Iraq's invasions of Iran and Kuwait and claim over the United Arab Emirates; and Israel's occupation of Palestinian and neighbouring Arab territories and reluctance to negotiate the return of some of them.

Meanwhile, while three are nuclear states – China, India, and Israel – the remaining two are aspiring to achieve a nuclear capability. By 1991 Iraq had come very close to being able to produce nuclear bombs within the next five years, only to be thwarted by the United Nations' efforts to dismantle all its weapons of mass destruction as a condition of the cease-fire that it signed to end the Gulf War of 1991. This does not mean that the Iraqi Ba'thist regime has given up its aspirations altogether. As for Iran, it has reportedly made considerable progress towards acquiring nuclear technology, and if unhindered it is projected that it might be in a position to join the nuclear club by early next century, if it has not already obtained nuclear warheads from the Soviet stockpile left behind in Kazakhstan.

This is broadly where the major similarities between these states end, but it is the nexus between these similarities and certain fundamental dissimilarities among them that essentially defines and determines their individual geopolitical character and national behaviour, as well as internal and external constraints, and outside perception and treatment of them as clearly differentiated actors in the international system. It is largely in this context that their profiles in relation to their statist goals, weaknesses, and strengths can be assessed, and their individual courses of development as state actors can be determined on a long-term basis.

Differences

The five states clearly differ from one another in the nature of their domestic political order. Three of them are dominated by authoritarian political systems, though of different ideological bent. Whereas China is subject to managerial communist rule, Iran is in the grip of Islamic theocratic rule, and Iraq lives under an Arab Ba'thist dictatorship. In these states, politics are more personalized than institutionalized, with those in control of the instrumentalities of state power playing greater roles than the general public or political institutions in ensuring political stability and continuity. In each one of them, it is the ruling élite which has a determining role in arranging and manipulating domestic and external settings in such a way as to enable it to regulate the course of national change and development, and to limit the growth of political pluralism and civil society as it sees fit. Communist ideology (as in China), Shi'ite Islam (as in Iran), and Ba'thist socialism and Arab nationalism (as in Iraq) are deployed mainly as means of political legitimization and mass mobilization. In all three cases, the state is treated as "furthering the interests of the dominant" classes or élites, and as exploiting society for the benefit of these élites.[14]

The remaining two, India and Israel, on the other hand, have democratic orders, although Israel's democracy is more conditional than that of India, given its emphasis on the legitimacy and preservation of Israel as a Jewish state, which acts to the disadvantage of the country's non-Jewish, particularly Arab, inhabitants. Whereas India is the world's largest democracy, Israel is one of the world's smaller democracies, with a population of about 5 million. The force of constitutionalism, the rule of law, the separation of powers, tolerant political pluralism, and the inviolability of the right of the citizens ultimately to make and unmake governments are the dominant features of the state. As such, the state is treated "as fulfilling the programmes of democratically elected interests."[15] Consequently, each of these states has developed a strong civil society, where a clear break is made between politics and capital, and robust private sectors act as important counters to excessive intervention by public authorities in shaping the political, social and economic life of the electorate and in weakening or violating the rights of citizens through arbitrary use of power.

China

Each state has developed its own distinct mode of operation, and has differing resource capabilities to be used in pursuit of widely differing domestic and foreign policy objectives and priorities. China has combined an authoritarian political structure with a government-guided mode of market economic development, supported by increasing foreign investment and technological assistance, to build a fairly effective statist system of management. This has delivered an impressive, sustained rate of economic growth in China, with an annual average rate of about 10 per cent over the last decade, a strong manufacturing sector, and a growing middle class and consumerist society. China today enjoys not only one of the world's fastest-growing economies and an industrially- and technologically-backed resource capability, but also some of the associated social changes which could accelerate the development of a civil society as a precondition for wider liberalization in the long run. When combined with China's vast human resources as the world's most populated state, and growing nuclear-backed military strength, giving it a capability to project power beyond China's region, this augurs well for China to become one of the global powers of the twenty-first century. At the same time, China politically and socially is in a transitional phase. Its leadership remains deeply committed to pursuing its authoritarian communist governmental system. It has increasingly become assertively protective of its sovereignty and critical of those states, especially Western democracies, which proclaim a "one-China policy" but in reality pursue a multi-China policy by maintaining close ties with Taiwan and supporting Tibet's right to "self-determination." These considerations have caused diverse perceptions of China in the West. In general, three major perspectives have emerged about China's future.

One view foresees the possible development of China as an uncontrollable politically authoritarian but economically robust and militarily powerful giant, with not only an unwavering commitment to its sovereignty but also a capacity to engage in nationalist and aggressive expansionist actions. It points to the tensions that exist between the insecurity inherent in its political system and the societal shifts caused by its far-reaching economic changes, and the consequent demands that these may generate for greater public participation in the policy-making and policy-implementation processes. It envisages a post-Deng China being more assertive than timid.[16]

The second prognosis posits that the courses of political authoritarianism and economic liberalization which the Chinese communist leadership has adopted are likely to produce serious political contradictions and socio-economic disparities and dislocations, with a growing gap between the political leadership and the people, and between state and society. It asserts that unless the communist leadership decides to unleash a speedy process of political pluralization and democratization to create a polity which is governed by the rule of law and norms of civil society, China could collapse from within. If this were to happen, not only would the country be divided into numerous weak ethno-political entities, involved in internal conflicts, but also the world would have to cope with a massive, tragic trans-border refugee problem and serious threats to regional and for that matter world stability and security.[17]

The third view posits that despite the present contradictions between its mode of authoritarian governance and its mode of market social and economic development, China is most likely to take a course of change similar to those of the Republic of Korea and Taiwan. It projects that China may transform in the same way as those two have done: its processes of politically authoritarian market reforms and its transitional phase of national assertiveness in domestic and foreign policy arenas are likely to give way to the emergence of a China with a tolerant, pluralist, democratic order and sober, rational foreign policy behaviour. It argues that such a process of transformation is already evident, and that the Chinese communist leadership has demonstrated its awareness of the need not to engage in any transgression which could either result in a reduction in the spread and benefits of its market reforms to its population as an important base for national stability, or entangle China in external conflicts which would prove to be threatening to its domestic order and draining on its national resources. It is within the limits of this consideration, and the fact that China has always laboured under its own formidable weight, that one can remain fairly confident that just in the same way as the passing of Mao led to no massive domestic chaos, so too the death of Deng may equally bring no serious disturbances, and China may experience a more peaceful transformation than many of its critics have predicted. As such, China could be expected to develop those attributes of a strong state which would make its transformation relatively painless for itself and free of major security risks for the international system.[18]

Of course, while reflecting different disciplinary perspectives, analysts have proffered various approaches as to how to deal with China during its transitional phase. Some, who predominantly belong to the Western realist school of thought and who have viewed China as an emergent but potentially uncontrollable major power of the next century, have called for a US-led strategy to contain China and pressure it to develop a domestic order and foreign policy posture which would pose no serious challenge to the post-Cold War and post-Soviet configuration of forces in world politics and, by the same token, would be in conformity with Western values and interests. Such analysts have suggested various policy prescriptions for achieving this objective. The prescriptions range from the need to develop some sort of deterrent, to some kind of regional balance of power, to economic containment.[19]

One the other hand, analysts who are concerned about a possible destabilization of China and the effect that the realists' alarmist views might have on Western attitudes towards China, and the negative impact that this could in turn bring to bear on China, seriously question the realists' policy prescriptions. They view the realists' preferences for containment as being based on a Cold War mentality, with little relevance to the post-Soviet world, but with sufficient gusto to make the course of China's transition more painful and hazardous than might otherwise be the case. They call for a better understanding of China in the context of its historical development and present transitional phase, and proffer constructive engagement as an appropriate approach to helping the country achieve a transformation which would be conducive to the evolution of a more peaceful and safer world.[20]

This approach is also generally shared by the analysts who see the course of China's future development in more positive terms, and contend that China's transition may well follow the path of its newly-democratized neighbours. They caution against any policy approach which could drive China away from such a course and pressure it into a direction that could imperil China's viability and regional and international peace and security.[21]

The case of China is indeed a highly complex one. While the ruling communist élite is determined to control the future of the country, the very process of social and economic reform that it has pursued so vigorously over the last two decades is bound to foster the growth of civil society and political pluralism, narrowing the options of the élite. As the situation stands, the chances are that China may vacillate between being defensive and assertive in its domestic and foreign policy, but eventually take a direction similar to that of the Republic of Korea and Taiwan. But of course, for China to move in this direction depends not just on how the country's Communist Party readjusts to the new realities of China, but also on how China is treated by the outside world, especially those states which fear the emergence of China as a superpower in the coming decades.

India

There are currently two views predominant about India. One provides a fairly bleak assessment of the country's future, projecting India as becoming increasingly ungovernable from within and vulnerable to the outside. It points to the country's chronic national divisions, ethno-nationalist secessionist demands, social and economic problems – including 300 million of its citizens living below the poverty line and twice as many illiterate or semi-literate, or suffering from curable diseases – and growing, endemic corruption (especially at the political level), as well as foreign policy complications, encompassing its conflict with Pakistan, its uneasy relations with its other neighbours, and the fears of these neighbours of a perceived hegemonic India.[22] It combines this with India's loss of the Soviet Union as its main Cold War strategic ally and its inability to find a new and solid niche for itself as an effective and acceptable regional power in the international system, where its relations with the United States continue to remain on a low key in the post-Cold War era, to substantiate a thesis that the country's progression into the twenty-first century is likely to be as crisis-ridden as its existence since its independence in 1947.

The other prognosis claims that despite all its problems, India is well set on a course to emerge as one of Asia's most stable powers, as its third formidable economic power after China and Japan and second military power after China, and as potentially the world's fifth largest power in the coming decades. To substantiate this projection, analysts stress a number of relevant factors. The first is the robust nature of India's democratic system, legal-constitutional arrangements, and tolerant pluralism. The second is the growth of one of the world's fastest-expanding, best-educated, entrepreneurial and articulate middle classes, with considerable disposable income, whose size today is estimated from 180 million to 350 million, and which "could act as both a stabilizing factor and a factor of change in Indian politics,"[23] and constrain government excesses (as it did during Prime Minister Indira Gandhi's state of emergency in the 1970s). The third is the economic liberalization of the 1990s, which has so far brought India an impressive average annual growth rate of about 6 per cent[24] and a considerable inflow of direct foreign investment, with 42 per cent of it coming from the United States.[25] The fourth is the corrective mechanisms that are inherent in Indian democracy to ensure the viability of the system and cushion people against individual and organized excesses. The fifth is India's "looking east" strategy to link up to the security arrangements and economic dynamism of various regional fora, such as the Association of South-East Asian Nations (ASEAN), and the Asia-Pacific Economic Cooperation Forum (APEC)[26] – a strategy that many analysts believe goes a long way to compensating for the loss of the Soviet Union, and for the lack of progress in building the South Asian Association for Regional Cooperation (SAARC) into a meaningful forum for regional economic cooperation. The sixth is India's endeavour to improve relations with China, and the peace dividends from which both sides have benefited – an issue which may strongly continue to hold India back from joining any alliance which may seek to counterbalance China. The seventh is India's reasonable management of the forces of globalization, through either indigenizing them or influencing them in such ways as to adapt them closely – whether in the fields of finance, trade, mass communications (such as satellite television), corporate investment, high technology, or the silicon industry in Bangalore[27] – to its own priorities and policy goals either through governmental processes or private sector mechanisms.

Thus the overall prognosis is that should India continue its present course of change and development, it has sufficient internal cohesion, national strength, and geopolitical assets to be able to cope with current levels of pressure from below and above, and march forward with considerable confidence as a relatively significant sovereign statist player into the next century. This may be so even despite a degree of political extremism to which it may be prey under such political forces as the Hindu Bharatiya Janata Party (BJP).[28] This is not to say that India is going to be a zone of peace and stability; far from it. The Indo-Pakistan disputes, the Muslim secessionist movement in Jammu and Kashmir, and similar movements elsewhere, especially in the north-east of the country, may remain in place for the foreseeable future. But what it does intimate is that, short of major structural changes in regional and international politics, India on the strength of present indicators stands to develop as a strong, nationalistic, but not necessarily aggressive power. It is this view which is more likely to stand the test of time than the one that offers a negative projection of India.

Iran

The same cannot be said about the Islamic Republic of Iran, which is unique in so far as it is the only theocratic state of its kind in the international system, purportedly governed by the rules of Shi'ite Islam as distinct from the mainstream Sunni Islam. The Iranian theocratic order, founded by the leader of the anti-Shah revolution of 1978–1979,[29] Ayatollah Khomeini, and carried through by his followers, has given rise to a state whose complex attributes are not always easily discernible through the application of the normal criteria of what constitutes a weak or strong state. Nonetheless, the nature of its regime and the kind of polity that it has sought to engender ultimately reveal it to be not much more than an authoritarian state, ruled by a Shi'ite oligarchy made up of a mixture of selected and elected leaders.

Despite its oil riches, the goal promised by Ayatollah Khomeini of transforming Iran into a model Islamic state is far from being realized. Even according to Iranian official sources, a majority of Iranians continue to suffer from poor social and economic conditions, underlined by rising inflation (estimated to be at an annual rate of 50–100 per cent) and unemployment and underemployment (estimated to be 30–50 per cent), shortages of basic commodities, a high cost of living, growing disparity between rich and poor, insufficient infrastructural, educational and medical development, and lack of foreign investment, as well as large-scale corruption and human rights violations. While its national consumption has sharply risen, with a doubling of its population since the revolution, its national productivity has made no corresponding progress.

At the same time, there are two other factors which further complicate the Iranian situation. The first is the continued division within the country's oligarchical theocratic leadership between Islamic traditionalists (presently headed by the Speaker of the National Assembly, Nateq Noori, and supported by the supreme Iranian religious-political leader, Ayatollah Ali Khamanei), who stress the preservation of ideological purity above all else as the foundations of political legitimation, and the Islamic reformists, led by President Hashemi Rafsanjani, who strongly favour an interactive relationship between ideology and what is pragmatically required to build and protect Iran as an effective state. The second is Iran's continued challenge to the forces of status quo and the connection that exists between this and the traditional interventionist diplomacy which outside powers, especially the United States, have sought to maintain in the region.

The overall effect has been that Iran today is in the grip of serious economic difficulties, ideological malaise, and a notable degree of foreign policy stagnation.[30] Assessing the future of the country within the parameters of these factors, an argument can be mounted that Iran's viability as a sovereign nation-state could come under severe threat from both within and outside. Unless its leadership succeeds in turning around the economy, implementing serious social and market reforms, and changing foreign policy direction, thus ending the country's international isolation, Iran's future is pregnant with potential for massive political and social unrest.[31] And there is a possibility that this could either erode its capacity to defend its statist goals or stimulate its leadership in the direction of an aggressive nationalist universalism as a means of regime preservation.

On the other hand, there is a strong body of opinion that such a prognosis overstates Iran's problems, for there are some underlying currents of stability in Iranian politics and society which could easily militate against the forces of destabilization of the country, and help it to pull through its difficulties so that it can remain an effective sovereign actor into the next century. It is important to note that in spite of all their limitations, Iranian politics are by no means either monolithic or mono-organizational: Iran has a lively constitutionalism of its own, featuring a robust electoral and parliamentary system; an active private sector; a sizeable oil-based middle class; and sufficient resources (including defence capability); as well as favourable geopolitical settings. This has provided for widespread public participation and regulated order, and a considerable amount of political pluralism within the bounds of political factionalism, civil freedoms, and market forces which have developed within the parameters set by what is theocratically legitimate and what is pragmatically necessary.[32]

Furthermore, despite all its shortcomings, the Iranian economy is not beyond corrective measures. With an annual growth rate of about 6 per cent since the early 1990s and a relatively small foreign debt of about US$18 billion,[33] as well as expanding trade ties with the Russian Federation, the Central Asian republics, China, Japan, and some Europeans countries, and possible increases in its oil revenues, Iran has the potential to improve its economic outlook substantially in the coming years. In addition, while demonized by the United States and shunned by America's Arab friends and allies in the region,[34] Iran has worked hard to assume a central role in the development of the regional Economic Co-operation Organization (ECO), joining it with Turkey, Central Asian republics, Afghanistan, and Pakistan. Also, it has managed to forge close links with those states which share its concerns about America's post-Cold War hegemonic role in world politics; these include, most importantly, the Russian Federation, China, and India, with the first two now acting as Iran's major arms suppliers.

A skilful manipulation of these settings by the Iranian leadership could comfortably enable it not only to weather challenges from below but also to resist pressure from above, as it has done so far, and enforce its statist goals in order to maintain its position as a sovereign actor in the international system on a long-term basis. It is this prognosis which appears to be more credible than the one which emphasizes the weaknesses of Iran and anticipates possible structural shifts in the country's statist position.

Iraq

As for Iraq, in contrast to all the other countries under study it presents a fairly clear case of a state which has markedly weakened since the beginning of the 1990s. Although in the past President Saddam Hussein based his dictatorial system of governance on Iraq's oil riches to build a powerful state economically and militarily, with a noticeable degree of geopolitical clout in regional politics and an assured place in the international system, this has not been so in the 1990s. Following Iraq's invasion of Kuwait in August 1990 and the subsequent reveral of the invasion by a UN-backed but American-led international coalition seven months later, Iraq was forced to pay a very heavy price for both its invasion and its military defeat.

The Western members of the international coalition, more specifically the United States, and the United Nations declared Iraq's Kurdish territory north of the thirty-sixth parallel a "safe haven" to protect Iraq's rebellious Kurdish minority against Saddam Hussein's repression, with a "no-fly" zone for Iraqi planes over the area. They similarly imposed an air exclusion zone over southern Iran, covering an area up to the thirty-fourth parallel – a limit which in mid-1996 was extended further to the thirty-second parallel, partly to protect the Iraqi Shi'ites, who are concentrated in the south and had joined the post-war revolt against Saddam Hussein, and partly to reduce any chances of more Iraqi threats against Kuwait and other member states of the pro-Western Gulf Cooperation Council (GCC).[35] Furthermore, they empowered the United Nations to undertake an extended mission to destroy, without any impunity, all Iraq's weapons of mass destruction and circumvent its capacity to produce any in the future. In so doing, in the context of Iraq's demographic divisions, they also made northern Iraq vulnerable to Turkish and Iranian intrusions in pursuit of leverage against their respective Kurdish opposition groups.[36]

All this, together with the widespread infrastructural damage that the war inflicted upon Iraq and the devastation that the United Nations' comprehensive regime of economic sanctions has brought to the country, has substantially weakened its domestic structures, virtually destroyed its middle class, and rendered it a divided state, functioning only partly under the sovereignty of the Baghdad government but largely under the shadow of the United States and the United Nations. Although the United Nations has recently lost its control of the safe haven on the ground in the north to an Iraqi-backed Kurdish faction, and also signed an "oil for food" agreement with the Iraqi government to allow it to sell a limited amount of oil to meet the humanitarian needs of the Iraqis and pay war reparations to Kuwait, Iraq continues to the present date to be subjected to severe limitations on the exercise of its political and territorial sovereignty. As a result, it is likely to remain a fairly weak state for the foreseeable future. Having said this, it is important to stress that what has undermined the Iraqi state is not necessarily the pressure which may have arisen from below or above, for the Iraqi regime coped with such pressure quite effectively prior to the 1990s. It is rather a consequence mainly of Iraq losing its income from oil due to its aggression against a state in a zone where the world's only post-Cold War superpower continues to maintain vital geopolitical interests.

Israel

Israel presents a total contrast. After India, it is the only other state with a democratic system in the group of countries under study. It is a Westphalian state, underlined by a highly institutionalized, legal-rational and pluralist political order, a robust civil society, a high level of social and economic development, and a high standard of living, as well as an impressive level of industrial-military resources (including nuclear capabilities). Despite its relatively small territorial and demographic size and considerable social divisions, it has undoubtedly grown to be a powerful state actor in the region.

However, certain important qualifications are in order. Israel is as much of a confessional entity as it is a secular and democratic state in its operations. It is heavily influenced by Judaism as the foundation of state legitimacy and identity. The delicate balance that has been forged between the two has transformed Israel into more of a confessional democracy than anything else. This means that its system is not as participatory as would be the case with a liberal democracy. It is in some ways quite exclusive, obliging the state to cater more for its Jewish citizens than non-Jewish (most importantly Arab) inhabitants. The result has been an underlying tension that has characterized the development of the Israeli state since its inception in 1948 – a tension which has at times erupted into open conflict, affecting state cohesion and functions.

Further, Israel's strength as a political and territorial actor is not entirely domestically resourced. In a distinct way, Israel is a rentier state, dependent heavily on outside, more specifically American, assistance. Whereas between 1949 and 1990, US grants and loans to Israel totalled over US$49 billion,[37] from 1991 the annual amount registered a dramatic rise, reaching a little more than US$5.5 billion dollars in the fiscal year of 1996.[38] This has been in addition to the US$2–3 billion that has been donated annually by private Jewish sources in America for many years. Altogether the American aid – from both official and private sources – has come to account for about 10–15 per cent of Israel's annual income. This, plus other benefits that it reaps from its strategic alliance with the

United States, has proved to be critical to Israel's ability to maintain its domestic order and at the same time acquire a level of social, economic and military resourcefulness[39] enabling it to emerge as a strong actor in the region.

A further associated complicating factor is that, ever since its foundation, Israel has existed as a confessionally/territorially/security-driven actor in a very hostile regional environment. This has intertwined Israel's sovereignty with Judaism, and the need for a certain amount of territorial expansion as an important imperative for enforcing the viability of the Israeli state. This in turn has occasioned the country to live in a state of perpetual regional insecurity and isolation. Thus the task of protecting and asserting its sovereignty against those whose territories it has occupied and whose enmity it has experienced – as in the case of the Palestinians and some of Israel's other Arab neighbours – has produced a powerful nexus between Israel's conditional democratic order and foreign policy behaviour. No matter what Israel's legal-constitutional arrangements and constraints, democratic values and practices, and norms of civil society may be, to maintain its position as a viable state, Israel has necessarily had to bear the brunt of being a somewhat expansionist power. For this it has had to be naturally a vigilant and, if required, a forceful actor, as it has been on numerous occasions, with its massive military incursion into Lebanon in April 1996 as one of the latest examples.

This means that the future of Israel will depend very much on developments in three main areas. The first relates to how Israel is likely to manage the nexus between its domestic setting and foreign policy position. If there is any serious disruption in the balance between the two, Israel is likely to face painful stresses and dilemmas. The culture of internal democracy and expansionist foreign policy has created a political environment in which it is neither simple nor viable for Israel to settle easily its conflicts with Palestinians, in particular, and the Syrians and Lebanese, in general, on the basis of land for peace. Thriving on such a culture, the right-wing Israeli Prime Minister, Benjamin Netanyahu, who was elected in May 1996, is well placed to drag out the implementation of his Labour predecessors' peace deals with the Palestinians and refuse to negotiate a total withdrawal from the Golan Heights, in a clear expectation that the nexus between Israel's domestic and foreign policy provides him with the necessary space of legitimacy to do so.

The second main area concerns Israel's management of its special alliance with the United States. Although at present there is nothing major to indicate that the nature of the alliance is about to change, Israel cannot take this for granted. Both regional and international politics are in a transitional phase. Furthermore, if Israel prevents the present Middle East peace process from reaching its goal of a final settlement of the

Palestinian problem, the United States may at last conclude that it has created a power over which it has lost control. This could result in all kinds of changes, including ones which may prompt the United States to rationalize its relations with Israel in the long run. A foretaste of this became evident when President George Bush refused in 1991 to provide a US$10 billion loan guarantee for Israel in an attempt to force its hard-line Likud Prime Minister, Yitzhak Shamir, to agree to a Middle East peace process. Any serious disruption in the relationship could prove to be more costly for Israel's democracy and regional policy than can be anticipated at this point.

The third area concerns the possibility of changes in Israel's domestic politics that could decouple its internal situation from its foreign policy position. Although for the time being Israeli democracy is firm, the increase in right-wing extremist religious parties and groups, which have succeeded in exerting far greater influence in Israeli politics than their size would normally allow and which have done so by thriving on Israel's conflict with the Palestinians and its other Arab neighbours, has already induced some potentially dangerous shifts in Israeli politics. Not only has political assassination found its way into Israel's political life, as with the gunning down of Prime Minister Yitzhak Rabin in November 1995, but also Israel has become more and more vulnerable to antisecularist activities. If the situation is not contained, it could weaken the forces of political centralism and make Israeli politics vulnerable to volatile shifts. In such an event, no one can rule out the possibility of the stimulation of Israel towards a more nationalistic/aggressive posture.

As such, while Israel at present is a strong state, with a promising capacity to grow in this way into the twenty-first century, there are certain underlying tensions and currents of instability within its domestic order, as well as between this and its foreign policy circumstances, which could change the situation. How Israel is going to manage these tensions and currents in the coming years is going to be very critical to determining its future.

Conclusion

If there is one point that emerges clearly from this study it is that the state, and statism, remain dominant features of the five states under focus. This is not to say that the nature of these states has not changed, or that they are not confronted by a cobweb of subnational and national difficulties, and international challenges, with the potential to weaken their individual sovereignty. Nor does it deny that the major challenge to these states (especially China and India) may stem from their economies, where market forces are set to weaken or limit their role as institutionalized actors. What it does suggest is that, although there are strong and weak states in the international system, all the states examined in this study (with the partial exception of Iraq) have so far successfully managed, in distinct ways and under varying internal and external circumstances, to change and develop in such a manner as to avoid an erosion of their sovereignty due to pressure arising from below and above, and are well positioned to protect their individual status as sovereign political and territorial states into the next century. Even with regard to Iraq, the weakening of the country's sovereignty has not come about as a result of pressure from forces of either domestic change or globalization, but mainly as a result of exogenous coercion. Otherwise, prior to the 1990 Iraqi invasion of Kuwait, the dictatorial regime of Saddam Hussein had successfully managed to build a credible state. At present there is little to indicate that any of the other four states is pressured towards forfeiting its statist goals and claims.

Although no universal conclusion is intended to be drawn from the study, it is clear that the nation-state is also set to underwrite the structure and define the operation of the international system beyond this century. It is around this imperative that proponents of a new world order, based on the primacy of humane governance or a variant of it, will need to work out their conceptual formulations if they are to have tangible success. Similarly, it is within the parameters of this reality that the United Nations would need to be reformed, with a capacity to be able to accept the existence of states as the underlying blocks of a world system on the one hand, and help to build the necessary conditions for the emergence of a global regime of humane governance in order to enable states to meet the growing challenges of a fast-changing world on the other. This would require a restructuring of the United Nations along lines which could enable it to fulfil two important functions simultaneously: to act as a global counselling body to help its member states manage their individual affairs and developments more effectively but within a framework which would promote global peace and stability; and to have the necessary resources and capacity to be able to intervene in those situations where internally- or externally-based developments in a certain state or states threaten the well-being and security of other states, and for that matter the international system.[40]

Notes

1. See Joseph A. Camilleri and Jim Falk, *The End of Sovereignty? The Politics of a Shrinking and Fragmenting World*. Aldershot: Edward Elgar, 1992.

2. See Zbigniew Brzezinski, *Out of Control: Global Turmoil on the Eve of the Twenty-first Century*. New York: Collier Books, 1993, esp. Parts III–V.
3. For early assessment of the ideas, see Richard A. Falk, *This Endangered Planet: Prospects and Proposals for Human Survival*. New York: Vintage Books, 1972.
4. For a discussion of the Hobbesian view, see Hedley Bull, *The Anarchical Society*. New York: Columbia University Press, 1977.
5. Richard Falk, *On Humane Governance: Toward a New Global Politics*. Pennsylvania: Pennsylvania State University Press, 1996, p. 2.
6. Ibid., p. 212.
7. Samuel P. Huntington, "The Clash of Civilizations," *Foreign Affairs* (1993), pp. 29–49.
8. Brzezinski, op. cit., Part 5.
9. See Paul Dibb, *Towards a New Balance of Power in Asia*. Adelphi Paper 295, Oxford: Oxford University Press, for the International Institute for Strategic Studies, 1995.
10. G. John Ikenberry, "The Myth of Post-Cold War Chaos," *Foreign Affairs*, May/June 1996, pp. 79–91.
11. See James L. Richardson, "Asia-Pacific: The Case for Geopolitical Optimism," *The National Interest*, Winter 1995, pp. 28–39.
12. For details, see Georg Sørensen's discussion in Chapter 2.
13. For a comparative study of their defence expenditures, see *The Military Balance, 1994–1995*. London: Brassey's, for the International Institute for Strategic Studies, 1994; *The Military Balance, 1995–1996*. London: Brassey's, for the International Institute for Strategic Studies, 1995.
14. A Marxist variant of this is detailed in John Waterbury, *Exposed To Innumerable Delusions: Public Enterprise and State Power in Egypt, India, Mexico, and Turkey*. New York: Cambridge University Press, 1993, p. 17.
15. Ibid.
16. For example, see Gerald Segal, *China Changes Shape: Regionalism and Foreign Policy*. Adelphi Paper 287, London: Brassey's, for the International Institute for Strategic Studies, 1994; Denny Roy, "Consequences of China's Economic Growth for Asia-Pacific Security," *Security Dialogue*, June 1993, pp. 181–91; Paul Dibb, op. cit.
17. For a discussion of this view, see Shirly WuDunn, *China Wakes: The Struggle for the Soul of a Rising Power*. New York: Times Books, 1994; W. J. F. Jenner, *The Tyranny of History: The Roots of China's Crisis*. New York: Penguin Books, 1994.
18. See Bruce Cumings, "The World Shakes China," *The National Interest*, Spring 1995, pp. 28–41; William H. Overholt, "China after Deng," *Foreign Affairs*, May/June 1996, pp. 63–78.
19. See Paul Dibb, op. cit., pp. 56–73.
20. For example, see James L. Richardson, op. cit.
21. For example, see Kenneth Lieberthal, "A New China Strategy," *Foreign Affairs*, November/December 1995, pp. 35–49.
22. For a discussion of these issues, see Pranay Gupte, *India: The Challenge of Change*. London: Methuen – Mandarin, 1989; Atul Kohli also provides a detailed discussion in *Democracy and Discontent: India's Growing Crisis of Governability*. New York: Cambridge University Press, 1990.
23. See M. S. Dobbs-Higginson, *Asia-Pacific: Its Role in the New World Order*. Melbourne: Minerva, 1995, p. 188; "India Seeks More Investment in South-East Asia," *Reuters News Service*, Art. No. 000459326155, 25 May 1994.
24. For details, see Walter Andersen, "India in 1995: Year of the Long Campaign," *Asian Survey*, February 1996, pp. 172–4.
25. Sandy Gordon, "India and Asia-Pacific Security," in Gary Klintworth (ed.), *Asia-Pacific Security: Less Uncertainty, New Opportunities*. Melbourne: Longman Australia, 1996, p. 66.

26. Ibid., pp. 72–5.
27. For an informed piece about Bangalore as India's market-driven success, see John Stremlau, "Dateline Bangalore: Third World Technopolis," *Foreign Policy*, Spring 1996, pp. 152–68.
28. See M. S. Dobbs-Higginson, op. cit., pp. 181–211.
29. For a detailed discussion of the revolution, see Amin Saikal, *The Rise and Fall of the Shah*. Princeton: Princeton University Press, 1980.
30. See Hazhir Teimourian, "Iran's 15 Years of Islam," *The World Today*, April 1994, pp. 67–70.
31. See James Willie, "Iran – The Edge of the Precipice," *Jane's Intelligence Review*, April 1994, pp. 176–7.
32. For a detailed discussion of some of these issues, see Mohsen M. Milani, *The Making of Iran's Islamic Revolution: From Monarchy to Islamic Republic*. 2nd ed., Boulder: Westview Press, 1994, esp. chs. 8–11.
33. *The Military Balance, 1994–1995*, op. cit., p. 127.
34. See Amin Saikal, "The American Approach to the Security of the Gulf," in Wolfgang F. Danspeckgruber and Charles R. H. Tripp (eds.), *The Iraqi Aggression Against Kuwait: Strategic Lessons and Implications for Europe*. Boulder: Westview Press, 1996, pp. 179–93.
35. For details, see Ofra Bengio, "The Challenge to the Territorial Integrity of Iraq," *Survival*, Summer 1995, pp. 74–94.
36. George Joffe, "Iraq's Strategic Role," *Middle East*, May 1993, pp. 221–4.
37. For details and breakdown of grants and loans, see Camille Mansour, *Beyond Alliance: Israel in US Foreign Policy*. New York: Columbia University Press, 1994, p. 190.
38. *Washington Report on Middle East Affairs*, August/September 1996, p. 104.
39. For statistical data about Israel's rate of economic growth and military strength, see *Statistical Yearbook 1993*. New York: United Nations, 1995, p. 160; *The Military Balance, 1994–1995*, op. cit., pp. 132–3.
40. I am very grateful to Professors Atul Kholi, Georg Sørensen, and James Richardson, Dr William Maley, and Mr Greg Fry for reading an earlier draft of this paper.

5

The problem of the failed state in Africa

Charles Abiodun Alao

Introduction: Of "states" and "failure"

The problem of state failure has recently become prominent in global vocabulary. While there may still be controversy as regards the appropriateness of this term, there seems to be little doubt as to what constitutes its characteristics. A state may be said to have "failed" when:

> ... as the decision-making centre ... the state is paralyzed and inoperative... As a symbol of identity, it has lost its power of conferring a name on its people ... as a territory, it is no longer assured security and provisionment by a central sovereign organization. As the authoritative political institution, it has lost its legitimacy, which is therefore up for grabs... It no longer receives support from nor exercises control over its people.[1]

Most of the states that have recently collapsed are in Africa, where the historically weak state structures were further weakened by colonialism and the activities of the élite class that took over the mantle of leadership at independence. This chapter takes a look at the problem of state failure in Africa, investigating the forces that underlie it and why these have been on the increase in the continent. It also considers the consequences, and what can be done to arrest this situation.

"Peculiar" characteristics of the state system in Africa

Africa has always been at the receiving end of global vicissitudes. Throughout its history, it has had to cope with successive pillaging, including African states pillaging each other. The devastation caused by the slave trade was followed by the exploitation of colonialism, which subsequently gave way to neo-colonialism and all its attendant implications. At independence, African countries also became members of an international system which they had taken no part in creating.

At the roots of most of the recent cases of state failure in Africa is the process of state formation. People of different ethnic, political and religious affiliations were brought together by colonialism to form states. So markedly was this policy adopted by the erstwhile colonial powers that, of all the countries in the continent, only the former Somali Republic was ethnically homogenous, and even this country was bedevilled by divisions along clan lines.[2] Thus at independence "the historical memory of these people is limited only to the common experience of a single colonial ruler and their collective struggle for independence."[3] In the post-independence years this was to make the establishment of harmonious citizenry extremely difficult.

Closely related to this is the difficulty created by the artificial nature of Africa's national boundaries, which divide individual ethnic groups between two or more nations. Apart from creating boundary problems between neighbouring countries, agitation for self-determination by partitioned ethnic groups and attempts at "reunification" further undermined weak state structures. Although at independence African countries realized the potential crisis of these boundaries, they nevertheless decided to respect them. This position could have been influenced by African leaders' traumatized perception of the violence that followed the partition of South Asia in 1947, and the fear that many of them may not have countries left to rule if boundaries were redrawn.[4]

A third characteristic is rooted in the nature of the economy African countries inherited at their independence. So much has been written on the subject that a summary will suffice.[5] The colonial incorporation of the African economy into the European capitalist framework created many structural deficiencies, making the economies "susceptible not only to internally generated crises ... but also to dislocations arising from the crises of global capitalism as refracted into the local economies."[6] This makes the economies too structurally weak to withstand the challenges of nation-building.

A final issue worth considering is the nature of the élites that took over the leadership of these countries at independence. In virtually all cases, these "inheritance élites" were more concerned with the desire to perpetuate themselves in power than to advance the interests of their fledging nations. This is largely because of the attraction of power and the fear of what life would be like outside office. The perpetuation was implemented through suppression, corruption, and the exploitation of primordial allegiances. In all the failed states, the role of the "élites," some of whom became warlords in their respective countries, has been redoubtable. It is no mere coincidence that all those who emerged as warlords in recently collapsed nations had played important political, economic, or military roles in the affairs of their respective countries before the collapse.

All the "peculiar" characteristics identified above are quite important in appreciating the problem of recent state failure. The first "wave" of failed states in the continent came towards the end of the second decade of independence. This was "when regimes that had replaced the original nationalist generation were overthrown, carrying the whole state structure with them into a vacuum."[7] States that collapsed during this phase include Chad and Uganda. The second wave came in the late 1980s, and continued into the 1990s. The concentration of this chapter is on the latter wave, because it has implications that could spread into the coming century, and also because most of the states affected by the first wave are now well on the path of recovery.

The causes of state failure in post-Cold War Africa

The meaning of the end of the Cold War has been widely interpreted, ranging from Francis Fukuyama's *End of History* to Samuel Huntington's *Clash of Civilization.*[8] Some of these implications as they relate to Africa have also received attention from scholars, the best known perhaps being Robert Kaplan's *The Coming Anarchy.*[9] While the debate rages on, what is certain is that, for Africa, the end of the Cold War has not resulted in the much-anticipated "peace dividend." In fact, there have been far more conflicts in the continent. Again, unlike during the Cold War, when the conceptualization of conflicts was easily fixable in the Cold War paradigm, post-Cold War conflicts have been more difficult to conceptualize.

"State failure" is an umbrella for various tendencies which are not always the same, but are united in demonstrating the inability to control. For example, the situation in Somalia, where warlords hijacked the initiative from a collapsing government, is different from Rwanda, where in 1994 there was a systematic state-induced massacre. Although the problem of "state failure" or threatened failure in Africa has gained momentum since the end of the Cold War, it was not entirely created by it. All that seems to have happened is that the end of the Cold War created legacies which shook the foundation of many governments, and those which could not stand the pressure ultimately collapsed. The post-Cold War disentanglement of superpower rivalry from African conflicts also meant that many of these conflicts had to seek "local" resources for their continuation. The pressure this brought on some countries hastened their disintegration.

For Africa, some of the interrelated causes of state failure in the post-Cold War period include the weakness of inherited state structures and their difficulties in coping with the post-Cold War transition; the downward plunge in the economic fortune of most African states; and the drastic rise in ethno-nationalism.

Weak state structures and the demands of "transition"

The inability to establish viable institutional structures after independence meant, among other things, that few African countries had strong democratic traditions. Most either had military regimes or were operating a one-party system. Even many of those professing democracy were de facto one-party states, as the ruling party always employed the "advantage of incumbency" to win successive elections. Apart from this, there was an absence of the social and economic structures that could enhance harmonious citizenry. For instance, in most countries the issue of accountability by holders of public offices was absent. While all these aberrations were condoned by the structures in place during the Cold War, the shift in global focus from "aid for ideology" to "aid for accountability" meant that many Africa countries had to "transform." The transition into the phase of accountability, democratic values, and institutional restructuring created a lot of difficulties, and it brought some African countries close to disintegration, especially those where the structures were already too weak to withstand the change.

The downward plunge in economic fortunes

Another cause for state failure in Africa has been the rise in the poverty level. Africa is currently the poorest continent in the world, with a debt of about US$135 billion as at February 1996.[10] This chapter does not attempt to consider the causes of Africa's economic problems, but rather their consequences, especially as they relate to state collapse. The main creditors of African states – the IMF and the World Bank – have always imposed the Structural Adjustment Policy (SAP) on countries as a means of solving their balance of budget problems. So much has been written on the effects of SAP on Africa that it serves no purpose going into any details here.[11] However, a major criticism that has often been levelled against these institutions is their introduction of "exactly the same structural adjustment package to all third world states irrespective of regional or national peculiarities and variations."[12] The standard IMF/World Bank package includes:

public sector enterprises' rationalization, which usually entails their abolition, privatization and commercialization; the liberalization of trade and payments; the deregulation of prices and interest rates; the removal of subsidies and the introduction of cost recovery measures; the vigorous pursuit of demand management and the introduction of measures to strengthen the supply base of the economy; the sharp reduction of public sector expenditure with a view to balancing the national budget; civil service reform and rationalization; and local currency exchange rate realignment which in all cases translates to massive devaluation.[13]

SAP has many effects associated with state failure, but two are discussed here. The first is its impact on socio-economic life. In all African countries, the implementation of SAP has resulted in a drastic reduction in the quality of life. Conditionalities like the removal of subsidies and the devaluation of currency have widened the poverty level and completely eliminated the middle class in some states. Other effects have been an increase in the army of jobless and discontented masses who are unable to make a meaningful living out of the depressed economy. This has also resulted in the destruction of the moral fabric of society. The restlessness that eventually emerged out of the brutalization and dehumanization of these populations was to combine with other factors to increase the propensity for the ultimate collapse of many countries.

A second direct link between SAP and state failure in Africa arises from the fact that most of the conditionalities often imposed by the IMF and the World Bank would require an authoritarian government to see them through. For example, because of the problems inherent in implementing policies like the removal of subsidies and the reduction of public sector expenditure, democratic government, with all the structures of checks and balances in place, would be reluctant to effect them. Thus, even if unwittingly, the IMF and the World Bank have through their policies encouraged the perpetration of authoritarianism in many African states. The link between authoritarianism and state failure is easily established, as authoritarian leaders often adopt policies to ensure their perpetual stay in power – leading to opposition from discontented groups.

The rise of ethno-nationalism

With the end of the Cold War has come a drastic increase in ethnic nationalism in Eastern Europe and Africa. This has been further exacerbated by the drastic reduction in the socio-economic well-being of most countries in the African continent. There is a debate as to whether the rise in ethnic nationalism is a cause or consequence of state collapse. In a recent study, Chris Smith and Dylan Hendrickson argue that the "phenomenon of ethnic divisions and tensions ... is perhaps best understood ... not as the cause of conflict, but as its consequences."[14] Experiences in Africa, however, seem not to support this position. Ethnic division could act both as a cause and as a consequence of conflict and eventual state collapse. For example, oppressive leadership could lead to ethnic division, which in turn could bring oppressed sections of a country together to challenge the central government. This was, at least to an extent, the beginning of the disintegration of Liberia. This tendency has increased in post-Cold War Africa, as the Cold War politics which had implicitly endorsed repression have disappeared.

Political fragmentation, however, may not necessarily translate as an ethnic phenomenon. On the contrary, it is indeed ironic that one of the countries which has experienced enormous fragmentation – Somalia – is perhaps the only country in the continent that is ethnically homogenous. An explanation for this has, however, been found in the country's complex clan system, which by and large operated along pseudo-ethnic lines. On the whole, political fragmentation along ethnic lines has been at the root of all state collapse in Africa. This is largely because ethnicity is the easiest and quickest process by which emotions could be harnessed to challenge what is often seen as an attempt to marginalize a group.

The political "bill of health": The "failed" and "failing" states in Africa

Three African states – Somalia, Liberia, and Rwanda – have collapsed in the last half a decade, while the socio-economic and political problems facing at least 20 others make complete collapse a distinct possibility. In a 1993 study, Nellier categorized these states as being in either "serious" or "maximum" danger of collapse.[15] In the "serious" category are Algeria, South Africa, the Sudan, Cameroon, Madagascar, Malawi, Kenya, Djibouti, Nigeria, the Niger, Togo, and Mali, while those on the "maximum" danger list are Angola, Mozambique, Rwanda, Burundi, the former Zaire, Ethiopia, Chad, and Sierra Leone. Although the concentration of this section is on the three states that have collapsed, there is a discussion, too, of some of the states in Nellier's "serious" and "maximum" categorization.

The political and socio-economic developments which ultimately resulted in state failure bring out some complexities. The Somali Republic owes its collapse to a number of factors, including the decline of external patronage that had sustained the corrupt and repressive regime of Siad Barre; the intense (largely man-made) famine that ravaged the country; the domestic opposition to the government's internal repression; and the country's defeat in the Ogaden war against Ethiopia. All these kept the country tottering on the brink of total collapse, such that by the end of the 1980s Somalia could be said to be on a life-support machine. The fact that most neighbouring countries, especially Ethiopia, Djibouti, the Sudan, Kenya, and Eritrea, were either recovering from wars or had serious domestic problems, too, did not help the Somali case. By 1991, the government of President Barre had collapsed. The competition to fill the vacuum resulted in a breakdown of law and order. Two "warlords" – Mohamed Farah Aideed and Ali Mahdi – among others, tore the country apart. The situation eventually deteriorated, to the extent that relief materials could not get to the starving population. It was this that eventually resulted in the concern of the international community.[17]

Liberia's gradual descent to its ultimate collapse began in December 1989, when Charles Taylor led the National Patriotic Front of Liberia (NPFL) to challenge the oppressive regime of the late President Samuel Doe. The initial NPFL recruits were taken from the Gio/Mano ethnic group, a group that had suffered enormous persecution under the government of President Doe.[18] The badly organized armed forces of Liberia could not counter the insurgent attack, and within weeks the government had collapsed and carnage had started in the country. The unparalleled nature of the destruction to life and property resulted in the despatch of a regional peace-keeping mission (named the ECOWAS Monitoring Group, ECOMOG).[19]

The war has now graduated from the initial ideological conflict to a complex intermix of personality and economic war. There are presently eight factions, formed along ethnic and religious lines.[20] ECOMOG, too, has become embroiled in the controversy, while a United Nations Observer Mission brought in to assist ECOMOG also found itself in a number of practical difficulties. Already the warring factions have signed 14 unsuccessful peace agreements. Finally, an accord established a "Council of State" – comprising the leaders of the major factions – to rule Liberia until May 1997, when an election took place in the country.

But the country that brought the ramifications of state failure to global attention was Rwanda, where within weeks of the outbreak of an ethnic conflict between the two major ethnic groups, almost half a million people had died and more than a million others had been displaced. In a way, Rwanda was a state that collapsed in instalments, and the roots of the 1994 crisis are deeply seated in the country's post-colonial politics. The nation is composed mainly of two major ethnic groups – the Hutus and the Tutsis.[21] The Hutus, about 80 per cent of the population, controlled the affairs of the country. Rivalry and tension between the two groups pre-dated independence, as the first clash between them took place in 1959. In a second attack that took place a year after independence in 1963, about 10,000 Tutsis were killed, while those who remained at home were ostracized and prevented from joining the army. Many of them fled to Uganda, where they eventually formed the Rwandan Patriotic Front (RPF), which opposed the Hutu-led government in Rwanda. They were later to receive considerable support from the government of President Yoweri Musoveni of Uganda.[22] All these made Rwandan politics inextricably linked with those of its neighbours, especially Uganda, Burundi, and the former Zaire.

The immediate catalyst of the Rwandan tragedy was the assassination in a plane crash of Juvenal Habyarimana and Cyprien Ntaryamira, Presidents of Rwanda and Burundi respectively. The Hutu-dominated Rwandan army accused the RPF of the assassination, a charge the latter denied, accusing in turn the Hutu Presidential Guards of killing the President to express their displeasure at his conciliatory policies towards the Tutsis.[23] Once the death was announced, Hutu soldiers went on a killing spree, targeting Tutsis and Hutu politicians believed to have political sympathy for the RPF.[24] This also resulted in a massive exodus of people from Rwanda into neighbouring countries, especially the former Zaire, where a cholera epidemic was to claim many lives.[25] The RPF marched towards the capital, Kigali, and by the end of July 1994 had captured the city and formed a new government.[26]

Apart from Somalia, Liberia, and Rwanda, a number of countries could be categorized as "wounded" states. In most cases, nations in this category are those which could collapse because of the serious political and economic problems that confront them. While it will not be possible here to go into a detailed discussion of the situation in these states, a brief mention of the important ones may be in order. In Nigeria, the "historical accidents of cultural pluralism and exploitative colonialism [have been compounded] by accountability and moral vacuum that had dogged its public service."[27] The country's uncoordinated search for a workable nation-building agenda was dealt two major blows in quick succession with the nullification of the 12 June 1993 election, and the incumbent government's hanging of nine minority human rights activists in November 1995. These two events brought Nigeria to the tribunal of international attention and led the nation down the path of collapse.

In 1996, Major Pierre Buyoya's military coup in Burundi caused considerable anxiety, largely because of the grave political situation in the country, and also because the Rwandan experience had shown how fast the explosion in the Great Lakes region could spread. Burundi has been facing a civil war since 1993, when Hutu rebels attacked the central government under the leadership of a Tutsi President. Although reliable figures are not available, it is estimated that more than 150,000 people have so far died. In the few months before the Buyoya coup, the former President Ntibantunganya was obviously losing his grip on power. The army, in particular, was getting uncomfortable with his policies. It was this gradual slide towards "another Rwanda" that Buyoya (a Tutsi) used to justify his July 1996 coup. He claimed that the coup was to prevent a *putsch* by Tutsi extremists from plunging the country into its worst crisis.[28] Although neighbouring countries have disagreed with him,[29] Buyoya has remained defiant that he would not "sacrifice" the lives of his people "for the sake of democracy."[30] Other countries like Sierra Leone, Senegal, Mauritania, Mali, and the Niger all face domestic instability of different magnitudes.

The security implications of failed states

There are many security complications associated with failed states. Some of those identified for discussion here include foreign involvement and its implications on national sovereignty; human casualties and their impact on security; mass migration and refugee influx; exportation of conflict and border incursion; proliferation of light weapons; the destruction of economic infrastructures; and the establishment of regional/continental conflict management strategies.

Foreign involvement and the erosion of sovereignty

With the collapse of states often comes urgent international response, either in the form of humanitarian actions and/or peace-keeping missions. This always results in the erosion of sovereignty of the affected states. International involvement always attract a mixture of appreciation and hostility. In Liberia, despite the total collapse of all infrastructures of governance, there are still many indigenes of the country who insist on retaining their consciousness of pride, honour, and independence. Some even want the extent of the interference of the regional peace-keeping force to be properly defined.[31] Rwanda expelled 39 non-governmental organizations from the country, accusing them, among other things, of interfering in the country's independence. In Somalia the initial affection that greeted "Operation Restore Hope" later changed, when warlords whipped up the emotion of sovereignty to reject all forms of foreign interference.

The implications of this are numerous. For example, it often creates a dilemma for the international community as to whether they should respect "sovereignty" in the quest to arrest an imminent human tragedy. The inability to resolve this dilemma quickly could cause delay and result in more loss of lives, while a wrong interpretation of the situation could lead to a faulty or inadequate response. Another security consequence of international involvement and the loss of sovereignty is the controversy it often creates among the nationals of the affected state. For example, the question of what should be the attitude towards ECOMOG has been as much of a problem between the Liberian warring factions as the original ideological cause of the conflict.

Human casualties and their impact on security

Perhaps the best-known security implication of state failure in Africa is its human casualties. Although accurate figures are very rarely available, it is believed that up to 200,000 people have died in the Liberian war. Somali figures are equally as high. The collapse of these countries also resulted in the death of foreigners who had gone into the conflicts to pacify the warring sides. But the country that brought the human cost of state collapse to the fore of global attention was Rwanda, with several hundreds of thousands killed. The consequences of the massive loss of lives for security are enormous. As the citizens of a country represent its first line of security, large-scale casualties deprive the country of not only those who can defend it in times of aggression, but also of those who can contribute manpower to its economic development. For Liberia, Somalia, and Rwanda, a complete generation has been depleted, such that even when peace eventually returns, getting the necessary manpower to ensure nation-building could create fresh problems.

Migration and refugee influx

Closely related to the casualty problem is the effect of population displacement and the influx of refugees. In Liberia, several hundreds of thousands were displaced both within and outside the nation. Inside the country there has been mass movement from the countryside to the capital, Monrovia. At one stage it was speculated that the capital contained more than a million inhabitants – nearly a third of the country's population. With such a congested and destroyed infrastructure came health risks which have been difficult to contain, despite the extent of the humanitarian assistance. Apart from the problem of internal displacement, more than a million Liberians are now refugees in neighbouring Sierra Leone, Guinea, Ghana, and Nigeria. For some of these countries, especially Sierra Leone and Guinea, their already limited national resources were further depleted by the influx of Liberian refugees, heightening the propensity for internal tension within these states. The situation in Rwanda was the most serious. Up to a million people moved to neighbouring countries, especially the former Zaire, in what humanitarian agencies described as the worst mass migration in recent history. The outbreak of a cholera epidemic created further problems in the refugee camps. Somali refugees are in the neighbouring nations of Ethiopia, Kenya, and Djibouti.

There are a number of major security problems associated with a refugee influx, especially in the depressed economy now prevailing in most African nations. First, the competition between the refugees and their hosts over scarce resources often results in conflict. The oft-cited traditional hospitality of African people towards foreigners has now been proven to be resource-availability dependent. Second, there have been cases where refugees have exploited their hosts' hospitality to launch attacks on their home states. As it is difficult for host states to monitor the activities of refugees, tension often ensued between the host nation and the refugees' home states. The recent problem in the Rwandan refugee camps in the former Zaire brings out some of the security implications of this problem.

Proliferation of light weapons

The problem of light weapon proliferation first became pronounced in the aftermath of the wars of liberation in Africa, especially in the southern part of the continent. In recent years, however, the problem has become more associated with failed states. In Somalia, Liberia, and Rwanda, one of the greatest security problems is how to control the light weapons which have found their ways into illegal hands. With the collapse of these countries, all armed factions eventually obtained arms to continue the factional fighting. In some states, especially Liberia and Somalia, warlords purchase arms from different sources to sustain their factions. Once the proliferation has become large-scale, as it is in all these countries, control is difficult. In Liberia, all the efforts of ECOMOG and UNOMIL (United Nations Operations to Liberia) to disarm the factions have been ineffective. One of the consequences of this massive proliferation is the increase in armed robbery, which could continue long after the cessation of the conflicts in these countries.[32] Another consequence is the possibility of the problem spreading to neighbouring countries.

Destruction of economic infrastructure

In all cases, the destruction of physical economic infrastructures is an integral part of state collapse. Here again actual figures are not available, but the implications have been enormous. The war in Liberia, for example, left major installations such as airports, seaports, roads, bridges, and other transportation networks completely destroyed. Similarly, industries such as mining and iron and steel production have been rendered ineffective. The country's rubber plantation at Firestone, reputed to be the largest in the world, has stopped production. The same applies to Somalia, where structures have either been destroyed or fallen under the control of war-lords who collect taxes to pay their armies. The situation in Rwanda is the same, as many parts of the country were destroyed in the fighting that began immediately after the assassination of the President. However, things seem to be getting better in Rwanda.

Another dimension to the destruction of the economic infrastructure has been the looting activities of warlords. This has been most prevalent in Liberia, and to an extent in Somalia. In Liberia, all the warring factions have carved the country into economic spheres of influence, and illegal mining of iron and diamonds is rampant. The money made from this has been used to finance the war. The situation painted here has a number of security implications. First, it is putting in serious danger the chances of post-war recovery, a situation which, in turn, could create a vicious cycle of conflict. Second, it is prolonging the civil wars, as competition over areas of economic interest often leads to the destruction of such areas.

Exportation of conflict and border incursion

As ethnic groups in Africa do cut across national boundaries, the implications of state failure often result in the exportation of conflict to neighbouring nations. Liberian warring factions often make incursions into the neighbouring countries of Guinea and Sierra Leone, threatening the lives and property of their inhabitants. One of the Liberian warring factions, the United Liberian Movement for Democracy (ULIMO), was in fact formed in Guinea.[33] Apart from military incursions, the collapse of Liberia has resulted in a civil war in Sierra Leone, with the NPFL of Liberia arming a rebel movement – the Revolutionary United Front (RUF) – to destabilize the government of former President Joseph Momoh. In the Gambia, the Liberian conflict resulted in the overthrow of the government of President Dauda Jawara, thereby ending the history of democratic rule in the country.[34]

There is also an inseparable link in the causes of the conflict in Rwanda and that in neighbouring Burundi. The problem in the two countries is rooted in the unending rivalry between the two main ethnic groups – the Hutus and the Tutsis – for power and resources. The similarity in the social composition almost automatically makes the conflicts in the two countries contagious. As mentioned earlier, a major crisis has been brewing in Burundi since the Rwandan explosion of 1994. The situation is slightly less serious in Somalia, due largely to the ethnic uniformity of the country and the fact that most of the neighbouring countries had other important reasons to embark on inter- and intra-factional squabbles.

Establishment of regional/continental security strategies and their socio-economic and military implications

In the face of insecurity and instability resulting from failed states, regional and subregional organizations (the OAU and the Economic Community of West African States – ECOWAS) have found it necessary to interfere to restore some measure of stability in the targeted states. This has had immense implications. The best example here is the ECOMOG involvement in Liberia. This establishment of regional mediatory efforts has both negative and positive sides. On the negative side, it could create discontent among the citizens of countries bearing the brunt of such an arrangement. For example, the entire ECOMOG operation has caused opposition within Nigeria, as its citizens question the wisdom of such an involvement at a period of dire economic need for the country. On the positive dimension, however, is the shared sense of responsibility to resolve regional problems locally, especially when the end of the Cold War has led to a reduction of foreign interest in Africa.

Democratization after state collapse

A crucial question concerns the process of democratization after state collapse. The speed at which such states should embark on the process of democratization, and the form the democracy should take, have been important issues. One noticeable feature of the states that have achieved some degree of success in democratic reform after collapse is that, in all cases, a faction had emerged as an undisputed winner, and had imposed its own form of democratic values on the country. Examples of this include Chad, Ethiopia, and Uganda. In all these cases, the dominant group incorporated other elements into the ruling coalition. "While power sharing may not qualify for democracy in the true definition of the word, particularly as it works against a major quality of democracy, accountability, it has proved to be the first step."[35]

Of all the countries that have put in place a version of democracy after the collapse of state structures, Uganda, under Yoweri Musoveni, presents an interesting case. On his assumption of power, Musoveni initiated an agenda that emphasized democracy, security, national unity, and the restoration of the economy. This led to the creation of a "no-party" democracy that is now operational in the country. Under this scheme, the "Resistance Committees" organized in rural areas during the war against the Obote regime were institutionalized after the National Resistance Movement assumed power. Thus representation in government for people in rural areas is effected through these committees. This unique method gives the people the impression that they are being represented in the management of the state, thereby having a version of democracy without having political parties. While this method has both adherents and critics, what it shows clearly is that once a state has collapsed additional tools may be required to handle transition to democracy

The United Nations in Africa's "divided" nations

The increase in the number of failed and weak states in Africa has forced the United Nations to have greater involvement in the continent. This has been evident in three main ways: physical presence through the despatch of personnel (military and/or civilian peace-keeping missions); the despatch of teams to investigate and offer suggestions on states that are at the highest risk of collapsing; and the involvement of UN agencies in the socio-economic life of failed states. In all three spheres the United Nations has been criticized, either for coming in too late, or for doing too little even after its entrance. So pronounced have been the criticisms against the United Nations that some commentators have argued that the plight of the affected countries could have been less severe if the organization had not intervened. This section provides a critique of UN activities in these countries.

In Liberia, the United Nations got in late. This was largely because the crisis began at a time when the organization was preoccupied with the Iraqi invasion of Kuwait. The initial involvement of the United Nations in the Liberian civil war was thus to give the ECOWAS peace initiative all the support it needed to arrest the situation in the country. When, however, the ECOWAS peace efforts could not solve the problem with despatch, the United Nations began a more active involvement in the conflict. Under the Cotonou Agreement signed by the Liberian warring factions in July 1993, the United Nations was invited to monitor the cease-fire and disarmament processes. The United Nations was to work with ECOMOG, with the latter taking on the military aspects of the exercise and the United Nations monitoring activities to ensure impartiality.[36] This ECOMOG/UN arrangement is particularly important, as it was the first time that the United Nations and a regional organization had worked together to pacify a civil society.

On the whole, UNOMIL has been only partially successful. First, the relationship between ECOMOG and UNOMIL has never been cordial. They see each other more as rivals, instead of allies in a common cause.[37] ECOMOG soldiers are particularly resentful of UNOMIL because of what they perceive as the arrogant tendencies of the United Nations team; while UNOMIL, on its part, criticizes ECOMOG's peace-keeping methods. Second, UNOMIL has suffered from the general cash shortage affecting the United Nations. On several occasions, the UN Secretary-General complained that the Liberia operation ran the danger of being stopped if there was no financial assistance to continue the project. Finally, there are allegations from Liberians that UNOMIL officials do not sympathize with the prevailing socio-economic poverty in the country. Many Liberians allege that UNOMIL officials are fond of driving expensive vehicles around the capital.[38] It was thus not surprising that the organization was a target of much attack during the April 1996 re-emergence of conflict in Liberia.[39]

The criticism against the United Nations in Somalia was more profound. The timing, the extent, and the sincerity of the involvement have been criticized.[40] Where it was not considered inadequate, it was seen as being late. First, the withdrawal of UN officials after the fall of President Barre on the grounds of insecurity was roundly condemned. The refusal of the United Nations to respond to the gathering tragedy in Somalia during this period was seen as showing a lack of concern for the plight of the Somalians. When eventually the United Nations acknowledged the tragedy in the country, with the passing of UN Security Council Resolution 733 of January 1992, it still did not follow this up with full commitment. The despatch of the UN Secretary-General's special representative, James Jonah, to Somalia was seen as aggravating the problem, as he was alleged to have allowed the visit to be manipulated by the late General Mohamed Farah Aideed, to the objection of other factions and neutral Somalians.[41]

The next two UN Security Council resolutions on Somalia (Resolutions 746 of March 1992 and 751 of April 1992) did not advance the ending of the conflict in any way. The first merely called on the warring factions to respect the lives of relief workers, while the other agreed in principle to send in a UN security force. However, it took another four months before the US airlift began. Even after this, no impressive international presence was achieved until December 1992. This failure to act decisively to implement the Security Council resolutions has proved disastrous in Somalia.

The UN's reaction to the Rwandan crisis was similar to that in Somalia. Against the background that the United Nations had a mission in the country before the outbreak of the 1994 violence, many expected the organization to have a more articulate and organized response to the outbreak of violence in the country.[42] Among others, two initial errors by the United Nations are worthy of note. The first was that the United Nations Mission in Rwanda (UNAMIR) stuck to its initial mandate of not using force even after the massacre of the Tutsis by the Hutus had begun. This affected the credibility of the force, as it was seen as the UN's implicit endorsement of the Hutu actions. The problem was compounded by the UN Secretary-General's decision to withdraw all but 270 of the UN soldiers. To reduce the strength of the force at a time when a reinforcement was needed was seen by many as being unjustifiable. Secondly, the United Nations may have again unwittingly added to the initial confusion by its announcement on 8 April 1994 that the Tutsi RPF (Rwandan Patriotic Front) had left its Mulundi base and was expected to move on to Kigali the following day. This report was false, but its announcement – coming from the credible UNAMIR – could have led the Hutu militias to increase the killings.

The involvement of the United Nations in despatching missions to weak states has resulted in UN mediation missions visiting countries like Burundi and Western Sahara. These missions have often faced financial problems, but the action has been largely successful. Its most important advantage is that it keeps the situation in these countries under constant watch, thereby preventing conflicts from emerging. The activities of the UN agencies have mostly been in countries that are either at war or where there have been natural tragedies like famine. These activities have again been remarkable, and have done a lot to make life bearable for affected populations all across Africa. The basic problem, however, is shortage of funds, especially with the ever-increasing complex emergencies in the continent. Although these agencies are already being supported by other non-governmental organizations from Western European countries, their activities have not yet equalled the extent of the devastation.

Reducing the risks of failure: Some policy recommendations

The increase in the number of states that are structurally weak makes it necessary to proffer suggestions on how to reduce what now seems to be one of the major problems facing the international community. A major solution often advanced is the need to reduce or cancel the debt burden on African countries. Although there can be no doubt that the debt problem is linked with state failure, and that the cancellation could resuscitate some of the "wounded" states, debt relief could only be helpful if it came as a part of a package. Experience across the continent has shown that there are no guarantees that the resources saved as a result of debt relief would go into development of the state. However, countries that have completely collapsed would need financial assistance. There could be a vicious cycle of violence if they are to confront the problems of post-war reconstruction amidst the debt burden that presently weighs on their shoulders.

A second suggestion is the need to give assistance to African countries in their search for enduring democratic traditions. This could be done by ostracizing the military and undemocratic regimes in the continent. In the same vein, regimes known to be violating the human rights of their citizens should be tagged pariah states. This will give autocratic leaders the message that they cannot oppress their people with impunity. A final suggestion is the establishment of a committee of respected African statesmen to mediate in brewing African conflicts. Since the OAU Mediation Committee that was established for this assignment has failed, a committee of elder statesmen may offer a better chance. With the ranks of such people increasing, the chances of success become higher. Respected leaders like the Mwalimu Julius Nyerere of Tanzania, Kenneth Kaunda of Zambia, and Olusegun Obasanjo of Nigeria (if and when he is released from jail) could be in this committee.

Conclusion

It is difficult to make any major predictions on the future of the African states that have collapsed. Rwanda seems to be settling down, although the development in Burundi does not augur well for the entire Great Lakes region. The West African leaders have developed a fresh agenda for Liberia.[43] Under the new scheme, disarmament began in November 1996 and an election took place in May 1997. To prevent a relapse into violence, any warlords who violate this arrangement would be banned from travelling within the region and would be recommended to be tried by a war crimes tribunal. The latest agreement goes further than previous versions, but after 14 agreements have failed, it would be naïve to believe that this latest one will make a difference. However, a national government comprising all the warring factions could be the only guarantee of enduring peace in the country.

Those who thought that Somalia's problem could take a positive step towards peace with the death of Mohamed Farah Aideed in July 1996 should now see that their optimism was misplaced. The country has not even stopped intra-clan struggle. The appointment of Aideed's son, Hussein, as the clan leader has now introduced a new dimension to the problem: a clash between the older members of the clan who rejected him on the grounds of his youth, and the younger elements who see his appointment as a way of reducing the generational gap between the leaders and the led.[44]

On the whole, it may be said that Africa is entering the twenty-first century as a continent that is still badly divided and structurally weak. The defence and security problems that could confront the continent in the coming century will largely be the legacies of this present century. Economically, Africa will have to use its limited resources to address its apparently limitless problems. Politically, efforts to establish enduring democratic institutions will have to continue. However, it would appear that the greatest challenge the continent will face in the coming century will be that of preventing more state collapse while reconstructing failed states on a slender budget. The continent looks up to the United Nations and its dominant actors to assist in this endeavour.

Notes

1. I. William Zartman, "Introduction: Posing the Problem of State Collapse," in I. William Zartman (ed.), *Collapsed States: The Disintegration and Restoration of Legitimate Authority*, Boulder and London: Lynne Rienner Publishers, 1995.
2. Some studies which discuss this topic as well as its implications for the post-independent state include Kenneth Ingham, *Politics in Modern Africa: the Uneven Tribal Dimension*, London: Routledge, 1990; Antoina Lema, *Africa Divided: The Creation of Ethnic Groups*, Lund: Lund University Press, 1993; Okwudiba Nnoli, *Ethnicity and Democracy in Africa: Intervening Variables*, Lagos: Malthouse Press, 1994; and Ehosa Osaghae, *Ethnicity and Its Management: The Democratization Link*, Lagos: Malthouse Press, 1994.
3. Simeon Ilesanmi, "The Myth of a Secular State: A Study of Religious Politics with Historical Illustration," *Islam and Christian-Muslim Relations*, vol. 6, 1, 1995, p. 111.
4. Jeffery Hebst, "Is Nigeria a Viable State?" *The Washington Quarterly*, vol. 19, 2, Spring 1996, p. 152.
5. Perhaps the best-known study in this respect is Walter Rodney, *How Europe Underdeveloped Africa*, Washington, DC: Howard University Press, 1981. Other studies include Koponen Juhani, *Development for Exploitation: German Colonial Policies in Mainland Tanzania, 1884–1914*, Helsinki: Finnish Historical Society, 1995; Bruce Fetter, *Colonial Rule and Regional Imbalance in Central Africa*, Boulder: Westview, 1983; Bill Guest and John Sellers, *Enterprise and Exploitation in a Victorian Colony: Aspects of the Economic and Social History of Colonial Natal*, Pietermaritzburg: University of Natal Press, 1985.
6. Adebayo Olukoshi, "Structural Adjustment Programmes in West Africa: An Overview," in Adebayo Olukoshi, Omotayo Olaniyan, and Femi Aribisala (eds.), *Structural Adjustment in West Africa*, Lagos: Pumark, 1994, p. 28.
7. I. William Zartman, op. cit., p. 2.
8. See Francis Fukuyama, "The End of History?" *The National Interest*, (16) 1989, and Samuel Huntington, "The Clash of Civilization," *Foreign Affairs*, Summer 1993.
9. Robert Kaplan, "The Coming Anarchy," *The Atlantic Monthly*, February 1994.
10. *West Africa*, 12–18 February 1996, p. 217
11. For more on the impact of SAP in Africa, see (among others) T. Nkandiwire and A. Olukoshi (eds.), *The Politics of Structural Adjustment in Africa*, Dakar: Cordesria

Books, 1994; Havevik Kjell, *IMF and the World Bank in Africa: Conditionality and Its Impacts*, Uppsalla: SIIA, 1987; Adedotun Phillips and Eddy Ndekwu (eds.), *SAP in a Developing Economy*, Ibadan, 1987.

12. Adebayo Olukoshi, "Structural Adjustment Programmes in West Africa," p. 28.
13. Ibid., p. 29.
14. Chris Smith and Dylan Hendrickson, *The Dynamics of Security and Development: State Failure and Emerging Patterns of Conflict*, submitted to the Defence Evaluation and Research Agency, March 1996, p. 27.
15. J. Nellier, "States in Danger," mimeo, cited in Smith and Hendrickson.
16. Since 1993, when Nellier's study was published, there have been obvious shifts in this categorization. For example, with the establishment of some form of order in Mozambique, the country is no longer in the "maximum" categorization, while Nigeria seems to have slopped into the "maximum" danger list.
17. I. M. Lewis, *Understanding Somalia: Guide to Culture, History, and Social Institutions*, London: LSE, June 1993.
18. Doe was from the Krahn ethnic group. The root of his hatred of the Gio/Mano people was the abortive coup organized against him by the former commander of the armed forces of Liberia, Thomas Quiwonkpa, who was of the Gio/Mano ethnic group.
19. The team was initially composed of troops from Nigeria, Ghana, Sierra Leone, Gambia, and Guinea. At different stages, a number of other countries like Senegal, Uganda, and Tanzania contributed troops to the mission. Nigeria's contribution has always remained the largest, and this has give the ECOMOG operation distinct Nigerian traits.
20. These factions are the National Patriotic Front of Liberia (NPFL), the Central Revolutionary Council of the National Patriotic Front of Liberia (CRC-NPFL), the United Liberation Movement of Liberia Kromah (ULIMO K), the United Liberation Movement of Liberia Johnson (ULIMO J), the Liberian Peace Council (LPC), the Boni County Council (BCC), the Lofa Defence Force (LDF) and the Liberian National Congress (LNC).
21. There is another ethnic group, known as the Twa, but this group is small and has not contributed much to the crisis that started unfolding in 1994.
22. The Tutsi refugees had earlier assisted President Musoveni in his guerrilla war that ultimately deposed the government of former President Obote. There were rumours later that Musoveni's support for the RPF was predetermined by the fact that he himself is originally a Tutsi. This was, however, emphatically denied.
23. The late President was killed on his way from Tanzania, after attending a meeting on the resolution of the conflict in his country. He had earlier shown willingness to share power with the Tutsis.
24. For more detailed information on the outbreak of the conflict, see Lindsey Hilsum, "Rwanda: The Day the Genocide Started," *BBC Focus on Africa*, July–September 1994, pp. 6–8.
25. For more on the involvement of neighbouring countries in the Rwandan problem, see Jinmi Adisa, *The Comfort of Strangers: The Impact of Rwandan Refugees on Neighbouring Countries*, Nairobi and Ibadan: UNCHS and IFRA, 1996.
26. See, for more on the Rwandan problem, Abiodun Alao, "The Rwandan Crisis – Incident, Prelude, or Warning?," *Jane's Intelligence Review*, vol. 6, 10, October 1994.
27. Simeon Ilesanmi, op. cit., p. 105.
28. See "Sanctions Slapped on Buyoya," *Africa Today*, vol. 2, 5, September/October 1996, p. 9.
29. The neighbouring countries have now imposed an economic sanction on the Buyoya government, and the OAU has given the countries an implicit endorsement.
30. See "Sanctions Slapped on Buyoya."

31. This takes the form of persistent calls for a "Status of Forces Agreement."
32. An example of this could be seen in the case of Nigeria after the end of the country's civil war in 1970. The proliferation of weapons resulted in a massive increase in cases of armed robbery, and the Federal Government of Nigeria was forced to promulgate a decree ordering execution by firing squad of those found guilty of armed robbery.
33. This was the original ULIMO, before it broke into two factions. The main ethnic group in the original ULIMO is the Madingos, and this group also formed a major percentage of the ethnic group in Guinea.
34. Those who planned the coup that overthrew the government of President Jawara conceived the plan while they were serving as part of the Gambian contingent in ECOMOG, and executed it immediately they got back to their country.
35. Sola Akinrinade, "Democracy and Security in Africa: Towards a Framework of Understanding." Paper presented at the African Security Seminar Series, Department of War Studies, King's College, London, February 1997.
36. It should be noted that at this time ECOMOG had become unpopular with some of the Liberian factions, especially the NPFL, which has accused the regional peace-keeping mission of being partial towards other factions.
37. Evidence gathered on my research visits to Liberia.
38. Discussions with Liberians during my field trips.
39. UNOMIL head office in the exclusive Mamba Point district of Monrovia was destroyed and looted. Expensive UN vehicles were driven to the borders of neighbouring towns, where they were sold at ridiculous prices.
40. For what appears to be a damming report of the United Nations' involvement in Somalia, see "Somalia Beyond the War Lords: The Need for a Verdict on Human Rights Abuses," *Africa Watch*, vol. V, 2, 7 March 1993.
41. To register their objection, the airport in Mogadishu was shelled during his visit and had to be closed down for almost two weeks, a situation which again complicated relief operations.
42. The United Nations Mission in Rwanda (UNAMIR) had been in the country since October 1993 to keep peace between the RPF and the government forces.
43. At a meeting in August 1996, held at the Nigerian capital of Abuja.
44. See "Somalia After Aideed," *Africa Today*, September/October 1996, p. 12.

6

Conclusion

Atul Kohli and Georg Sørensen

The chapters in this section have sought to assess how the state system is changing and the implications of these changes, both for patterns of conflict and for management of conflict – especially the role of the United Nations. These are big issues, and many people are contemplating them. Based on these four chapters, we offer some tentative but important conclusions.

- First, states are not going away. In spite of pressures from "above" and "below," and in spite of the unleashing of markets globally, what is really happening is that states, instead of shrinking, are mainly refocusing. That is, instead of talking about states "losing out" in current developments, what happens is that states are changing – growing even stronger in some respects and weaker in others.

- It is misleading to speak of a "world order," the term made popular by President Bush in 1990. We do not have a world order in the sense of a universal order where all individuals have equal rights. What we do have is an international order, based on a system of sovereign states. States are the basic units in the international system. International law is written for, about, and by states. Individuals also have rights, of course, but they have them primarily through states. That is why individuals without states (stateless), and individuals in malfunctioning, failed states, are in a very critical situation.

- Aside from the issue of the world becoming more or less statist, the international system of states consists of a variety of types of states.

While post-modern states in parts of the North develop new forms of intense cooperation, severe domestic conflict plagues the unsubstantial states in parts of the South. At the same time, modernizing states in parts of Asia are involved in intense arms races and balance-of-power rivalries. There are some indications of a more regionalized, segregated world, moving in qualitatively different directions.

- The major global power, the United States, is not likely to provide constructive leadership that will facilitate the emergence of a multipolar, multilateral, cooperative international order. That poses severe problems for international cooperation in general and for the United Nations in particular. Without support from the predominant power in the system, the United Nations faces severe limitations in its capacity for constructive conflict resolution and management.
- A number of existing/emerging powers will continue to assert themselves. China, India, Iran, Iraq, and Israel are of paramount importance in their respective regional contexts, and their actions can have repercussions for the entire system. These states will remain highly sovereignty/security-conscious, occasionally cooperative, but also occasionally belligerent.
- Problems of failed states have deep structural roots and are neither likely to vanish, nor readily be dealt with. There was state failure earlier, during the Cold War, but the problem has become more acute since 1990. The withdrawal of the United States and the former Soviet Union from the third world has had the side-effect of intensifying domestic conflict, which has also been fuelled by demands of drastic economic and political reforms.

Overall, the global picture that emerges is not very optimistic. It is certainly not the "end of history," though it is also not an impending "clash of civilizations." The more nuanced view suggests that conventional inter-state conflicts will coexist with a variety of newer conflicts in the twenty-first century (intra-state implosions; ethnic conflicts, even in well-established states; economic conflicts). The weakest, unsubstantial states with their high levels of domestic conflict will present an increasing dilemma for the United Nations, because large-scale domestic conflict presents an awkward problem for a collective security system based on sovereign states.

While it will be fruitful for the United Nations to open up a more intensive dialogue with representatives from societies, including non-governmental organizations, the core basis for the United Nations will continue to be a compact with leading states. Without such a basis, the United Nations will not be able to perform its several tasks. Given the fact that the international system remains in basic respects a system of sovereign states, the United Nations will not become a global manager in the sense of a quasi-world government to which member states cede substantial elements of sovereignty.

Yet the United Nations will not go the other extreme either. It will not be reduced to a global council which is powerless in the conventional sense and which exercises influence only through prestige and the quality of its ideas. Our analyses suggest a role for the United Nations which is somewhere in between – we might call it global coordinator. The United Nations will remain crucially dependent on member states, but given the complexity of international conflict after the Cold War, many member states are now willing to let the United Nations play a more predominant role in certain areas.

One of these areas concerns humanitarian intervention in failed states. Furthermore, any sustainable solution to the problem of failed states, be it in terms of changing borders and creating new sovereign entities, or in terms of new forms of democratization with minority guarantees, will have to substantially involve the United Nations. And there is a host of other issues in the larger area, or different conflicts identified above, where a strong role for the United Nations will be necessary.

Maybe this is the core challenge for the United Nations in the next century: to maintain and build on support from the international system of sovereign states while also utilizing that basis to build a stronger and more efficient – and in some respects more independent – position as global coordinator.

Transnational civil society actors and the quest for security

7

Introduction

Volker Rittberger, Christina Schrade, and Daniela Schwarzer

A crucial characteristic of the international political system, distinguishing it clearly from domestic systems of political organization, is the fact that there is no central authority with a legal competence and the material resources to guarantee the compliance of states and other actors with international norms and rules. The absence of a government with a legal monopoly of physical force in the international system leads realist theorists of international relations to the conclusion that the international system necessarily has to be a self-help system made up of unitary state actors. Order, in this context, results exclusively from the balance-of-power (or threat) mechanism, but not from cooperatively constructed systems of norms and rules among international actors.

This theoretical view of international politics, especially prominent during the Cold War, has come under increased attack in recent years. Critics of the realist view have argued that the international system today is not exclusively constituted of state actors competing for power and autonomy, and constrained by prudence or overwhelming (threat of) force only. On the contrary, based on unambiguous empirical evidence, there now exists a consensus that international politics – even in the absence of a central governing authority – is becoming increasingly rule-governed and non-anarchical. States do not operate in a space void of norms and rules, but rather in a social construction that has "material consequences and constrains action as well as perception."[1]

The concept that has been coined to describe this system is that of international or global "governance without government."[2] According to these authors, governance with or without government "refers to purposive systems of rule or normative orders," which are "the result of several ... efforts of social engineering. In the case of governance without government, obligations do not emanate from a hierarchical norm- and rule-setting and -enforcement process (government), but from voluntary agreements to play by a set of rules which are binding," not because of the threat of physical force but because of the perceived legitimacy of the rules and their underlying norms. Governance without government, therefore, is the "result of non-hierarchical, voluntary self-organization,"[3] based on institutionalized regulatory arrangements as well as on less formalized norms, rules, and procedures for interaction in recurring problematic social situations, which induce state (and non-state) actors in the international arena "to get things done without the legal competence to command that they be done."[4]

The terms "complex international governance"[5] or "regulated anarchy"[6] have been introduced as alternative labels to "governance without government" in order to emphasize the diversity and complexity of coexisting "steering" and "control mechanisms"[7] in contemporary international relations.

International regimes are, although the most important, only one of several mechanisms of collective self-regulation by states and other international actors.[8] Nevertheless, neoliberal regime theory, like realist theory, focuses on national governments as central actors in international governance: "international regimes seem to ... serve the specific interests of states and governments."[9] Regime theory, therefore, largely neglects non-governmental actors in the analysis of international governance.[10] This state-centric analytical bias was criticized in the first debate on transnationalism in the 1970s.[11] The end of the East–West conflict, however, initiated a second debate about the role of non-governmental actors.[12] In the context of an increasingly globalized system, the activities and impact of non-state actors in realms which were formerly exclusively the object of sovereign state action have intensified remarkably. This phenomenon has forced political scientists to pay more attention to non-state actors in the analysis of international politics, particularly to the question how non-governmental organizations (NGOs), transnational corporations (TNCs), governments, and intergovernmental organizations "grope, sometimes cooperatively, sometimes competitively, sometimes parallel towards a modicum of 'global governance.'"[13] The question of who are the relevant actors of international politics and how complex international steering mechanisms can become is now being discussed in this light.

The UN21 project pays tribute to the growing density, public visibility, and influence of non-governmental actors in international governance. In accordance with the differentiation between the state on the one hand, and the economy or market as well as civil society on the other,[14] the UN21 project has initiated research on non-governmental actors. In particular, attention is given to transnational (business) corporations as the central actors of the world market sphere. Operating legally across borders, the principal aim of these "market forces" is legitimate (legal) profit-making. Research also focuses on another set of non-governmental actors, constituting what is frequently termed an emerging "global civil society."

A first step toward constructing our analytical framework will be to elaborate a working definition of the concept of global civil society – a concept very much in vogue these days but seldom defined by those who use it. Next, we will distinguish three types of civil society actors according to their principal aims and strategies. Having thus laid the conceptual groundwork for the analysis of societal actors, we will turn to the issue area – international security – that was chosen as the focus of the research agenda for 1996. Using a three-level security concept, it will be shown that certain types of civil society actors concentrate their activities on one level of security more than on another, and that each of the actor types analyzed in the chapters by Koch, Morrison/Blair, Smith, and Williams[15] is especially relevant to one specific level of security. The following part of this chapter summarizes the findings of the four studies by comparing the strategies, challenges, and problems of the three types of civil society actors in the security area. Finally, we will ask what impact their activities have on the three levels of security, and how far they can be held to contribute to the democratization of international politics.

The concept of an emerging global civil society

The concept of civil society

Initially developed in the context of the nation-state, the concept of civil society has increasingly been applied to the analysis of international relations. Before assessing the validity of this concept in a global context, it seems reasonable to trace its defining characteristics in its initial national context.

According to Walzer,[16] "the words 'civil society' name the space of uncoerced human association and also the set of relational networks – formed for the sake of family, faith, interest, and ideology – that fill this space." This definition emphasizes three relevant aspects. The first one is uncoerciveness: the protection of the societal sphere from governmental encroachment and the possession of a degree of autonomy necessary for independent action. Indeed, by definition, civil society operates outside state institutions within a public sphere which is not monopolized by the state: civil society is "a sphere of social interaction distinct from economy and the state, composed above all of associations (including the family) and publics."[17] The second aspect crucial to the concept of civil society which can be deduced from Walzer's definition is the notion of shared basic values and identity. There is no civil society without common norms and codes of behaviour which shape the interaction of its members. Crucial to the existence of a civil society is "a set of fundamental principles which define the nature and purpose of social actors."[18] The notion of "human association" can be identified as a third characteristic. Group-building, formal or informal, interaction, and networking are the structural characteristics of civil society.

Towards a transnational or global civil society?

The acknowledgement of the growing importance of societal actors operating across state boundaries has led to the introduction of the notion of an emerging transnational or global civil society in academic and political discourse.[19] Bearing in mind the definition cited above, the question arises of whether the concept of civil society, initially linked to the framework of the nation-state and hence corresponding to the national territory and political community, can be applied to the phenomena we witness on the global level. Does the way in which non-state actors expand and connect their activities across state boundaries imply the emergence of a global civil society? Can the emergence of a common identity and common values, which are crucial to the concept of civil society, be observed on the global level?

Taking into account the increasing scope and density of transnational activities (the conditions and implications of which we will discuss later), we can assume that at least some conditions are fulfilled in order to be able to speak of an emerging transnational or global civil society. The fact that individuals increasingly and continuously interact cross-nationally, and organize themselves in international non-governmental organizations (INGOs), corresponds to the aspect of human association, the structural characteristic of civil society observed in the nation-state context. These group formation processes and their increasing frequency and density clearly take place outside state institutions. Although contact and interaction with state institutions is not excluded, and in many cases even intentionally pursued, INGOs are largely autonomous actors. However, governments sometimes use the form of an INGO for the purpose of either hiding their pursuit of unseemly objectives or pursuing publicly declared goals more efficiently; in these instances, the literature refers to the instrumentalization of this institutional form as a "quasi-autonomous non-governmental organization" (quango).

It may have been exactly this aspect – the widening and deepening of transnational communication and interaction among societal groups and their organizations – which led scholars of international relations and of sociology alike to study the space between the state and the economy on the international level, and to introduce the concept of civil society to this level.

The formal and informal cross-national group-building processes support the development of common norms and values which transcend national boundaries. Examples include the promotion of human rights and environmental protection, as well as sustainable development and women's rights. These are seen as constituting the basis of "a healthier and more sustainable world civilization [based on] values of empowerment, i.e. egalitarian, people-centred forms of social action."[20]

Thus, although it is evident that "national loyalties are not being superseded by global or regional loyalties,"[21] the fact that something like a "global consciousness" is developing, that "people's identification with and ideational support for global causes and global conceptions of citizenship"[22] is growing – even if not in a linear and universal process – allows us to speak of an emerging transnational or global civil society.

The conditions for increasing transnational INGO activities

One question that has frequently been asked concerns the conditions for the emergence of transnational interaction. We will briefly outline the explanations that have been put forward.

First, whereas INGOs were often highly restricted in their international action in the era of the Cold War and a bipolar world system, they can now operate relatively freely across former rather tightly closed systemic borders. This fact alone, however, cannot account for the increase in INGO activity. The end of the East–West conflict and the receding urgency of the nuclear threat have also contributed to a growing awareness of globalizing non-military problems. The emergence of a "world without borders" has given these issues, formerly considered to be part of "low politics" (in other words, not vital to the immediate survival of states), a more prominent status.

Secondly, increasing autonomous action of societal actors across state boundaries can be explained as a functional response to the incompetence or unwillingness of states to cope with these problems in the changing global system in which the sovereignty of national governments is reduced.[23] What is crucial, in this context, is that problems are perceived as requiring transnational solutions which, however, national governments or international organizations fail to provide commensurate to the needs. Lipschutz[24] observes "a growing element of global consciousness in the way the members of global civil society act," which may explain why citizens commit themselves to the pursuit of ends from which they themselves may not even benefit directly.

In addition, public funding of INGO activities has increased following the end of the Cold War. For example, "Western European governments ... place a considerable amount of money at the disposal of the European Community Humanitarian Office ... especially to finance humanitarian activities of NGOs."[25] Nevertheless, as we will show later, this does not mean that there is no INGO competition for funding.

A further critical element for the increase of INGO activity is technological innovations, such as the vast expansion and accessibility of information and communication systems, and increased mobility of people due to better transportation systems. Opening up new channels for the exchange of information and the possibility of coordination, new communication technologies such as the World Wide Web, electronic mail, and access to databases facilitate close cooperation between actors over long distances. The possibility of communication without delay and at low cost has indeed revolutionized the possibilities for cooperation regardless of location and time. In addition, INGOs use the Internet to communicate with a broader public by providing information and also by stimulating responses – through using interactivity in their Web sites, for example. Non-governmental societal actors have thus successfully taken advantage of these opportunities to coordinate their activities better, to reach a broader public, and to expand discourses on the issues of interest to them.

The consequences of increasing INGO action

The effects of increasing INGO action leading to the emergence and, in the long run, establishment of a global civil society are not only limited to the societal level. Increasing transnational self-organization, interest articulation, and aggregation according to shared values and preferences could cause important changes in world politics, such as the decline of historically established structures and lines of conflict. Non-state actors both develop programmes and provide services to tackle global problems, such as environmental degradation, human rights abuse, and social disparities, which national governments or international organizations cannot or will not provide. They are often considered the motors which could, in the long run, advance the democratization of international politics as they experiment with new forms of public participation and thus "develop tactics that enable influence attempts by groups and individuals that are otherwise disenfranchised from bilateral or multilateral decision processes."[26] In addition, INGO action has introduced a higher degree of accountability into intergovernmental settings, given the continuous and structured monitoring of (inter)governmental activities by INGOs and their efforts to ensure broad public communication.

On the other hand, it must also be noted that the emergence of a global civil society is by no means an automatic guarantee of peace and security in the world, and that not all civil society actors share democratic and liberal values. On the contrary, "the effect may be the opposite: the emergence of a neo-medieval world with high levels of conflict and confrontation."[27] The growing illicit activities of powerful actors, such as transnational criminal organizations or terrorist groups, not only undermine civil society but also constitute a serious threat to individual, national and international security. Moreover, the democratic quality of civil society can easily be questioned. Although there are internal democratic mechanisms in the organization of some INGOs, their constituencies are certainly not representative samples of the global population, and INGOs cannot easily be made accountable for their actions by a broader public or (inter)governmental institutions.[28]

Classification of civil society actors

Having discussed the phenomenon of an emerging global civil society, another crucial question arises: is it possible to group the vast range of societal actors according to analytically useful criteria? Or, to put it differently, is it possible to construct distinct types of civil society actors, which can be examined separately and compared with one another?

Among very different imaginable analytical approaches to classifying societal actors,[29] we have chosen to construct a typology based on their main objective combined with their overall mode of operation. Although we have geared this typology of INGOs to the security sector, it may be valid for the analysis of non-state actors in other issue areas as well. Three types of actors emerge from this approach.

Advocacy organizations

The first group can be labelled advocacy organizations.[30] The term "advocacy organization" already implies that these actors concentrate on influencing the process of agenda-setting, policy-making (input functions), and implementation (output function) on the international or national level according to their specific programme goals.[31] To these ends the strategies of advocacy agencies comprise four major components.

One starting point is to inform the public about the importance and urgency of their cause. Media coverage is an important vehicle to achieve public awareness, which is a precondition for the second element: the mobilization of public pressure on national governments and international organizations, for example to abide by established rules or develop new ones. Advocacy organizations can also attempt to further their aims by a third method: creating pressure on decision makers through other governments which are not directly involved in the issue at stake.[32] The final way is by seeking direct contact with decision makers. This lobbying process includes offering know-how and information to decision makers in order to facilitate and encourage policy change, retrieval of information, and, of course, the direct attempt to convince decision makers of the pursued goals.

The main target groups of advocacy organizations are thus national and international public audiences, key decision makers in parliaments and governments, and national delegates to, and officials of, international organizations. The transnational nuclear disarmament organizations analyzed in the chapter by Jackie Smith can be assigned to this class. Some of the INGOs active in support of international peace-keeping, which are the focus of Alex Morrison's and Stephanie A. Blair's chapter, equally belong to this group. Others are clearly part of the next actor group: service organizations.

Service organizations

The second category of civil society actors encompasses organizations which can be referred to as service organizations.[33] Their activities focus on providing services to other organizations or groups of individuals, and on implementing specific programmes. In performing these tasks, service organizations often interact with (inter)governmental agencies, be it that they are financially supported by them, that they are their subcontractors, or that they depend on them to guarantee their own safety.

The INGO community analyzed in Roland Koch's (1997) paper on complex humanitarian emergencies belongs to the category of service organizations.[34] Their service functions include providing resources for disaster relief, shelter and food in cases of mass migration, and technical assistance, as well as intercommunal peace-building assistance immediately following civil war. In this sense, humanitarian assistance organizations provide peace-keeping services as well. Of course, many service organizations also perform advocacy functions. Contractual relationships with donor governments, for example, often provide service NGOs with opportunities to influence donors to adopt their approaches. Another example given by Koch is the efforts of the French NGO Médecins Sans Frontières to promote the idea of a UN resolution securing better access for INGOs in humanitarian emergencies. But in comparison to advocacy organizations, their focus remains on service delivery, while achieving policy change on the international level remains a secondary task.

Illicit autogoverning organizations

The third class of societal actors, illicit autogoverning organizations, differs from the other two in that these actors try to create a sphere of action with norms and rules of their own, in which the impact of national and international legal systems is restricted. Actors within this third group pursue organization-specific, self-serving aims by creating their own autonomous transnational system of governance, and by trying to insulate it against governmental or intergovernmental interference.

It is to this group of non-governmental actors in the security sector that the "dark side" of the emergence of a global civil society can be traced. A prominent example of this group of actors is terrorist organizations. The chapter by Phil Williams also analyzes the growing array of transnational criminal organizations (TCOs). As the latter generally focus on illegal profit-making, but at the same time sustain their "business" activities by not only taking over single societal functions but also establishing complete quasi-autonomous systems of rule,[37] they hold somewhat of a "mid-position" between market forces and civil society. Despite their hybrid nature, we found TCOs to be too important an actor group in the security sector not to be dealt with in some detail.

Of course, organizations of the third type also – at times – try to influence governments in favour of their specific interests, but this is rather a complementary strategy. Moreover, they rarely try to mobilize public pressure, for the goals they pursue are not suitable for attracting broad public support or, in the case of criminal organizations, they must even be kept hidden from the public.

Levels of security and civil society actors

Just as the concept of global civil society, the term "security" is multi-faceted and used accordingly in public and scientific discourse – often, however, without sufficient clarification as to which meaning is implied. As Helga Haftendorn pointed out:

The term "security" is as ambigous in content as it is in format: is it a goal, an issue area, a research programme, or a discipline? There is no one concept of security ...[38]

It is essential, therefore, to get a better analytical grasp of the concept of security before investigating the role of non-state actors in promoting or jeopardizing security. To this end, we suggest not to search for one encompassing generic definition of security (an effort which is bound to fail), but to separate analytically three levels of security: a macro, a meso, and a micro level.

The concept of security on the macro level addresses such problems as inter-state armed conflicts or the proliferation and threat of weapons of mass destruction. But in addition to the traditional definition of security as "the absence of military threat or ... the protection of the nation from external overthrow or attack,"[39] the concept of security on the macro level has come to encompass threats to the well-being of states and societies such as environmental degradation and economic shocks. In other words, the definition of security on the macro level has been extended, now comprising "a certain minimal enjoyment of economic welfare"[40] and ecological stability.

But even this extended concept does not fully grasp the meaning of security today. We need to add what can be called the meso level or societal level of security. Indeed, this is the level on which – after the end of the bipolar system – security seems to be especially precarious. The very physical security of populations is threatened by brutal civil wars of an ethnopolitical nature (such as Afghanistan, and the former Yugoslavia), and resulting mass migration and famines (Rwanda and Somalia). International relief organizations refer to such situations as "complex humanitarian emergencies."[41]

Finally, we also have to consider security on the micro level. The classical understanding of the individualized concept of security is the guarantee of individual personal, civil and political rights *vis-à-vis* the government. Apart from this political understanding of individual security, social and economic dimensions (social and economic security) have to be incorporated into a wider concept of security on the individual level.

In addition, challenges and threats on the part of the state towards individual security, and risks to personal safety emanating from transnational non-state actors, are increasingly perceived as alarming. In particular, the expansion and intensification of transnational criminal activities (such as drug trafficking, or the extortion of "protection money" from legitimate business enterprises) and terrorism are prominent issues in the debate on individual security in the context of globalization.

An interesting point is that the end of the East–West conflict seems to have caused a shift in the relevance and urgency assigned to security problems on the macro level in comparison with security problems located on the meso and micro levels; and shifts in the level of societal activity within the three sectors. In the era of the bipolar international system, public attention and societal activity were clearly concentrated on macro-level security problems, most prominently the nuclear threat to international security resulting from the military competition between East and West. In this context, transnational NGO activities concentrated on the macro level of security – in other words, inter-state security issues – as the example of transnational nuclear disarmament organizations illustrates. Opportunities for INGOs to perform humanitarian relief functions on foreign territory were severely constrained by the governments on both sides.

Since the end of the East–West conflict an increasing scope of activities among societal actors on the meso and micro levels can be observed. A large number of new service organizations have been founded, existing service organizations have expanded, and transnational advocacy organizations like Pugwash have started to take up new issues which can no longer be attributed to the macro level of security alone, such as "environmental and development concerns along with more traditional security concerns."[42] One reason for this is an obviously increased public awareness of newly emerging security problems on the meso and micro levels, which have grown in number and gained in urgency. Examples of these newly emerging security problems are increasing threats to individual safety caused by the spread of transnational criminal networks, and complex humanitarian emergencies. According to Koch,[43] the reasons for the growing number of humanitarian emergencies lie in two related phenomena: the marginalization of some of the poorest countries in the context of economic globalization and drastic cuts in development aid; and the political fragmentation of such states and their eventual collapse, triggered by the retreat of the two former superpowers which had previously kept "friendly" élites in power.

On the basis of our three-level concept of security, we can now address the role of civil society actors in the security sector more specifically. To this end, we turn to the chapters by Koch, Morrison/Blair, Smith, and Williams. The transnational social movement organizations (TSMOs) against nuclear war studied by Smith are typical advocacy organizations, whereas the organizations analyzed by Koch mainly concentrate on service delivery in complex humanitarian emergencies, and therefore belong to the class of service organizations. Activities in support of international peace-keeping are carried out, according to Morrison/ Blair, by both types of organizations – primarily advocacy-oriented ones as well as primarily service-oriented ones. The transnational criminal organizations, finally, are representative of the third class of civil society actors, acting around and in defiance of the state and intergovernmental institutions to pursue narrowly defined group interests, the fulfilment of which entails damages to individuals as well as to society at large (in contrast to the collective values pursued by advocacy groups).[44]

Comparing adovocacy organizations, service organizations, and illicit autogoverning organizations in the security sector

In the following section we will compare the above-mentioned transnational actors on two dimensions. First, we seek to identify their specific prerequisites for successful action, success being defined in terms of the achievement of the actors' highly diverse goals. Second, we highlight the specific challenges, difficulties, and risks with which these actors are confronted in their operations.

Prerequisites for successful action

Advocacy organizations, service organizations, and illicit autogoverning organizations, affecting the security of individuals and collectivities at various levels, naturally act under very different conditions and, accordingly, need to meet different requirements for successful action.

Advocacy organizations

From Smith's analysis of the nuclear disarmament TSMOs, and from Morrison and Blair's investigation of networks of peace-keeping professionals, three crucial requirements for INGOs to achieve policy changes can be extracted. The first is securing access to, and facilitating dialogue with, key decision makers in national governments and international organizations. Gaining access to governmental élites and intergovernmental bodies is a particularly difficult task to achieve in the security sector, as foreign and security policy is traditionally considered to be the exclusive domain of national governments and too important to the immediate survival of the state to open it up to societal influence. Moreover, in the period of the Cold War, the readiness for communication between Eastern and Western decision makers concerning international security questions lying at the heart of the competition for power between the two groups of states was certainly much lower than in other issue areas.

Scientist-based advocacy organizations, which formed the basis of the transnational peace movement of later years, were the first organizations to establish regular forms of dialogue and information flow among nuclear scientists of Eastern and Western origin, as well as between nuclear scientists and political decision makers. Smith[45] shows how a

TSMO like Pugwash succeeded in gaining influence on the thinking of élite-level scientists and policy makers concerning the possibilities of nuclear disarmament. Favourable for direct access to decision makers is either "relevant expertise that decision makers need to make informed decisions" or a "prestigious membership" as in the case of Global Action.[46] Other more mass-based disarmament TSMOs profited from the scientific legitimation Pugwash granted, and from the contacts scientist-based organizations had already established to gain access to decision makers to further their cause. On the other hand, they built "cooperative ties with other like-minded organizations" to enhance their ideas.[47]

Morrison and Blair, in their analysis of transnational networks of peacekeepers, point to the International Association of Peacekeeping Training Centres (IAPTC) as another example of an INGO which has managed to exert influence on international decision-making about peace-keeping missions. Again, the "vital determining factor" for the success of this organization in influencing policy formulation has been its ability "to facilitate dialogue and information flow between key decision makers."[48]

The second crucial requirement for INGOs to achieve policy change is that they succeed in substantially raising the political costs of decision makers' objections to TSMO-sponsored policy changes,[49] be they disarmament proposals or the call for peace-keeping missions.[50] In order to create a sense of urgency for action, advocacy organizations have to be able to mobilize visible cross-border mass public support to create sufficient pressure on governments to keep their goal on the political agenda.

Within the transnational disarmament movement as a whole, the task of building broad constituencies for disarmament fell to national and transnational mass-based peace movement organizations. These actor groups could perform much better in this field than a TSMO like Pugwash, which is based on a smaller network of élite scientists. In the field of peace-keeping no mass-based transnational movement has yet emerged, and is not likely to emerge in the future, either.

Advocacy organizations promoting peace-keeping missions, however, have successfully employed the media to raise public awareness. Increased public awareness has increased the willingness among individuals to donate money. Furthermore, it has created pressure on decisions makers and thus raised the perceived costs of procrastination, thereby forcing decision makers to take action when they might otherwise have remained passive. As a recent example, Morrison and Blair point to the Canadian Prime Minister's decision to act to solve the desperate refugee situation in the former Zaire and Rwanda. "He said that the impetus for his desire to mobilize the international comunity was the scenes he witnessed on the television. He was successful in focusing the attention of world leaders on the plight of refugees. The cries for help, including military force, by many NGOs operating in Central Africa helped tremendously."[51]

The third important condition for achieving policy change is that INGOs supply know-how and resources to governments or international organizations to support such change, thereby reducing the costs and risks of cooperation among governments. One example, cited by Smith, is the verification agreement between the Soviet Academy of Sciences and the US-based National Resources Defense Council (NRDC), which was facilitated by Pugwash's intervention[52] and allowed for the monitoring of US and Soviet nuclear test sites by scientists of both sides. A further example is the Middle Power Peace Initiative by Global Action, "as non-aligned country leaders offered their own services for helping verify a complete ban on testing."[53]

Service organizations

The requirements for successful action faced by organizations focusing on the provision of services in complex humanitarian emergencies are, evidently, very different from the ones pertaining to advocacy organizations outlined above. Whereas advocacy organizations need to secure access to the decision-making élites, relief organizations need to secure access to the territory in which a complex humanitarian emergency has occurred, and to the affected segments of the population.[54] Secure and immediate access of service organizations is indeed a major problem, since most humanitarian emergencies occur in the context of ongoing civil wars or violent ethnopolitical conflicts.

A second important requirement for successful action is the ability to react instantaneously to emergency situations. Arriving as early as possible raises the probability of being able to supply effective assistance to the victims. In addition, being "first on the spot" has one effect especially important to the category of service-providing actors: the earlier an organization arrives and establishes itself in an emergency area, the greater its prospects for getting good media coverage of its activities, which is often a decisive advantage in the competition for private donations.[55]

Illicit autogoverning organizations

This third group of civil society actors is completely different from advocacy and service organizations in goals, modes, and implications of action. In contrast to advocacy and service organizations, whose central aim is to further collective immaterial interests or the welfare of others, the key objective of all transnational criminal organizations – as heterogeneous as they may be regarding their organizational structures – is the promotion of their main self-serving interest, which is illicit profit-making.

Indeed, TCOs differ so much from the two other actor types that the comparability of TCOs with TSMOs and and relief INGOs in the security area is not self-evident. It may seem awkward, or even on the verge of cynicism, to investigate the requirements for success for TCOs. Yet such an analysis can provide valuable academic as well as practical insights for policy development aiming at TCOs. It has explanatory power for the strategies transnational criminal actors rely on, and thus may serve as a basis for the development of counter-strategies.

From the main objective of TCOs, illegal profit-making, two requirements for successful activity can be deduced: TCOs have (1) to minimize their vulnerabilities to state attacks on, and control of, illicit activities; and (2) to enhance their "business" opportunities. Regarding the first point, it is evident that TCOs develop tactics to circumvent legal restrictions and to avoid law enforcement. The pursuit of large-scale illegal business activities without being discovered makes the creation of networks, contacts, and information infrastructures, guarded against infiltration by law enforcement personnel, a fundamental requirement for TCOs. Moreover, TCOs, which have "unfamiliar languages and cultures, operate in novel and unexpected ways, and entrench themselves within larger ethnic communities which are difficult to penetrate,"[56] prove to be especially well prepared to confront even specialized anti-crime agencies. Despite a transnational radius of action, TCOs usually operate from one home base, preferably in a country in which "both government and law enforcement are weak or acquiescent."[57] In order to sustain successful operations, TCOs need to create bonding mechanisms – be it on the basis of family, clan, ethnic ties, etc. – which on the one hand guarantee permanence within the TCO itself and, on the other hand, enable an entrenchment in society and the development of mutually profitable relationships with the political and economic élites.

The latter aspect of securing access to economic élites is also crucial for the second important prerequisite for "successful" action of TCOs, in other words, the extension of "business" opportunities. Moreover, it is important for TCOs to secure ways to "embed illicit products in licit"[58] without being discovered. This task has become a lot easier to achieve with the expansion of international trade and a globalized financial system. Another prerequisite is the ability to move funds to "safe havens beyond the reach of law enforcement" and to obscure the sources.[59]

Obstacles to effective action

In the preceding part of this chapter, we have identified and elaborated the prerequisites for successful action of advocacy, service, and illicit auto-governing organizations. We will now identify the obstacles and restrictive conditions which may prevent effective action by societal actors; and discuss the approaches they take to counter these challenges and, eventually, to overcome obstacles. We will first take a look at advocacy and service organizations. Both of them have to counter the challenge of limited resources and deal with problems emanating from the fact that – in contrast to states – they are non-sovereign actors. Illicit autogoverning organizations are treated separately at the end of this section, as the challenges they face, and the strategies they employ to overcome them, are completely different from those of advocacy and service INGOs.

Advocacy and service organizations

To a very high degree, the scope and success of INGO action depends on sufficient resources. Funding poses the first major difficulty for non-governmental advocacy and service organizations alike. Given the changing global security environment, with an increasing number of armed conflicts and a growing awareness of these conflicts, the demand for INGO action has increased. But this growing importance of INGOs has not been paralleled by an increase of their resources. On the contrary, the growing number of INGOs has lead to increased competition for scarce resources. An indicator of this increasing competition is the effort of INGOs to be the first on the scene – "ambulance chasing," as Natsios[60] calls it ironically – in order to receive the best media coverage and hence public attention and financial support.

Although advocacy organizations in general require fewer material resources than service NGOs, both rely on private donations from their members and from the general public. Service organizations generally receive governmental or intergovernmental financial or logistic support more easily. Advocacy organizations such as the disarmament TSMOs, which exert pressure on decision makers to adopt their goals, were – at least in earlier times – seen as trouble-makers and thus could not expect much funding from governments. Or, if governments favoured an INGO's aims, the organization risked being instrumentalized for governmental purposes. The danger of becoming dependent on governmental or intergovernmental funding, which would be detrimental to the credibility of advocacy organizations, is the main reason why these organizations try to work independently from governmental funding.

Service organizations, on the other hand, normally rely heavily on governmental and intergovernmental resources in order to perform their work.[61] Governments and international organizations have a specific interest in ensuring that non-governmental organizations provide services. An example is the considerable increase in joint action between INGOs and UN agencies after the end of the Cold War.[62] Generally speaking, there are two reasons for the interest in cooperating with INGOs. First of all, carrying out the services themselves would confront governments with much higher expenses than the sponsoring of INGOs. Secondly, especially in cases of armed conflict, some tasks can only be carried out by INGOs. Their independent, non-partisan status gives them a crucial advantage over governmental actors.

Scarcity of resources does not only show up in the financial sphere. The growing number of complex humanitarian emergencies demanding immediate and appropriate responses reveal limitations of time, information, and personnel. Of course, better funding could solve some of these problems. But the lack of information, in particular, cannot be countered as easily as that. It is obvious that successful action requires highly reliable, instant information which can only be secured by long-term observation or even prospective analyses, and an exchange of experience.

Limited resources on the one hand, and growing numbers of emergencies combined with more ambitious tasks on the other, have led to increased coordination and cooperation among INGOs, and between INGOs and other actors involved in an emergency. Coordination and cooperation can hence be identified as a functional response to the scarcity of resources and to the insight that the performance of every single actor is not as good as it could be. Indeed, cooperation and coordination seem crucial to avoid the waste of resources such as relief goods, and the duplication of efforts.

Cooperation can occur in the emergency situation itself, or it can develop in a long-term process – for example, after having discovered that there were deficits in spontaneous coordination and cooperation in the emergency situation. Ad hoc cooperation can involve very intensive interaction, implying sharing certain resources, or be limited to negative coordination only, simply to avoid duplicating efforts. Equally, long-term cooperation can be of different degrees, ranging from very loose personal contacts to institutionalized forms of cooperation.

Cooperation, especially in an emergency case, usually faces various constraints. Apart from competition for scarce resources, two other important obstacles to cooperation that apply to both advocacy and service agencies are the fear of being dominated by another group or a bureaucracy and thus losing independence,[63] and the lack of consensus among the different actors involved concerning approaches and strategies. Among organizations advocating nuclear disarmament, for example, repeated conflicts concerning approaches and goals arose between pacifists and non-pacifists, as well as between direct-action advocates and activists preferring less confrontational strategies.[64] This was partly due to the fact that actors' approaches remained strongly influenced by the context in which they operated, in other words the different national and regional framings of the anti-nuclear debates. "Because activists had to concern themselves with satisfying the domestic constituencies that supported their work, such a preoccupation with the nationally structured political opportunities is understandable."[65] Similar problems can be discerned in the field of humanitarian relief, where "conflicting strategies and objectives, or their abysmal absence ... frequently cancel each other out."[66]

One approach to overcoming the problems of ad hoc cooperation is the creation of professional networks. The studies of Morrison and Blair (1996) imply that it is actually through these networks of professionals – here in the area of international peace-keeping – that ways and means can be found to overcome the problems of cooperation over competition for scarce resources, a lack of consensus on ends and means, a lack of mutual trust, and so on. These "informal networks" encompass "groupings [that] may be transitory, intangible ... or may establish organizational mechanisms akin to those of highly structured, formal bodies."[67] They emerge around formal organizations without being part of any official structure. Informal networks are hence no "self-generating entities."[68] They are not specific to the area of international peace-keeping, either, but rather apply more generally.

The reason for the establishment of "informal networks" is not so much working towards the individual target of each actor involved. Rather their goal is to improve the overall performance of all actors involved by questioning strategies and instruments, and by exchanging background information and practical know-how. Informal networks allow organizations "to make maximum use of existing resources,"[69] to promote mutual education through information sharing, and to improve future performance thanks to mutual education. Additionally, they foster a "spirit of collegiality and friendship"[70] which helps to reduce mistrust and increases motivation. "Informal discussions lead to a new appreciation of the strengths of their respective organizations, an appreciation they take with them when they return to the field and which enables them to work more cooperatively with other organizations."[71]

Apart from the challenge of cooperation to overcome limited resources, a second type of challenge facing advocacy and service organizations derives from the fact that advocacy and service organizations as non-sovereign actors have to interact with sovereign actors, such as states. This confronts them with difficulties that differ in quality, due to the different goals pursued by advocacy and service organizations.

Transnational advocacy organizations generally have the advantage of not having to enter a specific territory physically to be able to pursue their goals. At least, this is true for nuclear disarmament organizations.[72] However, since advocacy organizations are non-governmental actors attempting to pressure national governments to adopt national and international policy change, the special challenge for these actors is to convince the broad public and national governments of the legitimacy of their causes and activities (a problem which relief NGOs do not have).

Service organizations are regularly and very directly confronted with the problem of state sovereignty when they have to secure physical access to a territory in order to perform their relief functions. Access, however, is often denied by the government of the state in question or by civil war factions, and it has only been a recent development that the Security Council has legalized external United Nations and NGO access[73] to sovereign territory for the purpose of humanitarian assistance.[74] But even if the delivery of humanitarian relief services is held to be legal under international law, service organizations might still not be able to perform their work because fighting groups within the territory may not accept their presence and the "operational staff runs into severe security problems,"[75] as was the case in Rwanda and elsewhere.

The problem of sovereignty and legitimate intervention has so far not met with a satisfactory collective response from the international community. Up to now, no consensus has been reached as to whether INGO activities can override national sovereignty claims in cases of emergency, although the latest UN resolutions on this issue clearly present a shift towards granting more rights to UN agencies and INGOs operating in foreign territory in humanitarian emergencies.

Illicit autogoverning organizations

None of the obstacles to effective action by advocacy and service organizations outlined above applies to illicit autogoverning organizations. The most important challenges these criminal organizations face are posed by national law enforcement agencies, and increasingly also by international or regional bodies which aim to prevent the activities of TCOs, and to investigate and finally destroy their networks. Williams considers the role of the United Nations in crime prevention to be crucial, "partly because of its long experience in this area and partly because of its global responsibilities."[76] Examples of UN bodies fighting transnational crime are the United Nations Crime Prevention and Criminal Justice Division and the United Nations Drug Control Programme (UNDCP). One of the latest UN initiatives, to which Williams attributes "a whole new dimension," was its organization of a World Ministerial Conference on transnational crime in Naples in 1994, bringing together ministers of the interior from 142 states. The conference resulted in a political declaration and action plan "designed to initiate more effective measures to prevent and control cross-border criminal activities."[77] Outside the United Nations framework, other intergovernmental bodies such as the OECD and the European Union have also established task forces and started initiatives to improve multilateral cooperation in the fight against trans-national organized crime.

In order to control these increasing "risks," three TCO strategies can be distinguished. The first one can be referred to as risk prevention, in other words the effort to maintain a "congenial environment through bribery and corruption."[78] A second strategy lies in the attempt to absorb the costs of law enforcement through defensive measures. This self-defence can be observed in stages, in which the state is determined to take measures against criminal organizations. Measures taken by TCOs in this context, such as monitoring telephone calls, resemble counter-intelligence. If all preventive and defensive measures fail, the third strategy aims at limiting the damage of an all-out attack by the state on the TCO. Maintaining the basic structures of the criminal organization is the main goal in this situation. TCOs try to achieve this by transferring assets, and by naming proxies to manage the organization.

Impact of increasing INGO action

In the last part of this chapter, we want to wrap up our analysis by asking what kind of impact the activites of societal actors have had, and continue to have, on security on the three different levels. We will start with the "dark side" of the globalizing civil society, TCOs, and then continue with societal organizations aiming at promoting security by supporting policy changes or by delivering services in emergency situations. A second question pertaining only to advocacy and service organizations refers to the extent to which these organizations contribute to the democratization of international politics and the emergence of a global civil society.

Williams's analysis of TCOs shows that transnational operations and contacts of societal actors cannot be seen as a process that, in and by itself, leads to more accountabilty, more democracy, and thus more security in the international system. These profit-seeking illicit networks do not contribute to stability and security, but challenge it constantly.

Impact on macro, meso, and micro levels of security

By denying the legal order established by states and international orga-nizations and promoting an alternative, illegal system of norms and rules, TCOs, just like terrorist groups whose main goal is the destruction of an existing political order, present a great risk to security and stability on all levels: they "pose challenges to national sovereignty, to individual mem-bers of society, to societies themselves, to the rule of law, to the effec-tiveness of some international norms and conventions, including those important to an emerging civil society, and to the viability and integrity of their home states."[79] On the micro level, they pose threats to the dignity and safety of individuals whether they are involved in criminal activity or not. On the meso level, they challenge the security and stability of states (for example, by undermining law enforcement institutions, challenging the state monopoly of the legitimate use of violence, or even creating a rival authority structure) and undermine civil society in the national context.[80] On the macro level, they may even be capable of weakening international prohibition regimes in the area of weapons of mass destruction. In addition, TCOs may get involved in ongoing inter- or intra-state conflicts for their own profit, such as through arms trafficking, and thus may raise the level of violence and insecurity.[81]

Having pointed out the risks to security caused by non-state actors, we can now ask what impact the activities of security-promoting societal actors have on peace building and on democratizing the international system. As Smith shows in detail, the efforts of TSMOs to gain influence on decision-making related to nuclear disarmament have been moderately successful. They have created "massive mobilizations"[82] and gained direct access to decision makers, enhancing macro-level security by, for example, helping the passage of an Anti-Ballistic Missile (ABM) Treaty and promoting an amendment conference to the Partial Test Ban Treaty.[83] Nevertheless, the transnational nuclear disarmament movement "failed to generate strong pressures for multilateral institution building."[84] If the TSMOs analyzed did not achieve as much as could have been expected, this can be explained by considering practical difficulties. As outlined earlier, the transnational peace movement, for example, faced coordination and fundraising difficulties which prevented activists from pursuing their goals more effectively. The main reason for the lack of interorganizational cooperation and coherence was an often-missing consensus on ends and means among the groups' members. Building a consensus on goals and strategies, in general, seems to be the task which becomes increasingly difficult to achieve the bigger the organizations' constituencies and the more complex the interorganizational networks grow. In addition, as Smith puts it, the TSMOs "faced serious limitations in their abilities to overcome challenges to transnationalism. They failed to free the nuclear security debate from the constraints of state-centred, bi-polar security paradigms in order to cultivate support for multilateral responses."[85]

Relief organizations have been able to professionalize their work in recent years, and by cooperating closely with UN agencies they have successfully operated in humanitarian emergencies. By delivering services, which otherwise probably would not have been supplied by national or international governmental institutions, they have contributed to alleviating human suffering and to re-establishing security on the micro and meso levels. Nevertheless, the major deficiency of service organizations remains that they most often merely react to already existing humanitarian emergencies. They are not yet capable of taking effective action to prevent such emergencies. On the one hand, this may indicate an incapacity to monitor developments in areas which are likely to be affected by humanitarian emergencies. On the other hand, overtaxing of INGOs active in humanitarian relief operations and lack of funding may also account for these deficiencies.

Impact on the democratization of the international political system

Concerning the emergence of a truly global civil society and the democratization of the international system, Smith considers "the expansion of formal organizations designed to promote transnational goals and values" as "a positive development for the realization of a stronger global civil society." Nevertheless "the transnational disarmament movement ... lacked extensive and strong transnational associations."[86] Up to the present day, "real" transnational actors have difficulties in gaining ground as they must "overcome the competing claims to citizens' loyalties made by national and subnational entities."[87] In addition, advocacy organizations such as Pugwash, and even disarmament TSMOs based on a broader constituency, have remained highly élite-centred and Western-biased. In that they "do not constitute representative samples of the global population, but are rather self-selected,"[88] they are clearly not representatives of a global civil society.

Despite these deficiencies, disarmament TSMOs still express views which are indeed shared by a broad public, and they have contributed to the development of new and democratic forms of global governance. The TSMOs described by Smith have expanded democratic participation in the politics of human security by "providing opportunities for individuals from many different countries to come together to engage in global problem-solving dialogues."[89] By bringing formerly unrepresented voices into the national policy-making processes and intergovernmental negotiations, and by "monitoring government behaviour in order to hold them accountable to their formal and informal agreements,"[90] TSMOs have made the domain of foreign policy more accountable to citizens and thus advanced the process of transnational democratization.

As in the case of transnational advocacy organizations, the democratic quality of the constituency of humanitarian relief organizations remains incomplete. It may be true that, overall, service organizations active in humanitarian relief are "getting closer to the internal UN headquarters decision-making process,"[91] but it is also true that real political leverage and the privilege of substantial funding are limited to the few largest service organizations,[92] which are all of Western origin. This oligopolistic trend, and the fact that Western organizations receive the lion's share of governmental funds for the provision of services in humanitarian emergencies, are certainly democratic weaknesses.

Nevertheless, humanitarian service INGOs have indeed contributed to democratization in that they cooperate closely with UN agencies and communicate people's needs to (inter)governmental institutions. By doing so, they facilitate the exchange of views on problems of international security and peace, as well as on humanitarian emergencies in different countries, and hence indirectly shape international and national policy-making. Finally, humanitarian INGOs, just like advocacy organizations, "introduce better transparency and accountability" to the political process,[93] and by doing so help to render state actions more suitable to people's actual needs. Thus, societal actors may indeed form an important basis of a more democratic and peaceful structure of conflict arbitration within the United Nations system.

In this context, the networking phenomenon has to be taken into account as well. The creation of networks linking INGOs with one another, but also with UN agencies and other international organizations, is a further indicator of an emerging transnational or global civil society. It implies that civil society encompasses a highly complex and dynamic network of individual and corporate actors which is again closely linked with (inter)governmental institutions.

Conclusion

In this chapter we have shown that, since the end of the Cold War, INGOs have played an increasingly important role in the sector of security. Three types of societal actors were distinguished according to their objectives and strategies, and the notion of three levels of security was put forward. We have discussed the conditions for successful INGO action, the obstacles that INGOs are confronted with, and their strategies to overcome these obstacles. In that regard we came across the aspect of cooperation and networking. These phenomena can be identified as a functional response to problems that arise when INGOs pursue their goals. The phenomenon of networking among INGOs up to now has not received sufficient attention from social scientists. The same applies to issues related to sovereignty or democratic legitimization. Here, the question of how INGOs can be integrated into the decision-making processes of international organizations becomes increasingly salient. Moreover, most of the research dealing with societal actors in international affairs has so far been centred on only one particular issue area, the most popular fields being environment, development, and human rights. The problem with this one-dimensional approach is that findings pertaining to a single sector, and sometimes even to only one INGO within this sector, can hardly be generalized to the vast range of actor types in the INGO community. What is needed, therefore, is more intra-sectoral as well as cross-sectoral comparisons of societal actor groups and strategies, resources, and networks, as well as their channels of influence and the specific challenges and obstacles they face. In this chapter on non-state actors in the field of security, we have attempted to take a first step toward constructing and applying such a comparative framework.

Notes

1. Ronnie Lipschutz, "Reconstructing World Politics. Emergence of Global Civil Society," *Millennium*, vol. 21, 3, 1992, pp. 389–411, 404.
2. Ernst-Otto Czempiel, "Governance and Democratization," in Ernst-Otto Czempiel and James N. Rosenau (eds.), *Governance without Government: Order and Change in World Politics*, Cambridge: Cambridge University Press, 1992, pp. 250–71.
3. Peter Mayer, Volker Rittberger, and Michael Zürn, "Regime Theory: State of the Art and Persepctives," in Ritterberger (ed.), *Regime Theory and International Relations*, Oxford: Clarendon Press, 1993, p. 393.
4. Ernst-Otto Czempiel, op. cit., p. 250.
5. Mayer, Rittberger, and Zürn, op. cit., p. 404.
6. Volker Rittberger and Michael Zürn, "Towards Regulated Anarchy in East–West Re- lations" in Rittberger (ed.), *International Regimes in East–West Politics*, London: Pinter, 1990.
7. James M. Rosenau, "Governance in the Twenty-first Century," *Global Governance*, vol. 1, 1995, pp. 13–43.
8. Mayer, Rittberger, and Zürn, op. cit., p. 402.
9. Lipschutz, op. cit., p. 397.
10. An exception is the work by Virginia Haufler, *Dangerous Commerce: State, Market, and International Risks Insurance*, Ithaca, New York/London: Cornell University Press; and Virginia Haufler, "Crossing the Boundary between the Public and Private: International Regimes and Non-State Actors," in Volker Rittberger (ed.), *Regime Theory and Inter- national Relations*, pp. 94–111.
11. R. O. Keohane and J. S. Nye, *Power and Interdependence. World Politics in Transition*, Boston: Little Brown, 1977.
12. Thomas Risse-Kappen, "Bringing Transnational Relations Back," in Risse-Kappen (ed.), *Non-State Actors, Domestic Structures, and International Institutions*, Cambridge: Cambridge University Press, 1995.
13. Leon Gordenker and Thomas Weiss, "Pluralizing Global Goverance: Analytical Ap- proaches," in Gordenker and Weiss (eds.), *NGOs, the United Nations, and Global Governance*, Boulder: Lynne Rienner, 1996, p. 17.
14. The root of this three-part model lies in Hegel's writings. The model has been used and developed by theorists such as Gramsci, Parsons, and Habermas. Ernst-Otto Czempiel, *Weltpolitik im Umbruch: Das Internationale System nach dem Ende des Ost-West-*

Konflikts, second edition, Munich: Beck, 1993, pp. 14–16, similarily differentiates between the worlds of the state, the economy, and the society. The model's crucial advantage in comparison to the approach defining two spheres (the state on the one side and societal and economic actors in opposition to it) is the fact that it allows us to assess independently the autonomous logics of market forces and civil society.

15. The titles of the papers concerned are: Smith, Jackie, 1997: *Global Civil Society, Social Movement Organizations, and the Global Politics of Nuclear Security*. Revised version of a paper prepared for the UNU Symposium, "The United Nations System in the Twenty-first Century: International Peace and Security," 8–9 November 1996, Tokyo, Japan, and published in this volume. Koch, Roland, 1997: *UN Agencies and Non-Governmental Organizations in Cross-Border Humanitarian Assistance*. Revised version of a paper prepared for the UNU Symposium, as above. Morrison, Alex/Blair, Stephanie A., 1996: *Transnational Networks of Peacekeepers*. Paper prepared for the UNU Symposium, as above. Williams, Phil, 1997: *The Dark Side of Global Civil Society: The Role and Impact of Transnational Criminal Organizations as a Threat to International Security*. Revised version of a paper prepared for the UNU Symposium, as above.

16. Michael Walzer, "The Concept of Civil Society," in Walzer (ed.), *Toward Global Civil Society*, Providence, RI: Berghahn Books, 1995, p. 7.

17. Jean Cohen, "Interpreting the Notion of Civil Society," in M. Walzer (ed.), *Toward Global Civil Society*, p. 37.

18. John Boli, "Organizing World Polity: INGOs since 1875," paper prepared for the thirty-sixth annual meeting of the International Studies Association, Chicago, 1995, p. 28.

19. The concept of "transnational sodalities" referring to "voluntary cross-national associations composed of nationally organized groups" has already been used in the 1970s to refer to this phenomenon. Volker Rittberger, *Evolution and International Organization: Towards a New Level of Socio-political Integration*, The Hague: Martinus Nijhoff, 1973, p. 33.

20. David L. Cooperrider and William A. Pasmore, "The Organization Dimension of Global Change," *Human Relations*, vol. 44, 8, 1991, p. 365.

21. M. J. Peterson, "Transnational Activity, International Society, and World Politics," *Millennium*, vol. 21, 3, 1992, p. 379. Peterson prefers to speak of an "international civil society" rather than of a global civil society as "countries and national borders remain real." His concept of an international civil society is that of "interlinked" national civil societies.

22. James V. Riker, "Inter-societal Linkages in a Global Civil Society: Transcending the State for Global Goverance?," paper prepared for the thirty-seventh annual meeting of the International Studies Association, San Diego, 1996, p. 6.

23. Ernst-Otto Czempiel, op. cit.

24. Lipschutz, op. cit., p. 399.

25. Koch, op. cit., p. 10.

26. J. Smith, op. cit., p. 34.

27. Lipschutz, op. cit., p. 419.

28. Andrew S. Natsios, "NGOs and the UN System in Complex Humanitarian Emergencies," in L. Gordenker and T. Weiss, op. cit., p. 71.

29. For other classifications compare e.g. William Cousins, *Non-governmental Initiatives. The Urban Poor and Basic Infrastructure Services in Asian and the Pacific*, Manila: Asian Development Bank, 1991.

30. The distinction of "advocacy" and "service" non-governmental organizations, which has been adopted from Gordenker/Weiss, "Pluralizing Global Governance," in op. cit., parallels the categorization of international organizations into "programmatic" and "operative" organizations, the former focusing on problem articulation, definition of

programmes and targets, and norm-setting (examples are the United Nations and the Organization for Cooperation and Security in Europe). The latter category concentrates on implementation and executive tasks (such as the World Bank or the UNHCR), cf. Volker Rittberger and Bernhard Zangl, *Interantionale Organizationen. Politik Und Geschichte*, second edition, Opladen: Leske and Budrich, 1995.

31. As we consider "education" to be a subfunction of "advocacy" we do not distinguish between advocacy and educational organizations, as do Weiss and Gordenker ("Pluralizing Global Governance," p. 38).
32. J. Smith, op. cit., p. 30.
33. Leon Gordenker and Thomas Weiss ("Pluralizing Global Goverance") refer to this class of actors as "operational organizations."
34. Although comparable to this group in terms of its targets, the International Committee of the Red Cross does not form part of this group of non-governmental actors. This is due to the special mandate assigned to it under international law and its highly formalized structure. Its special role might best be described as that of an "international organization, not an NGO, yet ... outside the UN system" which "more jealously guards its autonomy and prerogatives than any of the other international actors – UN or NGO – and resists coordination." Natsios, op. cit., 1996, p. 74.
35. Morrison/Blair, op. cit., p.12f.
36. Koch, op. cit., p. 14.
37. Although the negative consequences of these alternative illegal systems of rule are obvious, they also entail the provision of economic benefits to non-members, especially relevant in poorer countries. TCO activities may account for a considerable part of export earnings (e.g. through drug trafficking) and employment opportunities in these countries. P. Williams, op. cit.
38. Helga Haftendorn, "The Security Puzzle: Theory Building and Discipline Building in International Security," *International Studies Quarterly*, vol. 35, 1, 1991, p. 3.
39. Ibid., p. 4.
40. Joseph S. Nye, "Problems of Security Studies," paper presented at the fourteenth World Congress of the International Political Science Association, Washington DC, 1988.
41. Natsios, op. cit., p. 67, defines complex humanitarian emergencies by five characteristics: deterioration or collapse of governmental authority, ethnic or religious conflict and human rights abuse, food insecurity, macroeconomic collapse, and mass population movements.
42. J. Smith, op. cit., p. 17.
43. Koch, op. cit. p. 7f.
44. Nevertheless it has to be noted that actors in this group do not necessarily operate illegally. The defining characteristic remains the fact that they operate "around" the state or intergovernmental organizations to pursue more or less narrowly defined group interests. The International Olympic Committee, for instance, which sets its own norms and rules, is an example – taken from another issue area – of a legally operating actor belonging to this category. Compare with Volker Rittberger and Henning Boekle, "Das Internationale Olympische Komitee – eine Weltregierung des Sports?," *Die Friedenswarte*, vol. 71, 2, 1996, pp. 155–88.
45. J. Smith, op. cit., p. 13f.
46. Ibid., p. 29.
47. Ibid.
48. Morrison/Blair, op. cit., p. 18.
49. J. Smith, op. cit., p. 24f.
50. Morrison/Blair, op. cit., p. 18.
51. Morrison/Blair, op. cit., p. 12f.

52. J. Smith, op. cit., p. 31.
53. Ibid.
54. Morrison/Blair, op. cit., pp. 9, 32f.
55. Natsios, op. cit., p. 71.
56. P. Williams, op. cit., p. 6.
57. Ibid.
58. Ibid., p. 8.
59. Ibid., p. 7.
60. Natsios, op. cit., p. 71.
61. The financial dependency on governmental and intergovernmental as well as private donors is a problem that is being discussed controversially within the transnational relief service community as well as in scholarly circles, without a solution in sight.
62. Koch, op. cit., p. 32.
63. Koch, op. cit., pp. 20, 27; Natsios, op. cit., p. 78.
64. J. Smith, op. cit., p. 36.
65. Ibid.
66. Natsios, op. cit., p. 78.
67. Morrison/Blair, op. cit., p. 10.
68. Ibid.
69. Ibid., p. 27.
70. Ibid., p. 28.
71. Ibid., p. 30.
72. This is likely to be different, and more difficult to deal with, for environmental NGOs and human rights NGOs which are dependent on fact-finding missions in particular countries.
73. The UN Security Council resolutions since 1990 have supported INGO action by gradually removing the UN Charter's restrictions on UN-NGO assistance in humanitarian emergencies (Koch, op. cit., p. 32).
74. Compare with Koch, op. cit., p. 13ff.
75. Koch, op. cit., p. 33.
76. J. Williams, op. cit., p. 16.
77. Ibid.
78. Ibid., p. 7. Equally important can be the effort to gain public acquiescence through forms of patronage, for example the assistance provided to the people of Kobe after the earthquake by the Japanese Yakuza.
79. J. Williams, op. cit., p. 9.
80. Ibid., p. 10.
81. Ibid., p. 5.
82. J. Smith, op. cit., p. 35.
83. Ibid., p. 27.
84. Ibid., p. 35.
85. Ibid., p. 38.
86. Ibid., p. 31.
87. Ibid.
88. Ibid., p. 33.
89. Ibid., p. 32.
90. Ibid., p. 34.
91. Koch, op. cit., p. 21
92. The three largest NGOs active in humanitarian relief are CARE, World Vision, and Catholic Relief Services. Their combined budgets exceed US$1 billion annually (cf. Natsios, op. cit., p. 72).

93. Donini, Antonio, "The Bureaucracy and the Free Spirits: Stagnation and Innovation in the Relationship Between the UN and NGOs," in Gordenker/Weiss (eds.), *NGOs, the United Nations, and Global Governance*, p. 87.

BIBLIOGRAPHY

Boli, John (1995): *Organizing World Polity: INGOs since 1875*. Paper prepared for the thirty-sixth annual meeting of the International Studies Association, Chicago.

Cohen, Jean (1995): "Interpreting the Notion of Civil Society," in Walzer, Michael (ed.), *Toward a Global Civil Society*, Providence, Rhode Island: Berghahn Books, pp. 35–40.

Cooperrider, David L./Pasmore, William A. (1991): "The Organization Dimension of Global Change," *Human Relations*, vol. 44, 8, pp. 763–87.

Cousins, William (1991): *Non-Governmental Initiatives. The Urban Poor and Basic Infrastructure Services in Asia and the Pacific*. Manila: Asian Development Bank.

Czempiel, Ernst-Otto (1993): *Weltpolitik im Umbruch. Das internationale System nach dem Ende des Ost-West-Konflikts*, second edition, Munich: Beck.

Czempiel, Ernst-Otto (1992): "Governance and Democratization," in Czempiel, Ernst-Otto/Rosenau, James N. (eds.), *Governance without Government: Order and Change in World Politics*, Cambridge: Cambridge University Press, pp. 250–71.

Donini, Antonio (1996): "The Bureaucracy and the Free Spirits: Stagnation and Innovation in the Relationship Between the UN and NGOs," in Gordenker, Leon/Weiss, Thomas G. (eds.), *NGOs, the UN, and Global Governance*, Boulder, Colorado: Lynne Rienner, pp. 83–101.

Gordenker, Leon/Weiss, Thomas G. (1996a): "Pluralizing Global Governance: Analytical Approaches," in Gordenker, Leon/Weiss, Thomas G. (eds.), *NGOs, the UN, and Global Governance*, Boulder, Colorado: Lynne Rienner, pp. 17–47.

Gordenker, Leon/Weiss, Thomas G. (eds.) (1996b): *NGOs, the UN, and Global Governance*, Boulder, Colorado: Lynne Rienner.

Haftendorn, Helga (1991): "The Security Puzzle: Theory-Building and Discipline-Building in International Security," *International Studies Quarterly*, vol. 35, 1, pp. 3–17.

Haufler, Virginia (1993): "Crossing the Boundary between the Public and Private: International Regimes and Non-State Actors," in Rittberger, Volker (ed.) 1993, *Regime Theory and International Relations*, Oxford: Clarendon Press, pp. 94–111.

Haufler, Virginia (1997): *Dangerous Commerce: State, Market, and International Risks Insurance*, Ithaca, New York/London: Cornell University Press.

Keohane, Robert O./Nye, Joseph S., Jr. (1977): *Power and Interdependence. World Politics in Transition*, Boston, Massachusetts: Little, Brown.

Koch, Roland (1997): *UN Agencies and Non-Governmental Organizations in Cross-Border Humanitarian Assistance*. Paper prepared for the UNU Symposium "The United Nations System in the Twenty-first Century: International Peace and Security," 8–9 November 1996, Tokyo, Japan.

Lipschutz, Ronnie (1992): "Reconstructing World Politics. Emergence of Global Civil Society," *Millennium*, vol. 21, 3, pp. 389–411.

Mayer, Peter/Rittberger, Volker/Zürn, Michael (1993): "Regime Theory: State of the Art and Perspectives," in Rittberger, Volker (ed.), *Regime Theory and International Relations*, Oxford: Clarendon Press, pp. 391–430.

Michalski, Kristoph (ed.) (1991): *Europa und die Civil Society*, Stuttgart: Klett-Cotta.

Morrison, Alex/Blair, Stephanie A. (1996): *Transnational Networks of Peacekeepers*. Paper prepared for the UNU Symposium "The United Nations System in the Twenty-first Century: International Peace and Security," 8–9 November 1996, Tokyo, Japan.

Natsios, Andrew S. (1996): "NGOs and the UN System in Complex Humanitarian Emergencies," in Gordenker, Leon/Weiss, Thomas G. (eds.), *NGOs, the UN, and Global Governance*, Boulder, Colorado: Lynne Rienner, pp. 67–81.

Nye, Joseph S., Jr. (1988): *Problems of Security Studies*. Paper presented at the XIV World Congress of the International Political Science Association, Washington, DC.

Peterson, M. J. (1992): "Transnational Activity, International Society, and World Politics," *Millenium*, vol. 21, 3, pp. 371–88.

Riker, James V. (1996): *Inter-Societal Linkages in a Global Civil Society: Transcending the State for Global Governance?* Paper prepared for the thirty-seventh annual meeting of the International Studies Association, San Diego.

Risse-Kappen, Thomas (ed.) (1995): *Bringing Transnational Relations Back In: Non-State Actors, Domestic Structures, and International Institutions*, Cambridge: Cambridge University Press.

Rittberger, Volker (1973): *Evolution and International Organization: Toward a New Level of Socio-political Integration*, The Hague: Martinus Nijhoff.

Rittberger, Volker (ed.) (1990): *International Regimes in East-West Politics*, London: Pinter.

Rittberger, Volker (ed.) (1993): *Regime Theory and International Relations*, Oxford: Clarendon Press.

Rittberger, Volker/Boekle, Henning (1996): "Das Internationale Olympische Komitee – eine Weltregierung des Sports?," *Die Friedenswarte*, vol. 71, 2, pp. 155–88.

Rittberger, Volker/Zangl, Bernhard (1995): *Internationale Organisationen. Politik und Geschichte*, 2nd ed., Opladen: Leske and Budrich.

Rittberger, Volker/Zürn, Michael (1990): "Towards Regulated Anarchy in East-West Relations," in Rittberger, Volker (ed.), *International Regimes in East-West Politics*, London: Pinter, pp. 9–63.

Rosenau, James N./Czempiel, Ernst-Otto (eds.) (1992): *Governance without Government: Order and Change in World Politics*, Cambridge: Cambridge University Press.

Rosenau, James N. (1995): "Governance in the Twenty-first Century," *Global Governance*, vol. 1, pp. 13–43.

Smith, Jackie (1997): *Global Civil Society, Social Movement Organizations, and the Global Politics of Nuclear Security*. Paper prepared for the UNU Symposium "The United Nations System in the Twenty-first Century: International Peace and Security," 8–9 November 1996, Tokyo, Japan.

Walzer, Michael (1995a): "The Concept of Civil Society," in Walzer, Michael (ed.), *Toward a Global Civil Society*, Providence, Rhode Island: Berghahn Books, pp. 7–27.

Walzer, Michael (ed.) (1995b): *Toward a Global Civil Society*, Providence, Rhode Island: Berghahn Books.

Williams, Phil (1997): *The Dark Side of Global Civil Society: The Role and Impact of Transnational Criminal Organizations as a Threat to International Security*. Paper prepared for the UNU Symposium "The United Nations System in the Twenty-first Century: International Peace and Security," 8–9 November 1996, Tokyo, Japan.

8

Global civil society, social movement organizations, and the global politics of nuclear security

Jackie Smith

Introduction

The introduction of nuclear weapons to the military arsenals of states brought concerns for macro-level, or inter-state, security to the forefront of the international agenda. Throughout the Cold War period, nuclear weapons and their regulation remained a major focus of inter-state dialogue within the United Nations system. Because these weapons threatened human society in ways that no other human invention had done previously, governments were forced to think about military security in fundamentally different ways. In other words, nuclear weapons were inconsistent with the logics driving conventional deterrence strategies. In order to prevent a nuclear confrontation, states had to adapt their approaches to security.

Traditional analyses of international relations and institutions focus principally on governments and their agents to explain changes such as adaptations in international policies. This is particularly true when confronting issues of nuclear weapons and macro-level security, which represent the foundation of state sovereignty. However, closer examinations reveal that most international institutions have been shaped by extensive and complex interactions among governmental and non-governmental actors.[1] Non-state actors, including international non-governmental organizations (INGOs), have generated ideas, pressure, and public support for the formation of international institutions, and have occasionally exerted substantial influence on the shape of these institutions. In recent years, scholarly and policy-oriented debates have focused on how a growing number of INGOs interact with and influence international political institutions and global governance.[2] These debates reflect an increasingly widespread observation that some degree of "global civil society" does indeed exist outside of governmental and economic spheres, and at times influences global policies and practices.[3]

A growing body of evidence shows that NGOs and INGOs participate routinely in formal intergovernmental negotiations,[4] and that their work also serves to shape individuals' perceptions, beliefs, and behaviours. On issues of macro-level security, we likewise find extensive efforts on the part of non-state actors to promote changes in states' values and policies regarding nuclear weapons. Although the primary goal of this movement – nuclear disarmament – has not been achieved, and while steps towards this goal have been painfully slow, the movement clearly helped contain the superpower nuclear arms race during the Cold War and advanced changes in government security policies.[5]

Looking at the role of non-state actors in helping to bring about changes in global security thinking and action, we can ask more general questions about how global civil society might be affecting global political processes. What aspects of this emergent, more-or-less global civil society make it relevant politically? Does the activity of transnational civil society actors suggest that common identities and transnational loyalties are developing among participants in transnational activities? To what extent do these transnational affiliations require new thinking about global political processes?

This chapter examines two cases of transnational organizations – the Pugwash Conferences on Science and World Affairs, and Parliamentarians for Global Action – which promoted international steps to reduce the threat of nuclear war. The cases describe the contributions each group made to international nuclear security debates, and assess their impacts on global policy. An analysis is offered of what these cases suggest about the prerequisites for NGOs' impact on inter-state policies as well as the challenges of transnational association to promote policy change.

Global civil society, non-state actors, and global security politics

Global civil society is "the space of uncoerced human association and also the set of relational networks – formed for the sake of family, faith, interest, and ideology – that fill this space."[6] The proliferation and expansion of international NGOs and of transnational alliances among national and local NGOs signal the presence of a global civil society with deepening roots. Moreover, as the broader global society has expanded, so too has its politically engaged sector, or a public sphere "in which a rational-critical discourse can take place about how the interests of different groups are related to each other and to the actions of the state."[7] Global civil society, according to Falk, is a product of transnational activity which contributes to greater political democracy while serving as a counterbalance to state and market forces.[8] But global civil society remains in its infancy, as state and corporate interests remain predominant in global political affairs.

How do we recognize global civil society when we see it? Organizations are but one manifestation of it, and indeed they are typically its most readily observable element. Falk suggests six observable activities which might be used to assess the contributions of particular actors to the strengthening of global civil society: providing information not readily attended to in routine political considerations; advancing identities that transcend state boundaries; demanding greater accountability from political leaders; advancing non-violent strategies for change; promoting "reverse cooption" to "adapt the forms of ordinary international relations to serve the goals of global civil society"; and promoting constitutionalism, or forms of global governance that further the values of human rights, democracy, equity, and environmental protection. Organizations performing some or all of these tasks can be considered to be contributing to the development of global civil society.

Types of non-state actors

Non-state actors that help make up global civil society may be involved in a variety of activities, and only a small proportion of these actors routinely engage in politics.[9] Among the politically active subset of non-state actors, we find associations that resemble conventional interest groups which seek to advance the interests of a specific group of people within the existing policy framework. Another set of actors might be called advocates. Advocacy associations seek to advance the interests of marginalized groups (who may or may not be among the organizations' members) by changing "some elements of the social structure and/or reward distribution of society."[10]

Social change advocacy organizations provide the foundations for collective action on behalf of particular issues. Because such organizations lack the means of influence that distinguish governmental and economic actors, these groups must employ alternative means of influence if they are to affect policy. One principal resource such groups use is to mobilize a broad range of actors around certain change goals. Such mobilizing efforts produce social movements. I will now discuss the concept of social movements, and the relationships between movements and organizations. I then relate the language of social movements to the concept of "epistemic communities" as it has been used in international relations scholarship, since this term has been used to describe the kinds of organizations which I refer to here as transnational social movement organizations.

Transnational social movements and organizations

Transnational social movement organizations (TSMOs) constitute a subset of INGOs which are routinely engaged in this emerging global public sphere. TSMOs are organized across national boundaries to advocate some form of social and/or political change. Their routine involvement in politically motivated social change advocacy distinguishes them from recreational, professional, and other INGOs which may enter into political debates at times, but whose organizational missions prevent them from undertaking regular social change activity.

As nodes in much broader networks of individuals and organizations seeking a particular social change goal (social movements), TSMOs help frame global issues, mobilize broader publics around their social change frames, and promote activities in national, subnational, and transnational contexts to advance movement goals. TSMOs, moreover, help identify, frame, and disseminate important technical and scientific information that is relevant to policy debates, and their political orientation helps channel such information into and through policy processes.[11]

Over time, transnational social movements attract different clusters of organizational and individual actors which offer varying degrees of material, logistic, and solidary support for the movements' goals.[12] Often international and national NGOs – including church organizations and professional associations – participate in social movements, working alongside TSMOs and bringing the movement both an expanded legitimacy and broader constituencies.[13] Variations in the activation of adherents from the broader society (including governmental and economic realms as well as civil society) around a movement's goals produce "cycles" or "surges" of movement activity. The surges in movement activity can – if they generate substantial pressure – help realize changes in government policies (although not always in the direction sought by the movement), or repression.[14]

Because they are explicitly designed to advocate some kind of change, TSMOs can be expected to be active in political processes on a regular basis. Thus they are often in a better position to provide relevant information, interpretations of global problems, action strategies, and tools for action than are those actors which participate in a movement only sporadically.[15] In addition to TSMOs, other INGOs often join in movement efforts. For instance, committees of the World Council of Churches and of various professional associations engage in international human rights or peace movement work. Sometimes national and local NGOs and social movement organizations (SMOs) join international coalitions to promote a particular policy goal or influence intergovernmental conferences. Often individuals acting outside of formal organizations – including general citizens, media workers, celebrities, parliamentarians, and government officials – participate in movement activities by writing op-ed pieces, attending movement-sponsored events, signing petitions, or otherwise contributing to the advancement of movement aims.

Epistemic communities

Peter Haas has used the term "epistemic communities" to refer to networks of knowledge-based experts who help promote policy change by articulating and legitimating particular understandings of complex problems, thereby shaping the terms of policy debate on those problems.[16] Although this approach is correct in recognizing the important role that experts play in shaping public debates over policies addressing complex problems, it fails to explain variation in participation by different portions of the scientific community or to elucidate the conditions under which the policies advanced by a scientific community actually come to be reflected in public policy. As Risse-Kappen observes:

Decision makers are always exposed to several and often contradictory policy concepts. Research on transnational relations and, most recently, on "epistemic communities" of knowledge-based transnational networks has failed so far to specify the conditions under which specific ideas are selected and influence policies while others fall by the wayside.[17]

A further problem with the epistemic community approach is that political change is typically extremely slow, often requiring years of diligent monitoring and strategic intervention by policy entrepreneurs and networks of change advocates. Even in cases where scientific consensus on the nature of a problem and its appropriate solutions exists, significant time and energy must still be devoted to building political consensus. This process appears to demand the formation of organizational structures specifically devoted to political work. Indeed, Kubbig attributes much of the Pugwash organization's success to its leaders' ability to develop and sustain an organization that could facilitate routine interactions among members of the more diffuse epistemic community. He documents the very process by which key leaders actively cultivated a network of people they felt were particularly important to both illuminating the technical aspects of nuclear security questions and channelling this knowledge into government decision structures.[18]

Moreover, although the participation of scientists helped focus government attention on the problems nuclear weapons posed for human security, the "epistemic community" approach does not adequately explain the lengthy and interactive process that led to only gradual steps toward nuclear disarmament. Nor does it explain why the organized and concerted efforts of a transnational network of élite nuclear scientists could not prevent the nuclear arms race that emerged in the wake of the Second World War.[19]

Although the transnational disarmament movement contained scientific networks that resemble Haas's epistemic communities, the concept does little to help clarify this highly complex and diverse movement which went well beyond the scientific community. In contrast, sociological studies of social movements provide conceptual tools that have been tested in the study of national social movements to foster understanding of the conditions under which influential élites are mobilized around social change goals, and how their participation in broader social change efforts influences policy change.[20]

The transnational nuclear disarmament movement

Over the past five decades, transnational citizens' efforts to prevent nuclear war have generated formal social movement organizations, and these have attracted sustained support from the scientific community as well as from religious institutions. In addition, intermittent surges of support from more general publics, such as school or church groups and social clubs, and from social movement organizations working on goals other than nuclear disarmament, helped focus world attention on the problem of nuclear weapons, and prodded governments to consider concrete steps toward disarmament. A particularly important segment of the transnational nuclear disarmament movement has been the scientific community, which was perhaps reluctantly drawn to international peace work by its own responsibility for the development of nuclear weapons.

Transnational citizens' efforts to prevent nuclear war represented a new chapter in international peace activism, which, from the early nineteenth century, had emerged in various forms to oppose militaristic nationalism and promote non-violent means for resolving international disputes.[21] Efforts to combat nuclear weapons' development rose in urgency in the wake of the nuclear bombings of Hiroshima and Nagasaki at the end of the Second World War. Interestingly, the scientists who had helped to design and perfect the nuclear bomb became the core of the incipient anti-nuclear movement in the immediate post-war years.[22] Many remained active in the movement through subsequent decades, seeking to limit governments' reliance on nuclear weapons. Outside the scientific community, few truly transnational efforts flourished, at least until the late 1970s and 1980s, and even then efforts to build transnational organizations to work specifically on nuclear disarmament remained limited.[23]

This chapter focuses on the work of two TSMOs representing élite segments of the transnational nuclear disarmament movement: the Pugwash Conferences on Science and World Affairs, and the Parliamentarians for Global Action. Although relatively privileged members of the polity, scientists and parliamentarians were formally excluded from routine participation in decisions related to nuclear security policies. The Pugwash Conferences and Parliamentarians for Global Action provided mechanisms that allowed these two categories of individuals to engage in nuclear policy debates more than they could otherwise have done.

These groups made up a small piece of the much broader transnational nuclear disarmament movement, which encompassed a vast range of activists from many different social groups. As two of the stronger examples of transnational cooperation, these organizations should provide insights into the factors that contribute to building global civil society. As groups with a primary focus on formal inter-state negotiations and with relatively privileged access to key decision makers, these cases should help us better understand how intervention by civil society actors affects international policy-making processes.

Scientists against the bomb: Pugwash in the Cold War years

Even before they witnessed the actual explosions of nuclear weapons over Hiroshima and Nagasaki, prominent nuclear scientists became alarmed at the potential for misuse of these weapons by political leaders. When several scientists working on the US Manhattan Project realized that it was indeed possible to produce a nuclear bomb, they began to oppose further nuclear experimentation and to advise political leaders against their use.[24] Several leading scientific thinkers – including Albert Einstein and Bertrand Russell – even advocated the formation of a world government that would reduce the risks of nuclear war by providing multilateral mechanisms for non-violent conflict resolution and regulating nuclear weapons.

The scientific community of the 1930s and 1940s was one of the more internationally networked segments of society, largely because the norms of scientific enquiry encourage communication that transcends national divisions.[25] The war also helped nurture transnational cooperation among scientific communities in Allied nations, and frequently émigré scientists seeking refuge from the Bolshevik or Nazi regimes were part of Allied nuclear programmes. The war forced many scientists to confront directly questions related to politics, as here their own scientific work had very obvious (and potentially disastrous) implications for humanity. This served to politicize the scientific community and to generate an organizational foundation for post-war disarmament work.[26]

By mid-1945, Eugene Rabinowitch – a Russian émigré and biophysicist who had worked in Germany and Great Britain before coming to the United States – was advocating that, once the general public became aware of the nuclear bomb, scientists should begin organizing opposition to the threats posed by atomic weapons.[27] He was supported by a strong network of like-minded colleagues at Chicago's Metallurgical Laboratory (Met Lab), where the first controlled nuclear chain reaction was produced in 1941. Scientists' fears about the possible use of nuclear weapons in the Second World War had escalated as the end of the war neared, and as it became clear that a nuclear bomb was not needed as a deterrent against Nazi Germany, but that the United States might use the weapon against Japan. A committee of scientists working at the Met Lab began to assess the scientific, social, and political implications of their research on atomic energy. Rabinowitch wrote important sections of the committee's report, arguing that lasting security would demand strict controls on nuclear weapons' development and the immediate establishment of "an international administration with police powers which can effectively control at least the means of nucleonic warfare."[28]

Manhattan Project scientists sharing the sentiments voiced in the Met Lab report formed associations to promote nuclear disarmament immediately following the bombing of Hiroshima and Nagasaki. In November 1945, several of these local associations joined together to form the Federation of American Scientists (FAS).[29] The FAS soon had more than 3,000 members and included 90 per cent of the scientists who had worked on the nuclear bomb.[30] The new scientists' organization also quickly established a mechanism to help it expand awareness and dialogue about the social and political implications of the nuclear bomb: the National Committee on Atomic Information (NCAI) was established to distribute information on atomic energy to a broad public through more than 60 labour, civic, religious, and other social organizations across the United States. Rabinowitch and several of his Chicago Met Lab colleagues launched *The Bulletin of the Atomic Scientists* to foster even broader awareness and dialogue among experts and the public.

The scientific community, organized through the rapidly expanding and explicitly political FAS,[31] continued its efforts to press governments to abandon their reliance on nuclear weapons for security. Leading scientific figures used their access to the US Administration[32] to advance steps to reduce the threat of nuclear war. Their discussions with government officials helped generate a climate more favourable to arms control than might otherwise have developed.[33] One reason for scientists' success in influencing political leaders' thinking about arms control was the formation of a transnational organization, the Pugwash Conferences on Science and World Affairs, which brought together American, Soviet, and other nations' scientists to promote international communication focused on preventing nuclear war. This TSMO proved to be a crucial mechanism for the transfer of ideas about nuclear arms control and disarmament between the United States and the Soviet Union, especially at times when Cold War tensions prevented official discussions of these matters.[34]

Pugwash's mission statement urges scientists of the world to press governments to both acknowledge the threat to humankind posed by nuclear weapons and seek peaceful means of settling international disputes. The introduction of nuclear weapons fundamentally altered existing security strategies, and it meant that "the two sides needed to find a way of developing collective knowledge which could be converted into a binding policy that would prevent war."[35] The Pugwash Conferences sought to respond to this need by organizing efforts to influence governments, promoting communication among scholars, and carrying out public education work.[36] The organization's major activity consisted of conferences among scientists, who were invited based on considerations of their expertise as well as on their relationship to policy makers. In their selection of conference participants, Pugwash leaders made deliberate efforts to ensure that ideas generated in conferences would find their way to policy makers.[37]

The Pugwash Conferences began in 1957 in Pugwash, Nova Scotia, bringing together scientists from 10 countries. Since then, the organization has sponsored more than 200 gatherings. Each conference contributed to global civil society by providing a forum for relatively free discussion of issues of concern to humanity. This allowed participants gradually to develop relationships based on trust and openness, even when the Soviet government obstructed the truly free participation of their delegates to the Pugwash meetings.[38] This process is evident in the observations that early Pugwash meetings were difficult, and some Western participants reported frustration at their Soviet counterparts' unwillingness to engage in free intellectual exchanges exploring differences among them. However, this obstacle subsided over the years, and often Western participants would find their counterparts supporting positions they had rejected at earlier meetings.[39]

The Pugwash Conferences provided one of the few opportunities then available for scientists in the Eastern and Western blocs to exchange scientific and political information. Indeed, they provided a rare chance for scientists to consider the social and political implications of their research. While allowing participants opportunities to hear and share scientific papers on the conferences' disarmament themes, Pugwash more importantly helped cultivate informal dialogues and networking among scientists divided by political realities. These networks transcended state boundaries to expand international information flows, thereby broadening scientists' and political leaders' understandings of the Cold War conflict and of the nuclear dilemma, and increasing the opportunities for new solutions to emerge. Contacts generated through Pugwash helped generate other transnational networking that facilitated cooperation, such as a 1986 agreement between the Soviet Academy of Sciences (SAS) and the US-based National Resources Defense Council (NRDC), which allowed scientists to monitor American and Soviet nuclear test sites.[40]

The continuity of the Pugwash meetings was important in allowing participants to develop interpersonal ties, encouraging them to rely on these ties to improve communications during periods of heightened Cold War tension.[41] This reliance on interpersonal ties to facilitate rapid communication where the potential for conflict escalation is high is evident in an account provided by Frank von Hippel, a key Pugwashite who served as Chairman of the FAS. When Reagan announced his own Strategic Defense Initiative, which would have violated the Anti-Ballistic Missile (ABM) Treaty then in place, a group from the Soviet Academy of Sciences sent an open letter to their American counterparts in the FAS saying "You people convinced us that it would be counter-productive to have an anti-missile race. There were talks going on through Pugwash about these matters in the late 1960s. Have you changed your mind?" (von Hippel's paraphrasing of the SAS letter, quoted in Spencer).[42]

The Pugwash Conferences were mechanisms for transnational communication that filled the many gaps in inter-state communications channels. Because they convened routinely – regardless of the state of US-Soviet relations – the conferences served as "ice-breakers" when bilateral tensions prevented constructive intergovernmental dialogue.[43] And even at times when the Soviet government restricted its people's participation in other transnational exchanges, it allowed its delegations to attend the Pugwash meetings.[44] The effectiveness of the Pugwash meetings as communication channels was amplified by the conscious efforts made to ensure that ideas discussed in conferences were fed into policy circles. There is also evidence that political leaders came to look to Pugwash for expertise and ideas regarding nuclear policy.[45,46]

Pugwash after the Cold War

Especially in the years since the Soviet Union's demise, Pugwash's role has changed. Even in the late 1980s, the organization began rethinking the relationship between nuclear security and other global threats.[47] In September 1988, for instance, the Pugwash Council adopted its "Dagomys Declaration," which emphasized that poverty, energy consumption, and environmental degradation pose crucial threats to human security and peace, and that therefore "[w]ithout reducing our commitment to arms reduction and war prevention, we must recognize that environmental degradation and large-scale impoverishment are already facts and can lead to massive catastrophe even if nuclear war is avoided."[48]

As the primacy of the nuclear threat has subsided, and as concerns about other global dangers have arisen to threaten global security, the range of issues on Pugwash's agenda has expanded to include environmental and development concerns along with more traditional security concerns.[49] This expanded agenda reflects the recognition among Pugwash members that the threat of nuclear war is no longer the principal threat to human security, and that problems such as continued environmental degradation and economic inequalities are likely to be the source of future global conflicts. Pursuing their goal of helping governments find ways to avoid war, Pugwash Conferences have incorporated themes such as "Global Action on the Energy/Climate Interaction" and "Developing in Peace" to complement their more traditional concerns.[50]

Despite its expanded programme agenda, Pugwash's principal goal remains that of promoting a nuclear-weapons-free world. The bulk of attention at its annual conferences is paid to issues related to nuclear weapons and their elimination. And the organization's major research initiatives and related publications are heavily directed toward nuclear concerns, with the most recently published titles including *Verification: Monitoring Disarmament* (1991), *A Nuclear-Weapons-Free World: Desirable? Feasible?* (1993), and *Conversion of Military Research and Development in the Former Soviet Republics – the Future of their Nuclear Weapon Complex* (1993; 1994; 1995).[51]

This internal dilution of Pugwash's anti-nuclear message has been paralleled by external factors that have helped diminish Pugwash's predominant voice in international nuclear disarmament policy. Pugwash's prominence has faded with the Cold War, and this is due in part to the emergence of a much wider range of scientifically-based TSMOs.[52] As one of a number of organizations that help mobilize scientific expertise for social purposes, Pugwash must compete with other professional voices seeking to steer national security policies.

Activating national legislators: Parliamentarians for Global Action

Parliamentarians for Global Action is a New York-based transnational organization of over 1,000 members of parliament from more than 80 countries. The organization was formed in the late 1970s by a network of MPs who were members of the World Association for World Federalism.[53] It has worked since then to support multilateral institutions for peace and disarmament, and more recently has expanded to include work for democracy, development, and environmental protection.

A major premiss of its founders was that nations' foreign policy decisions are the products of fairly secretive and insulated processes which are dominated by the executive. Even under democratic regimes, decisions about foreign policy are less transparent and less accountable to elected legislators and their constituents than those on other issues.[54] Partly because of this, negotiations among governments are even further insulated. What goes on behind the closed doors of official conference rooms in Geneva, Brussels, and New York remains largely inaccessible to many who are affected by the outcomes of those negotiations. By organizing MPs around global change issues, Global Action seeks to empower these members to be more active in shaping their nations' foreign policies. Its various activities serve to educate MPs about complex global issues and policy choices, to involve them in coordinated parliamentary initiatives designed to press governments to adopt internationalist policies, and to provide them with a valuable global network of MPs which gives members a sense that they are not alone in their efforts as well as more concrete cooperative benefits.

As the Pugwash scientists' expertise enhanced that organization's ability to win the attention of government officials, Global Action's membership likewise gives it atypical access (however sporadic) to the highest levels of some governments, and it has used this access to raise new issues in the global arena as well as to press governments to take certain actions or positions. Its years of work in the area of peace and disarmament, the creative ideas it has brought to disarmament negotiations, and the influence it has been able to wield have earned it a reputation which further facilitates its access to officials and government delegates.[55]

Like Pugwash, Global Action's principal routine activity is its annual Parliamentary Forum, which brings together members of the organization who wish to engage in dialogues about how to address contemporary global problems with their counterparts from around the world. The Parliamentary Forums provide opportunities for many MPs to learn about and consider positions on foreign policy issues which lie outside their routine legislative work. As routine gatherings, these meetings foster the development of individual relationships among participants, who enjoy the chance to compare legislative experiences, seek advice from colleagues working on similar issues, and learn about how colleagues from other nations interpret global problems. The ties cultivated through participation in Global Action events have, in many cases, persisted after members leave the organization, and they can become particularly influential when Global Action members move on to accept government positions.[56]

In addition to its annual forums, Global Action mobilizes its members to participate in delegations to intergovernmental conferences or to meet with heads of state. This was a frequent strategy used in the campaign for an Amendment Conference to the Partial Test Ban Treaty (described below); delegations were dispatched at critical times to press government officials to help advance the campaign. Although political risks dampened officials' interest in taking on Global Action's requests, often the fact that legislators from other nations were interested enough in their governments' position on an issue to travel halfway around the world to discuss it could convince political leaders to at least consider the proposal. Global Action also offered logistical support to political leaders agreeing to work with its campaigns, and this helped reduce the costs associated with taking on a proposal like advancing a call for an Amendment Conference.

Another strategy of Global Action is to organize meetings of delegates during routine inter-state gatherings, such as UN General Assemblies or global conferences, meetings of the Conference on Disarmament, and so on. These unofficial meetings provide opportunities for delegates to consider ideas that lie outside the formal negotiating agenda. They can learn details about a proposal, query experts about the feasibility of a proposal, learn the views of other nations' delegates (and thereby judge the likelihood of a proposal gaining wider support), and discuss political opportunities and obstacles surrounding a proposal with Global Action staff (who spend a much larger proportion of their time than delegates can ever hope to spend considering these questions).[57]

Like the Pugwash meetings, these private, informal meetings allowed participants to take the risk of raising new ideas or considering positions which would be forbidden within the constraints of their normal professional and diplomatic routines. Such meetings allow officials to interact in an unofficial setting where they can be more frank and tentative than they can in normal diplomatic settings.[58] Global Action's strategy helps overcome many obstacles to change posed by bureaucratic and political realities:

[Global Action President Ólafur] Grímsson developed the theory of what he believed was [Global Action]'s new approach to international relations. In his view, virtually all of the usual global actors were paralyzed. The superpowers were constrained by their enormous bureaucracies from taking new or risky initiatives for peace. The other governments were afraid to confront the superpowers because they would be embarrassed by a failure. The international organizations were staffed by bureaucrats more concerned with protecting their careers than with making policy; this focus ensured that they made no waves because in these organizations, causing any offence can jeopardize a career. So in the entire diplomatic world, Grímsson reasoned, it was nearly impossible for anyone to try anything new. [Global Action] could become "the guys who can afford to lose face, the ones who are in the business of being turned down ... [Global Action] accepted the role that the monks played in the Middle Ages. We could speak to the princes who couldn't speak to each other."[59]

Thus, Global Action helps remove the obstacles posed by diplomatic procedure to make interactions among government officials more conducive to real problem-solving efforts than is typically the case. Through these contacts, government officials responding to Global Action's initiatives are less at risk if a proposal should fail: they can always deny their association with a non-governmental organization and can, through its non-official partner, test the waters before acting.

Global Action and nuclear disarmament politics

Global Action's Deputy Secretary-General, Aaron Tovish, was preparing for the 1985 NPT (Non-Proliferation Treaty) Review Conference when he discovered a new means of raising the test ban issue: he noticed that – while the NPT treaty is basically impossible to amend – the amendment procedure contained in the Partial Test Ban Treaty (PTBT) allows for a third of the state parties to issue a call for a conference to amend the treaty, even over the objections of the "depository governments," the United States, Britain, and the USSR. He recognized that such an amendment process might be used to extend the treaty to include a ban on underground tests, thus making it a comprehensive nuclear test ban treaty.[60] In short, if Global Action could convince a handful of states to raise the conference call, it could gain the momentum to convince the requisite 39 countries to stand up to the depository states and back the Amendment Conference idea. As Tovish and his colleagues were to discover, however, convincing states to defy the American and British resistance to a comprehensive test ban was no easy task.

It took six years to move from the initial action of the campaign in 1984 to the conclusion of the Amendment Conference. Moreover, the Amendment Conference did not result in the actual extension of the PTBT, but rather a decision to allow the Amendment Conference to be reconvened in the future.[61] This result – if not the six-year delay in bringing the conference to fruition – was completely consistent with Global Action's expectations. As Tovish recalled, "we had no illusions with the Partial Test Ban Treaty Amendment Conference: [we knew] that the United States would go down to the wire against it. That was absolutely clear from the beginning."[62] But the amendment procedure "was a way for the rest of the world to register the fact that they cared so much about this issue that they were prepared to use unorthodox methods, and prepared to even have a conference that was technically a failure if you look at the result, simply to underscore where the problem was."[63] The fact that – despite strong US opposition – one-third of the parties to the PTBT successfully initiated the call for an Amendment Conference, and that 74 of 95 countries voting on the final decision of the Amendment Conference favoured the extension of the conference (leaving only the United States and Britain opposed), said to the United States that "it is totally unacceptable that you are stonewalling the test ban issue. And we will continue to harass you on this by whatever means necessary until you come around on this."[64] Thus the campaign did ultimately serve to communicate to the nuclear weapons states, particularly the recalcitrant United States, that it could not simply ignore the test ban issue and hope for it to go away on its own.

This sentiment was further reinforced after the Amendment Conference by Global Action's work to support annual UN General Assembly resolutions supporting a comprehensive test ban.[65] A more instrumental action was to encourage the PTBT Amendment Conference President, Ali Alatas, to call a special meeting of the conference in 1993 to mark the thirtieth anniversary of the PTBT.[66] Global Action met with relevant US government officials to ensure that they would not oppose the meeting outright – indeed, that they might attend it – and to convince Alatas that he would not be embarrassed by issuing the call. Global Action had worked to bring pressure on the Administration through its Congressional contacts, through the media, and through direct meetings with the Administration. Its major goal was to both sway the Administration away from the position of the previous Administration and to give it a chance to say no to a special meeting before Alatas made his call public. When the United States expressed no direct opposition to a meeting, Global

Action advised Alatas to go ahead with the special meeting. So the issue of a comprehensive test ban (CTB) was again revived for international debate.

One immediate consequence of the special meeting of the parties to the PTBT was to press the Conference on Disarmament (CD) to initiate negotiations on a CTB within that forum.[67,68] Thus, by late 1993 there were three simultaneous "tracks"[69] on which CTB negotiations were proceeding, and Global Action, Alatas, and many of the non-aligned states saw this as a means of keeping the pressure on the nuclear weapons states (NWS) to make real progress on a CTB.[70] Global Action kept a watchful eye over all of this, taking any action it deemed necessary to facilitate progress, and being careful not to derail any progress that might be under way.[71] In mid-1994, a Global Action delegation to the Non-Aligned Movement's foreign ministers' meeting in Cairo met with 17 delegations in order to promote its draft UN resolution for a "step-by-step reduction of the nuclear threat."[72] The proposal was drafted as a model UN resolution which would state clear and limited objectives towards nuclear disarmament and establish a foundation for negotiations on the NPT extension, and it moved more quickly from idea to actuality than any other Global Action proposal, according to International Committee Chair and long-time Global Action member Ólafur Grímsson.[73,74]

Global Action after the Cold War

The end of the Cold War brought new attention to a host of global concerns that were previously submerged by Cold War confrontation. The corresponding emergence of new democratic institutions has also brought an influx of members into the organization, and these members come from regions heretofore unrepresented in Parliamentarians for Global Action. As a consequence, the organization has been challenged to take up new issues and develop its staff to accommodate these new concerns. This has meant the development of new programmes, such as the East Asia Conflict Resolution Programme and the Democracy and Africa Programme. Each of these new programmes represents a response to a changed global context.

Throughout the 1980s, Global Action's efforts focused primarily on advancing nuclear disarmament, and very little attention was devoted to other issues. But by 1990 the Cold War had clearly ended and new issues appeared to be taking on greater significance in global affairs, and larger numbers of Global Action's members brought these issues into the organization's agenda. At the same time, funding for disarmament work was disappearing as many funders saw the end of the Cold War as a signal to shift to other issues.

Because its new members come from dramatically different cultural and political backgrounds, Global Action has had to expend more effort to integrate these members. This has meant everything from expanding its translation services to diversifying its meeting sites and adapting its political strategies and focii. With growth has come growing pains. Long-time members have seen the growth of the organization and the expansion of its activities as taking away from its political impact.[75] New members have expressed their frustrations with the organization's failure to provide its materials in languages other than English, and with the limited translation at meetings. The international secretariat has had to focus more urgently on hiring multilingual staff. All of this comes at a time when recession and global political changes have brought dramatic changes in the amount and nature of funding available for peace-related action.

TSMOs and global security politics

Although TSMOs devote their energies towards promoting social and political change, their change goals are rarely met, and the impacts of their work are difficult to substantiate. First, it is impossible to disentangle the efforts of social movement actors from the myriad other factors shaping political decisions. Second, a single TSMO is but one of a large number of actors involved in a political movement. While Pugwash or Parliamentarians for Global Action may have spoken with louder voices because of their distinct memberships and access to decision makers, the fact that policy makers paid any heed to their proposals cannot be interpreted without acknowledging the broader movement and popular protests that reinforced the disarmament goals advanced by these groups. The two cases examined here, however, can be quite clearly linked to at least two concrete political developments. Pugwash has been shown to have clearly helped shift the strategic thinking of Soviet nuclear policy advisers, enabling the passage of an ABM Treaty. And it is safe to say that an Amendment Conference to the Partial Test Ban Treaty would not have happened without Global Action's efforts to introduce and pursue the idea.[76]

What conditions allowed these TSMOs to have the impact they did on global security politics? Kubbig identifies three conditions which allowed Pugwash to enjoy the success it saw in shaping nuclear security policy. First, it mobilized around the nuclear question before there had been much public debate or understanding of the implications of nuclear technology for security policy. This allowed the organization to frame the terms of the debate as it emerged. Second, Pugwash generated lasting networks of communication by providing a persisting organization that could organize routine international gatherings to reinforce these networks. Moreover, the ability of the organization to survive over the long term was crucial, since changes in Pugwash participants' views were often observable only after a number of years. Thirdly, the Pugwash strategy was designed to help the participants identify common interests and provided incentives for governments to both pay attention to the conferences and allow the organization to operate fairly freely. This enabled it to continue meetings even when bilateral tensions cut off official dialogue.[77]

Similarly, Global Action emerged at a time when the superpowers were embarking on a stalemate, and new ideas were needed to rekindle nuclear disarmament efforts. The group was formed on the eve of the mass mobilizations against the nuclear arms race, and its effort to mobilize a constituency that most disarmament groups did not explicitly target gave it a propitious niche in the budding anti-nuclear movement. Second, Global Action's leaders were able to generate a durable organization that could withstand years of disappointment in order to see the long-term effects of its pressure. The organization's consistent presence in relevant diplomatic circles, its reputation for providing useful and innovative information and ideas, and its dogged persistence were key to advancing its objectives. Finally, Global Action, like Pugwash, adopted the approach of identifying common goals such as avoiding nuclear war. By helping participants and government targets focus on such fundamental, common values, they helped attract greater cooperation from a wider range of participants than they would have achived with a more narrowly focused strategy.

Conditions affecting TSMO impacts

Drawing from these two cases, one might expand upon and refine Kubbig's conclusions about the conditions shaping these TSMOs' impact on policy to make them more generalizable to other kinds of social change organizations. First, a group's impact will depend in large part on its access to key decision makers. Some direct or indirect channel must be open to the organization to transfer its ideas to central actors. Of course, many social movement actors must work to help open such channels by demonstrating public concern about an issue. But having some relevant expertise that policy makers need to make informed decisions will greatly increase an organization's access to decision makers. Or, as in the case of Global Action, having a prestigious membership can create various types of incentives (for example, to appeal to the constituents who elected an MP, or to benefit from a public appearance with a popular figure) for officials to pay attention to an organization. Organizations without a direct link to the policy process must be more creative in finding ways of advancing their ideas. One common way is to build cooperative ties with other like-minded organizations.

While access is perhaps the most important condition for an organization's success, the organization must be able to facilitate information flows among delegates. This means it must be present at intergovernmental meetings with good ideas about how to encourage delegates to consider an idea or to facilitate discussion among delegates. Groups with access to solid technical expertise and financial resources to provide incentives (such as meals) for delegates to attend their events are likely to be most effective as conduits of ideas and information. Advocates who consider the needs and capabilities of the individual delegates themselves, and who cultivate personal relationships with key delegates, also appear more effective in facilitating information exchange.

Thirdly, TSMOs' impacts on policy change are more marked when they account for decision makers' perceptions of the costs and benefits of a particular policy and seek to alter those cost-benefit calculations. This is what Pugwash sought to do as it pressed Soviet scientists to rethink their notions of nuclear defensive systems. And by cultivating ties with reformers among the Soviet élite, Pugwash helped condition the perceptions of Soviet hard-liners about the likelihood that they could challenge Gorbachev's move towards accommodation with the West.[78] Parliamentarians for Global Action likewise affected the perceived costs the United States would face if it continued to resist a PTBT Amendment Conference by mobilizing key governments in support of the conference.

One important way in which TSMOs alter the cost-benefit assessments of governments is by enhancing the transparency of international negotiations. The Pugwash Conferences were especially important venues for the sharing of information on nuclear strategies and scientific capabilities. They allowed for informal dialogue and explorations of strategic ideas outside of formal, diplomatic circles characterized by stringent responsibility and accountability norms that stifle creative searches for solutions to collective problems. And when official actions like Reagan's announcement of the Star Wars initiative contradicted understandings reached in unofficial circles, these channels remained open to provide important means of reassuring Soviets of American scientists' adherence to the shared understandings of ABM defences reached at Pugwash meetings, thus preventing more serious escalation of bipolar tensions over the Star Wars proposal.

Finally, TSMOs can help introduce new resources into multilateral political processes. An important illustration of this capacity is the SAS-NRDC verification agreement. In the absence of the US government's willingness to seek a means of overcoming its key stated reason for opposing a comprehensive nuclear test ban, these elements of global civil society demonstrated that a test ban could technically be verified, and they offered governments resources to carry out such verification. A similar offer to help verify a test ban was raised in Global Action's Middle Power Peace Initiative, as non-aligned country leaders offered their own services for helping verify a complete ban on testing.[79] Proposals like this reduced the costs and risks of cooperation, thereby making agreement more likely.

TSMOs and global civil society

Global civil society remains in many ways elusive, and its strengths lie only in the ability of its participants to overcome numerous obstacles to achieving transnational cooperation. The expansion of formal organizations designed to promote transnational goals and values represents a positive development for the realization of a stronger global civil society. But these associations must still overcome the competing claims to citizens' loyalties made by national and subnational entities. The transnational disarmament movement discussed here lacked extensive and strong transnational associations, and was principally comprised of sporadically-utilized transnational links among much stronger national movements.[80]

Transnational organizations such as the TSMOs examined here helped foster global civil society primarily by providing opportunities for individuals from many different countries to come together to engage in global problem-solving dialogues. The conferences sponsored by these organizations allowed transnational interpersonal ties to develop and flourish with routine organizational gatherings. These ties among individuals with key positions in policy circles helped generate dialogue that could facilitate the emergence of shared understandings about global problems. Dialogues based on the premiss that participants shared at least the basic goal of averting nuclear catastrophe formed the basis for the development of transnational identities. As the organization becomes more central to participants' own daily routines, their loyalty to the organization is likely to displace other loyalties, or at least to transform them.

In order for transnational organizations to facilitate the emergence of transnational identities and loyalties, they must first and foremost develop organizational structures that maximize communication among individuals from different countries. Routine conferences, newsletters, teleconferencing, and other activities that allow members from different countries to interact with one another are best able to challenge excessive nationalism and to cultivate a sense that many of the world's problems – perhaps nuclear weapons in particular – demand collective global responses.

Transnational organizations must work to counter the more particularistic interests often pursued by states, which typically act to defend state sovereignty even at the expense of human interests, and economic actors, which pursue economic benefit with little regard for the costs imposed on the wider society and environment. They must also work against limitations on people's time, their ability to understand complex global issues, and their ability to empathize with others who do not share their life experiences. Overcoming these obstacles is likely to demand a range of different activities.

Both Pugwash and Parliamentarians for Global Action possess organizational features that assist them in overcoming some of the obstacles to cultivating transnational loyalties. Their focus on particular professional groups certainly helps them in this work. Members share many common experiences, and can benefit from interpersonal linkages which will allow them to learn from colleagues in other countries. Moreover, the specific professions these groups organize are particularly susceptible to transnational loyalties and identities, since their high degrees of specialization in their fields may mean that they have more in common with their professional colleagues than with many individuals with whom they share a nationality. At least in the scientific field, transnational dialogue is considered an essential element of the scientific method.[81]

Implications for democracy

Oganizations like Pugwash and Parliamentarians for Global Action are especially susceptible to the criticism that they fail to manifest truly democratic practices. One obvious democratic deficit is the fact that these groups do not constitute representative samples of the global population, but rather are self-selected. Indeed, many advocacy groups – and perhaps transnational ones in particular – tend to involve only a small number of highly motivated activists in routine decision-making, becoming oligarchies with few if any mechanisms for representative input from and accountability to a grass-roots membership base.[82] Moreover, the demands of transnational activism mean there is limited cultural and socio-economic diversity among transnational movement organizations. Given this, can the claim be made that these groups contribute to the development of civil society and a more democratic global order?

Although they appear to lack internal democracy and fail to represent truly the views of a broad cross-section of society, both Pugwash and Parliamentarians for Global Action perform tasks that are essential to the operation of more democratic global institutions. They do so by providing information to a broader public than might otherwise have access to information related to nuclear security policies; cultivating transnational identities which help individuals perceive common stakes in political decisions occurring beyond the national level; monitoring the behaviour of governments in order to hold them accountable to their formal and informal agreements; and developing tactics that enable groups and individuals who are otherwise disenfranchised from bilateral and multilateral decision processes to attempt to influence policy. Thus, in the aggregate, TSMOs – even those organized in a highly undemocratic manner – contribute to global democracy. We can conclude from these observations that transnational movement actors such as those described here contribute to the evolution of new forms of democratic global governance, but they remain imperfect.

Challenges to transnationalism

Early statements by scientists who became central to the formation of Pugwash, including Albert Einstein, Leo Szilard, and Eugene Rabinowitch, emphasized that nuclear weapons demanded the formation of a world government capable of effectively containing the spread of nuclear weapons technology and of promoting collective security to reduce the incentives for states to develop such weapons. These sentiments were, however, fairly quickly abandoned in favour of the more limited objective of preventing and containing a nuclear arms race. In hindsight, the shift of attention from multilateral institution-building towards arms control solutions might have inhibited the development of transnational cooperation for more comprehensive and enduring structures for global security. Moreover, it demonstrates an important obstacle to the formation of the common identity and transnational loyalty that is critical to a strong global civil society.

The transnational nuclear disarmament movement did not generate strong pressures for multilateral institution-building, in part because of the failure to overcome national influences on mobilizing opportunities and strategies. Cortright and Pagnucco demonstrate how this obstacle manifested itself in limited transnational cooperation (at least between American and European groups) around the nuclear freeze efforts and those of INF (intermediate-range nuclear forces).[83] As Risse-Kappen observed, "concepts such as common security were rather alien to a [US] political culture emphasizing pluralist individualism at home and sharp zero-sum conflicts with ideological opponents abroad."[84] The bilateral arms control framework inherent in the nuclear freeze proposal fitted neatly into US policy frameworks, and it did not require extensive amounts of knowledge on the part of the public the movement sought to mobilize.

What the freeze could not do was expand US foreign policy debates beyond a simple bilateral arms control paradigm to incorporate more multilateral and institutional responses to global conflict. Thus, despite the massive mobilizations of the 1980s around foreign policy concerns, the post-Cold War era had inherited a US public unaccustomed to multilateral security thinking, uninformed about the United Nations, and therefore unable to hold its government's foreign policy accountable to a broader public interest. Instead, it is easily swayed by multilateralism's opponents in Congress.

Movement organizations outside the United States also faced strong limitations to their ability to transcend national political frameworks to cultivate transnational interests, loyalties, and identities. Strategic choices reflected activists' perceptions about appropriate mobilizing strategies for their national contexts. Because activists had to concern themselves with satisfying the domestic constituencies which supported their work, such a preoccupation with nationally structured political opportunities is understandable, if short-sighted. The experience of the 1980s' freeze movement, however, is not much different from earlier inter-war peace mobilizations that similarly broke down along nationalist lines. For transnational efforts around multilateral problem-solving efforts to succeed, activists should be mindful that their national struggles take place within a larger international political context. In other words, multiple national decision arenas operate within and interact with a global intergovernmental decision arena. Effective strategies must seek to relate these interdependent decision processes.

In addition to differences in political strategies based upon participants' national political contexts, transnational peace movement cooperation was limited because of conflicts among activists about appropriate strategies and priorities as well as over resources. Wittner's and Atwood's discussions of transnational nuclear disarmament efforts detail the conflicts that arose repeatedly to divide peace activists. Pacifists favoured strategies and goals that non-pacifists found unrealistic or utopian. Activists favouring direct action strategies found less confrontational strategies unacceptable. Other elements of the movement bent over backwards not to appear sympathetic to the Soviet line, while some chose to overlook blatant Soviet attempts to manipulate the movement for its own purposes. These kinds of tensions routinely produced conflicts between organizations and individuals in the movement, inhibiting sustained and strategically coordinated efforts. Conflicts whcih arose over the definitions of the nuclear problem also divided movement efforts. Major segments of the movement linked nuclear disarmament with social and economic justice concerns, while others sought to focus strictly on the dangers of nuclear arms races and deterrence strategy. Improved communications, such as those available to contemporary movements, might prevent these kinds of conflicts from crippling future transnational disarmament efforts. Nevertheless, disarmament advocates might benefit from more historically informed and strategic thinking about how to frame at least some struggles in ways that can promote cooperation among the necessarily diverse elements of a transnational movement.

Conclusions

Global integration – whether caused by the expansion of economic interdependencies, the proliferation of international institutions, or the expansion of threats to human well-being beyond national borders – demands new forms of public participation in both national and transnational decision-making processes. Cultivating a healthy global civil society is the only path to such participation. The preceding analysis of transnational disarmament organizations illustrates that such groups can promote transnational identities and activities which can shape global policies and dialogues. But the cases also revealed persisting gaps in the development of a robust civil society that transcends national loyalties.

Conditions affecting the success of these TSMOs were their access to decision-making processes, their skilful and strategic use of information, their ability to interpret and respond to policy makers' cost-benefit calculations within a given negotiating context, and their abilities to introduce new resources into negotiations. We can expect that groups which lack the élite memberships shared by both Pugwash and Parliamentarians for Global Action will face more serious difficulties in achieving the kinds of impacts these groups have enjoyed. Also, the post-Cold War proliferation of issues demanding the attention of global political leaders makes the single-issue focus these groups shared more difficult to maintain. Each organization has expanded its issue agenda, thereby dividing its resources across a number of campaigns rather than focusing all its efforts on the nuclear issue.

Despite their relative advantages (when compared with other TSMOs), even these two groups faced serious limitations in their abilities to overcome challenges to transnationalism. They failed to free the nuclear security debate from the constraints of state-centred, bipolar security paradigms in order to cultivate support for multilateral responses to the nuclear security dilemma. One possible reason for this problem is that most TSMOs focus on achieving particular policy change goals rather than viewing their work as building a global civil society. A more conscious effort on the part of leaders to cultivate the ideas and practices that strengthen global civil society, empowering citizens to participate in political decisions that take place beyond national political institutions, may do more to advance causes such as peace and disarmament than do efforts focused purely on specific policy change goals.[85]

Notes

1. Chatfield, Charles, forthcoming, "Intergovernmental and Non-governmental Associations to 1945," in *Solidarity Beyond the State: The Dynamics of Transnational Social Movements*, Charles Chatfield, Ron Pagnucco, and Jackie Smith (eds.), Syracuse, New York: Syracuse University Press; and Robbins, Dorothy B, 1971, *Experiment in Democracy: The Story of US Citizen Organizations in Forging the Charter of the United Nations*, New York: The Parkside Press.
2. Smith, Jackie, Ron Pagnucco, and Charles Chatfield (eds.) forthcoming, *Solidarity Beyond the State: The Dynamics of Transnational Social Movements*; Weiss, Thomas G. and Leon Gordenker (eds.), 1996, *NGOs, the United Nations, and Global Governance*, Boulder, Colorado: Lynne Reinner; Sikkink, Kathryn, 1986, "Codes of Conduct for Transnational Corporations: The Case of the WHO/UNICEF Code," *International Organization*, vol. 40, pp. 815–40; Willetts, Peter, 1996, *The Conscience of the World: The Influence of NGOs in the United Nations System*, London: C. Hurst.
3. Falk, Richard, 1992, *Explorations at the Edge of Time: Prospects for World Order*, Philadelphia: Temple University Press; Peterson, M. J., 1992, "Whalers, Cetologists, Environmentalists, and the International Management of Whaling," *International Organization*, vol. 46, pp. 147–86; Walker, R. B. J., 1995, "Social Movements/World Politics," *Millennium*, vol. 23, pp. 669–700; see, e.g., Wapner, Paul, 1996, "Bringing Society Back In: Environmental Governance and World Sociology," International Studies Association, San Diego, California; and Wapner, Paul, 1996, *Environmental Activism and World Civic Politics*, New York: City University of New York Press.
4. Clark, Ann Marie, 1995, "Non-Governmental Organizations and their Influence on International Society," *Journal of International Affairs*, vol. 48, pp. 507–25; Princen, Thomas, 1994, "NGOs: Creating a Niche in Environmental Diplomacy," in *Environmental NGOs in World Politics*, Thomas Princen and Matthias Finger (eds.), pp. 29–47, New York: Routledge; Rowlands, Ian H., 1992, "The International Politics of Environment and Development: The Post-UNCED Agenda," *Millennium*, vol. 21, pp. 209–24; Sikkink, op. cit.
5. Cortright, David, 1993, *Peace Works*, Boulder, Colorado: Westview; Meyer, David and Sam Marullo, 1992, "Grassroots Mobilization and International Change," in *Research in Social Movements, Conflict, and Change*; Risse-Kappen, Thomas, 1994, "Ideas do not Float Freely: Transnational Coalitions, Domestic Structures, and the End of the Cold War," *International Organization*, vol. 48, pp. 185–214; Wittner, Lawrence, 1997, *Resisting the Bomb: A History of the World Nuclear Disarmament Movement, 1954–1970*, vol. 2, *The Struggle Against the Bomb*, Stanford, California: Stanford University Press.
6. Walzer, Michael (ed.), 1995, *Toward a Global Civil Society*, Oxford: Berghahn Books, p. 7.
7. Calhoun, Craig, 1994, *Neither Gods Nor Emperors: Students and the Struggle for Democracy in China*. Berkeley: University of California Press, p. 190.

8. Falk, Richard, 1993, "The Infancy of Global Civil Society," in *Beyond the Cold War: New Dimensions in International Relations*, Geir Lundestad and Odd Arne Westad (eds.), New York: Oxford University Press, p. 233.

9. The activities of nominally apolitical non-state actors, however, can have political relevance, since such organizations provide the infrastructures for mobilizing individuals around political issues. Also, organizations such as churches, whose primary purpose lies outside the political realm, frequently become involved in political campaigns that advance values consistent with those of the organization.

10. McCarthy, John D. and Mayer Zald, 1977, "Resource Mobilization in Social Movements: A Partial Theory," *American Journal of Sociology*, vol. 82: p. 1217.

11. Smith, Jackie, 1995, "Organizing Global Action: Transnational Social Movements and World Politics," doctoral dissertation, University of Notre Dame; and Smith et al., forthcoming, op. cit.

12. At the same time, these movements often generate organized opposition to such goals, and this opposition takes the form of a movements, earning it the label "countermovement." See Meyer, David and Suzanne Staggenborg, 1996, "Movements, Countermovements, and the Structure of Political Opportunity," *American Journal of Sociology*, vol. 101, pp. 1628–60.

13. Because many churches are already transnational in character, these may be more likely sites of transnational movement-building than are other social infrastructures that lack transnational organizational structures.

14. Marullo, Sam, 1993, "The Surge Phase in Social Movement," in *Polite Protesters: The American Peace Movement of the 1980s*, John Lofland (ed.), Syracuse, New York: Syracuse University Press; Tarrow, Sidney, 1989, *Democracy and Disorder: Protest and Politics in Italy, 1965–1975*, New York: Oxford University Press.

15. On the emergence of a formally organized and professionalized social movements sector, see McCarthy, John and Mayer Zald, 1987, "The Trend of Social Movements in America: Professionalization and Resource Mobilization," in *Social Movements in an Organizational Society*, Mayer Zald and John D. McCarthy (eds.), pp. 393–420, New Brunswick, New Jersey: Transaction.

16. Haas, Peter, 1992, "Introduction: Epistemic Communities and International Policy Coordination," *International Organization*, vol. 46, p. 2.

17. Risse-Kappen, op. cit., p. 187.

18. Kubbig, Berndt W., 1996, *Communicators in the Cold War: The Pugwash Conferences, the US-Soviet Study Group, and the ABM Treaty*, Peace Research Institute Frankfurt, p. 44.

19. See also Evangelista, Matthew, 1995b, "Transnational Relations, Domestic Structures, and Security Policy in the USSR and Russia," in *Bringing Transnational Relations Back In: Non-State Actors, Domestic Structures, and International Institutions*, Thomas Risse-Kappen (ed.), pp. 146–88, New York: Cambridge University Press.

20. Jenkins, J. Craig and Charles Perrow, 1977, "Insurgency of the Powerless: Farm Worker Movements," *American Sociological Review*, vol. 42, pp. 249–68; Moore, Kelly, 1994, "The Development of New Channels of Political Access: Public Interest Science Organizations in America, 1955–1990," American Sociological Association, Miami, Florida; see, e.g., Tarrow, Sidney, 1988, "National Politics and Collective Action," *Annual Review of Sociology*, vol. 14, pp. 421–40.

21. See Chatfield, forthcoming, op. cit., p. 44.

22. Wittner, Lawrence, 1993, *One World or None: A History of the Nuclear Disarmament Movement Through 1953*, vol. 1: *The Struggle Against the Bomb*, Stanford, California: Stanford University Press.

23. Atwood, David, forthcoming, "Mobilizing Around the United Nations Special Session

on Disarmament," in *Solidarity Beyond the State: The Dynamics of Transnational Social Movements*; Cortright, David and Ron Pagnucco, forthcoming, "Limits to Transnationalism: the 1980s' Freeze Campaign," in *Solidarity Beyond the State: The Dynamics of Transnational Social Movements*; Wittner, 1993, op. cit.; Wittner, 1997, op. cit. The International Liaison Committee of Organizations for Peace was formed in 1949 as a coalition of national pacifist and world federalist organizations, and it included other NGOs (Wittner, 1993, op. cit., p. 167). In 1963, the International Confederation for Disarmament and Peace emerged as a Western competitor to the Soviet-led World Peace Council (Wittner, 1997, op. cit.). Atwood (forthcoming) and Cortright and Pagnucco (forthcoming) describe international peace movement coalitions emerging around the UN Special Sessions on Disarmament and the nuclear freeze campaign, respectively. Both of these latter studies conclude that efforts to coordinate transnational nuclear disarmament activities were rather limited, in part because of Cold War geopolitical dynamics.

24. Wittner, 1993, op. cit., pp. 9–11.
25. See Haas, op. cit.; Spencer, Metta, 1995, "'Political' Scientists," *The Bulletin of the Atomic Scientists*, July/August, p. 62.
26. Wittner, 1993, op. cit., pp. 44–5.
27. At this time, the scientists most involved in nuclear research were part of the US government's Manhattan Project, and were thus closely linked to US policy makers and committed to wartime secrecy as a means of preventing Germany's development of a nuclear bomb. Efforts to educate the public about the dangers of nuclear war came only after their use in 1945 (Wittner, 1993, op. cit.)
28. Quoted in Wittner, 1993, op. cit., pp. 23–4.
29. Ibid., pp. 59–60.
30. Ibid., p. 60.
31. There was some debate within the scientific community about the appropriateness of a scientific association taking on political issues, but this view was largely eclipsed by a membership concerned with creating an organization that would limit the dangers of nuclear energy (ibid., p. 60). On the formation of explicitly political scientist-based organizations and their role in social movements, see Moore, Kelly, 1996, "Organizing Integrity: American Science and the Creation of Public Interest Organizations, 1955–1975," *American Journal of Sociology*, vol. 101, pp. 1592–1627.
32. Several leading scientists involved in nuclear research helped form the Presidential Science Advisory Committee (PSAC), which actively consulted with the Eisenhower and Kennedy Administrations about nuclear security and arms control policies (Adler, 1992, op. cit.).
33. Adler, Emanuel, 1992, "The Emergence of Cooperation: National Epistemic Communities and the International Evolution of the Idea of Nuclear Arms Control," *International Organization*, vol. 46, pp. 101–45.
34. See Kubbig, 1996, op. cit., p. 4.
35. Ibid., p. 3.
36. Ibid., p. 8.
37. Ibid.
38. Rotblat, Joseph, 1972, *Scientists in the Quest for Peace: A History of the Pugwash Conferences*. Cambridge, Massachusetts: MIT Press.
39. Ibid.; Spencer, 1995, op. cit.; Wittner, 1997, op. cit.
40. Evangelista, Matthew, 1995b, "Transnational Relations, Domestic Structures, and Security Policy in the USSR and Russia," in *Bringing Transnational Relations Back In: Non-State Actors, Domestic Structures, and International Institutions*, p. 170; and Spencer, Metta, 1994, "Scientists and Weaponeers," unpublished typescript, Toronto.

This demonstration of the feasibility of bilateral verification of a test ban came about after Frank von Hippel, an American physicist, discussed the idea of verifying the Soviet's unilateral testing moratorium with Yevgency Velikhov at a Pugwash Conference in Copenhagen in 1985. The idea was one that several peace groups were already considering: Parliamentarians for Global Action, a TSMO, had commissioned a report detailing the design of such a verification system. At the same time, the NRDC was exploring the same idea. Parliamentarian for Global Action helped organize a delegation to push the idea forward and, after a number of meetings between Global Action, the NRDC, and Soviet scientists and political leaders, the monitoring agreement was realized (Schrag, 1992, op. cit.; see Spencer, 1995, op. cit.). The SAS-NRDC agreement was significant in that it debunked the principal American objection to a Comprehensive Test Ban Treaty, namely, that it could not be adequately verified.

41. Kubbig, 1996, op. cit.
42. Western scientists believed that ABM systems would propel an international nuclear arms race, since they would encourage the proliferation of more accurate offensive nuclear weapons that could easily overcome any ABM defences. ABM systems might also induce any nation possessing them to initiate a nuclear exchange. On the other hand, Soviet scientists (at least overtly) supported their government's position that ABM systems were defensive, and thus morally acceptable alternatives to the West's offensive systems. The Soviets' views gradually came to resemble those advanced by Western Pugwashites. Kubbig, 1996, op. cit; Spencer, 1995, op. cit.
43. Kubbig, 1996, op. cit.
44. Ibid.
45. Adler, 1992, op. cit.; Evangelista, 1995b, op. cit.; Kubbig, 1996, op. cit.; Risse-Kappen, 1994, op. cit.; Spencer, 1995, op. cit.
46. Spencer's interviews with scientists involved in the Pugwash movement, moreover, convinced her of another important outcome of these meetings: they enabled discourses that could challenge state-dominated strategic thinking by allowing Soviet scientists to see their own peers and colleagues interact with foreigners. This allowed them to see both how their colleagues presented their views to people outside their own restrictions and the reactions of non-Soviet scientists' to their views (Spencer, 1994, op. cit.).
47. This shift mirrors that found among US-based peace movement organizations, which between 1988 and 1991 abandoned strict arms control/nuclear disarmament approaches to adopt a broader range of interrelated security concerns (see Marullo, Sam, et al., 1996, "Frame Changes and Social Movement Contraction: US Peace Movement Framing After the Cold War," *Sociological Inquiry*, vol. 66, pp. 1–28).
48. Student Pugwash-USA, 1996, "Dagomys Declaration of the Pugwash Council." World Wide Web document. URL http://www.spusa.org/pugwash/pugwash/senior-pug/declaration.html.
49. Pugwash had begun to engage questions about conventional and biological weapons security during the 1970s and 1980s.
50. Pugwash, 1996a, "1996 Conference Lahti, Finland." Web site maintained by Paul Guinnessy.
51. Pugwash, 1996b, "Descriptions of the Pugwash Conferences on Science and World Affairs." Web site maintained by Paul Guinnessy. URL http://www.qmw.ac.uk/pugwash/statements/statement 0996.html.
52. Kubbig, 1996, op. cit.
53. Roche, Douglas, 1983, *Politicians for Peace*, Toronto: New Canada Press.
54. Pagnucco, Ron and Jackie Smith, 1993, "The Peace Movement and the Formulation of US Foreign Policy," *Peace and Change*, vol. 18, pp. 157–81.
55. Examples of the political relationships Global Action has developed extent across vari-

ous parliaments and government ministries as well as United Nations agencies. At a recent meeting between Global Action members and ambassadors to the Non-Proliferation Treaty Review Conference preparatory committee meeting, for instance, the Mexican ambassador for disarmament Miguel Marín-Bosch noted the significance of his long and close relationship with the organization. On the other hand, the American ambassador Thomas Graham remarked that he had not had a long relationship with the organization, but rather over the last few years he had had an "intense" one (see Global Action, 1995, "The Extension of the NPT: Problems and Possibilities – Parliamentary Briefing by Ambassadors and Discussion," in *Parliamentarians for Global Action 1995 United Nations Parliamentary Forum*, New York, 1995.

56. Johansen, Robert, 1995, interview in *South Bend*, 26 May; and Tovish, Aaron, 1995, "Interview." Parliamentarians for Global Action Deputy Secretary-General (ed.), New York, 1995.

57. For a discussion of the importance of such unofficial conferences in helping delegates to reach consensus on new policies, see Hovey's discussion of how the Quakers used them to advance the recognition of conscientious objection as a human right (Hovey, Michael, 1997, "Interceding at the United Nations: The Right of Conscientious Objection," in *Solidarity Beyond the State: The Dynamics of Transnational Social Movements*); and Levering's analysis of the Neptune Group's work to advance the Law of the Sea Convention (Levering, Ralph A, 1997, "Brokering the Law of the Sea Treaty: The Neptune Group," in *Solidarity Beyond the State: The Dynamics of Transnational Social Movements*).

58. cf. Berman, Maureen and Joseph Johnson, 1977, "The Growing Role of Unofficial Diplomacy," in *Unofficial Diplomats*, Maureen Berman and Joseph Johnson (eds.), pp. 1–34, New York: Columbia University Press.

59. Schrag, Philip G., 1992, *Global Action Nuclear Test Ban Diplomacy at the End of the Cold War*, Boulder, Colorado: Westview, pp. 46–7.

60. Tovish, 1995, op. cit.

61. Schrag, 1992, op. cit.

62. Tovish, 1995, op. cit.

63. Ibid.

64. Ibid.

65. cf. Xinhua, 1992, "UN Committee Calls for Amendment of Partial Nuclear Test Ban," *Xinhua General Overseas News Service*.

66. Global Action, 1992, "New Directions Explored at Non-Aligned Summit: MP Delegation Focuses on Peace-keeping and Disarmament," *Parliamentarians for Global Action Newsletter*, October, pp. 1–2.

67. Dayal, Jaya, 1993, "Disarmament: UN Moves Closer to Total Ban on Nuclear Testing," *Inter-Press Service*, 11 August; and *UN Chronicle*, 1993, "Conference Goal: Comprehensive Test Ban," in *UN Chronicle*, December, p. 64.

68. The NWS favored negotiations within the CD, and the progress of the Amendment Conference is likely to have pushed them to take action on this in order to head off further action in this forum.

69. Negotiations were proceeding among nuclear weapons states as well as in the CD and among PTBT parties (Dayal, 1993, op. cit.).

70. Global Action more recently has modified its strategy in response to the fact that a CTB is unlikely to precede the extension conference and sees the continuation of the multitrack CTB negotiations – particularly the Amendment Conference – as necessary for sustaining the momentum for a CTB after April 1995 (Global Action, 1994a, "Step-By-Step Progress: PGA Proposal Put on UN Agenda," *Parliamentarians for Global Action Newsletter*, December, p. 2.

71. Global Action, 1993a, "Special Report: Nuclear Test Ban," *Parliamentarians for Global Action Newsletter*, September, pp. i–iv; and Global Action, 1993b, "Summary of Progress on CTB," *Annual Report*, pp. 21–2.
72. Global Action, 1994b, "Step-By-Step Reduction of the Nuclear Threat: High-Level Delegations Consider PGA's Proposal in Cairo and New York," *Parliamentarians for Global Action Newsletter*, June, p. 9.
73. Grimsson, Olafur, "Statement to 1995 Parliamentary Forum at the United Nations," New York, 1995.
74. The Step-By-Step resolution (UN Res. A/C.1/49/L.25) was sponsored by Brazil, Colombia, Egypt, India, Indonesia, Malaysia, Mexico, Nigeria, and Zimbabwe, which were later jointed by Tanzania and Ecuador. It passed in the UN General Assembly by a vote of 91 to 24 with 30 abstentions (Global Action, 1994a, op. cit.).
75. Graham, Kennedy, 1995, "Interview." Parliamentarians for Global Action Secretary-General (ed.), Cambridge, UK; and Tovish, 1995, op. cit..
76. One can still question how much closer these events brought us to both groups' ultimate goal of nuclear disarmament, but this question will probably always be open to speculation.
77. Kubbig, 1996, op. cit., p. 45.
78. Risse-Kappen, 1994, op. cit.
79. Schrag, 1992, op. cit.
80. Wittner, 1993, op. cit.; and Wittner, 1997, op. cit.
81. The same can increasingly be said of policy-making communities.
82. cf. Michels, 1978, op. cit.
83. Cortright and Pagnucco, forthcoming, op. cit.
84. Risse-Kappen, 1994, op. cit., p. 187.
85. I am grateful to Metta Spencer and Lawrence Wittner for sharing their unpublished research with me; to Dorinda Dallmeyer for providing ideas at the early stages of this project; to Volker Rittberger for providing the impetus to consider the questions addressed in the paper and for recommendations on improving an initial draft; and to Diana Zoelle for her comments on an early version.

BIBLIOGRAPHY

Adler, Emanuel. (1992) "The Emergence of Cooperation: National Epistemic Communities and the International Evolution of the Idea of Nuclear Arms Control." *International Organization*, vol. 46, pp. 101–45.

Atwood, David. (Forthcoming) "Mobilizing Around the United Nations Special Session on Disarmament." In *Solidarity Beyond the State: The Dynamics of Transnational Social Movements*, Jackie Smith, Charles Chatfield, and Ron Pagnucco (eds.), Syracuse, New York: Syracuse University Press.

Berman, Maureen and Joseph Johnson. (1977) "The Growing Role of Unofficial Diplomacy." In *Unofficial Diplomats*, Maureen Berman and Joseph Johnson (eds.), New York: Columbia University Press.

Calhoun, Craig. (1994) *Neither Gods Nor Emperors: Students and the Struggle for Democracy in China.* Berkeley: University of California Press.

Chatfield, Charles. (Forthcoming) "Intergovernmental and Non-governmental Associations to 1945." In *Solidarity Beyond the State: The Dynamics of Trans-*

national Social Movements, Charles Chatfield, Ron Pagnucco, and Jackie Smith (eds.), Syracuse, New York: Syracuse University Press.

Clark, Ann Marie. (1995) "Non-governmental Organizations and their Influence on International Society." *Journal of International Affairs*, vol. 48, pp. 507–25.

Cortright, David. (1993) *Peace Works*. Boulder: Westview.

Cortright, David and Ron Pagnucco. (Forthcoming.) "Limits to Transnationalism: the 1980s' Freeze Campaign." In *Solidarity Beyond the State: The Dynamics of Transnational Social Movements*, Jackie Smith, Charles Chatfield, and Ron Pagnucco (eds.), Syracuse, New York: Syracuse University Press.

Dayal, Jaya. (1993) "Disarmament: UN Moves Closer to Total Ban on Nuclear Testing." *Inter Press Service*, 11 August.

Evangelista, Matthew. (1995a) "The Paradox of State Strength: Transnational Relations, Domestic Structures and Security Policy in Russia and the Soviet Union." *International Organization*, vol. 49, pp. 1–38.

Evangelista, Matthew. (1995b) "Transnational Relations, Domestic Structures, and Security Policy in the USSR and Russia." In *Bringing Transnational Relations Back In: Non-State Actors, Domestic Structures, and International Institutions*, Thomas Risse-Kappen (ed.), New York: Cambridge University Press.

Falk, Richard. (1992) *Explorations at the Edge of Time: Prospects for World Order*. Philadelphia: Temple University Press.

Falk, Richard. (1993) "The Infancy of Global Civil Society." In *Beyond the Cold War: New Dimensions in International Relations*, Geir Lundestad and Odd Arne Westad (eds.), New York: Oxford University Press.

Global Action. (1992) "New Directions Explored at Non-Aligned Summit: MP Delegation Focuses on Peace-keeping, Disarmament." *Parliamentarians for Global Action Newsletter*, October.

Global Action. (1993a) "Special Report: Nuclear Test Ban." *Parliamentarians for Global Action Newsletter*, September.

Global Action. (1993b) "Summary of Progress on CTB." *Annual Report*.

Global Action. (1994a) "Step-By-Step Progress: PGA Proposal Put on UN Agenda." *Parliamentarians for Global Action Newsletter*, December.

Global Action. (1994b) "Step-By-Step Reduction of the Nuclear Threat: High-Level Delegations Consider PGA's Proposal in Cairo and New York." *Parliamentarians for Global Action Newsletter*, June.

Global Action. (1995) "The Extension of the NPT: Problems and Possibilities – Parliamentary Briefing by Ambassadors and Discussion." In *Parliamentarians for Global Action 1995 United Nations Parliamentary Forum*, New York.

Graham, Kennedy. (1995) "Interview." Parliamentarians for Global Action Secretary-General. Cambridge, UK.

Grímsson, Olafur. (1995) "Statement to 1995 Parliamentary Forum at the United Nations." New York.

Haas, Peter. (1992) "Introduction: Epistemic Communities and International Policy Coordination." *International Organization*, vol. 46, pp. 1–35.

Hovey, Michael. (1997) "Interceding at the United Nations: The Right of Conscientious Objection." In *Solidarity Beyond the State: The Dynamics of Trans-*

national Social Movements, Jackie Smith, Charles Chatfield, and Ron Pagnucco (eds.), Syracuse, New York: Syracuse University Press.

Jenkins, J. Craig and Charles Perrow. (1977) "Insurgency of the Powerless: Farm Worker Movements." *American Sociological Review*, vol. 42, pp. 249–68.

Johansen, Robert. (1995) Interview. South Bend, 26 May.

Kriesberg, Louis. (1991) "Formal and Quasi-Mediators in International Disputes: an Exploratory Analysis." *Journal of Peace Research*, vol. 28, pp. 19–27.

Kubbig, Berndt W. (1996) *Communicators in the Cold War: The Pugwash Conferences, the US-Soviet Study Group, and the ABM Treaty*. Peace Research Institute, Frankfurt, p. 44.

Levering, Ralph A. (1997) "Brokering the Law of the Sea Treaty: The Neptune Group." In *Solidarity Beyond the State: The Dynamics of Transnational Social Movements*, Jackie Smith, Charles Chatfield, and Ron Pagnucco (eds.), Syracuse, New York: Syracuse University Press.

Marullo, Sam. (1993) "The Surge Phase in Social Movements." In *Polite Protesters: The American Peace Movement of the 1980s*, John Lofland (ed.), Syracuse, New York: Syracuse University Press.

Marullo, Sam, Ron Pagnucco, and Jackie Smith. (1996) "Frame Changes and Social Movement Contraction: US Peace Movement Framing After the Cold War." *Sociological Inquiry*, vol. 66, pp. 1–28.

Michels, Robert. (1978) *Political Parties: A Sociological Study of the Oligarchical Tendencies of Modern Democracy*. Gloucester, Massachusetts: P. Smith.

McCarthy, John D. and Mayer Zald. (1977) "Resource Mobilization in Social Movements: A Partial Theory." *American Journal of Sociology*, vol. 82, pp. 1212–41.

McCarthy, John and Mayer Zald. (1987) "The Trend of Social Movements in America: Professionalization and Resource Mobilization." In *Social Movements in an Organizational Society*, Mayer Zald and John D. McCarthy (eds.), New Brunswick, New Jersey: Transaction.

Meyer, David and Sam Marullo. (1992) "Grass-roots Mobilization and International Change." *Research in Social Movements, Conflict, and Change*.

Meyer, David and Suzanne Staggenborg. (1996) "Movements, Countermovements, and the Structure of Political Opportunity." *American Journal of Sociology*, vol. 101, pp. 1628–60.

Moore, Kelly. (1994) "The Development of New Channels of Political Access: Public Interest Science Organizations in America, 1955–1990." Miami, Florida: American Sociological Association.

Moore, Kelly. (1996) "Organizing Integrity: American Science and the Creation of Public Interest Organizations, 1955–1975." *American Journal of Sociology*, vol. 101, pp. 1592–1627.

Pagnucco, Ron and Jackie Smith. (1993) "The Peace Movement and the Formulation of US Foreign Policy." *Peace and Change*, vol. 18, pp. 157–81.

Peterson, M. J. (1992) "Whalers, Cetologists, Environmentalists, and the International Management of Whaling." *International Organization*, vol. 46, pp. 147–86.

Princen, Thomas. (1994) "NGOs: Creating a Niche in Environmental Diplomacy." In *Environmental NGOs in World Politics*, Thomas Princen and Matthias Finger (eds.), New York: Routledge.

Pugwash. (1996a) "1996 Conference, Lahti, Finland." Web site maintained by Paul Guinnessy. URL http://www.qmw.ac.uk/pugwash/archive/describe.html (3 February).

Pugwash. (1996b) "Description of the Pugwash Conferences on Science and World Affairs." Web site maintained by Paul Guinnessy. URL http://www.qmw.ac.uk/pugwash/statements/statement0996.html (3 February).

Risse-Kappen, Thomas. (1994) "Ideas do not Float Freely: Transnational Coalitions, Domestic Structures, and the End of the Cold War." *International Organization*, vol. 48, pp. 185–214.

Robbins, Dorothy B. (1971) *Experiment in Democracy: the Story of US Citizen Organizations in Forging the Charter of the United Nations*. New York: Parkside Press.

Roche, Douglas. (1983) *Politicians for Peace*. Toronto: New Canada Press.

Rotblat, Joseph. (1972) *Scientists in the Quest for Peace: A History of the Pugwash Conferences*. Cambridge, Massachusetts: MIT Press.

Rowlands, Ian H. (1992) "The International Politics of Environment and Development: The Post-UNCED Agenda." *Millennium: Journal of International Studies*, vol. 21, pp. 209–24.

Schrag, Philip G. (1992) *Global Action Nuclear Test Ban Diplomacy at the End of the Cold War*. Boulder: Westview.

Sikkink, Kathryn. (1986) "Codes of Conduct for Transnational Corporations: The Case of the WHO/UNICEF Code." *International Organization*, vol. 40, pp. 815–40.

Smith, Jackie. (1995) *Organizing Global Action: Transnational Social Movements and World Politics*. Doctoral dissertation, University of Notre Dame.

Smith, Jackie, Ron Pagnucco, and Charles Chatfield (eds.) (Forthcoming) *Solidarity Beyond the State: The Dynamics of Transnational Social Movements*. Syracuse, New York: Syracuse University Press.

Spencer, Metta. (1994) "'Scientists and Weaponeers'." In *Unpublished Typescript*. Toronto.

Spencer, Metta. (1995) "'Political' Scientists." *The Bulletin of the Atomic Scientists*, July/August, pp. 62–8.

Student Pugwash-USA. (1996) "Dagomys Declaration of the Pugwash Council." World Wide Web document. URL http://www.spusa.org/pugwash/pugwash/senior-pug/declaration. html.

Tarrow, Sidney. (1988) "National Politics and Collective Action." In *Annual Review of Sociology*, pp. 421–40.

Tarrow, Sidney. (1989) *Democracy and Disorder: Protest and Politics in Italy, 1965–1975*. New York: Oxford University Press.

Tovish, Aaron. (1995) "Interview." Parliamentarians for Global Action Deputy Secretary-General. New York.

UN Chronicle. (1993) "Conference Goal: Comprehensive Test Ban." *UN Chronicle*, December.

Walker, R. B. J. (1995) "Social Movements/World Politics." *Millennium*, vol. 23, pp. 669–700.

Walzer, Michael, (ed.) (1995) *Toward a Global Civil Society*. Oxford: Berghahn Books.

Wapner, Paul. (1996a) "Bringing Society Back In: Environmental Governance and World Sociology." San Diego, California: International Studies Association.

Wapner, Paul. (1996b) *Environmental Activism and World Civic Politics*. New York: City University of New York Press.

Weiss, Thomas G. and Leon Gordenker (eds.). (1996) *NGOs, the UN, and Global Governance*. Boulder: Lynne Reinner.

Willetts, Peter. (1996) *The Conscience of the World: The Influence of NGOs in the United Nations System*. London: C. Hurst.

Wittner, Lawrence. (1993) *One World or None: A History of the Nuclear Disarmament Movement Through 1953*. Vol. 1. *The Struggle Against the Bomb*, Stanford, California: Stanford University Press.

Wittner, Lawrence. (1997) *Resisting the Bomb: A History of the World Nuclear Disarmament Movement, 1954–1970*. Vol. 2. *The Struggle Against the Bomb*, Stanford, California: Stanford University Press.

Xinhua. (1992) "UN Committee Calls for Amendment of Partial Nuclear Test Ban." *Xinhua General Overseas News Service*.

9

The dark side of global civil society: The role and impact of transnational criminal organizations as a threat to international security

Phil Williams

Introduction

For many years, globalization, interdependence, and the rise of transnational non-state actors have been seen exclusively as positive developments in international relations. Some observers even suggested that such forces were so powerful that the traditional Hobbesian paradigm which treats international anarchy and its concomitants, the struggle for power and the search for security, as the driving forces in relations among states was increasingly outmoded and irrelevant. Whether or not this is the case is a matter of continuing dispute. What is far less contentious, however, is that globalization and interdependence have not only encouraged the emergence of "upright global citizens" but have facilitated the rise of transnational criminal organizations which pose new challenges to both national and international security.

Organized crime, of course, is not only one of the world's oldest professions, but has almost invariably involved both the crossing of borders and a challenge to political authority. This is exemplified in both smuggling and maritime piracy. Similarly, the rise of organized crime in the United States during Prohibition involved not only domestic production but also the smuggling of alcohol into the country. Even with these antecedents, however, the rise of transnational criminal organizations has been striking in both scope and impact. Yet, it should not really be surprising. Just as modern corporations have become global in the scope of

173

their activities, so have criminal enterprises. They have responded to new opportunities, incentives, and pressures at both the national and global levels, and have been able to exploit resources such as transnational ethnic networks in ways that have made them very difficult to counter or contain.

If transnational criminal organizations (TCOs) can be regarded as the illicit counterpart of transnational corporations in their search for profit, they also have many of the characteristics of transnational professional associations and rely fundamentally upon network structures. As ruthless profit-seeking illicit networks, they pose a major challenge for governance at both the national and global levels. They are also a manifestation of a deeper crisis of governance and the reflection of a long-term secular decline of the state.[1] Indeed, as both a symptom of the crisis of governance and phenomena that exacerbate this crisis, TCOs have become a source of great anxiety.

Against a background of growing consternation about the extent of transnational organized crime and the threat posed to national and international security this paper sets out to:

- elucidate the conditions that have given rise to a new form of geopolitics in which TCOs play a major role;
- identify some of the major characteristics of TCOs, with particular attention to their structures, range of activities, and strategies for managing the risks they face from law enforcement;
- identify and explore some of the leading TCOs, with emphasis on the scope of their domestic and transnational activities;
- delineate the ways in which TCOs threaten national and international security, and assess the extent of this threat.

The emergence of transnational criminal organizations

The emergence of TCOs resulted from a convergence of long-term secular trends with a series of distinct historic developments and upheavals, such as the collapse of the Soviet Union, the end of the Cold War, and the opening up of the barriers between East and West. The long-term secular trends embraced both globalization and the crisis of state authority and legitimacy that manifested itself most obviously in the collapse of the communist states of the Soviet bloc but was certainly not confined to this region.

Globalization

Globalization is clearly a long-term process, but one which has accelerated with advances in technology, transportation, information, and communications. It refers to the development of trade, financial, information and communications systems that are global in scope and have led many in the corporate world in particular to embrace the idea of a "borderless world" in which national sovereignty is both anachronistic and increasingly notional. Operating transnationally in the new global market has become a central characteristic of the modern corporation. But the very things which have made it possible to move goods, people, and money through the global economy have also facilitated the movement of "dirty money" and contract killers as well as the transportation of drugs, arms, and illegal aliens. Just as borders no longer provide an impediment to licit business activity, they are no longer a barrier to illicit activities. In short, globalization has provided new opportunities and capabilities for TCOs. As far as criminal organizations are concerned, borders and the formalities of sovereignty remain important only in terms of hindering government responses to criminal activities. While transnational criminals and terrorist groups operate in what is, in effect, a borderless world, law enforcement still operates in a bordered world.

There are several components of globalization which provide new opportunities for criminal organizations: the vast growth in mobility across borders facilitates criminal movement, while modern migration patterns and diasporas have resulted in the creation of ethnic networks that provide cover and recruitment opportunities for ethnically based criminal organizations; the growth of international trade has provided new opportunities to embed illicit products in licit, making them difficult for law enforcement to discover and confiscate; the growth of a global financial system with multiple points of access has provided new opportunities to launder the proceeds of illicit activities; the emergence of global cities has provided innumerable opportunities for the development of criminal contacts as well as a criminal cosmopolitanism, in which groups and individuals from different nations come together for specific criminal enterprises; and the emergence of both national and global information infrastructures offers opportunities for criminal groups to engage in new forms of extortion and other computer crimes. In short, a globalized world is one replete with opportunities for criminal organizations to advance their illicit activities. Moreover, such opportunities are likely to increase rather than decrease in the future.

One of the consequences of globalization has been a contraction in the domain of state authority. Resulting from long-term secular trends, this contraction is irreversible. States, in effect, have lost control of global markets. This is reflected in the development of parallel or informal economies, the rise of grey and black markets, and the inability of states to prevent flows of illicit products across their borders or to stem the tide of illegal migration. It is also reflected in the growing concerns over the theft of intellectual property, the growth of transnational software piracy, and counterfeiting of both products and currencies. In essence, globalization involves an assault on state authority and sovereignty from above. If this provides one set of opportunities for TCOs, these groups also benefit from regional and ethnic conflicts and the crisis of state authority that exists in large parts of the world.

The crisis of state authority

Simultaneously with the attack from above, there has been an erosion of legitimacy and authority at the national level, an erosion which has increased the number of weak states in the international system. This is not to claim that state weakness is a new phenomenon. Diego Gambetta, for example, has argued that it was the weakness of the Italian state which allowed the Mafia to develop in Sicily during the nineteenth century. With the state incapable of providing protection and arbitration for business, the Mafia developed to fill the vacuum.[2] More recently, as Francisco Thoumi has argued, the weakness of the Colombian state and its lack of control over some of the territory nominally under its jurisdiction were major factors in explaining the rise of Colombia as the corporate headquarters of the South American cocaine-trafficking industry. In his view, state weakness gave Colombian drug-trafficking organizations a comparative advantage over their counterparts in Peru and Bolivia.[3]

Perhaps the most dramatic examples of state weakness providing ideal conditions for the rise of criminal organizations, however, are to be found in the states of the former Soviet Union. The collapse of the Soviet state was a major factor in the upsurge of organized crime in the Russian Federation and other former republics, providing both unprecedented opportunities for criminal organizations and incentives and pressures for citizens to engage in criminal activities. Simply highlighting state weakness, though, is inadequate. There are several distinct aspects of weakness which are particularly relevant to the rise of criminal organizations and therefore require elucidation. The first is what might be termed a lack of capacity to impose order on the population. In periods of upheaval many of the normal conventions that govern the behaviour of citizens disappear or at the very least are severely weakened. As Durkheim argued almost 50 years ago, most societies have regulatory mechanisms to restrain criminal behaviour through both formal sanctions and social norms, "but when society is disturbed by some painful crisis or by beneficent but abrupt transitions" it becomes incapable of enforcing restraint – at least temporarily.[4] The lack of an appropriate legal framework and weaknesses in law enforcement capabilities can provide an environment in which criminal organizations can operate with impunity, secure in the knowledge that the government is unable to take effective action against them.

The second dimension of state weakness – and the one emphasized by Gambetta – is what might be termed a regulatory vacuum. One of the responsibilities of the state – at least in modern capitalist societies – is to provide a legal framework for business activity. In the absence of such a framework, there is no protection and no contract enforcement, a condition which allows organized crime to become a surrogate for government.[5] This has certainly been the case in the Russian Federation, where the attempt to move towards a market economy preceded the development of appropriate regulatory and legal provisions. In these circumstances, some businessmen turned to criminal organizations to collect outstanding debts or settle disputes. Recourse to these unorthodox methods had two consequences: it gave criminal organizations an entry into the business world, thereby creating a seamless web between the licit and the illicit, and it encouraged legitimate businesses to resort to increasingly ruthless methods against their competitors.

Another form of weakness – and one that, in spite of its importance in relation to the growth of criminal organizations, is often overlooked – occurs when the state is incapable of continuing to make provision for its citizens. Whereas other dimensions of weakness offer opportunities for criminal behaviour, this type of weakness creates pressures and incentives for citizens to engage in criminal activities. Amidst conditions of economic hardship caused by unemployment and hyperinflation, there is a tendency to turn to extra-legal means of obtaining basic needs. Illicit means of advancement offer opportunities that are simply not available in the licit economy. Moreover, the growth of criminal organizations can take on its own momentum as members of criminal gangs flaunt their wealth and power, thereby creating a desire for emulation on the part of those who have little future in the licit economy.

With the demise of the Soviet Union, two other dimensions were also important. The first was the decline in status and the collapse in morale of some of the central institutions of the state, such as the military, the intelligence services, and the scientific establishment. The result was that corruption in the Russian military became endemic, encouraging a haemorrhaging of weapons of all kinds out of military bases and into the hands of organized criminals and terrorists.[6] Furthermore, many of those who left the military and the KGB had little to offer other than their special skills in violence – skills which for reasons identified above were in high demand in the business world. Not surprisingly, many of the contract killings that occur in Russia have the hallmarks of former KGB agents. As for the scientific establishment, the worsening in pay and conditions, combined with the loosening of security and safeguards, has resulted in a highly disturbing increase in the number of nuclear smuggling incidents.[7] The second unique dimension of the Soviet collapse was the fragmentation of the Soviet Union into independent states, a development which resulted in the replacement of a "common judicial space" with a system characterized by a "lack of border controls, no consistent legal norms, and limited coordination among the justice systems of the successor states."[8] Although efforts have been made to overcome these weaknesses and devise effective law enforcement coordination mechanisms, much remains to be done. In the meantime, the advantages remain with the criminal organizations.

None of this is meant to imply that the state system has lost its hold. In some cases of civil strife there has been an almost complete failure of the state and a reversal to tribalism and ethnicity as the basis for political action. Yet even here the conflict generally centres around the form the state should take in terms of either its territorial or ethnic composition. In these cases the problem goes beyond weakness and involves what is, in essence, a contested state.

Whatever the particular circumstances, the "balkanization of nation-states in which culture is pitted against culture, people against people, tribe against tribe" offers additional opportunities for transnational organized crime.[9] One of the great strengths of TCOs is their ability to exploit developments of all kinds in many different ways. Ethnic conflicts, for example, offer numerous opportunities for trafficking in arms and encourage "arms for drugs" deals as ethnic groups seek ways of acquiring the means to continue the armed struggle. Linkages between the warring parties and criminal organizations willing to take the risks of dealing with them tend to be mutually beneficial. In some cases, however, the criminal organizations are cut out as the participants in conflict engage in criminal activities of their own, a phenomenon one journalist has described as "fighters-turned-felons."[10] Indeed, this phenomenon seems likely to grow as ethnic factions, insurgency movements, and terrorist groups all find it more difficult to obtain state sponsorship for their activities. Criminal endeavours provide a substitute which enables them to finance and sustain their political struggles. This has been reflected in the number of Tamils who have been arrested in Europe and North America for drug trafficking. While some might have been in the drug-trafficking business simply for profit, others were "clearly linked to fund-raising for the Tamil Tiger separatists."[11] In Angola, in contrast, the criminals have both gone into business for themselves and established links with organized crime: "UNITA [National Union for the Total Independence of Angola] insurgents have raised money by selling off poached elephant ivory and by throwing open state-owned diamond fields to smugglers who cut UNITA in on profits."[12] Elsewhere, even closer relationships have been forged between criminal organizations and revolutionary or guerilla movements. Ideological antipathies have been no barrier to alliances of convenience.

Although instability and conflict can pose problems for criminal organizations, compelling them, for example, to develop alternative trafficking routes, for the most part these organizations flourish amidst such
conditions. This is evident in the two states that are the largest producers
of opium – Myanmar and Afghanistan – both of which are torn by ethnic
and tribal splits and are home to major drug-trafficking organizations. If
"the links between war and crime are growing stronger in the 1990s,"[13]
however, this also reflects the underlying crisis of governance at both
national and global levels.

The end of the Cold War

The rapid rise of transnational organized crime also seemed, if not to
coincide with, at least to follow very closely the end of the Cold War. The
removal of the division between East and West in Europe allowed the
globalization processes discussed earlier to become more truly global,
and encouraged criminal enterprises as well as licit businesses to move
much more freely into the former Soviet bloc. Yet the end of the Cold
War provided the occasion for, rather than the cause of, the rise of TCOs.
Indeed, in some respects the Cold War itself had been an important
incubating chamber for transnational organized crime in the West. One
result of the preoccupation of Western governments with the Soviet
threat was tacit support for political parties which were closely linked to
criminal organizations but were staunchly anti-communist. The linkages –
most obvious in Italy and Japan – were either overlooked or quietly
condoned, because they helped to ensure that anti-communist governments stayed in power. In the final analysis, corruption was preferable
to communism. Anti-communism was not synonymous with support for
organized crime but it muted opposition to criminal organizations in
several countries, thereby facilitating the creation and maturation of
symbiotic relationships between organized crime and the political and
economic élites. From this perspective, the end of the Cold War was important less because it facilitated the rise of transnational organized crime
than because it allowed governments to take off the blinkers. There was
no longer any reason for turning a blind eye to corrupt or collusive relationships between organized crime and government leaders.

At the same time, the end of the Cold War also removed the pre-
occupations that had blinded authorities in the West to non-traditional
and non-military threats to security. In addition, it removed much of the
rationale for maintaining large security establishments and intelligence
agencies, thereby precipitating what some observers regard as a frantic
search for a new enemy. To a degree organized crime has fulfilled this
role, especially for intelligence establishments. To conclude from this that

the threat posed by TCOs is an artificial contrivance would be a mistake. Nevertheless, it does underline the importance of conceptualizing the phenomenon in ways which neither exaggerate nor underestimate the challenge to security.

Transnational criminal organizations: Structures, strategies, and activities

TCOs are as varied as legitimate economic enterprises in terms of their size, structure, range of activities, and degree of sophistication. There is no single model of transnational criminal organization. The groups come in various shapes and sizes, and with their own skills and specializations; they operate in different geographical domains and different product markets; they use a variety of tactics and mechanisms for circumventing restrictions and avoiding law enforcement; and they vary considerably in the scope of their activities. If "the complexity of transnational organized crime does not permit the construction of simple generalizations," however, these organizations do share some common features, including a willingness to use violence and corruption to protect and promote their enterprises.[14] It is this willingness, combined with their involvement in theft and in the trafficking of either illicit products or licit products in illicit ways (such as smuggling cigarettes across borders), that differentiates them from licit businesses. At the same time, TCOs resemble transnational corporations in at least some respects. One of the similarities is that they both operate from a home state and are active in one or more host states. For the criminal organizations, these host states are usually characterized by surplus wealth which helps to create significant markets for illicit products and a plethora of relatively accessible targets for financial fraud. Even when these states have well-developed law enforcement agencies equipped to deal with indigenous criminal organizations, the agencies are often less effective against criminal organizations which have unfamiliar languages and cultures, operate in novel and unexpected ways, and entrench themselves within larger ethnic communities that are difficult to penetrate. The United States and the countries of Western Europe are particularly important as host states. The famous bank robber Willy Horton once commented that he robbed banks because that was where the money was kept. Modern TCOs operate in advanced industrialized or post-industrialized societies because that is where the wealth is – and that is where they also find the most lucrative markets for their illicit products and the most lucrative targets for their criminal schemes.

At the same time, TCOs generally operate from a home base in which both government and law enforcement are weak or acquiescent. Criminal organizations attempt to perpetuate these conditions using corruption and bribery as well as threats and intimidation. Although Louise Shelley is correct to argue that "transnational organized crime groups thrive in different political environments" and "can be based in a collapsing superpower, the less-developed region of a developed democracy, and in a formerly stable democracy," the common feature of these environments is state weakness or acquiescence.[15] In this sense the environments are less diverse than first appears.

The other way in which TCOs vary is in the scope of their criminal activities. The range here stretches from Colombian drug-trafficking groups which focus solely on one category of products (even while diversifying within that category) to groups which not only traffic in multiple commodities but also engage in various other activities, such as fraud, extortion, counterfeiting, and piracy. These groups with wide criminal portfolios engage in "such widely publicized activities as drugs and arms trafficking, smuggling of automobiles and people, and trafficking in stolen art. They also engage in such insidious activities as smuggling of embargoed commodities, industrial and technological espionage, financial market manipulation, and the corruption and control of groups within and outside of the legal state system."[16] Where all the successful criminal enterprises converge is in the laundering of money. This is the equivalent of profit-taking by legitimate enterprises, but involves the movement of funds to safe havens beyond the reach of law enforcement, as well as efforts to obscure the source and ownership of the money.

Most criminal organizations also have some kind of bonding mechanism that provides a basis for trust and helps to guard against infiltration by law enforcement personnel.[17] Such mechanisms range from ethnicity to common experiences in youth gangs, military service, or prison. In some cases, such as Italian criminal organizations, the "networks of affiliation"[18] are based on family; in the Chinese case the underlying glue is *guanxi*, the notion of reciprocal obligation which can span generations to facilitate all kinds of business transactions, whether licit or illicit.[19] The essential point, however, is that most enduring criminal associations have affective as well as instrumental dimensions. This notion is challenged somewhat by a recent and comprehensive analysis of organized crime in the Netherlands, which drew a picture of a loose, fluid network of individuals who came together for specific criminal endeavours and then moved on to other associations.[20] Nevertheless, if specific groupings are successful then they are likely to endure. In such cases, shared criminal experiences provide their own bonding. Certainly, the most powerful organizations have bonding mechanisms which provide trust and enable them to operate with a degree of permanence that allows them to become entrenched in the society and develop close and mutually profitable relationships with the political and economic élites.

Similarly, all criminal organizations are concerned to a greater or lesser degree with managing and controlling the risks posed to them by governments and law enforcement agencies. There are three kinds of strategies for achieving this – preventive strategies, control or defence strategies, and absorption strategies. The balance among these not only varies from one organization to another, but can also change over time within the same organization. Some of the more powerful and effective criminal organizations have become extremely adept at risk prevention, particularly in their home states. They are able to maintain a congenial environment through bribery and corruption, as well as through forms of patronage that create a sympathetic public. Perhaps the most striking example of actions designed to elicit public support involved the assistance provided by the Yakuza to the people of Kobe after the earthquake. In circumstances where an acquiescent state becomes more aggressive towards its criminal organizations, more emphasis is placed on risk control, defensive measures, and the capacity to absorb the costs inflicted by law enforcement. The Cali cartel, for example, acquired electronic equipment from Israel which enabled the leaders to monitor all telephone calls to and from the city of Cali. The cartel had also infiltrated government and law enforcement agencies, with the result that it was able to obtain very good counter-intelligence. In the final analysis, such measures were insufficient to keep the leaders from capture and imprisonment. Yet in one sense this merely brought into play the third tier of risk management efforts, those measures designed to limit damage to the integrity of the criminal organization. In the Cali case these would include arrangements for proxies to manage the business, and the transfer of assets to relatives so that they could not be seized by law enforcement agencies.

While other organizations may be less sophisticated than the Cali cartel in their risk management efforts, they are certainly not oblivious to the risks they face. Nigerian drug-trafficking organizations, for example, increasingly employ couriers who do not fit the profile developed by law enforcement. Moreover, the reliance of most organizations on network structures with integral cells that are highly specialized and operate on a need-to-know basis also serves to limit the inroads that law enforcement can make. Network structures also have the advantage of being highly resilient: they can be reconstituted and revitalized in the aftermath of law enforcement actions against the criminal organization. This is particularly the case where these networks are loosely coupled: such arrangements provide ample opportunities to limit damage.[21]

Variations in the sophistication and extent of risk management efforts by TCOs depend in part on the size of the organization. The larger and more extensive the organization, the more obvious it is as a target for law enforcement and the greater its need for a comprehensive strategy of risk management. Many organizations, however, are relatively small and somewhat restricted in the scope of their activities. Indeed, part of the difficulty in responding to transnational organized crime is the relative paucity of large, monolithic, centrally-directed, hierarchical organizations. The traditional Italian Mafia model that prevailed for so long in law enforcement circles in the United States has limited relevance for understanding the multiplicity of organizations, ranging from structured business enterprises to highly fluid and dynamic networks that are constantly coalescing or moving apart as circumstances dictate.

Even small criminal organizations are increasingly establishing links with one another and with their larger counterparts. Some of the newer criminal organizations provide services to those which are more entrenched. In essence they become service organizations. If successful in this role, however, they often graduate into being more powerful and professional groups in their own right. The Albanian groups which operate in central Europe are a case in point. Having provided support for Italian criminal organizations, they are increasingly in business for themselves.[22] This is not to suggest that they have broken their links with the Italian Mafia groups. Indeed, one of the most striking features of the last few years has been the growing linkages among criminal organizations. These range from one-off spot transactions at the most basic to fully fledged strategic alliances at the other extreme. Most linkages are somewhere in the middle, and can best be described as tactical alliances. Strategic alliances are characterized not only by sustained patterns of cooperation but also by the expectation that such cooperation will continue. The rationale for strategic alliances is that they help to share risk, allow entry to new markets, create predictable supplier relationships, and coopt potential or actual competitors.[23] In addition to cooperating with one another, criminal organizations also establish links with terrorist and insurgency groups, and frequently with governments. Indeed, the more successful ones generally have a symbiotic relationship with the government in the home state.

In short, TCOs are sophisticated in their operations and act rationally both to enhance their business opportunities and to minimize their vulnerabilities. Moreover, the organizations are often characterized by entrepreneurial skills of a high order, by efficient and effective management systems based on generous financial inducements and severe penalties, and by the development of effective intelligence and counter-intelligence capabilities. Not surprisingly, they also display considerable resilience against law enforcement efforts to disrupt and destroy them.

The next section looks more closely at some of the leading examples of such organizations.

The major transnational criminal organizations

Italian Mafia

Until very recently the notion of organized crime was almost synonymous with the Italian Mafia, whether in Italy itself or in the United States. In fact, the fortunes of these two distinct criminal organizations have been very different. The Italian Mafia in the United States has declined in importance, partly because of the inroads made by the FBI, using electronic surveillance techniques and increasing use of informants, partly because of the growing assimilation of Italian-Americans into the economic, political, and social mainstreams, partly because of the rise of ruthless competitors in the form of other ethnic criminal organizations, and partly because of the "altered structure of urban politics and policing" which has reduced the opportunities for corruption.[24] In addition, a continued reliance on brute force rather than sophisticated business strategies has placed the Mafia at a competitive disadvantage when compared with groups such as Colombian drug traffickers, who often display considerable business acumen. Indicators of this decline include a drop in membership of the five New York Mafia families from 3,000 in the early 1970s to 1,200 in the mid-1990s, and the fact that 12 Philadelphia mafiosi requested representation by the public defender rather than using more expensive mob lawyers.[25] The extent of this decline, however, has been a matter of considerable controversy, with some very experienced observers claiming that celebrations of the Mafia's demise are premature to say the least. The willingness of Russian criminal organizations engaged in fuel gasoline scams to share the proceeds with Italian criminal groups in New York suggests that the Mafia is still a force to be reckoned with. If Italian criminal organizations remain an important component of what one commentator has termed a new criminal mosaic, however, they are no longer clearly the overwhelming or dominant presence.[26] Chinese, Colombian, Dominican, Vietnamese, African-American, Russian, Albanian, Jamaican, and Nigerian organizations have all become participants in a much more complex and competitive criminal environment.[27] In some cases these new groups are both more ruthless and more violent than the Italians. They are also more difficult targets for law enforcement agencies, which spent years developing expertise on Italian criminal organizations and were able to use the Rico statute and electronic surveillance to very good effect. The overall result has been that Italian organized crime in the United States has had to accommodate the new-comers. To some extent it has been surpassed by them.

In Italy, in contrast, the Mafia continues to dominate the criminal world in what still remains its exclusive domain. Yet even here it has suffered some major setbacks. Although the term "Italian Mafia" is used very widely, in many respects it is inadequate to describe an organized crime world that encompasses four distinct groups.

- The Sicilian Mafia or Cosa Nostra, which consists of around 180 criminal groups and 5,000 men of honour, and since the early 1980s has been dominated by the Corleonesi family.[28]
- The Neapolitan Camorra, which has "a fragmented and widespread structure, made up of a number of gangs which easily band together and then split up, sometimes peacefully, but more often after bloody wars."[29] The Camorra engages in various criminal activities, ranging from extortion to Euro-fraud, drug trafficking, and cigarette smuggling. The Camorra also exerts considerable influence on municipal councils, with the result that 32 of 75 councils in Campania had to be dissolved.[30]
- The Calabrian 'Ndrangheta, a federation of families engaging in contraband tobacco smuggling, drug trafficking, and kidnapping, consists of 160 criminal groups with over 6,000 personnel.[31] Factional differences within the 'Ndrangheta made Calabria the most violent region in Italy, and led in the early 1990s to the creation of a "provincial commission" to provide peaceful arbitration among the various factions.[32] The 'Ndrangheta has also established very close links with the Cosa Nostra. In addition, as one close observer has noted, it has developed extensive international operations and is active in Canada, the United States, Australia, and the Russian Federation.[33]
- The "Sacra Corona Unita" in Apulia, which is based on breakaway factions from the Camorra and 'Ndrangheta and is less powerful than the other three branches.

While each organization has its own specialization, all four are founded upon the law of silence (*omerta*) and upon close associations that are partly functional, partly personal and familial, and partly based on fear. Of the four groups the Sicilian Cosa Nostra remains the most powerful, and has successfully transformed itself from a predominantly rural phenomenon to a transnational criminal enterprise based on "industrial and business cultures."[34] Although many of its activities are still regional and its power base remains Sicily and southern Italy, the Cosa Nostra has spread its influence to the United States, Germany, and other European countries. It is in Italy itself, however, that the Cosa Nostra has had the greatest impact, partly because, in the aftermath of the Second World War, it succeeded in establishing a remarkably durable symbiotic relationship with segments of the political élite. "The Mafia entered the world of politics, commerce, and public administration as a direct participant" providing political support for politicians who, in turn, helped to ensure a continuing flow of contracts, franchises, and jobs.[35] The symbiosis between the Mafia and the Christian Democrats allowed the Cosa Nostra to flourish.

For a variety of reasons, this collusive relationship began to unravel during the 1980s. Factional fights within the Mafia itself, the defection of Tommaso Buscetta, the investigations of magistrates like Falcone and Borsellino who could be neither bought nor intimidated, and the Maxi trials led the Cosa Nostra in particular to conclude that its protectors had reneged on their agreement. The result was a war against the Italian state. After the assassinations of Falcone and Borsellino, the Italian state initiated "its most vigorous anti-Mafia campaign in decades. The Italian parliament quickly passed many of the tough anti-Mafia measures Falcone and Borsellino had been pushing for years: greater incentives and protection for Mafia witnesses, tougher prison conditions for Mafia defendants, streamlined procedures in Mafia trials ... the results of the next two years were nothing short of revolutionary."[36] Great inroads were achieved. Against a background of popular revulsion against the Mafia and its political allies, the Church issued its own condemnation of organized crime. The arrest in January 1993 of Salvatore Riina, the apparent leader of the Cosa Nostra, was a remarkable development, while the arrest in June 1996 of the killer of Judge Falcone revealed that the anti-Mafia campaign was even more sustained than had been expected. If the Cosa Nostra was the primary target, the other Mafia organizations were certainly not immune. In June 1994 Biagio Cave, the acting boss of the Camorra, was arrested, and on September 20 1994 Antonio Gava, the Minister of the Interior from 1988 to 1991, was arrested on the grounds that he had developed close links with criminal enterprises, especially the Camorra. During the first half of 1996 further inroads were made against organized crime, including a major assault on the Camorra. In short, the "clean hands" campaign and the associated measures against organized crime represented the most comprehensive and sustained assault on the Italian Mafia since the time of Mussolini.

One result of all this has been an erosion of what were once sacrosanct norms and conventions. Wives and families of leading *pentiti* have become targets of vendettas. The violation of the traditional norm prohibiting violence against family members can be understood as a response to the violation of the rule of silence. Nevertheless, it suggests a system in disarray. There has also been a significant deterioration in the political power of the Mafia – and a closely associated decline in profit levels. A comprehensive assessment in *Il Mondo* suggested that falling revenues from drug trafficking, a sharp drop in public works spending, stagnation in the market for new construction, increased asset seizure by courts, penitent information that made it possible for law enforcement to target Mafia assets, and increasing legal expenses (with over 1,000 people under arrest for association with the Mafia) had combined to create unprecedented financial problems.[37]

If these setbacks for the Mafia have been very real, Italian organized crime should not yet be counted out. Patron-client relations are deeply embedded in Italian political life, and although old political affiliations have dissolved, new ones can be created. The capacity of criminal organizations to continue to infiltrate local government should not be ignored. Moreover, according to one report the Cosa Nostra has "taken two important steps to protect itself: it has established new procedures to limit what any single mobster knows about the organization, and it has forged new ties with Italy's other major organized crime gangs."[38] This latter development has been characterized as "the syndication of Italian organized crime, a form of internal pax mafiosa directed at maximizing profit and minimizing conflict."[39]

In addition, the Mafia continues to operate extensively in other countries in Europe. In 1994, for example, members of Italian organized crime groups accounted for about 5.7 per cent of organized criminals arrested in Germany.[40] Equally significant, both the Cosa Nostra and the other major criminal organizations have developed close ties with their counterparts in Colombia and the Russian Federation. The cooperative arrangements with the Colombian cartels allowed the latter to break into the European drug markets while allowing the Italians to diversify from heroin distribution and sales into the cocaine market, and to assist with money laundering. Such cooperation has several levels: "At the lowest level are simple buyer-seller deals involving relatively small investments, little advance planning, and relatively little interaction between the parties ... at the highest level is what might be called strategic cooperation, which encompasses the principles of long-term agreements, large-volume shipments of both drugs and money, and the creation of a specialized infrastructure to facilitate these flows."[41]

Italian criminal organizations have exploited the conflict in the former Yugoslavia and engaged in lucrative arms trafficking to the Balkans. Migrant trafficking from Albania and elsewhere in Eastern Europe has also increased considerably. Perhaps of even greater long-term significance have been the growing connections with Russian criminal organizations. These linkages have provided new opportunities for money laundering, trafficking in counterfeit currency, munitions trafficking, and drug smuggling. There have also been persistent reports that Italian criminal organizations have been active in acquiring nuclear materials from the former Soviet Union – although whether this was for their own use or for resale is not clear. Whatever the case, these foreign activities provide not only new sources of profit but also a cushion that can help the Mafia to absorb the losses and offset the setbacks within Italy. The Italian Mafia has proven very resilient in the past. In view of its extensive criminal activities, its vast, if diminished, earning power, and its known capacity to corrupt the political system, celebrations of its demise would be premature.

Russian organized crime

The rise of Russian organized crime has been remarkable. Although the Russian *mafiya* had antecedents in the black-market operators of the centralized economy, as well as in a criminal underworld dominated by thieves, crime in the Soviet Union was circumscribed and contained by the state. There were symbiotic relationships, but these were dominated by the state apparatus. The collapse of centralized power in the Soviet Union, however, changed fundamentally the relationship between the state apparatus and criminal organizations. Although some symbiotic relationships remain intact, organized crime rather than the state is now the dominant partner.

According to the published figures on Russian organized crime, there has been a constant growth in the number of criminal organizations. The figures have inexorably moved upwards from 3,000 in 1992 to 5,700 in 1994 and about 8,000 in late 1995 and early 1996. At first glance, these figures seem to reveal an ever-increasing threat from an expanding criminal empire. It is equally plausible, however, that the increase reflects looser criteria for categorizing groups as criminal organizations, and in particular the inclusion of small and unimportant street gangs; fissiparous tendencies in many Russian criminal organizations leading to fragmentation into smaller groups; threat inflation on the part of Russian law enforcement authorities anxious for more Western assistance; or simply increased visibility of criminal organizations as a result of more efficient policing and better intelligence analysis. Moreover, the official figures do not reveal the process of consolidation among individual organizations that has led well-informed observers to claim that there are about 200 major criminal organizations with widespread geographical and sectoral influence. According to a detailed analysis by Guy Dunn of Control Risks, there are six large groups in Moscow – three Chechen groups (the Tstentralnaya, Ostankinskaya, and Avtomobilnaya) who have about 1,500 members between them, the Solntsevskaya and Podolskaya organizations, and the Twenty-first Century Association – another four major groups in St Petersburg, two major gangs in Yekaterinburg (the Uralmashkaya and the Tsentralnaya), and nine major gangs in Vladivostok.[42]

Even with the consolidation process, however, organized crime in the Russian Federation is highly diverse and fractured, with ethnic divisions, divisions based on territorial and sectoral control and on generational splits, and divisions between those who have established symbiotic links with officials and those who do not enjoy such access. There has been some role specialization, with particular groups dominating specific spheres of activity (for example, Chechens dominate the petroleum trade, Azeri groups are particularly prominent in the drug business, and Georgians are heavily involved in burglaries and robberies). This specialization has been helpful in limiting conflicts – at least at times – and has not precluded cooperation when there were obvious benefits from joint activity. Cooperative arrangements include many groups contributing to a common pool of resources, the *obshak*, which is used to support the families of those in prison, for bribery and corruption, and to generate new enterprises. But there has also been enormous competition among the groups resulting from ethnic divisions, rival territorial claims, and personal animosities among criminal leaders. A major split has emerged between "thieves professing the code" and the new generation of criminals who do not respect established traditions, are more entrepreneurial, and, in some cases, have become "authorities" because of wealth rather than status accrued through time in prison. As a result the "thieves" have suffered considerable attrition. Overlapping this particular rift is a continuing struggle for dominance between the Russian or Slavic groups and those from the Caucasus.

In part these conflicts reflect the powerful internal bonding mechanisms that provide the basis for trust in a milieu without formal laws and rules, and that can be based on ethnicity, common experience in the military or security service, or the camaraderie of functionally based groups such as the "karate" or "sportsmen" organizations that are a feature of organized crime not only in the Russian Federation but elsewhere in the former Soviet bloc.

From the perspective of Russian law enforcement, this diversity is a weakness: competition is preferable to further consolidation. At the same time, the very diversity and complexity of Russian criminal organizations makes concerted action against them difficult. So does the fact that many of the groups have infiltrated licit business and established inroads in key sectors of the licit economy. In August 1995 the MVD All-Russia Scientific Research Institute estimated that criminal groups control over 400 banks and 47 exchanges. An even more pessimistic assessment was made by Professor Lydia Krasfavina, head of the Institute for Banking and Financial Managers, who estimated that 70 to 80 per cent of private banks in the Russian Federation are controlled by organized crime. While few analysts are able to elaborate precisely what "control" means in this context, it is clear that criminal organizations exert considerable influence over the banking sector as well as other parts of the Russian economy. Extortion has become pervasive, and contract killings are often used to remove those who resist or to settle disputes.

Drug trafficking in the Russian Federation has become a major activity, involving not only well-publicized links with Colombian cocaine traffickers, but also the supply of opium, heroin, and marijuana from Central Asia and the Golden Crescent. In addition, there have been several major cases involving large-scale trafficking in synthetic drugs. While much of the trafficking is carried out by individuals or small groups, there is clearly a great deal of activity structured and controlled by larger criminal networks. The networks in the Russian Federation itself are linked with those in Central Asia, and have become adept at both marketing and ensuring a regular supply of narcotics. In 1994 3,126.74 kilograms of all kinds of drugs were seized in 418 separate incidents; during 1995 6,457.30 kilograms were seized in 767 incidents.[43] If drug trafficking is a highly lucrative activity, some organizations combine it with other criminal activities such as car theft, prostitution, extortion, and fraud. One of the strengths of organized crime in Russian is that it has so many different dimensions and engages in such a wide range of activities.

The issue that has aroused the greatest trepidation is that of nuclear material smuggling. Lack of security at some nuclear facilities, as well as poor inventory management, has provided opportunities for disgruntled workers in the nuclear industry. The possibility that workers, either through economic need or intimidation, could offer weapons-grade material to criminal organizations provides the basis for nightmare scenarios that range from large-scale environmental damage to nuclear terrorism or nuclear extortion. What remains uncertain, however, is the extent to which nuclear material trafficking is a core activity of Russian criminal organizations. For the most part nuclear material trafficking has been the preserve of amateur smugglers rather than well-established criminal groups. Yet there is some evidence that criminal organizations have been involved on a limited basis in this activity. One arrest seems to have involved 12 members of the Solntsevskaya in possession of radioactive material, while in another case a group of criminals from Yekaterinburg was involved in the smuggling of large amounts of zirconium to the United States and Cyprus. Nuclear material trafficking is not yet a core activity of Russian organized crime – not least because the risks are high and the profits uncertain – but could become much more important, especially as more Russian criminal organizations become transnational in their operations.

There is some evidence of this already. In the United States, Russian criminals have been involved in fuel tax evasion schemes, health care and insurance fraud, extortion, car theft, and contract murders. While the primary location of Russian criminal organizations is Brighton Beach in Brooklyn, such groups are also active in Florida, California, and the Pacific North West. Cyprus has become a major recipient of the profits of Russian criminal activity, while there is considerable concern in London about money laundering through British financial institutions. Russian criminal organizations also have a limited presence in Germany, which has become a source of luxury cars for the Russian market, a battleground for inter-group rivalries, and a market both for illicit products and for licit products that have been obtained through illegal means. While German arrest figures indicate that only 1.8 per cent of those involved in organized crime in Germany are Russian – compared with 14.6 per cent Turks, 7.5 per cent Yugoslavs, and 5.7 per cent each for Italians and Poles – this figure might be deceptively small.[44] Russian linkages with other groups, as well as the difficulties facing German law enforcement in penetrating Russian criminal organizations, suggest that Russian criminal organizations in Germany might be rather more significant than the figures imply.

One of the problems for law enforcement agencies combating Russian criminal organizations is that these organizations operate from what is, in effect, a sanctuary or safe haven. And unless the Russian state is able to develop both a greater capacity and the will to tackle criminal organizations, the situation could worsen. If domination by the Communist Party is replaced by the domination of organized crime – something that Louise Shelley suggests is a real possibility – then the Russian Federation will become an even more important base for transnational criminal activities.

Chinese criminal organizations

If Russian criminal organizations are becoming increasingly transnational in scope, Chinese criminal organizations have had this characteristic for some years. The Chinese diaspora has provided global networks that have helped to facilitate both licit and illicit business. It has also provided an excellent environment for the overseas activities of Chinese triads based in Hong Kong and Taiwan. Details of these criminal societies make sobering reading. Law enforcement estimates suggest that there are currently about 50 triad societies (with at least 80,000 members) in Hong Kong. About 15 of these are very active. The largest triad is the Sun Yee On, with an estimated 25,000 members. The Wo group, including the Wo Hop To and at least nine other subgroups, has more than 20,000 members, while the 14K and its various subgroups also have over 20,000 members in Hong Kong. There are also two major triads based in Taiwan – the United Bamboo Gang with an estimated membership of over

20,000, and the Four Seas Gang, which has about 5,000 members. All these groups are augmented by a considerable, although uncertain, number of overseas members.

Details of triad membership, however, do not convey the unique duality in Chinese organized crime. On the one hand there are the formal organizational structures – triads, tongs, and street gangs – that provide a framework for Chinese criminal activities. On the other, it is clear that much Chinese crime is transaction-based rather than organization-based. Individuals and small groups come together for particular criminal activities, disperse, and reassemble according to needs and opportunities. This is not to deny the importance of the triads. Perhaps the best description is that they are like an alumni association – membership of a triad provides a degree of trust and allows members of the triad to work together and provide assistance even when they are not personally known. Although there is a formal structure, with a dragon head and specialists such as enforcers and administrators, many of the triads' criminal activities tend to take place amongst members who operate on an ad hoc basis and establish fluid networks that are based partly on triad membership and partly on *guanxi* – a concept of reciprocal obligation based on family and social relationships that can span generations.

This mixture of formal structure and informal activities complicates the tasks of law enforcement. It also makes it more difficult to identify career criminals and to differentiate between legal and illegal enterprises. Chinese businessmen tend to cross the line between licit and illicit activities – and back again – with great ease. An important consequence of this is the very considerable scope for independent criminal entrepreneurship. As one report on Asian organized crime activity in Australia noted: "Whatever criminal triads exist in Australia do not operate as branches that are subject to control from some overseas headquarters. Indeed, it may be overstating things to regard them as enduring entities at all. In recent years in Australia, loosely-organized syndicates appear to have been the predominant form in which Chinese organized crime has manifested itself. Some syndicate members may belong to a particular triad, others may belong to different triads, and some syndicate members may not have any triad connections."[45] This is not to deny that Chinese criminal networks engage in a wide variety of criminal activities in Australia. Among other things, they are the most important heroin importers. They operate almost exclusively at the wholesale level, however, leaving the drug retail business to others, including Vietnamese groups.[46]

In short, Chinese criminal enterprises are a curious mix of formal structures and informal networks. This encourages great flexibility and makes it possible to exploit new opportunities as they arise. In recent years, one of the most significant opportunities has stemmed from the desire of many Chinese to migrate from China to the West. While there has been considerable legal migration, a lucrative business has developed in bringing illegal immigrants to the United States and Western Europe. Most of the illegal migrants coming to the United States travel by air, often by circuitous routes, using false documentation – a requirement that has generated a cottage industry in the production of false passports, visas, and the like. About 10 per cent are smuggled in by sea, often enduring months of hardship and ill-treatment at the hands of the smugglers. In those cases where the migrants are unable to pay the remainder of the fee (and fees generally range from US$25,000 to US$30,000), they are made to work in sweat-shops or recruited into criminal activities such as drug trafficking or prostitution. With Hong Kong having reverted to the control of China in 1997, the number of illegal aliens could well increase. As it stands, there are estimates that about 100,000 Chinese illegally enter the United States every year. Nor is the United States the only destination. Spain is also popular: large numbers of Chinese citizens have appeared in Galicia.[47] As elsewhere, these aliens are often exploited by the criminals as "slave labour," or are pressed into serving as drug couriers or prostitutes, or forced to engage in other forms of crime. Alien trafficking to Spain is controlled primarily by members of the Sun Yee On triad. Heroin trafficking is largely controlled by 14K members, whereas prostitution, pornography, and trafficking in children are controlled predominantly by criminals from the Wo On Lok.

The comprehensive nature of these criminal activities, the difficulties faced by law enforcement in attempting to infiltrate closely-knit ethnic groups, and the Chinese takeover of Hong Kong in 1997 – resulting in a further exodus of members of criminal gangs – suggest that the Chinese organized crime problem is likely to increase rather than decrease. It has already spread to mainland China which, in recent years, has once again become a major consumer of heroin, most of which is smuggled across the border from Myanmar. In addition, as Professor Cai Shaoqing has noted, China provides enormous opportunities for criminal organizations as "old systems and ideas have broken down and new social guarantees and prevention forces are not yet in place."[48] China has a "transient population" of around 50 million people, many of whom become beggars, vagrants, and thieves. "Letting such a new parasite community grow makes it likely that it will form criminal gangs through connections with provincial and clan relationships, as well as to formal gangs such as 'Xinjiang gang' pickpockets and thieves, and the Northeast Gang who plunder on the railways."[49] The extent of the problem was evident in 1993, when Chinese authorities reported that they had disrupted over 150,000 criminal groups with over 570,000 members.[50] Although these figures may include political activists as well as criminals, they nevertheless reveal that Chinese criminal organizations are a problem inside China itself as well as elsewhere. As Chinese economic reform continues and China reclaims Hong Kong, these problems are likely to intensify. As they do, Chinese authorities will increasingly have to contend with deeply entrenched organizations. This is an area in which China may well be able to learn some important lessons from Japan.

Japanese Yakuza

The Japanese umbrella term for organized crime is Yakuza or Bor-yokudan (violent ones). Rather like the term Mafia, however, this encompasses a number of distinctive organizations. The most important of these is the Yamaguchi-gumi, which a few years ago had an estimated membership of over 26,000 individuals. The second largest gang is the Inagawa-kai, which had over 8,600 members, while the third largest organization, the Sumiyoshi-kai, had over 7,000 members.[51] These three groups have been the major target of an intense crackdown by Japanese law enforcement agencies, using anti-Boryokudan laws passed in the early 1990s and a strategy that encourages members of the groups to defect. The result has been a marked decline in membership of the Yamaguchi-gumi, Inagawa-kai, and Sumiyoshi-kai to about 34,600.[52] In addition, Japanese authorities reported that in 1993 they succeeded in dissolving 222 smaller criminal organizations with over 2,600 members.[53]

These successes not withstanding, the Yakuza remains active in a variety of criminal enterprises, including racketeering and extortion. Japanese criminal organizations make extensive use of front companies to penetrate the licit economy, especially in the areas of construction, finance and insurance, and real estate. The Japanese recession and its accompanying bankruptcies have provided new opportunities for criminal organizations to gain control over legitimate companies.

Japanese criminal organizations have also played a big role in the banking crisis. "According to a top Japanese police official, as many as 10 to 30 per cent of the non-performing loans of the banking sector can be attributed to the activities of front companies owned by the Yakuza. Organized crime takes over empty condominiums. Owners cannot oust these 'squatters' and find paying tenants. Deprived of rent, they cannot make their payments to banks, and therefore default."[54]

In spite of the inroads made by law enforcement agencies, therefore, the Yakuza remains a powerful force in Japanese economic and political life. And although Japanese criminal organizations have been less ambitious than many of their counterparts elsewhere in terms of their transnational activities, they have been involved in significant criminal activities across national borders, including the trafficking of methamphetamine into Hawaii and California as well as the smuggling of guns from the United States into Japan. In addition, the Yakuza has moved into gambling, fraud, and money laundering. Yakuza members have been deeply involved in the sex and drug trades, and have also invested heavily in real estate in Hawaii. Elsewhere in the United States, Japanese criminal organizations have also invested in real estate, especially golf courses, as well as in legitimate American corporations.[55] The Yakuza also has a significant presence throughout much of South-East Asia, where Japanese criminals have become a major force in the sex industry. This is certainly the case in the Philippines, which has also been used by the Yakuza as a base for production and smuggling of amphetamines and hand guns.[56]

Ironically, the same report that provided details of law enforcement successes against Japanese criminal organizations also acknowledged that these organizations "have stepped up their international activities in recent years. They have expanded into foreign countries with the aim of procuring firearms and stimulant drugs and securing funds through real estate investment."[57] One of the major targets for investment has been the Republic of Korea, where Japanese Yakuza organizations have purchased or invested in hotels, gambling establishments, and in at least one case a department store. "As their typical method of infiltration, Korean resident members of Yakuza organizations use their relatives in Korea. Of the total 90,000 Yakuza members in Japan it is estimated that about 9,000 or 10 per cent are Korean residents."[58] As part of what is clearly a more diversified criminal portfolio, Japanese criminal organizations have also helped smuggle Chinese illegal migrants into Japan.[59] Even though they are under considerable pressure in their home base, therefore, Japanese criminal organizations have developed an important reservoir of resources and profits through their transnational activities.

Colombian cartels

Unlike most other transnational criminal organizations, which tend to engage in a range of illegal activity, the Colombian cartels focus almost exclusively on drug trafficking. At the same time, they have diversified their markets to include Western Europe as well as the United States, and their products to include heroin as well as cocaine. Some of the major organizations within the drug industry in Colombia have amalgamated corporate and criminal cultures, using sound management principles such as specialization and division of labour while also employing classical criminal techniques of violence and corruption.

During the 1980s Carlos Ledher and other members of the Medellin cartel led the way in applying industrial-style transport to the drug-trafficking business, increasing the amounts that were transported into the United States by air. The Cali cartel took this a stage further, and applied successful business management techniques and meticulous accounting procedures to its activities. Although the Medellin cartel is still active in drug trafficking – and there have been allegations that the Ochoas are still running their drug business from prison – the killing of Pablo Escobar by government forces both highlighted and accentuated the shift in power from the Medellin cartel to the Cali cartel. For its part, the Cali cartel adopted a strategy of cooption rather than confrontation, and tried to establish a *modus vivendi* with the Colombian government based in large part on high-level corruption. Nevertheless the government, under pressure from the United States, initiated a major crackdown, resulting in the captivity or death of the leaders of the cartel. While the cartel has not been completely destroyed, the organization is clearly no longer the developing world's most successful transnational corporation. These successes against Medellin and Cali have not destroyed the drug industry in Colombia, but have neutralized – at least temporarily – the threat to the state posed by powerful criminal organizations with large disposable resources and a substantial capacity for both violence and corruption. Unfortunately they have also benefited the narco-guerrillas, who may come to pose and equally formidable threat to the government – although for different reasons.

Nigerian criminal organizations[60]

The emergence of Nigerian criminal organizations is often traced to the collapse of oil prices in the early 1980s and the dislocation that this caused to an economy that, by the late 1970s, had come to rely on oil for 95 per cent of its export earnings. Many sophisticated and college-educated Nigerians located in other countries were effectively deprived of their source of income. In some cases they turned to crime, with spectacularly successful results. Indeed, Nigerians have developed large-scale drug-trafficking activities and have been identified as second only to the Chinese in the import of heroin into the United States. Once again this was facilitated by the fact that they were able to operate from a relatively safe home base characterized by unstable government, a high level of corruption, and few resources to devote to the fight against organized crime. They have also proved to be very adept in finding alternative trafficking routes, concealment techniques, courier profiles, and choice of product, and have progressed from simply being couriers for other transnational criminal organizations to becoming major players in their own right. Although there is little evidence of a Nigerian cartel, a loose network of drug barons has been identified and it is clear that even the activities of couriers are carefully orchestrated, with the couriers themselves being trained in methods to avoid detection. In October 1996, the United States Department of Justice announced the arrest of 34 members of a transnational heroin network that was run largely by Nigerian women. The arrests were made primarily in Chicago, New York, and Detroit, but one person was also arrested in Bangkok and one in Pakistan. The key distributor of the heroin in the United States was a Nigerian woman who used her Chicago boutique as a front.

Nigerian criminal activities in the United States, however, have not been limited to drug trafficking. US Deputy Assistant Secretary of State Jonathan Winer recently described Nigerian criminal enterprises as "adaptable, polycrime organizations" active in at least 60 countries. "They launder money in Hong Kong, buy cocaine in the Andes, run prostitution and gambling rings in Spain and Italy, and corrupt legitimate businesses in Great Britain with their financial crimes."[61] There are also a large number of fraudulent proposals emanating from Lagos and directed at wealthy businessmen. It has been estimated that American lose US$250 million a year in "4-1-9 schemes, a term that refers to the section of the Nigerian criminal code dealing with advance fee frauds. Individual losses range from around US$10,000 to about US$4 million."[62] Those perpetrating the frauds are very skilled, ensuring that all the documentation looks official. In some cases they also point out that, although Nigerians have a reputation for engaging in scams, this particular offer is genuine. Nigerian organizations have also engaged in fraudulent activities related to credit cards, commercial banks, and government assistance programmes. They have proved adept at obtaining the documentation for false identities that have facilitated cheque kiting, student loan fraud, social services fraud, insurance fraud, and electronic funds transfer fraud.

The members tend to live modestly and ship money back to Nigeria, and although legislation has recently been passed against money laundering, it is far from clear that this is being vigorously implemented. Nevertheless, their success has bred imitation, and individuals and groups from Ghana, Benin, and Sierra Leone have also become involved in transnational crime, especially drug trafficking, leading law enforcement agencies in some countries to refer to West African criminal organizations rather than simply Nigerian groups.

Although law enforcement agencies have had some success in response to their activities, the Nigerian organizations have several built-in defence mechanisms. The use of a variety of different dialects, for example, reduces the usefulness of wire tapping and other electronic surveillance devices. In essence, they have a non-technological way of circumventing hi-tech law enforcement. The fact that the organizations tend to be based on family or tribal ties also makes them very difficult to infiltrate. While the threat they pose in terms of corruption and violence may be less than some of the other groups, they have opened up areas such as Southern Africa to drug-trafficking activity, often coming in from Brazil. This is reflected in cocaine seizures in South Africa, which increased by 250 per cent from 1994 to 1995. Moreover, South Africans are increasingly used as couriers, with the result that some of them are now in Brazilian jails. Rio de Janeiro has emerged as a major emporium for buying drugs, and some estimates suggest that Nigerian drug-trafficking and criminal groups employ over 1,500 people in the city. Reports also indicate that there are tribal specializations, with the Ibo providing the routes for the cocaine; the Ioruba, who are strongly represented in public administration, expediting bureaucratic channels; and the Haussa-Fulani, who are the richest tribal group, financing the operation.

Other criminal organizations

This survey has obviously not been comprehensive. Turkish drug-trafficking organizations which supply heroin to Western Europe from South-West Asia using the famous Balkans Route, and the variations on it that have been made necessary by the conflict in former Yugoslavia, have not been discussed. Nor have Jamaican posses, African-American criminal organizations, Mexican drug-trafficking families, Dominican organizations, or a variety of other groups. This should not be surprising. Transnational criminal organizations have become pervasive. In Belgium, for example, indigenous groups have links with Chinese and Italian groups as well as with Turkish networks, while in the Czech Republic law enforcement authorities complain that indigenous criminal groups have been relegated to "service" organizations for stronger organizations from elsewhere.[63] One member of the Czech criminal police has even claimed that 90 per cent of Yugoslavs in the Czech Republic deal in drugs, guns, and prostitution, while 90 per cent of Albanians are heroin and gun runners, 90 per cent of Vietnamese are tax evaders and black marketeers, most Chinese restaurants launder dirty money, and the Bulgarians steal cars and deal drugs.[64] Although there is some xenophobia in this statement, it encapsulates what has become in many countries a mosaic of transnational criminal organizations. The Albanian groups, for example, are active not only in the Czech Republic but elsewhere in central Europe and even on the east coast of the United States. In short, transnational criminal organizations have become ubiquitous. While their capacity to destabilize governments and their impact on national and international security vary considerably, they certainly present a challenge that cannot be ignored. The extent and nature of this challenge to security is the subject of the final section.

The threat to national and international security

When considering the impact of TCOs on national and international security, it is necessary both to identify the ways in which these groups threaten security and to assess the nature and extent of these threats. In undertaking these tasks there are several dangers that need to be avoided. The first is dismissal of these threats because they do not fit the traditional Cold War paradigm. For those observers and analysts accustomed to defining security exclusively in military terms, transnational criminal organizations can be relegated to a law and order challenge. The difficulty is that this treats the Cold War paradigm of security as immutable, ignoring challenges other than overt military actions or military threats. This is understandable but shortsighted: it overlooks the variety of ways in which, and the variety of levels on which, TCOs can inflict harm upon states, societies, and individuals.

The second danger is related to the first in complex ways. In order to convince sceptics about the seriousness of the threat from TCOs, it is tempting to characterize this threat as a direct assault on political stability, social well-being, and the integrity and soundness of financial institutions. As one report noted: "Organized crime poses a direct threat to national and international security and stability, and constitutes a frontal attack on political and legislative authority, challenging states in fundamental ways."[65] While such a characterization is in many ways very persuasive, it sacrifices subtlety and nuance for impact. It also makes an attractive target for critics like R. Thomas Naylor, who contends that in the post-Cold War world national security establishments have a desperate need for new enemies, and have elevated criminal organizations to a status they do not deserve.[66] Naylor argues that criminal organizations are rarely conceptualized properly. In his view, the leading criminal authorities are not chief executive officers of criminal enterprises, but providers of governance and arbitrators of disputes in the criminal world. There is much to this argument, and it is an important critique of what might be termed the "global organized crime school" which presents criminal organizations as large hierarchical monoliths that are moving to create global conglomerates of crime. Yet it is also possible to accept part of Naylor's argument without dismissing the threat to security.

This critique also underlines the need to be sensitive in one's portrayal of transnational organized crime. Treating organized crime as an unmitigated evil, for example, ignores the benefits that organized crime provides, benefits that extend well beyond the immediate members of the organizations. At least some of the money earned by criminal organizations has significant and beneficial multiplier effects in local, regional, and sometimes even national economies. Similarly, illicit trafficking can be a major source of export earnings for states which have little to provide in licit products. Moreover, organized crime often provides a form of employment when few other opportunities are available. In societies where large segments of the population do not have ready access to legitimate avenues of advancement, or where these avenues are simply not well developed, becoming a member of a criminal organization can appear very attractive. As suggested earlier, it is no coincidence that the rise of criminal organizations often occurs amidst conditions of poverty or as an accompaniment to social upheaval, economic dislocation, or political disruption. In such circumstances, the willingness and ability of criminal organizations to provide patronage to the local community sometimes elevates their leaders to the status of folk heroes.

None of this is intended to condone TCOs or their activities; it is simply that understanding them better is a prerequisite for implementing more effective preventive, control, and disruptive strategies against them. To the extent that TCOs emerge from specific conditions, for example, then changing the conditions should be a major element in preventive strategies elsewhere. Similarly, identifying their weaknesses can reveal better ways of combating them and reducing their effectiveness. Understanding the ways in which they manage the risks posed to them by law enforcement offers novel opportunities to exploit their risk management techniques against them.

Furthermore, acknowledgment of the benefits they provide does not obviate the fundamental reality that the positive results from their activities are greatly outweighed by the negative consequences. Although the threat from TCOs is sometimes more subtle than overt, it is hard to escape the conclusion that they pose challenges to national sovereignty, to individual members of society, to societies themselves, to the rule of law, to the effectiveness of some international norms and conventions, and to the viability and integrity of their home states. The linkages between criminal and terrorist organizations, the capacity of criminal organizations to benefit from civil war and ethnic strife, the extensive use of violence and corruption by TCOs, and the willingness of these groups to traffic in a wide range of products with little attention given to the consequences, all accentuate the emergence of TCOs as a threat to both security and stability.

In some respects, TCOs can be regarded as the AIDS virus of the modern state. While they tend to be most pervasive where the state is already weak, TCOs perpetuate that weakness using a mix of corruption and violence. While they use these tactics to a degree in their host states, their main efforts are directed at their home state in an effort to ensure that this remains a safe haven. The consequences are insidious. Just as the AIDS virus breaks down the body's immune system, powerful criminal organizations can break down the defence mechanisms of the state. Using corruption and the infiltration of licit institutions, they are able to create conditions that allow them to operate with impunity. In some cases criminal organizations are able to extend their networks into law enforcement institutions, thereby neutralizing and undermining these institutions. The capacity of criminal organizations to spread corruption can also distort the purposes that the state is supposed to serve. At worst, the state can become the servant of the criminal organization, placing the whims and desires of the criminal leaders above the needs of the citizens. It could be argued, of course, that organized crime differs from the AIDS virus in that it generally creates a symbiotic relationship with the state, but does not destroy it. Yet there may be an interesting parallel emerging here: there is some speculation in the medical community that the HIV virus is becoming less virulent. As it stands, when the host dies the virus too ceases to exist. Allowing the host to survive longer, therefore, also benefits the virus and can be understood as a sophisticated form of adaptation. To the extent that this occurs, the parallels between AIDS and organized crime will become even stronger.

This emphasis on the insidious rather than overt nature of the threat is not to deny that, in some cases, organized crime has initiated a direct assault on its home state. The two most obvious instances are in Italy and Colombia. In both cases, the criminal organizations created a rival authority structure and displayed a remarkable willingness to use force against the state and its agents. Not only did they challenge the state monopoly of the legitimate use of violence, but they also inflicted a level of harm exceeding that resulting from the activities of most terrorist groups.

In Colombia, the Medellin cartel assaulted the state apparatus, decimating the judiciary and killing police and military officers who were not readily susceptible to corruption. One result of this campaign of violence was that Colombia relinquished its extradition agreement with the United States, essentially acquiescing in what the traffickers wanted. At the end of the day, however, the Colombian state emerged triumphant: Pablo Escobar was killed and other leaders of the cartel were imprisoned. The threat from the Cali cartel was more insidious but still fundamental. Under pressure from the United States, the government moved against the Cali cartel and its key leaders were imprisoned or killed. Yet at best this was a tarnished victory, as it became clear that corruption had reached the highest levels of the Colombian political élite. Moreover, the inadvertent consequences of this success highlight the severity of the problem. In Colombia itself the big winners were the guerrilla organizations which also engage in drug trafficking. Another result of the weakening of the major Colombian drug-trafficking organizations was to enhance the position of drug-trafficking groups in Mexico – leading to a process of violence and corruption there that some observers referred to as the Colombianization of Mexico.[67] In the slightly longer term, Brazil too could well emerge as another "safe haven" for drug trafficking and other criminal organizations. With a state apparatus that lacks the capacity for effective action against organized crime and drug trafficking, and has traditionally been open to corruption and collusion, a countryside in which there are many remote areas that are difficult to patrol and police effectively, and a large part of its population ensnared in poverty, Brazil has an ideal set of conditions to emerge as a home state for indigenous criminal groups and as a host state for transnational organizations looking for new "sanctuaries."[68] The threat to the viability of the state in Brazil may still be nascent but is unlikely to remain so.

The assault on the state in Italy in some respects paralleled that in Colombia. In Italy, however, the challenge resulted from what the Mafia saw as an attempt by the government to renege on a joint understanding and to dismantle what had been a very cosy symbiotic relationship. In the event, the Mafia proved to be a far more formidable enemy for the Italian state than terrorist organizations such as the Red Brigade. Deploying its very considerable resources, the Mafia engaged in an extensive and bloody campaign that resulted in the deaths of politicians and, most significantly, several leading anti-Mafia magistrates. Ultimately, though, these actions proved counter-productive, creating a major backlash that helped to sustain an unprecedented counter-attack by the state. With the arrest of top Mafia leaders and the continued efforts to eliminate corruption, it appears that the state has emerged victorious. At the same time, the Mafia should not be written off. Large criminal organizations often display considerable resilience in the face of adversity. While Italian criminal organizations are likely to maintain a lower profile for some years, the possibility of future challenges to state authority cannot be ruled out. Indeed, such challenges may be inescapable. As one eminent criminologist has noted, "each crime network attempts to build a coercive monopoly and to implement that system of control through at least two other criminal activities – corruption of public and private officials, and violent terrorism in order to enforce its discipline."[69]

The recent history of both Italy and Colombia suggests that, when faced with overt challenges from organized crime, the state can mobilize sufficient resources to defeat the challenge. But it is certainly conceivable that in some cases the state will not emerge victorious from such confrontations. State vulnerability is even greater when criminal organizations attempt to obtain power through stealth rather than confrontation. In this connection, a real possibility for the future is that a large and powerful criminal organization will, in effect, become a shadow government, exerting control from behind the scenes. A prime candidate for this is the Russian Federation, where the old symbiotic relationship between the state apparatus and the black-market criminals – a relationship that was essentially under the control of the state – has been replaced by a new symbiotic relationship dominated by the criminal organizations themselves. It is not too large a step from the present situation to the emergence of a criminalized state. The problems this would pose for the international community are enormous. Efforts to integrate the Russian Federation into the global economic system would have to be reconsidered, while the implications for the implementation of existing arms control and disarmament agreements are rather chilling.

Even in the absence of a worst-case contingency of this kind, TCOs will continue to present major challenges to governments. In an age of global information and communications technology, and global trade and financial systems, national borders are more porous than ever. Nevertheless, states still try to regulate what comes in and out of their borders, regarding their capacity to do this as a fundamental attribute of sovereignty. Such efforts are negated by TCOs, which routinely penetrate societies nominally under the control of state authorities. Although states retain the symbols of sovereignty, their inability to control the trafficking of arms, people, and drugs into their territory means a real erosion of national sovereignty. In other words, in their attempts to circumvent government authority and obtain access to lucrative illicit markets, TCOs pose an indirect but fundamental challenge to the prerogatives that are an integral part of statehood.

Nor are the threats confined to states. TCOs pose threats to civil society and to individual well-being. One component of the threat to societies is drug trafficking. Peddling a product that creates its own demand, drug-trafficking organizations have developed sophisticated marketing techniques that target new customers as well as habitual users. Moreover, the illicit drug industry is extremely innovative, and in the years ahead greater emphasis is likely to be placed on synthetic drugs. The only concern is profit, and the impact on individuals who steal to feed overwhelming drug habits is ignored, as is the violence that frequently accompanies certain kinds of substance use. In addition, of course, there is the violence that accompanies drug trafficking as street gangs fight to control turf and obtain the profits that go with domination of a particular territory. While violence is the most obvious of the debilitating consequences resulting from drug trafficking and drug abuse, it is not the only one. Other adverse consequences include lost productivity, which in many societies has significant implications for economic competitiveness, as well as substantial costs in terms of health care and law enforcement.

Even when they are not trafficking in drugs, TCOs still introduce a higher level of violence into the societies in which they operate. On some occasions innocent citizens are inadvertently caught in violent exchanges and become the casualties of internecine warfare or succession struggles. In other instances, licit businessmen become the victims of extortion attempts by criminal organizations. Perhaps the most serious threats to individuals, however, come from those organizations which engage in what might be termed human commodity trafficking. This has several dimensions. The first involves the trafficking of illegal migrants. Although migration generally results from both push and pull factors, in many cases migrants are fleeing oppression and hardship. Lured by the prospect of a better life, they try to reach developed regions such as the United States and Western Europe by any means possible. This places them at the mercy of ruthless criminal organizations which not only charge exorbitant fees but also subject the migrants to considerable deprivation and hardship along the way. And if, on arrival, the illegal immigrant is unable to pay the remainder of the fee then he or she is made to work for the trafficking organization. This may take the form of sweat-shop labour; or it may require the immigrant to become involved in criminal activities such as drug trafficking or prostitution.

It is at this juncture that illegal migration overlaps with the other major dimension of human commodity trafficking – the abuse of women and children for sexual slavery. The sex trade has long been a staple of organized criminal activity. Most recently, it has involved the trafficking of women from central and Eastern Europe to work as prostitutes in Holland and other Western European countries. At the most fundamental level, human commodity trafficking of this kind is a gross violation of human rights and the essential dignity of human beings. When it involves the systematic abuse of children it is among the most heinous of crimes. And in so far as security depends on the maintenance of a safe and secure environment in which citizens can exercise their right to life and property without fear of violence, intimidation, or the danger of sexual slavery, then it is clear that TCOs pose both direct and indirect threats to individual security. These threats may be a long way from traditional military threats to national security, but for the victims they are far more immediate than the scenarios devised by military planners.

It has become commonplace to note that TCOs pose a serious threat to the integrity of financial and commercial institutions. Yet the nature of this threat is rarely enunciated with sufficient care. Although the possibility that TCOs might attempt to disrupt the global financial system cannot be excluded, especially if these organizations are placed increasingly on the defensive, the real threat is less one of destruction or disruption than it is of exploitation. The criminal organizations want to maintain the existing system while ensuring that they can continue to exploit its multiple points of access, its capacity for rapid and anonymous money transfers, and its lack of complete transparency. In order to facilitate their interactions with the "upper world," corruption of financial officers is a favorite tactic. If corruption becomes sufficiently pervasive it could undermine confidence in financial institutions at both national and global levels. Yet this threat should not be exaggerated, as even the BCCI affair had a limited impact. Similarly, although the movement of criminal capital can have destabilizing consequences in particular sectors or on specific firms, the system-wide repercussions are likely to be limited. The amount of money that is laundered through the global financial system is large in absolute terms but is minuscule when compared to the sheer volume of financial transactions occurring on a daily basis.

This is not to recommend complacency. The infiltration of the banking system is particularly troublesome in developing countries and those states attempting to make the difficult transition towards the creation of democratic institutions and market economies. This dual transition has provided new opportunities for criminal activity, especially in areas where criminal justice systems are weak, while emergent financial institutions are particularly vulnerable to infiltration by criminal organizations. If the prevailing assessment is correct and between 40 and 80 per cent of the Russian banking system is actually under the control of criminal organizations, this has serious implications for the attempt to integrate the Russian Federation into the global financial system. Penetration of the banks provides access to other financial institutions and to corporations. It paves the way for infiltration of licit businesses, intimidation of their owners, and distortion of their purposes so that they no longer serve either the public interest or that of their shareholders. And as criminal organizations become more deeply entrenched in the financial sector, the prospects for effective counter-action by governments are significantly reduced. Such dangers loom particularly large in states in transition and developing states. In both categories, the accumulation of criminal capital and the unfair advantages it confers pose serious obstacles to legitimate entrepreneurial activity. Criminal organizations have greater capital liquidity than their legitimate competitors, and are often able to exercise undue influence over the bidding for contracts. On the other hand, if criminal organizations want to become legitimate then the capital they have accrued can be very important in ensuring the success of their legitimate businesses.

If the threat to financial institutions can all too easily be exaggerated, TCOs clearly add a new obstacle to efforts to regulate the global political system and establish codes of conduct, principles of restraint and responsibility, and norms of behaviour. Regimes to inhibit the proliferation of nuclear, chemical, and biological weapons are highly dependent upon cooperation among suppliers and the ability to isolate rogue states which seek to obtain such capabilities. In this connection, alliances of convenience, particularly between rogue states or pariah states on the one hand and TCOs on the other, could seriously undermine control efforts. Once a trafficking network is in place and is functioning effectively, product diversification is easy. Organizations which traffic in drugs can as easily traffic in technology and components for weapons of mass destruction. Whether the recipients are terrorist organizations or pariah states, the danger is obvious: if non-proliferation and other regulatory regimes are to function effectively in the future, it will be necessary to curb the activities of TCOs.

Another form of threat, although one that as yet is largely unrealized, relates to the vulnerability of communication and information systems. The more technologically advanced states are becoming increasingly reliant on national and global information infrastructures that are subject to disruption and attack by terrorists and criminal organizations. Paradoxically, the greater the sophistication, the greater the vulnerability. So far most of the attacks against information infrastructures have been carried out by individual hackers whose primary aim is to demonstrate their capacity to overcome safeguards and entry barriers to computer systems. Yet specialists in information pranks, young and impressionable as many of them are, could all too easily be recruited into criminal organizations and transformed into specialists in information warfare, cyber-terrorism, and cyber-crime. As yet there is little evidence that this has occurred, but it is a logical development of the growing sophistication of TCOs and the growing reliance of business and governments on computerized information and communication systems. There have been several reports of companies in Britain meeting extortion demands in order to prevent the disruption or destruction of their computerized information systems. Similarly, the success of a hacker living in St Petersburg in the Russian Federation in removing funds from a Citibank account in the United States highlights the potential for large-scale fraud and embezzlement. It is only a small step from this to worrying about the vulnerability of key nodes in the global financial system. As suggested earlier, criminal organizations are more interested in exploiting this system than in disrupting it. Nevertheless, when thinking about the actual and potential threats posed by TCOs, such vulnerabilities should certainly not be ignored.

The implication of all this is that TCOs, by their very nature, undermine civil society, add a degree of turbulence to domestic politics, and challenge the normal functioning of government and law. While they are particularly effective where government is already weak or unstable, criminal organizations add further layers of instability. They also pose serious and still not fully acknowledged threats to the dignity and safety of individuals, especially women and children, to the sovereignty, security, and stability of states, and to efforts to provide conventions and norms for the management of the international system. Potentially they pose a threat to global and national information systems and to the effective functioning of financial and commercial institutions at national and global levels. Many of them are global in scope. They are also transnational actors *par excellence*, regarding national borders as minor inconveniences and national sovereignty as an irrelevance. They are growing in power and influence, and could become one of the most serious threats to national and international security in the next century. In the final analysis this should not be a surprise. Just as globalization has encouraged the emergence of upright and constructive global citizens, it has also facilitated the transformation of organized crime from a local and domestic phenomenon to a transnational challenge of the first order. Meeting this challenge requires states to overcome the traditional constraints of sovereignty in the area of criminal justice and create effective transnational law enforcement networks. Until they do, the world will continue to be both playground and target for those who exploit the benefits of global citizenship but are unwilling to observe its obligations.

Notes

1. Roy Godson and William Olson have popularized the notion of a crisis of governance. See, for example, their contributions to *Terrorism and Political Violence*, vol. 6, 2 (Summer 1994).
2. Diego Gambetta, *The Sicilian Mafia: The Business of Private Protection* (Cambridge: Harvard University Press, 1993).
3. Francisco E. Thoumi, *Political Economy and Illegal Drugs in Colombia* (Boulder: Lynne Reiner, 1995), pp. 172–3.
4. Quoted in Richard Lotspeich, "Crime in the Transition Economies," *Europe-Asia Studies*, vol 47, 4 (June 1995), pp. 555–90 at p. 569.
5. Frederico Varese has made the same argument as Gambetta, but in relation to the Russian Federation.
6. Graham H. Turbiville, "Organized Crime and the Russian Armed Forces," *Transnational Organized Crime*, vol. 1, 4 (Winter 1995), pp. 57–104.
7. See P. Williams and P. Woessner, "Nuclear Material Trafficking: An Interim Assessment," *Transnational Organized Crime*, vol. 1, 2 (Summer 1995), pp. 206–38.
8. Louise Shelley, "Transnational Organized Crime: An Imminent Threat to the Nation-state?," *Journal of International Affairs*, vol. 48, 1 (January 1995).
9. Benjamin R. Barber, *Jihad versus McWorld* (New York: Times Books, 1995), p. 4.
10. Charles Hanley, "Increasingly, guerrillas financed by drugs," *Toronto Star*, 29 December 1994, p. A19.
11. Ibid.
12. Ibid.

13. Ibid.
14. The quotation is from Shelley, op. cit.
15. Ibid.
16. Ibid.
17. For an excellent discussion of bonding mechanisms see Francis A. J. Ianni, *Black Mafia: Ethnic Succession in Organized Crime* (New York: Simon and Schuster, 1974).
18. I am grateful to Peter Lupsha for this phrase.
19. See Willard Myers, "Orb Weavers – The Global Webs: The Structures and Activities of Transnational Ethnic Chinese Criminal Groups," *Transnational Organized Crime*, vol. 1, 4 (Winter 1995) pp. 1–36.
20. See "Netherlands: International Connections of Organized Crime," *Amsterdam De Volkskrant*, 28 February 1996.
21. The concept of loose coupling is developed in Charles Perrow, *Normal Accidents* (New York: Basic Books, 1984).
22. Gus Xhudo, "Men of Purpose: The Growth of Albanian Criminal Activity," *Transnational Organized Crime*, vol. 2, 1 (Spring 1996), pp. 1–20.
23. See Phil Williams, "Transnational Criminal Organizations: Strategic Alliances," *Washington Quarterly*, vol. 18, 1 (Winter 1994), pp. 57–72.
24. See Peter Reuter, "The Decline of the American Mafia," *Public Interest*, No. 120 (Summer 1995).
25. Charles Rogovin and Frederick Martens, "The American Mafia is Alive and Kicking," *Trends in Organized Crime*, vol. 1, 3 (Spring 1996), pp. 35–6.
26. William Kleinknecht, *The New Ethnic Mobs* (New York: Free Press, 1996).
27. Ibid.
28. G. de Genaro, "The Influence of Mafia-Type Organizations on Business and Industry," *Trends in Organized Crime*, vol. 1, 2 (Winter 1995), pp. 36–42.
29. Ibid.
30. Ibid.
31. Ibid.
32. Ibid.
33. Ibid.
34. Adolfo Beria di Argentine, "The Mafias in Italy," in Ernesto Savona (ed.), *Mafia Issues*, pp. 19–32 provides an excellent overview of the various Mafias. The quote is from page 20.
35. See Alison Jamieson, "Mafia and Institutional Power in Italy," *International Relations*, pp. 1–23 at p. 3.
36. Alexander Stille, *Excellent Cadavers* (New York: Pantheon, 1995), p. 7.
37. See Enzo d'Antona, "The Mafia in the Red," *Il Mondo*, 11–18 September 1995, pp. 12–16.
38. Alan Cowell, "Italians Voting, With Mafia a Top Issue," *The New York Times*, Sunday 27 March 1994, p. 10.
39. Alison Jamieson, "The Transnational Dimension of Italian Organized Crime," *Transnational Organized Crime*, vol. 1, 2 (Summer 1995), pp. 151–72.
40. Ibid.
41. P. Clawson and R. Lee, *The Andean Cocaine Industry* (New York: St Martin's, 1996), p. 75.
42. See Guy Dunn, "Major Mafia Gangs in Russia," in *Transnational Organized Crime* (forthcoming).
43. These figures are based on official reports by the Ministry of Interior.
44. These figures are taken from a report by the BKA discussed in "A Chronic Problem," *Munich Focus*, 17 June 1996, p. 34. They refer to 1995. For the 1994 figures see *Orga-

nized Crime in the Federal Republic of Germany: Summary of the Situation in 1994 reproduced in "Global Proliferation of Weapons of Mass Destruction," Hearings before the Permanent Subcommittee on Investigations of the Committee on Governmental Affairs, United States Senate, 104th Congress. Second Session Part II, 13, 20, and 22 March 1996, pp. 741–57.

45. Report on Asian organized crime in Australia by Parliamentary Committee 1994.
46. Ibid.
47. "Heroin Trafficking Among Four Tentacles of Chinese Mafia," *El Mundo*, 27 March 1994, p. 71.
48. "Expert interviewed on criminal syndicates," *FBIS Daily Report*, 8 March 1995.
49. Ibid.
50. "Minister warns of international organized crime," *FBIS Daily Report*, 21 November 1994.
51. See Asian Organized Crime: The new International Criminal Hearings before the Permanent Subcommittee on Investigations of the Committee on Governmental Affairs, United States Senate, 102nd Congress, Second Session, 18 June and 4 August 1992, p. 125.
52. White Paper on Police 1994, reproduced in *Trends in Organized Crime*, vol. 1, 3 (Spring 1996), pp. 49–56.
53. Ibid.
54. See "Of Note: Asia," in ibid., p. 69.
55. See "Asian Gangs Greatest Future Organized Crime Threat," in *Organized Crime Digest*, vol. 15, 13 (28 September 1994), pp. 1–3 at p. 2.
56. David E. Kaplan and Alec Dubro, *Yakuza* (New York: Macmillan, 1986), p. 208.
57. See White Paper on Police 1994.
58. "Article Views Struggles with International Crime," *FBIS Daily Report*, 27 July 1995.
59. See White Paper on Police 1994.
60. This section draws heavily upon *Nigeria – A County Overview* (Johnstown, Pennsylvania: National Drug Intelligence Center, 17 March 1994).
61. Pat Griffith, "Nigerian scams costing Americans millions," *Pittsburgh Post Gazette*, 22 September 1996, p. A.10.
62. Ibid.
63. JS, "Attention Mafia," *Prague Respekt*, 21 May 1995.
64. R. B. Reilly, "Black Market Bonanza," *Prague Prognosis Weekly*, 4 June 1995, p. 2.
65. Discussion Guide for the Ninth UN Congress on the Prevention of Crime and the Treatment of Offenders (A/Conf. 169/PM1 and corr. 1), para 39.
66. R. Thomas Naylor, "From Cold War to Crime War: The Search for a New National Security Threat," *Transnational Organized Crime*, vol. 1, 4 (Winter 1995), pp. 37–56.
67. D. Farah, "Drug Lords' Influence Pervading Mexico," *Washington Post*, 4 April 1995, p. A1.
68. For a fuller analysis of the potential of Brazil in this area see Maria Velez de Berliner and Kristin Lado, "Brazil: The Emerging Drug Superpower," *Transnational Organized Crime*, vol. 1, 2 (Summer 1995), pp. 239–60.
69. R. J. Kelly, "Criminal Underworlds: Looking Down on Society from Below," in R. J. Kelly (ed.), *Organized Crime: A Global Perspective* (Totowa, New Jersey: Rowman and Littlefield, 1986), pp. 10–31 at p. 17.

10

The relations of UN agencies and non-governmental organizations in cross-border humanitarian assistance

Roland Koch

Introduction

The end of the Cold War has changed the voting behaviour of the Permanent Members of the UN Security Council in relation to cross-border humanitarian assistance. This has resulted in a new freedom of humanitarian action for UN agencies and humanitarian NGOs. They became partners in humanitarian interventions. The joint UN-NGO humanitarian interventions in northern Iraq, Cambodia, former Yugoslavia, and Somalia were at first accompanied by the hope in Western public opinion of witnessing the development of a new era of global peace and justice. However, the new mandates of UN peace missions in internal humanitarian emergencies have also raised great concern among third world UN member states, who feared an erosion of the doctrine of national sovereignty guaranteed in Article 2, 7 of the UN Charter. Some of these states are extremely reluctant to accept even the massive violation of human rights as a legitimation of UN interference in what they believe to be their internal affairs.[1] Nevertheless, public opinion pressure on Western European and North American governments and NGO lobbying have prompted the UN Security Council to introduce a new type of humanitarian mandate. Relief operations are to facilitate free cross-border access for UN humanitarian agencies and NGOs to provide comfort to the victims in humanitarian emergencies.

The positive image of humanitarian assistance as a symbol of global responsibility and justice, along with cutbacks in the formerly applied strategically-oriented development aid, led donor governments to shift their financial aid budgets from development aid to humanitarian aid by funding UN agencies and NGOs. This boosted the humanitarian industry to a turnover volume of US$8 billion in 1996, and raised the problem of the independence of NGOs. The suspicion developed that they may sometimes be instrumentalized by the political interests of donor governments. Confronted with such an exploding humanitarian market, some NGOs developed considerable bureaucratic structures with self-centred interests. The necessary operational conversion in many programmes of UN agencies and NGOs from long-term development to short-term emergency intervention contradicted their recently adopted policy of facilitating self-help in the development process.

The exaggerated expectations of a new and just world order which arose after the end of the Cold War were rapidly adjusted to reality by the dramatic increase in the number of complex humanitarian emergencies since 1990. According to Bennett/Kayetisi-Blewitt,[2] 28 complex humanitarian emergencies were identified by the United Nations in 1995, with about 60 million people affected. Natsios[3] defines complex humanitarian emergencies by five common characteristics: first, the deterioration or complete collapse of central governmental authority; second, ethnic or religious conflict and widespread abuse of human rights; third, episodic food insecurity, frequently deteriorating into mass starvation; fourth, macroeconomic collapse involving hyperinflation, massive unemployment, and net decrease in gross national product; and fifth, mass population movements of displaced people and refugees escaping conflict or searching for food. Deciding to intervene in one place always meant discriminating against other humanitarian emergencies. Political interests of donor governments became increasingly predominant – a fact which also endangers the claim to neutrality in humanitarian assistance of UN agencies and NGOs. Although both have considerable experience of cooperating after natural disasters, they now have great difficulties in dealing with emergencies in military conflicts. The security problems of operational staff can no longer be solved by appealing to the conflict parties to respect the UN-NGO humanitarian neutrality.

These changes in the political conditions for UN-NGO humanitarian assistance after the end of the Cold War have caused a series of problems for UN-NGO relations in humanitarian missions:

- the strategic problem of emergency intervention versus emergency prevention;
- the problem of insufficient information about cultural, ethnic, and political causes of conflicts due to the time restriction of emergency assessment;

- the problems of competition, media appearance, and leadership during relief implementation;
- the severe security problems when humanitarian missions are implemented in ongoing military conflicts;
- the problem of impartiality and neutrality of UN agencies and NGOs *vis-à-vis* all conflict parties.

Following this introduction, this chapter's structure first takes up the changes in this political conditions for UN-NGO humanitarian assistance after the end of the Cold War, and by that the end of ideological suspicion against humanitarian cross-border assistance. The marginalizing effects of globalization are looked at with regard to their dynamics in causing humanitarian emergencies. The networking of humanitarian NGOs is described, resulting in conformity over large-scale emergency interventions and the creation of oligopolistic structures. The chapter outlines, second, the gradual inclination of the UN Security Council to demand free access for cross-border humanitarian assistance by UN agencies and NGOs, evidenced in the Security Council resolutions on North Iraq, former Yugoslavia, Cambodia, and Somalia, thereby introducing a new UN mission mandate to enforce the right of access of humanitarian relief delivery to victims in humanitarian emergencies. Third, after scanning the basic problems of the UN system accepting NGOs as partners in humanitarian interventions, the operational problems of UN agencies and NGO relations in joint humanitarian missions are discussed. The doubtful emergency orientation is emphasized, as well as the inadequate sharing of information, and problems of leadership and neutrality in the humanitarian community. Finally, necessary transformations from reactive to preventive humanitarian intervention by UN agencies and NGOs are proposed.

The research method has involved the interpretation of standardized questionnaires and additional qualitative interviews with some 65 European humanitarian NGOs and European offices of UN agencies in 1994 and 1995. The questions centred around the experiences of UN-NGO cooperation in the missions to northern Iraq, Cambodia, Bosnia and Herzegovina, Somalia, and Rwanda. The interview partners mostly had personal experience in more than one mission, and could therefore describe modifications in UN-NGO interaction from crisis to crisis. The questions included the topics of cooperation with local NGOs and the problems of negotiations with conflict parties, national or local officials, and commanding officers.

The chapter's main thesis is that the changes in the political conditions of UN-NGO cross-border humanitarian assistance after the end of the Cold War induced an expansion of the humanitarian industry at such a great pace that humanitarian UN-NGO missions developed into large-scale poor-relief supply structures with oligopolistic and hierarchical tendencies at the cost of suppressing pluralistic, locally participating, self-help-oriented service NGOs.[4] This indicates that global civil society up to now lacks the necessary representative legitimization procedures. The present oligopolistic development of the humanitarian NGO community may facilitate UN-NGO interaction. It may also make it easier to present their analyses and proposals to the different UN bodies; and it may heighten NGO influence on governmental decision-making within member states, including a better public visibility and successful national fund-raising. But the more creative and innovative parts of the NGO community are the tens of thousands of smaller humanitarian NGOs. There are networks of local humanitarian NGOs developing in Latin American and, albeit less organized, in some African and South-East Asian regions. They need external support, or at least international public acknowledgment, to overcome national government constraints.[5] This chapter criticizes the negative effects of large-scale relief supply structures where refugees and internally displaced persons are quartered in huge camps, thus becoming virtually the possessions of humanitarian organizations and losing almost all possibility of self-determination. The chapter argues that it is preferable to empower the small local service NGOs, to decentralize humanitarian assistance, and to develop a strategy of preventive humanitarian interventions.

The term "UN agencies" designates a broad variety of UN bodies, programmes, and organizations dealing with humanitarian emergencies which differ greatly in their specific mandates as well as in their degree of constitutional or practically acquired autonomy inside the UN system. For the purpose of this chapter the United Nations High Commissioner for Refugees (UNHCR), with his lead function in all humanitarian missions with refugees, must be named first. In 1995 the number of refugees was estimated at 16.3 million people. In cases of internally displaced persons, who were estimated at 29.1 million plus 35 million people displaced by development programmes and environmental disasters,[6] it is mostly the United Nations International Children's Emergency Fund (UNICEF) and the United Nations Development Programme (UNDP) which take over lead functions, because they are usually already on the spot with their respective programmes. The International Organization for Migration (IOM) has been engaged in helping internally displaced persons in northern Iraq and in some African countries.[7] According to their specific mandates in health care and food supply, the World Health Organization (WHO), the World Food Programme (WFP), and the Food and Agricultural Organization (FAO) are sometimes occupied with humanitarian emergencies. To support communication and coordination among the UN agencies, the Department of Humanitarian Affairs (DHA) has been established in the UN Secretariat.

The term "humanitarian non-governmental organizations" covers a multitude of organizations which differ mainly by concentrating more on human rights advocacy or on humanitarian service delivery. Their level of action may be local, national, regional, or international. Shelton[8] points out the fact that before the First World War 400 such organizations were already established, accredited by the Union of International Associations under the condition that their objectives be in the interest of all nations and not involve profit. Borton's definition of NGOs even goes beyond the non-profit sector: "NGOs include profit-making organizations, foundations, educational institutions, churches and professional organizations, business and commercial organizations, cooperatives, and cultural groups as well as voluntary agencies."[9]

The staff members of NGOs can be non-professionals, volunteer professionals, or fully-paid professionals, and they may be motivated by professional, religious, or humanistic ethics. The NGOs' finances can derive from private donations and/or public subsidies. The degree of organization can vary from very loose social movements and networks to hierarchically structured centralized administrations. The service methods vary from careful self-help support to the formalized implementation of predetermined relief modules for a selected target population. Operational decisions can be taken very spontaneously, they can depend on global network consultations, or they may be directives from a governing body of an international parent NGO.

In this chapter the term "NGO" encompasses globally acting international and national humanitarian service NGOs, with professional relief standards, administratively well organized, and financed by private donations and public subventions to engage in humanitarian cross-border assistance. They act in humanitarian emergencies, using global networks or company decisions in the ways shown in Figure 10.1.

The functions of military forces in humanitarian UN missions are normally determined by the mandates of the Security Council, but sometimes they have been interpreted by the member government entrusted with military command of the mission. They can range from pure observer status to an enforcement mandate to secure the delivery of humanitarian aid, and involve anything from mediation between conflict parties to disarming them. It is strongly questioned by UN agencies and NGOs whether military enforcement can facilitate the humanitarian relief supply. Even the pure security function of the military forces in humanitarian missions is disputed.[10] The Security Council's assumption that the Bluehelmets' authority would be respected worldwide was evi-

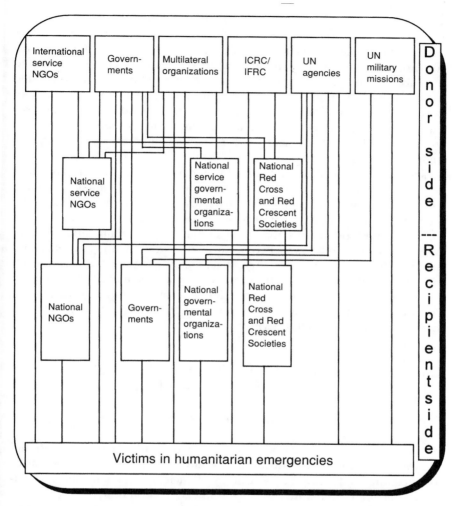

Figure 10.1 Cross-border humanitarian assistance by UN agencies and NGOs

dently erroneous. Because of the wide range of their mandates, humanitarian military UN missions have not been able to establish a neutral image with all conflict parties, and sometimes UN military forces have even become conflict parties themselves.

The cooperation between the military and UN agencies and NGOs in humanitarian emergencies extends over a wide variety of tasks. NGOs are dependent on the provision of air transport capacities for aid materials and staff members. Air transport can be bought by NGOs on the world market, but extra-large air transport capacity is scarce and thus military support in this area is highly esteemed. The same is true for heavy equipment to construct access roads, bridges, or sanitary systems for large refugee camps. Military support is also sometimes needed to establish autonomous communication systems. However, in the wide range of humanitarian services, like water and food supply, medical and psychological care, housing and administrative aid, education and training programmes, rehabilitation, and social reintegration, the military forces' contributions are clearly less effective compared to UN agencies' and NGOs' activities.[11]

The experiences in Somalia and former Yugoslavia have proved that the blend of military and humanitarian mandates is damaging to the objectives of both. The military objectives in Mogadishu, for example, were impeded by the attempt of belligerents to install weapon arsenals in hospitals and food distribution centres of NGOs; and humanitarian relief programmes had to be cancelled because of military offensives inside and around the city. Therefore, it might be called progress that the French commander of the United Nations operation in Rwanda in 1994, General Lafourcade, definitely refused to call it a humanitarian operation.[12] According to him, this was a military operation to prepare the ground for subsequent humanitarian activities.

Changes in the political conditions for UN-NGO humanitarian assistance after the end of the Cold War

End of Cold War limitations on humanitarian assistance

For nearly half a century after the Second World War, international security and peace were attributed by the leading powers of the East–West conflict to the deterrence strategy of nuclear armament. The second-strike capability on both sides guaranteed destruction of a potential aggressor, even if he was to succeed in destroying the other side in a first strike. So, on the basis of assumably rational decision-making on either side, military aggression would not pay. For the two blocs to wage war was tantamount to self-destruction.

Nuclear deterrence strategy, though, did not prevent wars globally. The world has seen many conventional wars fought by peoples on the periphery, sometimes even joined by the superpowers. The resulting humanitarian emergencies could only be met by NGOs, whereas the UN Security Council in most cases was blocked by the veto powers and nearly all other UN actions were constantly suspected of serving one side to the disadvantage of the other – a suspicion which, for the most part, limited

UN cross-border humanitarian assistance. Inside the United Nations system the ongoing East–West tensions impeded cooperation between UN officials and NGOs on these topics. "It was not possible to have any contact with non-governmental organizations in the Soviet Union, for example, because this would be seen as neo-imperialist intervention. On the other side, it was called communist intervention."[13]

The post-Cold War flexibility of the Security Council, with Permanent Members refraining from using their veto power against humanitarian intervention, allows the United Nations to act in two directions. First, the United Nations could give up its forced neutrality in humanitarian emergencies and differentiate between perpetrator and victims, although it was then dependent upon the members' willingness to provide sufficient military forces to put its words into actions. But neither the United Nations nor the member states seem to be well prepared to conduct such humanitarian peace-enforcement operations, and the humanitarian NGO community seems mostly unwilling to abandon neutrality, even in the case of military protection for humanitarian aid delivery. Second, the United Nations could try to address the underlying causes of humanitarian emergencies and thus develop an integrated approach to peace building, as it attempted in the Cambodian operation. This seems to be a promising strategy for the United Nations, but the growing number of complex humanitarian emergencies and the problems of financing such costly operations made it appear unrealistic.

With the end of the Cold War, UN-NGO cooperation in humanitarian assistance was – at least temporarily – freed from ideological suspicion; it was no longer seen as serving revolutionary movements, nor was it identified with the spread of capitalism, although there might still be a tendency not to look too closely at humanitarian emergencies if they are inside a traditional sphere of interest of one of the Permanent Members of the Security Council. In other areas, the United Nations gained more freedom of humanitarian action, and the major Western governments readily occupied this new field of international politics in an attempt to compensate internal legitimacy deficiencies.

Humanitarian emergencies as a result of globalization and marginalization

The most important change in the political conditions for UN-NGO cooperation in humanitarian assistance after the end of the Cold War – globalization – had been developing for years, but was somewhat obscured by East–West tensions. A rising number of multinational corporations gradually withdraw from national governments' control and formed a global market with hitherto unknown dynamic forces. New communication technologies have accelerated the flow of capital in a way that makes it seem omnipresent. Not only national taxation, but also social or ecological regulations to channel the economical dynamics – gained in many societies through long-lasting political struggles – are now proving more and more inefficient.

Globalization has actually developed a hierarchical division of economic involvement. An economic selection process is taking place within countries, marginalizing considerable parts of the population. The same is happening between countries, especially in North-South relations. The accelerating process of marginalization, and the almost total collapse of strategically oriented aid from and protection by the former leading superpowers and their allies, together resulted in a dramatic decline of political stability in the most affected areas. There is a considerable threat to global peace and security arising from the breaking up of states and societies. Internal military conflicts evolve out of violent distribution struggles and ideologically, religiously, or ethnically instrumentalized clashes between groups striving for economic and political participation or domination.[14]

The social fragmentation and marginalization in North and South are increasing, and with them the number of humanitarian emergencies. Governments in industrially developed countries have entered into hopeless competition for reducing social welfare systems and cutting back costly safety regulations, originally intended to protect employees, environment, and public interests.[15] State revenues are decreasing, state indebtedness is rising, unemployment rates are growing, and governments are losing important parts of their regulating power and legitimacy. The reduction of intra-state welfare systems apparently gives rise to some fictitious compensatory policies, especially by Western European governments. They place a considerable amount of money at the disposal of the European Community Humanitarian Office (ECHO), in order to support humanitarian UN agencies and especially to finance humanitarian activities of NGOs. To some NGOs this looks like an attempt to substitute the deficiencies of intra-state welfare systems, which neo-liberal-oriented governments refuse to finance any longer, with some symbolic poverty programmes in international humanitarian emergencies.

Global networking and oligopolistic tendencies of humanitarian NGOs

Creating networks and coalitions is one of the characteristics of modern globally active NGOs. To organize like-minded individuals and groups internationally is one of the strong capabilities of NGOs, and new communication technologies simplify the exchange of information and position papers. "Scaling up certain kinds of transnational efforts from neighbourhoods and regions to the global level, and scaling down to involve grass-roots organizations are no longer logistic impossibilities, but may be treated as institutional imperatives."[16] With the mutual dissolution of the East-West enemy images during the process of détente produced by the Conference on Security and Cooperation in Europe, humanitarian advocacy NGOs were the first to recognize the personal integrity and common interests of like-minded individuals and organizations on either side.

By the end of the 1980s new patterns of global civil society had evolved. The personal ties of NGO representatives had grown into international organizational networks, with rising public awareness of humanitarian emergencies as well as increasing public support of relief programmes. The scientific and professional advocacy NGOs in particular, like the Pugwash Conferences and the IPPNW (International Physicians for the Prevention of Nuclear War), supported the human rights movements in the German Democratic Republic and other Eastern European countries with publicity-gaining visits to protect their threatened exponents.

The successful spread of human rights movements created a global set of humanitarian values, and thereby prepared the ground for the global networking of humanitarian service NGOs. Although we can find these values and aims today in many NGOs all over the world and at all levels, from grass-roots self-help organizations to big international federations, cross-border humanitarian assistance by humanitarian service NGOs seems to be a Western concept: "... recognizable operational or advocacy operations with a combination of voluntary support and external funding that implemented discrete activities – are basically Western in origin."[17] Rieff found some evidence for a connection between modern secular humanitarian cross-border assistance and the Western religious missionary concept of the colonial past.[18]

Historically there is a long record of NGOs acting on a global level. Four hundred NGOs were accredited by the Union of International Associations before the First World War under the condition that their objectives were in the interest of all nations and did not involve profit.[19] Today, economic competition has reached humanitarian aid, and has transformed it partly into a humanitarian industry with big international trade fairs and mass production of various supply units. This facilitates humanitarian aid to serve governments' interests, because it can now be quantified and measured by industrial standards. It is not surprising that Borton,[20] in characterizing recent international NGO structures, includes profit-making organizations, business, and commercial organizations.

Networking provided humanitarian NGOs with an international

standing and access to executive levels of the UN system. The fact that the Secretary-General grants appointments to the heads of Oxfam or the International Rescue Committee as easily as he accepts visits from the presidents of the Socialist International or Liberal International[21] reflects the extent to which the big humanitarian NGO groupings have closed ranks with the United Nations headquarters. A senior UNDP official has called this a development into an "oligopoly," where eight major families or federations of international NGOs have come to control almost half the US$8 billion humanitarian assistance market.[22] The eight market leaders, which have an annual turnover of approximately US$300 million to US$600 million each,[23] are CARE, World Vision, Oxfam, Médicins Sans Frontières (MSF), Save the Children, Coopération Internationale pour le Développement et la Solidarité (CIDSE), Association of Protestant Development Organizations in Europe (APDOVE), and the European Secular NGOs Federation (Eurostep).

The recent trend towards oligopolistic structures in NGOs reflects not only the large scale of today's humanitarian missions and the increasing competition for funding. It also results from the historic shift from bilateral official development aid in the first two development decades to funding NGO aid programmes in the third decade. "This shift was only a part of the general privatization of what had been the public sector in the development world..."[24] By the end of the 1980s, development aid had been very much discredited in the eyes of the Western public. This is not the place to discuss the philosophy of development aid in the last decades, although it has to be emphasized that the concept of development was mostly manipulative treatment of Southern societies instead of giving them a secured space in which to develop their inherent capacities. The results were deformed economies, societies, and political systems[25] unable to cope with global market competition, or to resolve peacefully internal group conflicts, which eventually deteriorated into complex humanitarian emergencies.

It was anything but surprising that the governments of the industrialized countries after the end of the Cold War seized the opportunity of gaining new political credibility as donors in the growing number of humanitarian relief operations. Development aid was reallocated to NGOs offering humanitarian relief programmes. It did not take very long for some NGOs to find themselves dependent on the big humanitarian donor-governments' agencies, like the European ECHO. The bureaucratic structures of these governmental financing institutions required and promoted NGO networking. Donor cuts in development aid and a considerable increase in humanitarian emergency aid provoked a shift in UN agencies' and NGOs' actions. Humanitarian NGOs were more and more subcontracted by UN agencies and governmental and intergovernmental donors to carry out humanitarian assistance, which generally endangered the autonomy and the pluralistic approach of NGOs and fostered oligopolistic structures.

UN and NGO efforts to legalize humanitarian interventions

The legal framework of UN and NGO humanitarian interventions

The international legal basis of UN agencies' and NGOs' cross-border humanitarian assistance is not very strong. This chapter will trace the growing acceptance of cross-border humanitarian assistance by the international community in recent years. According to the treaties on humanitarian law, the Geneva Conventions and Protocols, even the Red Cross is bound to the consent of a government to allow the provision of humanitarian assistance to the civilian population in conflict areas. Sarooshi[26] argues that an arbitrary decision by a belligerent party or government to withhold relief supplies from a population in need would constitute a method of warfare which is prohibited in the Geneva Convention on the Protection of the Civilian Population in Times of War. Since Article 3 of this 1949 Geneva Convention makes it possible to offer humanitarian assistance in non-international conflicts, the International Committee of the Red Cross (ICRC) today accepts the consent of non-governmental conflict parties to deliver relief in the areas under their control.[27]

The UN Charter prohibits any intervention "in matters which are essentially within the domestic jurisdiction of any state."[28] Although all member states had to pledge themselves to achieve respect for the principle of equal rights and self-determination of peoples,[29] the Declaration of Human Rights of 1948 contained no permission for cross-border assistance in case of humanitarian emergencies. Three years before the end of the Cold War the International Court of Justice stated in 1986, in the case of Nicaragua, "... that the provision of strictly humanitarian aid ... cannot be regarded as unlawful intervention, or as in any other way contrary to international law."[30] Consequently the United Nations General Assembly accepted in its Resolution 43/831 (1988) the right of the victims to receive international aid in emergencies, and thereby accentuated the important role of humanitarian NGOs. Resolution 43/831 was strengthened by Resolution 45/100 (1990), with the inclusion of the concept of "corridors of tranquillity" in which conflict parties should refrain from exerting sovereign rights and allow free humanitarian intervention.

These two UN General Assembly resolutions were initiated by the French NGO Médecins Sans Frontières. Bettati[31] describes the efforts of

MSF to introduce the idea of an UN resolution securing better access for humanitarian relief NGOs to the then French Prime Minister, Chirac. But only after Rocard had been nominated French Prime Minister by President Mitterrand in May 1988 was the former MSF official and new Secretary of Health Kouchner charged to present the MSF proposal to the United Nations General Assembly. For UN Resolutions 43/831 and 45/100 Bettati was appointed editing consultant by the General Assembly. He transfered the regulations on free corridors for rescue ships in foreign territorial waters in international sea law into the concept of "land-corridors of tranquillity" for humanitarian cross-border relief.

The Security Council resolution on northern Iraq, 1991

Although there were repeated public opinion appeals to overrule of the principle of national sovereignty in cases of massive human rights violations like Tibet and South Africa, it was only in 1991 that the UN Security Council decided in its Resolution 688 that Iraq should allow immediate access by international humanitarian organizations to all those in need of assistance. The UN Security Council thereby sanctioned humanitarian intervention of allied forces without the consent of the Iraqi government. There had previously been considerable media pressure on the allies during the Gulf War in 1991. They were blamed in the European press for having done much to serve the rich ruling family in Kuwait and nothing to help the poor Kurd refugees fleeing Saddam Hussein's attacks in northern Iraq. Sir David Hanney, the UK Permanent Representative to the United Nations, called it a "CNN" factor which forced the governments into action by transmitting horrifying pictures of the 1.7 million Kurds being bombed by Saddam Hussein's airforce.[32]

Humanitarian assistance seems altogether very dependent on media coverage.[33] Donor governments tend to support relief programmes financially when the mass media give dramatic coverage to humanitarian emergencies. In the very special situation in northern Iraq, Western public opinion expected shortly after the end of the Cold War that the United Nations would be able to initiate a new global area of peace and justice. The Security Council decided to endorse the safe areas with refugee camps for the Kurdish population, already established by the Desert Storm allied forces. The protest of the Iraqi government could not halt the Security Council's decision to implement humanitarian assistance for the first time in a case of a massive internal humanitarian emergency.

To many third world governments, the Security Council's Resolution 688 (1991) seemed to be very dangerous. They feared that this decision could serve as a precedent for future interventions by big military powers. China and India abstained from voting. Cuba, Yemen, and Zimbabwe voted against it. The watershed Resolution 688 had stirred up much anxiety inside the United Nations. Thus the UN military unit to protect the Kurd refugee camps was not immediately deployed under Resolution 688, but had to wait for an additional special Memorandum of Understanding negotiated with the Iraqi government by the Aga Khan as representative of the Secretary-General. Nevertheless the Security Council Resolution 688 contained for the first time the official recognition of cross-border humanitarian assistance by NGOs in cooperation with UN agencies.

The Security Council resolution on former Yugoslavia, 1992

A second approach to legitimizing humanitarian cross-border actions by UN agencies and NGOs was made by the Security Council in its Resolution 776 (1992) on Bosnia and Herzegovina. In the case of northern Iraq, there was a strong political and military commitment by the United States and their allies against Saddam Hussein. His violations of Kurdish human rights, which induced a mass flight to Iran and Turkey, had been defined by the Security Council as a threat to international peace and security. In the second case, that of Bosnia and Herzegovina, there was at first no strong political and military commitment against the human rights violations of the Serbs, either by Western Europe or by the United States. The mandate of the UN military mission, UNPROFOR, was to encompass the military protection of the delivery of humanitarian relief. But it was simply not possible to combine the neutral presence of a buffer between the lines of Serbs and Bosnians with the task of enforcing the transit of humanitarian supplies, not to mention the lack of military strength to accomplish the latter.

Consequently the UNPROFOR protection efforts were all too often stalled, with the result that long convoys of UN agencies' or NGOs' aid trucks, accompanied by UNPROFOR units, were held up by some local Serb commanders. The combination of NATO airstrikes on Serb positions and Bluehelmets on the ground ended with Dutch UNPROFOR soldiers being taken hostage during the Serb aggression against the safe area of Srebrenica. There, the UN hostages had to witness the liquidation of Muslim civilians. Asked if he felt humiliated by these events, the UN Secretary-General Boutros Boutros-Ghali answered, "Yes, we feel humiliated, yes, we feel frustrated, but if we want to achieve peace, we have to accept that."[34]

The United Nations' humiliation in Bosnia and Herzegovina results from the false assumption that UN Bluehelmets are able to fulfil a humanitarian aid enforcement mandate.[35] This implies a police function on the basis of international public law which does not exist and does not therefore apply to United Nations peace-keeping forces. The Bosnian case made it appear very doubtful that air strikes can give military protection to aid convoys of UN agencies and NGOs. The enforcement of transit of humanitarian supplies requires sufficient UN ground forces to be able to urge the belligerent parties to comply with the negotiated access agreement.

The attempt of the UN Security Council to establish an international court in February 1993, and make the Serb military leaders appear there for violation of human rights, turned out to be impracticable for political reasons. The presiding judge, Richard Goldstone, deplored publicly the fact that even the post-Dayton IFOR (Implementation Force in Croalia and Bosnia and Herzegovina) troops avoided arresting leading war criminals, such as Mladic and Karacic. The actual situation in Bosnia and Herzegovina partly resembled the earlier UNTAC experiences in Cambodia. "Fear of escalation and lack of means to respond lead the United Nations force commander to avoid armed confrontation. This eventually favoured the interests of the factions whose acts of violence went unchecked. It directly caused the failure of phase two of the operation, the disarmament and demobilization phase, and resulted in an armed election during which the United Nations was not in control of the security conditions."[36]

The problem is not only the dilemma of creating a neutral humanitarian space or carrying out the just punishment of human rights' violators. It is rather the lack of a secured development space in which the non-violent civil movements could construct a democratic political system stabilized by a participating, unintimidated internal citizenship supported by the presence of external UN and NGO partners.

The Security Council resolution on Somalia, 1992

In his Agenda for Peace, UN Secretary-General Boutros Boutros-Ghali stressed the necessity of military enforcement of humanitarian aid delivery, should it be prevented by belligerent parties.[37] But the third case in which the Security Council decided on a humanitarian intervention – the Somalia operation – demonstrated a major deficiency of this policy. The organizational structure of the United Nations was not prepared to handle this type of humanitarian intervention in a dissolving society and a failed state, like Somalia at that time.

The UN Secretary-General did not succeed in installing an appropriate leadership for the Somalia operation. At the outbreak of the humanitarian emergency in Somalia in the summer of 1992, the local UNDP representative in Nairobi was charged with the responsibility for the relief operations, according to usual UN organizational provisions. In September 1992 he was replaced by a senior official of UNICEF, who was appointed relief coordinator for Somalia. A few weeks later, the Secretary-General nominated a Horn of Africa expert, the Algerian Ambassador Sahnoun, as his special representative to take on the overall leadership of the relief operations. In October 1992 the Secretary-General appointed the former executive head of CARE, USA, Philip Johnson, as operational manager to organize the UN-NGO humanitarian action in Somalia. After Ambassador Sahnoun went into the troublesome and time-consuming business of negotiating humanitarian access with the Somalian warlords, the Secretary-General appointed in November 1992 a new special representative, the Iraqi Ambassador Kittani.

In the Somalia operation the United Nations had not only to cope with personnel problems but also with information deficiencies. At the time Kittani was appointed the food emergency in Somalia was already reducing. Especially in the southern city of Baidoa, where according to MSF in August 1992 hundreds of inhabitants had been starving because they had no food and no water, the situation of aid delivery had definitively improved in November 1992. In the capital city of Mogadishu the situation with regard to humanitarian assistance had always been somewhat better. Nevertheless, immediately upon his arrival in Somalia Kittani sent a dramatic description of the situation in Mogadishu to the Secretary-General, summarized by Jonah: ". . . utter chaos in the city and the increasing reluctance of warlords to permit United Nations relief operations. At the same time roaming armed gangs had stepped up their banditry. It was increasingly evident that only a small portion – 20–30 per cent – of relief supplies was reaching the most vulnerable groups. The entire population was threatened with starvation."[38] The Secretary-General informed the Security Council of Kittani's assessment, which eventually led to Security Council Resolution 794 in December 1992 to enforce militarily the delivery of humanitarian relief by the United Nations Task Force (UNITAF) under the provision of Chapter VII of the UN Charter.

The security conditions in Somalia in summer 1992 had led the humanitarian organizations to engage private armed security guards. According to credible information about humanitarian NGOs active in Somalia, the appearance of UNITAF in Somalia improved the access of humanitarian aid to victims considerably. But security conditions worsened when the American commander of UNITAF was drawn into clan infighting with the aim of arresting General Aidit. A senior official of a German humanitarian NGO in Somalia had previously advised his staff to gather under the UN flag in case of fighting. After the expansion of the UNITAF mandate, he advised his staff to flee the UN flag in case of fighting. There is no doubt that all UN agencies in Somalia were compromised in their relief operations by UNITAF actions, and that some operational coordination instruments between UN agencies and NGOs were damaged.

These three decisions of the Security Council (northern Iraq, former Yugoslavia, and Somalia) in support of enforcement of humanitarian relief delivery do not yet constitute a new international humanitarian law, but they demonstrate a clear shift from the toleration of human rights violations under the cover of national sovereignty to the recognition of the right of victims to receive cross-border relief from UN agencies and the NGO community. Sir David Hannay, the United Kingdom Permanent Representative to the United Nations, argued that the Security Council, in discussing future peace-keeping operations to enforce humanitarian intervention, had to learn not to say "no," but to say "not yet," and in the meantime must define clear-cut criteria for humanitarian intervention.[39] For hundreds of thousands of Tutsis in Rwanda this argument was a death sentence, because the Security Council, in the light of the Somalian experience, was not willing to decide on an operation to Rwanda in spring 1994. The Security Council was well informed by the reports of Belgian UN observers about what was happening in Rwanda after the death of the Presidents of Rwanda and Burundi, Juvenal Habyarimana and Cyprien Ntaryamira, but in April 1994 a Security Council decision endorsing preventive humanitarian intervention to protect the Tutsi population from the genocide publicly prepared and carried out by the Hutu militia was not yet possible.

The problems of United Nations and NGO interaction and cooperation in humanitarian interventions

Humanitarian assistance in complex emergencies constantly requires a lot of professional problem-solving capacity. The description of the daily overload of NGO and UN agencies' operational staff dominated all interviews conducted in this research. There are also some general NGO characteristics which sometimes make cooperation between UN agencies and NGOs particularly difficult; these will be dealt with in this chapter after sketching the process of organizational recognition of humanitarian NGOs by the UN system. The special NGO characteristics result mostly from their social movement background. Many of them seem to cultivate a fundamental criticism of all bureacratic structures, with a tendency to ignore the process of conflict resolution in political systems, focusing only on suffering refugees and emergency reaction. In addition, most NGOs maintain a strong feeling of independence – they generally refuse leadership, and to some extent even avoid cooperation and information sharing. The widely perceived high moral self-image of NGOs values humanitarian aid above all interests of conflict parties, and overrates the rare chances to remain neutral in humanitarian emergencies.

The problem of organizational recognition of NGOs by the United Nations

After the end of the Cold War in 1989–1990 the UN-NGO organizational interaction became greatly intensified. The ICRC (International Committee of the Red Cross) was granted observer status by the General Assembly of the United Nations in 1990, and the serving president of the Security Council holds discrete monthly meetings with ICRC representatives.[40] Thus formal and informal contacts permitted the exchange of views on problems of international security and peace, as well as on humanitarian emergencies in different countries.

In confirming the trend that NGOs are getting closer and closer to the internal UN headquarters decision-making process, Donini[41] cites the example of the Interagency Standing Committee (IASC), which is chaired by the Undersecretary-General for Humanitarian Affairs. The main coalitions of humanitarian NGOs participate in IASC meetings, including InterAction, the International Council of Volunteer Agencies (ICVA), the ICRC, and the International Federation of Red Cross and Red Crescent Societies (IFRC).

The Department for Humanitarian Affairs (DHA) holds regular meetings in New York and Geneva to foster UN contacts with the main operational NGOs in humanitarian relief: the International Rescue Committee, CARE, World Vision, Save the Children Federation, MSF, Oxfam, and so on. "Given the importance of humanitarian NGOs in the mobilization of the international response to complex emergencies, having them on board when priorities and problems are thrashed out is no small advantage for all concerned. It also helps to introduce better transparency and accountability and to ease misunderstandings with other parts of the international response, such as the military."[42]

Several committees and subsidiary bodies of the General Assembly have since allowed humanitarian NGOs to take the floor and circulate documents. Sometimes they have even been invited to participate in preparatory formulations of General Assembly resolutions on humanitarian assistance. "UN Secretariats and NGOs are often confronted with a common problem, namely persuading governments to adopt a particular course of action, whether it be allowing food convoys to reach refugees, or ratifying the convention on the elimination of all forms of discrimination against women. NGO coalitions are powerful allies of the United Nations in such matters, and vice versa. NGO coalitions are perhaps increasingly essential partners in the advocacy roles that are needed to ensure that governments make decisions in the global public

interest and carry out the obligations that result from international conferences and conventions."[43]

But some member governments and United Nations officials are not at
all delighted by the close UN-NGO interactions. "The NGO world is
nothing if not independent-minded, which is a virtue because how else
could even the most recondite human cause find a group to defend or
attack it. The growth in the numbers of non-governmental organizations
appearing on the international scene, especially because so many have
solely national or local bases, has somewhat overwhelmed ... the United
Nations mechanism ..."[44] A working group of the UN Economics and
Social Council (ECOSOC) has recently decided to limit the regulations of
access for NGOs. In the very sensitive Commission on Human Rights, the
irritation of governments being accused publicly of violations of human
rights has led to defensive reactions: "... les communications et plaintes
des ONGs ne sont pas bienvenues dans les réunions intergouverne-
mentales et une tendance négative voire régressive s'observe dans un
nombre croissant d'Etats membres des Nations Unies à propos des ONGs
... certains d'Etats sont passés de la critique à la ménace. Le document
de travail fourni par le mouvement des Non-Alignés au groupe de travail
sur l'amélioration de la Commission [des Droits de l'Homme R. K.] con-
tenait tout un chapitre très restrictif sur les ONGs."[45]

According to Donini,[46] the General Assembly has recently refused
observer status to InterAction. There have been remarks made to the
effect that an increasing presence of NGOs could change the nature of
the organization. Other UN scholars[47] found that it would hardly be
manageable for United Nations organs and subsidiary bodies to listen to
representatives of hundreds of NGOs or to read every NGO's position
paper in addition to the numerous official documents. Considering the
multitude of humanitarian NGOs, so greatly differing in size, aims, and
strategies, the problem of organizational recognition of them has developed into a very difficult task for the UN to fulfil.

The problem of emergency reaction versus emergency prevention

The criteria for humanitarian UN-NGO interventions seem to be quite
clear. There is no preventive humanitarian intervention. The UN-NGO
humanitarian cooperation is restricted to manifest emergencies, not to
pre-crisis situations. Humanitarian missions are only reactive; to a much
lesser degree they are curative in some post-conflict situations,[48] but they
are not at all preventive. Humanitarian space is at the moment limited to
well-organized refugee camps, where all sorts of humanitarian organizations can show their professionalism in dealing with misery. There is a
lack of a UN-NGO strategy to secure humanitarian space before people

turn into refugees. If internal conflict resolution on the basis of the respect of human rights cannot be achieved by the respective government, or if a government no longer exists to accomplish this, conflicting groups need arbitrating partners to be offered by humanitarian NGOs and UN agencies.

It is still very doubtful whether the United Nations and the NGO community actually have the authority, the strength, and the will to pursue an alternative strategy of non-military preventive humanitarian intervention. Preventive humanitarian missions trying to avoid potential humanitarian emergencies will have more difficulties in gaining public and governmental subsidies. Peoples and donor governments are more apt to contribute aid donations to victims of televised atrocities. To overcome the problem of financing such an alternative strategy, one could refer to the experience of countries which oblige their citizens to take out fire insurance for their houses or to contribute to a social security system. One proposal would be to motivate citizens and professionals of all countries to sign up for some sort of social action year and long-term sponsorship relations with colleagues in marginalized areas.[49]

At present, it seems to be much easier for UN agencies and NGOs to restrict humanitarian assistance to well-known reactive emergency missions. National emergency and traffic laws give right of way to all sorts of ambulances and rescue services. The basic idea – that saving human lives has priority over compliance with bureaucratic rules and regulations – corresponds to the general philosophy of most humanitarian NGOs. The international application of this basic concept was the idea of French doctors (MSF) and the many subsequent organizations which adopted the suffix "without borders." They claimed free cross-border access to emergency victims, ranking human rights higher than state sovereignty – a position which cannot so easily be adopted by UN agencies. "Operations such as Provide Comfort and Restore Hope and many cross-border operations mounted by non-governmental organizations and even a few governments in places like Eritrea and Tigray indicate that humanitarian action precedes codification in international law. Human life takes precedence over artificial legal constructs that are used to justify using food and medicine as weapons by belligerents, whether they are recognized governments or insurgents in armed opposition."[50] The "without borders" approach may prove to be even more useful if it were extended to non-military preventive humanitarian action and applied jointly by UN agencies and the NGO community.

The problem of establishing access to the victims has to be solved in any humanitarian intervention. This becomes even more difficult in internal conflicts. The "without borders" approach justifies the intervention on life-saving emergency grounds. Nevertheless, NGOs and UN agencies have to negotiate access with some political or military authority which may not agree to this moral argument. With the concepts of "corridors of tranquillity" or "safe zones," NGOs and UN agencies tried to gain at least a limited freedom of movement for humanitarian assistance. The experiences in northern Iraq, Bosnia and Herzegovina, and Somalia showed that safety zones or corridors are not easy to secure militarily, but the idea does not necessarily apply uniquely to the reactive emergency strategy. It may be more suitable to establish free access for humanitarian organizations in a preventive mission. It can help to create secured humanitarian spaces inside a country without totally questionning its national jurisdiction. Even if this sounds very hypothetical, such an alternative strategy of preventive humanitarian crisis intervention may be accepted one day by governments accused of human rights violations in order to restore political stability. It could be negotiated with countries like China, perhaps in the same way as this country accepts "capitalistic" industrial development zones at the moment.

The problems of information sharing and of an early-warning system

Acting in humanitarian emergencies means working under great pressure. Their prevailing function as humanitarian fire brigades gives the UN agencies and NGOs little time for preliminary investigations in any given case. All large organizations have assessment teams ready to start at a moment's notice, which at best are trained to evaluate the basic needs of the victims, the amount of relief goods necessary, the logistic problems in the air and on the ground, and the security conditions for operational personnel. They have no time and mostly feel no obligation to go into the details of how the conflict originated and evolved, the political or economic structures in the crisis area, self-help capabilities, cultural and religious particularities, and ethnic or regional disparities. The special NGO characteristics of a strong feeling of independence and the tendency to focus only on suffering refugees leads them to screen out all these political implications of humanitarian emergencies. The service NGOs find themselves in the dilemma of being rated according to their ability to minimize overhead expenses and at the same time being accused of insufficient preparatory and accompanying analysis. But the field personnel are totally preoccupied with the daily overload of operational action, and have neither the time nor the necessary perspective for reflections on underlying causes of conflicts or on the long-term consequences of their efforts.

UN agencies and NGOs have contracted specialists and acquired high-level technical standards in recent years, and have thereby professional-ized their humanitarian services to a great extent. Nevertheless, in cases like the Rwandan events in 1994, they were overwhelmed by the sheer numbers of refugees pouring into Goma within a few days. And equally the coordinator in charge, the UNHCR representative, was overwhelmed by the sheer number of NGOs rushing into Goma shortly thereafter. What counts to them is to be there as professionally and as quickly as possible. The media cover only the first, the biggest, and the most professional-looking actors on the scene.

"The rash of recent emergencies has created the impression that NGOs are in the business of ambulance chasing as they appear on the scene in large numbers to provide assistance."[51] But it is not so much a direct competition between humanitarian organizations – as we can observe between ambulance services on our roads – as the "high premium on early and visible involvement in relief operations," as Natsios[52] charac-terizes it. "To attract private contributions to Rwanda programmes the NGOs must make use of news events and media coverage, which raise public awareness in a way that no paid advertisement could ever achieve. The more dramatic the event, the greater the media coverage and the greater the ease of fund-raising around it."[53]

Those UN agencies and NGOs which had worked before in the same area on development projects, and which cooperated with indigenous counterparts, have normally accumulated a lot of background informa-tion. To promote the scientific review and exchange of that information, the Oslo Conference of the UNHCR and NGOs in June 1994 requested the establishment of an emergency early-warning system: "It was consid-ered that coordinated emergency preparedness and response are directly dependent on the capacity of the UNHCR, NGOs, and other concerned actors to assess and take full advantage of early-warning information... However, it was noted that the impact of early-warning systems is often limited by availability of training and contingency plans as well as by the absence of inter-agency information-sharing structures... UNHCR should take further steps to develop effective inter-agency early-warning information-sharing systems... It should allow for an assessment of political, economic, and social conditions and risks in the affected coun-tries."[54]

This kind of information sharing could well be used to develop pre-ventive humanitarian interventions by UN agencies and NGOs. Human-itarian politics need not be reduced to emergency preparedness, and humanitarian NGOs need not have to depend on sensational journalism to increase their funding prospects. There is no doubt about the effectiveness of "relief pornography,"[55] but this type of sensational journalism does not contribute to public information about the conflicts and impedes the necessary structural transformation from acting as humanitarian fire brigade to non-military preventive humanitarian intervention.

The leadership problem

To many humanitarian NGOs the concept of leadership seems to be taboo, perhaps as a result of their social movement background. According to their cultivated self-image, every member should be able to participate with equal rights, actively and individually – in contrast to the hierarchically structured political parties and associations. They cling to the passed-on virtue that everybody should feel responsible for achieving a common goal. Although there is sometimes a strong founding personality, the historical merits of whom are respected, the organizations foster an image of self-guidance and independence which remains essential to them. Even if they have grown into large-scale organizations today and cannot avoid becoming bureaucratic and hierarchical, this ingrained feeling remains a strong orientation. So we find amongst the humanitarian NGOs many which are very reluctant to submit themselves to coordinating structures, and refuse to accept leadership by any other organization during relief operations. For some reason or other, this applies also to UN agencies, which show strong reservations towards coordination from the Department of Humanitarian Affairs (DHA) or any other UN Secretariat unit.

Considering the great number of UN agencies and NGOs coming into an emergency area, coordination seems to be necessary to avoid waste of relief goods, competition, and duplication. But coordination also consumes time and money, and large intergovernmental donors such as the European Community Humanitarian Office limit the proportion of funds to be spent in this field to 1 per cent of the total contribution. Some NGOs even admit to diverting money from development projects to subsidize overhead expenses of emergency projects. The reluctance to coordinate is exemplified by the typical argument of a UNICEF official: "UNICEF's priority is saving lives, not coordination," or by the experience of James Ingram, the former executive director of the World Food Programme (WFP): "Our experience at WFP was that centralized coordination imposes a heavy additional workload at WFP country and headquarters offices. A great deal of time of key operational officials, who are a very scarce resource, is spent in attending coordination meetings. The appearance of improved coordination at the centre does not necessarily lead to more effective and timely interventions in the field."[56]

Nevertheless, the professionalism and experience of some UN agencies were honoured in the acceptance of their function as lead agency in the field. When refugees have to be cared for, this role is mostly taken over by the UNHCR. In the case of the former Yugoslavia, with mostly internally displaced persons, it was ECHO which handled the accreditation of NGOs and coordinated the selection of operational sites. What becomes evident in the discussion of the no-leadership approach is the strong position of experienced practitioners with a "rough-and-ready, roll-up-the-sleeves" attitude,[57] which might indicate a discriminatory attitude towards any attempts at theoretical analysis of causes of conflicts or of long-term effects of relief delivery. The no-leadership approach somehow clings to emergency activism which is perceived to be spontaneous, totally independent, and impartial.

The practical coordination problems in extremely difficult situations like Goma proved to be not as major as was expected in the initial phase, mainly because the professionalism of the operating NGOs was generally recognized by the UNHCR as lead agency. This did not apply to theoretical reflections on and evaluations of the actions, which required time and perspective.[58] Not only analyzing humanitarian assistance but also the process of implementing results of such reflections and evaluations may need more guidance by the lead agency towards participating UN agencies and NGOs.

The security problem

United Nations and NGO humanitarian assistance in ongoing military conflicts has to rely on access negotiations with some local military authorities in order to secure basic security for the operational staff. The participants in the NGO-UNHCR Conference in Oslo (1994) accepted "the potential usefulness of the designation and establishment of safe zones and humanitarian corridors," but at the same time seemed to be worried "about the capacity of these measures to provide the minimum level of security."[59] Humanitarian relief is not always provided in neutral zones or in areas free of military power. More and more, UN agencies and NGOs have had to accept working in ongoing internal wars, where it may remain difficult to discern civilians and combatants.

This leads not only to substantial security risks to the personnel, but also endangers the delivery of relief goods to the point where they do not reach the affected population at all. "The international aid provided by the United Nations and voluntary agencies has become a major (and in some areas the only) source of income and as such the target of all the 'authorities,' who may sometimes be no more than two or three bandits with guns."[60] This situation raises several questions. When to pull out? What would this do to the local NGO partners and to the victims left behind? The main problem of the emergency approach remains that of security, which cannot be resolved completely by hiring private armed guards, nor by UN military enforcement of humanitarian relief even if there are sufficient ground forces.

The UN High Commissioner for Refugees, Sadako Ogata, admitted to a controversial debate on the military protection of humanitarian assistance inside the UNHCR. "The resort to military cover for humanitarian activities has caused some soul-searching in the UNHCR. There are understandable and obvious differences between the humanitarian aims of UNHCR and the political objectives of the Security Council. Directly linking the two could at least potentially jeopardize our neutrality and impartiality and affect our ability to work in security and confidence on all sides of the front line. But the security conditions on the ground left us with little choice, and we have had to receive military protections for our convoys in many parts of Bosnia and Herzegovina. Indeed, even the International Committee of the Red Cross has requested – and received – the protection of UN peace-keeping forces for its convoys of released prisoners."[61]

The neutrality problem

Neutrality was historically the only way to gain access to all victims of international wars, and thus constituted the basic rule in the Geneva Conventions for Red Cross humanitarian assistance. The signatory governments partially renounced their sovereignty, allowing the Red Cross to provide humanitarian relief on all sides under very restrictive rules and regulations. Because of their humanitarian aims, many NGOs tend to claim the same approach and thereby hope to acquire a status under international law similar to that of the Red Cross movement. But sometimes they overlook the fact that neutrality does not provide for the distinction between aggressors and victims of aggression. Besides, even so-called neutral relief can have a great impact on belligerent parties. It may give legitimacy to local military authorities. To use the roads or airstrips they control can contribute to recognition as a "beligerent" party to the conflict. The distribution of food and medicine can give them resources to recruit military personnel. According to Smith,[62] these effects could be reduced by what she calls "informed intervention": "What can be achieved is an informed intervention that, if carefully designed and undertaken, can result in fairness and balance. The shift in thinking and in the identification of goals – from neutrality to balance – is crucial to the success of future humanitarian work in armed conflicts."[63] But even the strategy of balancing relief programmes among all sides is not always perceived as impartial by all belligerent parties.

The operational staff of UN agencies and NGOs have severe psychological problems remaining neutral or balanced in the face of massive human rights violations. This requires a great deal of internal repression. Being constantly confronted with atrocities against civilians, they cannot switch off their individual ethics permanently. It is not a solution for them to perceive themselves as neutral and unpolitical, and to concentrate on the treatment of fighting casualties and starvation. The neutral approach allows conflict parties to instrumentalize humanitarian UN agencies and NGOs. Causing casualties and refugees subjects humanitarian organizations to extortive demands by belligerents to keep the flow of money and supplies pouring in.

The decision to pull out of Goma because it more and more turned into a supply station for the Hutu militia, with the refugees serving as hostages, became very hard for NGOs. The discussion on that reflects some of the problems of neutrality. "If we leave, however we justify it to ourselves in terms of not collaborating with criminals, what it means on the ground is that we are abandoning the innocent civilian population to its fate. They are in no position to do anything to change their leaders, if they wanted to. It seems to me that what is truly unacceptable is for us – I mean all of us, both within the UN system and NGOs – to abandon them. I believe that morally there is nothing for us to do except stay."[64] In Goma MSF and other NGOs nevertheless decided to pull out after the refugee camp fell under the complete control of the Hutu militia, which had directed the Tutsi genocide in 1994. The closure of the Goma camp in the course of military conflict between the East Zairian rebels and the Zairian government in late 1996 produced a new wave of Hutus fleeing further into Zaire, and at the same time freed a large number of Rwandan refugees. UN and NGO neutrality in the Goma case meant collaboration with war criminals and prolongation of the misery of refugees taken as hostages by the Hutu militia in the camp. To break with humanitarian neutrality enabled hundreds of thousands of them to return home to Rwanda.

The Red Cross movement deserves the greatest respect for the neutral relief it offers to all sides on the basis of the Geneva Conventions and Protocols, but it would be a big mistake for UN agencies and NGOs to confine their assistance to that based on neutrality. Public awareness of causes of conflicts allows partisanship in conflict prevention. To organize biased UN and NGO humanitarian intervention on the side of those discriminated against may be a solution. A better public understanding of conflict causes could eventually lead governments and intergovernmental organizations to act politically and address underlying conflict causes, instead of waiting for them to become humanitarian emergencies. "Pour beaucoup des gouvernements et pour une bonne partie de la communauté internationale, l'action humanitaire est devenu un substitut à l'action politique. Comme on ne sait pas quoi faire sur le plan politique ou que l'on ne veut pas agire, on se réfugie dans la domaine de l'humanitaire, ce qui, à notre avis, est d'une extrême gravité et pour les humanitaires et pour les politiques."[65]

Conclusion

The relations between UN agencies and NGOs in the field of humanitarian assistance have undergone substantial changes after the end of the Cold War.

First, the UN agencies and NGOs have gained considerable freedom of joint action, with UN humanitarian assistance becoming at least temporarily unchained from ideological suspicions. In some of its resolutions since 1990, the Security Council carefully removed the UN Charter's restrictions on humanitarian assistance in internal conflicts.

Second, the growing marginalizing effects of globalization have contributed to a considerable increase in complex humanitarian emergencies. At the same time, cutbacks in strategically oriented development aid have enabled donor governments to shift funding of UN agencies and NGOs from development aid to humanitarian assistance. Both these factors led to a fast-expanding humanitarian market to which big internationally acting service NGOs responded with networking and the emergence of oligopolistic structures. On the one hand they have thus become respected partners of UN agencies, but on the other hand they have excluded smaller self-help-oriented local service NGOs from this market.

Third, focused on large-scale supply structures for masses of refugees or internaly displaced persons, the humanitarian community tends to overlook the self-help capacities of victims in humanitarian emergencies, and to acquire some kind of humanitarian professional "property right" over them.

Fourth, the UN and NGO humanitarian cross-border interventions have been restricted to an emergency reaction approach, which necessarily obscures the causes of conflicts and gives little time for preliminary investigations of political or economic structures in the crisis area, cultural and religious particularities, and ethnic or regional disparities. In addition there is a lack of an effective inter-agency early-warning information-sharing system.

Fifth, the UN agencies and the NGOs overrate the chances for relief operations to remain neutral in complex humanitarian emergencies. Their operational staff therefore run into severe security problems. The recent experiences, with the problems of where and when to go in and where and when to pull out, clearly demonstrate the limits of the neutrality concept in humanitarian intervention.

Sixth, the main deficiency in UN and NGO cross-border humanitarian assistance is the lack of a preventive humanitarian intervention strategy. To prevent humanitarian emergencies, the evolving global civil society has to convince national governments,[66] if necessary, to accept external UN and NGO support of peaceful arbitration of conflicts.

Notes

1. Compare the voting behaviour of China, India, Cuba, Yemen, and Zimbabwe on the Security Council Resolution 688 of 1991.
2. Bennett, J./Kayetisi-Blewitt, M. "Beyond 'Working in Conflict': Understanding Conflict and Building Peace," in *Network Paper 18*, Relief and Rehabilitation Network of the Overseas Development Institute, London, November 1996, p. 6.
3. Natsios, A. S. "NGOs and the UN System in Complex Humanitarian Emergencies: Conflict or Cooperation?," *Third World Quarterly*, vol. 16, 3, 1995, p. 405.
4. cf. Summerfield, D. "The Impact of War and Atrocity on Civilian Populations: Basic Principles for NGO Interventions and a Critique of Psychosocial Trauma Projects," in *Network Paper 14*, Relief and Rehabilitation Network of the Overseas Development Institute, London, April 1996, p. 23.
5. cf. Fondation Pour Le Progrès De L'Homme, *Expériences et réflexions sur la reconstruction nationale et la paix*, Kigali, 1994.
6. IFRC. *World Disasters Report 1996*, International Federation of Red Cross and Red Crescent Societies, Oxford, 1996, pp. 131 and 135.
7. Cuny, F. C. "Assistance in the Post-Cold War Era," in Weiss, Thomas G./Minear, L. (eds.), *Humanitarianism Across Borders*, Boulder, 1993, p. 168.
8. Shelton, D. "The Participation of Non-governmental Organizations in International Judicial Proceedings," *American Journal of International Law*, vol. 88, 3/4, 1994, p. 622.
9. Borton, J. et al. *NGOs and Relief Operations: Trends and Policy Implications*, ESCOR Research Study R47774, London, June 1994, p. 71.
10. cf. Donini, A. "The bureaucracy and the free spirits: stagnation and innovation in the relationship between the UN and NGOs," *Third World Quarterly*, vol. 16, 3, 1995, p. 434, and Fuchs, P. "Emergency coordination: a problem of humanitarian agencies or rather of politicians and generals?," *Transnational Associations*, 2/1996, p. 83.
11. cf. Donini, A., op. cit., p. 434f.
12. Lafourcade, J.-C. Lecture about Operation "Turquoise" in Rwanda, 1994, during a workshop held at the University of Aix-Marseille in March 1995.
13. Boutros-Ghali, B. Interview in *The New York Times*, 3 January 1995, p. 3; quoted in Gordenker, C./Weiss, Th. G., "Pluralizing Global Governance: Analytical Approaches and Dimensions," *Third World Quarterly*, vol. 16, 3, 1995. p. 264.
14. cf. Duffield, M. *Complex Political Emergencies – An Exploratory Report for Unicef*, unpublished manuscript, March 1994, p. 107ff.
15. Groupe De Lisbonne. *Limites à la Compétitivité, Pour un nouveau contrat mondial*, La Découverte, Paris, 1995, p. 18ff.
16. Gordenker, C./Weiss, Th. G., op. cit., p. 365.

17. Donini, A., op. cit., p. 430.
18. cf. Rieff; D. "The Humanitarian Trap," *World Policy Journal*, vol. XII, 4, Winter 1995–1996, p. 6.
19. Shelton, D., op. cit., p. 622.
20. Borton, J. et al., op. cit., p. 71.
21. Donini, A., op. cit., p. 424.
22. Donini, A., op. cit., footnote 21, p. 429.
23. Ibid., footnote 22, p. 429.
24. Rieff, D., op. cit., p. 3.
25. cf. Koch, R. *Entwicklungsschutz statt Entwicklungshilfe,* Saarbrücken, 1993, p. 26ff.
26. Sarooshi, D. "Humanitarian intervention and international humanitarian assistance: law and practice," *Transnational Associations*, 2/1996, p. 86f.
27. Sarooshi, D., op. cit., p. 98.
28. United Nations Charter: Article 2.7.
29. Ibid., Article 55/56.
30. International Court of Justice: Reports 1986, No. 14, p. 114.
31. Bettati, M. "Le droit d'assistance humanitaire," in *Conflits, Développements et Interventions Militaires: Role, Position et Expérience des ONG*; Brussels, 1994, p. 36.
32. Hannay, D. Lecture at the German Society of the United Nations, Bonn, 11 April 1994, unpublished manuscript, p. 9.
33. cf. Rieff; D., op. cit., p. 7.
34. Boutros-Ghali, B. Interview in *Die Zeit*, 29 September 1995, p. 9.
35. Stedman, S. J. "Alchemy for a New World Order, Overselling 'Preventive Diplomacy,'" *Foreign Affairs*, May/June 1995, p. 17.
36. Chopra, J. *United Nations Authority in Cambodia*. Occasional paper of the Watson Institute for International Studies, No. 15, Providence, Rhode Island, 1994, p. 17ff.
37. Boutros-Ghali, B. "An Agenda for Peace," United Nations, New York, 1992, p. 68.
38. Jonah, J. O. "Humanitarian Intervention," in Weiss, Th. G./Minear, L. (eds.), op. cit., p. 76.
39. Hannay, D., op. cit., p. 6.
40. Donini, A., op. cit., p. 424.
41. Ibid., p. 424.
42. Ibid., p. 425.
43. Ritchey, C. "Coordinate? Cooperate? Harmonize? NGO policy and operational coalitions," *Third World Quarterly*, vol. 16, 3, 1995, p. 517.
44. Ibid., p. 519.
45. Zoller, A. C. "Tendences actuelles au seins des Nations Unies concernant les droits des organisations non-gouvernementales," in Fondation Pour Le Progrès De L'Homme, *Expériences et réflexions sur la reconstruction nationale et la paix*, Kigali, 1994, p. 111. "... Communications and complaints from NGOs are not welcomed at inter-governmental meetings. Furthermore, a negative, regressive tendency is now seen in an increasing number of United Nations member states concerning NGOs... Certain states have gone from criticism to menace. The working document provided by the Non-Aligned Movement to the working group on improvement of the Commission [of Human Rights R.K.] contained a full chapter on NGOs which was very restrictive."
46. Donini, A., op. cit., footnote 10, p. 438.
47. cf. Childers, E. B./Urquhart, B. "Renewing the United Nations System," *Development Dialogue*, 1994, 1, p. 175.
48. cf. Fuchs, P. "Emergency coordination: a problem of humanitarian agencies or rather of politicians and generals?," *Transnational Associations*, 2/1996, p. 82.
49. cf. Truger, A. "Das International Civilian Peace-keeping and Peace-building Program (IPT)," *Österreichische Zeitschrift für Politik ÖZP*, 24, 1995, 4, p. 465ff.

50. Weiss, Th. G./Minear, L. (eds.), op. cit., p. 60.
51. Natsios, A. S., op. cit., p. 409.
52. Ibid.
53. Ibid.
54. Oslo Declaration and Plan of Action: Partnership in Action (PARinAc) UNHCR-NGO Conference on Emergency Preparedness and Response, Oslo, 1994, p. 24.
55. Natsios, A. S., op. cit., p. 409.
56. Ingram, J. "The Future of Assistance," in Weiss, Th.G./Minear, L. (eds.), op. cit., p. 181.
57. Gordenker, L./Weiss, Th. G. "Pluralizing Global Governance," *Third World Quarterly*, vol. 16, 3/1995, p. 369.
58. cf. Bennett, J./Kayetisi-Blewitt, M., op. cit., pp. 23–32.
59. Oslo Declaration and Plan of Action, op. cit., p. 21.
60. Boutros-Ghali, B. Letter to the President of the Security Council, 24 November 1992, in United Nations, *The United Nations and Somalia*, Blue Books Series, vol. VIII, 1996, p. 208.
61. Ogata, S. *Refugees and World Peace*, lecture at United Nations University, Tokyo, on 7 January 1993, unpublished manuscript of UNHCR, p. 6.
62. Smith, G. E. "Relief Operations and Military Strategy," in Weiss, Th. G./Minear, L. (eds.), op. cit., p. 98.
63. Ibid.
64. Jessen-Petersen, S. UNHCR official quoted in Rieff, D., op. cit., p. 9.
65. Fresnard, J. "L'action non-gouvernemental," in *Conflits, Développements et Interventions Militaires: Role, Position et Experience des ONG*, Brussels, 1994, p. 55. "For many governments and for a good many in the international community, humanitarian action has become a substitute for political action. Either because it is difficult for them to know what to do at the political level, or because they do not want to act, they simply take refuge in the humanitarian area. This is in our opinion extremely grave for both the humanitarians as well as the politicians."
66. cf. Chesneaux, J. "Les ONG, ferment d'une société civile mondiale?," *Transversales Science Culture*, No. 24, 1995, p. 18.

BIBLIOGRAPHY

Bennett, J./Kayetisi-Blewitt, M. "Beyond 'Working in Conflict': Understanding Conflict and Building Peace," in *Network Paper 18*, Relief and Rehabilitation Network of the Overseas Development Institute, London, November 1996.

Bettati, M. "Le droit d'assistance humanitaire," in *Conflits, Développements et Interventions Militaires: Role, Position et Expérience des ONG*, Brussels, 1994.

Borton, J. et al. *NGOs and Relief Operations: Trends and Policy Implications*, ESCOR Research Study R47774; London, June 1994.

Boutros-Ghali, B. "An Agenda for Peace," United Nations, New York, 1992.

Boutros-Ghali, B. Interview in *Die Zeit*, 29 September 1995.

Boutros-Ghali, B. Interview in *New York Times*, 3 January 1995.

Boutros-Ghali, B. Letter to the President of the Security Council on 24 November 1992, in United Nations: *The United Nations and Somalia*, Blue Books Series, vol. VIII, 1996.

Chesneaux, J. "Les ONG, ferment d'une société civile mondiale?," *Transversales Science Culture*, No. 24, 1995.

Childers, E. B./Urquhart, B. "Renewing the United Nations System," *Development Dialogue*, 1994, 1.

Chopra, J./Weiss, Th. G. "Sovereignty is No Longer Sacrosant: Codifying Humanitarian Intervention," *Ethics & International Affairs*, vol. 6, 1992.

Chopra, J. *United Nations Authority in Cambodia*. Occasional paper of the Watson Institute for International Studies, No.15, Providence, Rhode Island, 1994.

Civicus. *Citizens Strengthening Global Civil Society*, Washington, 1994.

Clark, J. "The State, Popular Participation, and the Voluntary Sector," *World Development*, vol. 23, 4, 1995.

Cuny, F. C. "Assistance in the Post-Cold War Era," in Weiss, Th. G./Minear, L. (eds.), *Humanitarianism Across Borders*, Boulder, 1993.

Donini, A. "The bureaucracy and the free spirits: stagnation and innovation in the relationship between the UN and NGOs," *Third World Quarterly*, vol. 16, 3, 1995.

Duffield, M. *Complex Political Emergencies – An Exploratory Report for UNICEF*, unpublished manuscript, March, 1994.

Edwards, M./Hulme, D. *Beyond the Magic Bullet, NGO Performance and Accountability in the Post-Cold War World*, West Hartford, Connecticut, 1996.

Fondation Pour Le Progrès De L'Homme. *Expériences et réflexions sur la reconstruction nationale et la paix*, Kigali, 1994.

Fresnard, J. "L'action non-gouvernemental," in *Conflits, Développements et Interventions Militaires: Role, Position et Experience des ONG*, Brussels, 1994.

Fuchs, P. "Emergency coordination: a problem of humanitarian agencies or rather of politicians and generals?," *Transnational Associations*, 2/1996.

Gershmann, C. "The United Nations and the New World Order," *Journal of Democracy*, July 1993.

Gordenker, C./Weiss, Th. G. "NGO Participation in the International Policy Process," *Third World Quarterly*, vol. 16, 3, 1995.

Gordenker, C./Weiss, Th. G. "Pluralizing Global Governance: Analytical Approaches and Dimensions," *Third World Quarterly*, vol. 16, 3, 1995.

Groupe De Lisbonne. *Limites à la Compétitivité, Pour un Nouveau Contrat Mondial*, La Découverte, Paris, 1995.

Hannay, D. Speech at the German Society of the United Nations, Bonn, on 11 April 1994, unpublished manuscript.

IFRC. *World Disasters Report 1996*, International Federation of Red Cross and Red Cresent Societies, Oxford, 1996.

Ingram, J. "The Future of Assistance," in Weiss, Th. G./Minear, L. (eds.), *Humanitarianism Across Borders*, Boulder, 1993.

International Court of Justice. Reports 1986, No. 14.

Jahn, B. "Humanitäre Intervention und das Selbstbestimmungsrecht der Völker. Eine theoretische Disskussion und ihre historischen Hintergründe," *Politische Vierteljahresschrift PVS*, H. 4, 1993.

Jessen-Petersen, S. Quoted in Rieff, D., "The Humanitarian Trap," *World Policy Journal*, vol. XII, 4, Winter 1995–1996.

Jonah, J. O. "Humanitarian Intervention," in Weiss, Th. G./Minear, L. (eds.), *Humanitarianism Across Borders*, Boulder, 1993.

Koch, R. *Entwicklungsschutz statt Entwicklungshilfe*, Saarbrücken, 1993.

Martens, J. "Mehr Einfluß für unabhängige Gruppen? Die Vereinten Nationen prüfen ihr Verhältnis zu nichtstaatlichen Organisationen," *Der Überblick*, 3/1994.

Minear, L. et al. *United Nations Coordination of the International Humanitarian Response to the Gulf Crisis, 1990–1992*, Occasional Paper 13, Thomas J. Watson Jr. Institute for International Studies, Providence, Rhode Island, 1992.

Minear, L. et al. *Humanitarian Action in the Former Yugoslavia: The UN's Role, 1991–1993*, Occasional Paper 18, Thomas J. Watson Jr. Institute for International Studies, Providence, Rhode Island, 1994.

Natsios, A. S. "NGOs and the UN System in Complex Humanitarian Emergencies: Conflict or Cooperation?," *Third World Quarterly*, vol. 16, 3, 1995.

Ogata, S. *Refugees and World Peace*, speech at the United Nations University, Tokyo, on 7 January 1993, unpublished manuscript of UNHCR.

Olsen, G. R. "North–South Relations in the Process of Change: The Significance of International Civil Society," *The European Journal of Development Research*, vol. 7, 2, December 1995.

Oslo Declaration and Plan of Action: Partnership in Action (PARinAc), UNHCR-NGO Conference on Emergency Preparedness and Response, Oslo, 1994.

Rieff, D. "The Humanitarian Trap," *World Policy Journal*, vol. XII, 4, Winter 1995–1996.

Ritchey, C. "Coordinate? Cooperate? Harmonize? NGO policy and operational coalitions," *Third World Quarterly*, vol. 16, 3, 1995.

Sarooshi, D. "Humanitarian intervention and international humanitarian assistance: law and practice," *Transnational Associations*, 2/1996.

Shelton, D. "The Participation of Non-governmental Organizations in International Judicial Proceedings," *American Journal of International Law*, vol. 88, 3/4, 1994.

Smith, G. E. "Relief Operations and Military Strategy," in Weiss, Th. G./Minear, L. (eds.), *Humanitarianism Across Borders*, Boulder, 1993.

Spiro, P. J. "New Global Communities: Non-governmental Organizations in International Decision-making Institutions," *The Washington Quarterly*, vol. 18, 1, Winter 1995.

Stedman, S. J. "Alchemy for a New World Order, Overselling 'Preventive Diplomacy,'" *Foreign Affairs*, May/June 1995.

Summerfield, D. "The Impact of War and Atrocity on Civilian Populations: Basic Principles for NGO Interventions and a Critique of Psychosocial Trauma Projects," in *Network Paper 14*, Relief and Rehabilitation Network: Overseas Development Institute, April 1996.

The Commission on Global Governance: *Our Global Neighbourhood*, Oxford, 1995.

Truger, A. "Das International Civilian Peace-keeping and Peace-building Programme (IPT)," *Österreichische Zeitschrift für Politik ÖZP*, 24, 1995.

United Nations. *The United Nations and Cambodia*, Blue Books Series, vol. II, 1995.

United Nations. *The United Nations and Somalia*, Blue Books Series, vol. VIII, 1996.

Wapner, P. "Politics Beyond the State: Environmental Activism and World Civic Politics," *World Politics*, 47, April 1995.

Weiss, Th. G./Minear, L. (eds.). *Humanitarianism Across Borders*, Boulder, 1993.

Zoller, A. C. "Tendences actuelles au seins des Nations Unies concernant les droits des organizations non-gouvernementales," in Fondation Pour Le Progrès De L'Homme, *Expériences et réflexions sur la reconstruction nationale et la paix*, Kigali, 1994.

11

Transnational networks of peacekeepers

Alex Morrison and Stephanie A. Blair

Introduction

The end of the Cold War brought about a number of desirable outcomes, among them the fall of communism and the move towards democratic systems of government in many countries around the world. As attention shifted from the East–West struggle, it is now focused on an increasing number of conflicts characterized by astonishing levels of brutality and inhumanity. It is perhaps not surprising that shortly after the East–West struggle ended, the number of peace-keeping missions increased exponentially. For various reasons, however, the United Nations has not been able to act in all cases of need, with the result that the burden has been shared by other international organizations such as NATO, the OAS (Organization of American States), and the OAU (Organization of African Unity). Into this breach have also come the additional efforts of thousands of NGOs devoted to aiding their fellow citizens. "To fill the gap, to take humanitarian action where huge international agencies could not go, a flood of NGOs sprang up, private aid agencies that could work at the grass-roots level, especially in third world countries, with more flexibility and local awareness than large international bureaucracies."[1] As the number of such organizations increases along with the growth in international attention and action, informal national and international networks have emerged between and among them, with the result that peace-keeping has and is experiencing a significant cooperative contribution from informal groupings of individuals. This so-called "third sector" of international politics, also referred to as "non-state actors" or "global civil society," is bringing a new dimension to peace-keeping policy and practice.

This practically-oriented chapter will examine the informal groupings which have emerged amongst members of the "third sector" and the global environment which has led to their emergence, and will also outline their characteristics and perceived effects. It will serve to illustrate emerging examples of informal cooperation and coordination amongst peacekeepers which are aimed at furthering effectiveness and efficiency. Illustrations will draw heavily on the experience of the Pearson Peacekeeping Centre (PPC), a peace-keeping research, education, and training facility established by the government of Canada in 1994.

The aim of peace-keeping

The true aim of peace-keeping is the saving of lives and the alleviation of suffering. All individual, organizational, national, and international actions must be directed towards the accomplishment of that task. As the aim is at one and the same time broad and yet specific, it follows that peace-keeping itself must be so defined and implemented.

Defining the peacekeeper

Before we can appreciate the role played by informal networks of peacekeepers, we must first identify those about whom we speak; and, to understand who is likely to be considered as a "peacekeeper," we must first understand what is meant by the term "peace-keeping."

Despite many studies which have examined the concept of "peace-keeping," most have merely explained the author's opinion of what peace-keeping entails. There have been relatively few attempts to define the term. Some authors have taken up the challenge, including the United Nations Secretary-General Boutros Boutros-Ghali, who wrote in his Agenda for Peace that:

Peace-keeping is the deployment of a United Nations presence in the field, hitherto with the consent of all the parties concerned, normally involving United Nations military and/or police personnel and frequently civilians as well. Peace-keeping is a technique that expands the possibilities for both the prevention of conflict and the making of peace.[2]

Michael Pugh, Jeremy Ginifer, and Eric Grove, in *Maritime Security and Peace-keeping: A Framework for United Nations Operations,* have written about "ideal" peace-keeping, characterizing it as:

a peaceful intercession by impartial military-naval personnel, police, or civilians as part of multinational formations, on the basis of the consent of the hosts and parties to conflict and under international organization and direction, normally when hostilities are in abeyance.[3]

The British Army publication *Wider Peace-keeping* places peace-keeping within the category of peace support operations, and defines the term as:

Operations carried out with the consent of the belligerent parties in support of efforts to achieve or maintain peace in order to promote security and sustain life in areas of potential or actual conflict.[4]

In an Adelphi Paper, Mats Berdal has noted that peace-keeping "has traditionally been used to describe various forms of legitimized collective intervention aimed at avoiding the outbreak or resurgence of violent conflict between disputants."[5] The United Nations' own history of peace-keeping offers the following definition: "[A]n operation involving military personnel, but without enforcement powers, undertaken by the United Nations to help maintain or restore international peace and security in areas of conflict."[6]

In 1994, on its establishment, the Pearson Peacekeeping Centre (PPC) took issue with the popular perception of peace-keeping as a strictly military activity and sought to enlarge the definitional boundaries to include a much wider range of activities. Consequently, the PPC defines peace-keeping as:

Actions designed to enhance international peace, security, and stability which are authorized by competent national and international organizations and which are undertaken cooperatively by military, humanitarian, good governance, civilian police, and other interested agencies and groups.

This definition is intentionally broad in scope, and is meant to encompass actions ranging from inter-personal conflict resolution through classical inter-positional peace-keeping, operations under Chapter VII (enforcement) of the Charter, and democratic development measures to post-conflict reconstruction and development.

As a result of this wide-reaching definition, the definition of "peace-keepers" is equally inclusive, encompassing what is referred to at the PPC as the "New Peace-keeping Partnership":

The term applied to those organizations and individuals that work together to improve the effectiveness of modern peace-keeping operations. It includes the military; civil police; government and non-governmental agencies dealing with human rights and humanitarian assistance; diplomats; the media and information specialists; and organizations sponsoring development and democratization programmes.[7]

Thus, when this chapter refers to peace-keeping missions and to peace-keepers individually and/or collectively, such reference will be taken to include all members of the New Peace-keeping Partnership unless otherwise specified.

So that there is no mistake about the position from which we approach the topic of this chapter, let us emphasize that peace-keeping is a success. Despite some setbacks due to narrow political aims, it has saved human beings from the scourge of war, and remains the only internationally accepted conflict resolution tool. Owing to a constantly changing global environment, peace-keeping broadly defined has evolved into an increasingly complex and comprehensive response by the international community. Operating within the formal world of nation-states, and called upon to act at appropriate times, peace-keeping is able to contribute to global civil society as a response to the needs of human beings in times of crisis. The groups which contribute to peace-keeping are able to work within the established norms of international society but also are able to mobilize opinion and shape policy within informal groups, thus their actions and influence contribute to global civil society and global governance.

The new global environment

Unfortunately the world remains a dangerous place, and the end of the Cold War notwithstanding, we still have to remain "on guard." There have been changes to the threats that the international community faces: we have instability through regional, ethnic, religious, and cultural disputes; we have states that are artificial and therefore inherently unstable. All of this is a reminder to the world community that we cannot let down our vigilance and we must be ready and able to meet the large number of international crises on which the world community is asked to act. It must be kept in mind that peace-keeping encompasses more than just the "hard-edge" activities seen in Croatia and Bosnia and Herzegovina, which require combat-capable troops ready to defend people in the protected areas. It is also about humanitarian measures, such as those seen in Somalia, Rwanda, Burundi, and the former Zaire.

Peace-keeping operations have undergone a transformation. With the end of the Cold War, members of the Security Council have begun to act as was originally envisaged by the drafters of the UN Charter. The increased cooperation in the Council has, in turn, led to a proliferation of demands placed upon the organization. It is widely acknowledged that peace-keeping operations during the Cold War were largely a means of reducing the potential for direct confrontation between the United States and the Soviet Union. During that time, the United Nations undertook a number of peace-keeping missions which fell within the category of "classical peace-keeping": the use of inter-positional forces to monitor a cease-fire with the consent of the parties to the dispute, and use of force only for self-defence, as in the case of the United Nations Force in Cyprus (UNFICYP). These early missions were typically military in scope, overt and direct in nature. However, "The United Nations has played a useful and often behind the scenes part in preventive diplomacy and conflict resolution/settlement in line with Chapter VI of the Charter. As well, the United Nations invented peace-keeping as a means of insulating local wars, most of them in the third world, to prevent superpower entanglement and consequent globalization of the conflict."[8]

The end of the Cold War heralded a new era in peace-keeping, with increased expectations. Between 1989 and 1992 the United Nations authorized 13 new missions.[9] As the Security Council emerged from the deadlock imposed by the Cold War to meet the demands of the international community to respond to the proliferation of conflicts which resulted from the end of the superpower rivalry, the mandates of these new missions became more ambitious. There are as many types of peace-keeping missions as there are conflicts. The increased duties of the peacekeepers extended to the provision of humanitarian relief, as in UNPROFOR in the former Yugoslavia and UNOSOM I and II (UN Operations in Somalia); the monitoring of transitions to democracy and self-determination, as in UNTAG (United Nations Transitional Assistance Group) in Namibia, UNTAC (United Nations Transitional Authority in Cambodia), UNOMSA (United Nations Observer Mission in South Africa), and ONUVEH (UN Electoral Observer Mission to Haiti); and the monitoring of human rights, as with the experience of MICIVIH (International Civilian Mission in Haiti) and MINUGUA (United Nations Verification Mission in Guatemala). The effectiveness of these operations derives from a combination of factors, foremost being the presence of UN peacekeepers as a physical extension of the will of the international community.

The end of the Cold War has enabled, and indeed allowed and encouraged, many organizations, previously unable to operate freely as they were constricted by the confines of the bipolar world, to gain access to formerly inaccessible conflicts and populations. These organizations have moved to fill the void created by the absence of superpower rivalry and international interest. Where bipolar proxy wars had contributed to the stability of many fragile nations and governments, the post-Cold War era is now witnessing the toppling of those suddenly vulnerable states. The international community, composed of international and regional organizations and many NGOs and INGOs, is now faced with providing security and services in accordance with the letter and spirit of the UN Charter for many of the world's peoples. Many states which are wrought by conflict and war are unable, unwilling, or incompetent to provide even the most basic of services to their most needy citizens – the victims of the very conflicts which are being waged within their communities and homes. Many non-state actors are now finding themselves as the providers of these services.

Technological advancements have assisted organizations which come to the aid of the vulnerable and fragile. These developments have improved response time, permitting rapid logistical deployments, and increased communications and information accessibility, which assists in the promotion of awareness of global problems and conflicts. This increased awareness assists in bringing the issues to the attention of decision makers, thus putting pressure on all members of the international community to act. This in turn has the potential to lead to increased cooperation. These technological developments also serve to assist many NGOs reliant upon public fund-raising to highlight the urgency and gravity of a particular situation, thus probably increasing income.

As the complexity and scope of current missions increase in response to the changing global security environment, those who react to these crises have done so with increased resources and with greater efficiency and effectiveness. In spite of this increase in resources, however, there is greater competition for resources, both from the peace-keeping partners and among those nations in need of assistance.

It is our contention that the United Nations cannot and will not (as member states frequently lack the requisite political will) be all things to all people. The leaders of the organization have learned that they must pick and choose where they will be involved and to what extent. However, everywhere the United Nations, *qua* the United Nations, will not act, there still remains a requirement for coordination of international conflict resolution mechanisms. Key to this coordination is a willingness to share resources of all types. Coordination may be both formal and informal, and the need for it has led to the creation of ad hoc as well as formal networks.

The guiding principles behind the establishment and operation of peace-keeping missions have remained constant since the creation of

UNEF (United Nations Emergency Force) I, and are still applied even though the scope of peace-keeping has greatly expanded. They include consent, impartiality, non-use of force (except in cases of self-defence), international political support, international legitimacy, multinational composition, and persuasion.[10] The United Nations remains, and rightly so, an organization which is cautious and conservative; but it still bears the primary responsibility for the maintenance of international peace, security, and stability.

Rittberger et al. (Chapter 7) do, however, offer the following caution: "It must also be noted that the emergence of a global civil society is by no means an automatic guarantee of peace and security in the world, and that not all civil society actors share democratic and liberal values."

Informal networks of peacekeepers[11]

Having established the definitional framework for this chapter and discussed the evolution of peace-keeping in concert with the changing international situation, let us turn now to informal organizations themselves. They are not specific to peace-keeping missions, and are found universally in organizations of all sizes. Generally speaking, the larger the parent, the larger will be the informal group. There is not necessarily only one informal arrangement in each parent; quite the opposite – there will be as many informal networks as there are specific functions or groupings in the parent organization. The informal arrangement will quite often encompass an external component, in that individuals with a particular interest will seek out their counterparts in other organizations or agencies. By their very nature, such groupings may be transitory, intangible, and difficult to quantify or assess. On the other hand, they may establish organizational mechanisms akin to those of highly structured formal bodies.

Many believe that these informal networks can and do influence peace-keeping policy development and implementation, but hard evidence of results is not yet available to permit the unqualified acceptance of such an assertion. It is clear, however, that they offer a valuable, external contribution to the necessary continuing dialogue which seeks to advance peace-keeping policies and practices, mechanisms, modalities, results, and reassessments. As they are outside the formal decision-making processes, their members are not restrained by traditional political/diplomatic boundaries. Instead, they are able to exchange frank views and provide advice to one another "off-the-record," to superiors and subordinates alike.

Informal networks are not self-generating entities; they come from formal organizations. The actors involved in deciding which international and national crises receive attention and how action might be taken are diverse: some are institutions, while others are individuals. Outside of formal decision-making channels, each of the actors also contributes to the establishment of what we have termed an "informal information and resource sharing/exchange mechanism" (IIRSEM), and it is to this we refer when speaking of informal peace-keeping networks. The mechanism is not necessarily endowed with any degree of organizational stability, although it may well be. Its chief characteristic is that it lies outside of any formally recognized and constituted official structure. Mechanism membership may be fairly stable or greatly dynamic. Its institutional memory may be non-existent, or present through one long-term member or a combination of such members. Participants may not even think of acknowledging that they are part of such a mechanism. Their encounters with one another may be so brief that, while they may occur with regularity but not always with great frequency, the event of their happening is much less important than is the information acquired and the actions taken as a result of its acquisition. However, the main duty of the individual contributors to informal associations is to exercise their responsibility for formal decision-making. For the vast majority of their institutional life, they function within clearly defined boundaries with definite terms of reference, duties, and responsibilities. They communicate with their internal and external colleagues along well laid-out channels and according to approved mechanisms.

Utilizing Rittberger et al.'s classification of non-state actors in global civil society, while remaining within the context of informal networks of peacekeepers, it may prove useful to turn to an examination of advocacy organizations, service organizations, and autogovernmental organizations.

Advocacy organizations

According to Rittberger this term "implies those who concentrate on influencing the process of agenda setting, policy-making, and implementation." Within peace-keeping networks, it would include most NGOs referred to in Roland Koch's chapter, and also mentioned as informal groups in the following section, such as the International Association of Peacekeeping Training Centres (IAPTC). One of the mandates of these non-state actors is to educate the public about the importance and urgency of their cause. Media coverage is an important vehicle, as it has the ability to reach all sectors of the target audience, including decision makers. Most NGOs and INGOs now have their own public affairs departments to handle media campaigns, public information sessions to increase awareness, and direct mail campaigns to assist with fund-raising.

Their lobbying creates public pressure on national governments and international organizations, which serves in turn to prompt decision makers to change policy or implement the desired course of action.

A recent example of media influence coupled with public pressure and lobbying by NGOs was Canadian Prime Minister Chrétien's decision to act to solve the desperate refugee situation in the former Zaire and Rwanda. He said that the impetus for his desire to mobilize the international community was the scenes he witnessed on the television. He was successful in focusing the attention of world leaders on the plight of the refugees. The cries for help, including military force, by many of the NGOs operating in Central Africa helped tremendously.

Service organizations

Service organizations, according to Rittberger et al., implement specific programmes. In the context of the UNU research project on peace and security, these are addressed in Roland Koch's chapter. It is evident that peace-keeping itself could also be considered a service organization. Under UN Security Council resolutions, missions are mandated to perform functions such as maintaining a stable and secure environment, as in Haiti, and cooperating with humanitarian aid agencies in the delivery of their services, as in Somalia.

Autogovernmental organizations

This category refers to those who attempt to create a sphere of action with rules and norms of their own. Peace-keeping operations do not fall within this category, as they are established and operate within national and international frameworks.

Returning to a description of informal networks, perhaps the best example of an informal organization is that encompassed by the concept of the New Peace-keeping Partnership. The partners, as previously mentioned, are now acting together in a formal, structured manner as they have never done in the past. This formal linking was possible, we suggest, in overwhelming measure only because of the personal links forged between and among them in training institutions such as the Pearson Peacekeeping Centre and in field operations. The relatively recent practice of establishing combined civilian/military committees (CMOCs – Civilian Military Operation Centres; HIOCs – Humanitarian Integrated Operations Centres; and JCCs – Joint Consultative Commissions) as an integral part of contemporary peace-keeping missions has ensured much more positive and effective interdisciplinary and interorganizational cooperation. The multiplicity of informal links established among and between the members of these committees has, many individuals have contended, played a large role in the achievement of this effectiveness.

In peace-keeping situations, formal actions are taken by many organizations, including the following bodies.

- The United Nations. The UN Charter has given the Security Council responsibility for international peace and security. When the Council cannot act, the General Assembly may take action under the Uniting for Peace Resolution. The Secretary-General, assisted by, *inter alia*, the Under-Secretaries-General for Peace-keeping Operations, Political Affairs, and Humanitarian Affairs, and other members of the Secretariat, is responsible for implementing the decisions of the Security Council and General Assembly. The United Nations has been the executive agency for the vast majority of peace-keeping operations.
- The North Atlantic Treaty Organization. Since the end of the Cold War, NATO has assumed an ever-increasing role in various aspects of peace-keeping. It appears to be the only international organization, apart from the United Nations itself, with the training and interoperability experience to carry out peace-keeping missions. In all instances, however, it is connected to the United Nations through various overview or reporting mechanisms.
- The Organization of American States. The OAS is anxious to play a prominent role in international peace-keeping, but has so far been unable to perform up to its own expectations and those of others.
- The Organization of African Unity. The OAU has made a number of attempts at peace-keeping, and has achieved limited results.
- The Association of South–East Asian Nations. Increasingly, ASEAN members are searching for ways to play an organized part in peace-keeping.
- Peace-keeping missions. Each field operation has a more or less well-defined authority range.
- Peace-keeping training centres. These institutions, through their programmes, research, and publications, exert an influence on the conduct of current and future peace-keeping operations.
- National government foreign affairs and defence departments and their peace-keeping divisions. These organizations monitor international developments, determine national responses, and oversee their implementation.
- Humanitarian aid organizations. These organizations and their representatives (examples of which are the International Committee of the Red Cross, CARE, Médecins Sans Frontières, the UNHCR, UNICEF, and the World Health Organization) are usually in-theatre before the arrival of military peacekeepers and will be there long after the military have departed.

- "Think tanks" and private organizations. Brookings, the Rand Corporation, and the Canadian Institute of Strategic Studies are some examples.

Each of these organizations is bound by its mandate (as (re)interpreted from time to time), its operational and administrative structure, internal and external operating regulations, and the dictates of commercial confidentiality, as well as the inherent characteristic of virtually any group: that of taking action to guarantee the preservation and continued existence of the organization itself. It is within, between, and amongst these formal bodies that informal networks and groupings emerge.

We have chosen to classify informal networks according to two types. Type 1 encompasses activities ranging from individual communications which may involve two or more individuals from the same or different organizations, to organizations which, while they may be formalized in their structure, do not have a formal role in the peace-keeping decision-making process. They have been grouped together because they all involve, in some form or another, direct personal contact. This list is not exhaustive, but serves to illustrate the range and comprehensiveness of associations which are formed or may be formed in the future.

Turning now to levels of security and civil society actors, Rittberger et al. have identified three separate levels of security: macro, meso, and micro. We will attempt here to discuss these levels of security within the peace-keeping issue area. At the macro level the concept of security "has come to encompass threats to the well-being of states and societies such as environmental degradation and economic shocks," in addition to addressing traditional problems such as inter-state armed conflict. Peace-keeping missions conducted during the Cold War were specifically undertaken in an attempt to prevent outright conflict between the super-powers, entangled as they were in their proxy conflicts. The emergence of the traditional inter-positional model of peace-keeping, *à la* Cyprus and Suez, was developed to keep belligerents apart after a cease-fire was in place, while a resolution of the larger macro-level security issue at stake proceeded subtly. The meso level refers to the intra-state level, wherein the very physical security of populations is threatened by brutal civil wars of an ethno-political nature, resulting in mass migration and famines or complex humanitarian emergencies. During this post-Cold War era we are witnessing a relatively new phenomenon in this area, whereby states are increasingly not fighting between and amongst themselves, but are experiencing conflict inside their borders. More and more the victims of this often-times brutal conflict are civilians who suffer grievously, as illustrated by the situations in Bosnia and Herzegovina, Rwanda, and former Zaire. According to Rittberger et al., the classical understanding of the individualized concept of security, that of the micro level, "is the guarantee of individual personal, civil, and political rights *vis-à-vis* the government. Apart from this political understanding of individual security, social and economic dimensions (social and economic security) have to be incorporated into a wider concept of security on the individual level." The missions in Haiti illustrate attempts to establish democracy from the tyranny of dictatorial rule and the international community's dedication to alleviate human suffering.

An interesting point is that the end of the East–West conflict seems to have caused (1) a shift in the relevance and urgency assigned to security problems on the macro level in comparison with security problems on the meso and micro levels, and (2) shifts in the level of societal activity within the three sectors. In times of the bipolar international system, public attention and societal activity were clearly concentrated on macro-level security problems, most prominently the nuclear threat to international security resulting from the military competition between East and West. In this context, transnational NGO activities concentrated on the macro level of security – i.e. inter-state security issues. NGO opportunities to perform humanitarian relief functions on foreign territory were severely constrained by both sides.[12]

Dimensions

In a discussion of peace-keeping networks it must be borne in mind that it is states which contribute troops and civilian personnel to peace-keeping missions, thus states will remain the focus of the discussion, notwithstanding that NGOs participate enormously in peace-keeping, most often with funds from the home state (often NGOs are the catalyst which ensures that governments do the right thing). When considering peacekeeping missions some prerequisites for successful action are the fact that consent is highly desirable, but this condition is evolving as the concept of sovereignty is being eroded; an understanding of the specific challenges/difficulties and risks with which the actors will be confronted within their operations; and the actors' impact on security and their contribution to the establishment of a global civil society, as in Cambodia. The most important prerequisite is that of political will – on the part of the international community and by the parties to the dispute. Only when there is interdisciplinary cooperation among and between the military and civilian peacekeepers (the actualization of the New Peacekeeping Partnership), and among the parties to the dispute and between them and the peacekeepers, will there be a solid chance of success and of building true international peace, security, and stability.

Requirements for successful action by non-state actors can be determined by their ability to create policy change. Within advocacy organizations (such as the IAPTC), a vital determining factor is their access to decision-making élites, and the exercise of their collective influence through various UN member state missions in New York and through national governments to produce positive, effective, and efficient reforms within the Department of Peace-Keeping Operations (DPKO) and UN peace-keeping missions. As an organization the IAPTC is increasingly able to access and facilitate dialogue and information flow between key decision makers. All advocacy organizations within the conflict resolution spectrum which seek to achieve policy change strive substantially to raise the political and other costs of decision makers' procrastination and to create a sense of urgency. The recent examples of the former Zaire and Rwanda illustrate the urgent calls for practical and protective help from NGOs to states. "To this end advocacy organizations have to be able to mobilize visible, cross-border, mass public support to create sufficient pressure on governments to keep their goal on the political agenda."[13]

It has been noted previously that peace-keeping has been a tremendous success. It has saved literally millions of lives and has prevented injury, disease, and hunger on a much greater scale. The role of informal organizations in this success is a subject which necessitates much more research, discussion, and analysis than can be attempted in this chapter, which is largely descriptive in nature and does not attempt to assess the effectiveness of the organizational and individual relationships described in it. A cursory survey of a number of individuals indicates that while practical and long-lasting results are claimed, evidence is scanty at best. As more study is devoted to this topic, it will be necessary to establish effectiveness criteria which can then be applied in a systematic, objective manner. These criteria may be applicable to the complete cycle of activity or merely to one aspect. In any event, they should be used to compare the opinions of participants with perceived and actual results.

Informal networks: Type 1

Having addressed different classifications of global civil society or non-state actors, we shall now examine various network arrangements. Individual communication is perhaps the most important and influential informal association, yet the most difficult to quantify as to its effects. Called variously "networking" or "the old-boy network," lobbying or advocacy, among other labels, it entails the regular or occasional conversations or correspondence between and among individuals. Fact, speculation, rumour, and forecasts are exchanged and traded rapidly. In the course of the communication, decisions may be made to act in a certain manner and to act alone or in concert with others who may or may not be included in these discussions. Additionally, one or more of the parties to the discussion may decide to act or not to act without informing colleagues. Reports of these communications may be transmitted in a formal way to organizationally vertical or horizontal colleagues, thus structuring future decisions and actions. On the other hand, individuals may simply take it upon themselves to act without revealing, in any manner, the reasons for such actions. In sum, informal communications take place by many means and in many places.

Conferences, meetings, and seminars are important, not only for their own intrinsic value as an information exchange mechanism, but also for the value received from the activity which occurs "on the margins" of such events. In and of themselves, they facilitate sharing and exchange by means of the agenda items discussed, the papers presented, and the resultant question and answer sessions. Many times, however, a very real value is that these events provide a backdrop against which various players can meet informally to discuss and share or exchange information. New acquaintanceships are forged, existing relationships are strengthened, introductions are facilitated, and individual and collective promises and undertakings are made – many of which lead to actions and results which would not have occurred without these informal opportunities.

Organizations without direct association to the formal peace-keeping apparatus of the United Nations, NATO, the OAS, and so on constitute a third example of Type 1 informal networks. These groups may or may not have "formal" structures in place, but have no defined role within the formal decision-making structures of peace-keeping operations. The International Associations of Peacekeeping Veterans are one such group of organizations. These are veteran military peacekeepers who have banded together for a wide variety of reasons and to achieve various ends. The Soldiers of Peace International Association, based in Lyons, France, is in this group. It produces a newsletter, *The Blue Helmet News*, with a distribution of 5,000 copies, and grants membership to those who provide dates and locations of their peace-keeping service.

National associations of peace-keeping veterans are similar to the international groups. They (and there may be more than one in a particular country) seek to establish an atmosphere of recollective comradeship and support, and undertake memorial good works. As an example, there is the Canadian Peacekeeping Veterans Association (CPVA), again a military organization.

The IAPTC is yet another example of a Type 1 network. Founded in 1995 by the Pearson Peacekeeping Centre, it operates outside the normal structured apparatus of peace-keeping and is meant to provide exactly the type of atmosphere in which informal communication will thrive. It is not a directive association; rather, its membership represents a collaboration of interested agencies, institutes, and associated individuals focused on improving the effectiveness and efficiency of peace-keeping research, education, and training. Operating as an informal forum, the IAPTC provides and distributes information, facilitates refinement of the conceptual framework of peace-keeping, broadens contacts between and amongst various national and international organizations, and supports means to develop and refine common educational programmes, formal curricula, and training programmes.

The 1995 inaugural meeting of the IAPTC at the PPC was attended by 21 civilian and military individuals from 12 countries and from NATO. The 1996 gathering was attended by 62 persons from 20 countries, as well as representatives from Allied Forces Central Europe, the EU, the International Labour Organization, multinational forces and observers, the International Committee of the Red Cross, Supreme Headquarters Allied Powers in Europe, the United Nations (New York, Brindisi, Geneva, UNIDIR, Rome, Zagreb, and UN volunteers), and the Western European Union. This second meeting was held in Pisa, Italy, under the direction of Professor Andrea de Guttry of Scuola St. Anna. The main accomplishments of the second meeting included a reaffirmation that the IAPTC should remain, in accordance with its founding principles, an open and voluntary association; an agreement that members should facilitate an exchange of teaching staff, administrative personnel, and students between centres; a decision to publish an IAPTC newsletter in print and electronic format; a wish to make the IAPTC more widely known; and an agreement that the IAPTC would retain its non-directive character – in other words, that it would remain an informal information exchange and sharing mechanism. In line with this thought, the IAPTC has no permanent executive. The Pearson Peacekeeping Centre serves as a central secretariat and provides general guidance, in accordance with precedent and members' wishes, throughout the year.

Peace-keeping seminars are also planned, as well as the promotion of common training standards and guidelines. A Web site has been established, and the first edition of the newsletter was available earlier this autumn. The third gathering, coordinated by the Institute for Peace and Conflict Studies at the Foundation for International Studies in Malta, was held at the Institute in April 1997. The secretariat attributes the continuing growth in attendance numbers to the usefulness of this type of informal information exchange and the high regard in which it is held.

Gatherings of like-minded individuals are yet another example of Type 1 exchanges. These often take place within the formal structure of peace-keeping missions, involving military and civilian personnel alike. In the military portion of a mission it is common, for example, for signals officers of each contingent to gather to discuss common problems and strategies for dealing with them. The same could be said of medical officers, operations officers, and virtually every other classification within the mission. On the civilian side, the administrators of large agencies often meet regularly for informal exchanges; the same could correspondingly be said of other civilian occupations.

Finally, we wish to consider a plethora of organizations (of which only a few will be mentioned here) engaged in peace-keeping activities which also fit within the Type 1 category. They include the Canadian Council for International Cooperation (CCIC), the International Committee of the Red Cross, CARE, MSF, InterAction, and the various UN agencies such as UNICEF, UNESCO, and the UNHCR, the World Food Programme (WFP), and the World Health Organization (WHO). They are formal in their own sense, but their members forge their informal links in the same manner and for the same reasons as individuals from other organizations. They also form coalitions, which we suggest are another type of informal network.

The CCIC, for example, is a coalition of Canadian voluntary organizations "committed to achieving global development in a peaceful and healthy environment, with social justice, human dignity, and participation for all."[14] It supports the work of its members through "networking, leadership, information, training, and coordination, and represents their interests when dealing with government and others."[15] Similarly, InterAction is a coalition of over 150 US-based non-profit organizations working to promote human dignity and development in 165 countries around the world. Its diverse membership is active in programmes to ease human suffering and strengthen people's abilities to help themselves. It coordinates and promotes those activities and helps to ensure that goals are met in an ethical and cost-efficient manner. United Nations agencies are no different from any of the other groups listed here in their adoption of informal links and networks to accomplish their aims.

Informal networks: Type 2

A second type of informal network has also developed amongst peace-keepers, and involves shared information. It is distinguished from Type 1 in that the sharing does not necessarily involve personal contact. The World Wide Web, peace-keeping publications, and private organizations are examples of the second type of informal network.

Peace-keeping publications, be they journals, newsletters, academic papers, bibliographies, agency reports, books, media releases, position papers, studies, and so on, have long served as a nexus to connect and stimulate peace-keeping thought and debate. As with any subject, those who are a part of it soon become familiar with its latest positions, propositions, and proponents. Slowly, the readership evolves into a network of individuals who know the names, ideas, proposals, and activities of others in the field, whether or not they are personally acquainted with the individuals themselves. Through the printed – and widely distributed – word, debate takes place, information is shared, and new ideas are generated. Although extremely difficult to measure directly, it would be imprudent to think that this type of informal (and often faceless) exchange did not contribute, even indirectly, to formal policy processes.

Peace-keeping publications are an excellent medium of information exchange. Their pages are available to all, and can contain articles by all who are interested and/or involved in any aspect of peace-keeping. Of course, private individuals are freer to voice their opinions than are government employees, but even the latter may enjoy considerable writing freedom if it is made clear that the contents are an individual responsibility. Apart from books and proceedings of conferences, some of the main publications in the field are *Peacekeeping and International Relations*, published by the Pearson Peacekeeping Centre, *International Peacekeeping News* (University of Bradford), and *International Peacekeeping* (Kluwer).

As it has in myriad domains, the Internet has also brought a new dimension to informal sharing of information about peace-keeping. The many peace-keeping-related Internet sites sponsored by government departments, the United Nations, private organizations, peace-keeping institutes, study centres, and libraries demonstrate the rapidity with which this means of communication has inundated the field of peace-keeping. Not only can organizations make their information readily available to others as never before, but Internet "chat lines" and e-mail allow for fast, easy, and relatively inexpensive communication between individuals who, due to geography, would previously never have been able to communication so readily. Again, however, it is as yet difficult to measure the actual impact of this exchange on formal policy development.

The US Ambassador to the United Nations has repeatedly referred to the media as the "sixteenth member of the Security Council." This indicates the extent of the influence of media representatives and their product. International peacekeepers – policy makers and practitioners alike – have developed, from time to time, very close links with those in the media. It would be naive to assume that one does not influence the other. The same can be said of the relationship with information specialists and media employees of international organizations and peace-keeping missions.

Yet another example of a Type 2 participant is that of the private organization engaged in providing goods and services to peace-keeping missions; Brown and Root and Servair are two of the more prominent firms in this area. Their employees quickly learned the value of networking and establishing links with individuals at all levels of peace-keeping operations. In this way, they are able to determine what additional commercial opportunities may be available and how their performance is perceived by their employers.

The utility of informal networks

Given that there are so many formal organizations involved in peace-keeping operations, with formal channels for communication and decision-making advocacy undertakings, one might wonder why informal networks emerge. What services do they provide for the international peace-keeping missions of which they are a part? And what influence do they bring to bear, if any, on formal organizations? Unfortunately, as relevant as these questions are, there is little hard data available with which to answer them. The suggestions which follow, therefore, are observations which we propose as a point of departure for further study and discussion.

To begin, we know that the recent proliferation of peace-keeping missions and international humanitarian operations means that groups and individuals engaged in peace-keeping activities have increased in number and in the scope of their activities. At the same time, resources have not been made available in proportion to perceived demand. Many organizations find themselves in the same places at the same times, and – both in-theatre and in home countries – competing for the same limited resources. As there are no indications that they are prone to amalgamation in order to conserve, seemingly the best way to make maximum use of existing resources is through cooperation. More players are entering the scene, and there are alarming signs that the number of small "Mom and Pop" NGOs continues to grow. Paralleling this growth is the need for cooperation, coordination, and sharing of information between and among the parties. One method of achieving this, of course, is through formal links; another is through informal associations.

Second, informal networks offer opportunities for information sharing and exchange which are not available through formal structures, and which ultimately result in mutual education. In some instances, formal structures and lines of authority often inhibit the type of frank exchange enjoyed by those who participate in informal networks; while in other situations, formal structures exclude important peace-keeping players who, were it not for informal channels, would not have the opportunity to share information with other members of the New Peace-keeping Partnership.

Third, informal networks enable peacekeepers of all stripes to improve the future performance of their respective organizations. This is possible because the mutual education process which takes place within informal networks allows those who are a part of them to return with new ideas, policies, and practices which they in turn implement in their own activities, thereby improving the way they "do business."

A fourth benefit of informal networks is that they foster a spirit of collegiality and friendship amongst peacekeepers. "Collegiality" might seem a rather intangible benefit, yet its significance should not be overlooked. Friendship is a powerful motivating force, particularly for peacekeepers who work in difficult, strenuous, dangerous, and demanding conditions. In fact, it is even possible that informal networks generate friendships which develop because of frequent interactions. According to Otoman Bartos, who has studied what are termed "low-intensity friendships":

When individuals with similar values and similar beliefs interact frequently, they tend not only to become more similar, but also to become friends...

We gain further insights into similarity when we utilize the so-called "social exchange" theories. They view interaction as an exchange of so-called "extrinsic benefits," i.e., benefits that are valuable in themselves, such as material gifts, help, or advice. Exchange theoreticians ... argue that, if these exchanges are repeated and always are equal in value, the partners will grow fond of each other. Ultimately, they will become friends.[16]

While yet again it is difficult to determine the extent to which friendship is either the impetus for the creation of an informal network, or the result of informal networks, it is nonetheless less an important psychic reward, the impact of which deserves further study.

Finally, in the long term, informal networks offer a positive contribution to international peace, security, and stability.

Informal networks and the Pearson Peacekeeping Centre

The PPC was established by the government of Canada in February 1994 and commenced operation in April 1995. Named in honour of Lester B. Pearson, former Prime Minister of Canada and recipient of the 1957 Nobel Peace Prize for the establishment of UNEF I and the development of the concept of modern peace-keeping, its mission is to support and enhance the Canadian contribution to international peace, security, and stability through the provision of quality research, education, and training in all aspects of peace-keeping. To guide its activities, the PPC has formulated the concept of the New Peace-keeping Partnership (NPP), which was introduced earlier in this chapter. It is the NPP and the bringing together of military and civilian participants, plus mid- and high-level officials from all over the world, which makes the PPC unique.

The PPC conducts round tables, research, and seminars, produces a number of publications, and offers an extensive array of training courses. Subjects include issues such as interdisciplinary cooperation, peace-keeping negotiation and mediation, the maritime dimension of peace-keeping, the legal framework of modern peace-keeping, refugees and displaced persons, administration and logistics in modern peace-keeping, a general overview of modern peace-keeping, human rights in modern peace-keeping, military operations and modern peace-keeping, and peace-keeping management and command.

Within the PPC, informal networks have emerged as a direct result of the number and diversity of individuals who come to the Centre to attend courses and seminars. These individuals come from countries around the world and represent all the members of the NPP. It is common for the participants in each course to form close bonds with one another, due to the intensity of their work and the fact that they live together at the PPC for the duration of their studies. Outside class hours, participants meet informally to discuss issues related to their work. For some it is their first opportunity to sit down informally with their military or civilian counterparts and talk about the goals, projects, and programmes of their relative organizations. These informal discussions lead to a new appreciation of the strengths of their respective organizations, an appreciation they take with them when they return to the field and which enables them to work more cooperatively and effectively with other organizations. The experience in turn encourages participants to seek one another out when they are on a peace-keeping mission, because they better understand the role of the other person and organization, and they have a shared understanding upon which to build a better professional rapport.

The PPC believes that the kinds of links which are established amongst its alumni are so important to the continuing dialogue that must take place between all members of the NPP that it has developed an alumni newsletter. It not only provides former participants and faculty with information about activities of their colleagues, but also continues the exchange of information about civilian and military organizations. It is only through this type of sharing that modern multi-faceted peace-keeping operations will function in a manner which best protects human lives and offers hope of a better future.

Challenges and risks

What are the challenges and risks associated with and faced by organizations involved in peace-keeping? Rittberger et al. suggest that "advocacy and service organizations face the same three broad types of challenges to their work: funding, international cooperation and coordination, and legitimization/sovereignty questions."[17] Within the sphere of peace-keeping and conflict resolution, these questions are applicable to both formal and informal advocacy and service organizations and the many inherent combinations. Funding issues are influenced by sources, their legitimacy, and the competitive arena. For example, does government funding involve unwanted, unwarranted, or uncomfortable conditions?

The admirable notion of advancing international cooperation is faced with two other obstacles apart from competition for scarce resources, and cooperation and/or coordination: the fear of being dominated by another group or bureaucracy and thus losing independence; and the lack of consensus concerning approaches and strategies.

Non-state actors, such as service and advocacy organizations, must interact with the state as a sovereign actor. Service organizations are very often confronted with the doctrine of state sovereignty, when they have to secure physical access to a territory in order to carry out their services. Access, however, is very often denied by the state in question, and it is only recently that the UN Security Council has authorized external UN, plurilateral, and NGO non-permissive access to sovereign territory for the purpose of humanitarian assistance. But even if their actions are legalized, service organizations may not be able to perform their work as military groups often do not welcome their presence. Just as there are NGOs which feel that a military presence, however protective, will inhibit their good works, so are there military personnel who resent the perceived restrictive effect on their operations of NGO presence.

By delivering services which would otherwise not have been supplied by national or international governmental institutions, NGOs have contributed to the alleviation of human suffering and to reestablishing security on the micro and meso levels. There is no doubt that these organizations contribute to the democratization of international politics and the establishment of a global civil society. The measure of their success is a matter for further study.

Future contributions to global civil society

The existence of informal networks amongst military and civilian peace-keepers of such a diverse nature as those we examined in this chapter makes it clear that many people establish such networks and remain in contact for the exchange of information, resources, and psychic rewards outside of formal governmental and organizational channels. The proliferation of international non-state actors, or what is referred to as the "third sector" of international politics or "global civil society," is undoubtedly affecting international political processes. The difficult task, however, is to measure how and to what extent these actors are shaping issues of national and global concern.

One of the tasks of the UN21 research group is to scrutinize the status of various NGOs within the United Nations system to determine if the system should be "reformed to facilitate a more transparent and effective participation of NGOs as representatives of an emerging global civil society." On the fiftieth anniversary of the United Nations, many took the opportunity to reflect on the organization and offer comment on how it might refine and redefine itself to prepare for the challenges of the next 50 years. Is a redefinition necessary?

As the Cold War era came to an end, the long-hoped-for peace dividend did not materialize. Instead, we have witnessed an increase in the number and ferocity of low-intensity conflicts raging around the world. In an attempt to respond to these crises, the United Nations mandated an unprecedented number of peace-keeping missions. It also broadened the scope of these missions to include the delivery of humanitarian aid; response to natural disasters; care for refugees and the internally displaced; programmes of reconstruction and development; and, in some instances, the creation of domestic institutions usually reserved for sovereign governments. This has placed a large number of previously isolated and independent organizations in close proximity with one another. To fulfil their mandates, many of these organizations have sought creative solutions for resource sharing and increased cooperation and coordination. As we have seen, this may be something as simple as information dissemination, or something more elaborate, such as policy coordination and joint programme implementation. As these organizations come to play a greater role in assisting the United Nations to meet its mandate, it seems only sensible that the United Nations reflects, in its policies and its operation, the work that non-state actors undertake in this regard.

To further our understanding of informal networks, much additional research is needed to determine the impact and effects of non-state actors in this highly political field, and the mechanisms for bringing about these changes. The development and implementation of the concept of the New Peace-keeping Partnership needs examination in detail. In addition, practitioners must be prepared to share their experiences of informal networks with researchers, and to work closely with those who collect and analyze the relevant data. This collaborative effort has the potential to reach a new level of understanding.

Notes

1. Walker, John, *Orphans of the Storm: Peacebuilding for Children of War*, Toronto: Between the Lines, 1993.
2. Boutros-Ghali, Boutros, "An Agenda for Peace," 2nd edition with new supplement and related UN documents. New York: United Nations, 1995, p. 45.
3. Pugh, Michael, Jeremy Ginifer, and Eric Grove, "Sea Power, Security, and Peace-keeping after the Cold War," in *Maritime Security and Peace-keeping: A Framework for United Nations Operations*, Michael Pugh (ed.), Manchester: Manchester University Press, 1994, p. 16.
4. UK Army Field Manual, *Wider Peace-keeping*. The Army Field Manual Volume 5, Operations Other than War, Part 2. London: HMSO, 1995, pp. 1–2.
5. Berdal, Mats R., *Whither UN Peace-keeping?* Adelphi Paper 281 (October 1993), London.
6. United Nations, *The Blue Helmets: A Review of United Nations Peace-keeping*, 2nd edition. New York: United Nations, 1990, p. 4.
7. The Pearson Peacekeeping Centre, a division of the Canadian Institute of Strategic Studies, a non-governmental organization established by the government of Canada in 1994, serves the New Peace-keeping Partnership by proving national and international participants with the opportunity to examine specific peace-keeping issues, and to update their knowledge of the latest peace-keeping practices. As found in the promotional literature of the organization.
8. Molot, Maureen and Harald von Reikhoff (eds.), *Canada Among Nations*, Ottawa: Carleton University Press, 1994.
9. Durch, William, *The Evolution of UN Peace-keeping: Case Studies and Comparative Analysis*, New York: St. Martin's Press, 1993, p. 9.
10. United Nations, *United Nations Guidelines for Peace-keeping*. New York: United Nations Department of Peace-keeping Operations, 1994.
11. Please see Leon Gordenker et al., *International Cooperation in Response to AIDS*, New York: Printer Publishers, 1995, in particular pp. 18–20 for a concise explanation of networking. This work was particularly helpful in the preparation of this chapter.
12. Rittberger, Volker, Christina Schrade, and Danielas Schwarzer, "Transnational Civil Society Actors and the Quest for Security: An Analytical Framework and Overview." Prepared for the UNU Symposium "The United Nations System in the Twenty-first Century: International Peace and Security," 8–9 November 1996, Tokyo, Japan.
13. Ibid.
14. Canadian Council for International Co-operation, Ottawa, Ontario, Canada. Bye-laws, Preamble.
15. Ibid.
16. Bartos, Otomar, "Negotiation as Friendship Formation," *International Negotiation*, vol. 1, 1, 1996, p. 30.
17. Rittberger, Volker, Christina Schrade, and Daniela Schwarzer, op. cit.

Regional institutions, the United Nations, and international security

12

Introduction

Muthiah Alagappa

"... Under the Charter the Security Council has and will continue to have primary responsibility for maintaining international peace and security, but regional action as a matter of decentralization, delegation, and cooperation with United Nations efforts could not only lighten the burden of the Security Council but also contribute to a deeper sense of participation, consensus, and democratization in international affairs. Regional arrangements and agencies have not in recent decades been considered in this light... Today a new sense exists that they have contributions to make."

Boutros Boutros-Ghali, 1992

The ending of the Cold War reinvigorated the United Nations and simultaneously reinforced the trend toward security regionalism. The new-found unity of the Security Council enabled the United Nations to act in a relatively large number of conflicts, and in the process raised the expectations with regard to its "primary responsibility for maintaining international peace and security." The United Nations had several successes – the Gulf War, Cambodia, Mozambique, El Salvador, and Haiti – but there have also been several tragic failures – Somalia, Bosnia and Herzegovina, and Rwanda. These failures and the growing political, financial, and operational problems of the United Nations have greatly tempered the earlier enthusiasm and support for the organization. Unable to meet the ever-increasing demand for help, the United Nations has actively explored task-sharing and cooperation with other intergovernmental and non-governmental organizations as well as coalitions led by major global and regional powers. Regional institutions (regional arrangements and agencies) have been increasingly looked upon as one way of addressing the growing gap between demand and supply, and reducing the burden on the United Nations. In the words of Boutros Boutros-Ghali, "regional arrangements or agencies in many cases possess a potential that should be utilized."

The role of regional institutions (constituted under Chapter 8 of the UN Charter) in maintaining international peace and security has commanded renewed attention in the policy and intellectual communities from about the mid-1980s. Such interest has become more pronounced in the post-Cold War era. Regionalization of international politics, collapse of the Cold War security architecture, inability of any one state or organization to manage the post-Cold War world, the growth of regional powers and the desire on their part as well as other regional states to seek greater control over their strategic environment, and growth of economic regionalism are some of the reasons that underscore this growing interest and attention.[1] They inform, in various degrees, the attempt to broaden and deepen regional security arrangements and agencies in Europe, to update and revitalize those in Latin America and Africa, and to forge new ones in Asia.

Unlike in the formative years of the United Nations, when regional arrangements were seen as competing with and detrimental to the universal approach embodied in the organization,[2] it is now widely accepted that global and regional institutions can and should work together in promoting international peace and security. Regional actors have a deep interest in conflict management in their respective regions, and they can provide legitimacy, local knowledge and experience, and some resources, especially in the form of personnel. However, they also suffer several limitations, including a lack of mandate, difficulty in maintaining impartiality and forging common positions, limited resources, and organizational shortcomings. Regional institutions often require the support and involvement of the United Nations in managing conflicts. The United Nations has the mandate, legitimacy, structure, greater access to resources, and is often the most impartial and preferred means for extraregional involvement in local conflicts. Thus the need and rationale for task-sharing and cooperation between the United Nations and regional organizations is clear, and there have been several instances of such cooperation in the course of the last decade. The United Nation cooperated with NATO and the Organization for Security and Cooperation in Europe (OSCE) in Bosnia and Herzegovina, with ECOWAS (Economic Community of West African States) in Liberia, with the Commonwealth of Independent States (CIS) and the OSCE in Georgia, and with the OAS (Organization of American States) in Central America and Haiti. Such cooperation, however, has not always been smooth, and in several cases has been productive of tension.

Effective task-sharing and cooperation between the United Nations and regional institutions require, in part, an understanding of the possibilities and limitations of each as well as the development of principles, rules, and procedures to govern such a partnership. This has been difficult in practice. Regional institutions vary widely in terms of purpose, structure, and capacities. And often several regional and subregional institutions with overlapping responsibilities exist in a region. Further, the type and intensity of conflicts vary widely. It is impossible to decide in advance which would be the most appropriate regional institution for managing a specific conflict. This "choice" and consequently the basis for task-sharing and cooperation with the United Nations have often been ad hoc and quite distinct in each case, as demonstrated by the investigations in this volume of the experiences in Africa, Asia, and South America.

Although it is difficult to formulate and adhere strictly to a division of labour that would apply to each and every occasion, or even most of them, this does not preclude a general analytically oriented discussion of the basis for task-sharing and cooperation between the United Nations and regional institutions. Working on the hypothesis that task-sharing and cooperation between the United Nations and regional arrangements and agencies can contribute to the maintenance of international peace and security, this chapter seeks to develop an analytical framework to investigate the following questions. What are the roles and strategies available to regional institutions in managing peace and security? What are the possibilities and limitations of regional institutions in conflict management? What factors determine their effectiveness? What are the considerations that should inform the division of labour between the United Nations and regional agencies? Finally, how should coordination and accountability be achieved when regional institutions cooperate with the United Nations in maintaining international peace and security?

Definitions

We begin with definition and discussion of some key terms – regional arrangements and agencies; peace and security; and conflict management.

As observed by Gareth Evans,[3] there is no shared vocabulary and even the meanings of commonly used terms differ with audiences. It is therefore crucial to define and develop a common set of concepts to guide enquiry.

Regional arrangements and agencies

Considerable effort was made in the intellectual community in the 1960s and early 1970s to define regions and regional subsystems.[4] Comparatively less effort was devoted to defining regionalism.[5] And almost no effort was made to define regional arrangements and agencies. The UN Charter, which is the initiator of these terms, does not define them. Notwithstanding this, the meaning of "regional arrangements" is similar to that of "regionalism." Both relate to cooperation among regional states to enhance their national well-being through collective action. Building on this, regional arrangements or regionalism (these two terms are used interchangeably in this chapter) may be defined as "cooperation among governments or NGOs in three or more geographically proximate and interdependent countries for the pursuit of mutual gain in one or more issue areas." Although NGOs can undertake regional cooperation, the concern in this chapter and hence the ensuing elaboration is on cooperation among governments. Regionalism can be issue-specific – a collective self-defence arrangement (alliance) to confront a specific external threat, or a collective security arrangement to maintain order among member states, or a nuclear-free regime to regulate nuclear activities. Or it can encompass an issue area or a number of issue areas.[6] Often, as for example in the case of the OAS, the OAU, and ASEAN, it is a broad framework within which several specific regimes and accompanying bureaucratic organizations in a number of issues and issue areas can and do nest.[7] Regional agencies refer to formal and informal regional organizations (with physical and organizational infrastructures, staff, budgets, etc.) with responsibility for implementing regional arrangements. Regional agencies or organizations are usually coterminous with regional arrangements, but not necessarily so. The term "institutions" is used in this chapter to cover both arrangements and agencies.

Peace and security

Peace and security are difficult concepts to define. The United Nations, which has as its principle purpose the maintenance of international peace and security, neither defines these terms nor specifies the relationship between them. In the context of the United Nations, these two terms appear to be used rather loosely and often interchangeably. Peace and security carry distinct meanings within the academic community, but there is no agreed-upon definition of either of these concepts. The schism and debate between the proponents of negative and positive peace have been a central feature of peace studies.[8] Similarly, there is an ongoing debate in security studies over the definition of security. Realists define security as an international structural problem. Their focus is on international military threats to the political survival of the state. Others have argued for broadening the referent, scope, and approach to security.[9] We cannot and do not seek to resolve this debate, which is rooted in different world views.

The dependent variable in this chapter is security, defined as "the protection and enhancement of values deemed vital for the political survival and well-being of a community."[10] This definition is deeper and broader than realist definitions of security, but not indiscriminately so. The security referent in this definition is community, which usually, though not always, is the nation-state.[11] Communities at the subnational, regional, and global levels may also be referents of security. The definition excludes non-human entities like the international economic system or the ecological system as security referents in their own right, on the basis that security is for and about people who normally provide for their security by organizing themselves into communities. The focus on political survival and especially the well-being of a community allows the inclusion of non-conventional issues as security concerns, either because of their impact on political survival or because of their consequences for the well-being of the community. Such issues, however, must be vital. Only those concerns that are grave and urgent, and require the mobilization of a substantial part and ultimately, if necessary, all of a community's intellectual and material resources should be labelled as security concerns. This definition does not seek to include or exclude on the basis of specific issues, dimensions, nature and type of problems, threats, or means, but on the basis of gravity and urgency of an issue or problem. This approach sidelines the unresolvable debate between the proponents of narrow and broad conceptions of security. The definition also permits consideration of security at the intra-state and international levels, and does not limit the pursuit of security only to competitive means with emphasis on military power. For the purpose of this chapter, security is further delimited to include only political problems. This is necessary to keep the exercise manageable. It should be noted here that even this delimitation is much broader than allowed for by realists, and incorporates some features of the minimalist or negative definitions of peace.

Sources of insecurity

Most states are confronted with internal and international sources of insecurity. For analytical purposes these sources of conflict may be discussed separately, but in reality they are often interconnected. The international source of insecurity is rooted in anarchy, a condition that is taken by realists to be the fundamental fact of international political life.[12] In a system of sovereign states, there can be no central political authority. The structure of the system is necessarily anarchic, with each state retaining the right to judge its own cause and decide on the use of force. The incentives for aggression, risk of tension, conflict, and war in such a system are high.[13] In arming for their security, states set in motion a vicious circle. Attempts to increase the security of one state undermine the security of another, creating a security dilemma.[14]

This structural aspect, a "tragic consequence" of the desire for state autonomy, however, is only one of the two component layers that constitute the security dilemma.[15] The second component is more intentional and dynamic, a product of state policy rooted in the ideological beliefs and goals of the state, and in its orientation toward the international political and territorial status quo. A policy seeking revolutionary change, hegemony, or domination will intensify the struggle for power and sharpen the insecurity caused by the anarchic structure. Although these two layers of the security dilemma (structural and policy-driven) are often intertwined in practice, distinguishing them is analytically useful in investigating when, why, and how regionalism can promote international security.

Domestic sources of insecurity are rooted in problems of political identity, legitimacy, and socio-economic inequality. The idea of the nation as the basis of political community and the related construct of the nation-state have now become universal norms. But the nation is an "imagined community," and in many cases the idea of the nation on the basis of which the state is constituted is not deep-rooted.[16] Colonial states have in many cases been transformed into nation-states. The arbitrary state boundaries drawn by the colonial powers resulted in "multiethnic territorialisms" that had no political rationale for existence other than as dependencies of the metropolitan powers.[17] With the dissipation of the unity fostered by anti-colonial nationalism and experience of "internal colonialism," ethnic, racial, linguistic, and religious consciousnesses have been on the rise in some countries, contributing to disenchantment with the nation and nation-state rooted in the colonial state.[18]

Dissonance between power and legitimate authority is a second domestic source of conflict. This is relevant to states in which the normative and institutional frameworks for the acquisition and exercise of political power are not well established. In situations where the exercise of state power is not rooted in moral authority, the legitimacy of the regime (political system) as well as that of the incumbent government is likely to be contested by rival claimants to power on the basis of competing ideologies, promise of better performance, or greater force.[19] In the absence of accepted mechanisms and procedures to manage them, such competition is likely to translate into extra-legal and violent means, including *coups d'état*, rebellion, and revolution. Political legitimacy has been and is likely to continue to be an acute and persistent problem for most modern states.

Large and growing socio-economic inequality is yet another source of domestic conflict. However, although socio-economic grievances can fuel peasant rebellions or protests and strikes by farmers and industrial workers, their consequences are likely to be limited unless they feed into the conflicts over political identity or legitimacy. Often there is an overlap. Economically backward regions provide fertile ground for the development and support of separatist movements, or for political organizations which challenge the legitimacy of incumbent regimes and governments on the basis of competing ideologies or promises of better performance.

Insecurity and conflict at the international level are inherent in the principle of anarchy which underpins the international system, and cannot be resolved as long as sovereign political units (states or some other entities) exist. At the domestic level, the problems of political identity, legitimacy, and socio-economic grievances are rooted in the nation and state formation processes, and cannot be resolved quickly. Creation of political identities takes decades, if not centuries; the cultivation of political legitimacy is unending; and the attainment and maintenance of socio-economic equality requires continuous monitoring and action. These problems are not amenable to a once-and-for-all solution. Still, although the sources of conflict cannot be eliminated, they can nevertheless be managed and ameliorated.

Conflict management

Although in practice they overlap, for analytical purposes conflict management may be divided into three stages: prevention, containment, and termination. In conflict prevention, the goal is to forestall conflict situations and prevent the outbreak of hostilities or other forms of disruptive behaviour. Conflict prevention will require the redefinition of the identity, interests, and capabilities of the communities concerned.

In conflict containment, the goal is to deny victory to the aggressor and to prevent the spread of conflict. Denial of victory includes stopping aggressors short of attaining their full goal and persuading them to undo their actions. Preventing the spread of conflict includes stopping horizontal escalation in which other communities and issue areas become involved. It may also be directed to halt vertical escalation up the ladder of violence, including the use of weapons of mass destruction.

In conflict termination, the goal is to halt hostilities and bring them to a satisfactory conclusion through settlement or resolution. A satisfactory conclusion includes defeating the aggressor and re-establishing the status quo ante, achieving a compromise through splitting the difference, or removing the source of the conflict. Conflict settlement focuses on achieving an agreement to end the use of violence and resolve the more immediate and overt dimensions of the conflict.[20] Conflict resolution, on the other hand, seeks to remove the source of conflict altogether. This requires changes in the goals, attitudes, and perceptions of the conflicting parties. While these two aspects of conflict termination are not mutually exclusive, conflict resolution usually follows conflict settlement and requires long-range political and economic strategies to alter, if not transform, the underlying dynamics of the conflict. In a sense, this bring conflict management back to conflict prevention.

Regional institutions: Assets, roles, and strategies

Regionalism, in theory, should facilitate communications and socialization, information sharing, increase in consensual knowledge, increase in power through the pooling of resources, and collective action.[21] Based on these assets, regional agencies should be able to avail themselves of one or more of the following interconnected strategies: norm-setting, assurance, community-building, deterrence, non-intervention, isolation, intermediation, enforcement, and internationalization.

Norms can define identities of states as well as regulate their behaviour. Through norm-setting, regional institutions can influence the collective expectations and internal and international behaviour of member states in the political, economic, and security arenas. Assurance strategies can increase transparency, reduce uncertainty, limit and regulate competition, and thus help to build confidence and avoid the unintended outbreak and escalation of hostilities. The purpose of assurance strategies is to mitigate the security dilemma and minimize and regulate the use of force, not to eliminate them. Community-building strategies take this one step further and seek to eliminate the role of force in the resolution of political disputes. The culmination point is a security community in which "there is real assurance that the members of the community will not fight each other physically but will settle their disputes in some other way."[22] Deterrence strategies – collective security and collective defence – seek to deter aggressive behaviour on the part of member states as well as non-member states. Collective security comprising political, diplomatic, economic, and military measures is the more appropriate strategy for maintaining order among member states, since it is not directed against a specific country or group of countries which are identified as posing a threat.[23] Collective defence (alliances like NATO and the now defunct Warsaw Pact), based on an identified common threat, is more appropriate in dealing with external aggression. These two strategies are not, however, mutually exclusive, as illustrated by the provisions of the Rio Treaty. Assurance, community-building, and deterrence strategies are primarily concerned with conflict prevention, although many of the specific arrangements, particularly alliance and collective security, have a role in conflict containment and termination as well.

Non-intervention is an option when, for whatever reason, the regional institution does not seek to become involved in a particular conflict. Closely linked to non-intervention, but quite distinct, is isolation, the purpose of which is to prevent geographical spillover or widening of the conflict through the involvement of other parties. The intent in adopting these strategies may be to allow the protagonists to resolve the conflict among themselves, or to preserve a future intermediation role for the regional institution. Intervention refers to direct and active involvement in the conflict through the application of a regional organization's collective political, diplomatic, economic, and military power to contain and terminate the conflict. Intervention can be undertaken to enforce collective security and collective defence, or to keep the peace among the warring parties. Collective security and collective defence are implemented against an identified aggressor. Peace-keeping, the interposition of forces between belligerents to prevent further fighting, is undertaken to provide a cooling-off period and facilitate mediation efforts.

Intermediation and internationalization are two strategies applicable to conflict termination. Intermediation refers to a non-partisan and usually non-coercive approach to settlement. Regional institutions may urge conflicting parties to use regional or global mechanisms and procedures for pacific settlement of disputes, or they may attempt to play a more direct and active role by engaging in conciliation and mediation.[24] The strategy of internationalization becomes relevant when conflict prevention, containment, and termination are beyond the capabilities of the regional arrangements or when extraregional actors become involved. Through internationalization, regional organizations can mobilize the resources of external actors and organizations in support of their strategies, while denying the same resources to their adversaries.

The possible relevance of these strategies for managing internal and international conflicts, and enhancing the security of member states, is indicated in Table 12.1. Discussion in the ensuing sections highlights some critical aspects with regard to the possible roles and limitations of regional institutions in conflict management.

Regional institutions and conflict management

Conflict dynamics at the intra-state, intramural, and extramural levels vary substantially, as does the potential of regional institutions in conflict management. It is thus necessary to distinguish and discuss separately the conflict management roles and tasks of regional institutions by type of conflict. We begin with political conflict at the intra-state level.

Table 12.1 Regional institutions and security: A framework for analysis

Domestic Conflicts
Issues of contention: Identity, legitimacy, socio-economic grievances

	Tasks	Measures/Strategies
Conflict Prevention	1. Protection of individual and minority rights. 2. Support for socio-political development. 3. Support for economic development. 4. Early warning.	1. Norm-setting. 2. Redress by regional institutions. 3. Encourage and facilitate dialogue. 4. Preventive deployment. 5. Collective inducement and sanctions. 6. Regional economic cooperation. 7. Maintain a stable and conducive regional environment.
Conflict Containment	1. Prevent escalation. 2. Prevent torture, killing, and genocide. 3. Humanitarian relief.	1. Preventive deployment. 2. Enforce sanctions. 3. Isolate conflict. 4. Peace-keeping. 5. Internationalize conflict. 6. Humanitarian assistance.
Conflict Termination	1. End violence. 2. Negotiate and guarantee settlement. 3. Election monitoring. 4. Address underlying issues.	1. Encourage dialogue. 2. Intermediation. 3. Enforcement action. 4. Encourage and support long-range strategies for nation- and state-building. 5. Internationalization.

Table 12.1 (cont.)

Conflict Among Member States
Issues of concern: Security dilemma, specific issues in dispute, aggressive behaviour by member states

	Tasks	Measures/Strategies
Conflict Prevention	1. Ameliorate security dilemma. 2. Deter aggressive behaviour. 3. Build a society leading eventually to a community of nations. 4. Encourage dispute resolution.	1. Foster development of normative context that rejects threat and use of force as an instrument of state policy. 2. Build regimes – assurance and regulatory. 3. Regional dispute resolution mechanisms. 4. Collective security arrangement. 5. Regional integration measures.
Conflict Containment	1. Deny victory to aggressor. 2. Prevent escalation. 3. Humanitarian relief.	1. Enforce collective security arrangements. 2. Isolate conflict. 3. Peace-keeping. 4. Internationalization 5. Humanitarian assistance.
Conflict Termination	1. Stop armed conflict. 2. Negotiate and guarantee settlement. 3. Resolve dispute.	1. Encourage dialogue among parties to conflict. 2. Intermediation. 3. Enforcement action. 4. Internationalization.

Table 12.1 (cont.)

Conflicts with External Actors
Issues of concern: Security dilemma, specific issues in dispute, aggressive behaviour by external actors

	Tasks	Measures/Strategies
Conflict Prevention	1. Ameliorate security dilemma. 2. Deter aggressive behaviour. 3. Encourage dispute resolution.	1. Dialogue and negotiations. 2. Security regimes – assurance and regulatory. 3. Collective self-defence.
Conflict Containment	1. Deny victory to aggressor. 2. Prevent escalation. 3. Humanitarian relief.	1. Implement collective self-defence. 2. Internationalization. 3. Humanitarian assistance.
Conflict Termination	1. Defeat aggressor. 2. Negotiate settlement. 3. Resolve dispute.	1. Implement collective self-defence. 2. Internationalization. 3. Intermediation.

Domestic conflicts

Conflicts at the domestic level pose serious security problems for many countries, including some developed ones. Domestic conflicts often spill over into neighbouring countries and/or invite major power intervention, and threaten regional security as well. Yet the basis on which governments enter into regional cooperation often precludes any formal role for regional institutions in the management of domestic conflicts.

The principles of sovereignty and non-intervention form the cornerstones of regional arrangements like the Inter American system, the OAU, and ASEAN.[25] Based on these principles, regional institutions have either been deliberately excluded from domestic conflict management (the OAU and ASEAN), or accorded a role subject to the invitation of member states (ECOWAS and until recently the OAS). The sanctity of the principle of non-intervention, however, is now under challenge. A growing number of Western policy makers and scholars make the case for intervention by the international community on humanitarian grounds and to protect democratic regimes.[26] Although this case is contested in certain quarters, some change, particularly with regard to gross violation of human rights, may be in the offing.[27] Beginning in 1993, the OAS, in the light of its new goal of safeguarding democracy in the hemisphere, relaxed the commitment to the principle of non-intervention. In what has come to be known as the Santiago Commitment, the foreign ministers of the OAS member states pledged to adopt "timely and expeditious procedures to ensure the promotion and defence of representative democracy." The OAS has since condemned the coups in Guatemala, Haiti, and Peru and has applied economic sanctions to back its demand for return to democratic rule in these countries.[28] While the Santiago Commitment privileges the protection of democratic regimes over the principle of non-intervention, the latter is far from dead.[29] Humanitarian considerations and incipient rethinking of the basis of political community are also forcing a re-examination of the principle of non-intervention in Africa. Nevertheless, this still a crucial principle and it effectively precludes any direct intervention by regional and other international institutions until the outbreak of conflict.

Often the conflict-prevention role of regional institutions in relation to domestic conflicts has to be indirect, and relevant strategies may include norm-setting, development of collective regional identities which may mitigate internal identity conflicts, prevention of external meddling in domestic conflicts, and creation of a stable and conducive environment for economic development of member states. Early-warning systems, and mechanisms and procedures to encourage pacific settlement of domestic disputes, may also be part of the inventory. Once a conflict has erupted, regional institutions have the options of non-intervention, isolation, intervention, or mediation and conciliation. Non-intervention has been the preferred strategy of most regional institutions, for a variety of reasons: adherence to the principle of non-interference in domestic affairs; lack of invitation from the incumbent government; lack of capability; intractability of conflict; anticipated human and material cost especially if recent experiences have been negative (Britain's experience in Northern Ireland influenced its and several other EC members' approach to the ongoing conflict in Bosnia and Herzegovina; the OAU's experience in Western Sahara and Chad influenced its approach toward the Liberian conflict); difficulty in forging a common position (the EC in relation to the former Yugoslavia); difficulty in determining aggression and aggressor; tension between competing principles (territorial integrity versus self-determination in the case of the former Yugoslavia, or non-intervention versus the promotion of democracy in several Latin American cases); and a belief that external actors can have only a marginal impact on the resolution of domestic conflicts, and that these have to be resolved by domestic contestants even if the political, economic, and human costs are high. The OAU, for example, restricted its involvement to internal conflicts related to decolonization and apartheid. A common position was not difficult to formulate in these situations, but it did not intervene in the numerous other internal conflicts on the continent.

Concurrent with non-intervention, regional organizations often seek to isolate conflicts to prevent external interference and escalation, urging contestants to resolve the conflict by themselves. This has been the preferred option in ASEAN. In February 1986 when the Philippines was confronted with a critical situation which "portended bloodshed and civil war," the other ASEAN member states called upon all Filipino leaders to join efforts to pave the way for peaceful resolution.[30] But as demonstrated in the case of the Philippines, as well as by the ECOWAS experience in Liberia, isolation can be rather difficult. Domestic contestants will appeal and, in the absence of unanimity in the international community, are likely to receive external support.

Non-intervention in the context of endemic internal conflict, as in Africa, projects an image of regional institutions as irrelevant and useless. The OAU's reputation in and out of Africa has suffered much because of its reluctance to become involved in domestic conflicts. Such considerations are pushing it to become more involved. But intervention also carries its own limitations and dangers. Difficulty in forging and maintaining unity among member states, difficulty in maintaining the neutrality of the intervention force, limited authority and capability of regional institutions, lack of financial resources, and difficulty in arriving at and implementing an international settlement all limit the containment and termination roles of regionalism.

The above discussion suggests several observations. First, regional institutions are severely limited as an agent of domestic conflict management. Preclusion from domestic politics and the complex and intense dynamics of domestic conflicts severely limit their possibilities for conflict prevention. They may have a relatively greater role in conflict containment (isolation) and termination (mediation), but this is likely to be limited to a select few situations. Even then regional institutions may have to enlist the support of the United Nations or other external actors. Second, to the extent that regional institutions do have a role in domestic conflict management, because of their status quo character they are likely to favour the incumbent power-holders. Governments tend to support each other. As the former Tanzanian President Julius Nyerere is reported to have said, "The OAU exists only for the protection of the African heads of state."[31] Similarly, the primary rationale for the Gulf Cooperation Council is the protection of the incumbent monarchs and their conservative kingdoms.[32] Even non-intervention and isolation, as noted above, are likely to work in favour of the incumbent power-holders. Third, instead of containing and terminating domestic conflict, regionalism can also prolong and intensify it. By strengthening the hand of the government, as for example in Myanmar, regional support increases the persecution and insecurity of groups seeking political change.

For the most part, international actors and dynamics, including that at the regional level, will have only an indirect impact and will be relevant only to the extent that they influence the domestic political discourse and affect the power resources of the domestic contestants. In light of the many dilemmas and limitations, the optimal strategies of regional institutions in dealing with domestic conflicts would appear to be non-intervention, isolation, diplomatic pressure urging peaceful settlement of the dispute, offering of good services, and enlisting the support of the United Nations or a key external power.

Conflict among member states

Regionalism has its greatest value at the intramural level when the policy-driven power struggle component of the security dilemma has abated. In this situation, regional strategies can be effectively deployed to reduce the uncertainty inherent in anarchy and the misperceptions which can issue from it. Because of the commitment of member states to the status quo, regionalism can be particularly effective in conflict prevention. Through the construction of security regimes in the areas of confidence- and security-building and pacific settlement of disputes, and promoting defensive defence, it can mitigate the negative effects of anarchy. The resulting secure environment can foster cooperation in other issue areas, increase interdependence, alter the cost-benefit calculus in favour of

peaceful resolution of disputes, and contribute to the forging and consolidating of shared norms and values. This will further strengthen international society, and in the long run make for the development of a
pluralistic security community.

Regionalism is much less useful in coping with the policy-driven power
struggle component of the security dilemma. When the latter operates
unabated, as is the case when hostilities break out among member states
and most of the time at the extramural level, the collective power that
regionalism can bring to bear will be the crucial determinant of its role
in conflict prevention, containment, and termination. The power of the
regional organization should in theory be greater than that of individual
states, but the realization of this potential will be dependent upon the
unity of purpose among member states and their willingness to pool
national power and act collectively on the issue in concern. Even when
these stringent conditions are met, the power of the collective may still be
insufficient to redefine the interests and goals of the parties to the conflict.
Usually regional organizations are strong only in terms of diplomatic
power, which can be useful in mobilizing international support and
structuring international (especially United Nations) action.

To be effective in terms of deterrence, however, diplomatic power has
to be complemented with economic and military power. This will require
the regional organization to ally or align with one or more major powers
or seek the assistance of the United Nations. Though the diplomatic
power of a regional institution can be deployed to harness international
power in support of its policies, success will depend on the pattern of
relations among the major powers and the congruence of interest the
regional institution can establish with the target actor. The internationalization strategy will also constrain the freedom and flexibility of regional
institutions. Generally, the effectiveness of regional institutions in conflict
containment and termination is much more limited than its effectiveness
in conflict prevention. And because of its partisan role in conflict containment, its conflict termination role may be even more limited.

Conflicts with extraregional states

The security goal of regional institutions here is the protection of member
states from insecurity created by other states and organizations. There is
no sense of community at this level, and regional institutions would have
to deal with countries that are not necessarily committed to the status
quo. Some may even be categorically opposed and seek to overthrow it.
Regionalism could be perceived by these countries as directed against
them, provoking counter-groups and exacerbating the security dilemma.
In this situation it may not be possible to implement far-reaching assurance strategies. Limited regimes to avoid mutually undesirable outcomes,

such as that between the United States and the Soviet Union during the Cold War, and that between Israel and Egypt after the 1973 war, may, however, be possible.

Conflict prevention at the extramural level has to address both aspects of the security dilemma, with power being much more significant in the reduction of insecurity. In theory, regionalism can and should enhance the power (defined broadly to encompass military, economic, and diplomatic power) of the collective. In practice, regional institutions, especially among developing countries, seldom command the required power and/or a common threat perception for an effective alliance. They can seek to enhance their power through alliance or alignment with extraregional powers, as for example the ASEAN countries with China to contain the Vietnamese and Soviet threats. There is, however, the possibility that the interests of regional states may be overridden by those of the major powers. Beijing's own objectives of punishing Viet Nam and containing the Soviet threat overrode ASEAN's concerns and its peace proposals on several occasions. Even the EC has not been exempt from this. During the Cold War, American interests and policies frequently took priority over Western European concerns.

Though weak in military power, regional institutions may be relatively strong in diplomatic or economic power. If such power constitutes a critical mass, they can play a critical role in shaping the rules of the larger regional game, as with the EC in relation to Eastern Europe in the post-1989 period and ASEAN in relation to the Indochinese states. Even when the power of regional institutions does not constitute a critical mass, they may be able to take the initiative in constructing the larger regional order, as is currently the case with ASEAN's successful initiative in creating the ASEAN Regional Forum (ARF) to begin a dialogue on security matters in the Asia-Pacific region. But for this to be possible the status quo has to be acceptable or at least tolerable to all the major powers, and they must support, or at least not oppose, such initiatives. The abatement of the struggle for power among the major countries is a necessary precondition for such initiatives to succeed.

The diplomatic power of regional institutions can also be deployed to contain extramural conflict. It may be particularly useful in influencing UN debate and action. The arms embargo against the former Yugoslavia was sanctioned by the Security Council at the request of the EC. Indeed, the United Nations became involved in trying to negotiate an end to that conflict at the urging of the EC. Similarly, the support of the OAS was crucial in getting the Security Council to impose sanctions on Haiti. The OAU successfully pushed for UN sanctions against Taylorland in Liberia. Diplomatic power, however, is only enabling, providing regional institutions with the power of initiative. It cannot guarantee success. That will still depend on the disposition of non-member states, the dynamics of the larger international system, and the competence of member states in harnessing the power of external states in the service of their cause.

Effectiveness of regional institutions

As noted earlier, the roles, tasks, and strategies identified in Table 12.1 should in theory be available to all regional institutions. Their feasibility in practice and the effectiveness of regional institutions in conflict management, however, are contingent upon a number of factors, and therefore likely to vary considerably across institutions. Five factors – purpose, scope, and commitment to regional institutions; shared interest and common purpose in relation to the specific conflict; institutional capacity; resource availability; and legitimacy and credibility – appear to be crucial in determining the effectiveness of regional institutions.[33]

Purpose, scope, and commitment

In ascertaining effectiveness, one must begin with the purpose, scope, and commitment to regional institutions. This will determine whether and to what extent a regional institution can become involved in conflict management, and the roles and tasks that can it can undertake. The purpose and scope of all-inclusive multi-purpose regional organization like the OAS or the OAU will differ from subregional ones like ECOWAS and ASEAN, which in turn will differ from specific task-oriented institutions like NATO. Further, it is necessary to explore what roles and tasks are allowed or prohibited by the principles and purposes of the charters of these institutions, and whether practice has deviated from them. This will help ascertain their likely roles in conflict management and the legal basis for them.

Intimately connected to the purpose and scope is the identification with the institution and commitment to the norms, rules, and procedures to govern regional order. The stronger the identification and commitment from member states, the more effective will be the regional institution, and vice versa.

Shared interest and common purpose

Commitment of member states, however, will often vary by issue. Thus shared interest in a specific conflict and a common purpose with regard to strategy and outcome are crucial in the effectiveness of regional institutions. In the absence of these, even a strong regional organization like the EC will be inhibited from playing an effective role, as was the case in relation to Bosnia and Herzegovina.

Institutional capacity

This refers to the capacity of a regional institution to make decisions, as well as the existence of organs, rules, and procedures to implement them. Of concern here are the capacity and efficacy to collect, collate, and analyze data; the principles and procedures to make decisions; the necessary subsidiary organs to carry out these decisions; command, control, and communications capabilities; and administrative and logistics support.

Resource availability

Closely linked to institutional capacity is the availability of financial and manpower resources. Financial capacity is crucial. Obviously, no institution can function without financial capability. Manpower resources are also critical. They include trained mediators and negotiators, military and police forces, civilian administrators, and NGOs. Financial and manpower resources, and military strength, will determine the types of roles and tasks that a regional institution may be able to undertake.

Legitimacy and credibility

To be effective, regional institutions must command the respect and authority of the parties to the dispute in concern. For this to be the case, they must be perceived to be impartial and strong, and with a good track record. Recognition and support by other regional and global institutions, as well as cooperation with them, may also enhance credibility. Lack of coordination and especially competitive behaviour by other institutions may undermine legitimacy and credibility.

Strength in these areas will enhance the role and effectiveness of regional institutions in managing conflicts, but they by no means guarantee success. As noted in earlier discussion, although regional institutions have considerable potential, their actual role in conflict management is much more limited. Regionalism has to be viewed as part of a package that includes national self-help, regional and global balances of power, alliance with extraregional powers, and the UN collective security system. Often regional institutions will have to enlist the involvement and support of the United Nations or other extraregional actors.

Regional institutions and the United Nations

The UN Charter envisages a hierarchy, with the UN Security Council having the primary responsibility for maintaining international peace and security, and regional arrangements serving global interests as defined by the UN Security Council. It requires regional institutions to keep the Security Council fully informed of activities undertaken or contemplated with regard to the maintenance of international peace and security. The sole exception relates to the provision for collective defence under Article 51. Even here, the Security Council must be informed of the exercise of this right, which is allowed only until the Security Council takes action. In practice, however, the relationship between the United Nations and regional institutions has been rather loose and subject to considerable variation. Only rarely have the United Nations and regional institutions interacted as envisaged in the Charter. Regional institutions have frequently been used to circumvent and/or undermine the United Nations. This was especially the case during the Cold War, when the American- and Soviet-led regional alliances played the key role in maintaining international peace and security, with the United Nations relegated to playing a role only in peripheral areas. Even now the hierarchy envisaged in the Charter does not always exist. The United Nations is still not the key player where the security concerns of the major powers, especially the Permanent Five, are involved. It can act in support of them but not against them. The United Nations is not in a position to dictate to regional institutions or major actors, although it can deploy its moral authority and access to resources to influence them in certain situations.

The United Nations and regional institutions may on occasions be able to cooperate, one serving the interests of the other. At other times they may not be able to do so. In yet others, they may be in competition with each other. It should be noted here that tension is always present in the interaction between the United Nations and regional institutions, even when they are cooperating. While each may derive benefits from cooperating with the other, both will also incur costs, especially in terms of their purpose and autonomy. Often, each will try to preserve its autonomy while attempting to use the other to serve its purposes. This tension can only be managed, not eliminated. In light of this and other considerations, the actual relationship between the United Nations and regional institutions will vary by specific institution, issue, and context. A flexible approach is required. It is, however, necessary and possible to develop some general principles or criteria to facilitate a division of labour and ensure accountability when the United Nations and regional institutions deem it in their mutual interest to cooperate.

Division of labour

The earlier abstract discussion of conflict management suggested that conflict prevention is perhaps the strong suit of regional institutions. At the intra-state level, regional institutions can play an indirect role in conflict prevention as well as encourage pacific settlement of disputes. Regional institutions should be particularly strong in preventing the outbreak of conflicts among member states, and less so in preventing conflicts initiated by extraregional actors. Regional institutions are, for a number of reasons, likely to be less strong in conflict containment and even weaker in conflict termination. This suggests that regional institutions may have a comparative advantage and therefore should take the lead in conflict prevention, while the United Nations or other actors may be better able to take the lead in the other stages of conflict management. This functional division of labour, however, is an abstract one and may have to be modified in the context of each case.

Here, several other factors must be taken into consideration in ascertaining which institution is better placed to take the lead, and what kind of support should be provided by other institutions. Some of the critical factors to consider in this regard are identified below.

Depth of interest and consequences

Regional institutions will usually have greater interest, as they will be most affected by the outcome of regional conflicts. Further, a global institution like the United Nations may not have equal concern with all conflicts. It would therefore appear logical for regional institutions to take the lead. But this logic may be negated by other considerations.

Acceptability

This is a crucial factor, for non-acceptance by one or more parties to the conflict will undermine the success of the operation. As regional institutions are close to the event and their members are likely to have vested interests, it is difficult for them to remain impartial, at least not for long. Consequently they may be less acceptable to one or more parties to the conflict.

Institutional capacity

The organizational capacity to make decisions and implement them is critical. The components of this capacity have been identified earlier and will not be repeated here. A further capacity question to consider is whether the institution can handle an additional responsibility or whether it is already fully stretched, if not overburdened. What will be the consequences for the institution of taking on this new responsibility? Will its credibility be enhanced or undermined? Although it may be difficult to anticipate the consequences correctly, it is a question that must be given due consideration. Taking on a responsibility which is unlikely to succeed can damage the institution and negate its other positive benefits.

Resource availability

Which institution has or can harness the necessary financial, human, and military resources necessary to carry out the operation, and for how long? It is possible that one institution may be strong in one resource and weak in another. This will indicate which can provide what better.

Consideration of these factors would provide a basis to decide which institution should take the lead role and what support can be provided by the other institution. Often, however, the division of labour is not decided a priori. It evolves over time, sometimes fortuitously. Further, a multitude of institutions – global, regional, subregional, and extraregional – may be involved simultaneously, each taking the lead in different issues. Even within an issue, the lead role may pass from one institution to another over time and with the different stages of conflict management. In the case of the conflict in Nicaragua, for example, the United Nations, the OAS, the Contadora group, friends of the peace process (Peru, Argentina, Brazil, and Uruguay), the Esquipulas II group, and President Oscar Arias were all involved in negotiating and implementing a peace settlement. Further, the responsibility for monitoring elections, disarming the guerilla groups, and reconstruction were shared by several intergovernmental and non-governmental groups, and the division of labour was not clearly spelt out. Similarly, a somewhat different group of several institutions was involved in negotiating and implementing the peace settlement in El Salvador. No two arrangements will be the same. The key requirement is to remain flexible and make adjustments as required by the situation.

When the United Nations and regional institutions are cooperating in conflict management, the ultimate responsibility and hence ultimate political control must rest with the Security Council. All other responsibilities may be shared or delegated. The United Nations or a regional institution must take the lead role in managing a certain operation, with the other limiting itself to providing support. There should be no ambiguity as to who is in control of the operation. Otherwise not only will the success of the operation be hampered, but it may also aggravate tension between institutions, complicate the chain of command, and present enormous problems of coordination and accountability.

Accountability

Finally, when a regional institution is engaged in conflict management with the endorsement and support of the United Nations, it must remain accountable to the Security Council. Accountability means "the ability to ensure that a mission subcontracted by the international community to a powerful state (or regional institution) reflects collective interests and norms and not merely the national imperatives and preferences of the subcontractor."[34] Accountability applies to mission and objectives; principles governing the conduct of the operation including impartiality and use of force; and utilization of resources provided by the United Nations. The United Nations must retain an overview and not lose control of the operation. At the same time, however, it must not seek to micro-manage an operation that is being led by a regional institution. A proper balance between losing control and micro-managing has to be struck. Accountability, while its necessity is not in question, may be difficult to achieve in practice, especially if a major power is the driving force of a regional institution. The leverage available to the United Nations to ensure accountability is limited to its moral authority, and at times the resources that it can make available. The latter is only a consideration with respect to regional institutions in the developing world. For those which have the necessary resources, the UN's leverage lies only in its moral authority. It is therefore important to define clearly the mission, objectives, principles, and so on at the outset, and make UN endorsement and continued support conditional upon strict adherence to the initial terms. That changes to the initial terms can only be authorized by the Security Council must also be stipulated at the outset.

One or more of several measures may be employed to ensure accountability. One is to limit initial authorization of a mission to a specific, often limited, duration. Each extension will have to be re-authorized by the Security Council. This will provide an opportunity for the Security Council to exercise its overview and retain control over the mission. Second, UN personnel may be injected into the command-and-control system to provide guidance and assistance, as well as to report back to the United Nations. Third, a separate joint body comprising personnel from the United Nations, the regional institution, and other interested parties may be constituted to oversee the implementation of the mission. Fourth, the United Nations may appoint a special envoy to undertake the same function. The choice of measures will depend on the situation and the degree of overview sought. This cannot be determined without reference to context.

A related issue is the action to take if the terms set by the United Nations are violated, or if the delegated power and authority have been abused. Here the options available to the United Nations are very limited. It can withdraw its endorsement, but this may not be possible if the target institution has influence in the Security Council. The only option then would be not to re-authorize the mission. But for this to be possible, the initial endorsement must be for a limited duration and must expire at the opportune moment. Failing this, the United Nations may have to resort to mobilizing international norms and opinion through the General Assembly, and/or attempting to persuade the regional institution or actor to comply with the initial mission, goals, and principles.

Conclusion

The approach to international security in the post-Cold War world has to be multi-layered, comprising several arrangements and actors. No single arrangement or actor will be sufficient. Regional arrangements and the United Nations can each play an invaluable role in conflict management, but there are clear limitations to both. Task-sharing and cooperation between them will help overcome some of these limitations. An effective partnership between global and regional institutions depends on a good understanding of the possibilities and limitations of each, an effective division of labour, and accountability of the various institutions involved in managing a specific conflict. Although no firm basis can be applied to all occasions and a flexible approach is required, this chapter has set forth an analytical framework to investigate and understand the possible roles and limitations of regional institutions, identified factors that must be considered in the division of labour between global and regional institutions, and suggested some ways of ensuring accountability when regional institutions cooperate with the United Nations in maintaining international peace and security.

Notes

1. For an elaboration of these reasons, see Muthiah Alagappa, "Regionalism and Conflict Management: A Framework for Analysis," *Review of International Studies*, vol. 21, 4, 1995, pp. 359–87.
2. For a good account of the deliberation on regionalism versus globalism in the context of the formulation of the UN Charter, see Inis Claude, "The OAS, the UN, and the United States," *International Conciliation*, No. 547, March 1964, pp. 3–60. See also his *Swords into Ploughshares: The Problems and Progress of International Organization* (New York: Random House, 1971), pp. 102–17.
3. Evans, Gareth, "The United Nations: Cooperating for Peace," address to the Forty-eighth General Assembly of the United Nations, 27 September 1993.
4. For an overview of the effort to define a region, see Bruce M. Russett, "International Regions and the International System," in Richard A. Falk and Saul H. Mendlovitz (eds.), *Regional Politics and World Order* (San Francisco: W. H. Freeman and Company, 1973), pp. 181–7. On the effort to define a regional subsystem and specify the necessary and sufficient conditions for it, see William R. Thompson, "The Regional Subsystem: A Conceptual Explication and a Propositional Inventory," *International Studies Quarterly*, vol. 17, 1, 1973, pp. 89–117.
5. Among the few definitions of regionalism are those by Donald J. Puchala and Stuart I. Fanagan, and by Joseph Nye. See Puchala and Fanagan, "International Politics in the 1970s: The Search for a Perspective," *International Organization*, vol. 28, 1, 1974, p. 259; and Nye, *International Regionalism* (Boston: Little, Brown, 1968), p. vii.
6. On issues and issue areas, see Ernst B. Haas, "Why Collaborate? Issue-Linkage and International Regimes," *World Politics*, vol. 32, 3, 1980, pp. 364–7.
7. On "nesting" see Vinod Aggarwal, *Liberal Protectionism* (Berkeley: University of California Press, 1985), p. 27.

8. On negative and positive peace, and the debate among peace studies scholars, see Johan Galtung, "Violence, Peace, and Peace Research," *Journal of Peace Research*, vol. 6, 6, 1969; and Carolyn M. Stephenson, "The Evolution of Peace Studies," in Michael Klare and Daniel Thomas (eds.), *Peace and World Order Studies: A Curriculum Guide*, 5th edition (Boulder: Westview Press, 1989), pp. 9–19.

9. For a review of the debate, see Muthiah Alagappa, "Defining Security: A Critical Review and Appraisal of the Debate," in Muthiah Alagappa (ed.), *Asian Conceptions of Security: Ideational and Material* (forthcoming).

10. For elaboration of this definition, see Muthiah Alagappa, "Conceptualizing Security," in Muthiah Alagappa (ed.), *Asian Conceptions of Security: Ideational and Material*, forthcoming.

11. There is a growing body of literature that questions the effectiveness of the sovereign state and its continued relevance as the referent unit of security. It should be acknowledged here that the scope of state sovereignty in a number of issue areas, like human rights, monetary and financial matters, and production is becoming substantially limited; that non-state actors (subnational and international) have proliferated and in some cases play a central role in domestic and international regulation in the specific issue area of their concern; and that the state can protect as well as oppress its citizens. These developments, by no means uniform across states, should be given due consideration in analysis and policy-making, but they should not be interpreted as eclipsing the importance of the state. The sovereign state continues to be the most effective unit with respect to political identity and allegiance as well as to the fulfilment of the security and welfare functions, and it is the principal actor in the international system. The proliferation of secessionist movements, while reflective of the weakness of the constitution of specific states, is not indicative of the obsolescence of the state. On the contrary, it is a vindication of the state's continued vitality. The goal of the secessionist movements is to create new states in which the fit between ethno- or religious-nation and state will be closer and in which their ethnic or religious group will become the *Staatsvolk*, the dominant ethnic group which controls state power.

12. Kenneth N. Waltz, *Theory of International Politics* (New York: Random House, 1979), pp. 102–28.

13. Waltz, op. cit., pp. 91–2.

14. On the security dilemma, see John H. Herz, "Idealist Internationalism and the Security Dilemma," *World Politics*, vol. 2, 2, 1950, pp. 157–80; Robert Jervis, *Perception and Misperception in International Politics* (Princeton: Princeton University Press, 1976), pp. 72–6; and Barry Buzan, *People, States, and Fear: An Agenda for International Security Studies in the Post-Cold War Era* (Boulder: Lynne Rienner, 1991), chapter 8.

15. The two components of the security dilemma derive from Waltz's three-image analysis of world politics. He posits the third image (the structure) as describing the framework of world politics and as the permissive cause of war, and the first and second images (man and the state) as the forces of world politics, the immediate or efficient causes of war. See his *Man, the State, and War* (New York: Columbia University Press, 1959). Barry Buzan terms the two components as the power dilemma and the security dilemma, and their combination as the power-security dilemma. See his *People, States, and Fear: An Agenda for International Security Studies*, pp. 294–8.

16. Benedict Anderson, *Imagined Communities* (London: Verso, 1992), p. 6. See also Clifford Geertz, *The Interpretation of Cultures* (New York: Basic Books, 1973), pp. 317–19.

17. For a discussion of the formation of national-territorial states in the third world, see Anthony D. Smith, *State and the Nation in the Third World* (New York: St. Martin's Press, 1983), chapter 7.

18. The phrase "internal colonialism" is used by Michael Hechter in his *Internal Colo-*

nialism: The Celtic Fringe in British National Development (Berkeley: Transaction, 1975).

19. For an expanded discussion of the problem of political legitimacy, see Muthiah Alagappa (ed.), *Political Legitimacy in South-East Asia: The Quest for Moral Authority* (Stanford: Stanford University Press, 1995), chapters 1–3.

20. For the differences between conflict settlement and resolution, see C. R. Mitchell, *The Structure of International Conflict* (New York: St. Martin's Press, 1981), pp. 275–7.

21. This and the next section draw extensively on my article "Regionalism and Conflict Management" (see note 1).

22. On the security community, see Karl Deutsch, *Political Community and the North Atlantic Area* (Westport: Greenwood Press, 1957), pp. 5–7.

23. For a good discussion of collective security, see Claude, *Swords into Ploughshares*, pp. 245–85 (see note 2). For a summary of the theory of collective security, see Jerome Slater, *A Re-evaluation of Collective Security: The OAS in Action*, Mershon National Security Program Pamphlet Series No. 1 (Columbus, 1965), pp. 9–23.

24. On intermediation, the qualifications required, and the intervenor's repertory of practice, see Oran R. Young, *The Intermediaries* (Princeton: Princeton University Press, 1967), pp. 50–79.

25. For a good discussion of the evolution of the principle of non-intervention in the inter-American system, see G. Pope Atkins, *Latin America in the International Political System*, (Boulder: Westview Press, 1989), pp. 215–18.

26. See the collection of essays in Laura W. Reed and Carl Kayson (eds.), *Emerging Norms of Justified Intervention*, The Committee on International Security Studies, American Academy of Arts and Sciences (Cambridge, 1993).

27. On the growing force of the human rights regime in Latin America, see Sikkink, "Human Rights, Principled Issue-Networks, and Sovereignty in Latin America." On the weakness of the regime in Africa, see Claude E. Welch, "The OAU and Human Rights: Regional Promotion of Human Rights," in Yassin El-Ayouty (ed.), *The Organization of African Unity Thirty Years On* (Westport, 1994), pp. 53–76.

28. Richard J. Bloomfield, "Making the Western Hemisphere Safe for Democracy? The OAS Defense-of-Democracy Regime," *The Washington Quarterly*, vol. 17, 2, 1994, pp. 157–69.

29. Ibid., p. 162.

30. "ASEAN Joint Statement on the Situation in the Philippines," in *ASEAN Document Series 1967–1986*, issued by the ASEAN Secretariat in Jakarta (1986), p. 469.

31. Yassin El-Ayouty, "An OAU for the Future," in Yassin El-Ayouty (ed.), *The Organization of African Unity Thirty Years On*, p. 179.

32. According to R. K. Ramazani, "the overriding pre-GCC concern of Saudi Arabia with the security and stability of the House of Saud and other royal families" contributed to the creation of the GCC. See his *The Gulf Cooperation Council: Record and Analysis* (Charlottesville: University Press of Virginia, 1988), pp. 1–11.

33. For a similar discussion of a somewhat different list of factors, see Michael Barnett, "Partners in Peace? The UN, regional organizations, and peace-keeping," *Review of International Studies*, vol. 21, 4, pp: 420–4.

34. Jarat Chopra and Thomas G. Weiss, "The United Nations and the Former Second World: Coping with Conflicts," in Abram Chayes and Antonia Chayes (eds.), *Preventing Conflict in the Post-Communist World* (Washington, DC: The Brookings Institution, 1996), p. 529.

13

Regional arrangements, the United Nations, and security in Africa

Margaret A. Vogt

State of security regionalism

Collective security was first introduced in Africa in the early 1960s. Dr. Kwame Nkrumah, the first President of Ghana, conceived of the concept of an African High Command, a concept of collective defence, which Nkrumah proposed as an extension of his concept of an African Union Government. The African High Command was viewed as a military high command jointly operated by the newly independent African states, and consisting of air, land, and naval elements. Ghana recruited a corps of young Ghanian military officers to serve in this regional assignment.

Nkrumah and the members of the Casablanca Group (a group of socialist-leaning African states) were influenced by their fear of opposition to the independence of the new African states. They argued that the colonial powers, when they failed to adjust to the new economic dispensation of operating without their former possessions, might attempt to recolonize Africa or prevent any further moves to independence by those countries which had not yet attained their independence.[1] Nkrumah's argument appeared to be further supported by the events in the former Belgian Congo. Belgium sent its troops to the country without the authority of the Congolese government, purportedly to protect her nationals and other Europeans against the mutinous Congolese troops, who had carried out a rampage in Kinshasa.

The United Nations deployed a peace-keeping force in the Congo to protect the civilian population and facilitate the withdrawal of Belgian troops. The Congolese situation was further complicated by a constitutional crisis in the country which degenerated into the arrest and murder of the Prime Minister, Patrice Lumumba, even when UN forces were stationed in the Congo. The lessons of the Congo led Nkrumah and his associates to conclude that the danger of recolonization was real and that African security was best managed by African themselves.

Other African states, especially the 19 other independent African countries, including Liberia, Côte d'Ivoire, Sierra Leone, and Ethiopia, members of the Monrovia School, argued that threats to African security were most unlikely to come from extra-African sources, but from within Africa, especially over the definition of colonial boundaries.

The division between the Monrovia and the Casablanca groups of states almost prevented the consensus necessary for the formation of the OAU. A third grouping of states facilitated negotiations between the two ideological blocs, making the formation of the OAU possible. The consensus for the establishment of the regional organization was based on certain fundamental principles:[2] participation was to be based on a strict respect for and adherence to the sovereign equality of states; all states were to have equal representation in all organs, irrespective of their territorial size or their population; decisions were to be arrived at by consensus – the rule of consensus did not negate the expression of opposing views; but once agreed to, decisions were to be considered as binding even on those states which opposed the idea. It was only when a consensus decision was possible that the organization would act. Furthermore, the colonially defined boundaries were to be considered as sacrosanct. Although members recognized that the international frontiers of African states had been defined by the colonial rulers, the founding fathers of the OAU predicted that more problems and friction would be caused if member states were allowed to readjust their international boundaries. However, the founding fathers of the OAU did recognize that international boundary questions were a potentially divisive problem.

They therefore introduced into the OAU Charter the concept of a Commission on Mediation, Arbitration, and Reconciliation. This legal instrument was designed to be employed in the adjudication of disputes between states. Member states were to agree mutually and voluntarily to submit their conflicts for adjudication to the Commission. Since its formation, however, the Commission has never been presented with a case for adjudication; members prefer to submit their disputes to the jurisdiction of the International Court of Justice. One of the most important provisions of the OAU Charter, and one that provided the consensus which made the formation of the organization possible, is that which prevents the interference of external actors in the internal affairs of states.[3] Some analysts have argued that the concept of non-intervention was designed to prevent the exploitation by extraregional states of their military power and political influence to affect or undermine the security or political and economic development of African states. They argue that the concept of non-interference was not meant by the founding fathers to inhibit activities undertaken by fellow African states to resolve problems within the national boundaries of member states. Analysis of interventions in Africa's internal conflicts would show that in the post-independence period there have been more extra-African military interventions in African conflicts than interventions fully conducted and financed by African states.[4]

The Organization of African Unity that was established in May 1963 was a political grouping. It did not have the appropriate machinery for managing the security requirements of its members, and nor did it evolve a security agenda.[5] The Commission on Arbitration, Reconciliation, and Mediation was considered adequate to deal with the disputes over the definition of boundaries which were expected to dominate the African security landscape in the period after independence. There were disputes on border definition in the period following the independence of most African states, for example, between Ethiopia and Somalia, Somalia and Kenya, and Libya and Chad. However, it was the eruption of conflicts within states that posed the greatest challenge to the management capacity of the regional organization. The Congo crisis was the first in a line of crises that included a mutiny by the police force of the former Tanganyika. This necessitated the deployment of a multinational African police force in 1964, at the invitation of the government of then Tanganyika, to help contain that conflict.[6]

The civil war in Nigeria which started in 1966 was perhaps the most extensive of the internal security crises that confronted the post-colonial states of the continent. The concept of non-intervention was extensively debated with regards to the Nigerian crisis, which threatened the very survival of Africa's most populous country. While some African states, led principally by the then Tanzania and Côte d'Ivoire, granted recognition to Biafra in defiance of the general consensus on non-interference and support for Nigeria's territorial integrity, many African countries supported the Nigerian government in its campaign against the internalization of both the discussion and the management of the Nigerian civil war. Several other internal conflicts in various countries resulted in the deployment of foreign forces. Between 1976 and 1978, the French deployed troops into the then Zaire on two occasions to quell secession attempts in Shaba province. Civil war in Chad, stemming from a rebellion in the north of Chad which had continued through most of the colonial period, escalated radically following the overthrow of Tomabalbaye's government in 1977. The war in Chad resulted in the deployment of French forces to Chad in 1969, and later in 1979 and 1983.[7] From November 1981 to June 1982, a larger deployment of a multinational African force was sent to Chad, operating under an OAU mandate, and following the deployment of Libyan forces. This was proposed to the interim government of Chad (GUNT) as an alternative security arrangement to fill the vacuum that the withdrawal of the Libyan forces from Chad was expected to create. Confronted with a serious armed insurrection mounted by the former Minister of Defence, Hissen Habre, GUNT, under Goukoni Waddeyi, was persuaded to demand that Libya should withdraw its troops from Chad in exchange for the deployment of OAU peace-keeping troops.

The OAU, following earlier precedents, especially those set by the Nigerian civil war, avoided an extensive involvement in the internal security of its members, with the exception of Chad. The OAU intervention in Chad was an abysmal failure. The African multinational force was unable to deploy quickly and effectively to prevent an escalation of the crisis, which resulted in the overrunning of the country by Hissen Habre's forces, and the African peace-keeping force had to be withdrawn quickly.[8] There was confusion over the interpretation of the force's mandate and the purpose of its deployment.[9] The OAU's role in regional security management in the period following African independence remained largely political. Even with the eruption of wars of liberation against colonial rule in the former Rhodesia following the Unilateral Declaration of Independence, in the former Portuguese colonies, and against apartheid in South Africa, the OAU's response was limited to establishing the Liberate Committee which was to mobilize African and international political and financial support for the wars of liberation in Africa.

In the immediate post-independence phase the security issues which confronted the African continent were managed at different levels. Internal conflicts in some countries in the region were largely managed nationally, and the governments of the countries in crisis defined the parameters through which those crises were to be managed. In many cases, African states invested in the development of their military and other security forces. Often these were structured to respond more to internal crisis than to external threats. Internal crises in many countries in the region were dealt with largely by using national security resources, supplemented in some cases by the deployment of the military forces of some of the former colonial powers. There was often no distinction made between the nature and level of forces used for internal as opposed to external threat. The French have conducted the most numerous and extensive deployments of military forces in internal crises in many of their former colonies in Africa. France is the only colonial power with a provision in its national security structure and its concept of operation for the deployment of intervention forces to conflict situations in its former colonies, the Force d'Action Rapide. Most of the former colonies of France signed agreements which allowed the French government to provide support for the defence establishments of these countries.[10]

The post-Cold War period

The three decades after the independence of most African countries in the 1950s were characterized largely by disputes over the definition of the international boundaries of many African states. The most extensive of these boundary conflicts included the wars by Somalia against Ethiopia over the Ogadan and against Kenya in the northern region of Kenya. Siad Barre nursed the dream of a greater Somalia and the unification of settlements of Somali people in the Ogadan and northern Kenya; Togo and Ghana fought over the status of the UN trust territory in Togo; while Mali and Burkina Faso, Nigeria and Cameroon, and Uganda and the then Tanzania, to mention only some, had serious disputes over the definition of their international boundaries. As members preferred to take their disputes to the International Court of Justice than to the OAU's Commission on Mediation, Reconciliation, and Arbitration, the OAU had to plead that its members should give a first choice to home-grown African mediation before going to the international court. The organization adopted the use of ad hoc commissions of two or more heads of state to mediate these conflicts. Through the use of these ad hoc methods, the OAU was able to extract a concession from the states in dispute to allow the OAU the first attempt at mediation.

Internal conflicts in Africa

The African region exploded into conflicts following the collapse of the Soviet empire in 1990 and the ending of the Cold War. The assumed political stability of the African region and its post-colonial political systems came unravelled. This was a very dramatic change from the three decades following the independence of most African states in the early 1960s when, as discussed earlier, most conflicts in the region, with a few exceptions, were largely disputes over the definition of international boundaries. The colonial boundaries created by the European powers were often described as artificial, dividing families, tribes, and political systems that had been constructed following long periods of settlement, wars, and political negotiations. This is not to say that these empires and homelands were politically stable: a good number of them were in a constant state of inter-tribal war fighting over a wide range of issues, such as territory, strategic resources, water, or political succession. The successful imposition of new political systems in many parts of Africa by the colonial powers was made possible partly by the manipulation of the differences among African peoples, and also by the defeat of the Africans in colonial wars. Colonialism changed the social, political, and economic structures of Africa, introducing new systems and patterns of relationships. For almost a century of colonial rule, the Africans were regrouped under leadership systems which in most cases changed the role of the traditional political leadership and the patterns of relationship prior to colonialism.

More than half a century of colonial rule was dominated by the struggle of the colonial authorities to impose new political and economic systems on new groupings of people. At the time of independence in most parts of Africa, the imposition of colonial authority was still confronting challenges. The traditional political relationships were continued across colonial political boundaries, so that the region had two levels of political and economic systems: the one created by the Europeans and managed to meet their own political, economic, and security needs; and the political and economic relations amoung indigenous Africans. The period immediately following the independence of most states in Africa was characterized by the continuation of the colonial systems under African leadership. Authoritarian regimes were established in many countries in Africa, often with the endorsement and sometimes active military support of the former colonial powers. The argument proffered was that the West needed to promote regimes that would protect their security interest and prevent the expansion of communism in Africa.

When the Cold War ended, the former colonial powers became disinterested in continuing their support for authoritarian regimes. For the first time, the concept of "collapsed" or "failed" states was introduced into African political discussions. Central political authority came under tremendous challenge, and in some cases – such as in Ethiopia, Uganda, Somalia, Liberia, and Rwanda – armed opposition resulted in the collapse of central authority in those countries. In Somalia and Liberia, the reconstruction of the collapsed state system remains a problem. Apart from the crisis in countries which have experienced state collapse, most African countries have experienced some crises of governance in recent years, as the old assumptions made about who should exercise political control and the structure of power have come under question by groups within the system. In many cases the problems of governance went beyond the issue of political control, as many vital facilities of governance could not be provided in the hinterland, restricting central authority and public facilities only to the capital and some urban centres. In some of these instances, armed opposition spread in large parts of the country.

This was the case in Sierra Leone, where the Revolutionary United Front (RUF) led by Fode Sankho conducted an extensive guerrilla war which effectively undermined the country's security, forcing almost three-quarters of the rural population to migrate from their homes abroad and to the capital as internally displaced people. This was the situation until elections were held, which brought in a democratically elected government and fostered the commencement of dialogue with the rebels. In Mali, the Tuareg rebellion totally handicapped activities in many parts of the country until internationally supported negotiation and disarmament of the Tuaregs was commenced. The former Zaire provides another example of a state in a situation of collapse, in which central authority was narrowly restricted to the capital and largely sustained by a loyal armed force. Regional authorities assumed the overall economic and political control of the country from President Mobutu, who upon return from his convalescence in Europe appeared to lack the capacity to reassert a strong central authority. The various opposition parties appeared unable to agree on the formation of a central government.

More African countries are undergoing various forms of constitutional crises and institutional challenge, with a high possibility of collapse if these challenges are not properly managed. Nigeria and Algeria belong in this category. Care should be taken, however, not to interpret every sign of crisis and problem, even when they are widespread, as indicators of state collapse. Many states in all parts of the world are undergoing one form of mutation or another. This is not only true in the states of the former Soviet Union, including the Russian Federation itself, and countries like Viet Nam, El Salvador, and Cambodia which have witnessed long periods of civil war (in the case of Cambodia, some may argue that the state is still confronted by the serious danger of collapse[11]), but also in some mature democracies, where government has not been able to meet the aspirations of the people. This may describe the political crises which Italy and France have both confronted. In other words, the concept of "failure" or "collapse" is a relative one, and although all countries confront different levels of crisis, some have developed enduring institutions to manage such crises and some have not. These crisis-management institutions often include a well-oiled democratic process and a vibrant civil society which not only acts as a watchdog of government, but as an effective partner in the running of the democratic process.

The role of the OAU in internal conflicts

The concept of a security agenda for the OAU was first presented officially at the organization's Dakar summit in 1992, when the OAU Secretary-General suggested that the time was ripe for the introduction of an institutional frame within the organization for the management of conflicts in Africa. Ambassador Salim argued that the ad hoc approach used up until then was no longer viable. While the general principle of an expanded role for the OAU in regional and markedly internal conflicts was accepted, especially following the ECOWAS precedent in Liberia and the United Nations mission in Somalia, the impact which this would have on the sovereign authority of states over their domestic affairs still coloured the discussion.

The evolution of regional security regimes in Africa

The deterioration of security in Africa, especially the rise in the number and extent of internal conflicts, led to a reopening of the debate over the need for and modality of an OAU security agenda. The first major discussions on the issue of a role for the OAU and other regional organizations in internal conflicts were held in 1992 (an IPA seminar in Arusha on internal conflicts in Africa, and the Kampala discussions by the African Leadership Forum). At the IPA (International Peace Academy) seminar, the issue of internal conflicts was placed on the African agenda for the first time in an open forum. Participants concluded that, in spite of the non-intervention law, the OAU would be reneging in its responsibility if it failed to address the issue of the proliferating internal wars in Africa.

The next summit finally adopted the OAU Mechanism for Conflict Prevention, Management, and Resolution in 1993. The OAU mechanism provided for:

- a central decision-making body, the Central Organ, consisting of about 16 member states (the current chair, the past chair, and the incoming chair of the organization, and selected states representing the sub-regions of Africa), which meets at three levels: heads of state, ministerial, and ambassadorial;
- the Division of Conflict Management within the Secretariat, the implementing and secretarial agency of the mechanism.

The concept of the OAU mechanism is to provide the appropriate political leadership to the Secretary-General on an ongoing basis for the management of conflicts in the region; to provide the OAU with the appropriate tools to lead in organizing responses to the security challenges in Africa; and to mobilize resources, both from within Africa and from the international system, behind the objective of effective conflict management in the region.

Since the adoption of the mechanism, discussions on the direction of operationalizing the OAU peace-making instrument have centred on the development of the OAU's capacity to expand its role in the areas of conflict prevention, conflict mediation, peace operations, and military observers.

Conflict prevention

Conflict prevention involves the expansion of the organization's ability to predict potential conflicts, using a wide range of early-warning systems. In this regard, it is expected that partnership with the United Nations will expand the ability of the regional organization to tap into the extensive information resources available within the UN system. Partnership with a wide range of African institutions will also provide the OAU with points of entry into many African states, both for information collation and for the implementation of preventive measures. It is also expected that an increased relationship between the OAU and different levels of non-state actors and institutions would expand the scope of the organization.

The challenge facing the OAU in its efforts to establish an early-warning capability is the same as that faced by all international organizations: the fact that knowledge of impending conflicts does not always translate into the political will to act. The decision to intervene is more often based on the political calculation of states of where their interest lies. A more contemporary situation was the crisis in the former Zaire, where central authority had practically disappeared and civil war threatened to destroy the remaining thin threads of national cohesion, but the international community could not readily extract the consent of the government to undertake preventive deployment, even of a political mission.

Conflict mediation

Conflict mediation involves developing and expanding the OAU's capacity to perfect its act in an area where many believe the organization has been reasonably successful. Examples of previous activities include:

- the dispatch of OAU special envoys, and special representatives of the Secretary-General;
- the establishment of ad hoc commissions of heads of states on specific conflict situations (the summit vests the coordination of its intervention in specific conflicts in a group of heads of states who act on behalf of the whole and report accordingly). An ad hoc commission of Mozambique's neighbours contributed in applying pressure on the two

factions during the Mozambican peace talks and at implementation stages to ensure that they remained committed to the objectives of peace. In Somalia, Ethiopia was given the responsibility of coordinating the OAU facilitation, although some Somali factions perceived Ethiopia as an interested party.

The OAU has expanded the concept of political mediation to allow for the continuing role of its special envoys over an extended period so that they would have the opportunity to shepherd the process, hopefully to a logical and successful conclusion. Professor Canaan Banana has been the OAU special envoy to Liberia since 1992, while Ambassador Mohammed Sahnoun was recently appointed the special envoy of both the OAU and the UN Secretaries-General to the Great Lakes. Ambassador Bassole of Burkina Faso is the current OAU special envoy to Burundi, while a political office of the OAU was established in Western Sahara before being closed in December 1996. The next step is for the organization to develop the institutional and technical capacities to manage field missions.

Peace operations

Peace operations involve civilian political missions consisting of OAU political officers providing technical management and advisory support to peace negotiation teams and for the implementation of political decisions. Working with the special envoys, such political missions have monitored and facilitated peace constitutional talks in some countries, for example Congo (Brazzaville) and Sierra Leone. They have provided political support, observed electoral processes, and facilitated discussions between some governments and the opposition, again recently in Sierra Leone, where the OAU remained engaged in the negotiations between the rebel group and the government.

Military observers

The OAU has deployed military observer missions to Rwanda and Burundi. While these have had mixed results, the thinking is that the OAU has a comparative advantage in effectively preventing the escalation of conflicts through the use of its observers, subject to adequate funding, management, and organization. It has been argued that the presence of the OAU observers in Rwanda delayed the collapse of general security in that country, and that the transfer of the mission to UN responsibility and command, and the subsequent decision by the United Nations to pull the observers out at a critical phase of the crisis, contributed to the massacre that occurred in 1994. After the United Nations decided to withdraw from Rwanda, it was only the African component of the UN team that remained. In Burundi the OAU observer force, though very small and with limited reach, has remained in the country despite the imposition of sanctions and the withdrawal of other international organizations and governments.

To increase its ability to deploy observers more quickly into situations of conflict, the OAU has evolved plans to establish a standby arrangement through which identified units of the armed forces of its member states can be called upon for service in the shortest possible time, and with logistical stores to deploy a 100-man observer mission into a conflict situation within days.

The expansion of the OAU's activities to countries experiencing internal conflicts represents a radical departure from the original philosophy of the OAU Charter, which prohibits interference in the internal affairs of states. Some analysts have argued that the interpretation of interference as conceived by the founding fathers of the OAU refered to interventions organized and staged at the instigation of countries from outside the African continent, and was not meant to inhibit the responsibility of Africans to be "their brother's keepers." However, the history of the failure of the OAU to intervene in several situations of internal conflict, such as the Nigerian civil war, probably belies this redefinition of the concept of interference. Others have argued, as mentioned earlier, that the concepts of interference and intervention should be separated. Interference refers to interventions occurring without the consent of the governments affected, while intervention occurs when the regional organization makes a deliberate move, perhaps at the invitation of the affected state, but definitely with its blessing, to help resolved serious internal crises which may jeopardize the general security of the state.

Complementarity of roles

When it becomes necessary to mount an intervention into a conflict situation, either as a preventive measure or for peace-keeping or peace-making, at what level should such an intervention occur? Should all responsibilities for international peace and security remain the province of international organizations – particularly the United Nations, since that body already has the capacity and the framework to take such initiatives? Is there a role for a regional organization in the management of disputes occurring within the region? The question of the comparative advantage of the OAU in mounting peace-keeping missions in Africa, as opposed to the United Nations or subregional organizations, has been discussed, especially within the context of a joint task force. The OAU Secretary-General and the International Peace Academy have worked to help the OAU evolve ideas on the most appropriate way to make the OAU declaration on its mechanism applicable to the establishment of such a task force.

One school of thought in Africa argues that the OAU lacks the institutional structure, managerial capacity, and resource outlay to manage a peace-keeping operation properly. As a result it is argued that the United Nations should be left with that task, since it has the comparative advantage in this regard. Furthermore, as the concept of multi-functional peace operations has been expanded, sometimes necessitating the modification of mandates mid-operation and the use of enforcement action, it has been argued that the role of the OAU should be limited to the preparation of African forces for UN operations and to support UN efforts. Another school of thought argues that the experience of the Somali operation has reduced the political will of many Western Europeans and Americans in particular to deploy their ground forces in peace operations in Africa, especially under a UN command. More and more, Africa is being required to provide the manpower for UN peace operations, in an arrangement in which the logistical, technical, transport, and other support facilities will be provided by Western European and American states, perhaps through the United Nations and even possibly directly in a bilateral arrangement with the OAU.[12]

An understanding of the concept of comparative advantage in the management of conflicts is important in a region where several actors are increasingly becoming involved in the same conflict. Before the end of the Cold War, the options in the division of labour between the United Nations, regional organizations, and subregional organizations were clearly understood: the United Nations would mount military peace operations and deploy political missions, while the regional organizations concentrated on preventive political and diplomatic measures. In the post-Cold War era, with the proliferation of internal conflicts and the increasing intensity of conflicts, this division is no longer so clear.

For example, for reasons discussed earlier the OAU had limited its role to the facilitation of political mediation and reconciliation, and did not develop its security instruments. The attempt by the major powers to promote an OAU intervention in Chad failed, as had previous interventions by Nigerian forces in the past. The OAU mounted the peace-keeping force, even though it lacked the policy framework, technical support, and financial capability to manage a peace operation. The OAU peace-keeping force consisted of troops drawn largely from the states contiguous to Chad. Nigeria supplied the bulk of the troops and the force commander, and underwrote the cost of the operation, while France and the United States financed the participation of the Senegalese forces and those from the then Zaire. The OAU could not provide the communication and technical support for the force, as a result of which the troops could not be deployed in good time; and after deployment, they could not communicate with Addis Ababa on policy issues. There was also a confusion over the interpretation of the mandate, and the force commander failed to receive clear instructions from Addis Ababa until the OAU force was overrun by the rebel force and forced to withdraw.

The lessons of the Chadian intervention by the regional organization suggest that the use of states which are contiguous to the theatre of conflict compromises the perception of the force as impartial, as some parties accused troops from contributing states of sympathies towards some of the factions. Hissen Habre accused Nigeria of sympathies towards the provisional government of national unity (the GUNT), which was headed by Goukouni Waddeyi. On the other hand, the latter accused the OAU of reneging on its promise that the OAU force would provide the GUNT with security against the rebel group in exchange for the withdrawal of Libyan forces.

A similar deployment of OAU observers to Rwanda in the early 1990s utilizing troops from states contiguous to the country ran into similar problems, with some of the contiguous states supporting one or other of the factions. For example, the Rwandan Patriotic Front started its operations from Uganda. Kagame, the military commander of the Tutsi force, had served as the chief intelligence officer in Musuveni's army, while the then Zaire was accused of supporting the Hutus. The second OAU observer force was reconstituted with troops from other subregions, but was eventually withdrawn when the OAU could not finance the operation nor provide it with the requisite technical support. The Rwandan observer mission was then handed over to the United Nations, as discussed earlier.

Similar accusations of partiality by the troop-contributing states of ECOMOG (Economic Community Monitoring Group) did not result in the withdrawal of ECOMOG from Liberia. Attempts by ECOWAS to convince other states in the subregion to contribute troops, especially the francophone countries, have not succeeded in diluting the dominance by Nigerian troops; about 75 per cent of the 8,000-strong ECOMOG force is Nigerian, while Ghana provides the next largest number of troops. The United States financed Senegalese participation in ECOMOG in 1992, but Senegal quickly withdrew its forces when nine of its men were attacked and massacred by an NPFL (National Patriotic Front of Liberia) force. The deployment of troops from the then Tanzania and Uganda, financed by the United Nations, to increase the confidence of the Liberian factions in the impartiality of the force was attempted with the "expanded ECOMOG" in 1993. This still failed to prevent attacks on the peacekeepers by the various factions. The East African troops were withdrawn when their countries calculated that the mission exposed their troops to too much danger. As a follow-up to the implementation of the Liberian Peace Plan, based on the Abuja II Accord, some francophone countries (principally Cote d'Ivoire and Burkina Faso) have deployed technical support and medical contingents to Liberia.

The experiences of the United Nations in Somalia have affected the UN's approach to the division of labour with regional organizations in the management of international security. The complications which resulted from UNITAF's attempt to operate an enforcement mandate in Somalia, especially the failure to disarm the Somali militias forcefully, lead to the deaths of 18 American and 25 Pakistani soldiers in Somalia in 1993. This made the United Nations wary of operating multidimensional peace missions, especially when the organization has to enforce its mandate. UNITAF (the United Nations International Task Force in Somalia) was deployed by the United States and some of the Western European powers to assist the UN observer force that was unable to force its way through Somali militia factions to provide humanitarian support to people who were trapped behind fictional lines. Civil war erupted in Somalia following the collapse of the interim government established by the clan representatives after the defeat of the Said Barre regime and the routing of the Somali national army. The disappearance of central authority, as different factions asserted control over parts of the country, resulted in the collapse of the state system and the destruction of all national institutions.

This fear of entrapment in a complex civil war, similar to the experience in Somalia, inhibited the Security Council from authorizing an expansion of the UN presence in Rwanda in June 1994 when the conflict escalated beyond the control of the small UN intervention force. The Security Council ordered the UN force out of Rwanda when all information indicated that a serious security breakdown was imminent.

The United Nations then approached the OAU in 1994 to mobilize African peacekeepers for deployment to Rwanda. After protesting about the unacceptability of attempts to tribalize international peace-keeping, the OAU Secretary-General was able to get the immediate commitment of African countries to deploy 6,000 troops to Rwanda. However, their deployment was delayed for almost five months due to the lack of basic logistical and personal equipment required for the mission.

The Rwanda incident was perhaps the strongest indicator of the reluctance of European powers to commit forces to African theatres of conflict, although it is true that the United States in particular has resisted the deployment of US ground forces to Bosnia and Herzegovina, especially refusing to operate under UN command. The importance of the role of regional organizations in the management of international security, as provided for in Chapter VIII of the UN Charter, has become an important component in the thinking and planning for international security management. The UN Secretary-General argues for a complementarity in the roles of the United Nations and the regional organizations in conflict management. Such complementarity is reflected not only in the extensive consultation with regional actors on issues affecting their regions, but more recently in encouraging regional organizations to be more involved in the selection, preparation, and training of regional forces for UN operations. A critical aspect of the mission-planning functions of the Department of Peace-Keeping Operations and the Department of Political Affairs is the the support of regional organizations in the training and supply of their troops for peace operations. The strongest indication of this push for coordinated action in conflict situations was given recently by the appointment of Ambassador Mohammed Sahnoun as representative of both the OAU and the United Nations to the Great Lakes. Increasingly, the United Nations has conceded the lead in the political mediation of conflicts and in peace operations, especially in internal conflicts, to the regions. In the Great Lakes region, for example, the countries immediately contiguous to Burundi have served as the focal point for the negotiations and initiation of action to manage the conflict in that country. The ECOWAS states continued to take the lead in Liberia, with the United Nations coordinating international relief and the implementation of the disarmament and demobilization plan provided for in the peace accord.

The OAU has been engaged in laying the ground rules for its role in regional security management. The first-ever meeting of the chiefs of staff of African states took place in Addis Ababa in June 1996 to discuss common strategies for managing the security problems of Africa. This body concluded that the first stages in the development of African capacity should be in the standardization of training programmes, logistics, and communication resources for peace-keeping, development of a regional concept of operations, and the integration of planning at the level of the OAU. However, it is becoming evident that to be fully effective, major restructuring would be required at the OAU Secretariat. The current emphasis placed on the development of an early-warning capacity would remain fundamentally flawed if the system cannot quickly prevent the escalation of crises on the continent nor provide a clear road map towards their solution.

The OAU has still not overcome the contradictions that attended its formation. It is still difficult for the organization to gain an effective entry point into conflicts, even where these show the potential for affecting regional security. One example was the debate on a proposal by the United Nations for advance preparations for a rapid reaction force, with capability for enforcement action, to be deployed to Burundi if the crisis there were to deteriorate further. The Burundi government was opposed to the idea, and was able to prevent the OAU from arriving at a clear consensus in support of it. Eventually, Burundi's neighbours threatened to intervene forcefully to restore order if the slide towards decline were to continue, and mobilized international support in favour of a military and economic embargo of Burundi. Though the OAU has a special envoy of the Secretary-General in Burundi, the organization has not been able to expand its impact beyond playing a moderately restraining role, as discussed above, because it lacks the technical capability and the appropriate institutional back-up within the Secretariat to support the mission.

The OAU has not been able to mobilize the resources necessary to play a role larger than that of a supportive bystander in many of these conflicts. In Sierra Leone, the OAU dispatched its political experts to seek a platform for negotiation between the military government and the rebels. Yet the OAU initiative is hardly ever mentioned, because the organization lacks the resources to bring pressure on the belligerents. The involvement of the United States, Britain, the Commonwealth, and the United Nations received greater prominence because of the influence they wield on the parties to the conflict. However, the OAU has the advantage in its ability to retain the confidence of all the parties. Part of the problem may lie in the fact that the organization operates with great sensitivity to the particular government it is involved with, working strictly with official approval and careful not to be perceived as interfering in the internal affairs of the state in crisis.

The comparative advantage in the lead role which regional organizations can play in the negotiation of conflicts affecting their region is usually ascribed to the closeness of those organizations to the area of crisis, and the familiarity of the regional actors with the complexities and nuances of the conflict situations, including knowledge of the parties in conflict and the ability of the negotiators to exploit local cultural traditions which can help create the environment for parties to remain engaged in the negotiating process. The absence of an OAU input in the management of the crisis in Somalia was said to have undermined the UN efforts to achieve an understanding of the cultural complexities of the conflict, leading the United Nations to make false assumptions about what was required to manage the crisis.

The role of subregional organizations

However, it is not always the case that regional organizations have the comparative advantage. Where the incumbents are powerful, with independent resources to prosecute the conflict, relatively limited dependency on external support, and the ability to manage their international public relations, both international and regional organizations can have only limited impact on their positions. This was the case with the parties to the Angolan civil war which were accused of stalling the peace process by delaying the quartering of their forces. The United Nations and regional organizations can appeal for cooperation, but they have relatively limited effective weapons to use as pressure. In Mozambique, on the other hand, war fatigue among the people and the soldiers, the denial of assured support to RENAMO (Resistencia Nacional Mocambicana) from South Africa following the demise of the apartheid regime, coupled with pressure from their neighbours and incentives given by the international donor community, were sufficient to ensure that the two Mozambican factions remained engaged in the pursuit of peace until the demobilization of the fighting forces was completed and elections held.

Many of the conflicts in Africa have raised the possibility of enforcement action. Chapter 8 of the UN Charter, Article 52, vests the responsibility for the use of enforcement action in the United Nations, allowing regional organizations to act only with the permission of the United Nations. However, as a result of the problems caused by the use of enforcement action in Somalia and the former Yugoslavia, many have argued that the United Nations is not poised to conduct credible enforcement action. This is said to be partly because of its mode of operation. The United Nations does not have an integrated military command structure – urgent decisions on key issues relating to mandates, and by extension the concepts of operation, have to be discussed by the Security Council, whose decisions are based purely on the political perspectives of its members and their national interests. Secondly, the United Nations has no independent military resources, no large security force that can be used for deployment to theatres of conflict with flexibility and speed. It also does not have the necessary resources to use as back-up when such conflicts escalate. The United Nations has to depend on what its member states agree to make available, and this varies according to each conflict, as the contributing states have to approve the missions and the functions for which their forces are employed.

Proposals for providing the United Nations with rapid-reaction capability have been stalled by some Security Council members on the grounds that such a capability would be expensive for the international organization to sustain, and for reasons similar to those discussed above. This is apart from the political arguments about the impact of the use of UN forces for enforcement on the perception of the partiality of the United Nations in the eyes of the incumbents, as well as the confusion which may be caused in the minds of the people. The distinction between forces for peace-keeping and those for enforcement may become blurred. The concept of the United Nations prosecuting an assertive defence appears to some people to negate its role as an organization for the pacific settlement of disputes. For example, during the period in which ECOMOG instituted enforcement action in Liberia, the Nigerian Air Force was extensively employed in aggressive air operations to cut the supply lines of the factions and many civilian casualties resulted.

While complications akin to those experienced by the United Nations in operating enforcement action are likely to attend similar attempts by the OAU, the regional organization is presently even worse structured than the United Nations to handle peace operations. The political difficulties of establishing a framework for effective command and control may equally be a problem, especially given the tradition in the OAU that decisions are arrived at by consensus. However, the same sensitivity did not inhibit ECOWAS from mounting peace operations in Liberia and conducting enforcement action. ECOWAS's role was, however, facilitated by the hegemonic roles of some states, especially Nigeria and Ghana. The two countries provided the bulk of the initial force that went into Liberia. Nigeria in particular provided about 80 per cent of the force when ECOMOG's strength was increased to 12,000 during "Operation Octopus" in October 1992 before it was again decreased in 1993.

The sizes of the Nigerian and Ghanaian contingents were partially informed by the reluctance of some members of the Committee of Nine, principally Cote D'Ivoire, Burkina Faso, and Togo, to contribute troops to ECOMOG. However, there is an added problem of capacity among the regional states. Many of the states of West Africa have relatively small armies with the stronger emphasis in their security doctrine on internal security concerns. Since many have serious internal problems, they probably could not spare the men and the resources to deploy forces to Liberia. For example, in Togo governance was paralyzed for over a year from 1993 to 1994 due to political crisis. Opposition groups were demanding change to a democratic political process. Mali had a crisis with the rebellion by its Tuareg population, while Benin in 1991–1992 was just recovering from a serious constitutional crisis and the push for the institution of multi-party democracy. The West African countries have had the added complication of having to finance their participation in the Liberian operation.

Unlike UN peace-keeping, where the United Nations reimburses participants for their contribution to UN operations, ECOWAS did not have the resources to fund peace operations, and the Peace Fund for Liberia launched by the United Nations did not attract contributions adequate to meet the needs of that operation. Given the problem of human and material resources, only Nigeria and Ghana were in a position to provide the necessary resources for the Liberian operation. ECOMOG was more strongly perceived as a Nigerian operation when the overall command of the force came under a Nigerian commander, while the concept of operations for the force was largely directed from the Nigerian capital until the Committee of Nine and the chiefs of staff of the ECOMOG force-contributing states started to meet regularly from 1995. The lessons of Liberia suggest that it is at the level of the subregion that more assertive peace operations can be more easily initiated and successfully sustained in situations pertaining to the internal security of states. Only states which are directly affected by the impact of crises in their neighbourhood would be willing to invest the resources and maintain the staying power required for seeing the operation through.

The proliferation of internal conflicts, and the decision of the ECOWAS countries to send a multilateral subregional force to Liberia, established several precedents for the way the international system would view the role of the regional states in internal conflict situations. Indeed, the Liberian civil war suggested several new principles.

- Firstly, ECOWAS was established purely to facilitate economic integration and the economic development of the region. It is true that it had adopted a protocol on defence in 1976, but this economic grouping of states deployed a regional force into a civil war situation, thus blurring the edges in the definition of the organization as an economic organ and the group as a military instrument. ECOWAS argues that the expansion of its mandate to security questions represented a natural logic, in that security was a vital component of development; because the Liberian conflict had the potential for undermining the security of the entire region, as its impact on the security of Sierra Leone was to epitomize, and because it affected the lives of all the people of the region, the onus lay on ECOWAS to prevent the domino effect of the crisis in Liberia from destabilizing the entire region and to create a conducive atmosphere for economic development. The implication of the use of ECOWAS is that any organized grouping that is available within the region can be used to pursue a security agenda, and security responsibilities can be added to its schedule. The Intergovernmental Organization for Drought and Desertification recently decided to develop a security mechanism.
- Secondly, the concept of multilateral intervention in support of humanitarian action was also applied directly for the first time in relation to the use of the concept of peace-keeping. The ECOWAS states argued that their initiative in Liberia, and the attendant change of the ECOMOG mandate and concept of operations from peace-keeping to peace enforcement, was influenced by the need to respond to the humanitarian disaster in Liberia, the massacre of over 150,000 people,

and the complete collapse of law and order in that country as the government ceased to exist. The intervention of the subregional organization would and did, they argued, facilitate the dispensation of humanitarian assistance that was stymied by the state of anarchy. The same principle was to be applied by the United Nations in Somalia and the former Yugoslavia a few years down the line. The philosophy of international or regional intervention for humanitarian considerations also currently informs the involvement of the states of the Great Lakes in the crisis in Burundi, and the preparation by the United Nations and some Security Council members for an expanded capacity for rapid reaction to international crises.

- The ECOWAS states redefined the concept of non-intervention. Firstly, they argued that in a situation of anarchy where government had ceased to function, there was no longer sovereignty to protect. Secondly, the dimension of the killings relegated all sensitivity to the issue of sovereignty to second place: the primary objective was to stop the carnage. In Rwanda in 1994, when over 500,000 people were massacred within a matter of days, the members of the UN Security Council refused to describe the event as genocide because doing so would have created the compulsion to deploy an intervention force to stop the carnage.

- The Liberian operation also represents the first experience in which the United Nations participated in an operation in conjunction with the mandates of the subregional and regional organizations. At the initial deployment of ECOMOG in 1990, the UN's position on international intervention in Liberia was that, being a purely internal crisis, the organization lacked the jurisdiction to intervene. However, in 1994 UN military observers were deployed to Liberia to support the implementation of a peace accord which was concluded by ECOWAS and the Cotonu, later followed by the Accra and Abuja Accords. UNOMIL (United Nations Operations to Liberia) was deployed to support the implementation of the Liberian peace accord.

- While the United Nations did not enter into a joint operation with the ECOWAS states, Liberia provided for collaboration between the United Nations and the subregional organization in an arrangement which gave the security responsibilities over the protection of the UN operations to the subregional group. The United Nations thus had to depend on the security cover of ECOMOG for its operations. One cannot quite describe this arrangement as a partnership, and yet collaboration existed in that UN resources were deployed to implement a mandate which the organization did not negotiate. Though there has been some question about the sharing of responsibilities, and while the paucity of resources for the Liberian operations seriously handicapped the effectiveness of the UN input, the United Nations, especially following the eruption of renewed fighting in April 1996, has assumed a fuller role in the formulation of the Liberian peace accord. The second Abuja Accord, which is the current basis for the peace plan in Liberia, had a stronger input from the United Nations. Again, the United Nations has been called upon to implement an accord it did not negotiate.[13]

- The Liberian crisis equally redefined the conditions necessary for international intervention. ECOMOG was deployed even before a cease-fire was concluded and in defiance of one of the major parties to the conflict. Again, at different stages of the crisis, ECOMOG embarked on punitive military action to protect the integrity of its mandate, which was the protection of the civilian population. In November to December 1990, punitive measures were undertaken to create a "safe haven" in Monrovia, and an internationally protected zone. This was done to deny the warring factions access to strategic installations serving Monrovia, and to protect the internally displaced civilian population from constant threats of attack. Again, in 1992 enforcement action was taken to defend the integrity of Monrovia as a "safe area" following the NPFL-led attack on that city, and again for the same reason following the April 1996 spate of fighting.
- The ECOWAS intervention in Liberia has created a new perspective of the different role which subregional as opposed to regional organizations can play in managing conflicts in their neighbourhoods. Following the West African involvement in Liberia and their continued engagement in establishing the parameters for peace through the management of the peace accords, other African regional organizations have adopted a security agenda.

The SADC (Southern African Development Community) countries of Southern Africa, following the election of a post-apartheid government in South Africa, developed the defence arrangement of the states of the subregion. The SADC states not only plan to collaborate on the defence of their subregion, but also attempted to establish some ground rules to guide the conduct of members and prevent the eruption of conflicts. One such preventive measure adopted was the ultimatum given to Lesotho when the military attempted a coup in that country. The military was asked to pull back or punitive action would be taken against it; the Lesotho military complied. By this action, the SADC states reaffirmed their readiness to stand against unconstitutional changes of government.

Initiatives for conflict management in Africa

Discussions on an enhanced capability for the management of conflicts in Africa have been held at two levels. One set of initiatives is based on the presumption that the United Nations will continue to have the comparative advantage in mounting peace operations necessitating the deployment of troops to theatres of conflict, and these initiatives relate to how the UN's efforts can be enhanced. Another set of initiatives presume that the political will may not be present for an assertive UN role in Africa, and are thus focused on preparing and equipping African organizations for the management of security problems in Africa. As mentioned earlier, the trigger to the debate on the enhanced role of regional bodies was the experience of the United Nations in Somalia, and later in Rwanda. The absence of a quick UN response led to several proposals for the reform of the UN system.

One such proposal was provided by Nigeria and Britain. The two governments convened meetings of representatives of African governments and of some donor states in Africa during 1994 and 1995. Focusing on the relationships between the United Nations and the OAU, the Nigerian/ British initiative proposed UN support for the OAU in the development of the OAU's capability in early warning, with subregional organizations integrated into a layered system of information collation; they proposed the development of a common peace-keeping doctrine which should inform African peace operations. The British went a step further and organized a map-reading exercise in Addis Ababa in early 1996 among a number of representatives from selected African states. This was an initial attempt at the development of a common African doctrine for peace operations. The issue of a common doctrine was further discussed at the first meeting of African chiefs of staff. Other components of the proposal dealt with the preparation of African contingents for UN operations. In this regard, the Nigerian/British initiative suggested that the United Nations should establish forward logistical bases at some strategic points in Africa, where the United Nations will maintain strategic logistical equipment that can expedite the reaction time to emergencies in Africa. The United States further developed the concept of an advanced logistical facility, assisting and equipping the OAU to develop logistical stores that would support a force of 100 at a time of humanitarian emergency. The idea is for the OAU to have the capability in-house to deploy a force at the shortest possible notice.

The United Nations itself proposed concrete measures to enhance the capability of the OAU in conflict management. These include the posting of UN liaison personnel to the OAU, the expansion of the Economic Commission for Africa to handle political issues, a staff exchange programme with the OAU at various levels, and support for the OAU's efforts in training and preparing African contingents for peace-keeping.

The proposal by Canada, and in a modified form by Denmark, for a rapid-reaction capability to provide the United Nations with the capacity to react quickly to emergencies in Africa was not supported by the

Security Council, for reasons discussed earlier. Instead, the concept of an advanced headquarters was proposed. This would allow the United Nations to plan and prepare equipment to establish an operational headquarters in a theatre of conflict at the soon as conflict escalates and international intervention becomes imminent, and before a full mission is deployed. Even while planning for the advanced headquarters continued, the United States proposed the establishment of a 10,000-member All-African Crisis Response Force, drawn from a select number of African countries, which can be deployed at short notice into a crisis situation. This force is estimated to cost US$20 million to establish. The United States hoped to generate the interest of a conglomerate of donors and African countries to contribute financial and manpower support for the force.

While some African countries have expressed their support for the US idea, and their willingness to contribute troops, others rejected what was conceived as an American attempt to establish a peace-keeping force for Africa unilaterally, without consulting either the OAU or the subregional organizations. Other questions raised relate to the mandate that such a force would have. Who would authorize its deployment, into which conflict situations, and where would the command of the force be housed? How will such a force be sustained over time, and what will be the role of the United Nations and the OAU? The All-Africa Force, according to the US formulation, will have to receive Security Council and OAU approval before it can be deployed into a conflict, but does not have to operate under the mandate of either of these institutions. The force-contributing states would be required to earmark a battalion, which can be rotated. Such a battalion would be equipped and trained, and would conduct periodic joint training with other force-contributing states.

The situation in Burundi appears to be one of the driving forces behind the concept of such an All-Africa Force. The Americans argue that if the situation in Burundi were to erupt again, the force, perhaps with an SADC mandate and operating under Tanzanian leadership, would intervene to prevent a massacre. However, the adequacy of a 10,000-person force for the containment of an escalation in Burundi has been questioned. Some have argued that such a mission would require a force of not less than 30,000. The lessons of Liberia show that while it is easy for a multilateral operation to be launched, it is more difficult for such operations to be sustained and successfully extracted.

A conflict management mechanism for Africa

To be effective partners with the United Nations in international security management, the OAU has identified the need to develop an early-warning capability which, while not designed to replicate information that is already being collated at the UN Secretariat level, will concentrate on the collection of information that is specific to the Africa situation and would tap into the information network at the UN Secretariat level.[14] The most important functions of this early-warning capacity are the ability to analyze information that provides advance notification of potential conflicts and effectively exploit the appropriate entry points of intervention, especially in an intra-state conflict situation, and the adoption of the most effective strategies in dealing with the particular situation. In internal conflicts, the search for an acceptable point of entry is often a politically delicate task for the regional organization, as states are particularly sensitive to the impression that they have lost control of the situation within their boundaries.

At the beginning of the crisis in Liberia in 1989, as a result of an inadequate understanding of the strength and motivation of the rebel forces, and of the level of discontent of the Liberian people, there was a general presumption by the governments of the region that the Liberian situation could be easily contained. The initial force sent into Liberia was only 1,500 strong, with the mandate of evacuating the Liberian refugees, even when they were confronted by threats from the NPFL. In Sierra Leone, while the government of Valentine Strasser sought the assistance of the OAU to encourage the RUF to come to the bargaining table, they were reluctant to rely exclusively on regional initiatives. Strategic installations were being secured by Nigerian and Guinean troops, while a South African security force (Executive Outcomes) was employed to retrieve the diamond mines from the rebels and secure them. In Burundi, the UN Secretary-General and the heads of state of the region, based on the assessment of their newly developed early-warning mechanism, warned that another large-scale massacre was impending and called for the preparation of pre-emptive international action in the form of a rapid-reaction force that would be deployed to Burundi at short notice to enforce security if the need arose. The government of Burundi was strongly opposed to the idea, arguing that its sovereign rights would be violated.[15]

Peace-keeping and multilateral military operations

Can regional states bear the financial costs of peace operations in Africa? For example, by June 1995 the Nigerian government said it had spent about US$4 billion on peace-keeping in Liberia, discounting the amount spent by the United Nations and the contributions to the Special Fund for Liberia. The OAU in February 1997 announced that it spent 62 per cent of its special Peace Fund on preventive deployment and diplomacy in

Burundi. In 1996, of US$18.7 million that was available in the fund by December, US$9.6 million was spent on the observer mission in Burundi; US$1.5 million was spent on preventive diplomacy in Comoros, Congo, Gabon, Liberia, Mozambique, Rwanda, Sierra Leone, Somalia, and Togo. These interventions have practically depleted the Peace Fund. The Liberian experience suggests the importance of a multilevel management strategy between the United Nations, the regional, and the subregional organizations. At the continental level, the OAU capacity should be developed to coordinate subregional initiatives in the areas of planning, the development of doctrines, mandates, and common operational procedures, and the organization of periodic joint training at designated centres.

The United Nations certainly has the comparative financial and logistical advantage in the area of multilateral military operations in Africa, especially in peace-keeping. However, the experience of the past events in Rwanda and Liberia shows that there is still tremendous scope for OAU action and initiative at various levels, by the subregional bodies similar to ECOMOG intervention in Liberia, the SADC intervention in Lesotho, and by Angola in Sao Tome and Principe. The most realistic option for the OAU at this time is to perform a coordinating role in the preparation of African military and political forces for UN-sponsored military intervention in African crises. To perform this role effectively, the OAU would have to develop it capacity in the following areas.

- Development of the institutional framework at the OAU Secretariat level for the effective management of its Mechanism for Conflict Prevention, Management, and Resolution. Apart from the early-warning system discussed earlier, the capacity for political analysis of crises and the establishment of a well-developed military component at the OAU Secretariat to coordinate military operations and training have to be developed. Appropriate manning of the Secretariat, either through secondment from member states or through the recruitment of its own staff, is necessary. The Conflict Management Division at the OAU has developed tremendously recently, especially following the development of the early-warning system. In the immediate term, the secondment of serving military officers, as well as the recruitment of a few retired officers, would probably be the best option.

- The convening of regular meetings of the chiefs of staff, the chiefs of defence staff, or the appropriate heads of the armed forces of African countries, as they are variously designated, similar to the periodic meetings of the chiefs of staff of ECOWAS member states, would facilitate the coordination of planning for joint operations. The subregional bodies would continue with their regular coordination and meetings, while the regional meetings would perhaps occur quarterly.

The chiefs of staff of African states would discuss the earmarking and operation of contingents for UN military operations, assess the existing assets of it member states, and review the needs of their various forces. They would also deliberate on issues such as the doctrine that should govern the utilization of their forces, the concepts of operation, and the various types of mandates which would be required. The first in what is expected to become a series of such periodic meetings to discuss the coordination of plans, training, and the evolution of concepts of operation as well as standard operational procedures was held in June 1996.

- The OAU would coordinate with the United Nations and Africa's strategic allies the meeting of the needs of the African contingents for UN operations. Along lines suggested in the Nigerian/British initiative, the United Nations could create forward-deployed logistical stores in strategic regions of Africa, stockpiling the full range of non-lethal supplies and equipment for the mounting of an expanded peace-keeping operation (including the possibility of supplies for humanitarian support activities and for minimal peace enforcement).[16] These stores would be designed to service a minimum size of operation, such as one or two brigades or smaller, and the stores would be owned by the United Nations and manned by UN-employed personnel. The emphasis in the proposal is the development of a partnership between the United Nations and the regional organizations in which the United Nations will retain the primary responsibility for international security.[17]

Notes

1. In November 1958, Ghana and Guinea drafted a treaty, which was later also signed by Mali, providing for a Union of African States. On 7 January 1961, Ghana, Guinea, Mali, Morocco, Libya, Egypt, and the Algeria Provisional Government adopted the Casablanca Charter. The Charter provided for a joint military command and an African common market. See the background to the Charter of the OAU in *Africa Today* (Philadelphia: Lincoln University Press, 1996).
2. The section of the OAU Charter which defines the principles governing relationships between states is contained in Article 3 of the Charter, which deals with the fundamental principles that members were to abide by. Apart from the principles enunciated above, OAU members also committed themselves to the peaceful settlement of disputes through negotiation, mediation, conciliation, and arbitration; the unreserved condemnation of all political assassinations and subversive activities by neighbours; the emancipation of all African territories which were still dependent; and affirmation of the policy of non-alignment. See "The Organization of African Unity," in *Africa Today*.
3. The OAU Charter, in Article 3 on Principles, stipulates in sections 2 and 3 "non-interference in the internal affairs of States"; and "respect for the sovereignty and

territorial integrity of each State and for its inalienable right to independent existence." Ibid.

4. The interpretation of Article 3(2) of the OAU Charter, as analyzed by one of the drafters of the Charter, Dr. Talisman Elias, is extensively discussed in an article by Makumi Mwagiru, "'Who Will Bell the Cat?' Article 3(2) of the OAU Charter and the Crisis of OAU Conflict Management" (Institute of Diplomacy and International Studies, University of Nairobi, Kenya). The article is one of the *Kent Papers in Politics and International Relations*, published by the University of Kent at Canterbury, Graduate School of International Relations. The article refers to Elias's works in the *American Journal of International Law*, vol. 59 (1965), pp. 243–8, and to T. O. Elias, *Africa and the Development of International Law* (New York: Dobbs Ferry, 1972).

5. Mwagiru does argue that the OAU limited its jurisdiction in the management of African conflicts to inter-state and not intra-state conflicts. But then, the OAU equally limited its instruments of conflict management to purely political methods, through the use of preventive tools of mediation, and the possible use of juridical tools through arbitration. More militaristic and operational tools for conflict management, such as peace-keeping and peace observation, were avoided. The emphasis in the role which the OAU should play was placed on the peaceful settlement of disputes, with the assumption that such disputes in Africa can ultimately be peaceably resolved.

7. M. A. Vogt, "Nigeria and the World Powers," in M. A. Vogt and A. E. Ekoko (eds.), *Nigerian Defence Policy: Issues and Problems* (Lagos: Malthouse Publishers, 1990,) p. 78.

8. For an interesting account of the experiences of the Nigerian contingent and the difficulties posed by the confusing ambiguity of the mandate and the implications to the commander in the field, see R. Kupolati, "The Nigerian Contingent in the Organization of African Unity Peace-Keeping Operation in Chad," in M. A. Vogt and A. E. Ekoko (eds.), *Nigeria in International Peace-keeping, 1960–1992* (Lagos: Malthouse Press, 1993), pp. 144–55.

9. See also the account by the OAU Force Commander, G. O. Egiga, "Analysis of Operational Aspects of the OAU Peace-keeping in Chad," in M. A. Vogt and L. S. Aminu (eds.), *Peace-keeping As a Security Strategy in Africa: Chad and Liberia as Case Studies*, Vol. 2 (Enugu, Nigeria: Fourth Dimension Publishing, 1996), pp. 367–87.

10. For a table of defence and technical agreements between France and its former colonies, see John Chipman, "French Military Policies in Africa," Adelphi Paper No. 201, (London: International Institute for Strategic Studies), 1986, p. 23.

11. Michael W. Doyle: *Peacebuilding in Cambodia*, IPA Policy Briefing Series (New York: International Peace Academy, 1996).

12. African Crisis Response Group.

13. For a good discussion of the implications for the United Nations of its involvement in Liberia, see Funmi Olonisakin, "UN Cooperation with Regional Organizations in Peace-keeping: The Experience of ECOMOG and UNOMIL in Liberia," *International Peace-keeping*, vol. 3, Autumn 1996, pp. 33–51 (London: Frank Cass).

14. Plans for the construction of an early-warning capacity for the OAU are already being implemented with funding from the United States government. See *Summary Record of the Seminar for the Establishment, within the OAU, of an Early-Warning System on Conflict Resolution in Africa*, Addis Ababa, Ethiopia, 15–18 January 1996.

15. The report of the UN Secretary-General on the situation in Burundi, S/1996/116, on page 6 refers to the objection of the government of Burundi to the deployment of any form of foreign humanitarian operation that has a military component.

16. Nigerian/British initiative on conflict prevention and peace-keeping in Africa, April 1995.

17. These ideas are well explained in the recent Nigerian/British proposal. The proposal suggests the establishment of UN mobile logistics units that would visit troop-contributing states to enhance their capacity, especially in the area of heavy equipment and armoured personnel carriers. Another alternative is the establishment by potential troop-contributing states of partnerships with countries that can provide equipment.

14

Regional arrangements, the United Nations, and security in Asia

Shiro Harada and Akihiko Tanaka

Introduction

Economic dynamism in Asia is one of the most salient characteristics of the world system in the final decades of the twentieth century. Though some economists cast doubts about the future prospects of Asia's economic dynamism, the overwhelming majority of economists and businessmen seem to bet on optimism. In contrast, pessimism is quite prevalent in security affairs. "Realists" in international affairs predict that Asia will be the arena of a typical multipolar balance-of-power game in the coming decades. Distribution of power is undergoing a rapid change. Many territorial disputes are still unresolved. Nothing suggests that Asia may attain stability from the realist perspective. Even those who are inclined to accept the "liberal" view of international politics tend to suggest that Asia is very unstable by "liberal" standards. Democracies may not fight each other. But in Asia there are only a few democracies; important major powers are not democracies. Economic interdependence may prevent wars. But economic interdependence among Asian countries is lower than economic interdependence among Western European countries or that between Asian countries and North America. Multilateral institutions may prevent militarization of conflicts. But in Asia, multilateral institutions are still very embryonic and not well developed.

This chapter is not an attempt to repudiate such pessimistic views of

Asian security; in security affairs, pessimism may well be healthy. But we need to go beyond what pessimism deplores. We need to clarify desirable and possible courses of action in the current situation that has been historically created in Asia. Nothing is more valuable than learning from history for this purpose. This chapter, therefore, is an attempt to explore the historical experiences of Asia with respect to regionalism and conflict management, thereby indicating the possible sources of hope as well as limitations of regionalism which can be applied in Asia. It is true, as already indicated, that multilateral regional security frameworks in Asia are not well developed. Though small in number, however, some regional attempts existed in the past. We believe that useful insights can be drawn from their experiences.

In addition to this general context of the necessity of studying security regionalism, there is another and probably more pressing factor that became apparent in the post-Cold War period: the tendency of military conflicts to be localized. There are several reasons for this tendency,[1] but the most important is the likelihood of the global powers disengaging from regional conflicts which have little relevance to their vital national interests. The United States is still committed to maintaining its military presence in Asia.[2] But it is quite unlikely, whether good or bad, that the United States will become involved in every military conflict in Asia, except in the cases of its treaty commitments. Asian countries, therefore, are confronted with the challenge of devising some mechanisms to resolve regional conflicts on their own. If unilateral management of regional conflicts by global powers is neither likely nor desirable, Asian countries cannot but explore regional measures for managing and resolving military conflicts in the region. For this purpose, it is necessary to look back on past experiences.

In order to explore Asian experiences of security regionalism[3] and conflict management, we first examine various arrangements related to regional security in Asia, and secondly investigate the relationship between regionalism and the pattern of war termination in Asia. Third, by way of a case study, we look into the roles and functions that ASEAN played in the Cambodian war. Finally, we examine other regional arrangements which may be of use for conflict resolution and management in Asia.

State of security regionalism in post-war Asia

Before examining specific security regionalism in Asia, it seems useful to clarify the important criteria, or important dimensions, of any security arrangements. The first is the number of countries involved in an arrangement; in other words, whether the arrangement is bilateral or multilateral. "Regionalism" as a type of security arrangement, in this respect, is a multilateral mechanism based on a certain region. Based on this understanding, bilateral security arrangements may be excluded from the examination of security regionalism. But in the following, if only to give useful background to the security conditions in Asia, we would like to start with a discussion of bilateral arrangements in Asia. The second dimension of security arrangements is the sources of assumed threats: whether the assumed threats are external or internal. Some regional arrangements are created to cope with external threats, while others are essentially to cope with threats internal to the region. NATO during the Cold War, for example, was a security regionalism to cope with external threats, while the CSCE (Conference on Security and Cooperation in Europe) was one to cope with internal threats. The third dimension of security arrangements may be the salience of military means: how much importance is attached to military means and how much to non-military means? To use the same examples, military means were salient in NATO while non-military means were salient in the case of the CSCE. The fourth dimension is the degree of institutionalization: how much the process of managing conflicts is institutionalized.

Bilateral defence arrangements

In the early years following the Second World War, quite a few bilateral security arrangements were created to form two "hub and spokes" structures, with the United States and the Soviet Union as the respective hubs. Several other bilateral arrangements were added to this structure. Along with the evolution of Cold War politics, some of these disappeared while some still remain active.

In North-East Asia, the United States has bilateral defence treaties with Japan (1952; revised in 1960) and the Republic of Korea (1954). It also had a similar treaty with the Republic of China (1955–1979) until it established formal diplomatic ties with the People's Republic of China. Defence treaties exist between the former Soviet Union (USSR) and the Democratic People's Republic of Korea (DPRK) (1961; revised in 1993) and between the People's Republic of China (PRC) and the DPRK (1961). The USSR-PRC alliance formed in 1950 was a symbol of the "communist monolith" in the 1950s, but it expired in 1980 because China had no intention of renewing it; in fact, the alliance lost its substance long before because of the Sino-Soviet confrontation in the 1960s.

In South-East Asia, the US-Philippines defence treaty (1952) and the USSR-Viet Nam 'friendship' treaty (1978–1995), which stipulates "consultation" in emergency, can be pointed out. The former is still valid even after the US bases in the Philippines were withdrawn in 1992. The conclusion of the latter treaty was immediately followed by the Vietnamese invasion of Cambodia in late 1978 and the establishment of a government (People's Republic of Kampuchea) headed by Heng Samrin in January 1979. Then Viet Nam concluded a similar treaty of "peace, friendship, and cooperation" with the Heng Samrin government. In April 1995, the USSR-Viet Nam treaty was replaced by a new Russian Federation-Viet Nam friendship treaty signed in June 1994.[4]

Indonesia and Australia also concluded an agreement on security cooperation in 1995 – the first move to form a security alignment by Indonesia, which has led a non-aligned movement for many years – although both Australia and Indonesia insist that their agreement does not constitute a security treaty or military alliance.[5]

In South Asia, the US-Pakistan defence treaty (1959) and the USSR-India treaty of peace and friendship (1971) exist. The latter helped India to intervene in East Pakistan and conclude a similar treaty with new-born Bangladesh in 1972. But the practical validity of these treaties is now questionable. US-Pakistan relations have become worse since the Soviet withdrawal from Afghanistan,[6] while efforts to revitalize the security relationships have recently been made.[7] The USSR-India treaty was extended for another 20 years in August 1991, but soon afterwards the Soviet Union was dismantled and security cooperation with the United States began.[8] The relations between Bangladesh and India have worsened, especially over the water rights of the River Ganges, and Prime Minister Zia made it clear that his country would not extend the treaty of peace and friendship with India when it expired in 1997.[9]

Almost all bilateral arrangements are created to cope with external threats, have high military salience, and are institutionalized to a significant extent. Rather exceptional may be the recently formed Australia-Indonesia security arrangement, which is rather ambiguous about sources of threats and the means of security. But with the end of the Cold War, many bilateral security alliances lost clear and identifiable external threats. Efforts of redefinition and reaffirmation have been made, for example in the case of the Japan-US alliance. Prime Minister Hashimoto and President Clinton declared that the alliance was still valid to cope with the "instability and uncertainty" that persist in the region, and pointed out that the "tensions continue on the Korean Peninsula." Whether "external threats" are visible or not, these bilateral arrangements, along with each country's own defence efforts, continue to be the basic means of defence in Asia.

Multilateral defence arrangements

In addition to these bilateral arrangements, multilateral arrangements oriented towards external threats also exist in Asia. ANZUS, SEATO, and the Five Power Defence Pact are among them.

ANZUS was formed in 1951 by Australia, New Zealand, and the United States. Though tripartite, ANZUS is quite similar to other bilateral security arrangements which the United States concluded with Asian countries in the 1950s; it stipulates joint actions against "an armed attack in the Pacific area on any of the Parties," although the assumed external threat for ANZUS at its inception, at least to Australia and New Zealand, was "a re-armed Japan."[10] In the subsequent years, however, ANZUS acted as another Cold War alliance against the communist bloc. In the mid-1980s, when New Zealand under David Lange's government adopted a policy of not allowing any nuclear-armed or nuclear-powered ships to visit New Zealand's ports, the United States virtually terminated military cooperation with New Zealand. After the end of the Cold War, relations between the United States and New Zealand improved; security relations became normalized as Jim Bolger's government began to show willingness to change its nuclear policy.

The South-East Asia Treaty Organization (SEATO) was established by the 1954 Manila Treaty following the Geneva Conference on Korea and Indochina. It was a part of the US effort to create a group of mutual-security pacts against communism around the world (such as NATO and CENTO – the Central Treaty Organization), and SEATO was expected to be an Asian equivalent of NATO. The eight members were Australia, France, New Zealand, Pakistan, the Philippines, Thailand, the United Kingdom, and the United States. Its headquarters was established in Bangkok.

An important point is that the treaty could also be applied to the territory of non-member Indochinese states if they consented. As Cambodia and Laos chose neutrality, only the then South Vietnam was included in the area of treaty application. When the United States itself began to fight directly in Viet Nam in 1965, troops were also sent from four SEATO members (Australia, New Zealand, the Philippines, and Thailand) as well as from the non-member Republic of Korea. The significance of SEATO declined greatly as the Viet Nam quagmire deepened, and the strategic conditions is Asia changed in the 1970s with the Sino-American rapprochement and the general détente between Washington and Moscow. In 1977, SEATO was disbanded as it was considered meaningless, while the Manila Treaty per se is still in effect.

The Five Power Defence Pact was concluded in 1971. Since the independence of Malaya in 1957 (which became a part of Malaysia later in 1963), the United Kingdom, as the leader of the Commonwealth, had been committed with its defence. When the United Kingdom decided to withdraw from east of Suez in 1968, consultation began on how to defend Malaysia and Singapore, the latter having seceded from the former in 1965. Finally it was decided that Australia and New Zealand would fill a part of the former UK role in maintaining peace in Malaysia and

Singapore. Several related agreements are generically called the Five Power Defence Pact.

Regional defence conference

ANZUS, SEATO, and the Five Power Defence Pact were multilateral arrangements to cope with external threats using military means. The post-Second World War Asia had an attempt at another category of multilateral arrangements to deal with external threats by non-military measures: ASPAC.

The Asian and Pacific Council (ASPAC) was established at the initiative of the President of the Republic of Korea, Park Chung Hee, in June 1966. The nine members were the Republic of Korea, Japan, the Republic of China, South Vietnam, Thailand, Malaysia, the Philippines, Australia and New Zealand. Laos was an observer. Its broad geographical coverage is noteworthy. It aimed to preserve the integrity and sovereignty of member states in the face of communist threats, particularly from the People's Republic of China, which had become the world's fifth nuclear power in 1964. All but Laos were security partners of the United States. Reflecting the intention of Japan and others, it declared itself a non-military organization, and could do nothing more than give general support to efforts against communism. The member states thus did not share much beyond important relations with the United States and general anti-communist tones. The Republic of Korea wanted this conference to promote its security, but the other members did not show much interest. As the international situation in East Asia underwent a radical change because of the Sino-American rapprochement, the Council became insignificant and disbanded in 1973.

All in all, multilateral security arrangements to cope with external threats, whether military-oriented or not, did not play as significant a role in Asia as NATO did in Europe. SEATO and ASPAC were disbanded. The Five Power Defence Pact and ANZUS remain as valid security arrangements, but their roles are becoming similar to the Japan-US alliance in the sense that they serve as one of the basic mechanisms to cope with "instability and uncertainties" in the region.

Organizations for regional cooperation

In addition to the above regional arrangements to cope essentially with external threats, there are other types of regionalism relating to security in Asia. One of them is organizations for broad regional cooperation not necessarily created for security cooperation. ASEAN and SAARC are the cases in point; they have played de facto security roles to deal with internal and external threats by non-military means.

ASEAN[11] now seems to be the centre of Asian regionalism. It was established in 1967 by Indonesia, Malaysia, the Philippines, Singapore, and Thailand. Now it also includes Brunei Darussalam (since 1984) and Viet Nam (since 1995), while Cambodia, Laos, and Myanmar are also waiting for membership.

ASEAN started as a very "loose" grouping. Its members stressed that it was no more than a gathering of states, and did not set up a standing secretariat until 1976. According to the ASEAN Declaration (Bangkok Declaration) of 8 August 1967,[12] it is clear that it emphasized economic, social, and cultural cooperation rather than political cooperation. As they had experienced severe conflicts, such as territorial disputes between the UK/Malaya and the Philippines over Sabah and serious confrontation between Indonesia and Malaysia, the most important thing was to cooperate where they could and strengthen mutual confidence.

Nonetheless, ASEAN has in fact played political roles from the beginning, to deal with both internal and external destabilizing factors. Resumed disputes over Sabah in 1968 were contained through meetings of "ASEAN states," not ASEAN *per se*, until the problem was finally laid aside. In 1971, when improvement in US-PRC relations became clear, the meeting of "ASEAN states" issued the so-called Kuala Lumpur Declaration.[13] This intended to build a zone of peace, freedom, and neutrality (ZOPFAN) in South-East Asia, which meant neutralist security policy.

These informal political/security roles of ASEAN, "discovered" during the process of its evolution, were officially formalized in the Declaration of ASEAN Concord[14] issued at its first summit meeting in 1976, which provided for the political and security actions ASEAN should take. At the same time, the five ASEAN states signed the Treaty of Amity and Cooperation in South-East Asia,[15] which was the first attempt to institutionalize the peaceful settlement of disputes.

Toward external entities, ASEAN came to behave as a unit, as first in economic areas, but from the 1970s onwards also in political/security areas, because it increased the negotiating power of member states. On the one hand it began dialogues with the EC/EU, Australia, the United States, Canada, Japan, and so on, which became the basis of the ASEAN Post-Ministerial Conference from 1979 and finally led to the ASEAN Regional Forum in 1994. On the other, it issued statements supporting Resolution 242 of the Security Council after the Yom Kippur War through the Indonesian foreign minister.[16] This common diplomatic position was also seen later in dealing with the Cambodian war.

On 18 December 1995, the South-East Asia Nuclear Weapon-Free Zone (SEANWFZ) Treaty was signed by the seven ASEAN states plus Cambodia, Laos, and Myanmar. While its effectiveness is questionable because none of the nuclear powers is ready to sign the adjunct protocols, it is another example of the security role of ASEAN.

The South Asian Association for Regional Cooperation (SAARC)[17] was established in 1985 by Bangladesh, Bhutan, India, the Maldives, Nepal, Pakistan, and Sri Lanka. Although "peaceful settlement of all disputes" is mentioned in the preamble of its charter, it is not a security organization. The main goal is to accelerate the process of economic and social development in member states. Moreover, bilateral and contentious issues are not discussed in principle. Decisions must be made not by a majority rule but by unanimity, while non-interference in the internal affairs of states is respected; the former principle has worked in favour of India, while the latter has operated in favour of the other smaller countries.

In spite of these restrictions, SAARC has played de facto, if limited, security roles. First, the problem of terrorism was discussed at the first and second summit meetings, which led to the SAARC Regional Convention on Suppression of Terrorism at the third summit meeting in 1987. It became effective on 22 August 1988.

Second, SAARC meetings have provided opportunities for private consultations between leaders, especially India-Pakistan and India-Sri Lanka talks. One of the fruits of the former was the India-Pakistan bilateral agreements, the first in 16 years, concluded during the fourth summit meeting in 1988. The mutual ban on attacks on nuclear facilities was among them. The latter led to dispatch of an Indian peace-keeping force to terminate the civil war between the Sinhalese-dominant government and Tamil rebels in Sri Lanka, but it was unfortunate that the failure of the intervention worsened the bilateral relations.

The immense imbalance of power between India and the others, however, along with the long strife between India and Pakistan, challenges the security function of SAARC. Three out of 10 annual summit meetings have been cancelled. SAARC has facilitated functional cooperation and provided communication channels, but whether it can play more active security roles is yet to be seen.

Cooperative security arrangements

The last category of security arrangements is the security regionalism for "cooperative security," which deals with internal threats by basically non-military means. Two examples stand out: the TAC and ARF. The former tried to institutionalize peaceful settlement of disputes, though no formal institutions have been created to realize this goal. The latter does not aim to create such formal institutionalized processes, but attempts to realize peace and stability by increasing mutual confidence through sufficient communication.

The Treaty of Amity and Cooperation in South-East Asia (TAC)[18] was concluded by five ASEAN states in 1976, with the intention of expanding it to the whole of South-East Asia. It was a different framework from ASEAN, and was also made open to extraregional states by the amending protocol in 1987.[19]

The purpose of the treaty is "to promote perpetual peace, everlasting amity, and cooperation among their peoples" (Article 1). Its principles, listed in Article 2, are mutual respect for the independence, sovereignty, equality, territorial integrity, and national identity of all nations; the right of every state to lead its national existence free from external interference, subversion, or coercion; non-interference in the internal affairs of one another; settlement of differences or disputes by peaceful means; renunciation of the threat or use of force; and effective cooperation among themselves.

The most important point is that this treaty stipulates the institutionalization of pacific settlement of disputes. Articles 14 and 15 stipulate as follows.

Article 14: To settle disputes through regional processes, the High Contracting Parties shall constitute, as a continuing body, a High Council comprising a Representative at ministerial level from each of the High Contracting Parties to take cognizance of the existence of disputes or situations likely to disturb regional peace and harmony.

Article 15: In the event no solution is reached through direct negotiations, the High Council shall take cognizance of the dispute or the situation and shall recommend to the parties in dispute appropriate means of settlement such as good offices, mediation, inquiry, or conciliation. The High Council may however offer its good offices, or upon agreement of the parties in dispute, constitute itself into a committee of mediation, inquiry, or conciliation. When deemed necessary, the High Council shall recommend appropriate measures for the prevention of a deterioration of the dispute or the situation.

It would have been an epoch-making arrangement if the "High Council" had really worked as it is stipulated. But Article 16, which says that the Articles are applied only when "all the parties to the dispute agree," has virtually precluded the consideration of most sensitive issues that could threaten international security. In any case, the "High Council" itself has not been established yet.

Nevertheless, this treaty has now been enlarged to include seven ASEAN states, Cambodia, Laos, and Myanmar, and can be a basis of institutionalization of peaceful settlement of regional disputes in the future.

The ASEAN Regional Forum (ARF)[20] is the first comprehensive high-level consultative forum on political and security issues in the Asian-

Pacific region. Its first annual working session was held in 1994, participants at which were Australia, Brunei Darussalam, Canada, the People's Republic of China, Indonesia, Japan, the Republic of Korea, Laos, Malaysia, New Zealand, Papua New Guinea, the Philippines, the Russian Federation, Singapore, Thailand, the United States, Viet Nam, and the EU. Now the membership has increased in number to 21, with the participation of Cambodia (since 1995), India, and Myanmar (since 1996).

The ARF's major feature is dialogue, not institutionalization; it is very slow in institutionalizing security mechanisms. But it is far from meaningless. The first working session in Bangkok confirmed the importance of "the habit of constructive dialogue and consultation on political and security issues of common interest and concern," endorsed the purposes and principles of the TAC, and mentioned confidence-building and preventive diplomacy as goals to which it can contribute.

It has made steady progress. The second working session in Bandar Seri Begawan confirmed a gradual evolutionary approach in three stages: the promotion of confidence-building; the development of preventive diplomacy; and the elaboration of approaches to conflicts, with concentration on the first stage for the moment. It also accepted a two-track approach, which took not only governmental (Track I) but also non-governmental (Track II) activities into consideration, and agreed to set up an Inter-sessional Support Group (ISG) on confidence-building, an Inter-sessional Meeting (ISM) on search and rescue coordination and cooperation, and an ISM on peace-keeping operations as Track I activities. In the third working session in Jakarta a freer style of discussion was adopted to enable frank exchanges of opinion, and another ISM was set up on disaster relief. The topics of discussion were wide-ranging, including global issues like nuclear test bans, non-proliferation, and land mine problems, as well as regional issues like Korean and South China Sea problems.

Relationship with the United Nations

Regional security arrangements may be classified according to their relations with the United Nations: those which fall under "regional arrangements or agencies" in Article 52(1) of Chapter VIII of the UN Charter; those in charge of "collective self-defence" in Article 51 of the Charter; and the others.[21] The first type of organization is supposed to cooperate with the United Nations and take the primary responsibility for resolving conflicts in its own region. Regional organizations which regard themselves as a Chapter VIII entity include the OAS in America; the OAU in Africa; the OSCE in Europe; the LAS (League of Arab States) in the Middle East; and the CIS in the former Soviet Union. The second type of organization is a collective body to defend its members from external threats. NATO and the World Trade Organization (WTO) are examples.

Among the Asian regional arrangements discussed earlier, ANZUS, SEATO, the Five Power Defence Pact, and most of the bilateral security arrangements fall in the second category, while the others belong to the third category. The fact that Asia has no regional arrangements of the first category is characteristic of Asia, especially compared with other regions.

Wars in post-war Asia and their termination

In the previous section, as we examined the state of Asian security regionalism, it was shown that several regional arrangements do exist but that few of them are as institutionalized as NATO or the OSCE; nor are they closely related with the United Nations. What does this imply for conflict resolution?

Asia has been one of the most war-prone regions in the world in the post-war period. In our counting, 29 major (inter-state and intra-state) wars have taken place in Asia since 1945.[22] The following six were still continuing[23] at the end of 1996, all of which are intra-state wars: Burmese civil war (1948–); Moslem rebellion in Mindanao (1970–); communist rebellion in the Philippines (1972–); Cambodian war (1978–); Sri Lankan civil war (1983–); Kashmirian rebellions (1990–).

Of the remaining 23 cases, eight were concluded by exterminating or expelling one side of belligerents. Five were terminated without explicit agreement and three by one side's capitulation. Finally, the remaining seven wars were terminated by mutual explicit agreements.[24] Those seven wars were: the independence war of Indonesia (1945–1949), terminated by agreement mediated by the United Nations; Indochinese war (1945–1954), terminated by agreement at the Geneva Conference; first Kashmir war (1947–1949), terminated by agreement mediated by the United Nations; Korean War (1950–1953), terminated by agreement including the United Nations as a belligerent; first Laotian civil war (1959–1962), terminated by agreement; second Laotian civil war (1963–1967), terminated by agreement; second Kashmir war (1965), terminated by agreement mediated by the United Nations.

And partial termination was achieved by agreement in the Viet Nam War (1960–1975), the United States disengaged by agreement in 1973; and the Cambodian war (1978–), Vietnamese troops unilaterally withdrew in 1989, and all factions but the Khmer Rouge stopped fighting by agreement at the Paris Conference on Cambodia, including the United Nations, in 1991.

The first thing to note is that two-thirds of these wars terminated without mutual explicit agreement. This low rate of mutually agreed termination (30.4 per cent) is not peculiar to this region and is also seen in Latin America.[25] But most wars in Latin America were intra-state wars, which are generally harder to end with mutual agreement than inter-state wars.[26] Moreover, Asian inter-state wars themselves are not so often terminated by mutual agreement as those in other regions.[27]

Of the nine cases terminated (albeit only partly in the last two cases) by mutual agreement, none was successfully mediated by regional arrangements. This tendency contrasts with, for example, America and Africa, where the OAS and the OAU respectively try to mediate wars, although not always successfully. In five cases out of the nine in Asia, agreements were achieved by mediation of the United Nations or ad hoc international frameworks including great powers. Moreover, all of these terminated cases were followed by another breakout of hostilities. This means that confrontations in this region are so complicated and deep-rooted that their fundamental resolution is very difficult.

Should we conclude from this observation that Asian regionalism has been powerless to do anything but stand by and watch such intractable wars? Not necessarily. What ASEAN did in the Cambodian war could show that Asian security regionalism can play, if indirectly, a role in managing military conflicts. Furthermore, regionalism may be able to play more significant roles in less intense conflicts. To explore such possibilities, let us now turn to a case study of ASEAN's role in the Cambodian war.

ASEAN and the Cambodian war: A case study[28]

In the Cambodian war which stated in 1978, an Asian regional arrangement, ASEAN, played active security roles. It was also an example of collaboration between ASEAN and the United Nations.

ASEAN's commitment to the war can be divided into three phases. In the first period, when the United Nations failed to take effective measures, ASEAN tried to contain and eliminate the Vietnamese control of Cambodia. It supported the ousted government of Democratic Kampuchea, and tried to prevent the newly installed Phnom Penh regime from attaining legitimacy in international society. It also tried to make a UN-sponsored conference for peace successful, but in vain. In the second period, difference of policy among the ASEAN governments became wider as the war dragged on and the international environment changed. In the third period, a shift in the Thai position, as well as the withdrawal of the Vietnamese troops, gave ASEAN an opportunity to play the role of a rather neutral mediator. While ASEAN contributed much, it was superpowers which played a decisive role in the peace agreement, and it was the United Nations which mainly implemented the peace process.

ASEAN as a partial mediator

The whole of Indochina was under communist rule in 1975, but this did not mean peace in the region. The most tragic case was the Cambodian people, who suffered from the extraordinary atrocity of the Khmer Rouge regime in domestic politics. At the same time, confrontation between Cambodian and Viet Nam was also intensified. At the bilateral level, they had territorial disputes which caused a series of armed border conflicts. At the regional level, Viet Nam sought to control the whole region, which Cambodia could not accept. At the global level, Hanoi was supported by the USSR, while Phnom Penh was backed by the People's Republic of China.

Viet Nam consolidated its ties with the USSR by concluding a treaty of friendship and cooperation in November 1978. Then, on 25 December, large Vietnamese forces crossed the border into Cambodia with a front group called the Kampuchean National United Front for National Salvation, and quickly captured Phnom Penh on 7 January 1979. A Kampuchean People's Revolutionary Council headed by Heng Samrin was established there the next day. All the cities in Cambodia fell under the control of Viet Nam by the end of January, while the Khmer Rouge and other factions went on guerrilla campaigns.

On 12 January 1979, soon after the Vietnamese invasion, the ASEAN foreign ministers called for "the immediate and total withdrawal of the foreign forces from Kampuchean territory."[29] This stance was to be repeatedly confirmed and made clear in subsequent ASEAN meetings. Then the member states made efforts to have a favourable resolution passed by the UN Security Council, but failed because of a veto by the USSR in March.

Thus the United Nations became rather an arena than an actor. When the General Assembly began in September 1979, ASEAN governments actively and successfully moved to block the replacement of Democratic Kampuchea's seat in the United Nations by the Heng Samrin regime. This struggle over the UN seat was to be repeated every year. In November 1979 they also succeeded in gaining overwhelming support for a General Assembly resolution demanding an immediate withdrawal of all foreign forces from Cambodia.

In this way, ASEAN made clear its stance of refusing to accept the Vietnamese invasion, especially reflecting the fears of Thailand as a "front line" state which had experienced the temporary intrusion of Vietnamese troops in June 1980. Along with the People's Republic of China, which had been a patron of the Pol Pot regime and launched a punitive attack on Viet Nam, Thailand began to support the Khmer Rouge forces.

In October 1980, ASEAN governments secured a similar General Assembly resolution again, which also supported the staging of an international conference. The International Conference on Kampuchea was held at UN headquarters on 13–17 July 1981 and was attended by 83 nations, excluding Viet Nam, the USSR, and its allies.[30] ASEAN suggested a plan which included the following proposals: dispatch of UN peace-keeping forces; withdrawal of Vietnamese troops; subsequent disarmament of warring Cambodian factions; UN-supervised free elections, including the Heng Samrin party; international guarantees precluding Cambodia from becoming a threat to its neighbours; an interim government during the pre-election period; and a promise of development aid to Cambodia in exchange for a Vietnamese agreement about withdrawal. Through this plan, ASEAN seems to have attempted to realize total withdrawal of Vietnamese troops by accommodating its security interests. It is interesting that the essence of this plan would reappear in a final settlement plan a decade later.[31] However, China's goal at that time was more ambitious than that of ASEAN. It wanted to keep its influence through the rebuilt Pol Pot regime, and was against any compromise with the Vietnamese-installed government. The Chinese objection was supported by the United States, and the final draft of the resolution dropped the proposals for an interim government, development aid, and full disarmament of factions. Since Viet Nam and the Heng Samrin regime did not accept this resolution, ASEAN could not influence the course of the war.

The report of the conference was approved by the UN General Assembly on 21 October 1981, including a proposal to establish an ad hoc committee of the International Conference on Kampuchea. That committee was supposed to prepare for the reconvening of the conference, but this aim was not realized. In 1985 the Secretary-General himself went to South-East Asia and tried to mediate the war, with little success.

ASEAN's main concern was that the rise in international criticism of the genocide committed by the Khmer Rouge while in power might eventually lead to the ousting of the Pol Pot government from the United Nations. In reaction to such international pressure, ASEAN began to seek a joint government of the Khmer Rouge and two other factions led by Sihanouk and Son Sann. In June 1982, as a result of ASEAN's lengthy efforts, the Coalition Government of Democratic Kampuchea (CGDK) was formed, headed by President Sihanouk. Though it had no substance of "coalition," it could successfully get more support in the United Nations than ever.[32]

Divided ASEAN

In the following years, however, ASEAN was not free from a discordance of views among the member states. Thailand regarded Viet Nam, and the USSR, as main threats to South-East Asian security, and demanded total removal of their influence from Cambodia. This Thai position was supported by Singapore and the Philippines. For Indonesia and Malaysia, however, it was China which posed a potential threat to the region, and they preferred an early settlement of the war through negotiations. They actually made several unsuccessful peace proposals.[33] Although the ASEAN governments managed to maintain a common diplomatic position, this incongruity precluded any direct collective action, including military aid to the resistant forces. Moreover, as the war dragged on the discrepancy became wider, as typically shown in 1987, until Thai policy was changed in 1988.

The year 1987 was a turning point of the war. Viet Nam had adopted a new policy since the end of the previous year to improve its distressed economy, and the USSR under Gorbachev had begun reassessment of its economic and military aid to Viet Nam. On the battlefield, Viet Nam and the Heng Samrin regime, the People's Republic of Kampuchea (PRK), had maintained a great advantage since the successful sweeping of the enemies' bases in 1985, and the PRK's survival without the Vietnamese forces seemed possible. In this context, Hanoi and Phom Penh, supported by the USSR, began efforts to negotiate with the CGDK in late 1986, but did not succeed at first.[34]

In July 1987, Indonesia and Viet Nam reached an agreement to hold an informal and unconditional "cocktail party" of the "two sides of Kampuchea" in Indonesia for the first time (the Ho Chi Minh Agreement). It treated the PRK and the CGDK as equals, and classified Viet Nam as a concerned third party rather than a belligerent. But this agreement was contrary to the original ASEAN view that the war was an international war between Democratic Kampuchea and Viet Nam, and closer to the Vietnamese view that it was a civil war among Cambodian factions. Naturally, the hard-liners in ASEAN, especially Thailand, opposed such a formula and eventually killed it.

This stalemate was partially broken by the personal decision of Sihanouk. He met directly with the PRK premier, Hun Sen, in France in December 1987 and January 1988. But they differed on the timetable of withdrawal of the Vietnamese troops and dismantlement of the PRK regime, which could not be resolved in the absence of Viet Nam. ASEAN moved to revive the Ho Chi Minh Agreement, and Viet Nam accepted it under pressure from the USSR. In July, a Jakarta Informal Meeting (JIM) was held in Bogor, Indonesia, attended by the four warring factions and the other parties concerned: Viet Nam, Laos, and ASEAN. The PRK persisted in holding elections under its own regime, while the CGDK demanded elections under the interim government of four factions. The informal meeting ended without agreement.

Neutral ASEAN

In August 1988, the new Thai premier Chatchai Chunhavan, who had just replaced Prem Tinsulanonda, changed the country's policy toward Cambodia from unconditional support for the CGDK to a more practical peace-seeking. It led to a UN General Assembly resolution of 3 November 1988 which implied opposition to resurrection of the Pol Pot regime for the first time.[35] Another important change was rapid improvement in Sino-Soviet relations, as shown by the Chinese Foreign Minister Qian Qichen's visit to Moscow in December. These changes finally led to Hun Sen's informal visit to Bangkok on 25 January 1989, which broke the traditional ASEAN policy of isolating the PRK government.[36] However, a second JIM in February failed again because of Vietnamese attempts to exclude the Khmer Rouge.

Nevertheless, Viet Nam declared unconditional withdrawal of all its troops from Cambodia in April 1989, to be fully implemented by September. This Vietnamese move finally created an environment in which ASEAN could establish a new and more unified position of seeking peace and blocking a re-emergence of the Khmer Rouge regime; the Khmer Rouge was by then regarded not simply as a regional concern but as the party responsible for internationally condemned atrocities.

The Paris Conference on Cambodia convened on 30 July 1989, attended by four Cambodian factions, six ASEAN countries, Viet Nam, Laos, the P5 (the five Permanent Members of the UN Security Council), Japan, Australia, India, Canada, a representative of the non-aligned countries, and the UN Secretary-General. France and Indonesia co-chaired the conference. Despite these global efforts, Viet Nam, allied with the Heng Samrin government, and the CGDK again split over whether to include the Khmer Rouge in the interim government for elections, as well as over possible UN roles and the problems of Vietnamese settlers in Cambodia;[37] no agreements were achieved. The conference was indefinitely suspended in August. Moreover, when total withdrawal of the Vietnamese troops was completed, fresh battles between Phnom Penh and the three other factions began, and the latter secured some positions.

Nevertheless, efforts to achieve peace continued. At the informal meeting held in Jakarta in February 1990, Australia proposed that the four factions first set up a Supreme National Council (SNC) and then give its authority to the United Nations, aiming to avoid a split over an interim government. Although the meeting could not adopt a final agreement because of the intransigence of the Khmer Rouge, the proposal became a basis thereafter. At the following Tokyo Conference on Cambodia in June, the composition of the SNC was discussed, but the Khmer Rouge again blocked agreement by boycotting the conference.

It was the United States and China which finally broke this stalemate. In July 1990, the US Secretary of State James Baker, after meeting with the Soviet Foreign Minister Shevardnadze in Paris, stated that the United States would withdraw its tacit support for the CGDK seat in the United Nations, and that it was ready to begin negotiations with Viet Nam.[38] Washington, while supporting the Sihanoukists and KPNLF (Khmer People's National Liberation Front), no longer wanted to side with a scheme that might be seen as a tacit support for the Khmer Rouge. Congressional pressure was mounting on the Bush Administration. Furthermore, as the Cold War ended the United States no longer felt it necessary to bleed Viet Nam "white" and wanted an early settlement of the war.

The shift of the US stance forced China to reassess its unconditional support for the Khmer Rouge.[39] In its diplomatic isolation after the Tiananmen incident of 1989, Beijing found it increasingly more difficult to maintain a rigid policy of supporting the Khmer Rouge at all costs. It finally persuaded the Khmer Rouge to make concessions.

The peace process was accelerated. The UN Security Council agreed on a comprehensive peace plan, which was accepted by the Khmer Rouge in August. The UN-backed cease-fire was accepted by all parties in April 1991. Finally, comprehensive peace agreements were concluded at the resumed Paris Conference on 23 October 1991. The United Nations Transitional Authority in Cambodia (UNTAC) was established to implement the peace process, to which each of the six ASEAN governments dispatched personnel. Although UNTAC succeeded to a significant degree, it was not able to stop the resumed resistance of the Khmer Rouge completely.

Conflict management and ASEAN

What can we conclude about the roles of ASEAN in the conflict management and resolution process of the Cambodian war? First, ASEAN adopted a common partisan diplomatic position towards the external threat despite its internal incongruity, and successfully gained broad support in an effort to deny the Vietnamese complete victory on the battlefield and at the United Nations, where support came especially from

China and the United States. It contributed much to "containment" of this "extramural" war by the strategy of "internationalization," according to Alagappa's terminology.[40]

Second, it also played a more neutral mediator role in the late 1980s and through the 1990s, although it could not impose peace on warring parties by itself. Although ASEAN provided many opportunities for negotiation, it was the changes of policies by the United States and China which led warring parties to successful agreement. Thus ASEAN's contribution to the "termination" of the war may be judged to be rather limited, while the influence of external great powers was more decisive.

Third, ASEAN was not able to "deter" the Vietnamese aggression despite its collective diplomatic power. But this is nothing surprising. ASEAN is not a collective defence alliance, and the military power of the member states was limited. Furthermore, Cambodia was not a member of ASEAN.

Fourth, ASEAN was able to cooperate with the United Nations successfully in that they complemented each other in their efforts to contain and terminate the war. In terms of containment, ASEAN successfully used UN authority to justify its position through an anti-Vietnamese Cambodian seat and resolutions of the General Assembly, while disagreement among the P5 in the Security Council precluded a more active role by the United Nations itself. As for termination, ASEAN first seized the opportunity of peace and made a road to the Paris Conference, while the United Nations later embarked on implementation of the peace process, which was far beyond the capability of ASEAN.

In other words, ASEAN's experiences in the Cambodian war suggest useful roles that security regionalisms which now exist in Asia can play. Though such organizations cannot act like a "regional arrangement" as stipulated in Chapter VIII of the UN Charter, they can work closely with the UN Security Council and its member states. But it should be pointed out that the roles which ASEAN played also indicated inherent limitations to its activities; it could offer the opportunity of talks among the warring parties, but it could not force them to come to the table and impose peace plans. If global powers are less likely to get involved in regional conflicts henceforth, and if regional conflicts are to be resolved as early as possible rather than left alone until all warring parties become tired of killing, much stronger mechanisms than ASEAN or other currently available mechanisms, such as the ARF, may become necessary in Asia. Otherwise the United Nations, or the great powers themselves, must take their place.

Before discussing the possibilities of other security regionalisms, we would like to discuss the roles and functions that ASEAN fulfilled in regional conflicts other than those outside of ASEAN such as the Cambodian war. In terms of "intramural" conflicts, ASEAN seems to have successfully prevented these from escalating into open hostilities. In spite of underlying disputes, including the Sabah problem, no serious hostilities have been seen among the member states. As for "domestic" conflicts, however, ASEAN has done virtually nothing. With the rebellion of communists and Muslims in the Philippines among the list of ongoing wars, and the unresolved East Timor problem in Indonesia, its strategy has always been "non-intervention."[41] ASEAN is an association of sovereign states; it is not a supranational organization to give guidance to and, if necessary, intervene in the internal affairs of member states.

Other regional arrangements and Asian conflicts

As the case of the Cambodian war indicates, ASEAN has shown significant, if limited, capability to play a facilitating role in external wars; it has prevented the occurrence of "intramural" wars among its member states; but it has not shown any intention to intervene in civil wars or other instances of massive domestic violence in member states. What can we observe with respect to other regional arrangements?

The ARF seems to be repeating what ASEAN has done over the last 20-plus years in a much larger geographical context. First, it does not make any attempt to deter aggression forcefully nor resolve military conflicts once and for all. What it is seeking now is confidence-building by increasing the transparency of members' capabilities and intentions. This is going to be a long-term project which is, in all likelihood, not sufficient to help resolve short-term and pressing issues.

Second, its selection of subjects for discussion is reminiscent of ASEAN. The third session of the ARF held in 1996 discussed the issues of the South China Sea and the Korean Peninsula in addition to the South-East Asian Nuclear Weapons-Free Zone, issues of nuclear tests and a CTBT, and elimination of anti-personnel mines. The issue of the South China Sea may be compared to ASEAN's Sabah, while the Korean problem may be compared to ASEAN's Cambodia; the former is an issue internal to the members, while the latter is an issue external to its members but having a direct bearing on member states. Analogies should not be drawn too closely, but there are some similarities.

Third, the ARF process and the ASEAN process are similar if we look at what both of them do not deal with: internal affairs of member states. The ARF is silent about East Timor. It did not discuss the Taiwan Strait or Tibet. Nor does it discuss issues of insurgencies in the Philippines. Now that Cambodia has become an ARF member, it is not clear if the ARF addresses very much in case of an aggravation of Cambodian internal conditions.

In South Asia, regional countries are faced with several potential as well as actual conflicts. Conflicts among them include deep-rooted rifts between India and Pakistan and confrontations between Nepal and Bhutan over treatment of ethnic Nepalis in Bhutan. Intra-state conflicts include secessionist movements in India and Pakistan, to say nothing of the civil war in Sri Lanka.

SAARC seems more limited than ASEAN or the ARF. It cannot deal effectively with the civil war in Sri Lanka, let alone massive violence internal within India. It does not seem able to handle inter-state relations very effectively. A negative feedback between India–Pakistan rifts and SAARC makes management of these conflicts more difficult. Because of the confrontation, SAARC cannot strengthen its political/security roles, and is promoting only economic and functional cooperation. This is quite different from the case of ASEAN. As far as conflict management is concerned, the only thing SAARC can do seems to be to provide opportunities for informal and private exchanges of opinions.

Conclusion

Unilateral defence as well as bilateral security arrangements are the basic means of security to many countries in Asia. Few countries have shown willingness to depend totally on the United Nations or regional security arrangements. This is one of the reasons that "realism" continues to be the dominant mode of thinking in security affairs in Asia. But historical experiences indicate that some constructive regional efforts have emerged which can complement UN efforts: ASEAN's role in the Cambodian war was an example.

ASEAN, originally established for broad regional cooperation, has played de facto security roles through dialogues and a common diplomatic position. The significance of dialogues revealed by its success led to the establishment of the ARF, which aims at confidence-building in the Asia-Pacific region. The efforts of such mechanisms of "cooperative security" will be useful for creating an environment in which use of force is minimized and peaceful settlement of conflicts is preferred. There are reasons to believe that these security regionalisms in the ASEAN style will contribute to the enhancement of peace and stability in the region. But there are at least two deficiencies in Asian security regionalisms.

First, there are no regional frameworks to cope with an inter-state war if it really occurs. The ARF is a useful mechanism to create an environment in which war may become less likely, but it has no measures to cope with a war if it occurs. If a war takes place between major countries, it may be difficult for any regional arrangements to intervene; but it would at least be useful for the ARF or some other future regional security arrangements to think of the possibilities of mediating and intervening in wars between non-major countries. The current efforts of the ARF to increase cooperation in UN peace-keeping should be strengthened, with a view to creating a possible regional peace-keeping mechanism.

Second and more important, no frameworks exist in Asia to cope with civil wars or massive domestic violence. Inter-state wars can be very dangerous, but fortunately there are none going on in Asia. In contrast, all the ongoing wars in Asia are civil wars. Furthermore, as the earlier discussion has revealed, no regional frameworks are either interested in or capable of intervening in civil wars or domestic violence. This is one of the most difficult security issues in the world today. In Asia, sources of civil wars and domestic violence exist in major countries like India, Indonesia, and China. Though they are suffering from domestic strife, they are by no means "failed states." Realistically, no regional frameworks are capable of forcefully imposing solutions to domestic violence on these major countries. What can be done at most, then, is to create a forum to apply certain pressures on these countries in case their methods of handling domestic strife and civil wars become too extreme. It may be difficult to introduce such discussion into the current ARF, but the Track II discussion of Asian security should include desirable rules for military conduct even in domestic affairs. Fortunately, there are not many "failed states" in Asia. But as long as such possibilities exist in the nations in Asia, preparations to cope with atrocities in a failed state should not be neglected. It may be useful for this purpose to develop further the ARF discussion of UN peace-keeping.

The possible security roles for the United Nations in conjunction with security regionalisms are likewise limited in Asia. If an inter-state war occurs in Asia, theoretically the United Nations should be called in, as in other regions of the world. But if China, one of the Permanent Members of the Security Council, is directly or closedly involved in such a conflict, the United Nations may not be able to intervene directly. As for civil wars and internal disturbances, the United Nations could affect them indirectly. But as long as these civil wars and internal disturbances take place within more-or-less functioning states, which most states are in Asia, it is difficult for the United Nations to intervene directly. The conditions which limit the roles of security regionalisms in Asia thus also set similar limitations on the United Nations.

This does not, however, mean that the United Nations need not cooperate with regional security arrangements in Asia. On the contrary, the

United Nations and regional security arrangements need to explore possible cooperation, especially in the area of conflict prevention among states. It is important to make efforts to terminate currently ongoing conflicts, but in Asia it seems more important to prevent new hostilities, such as in the Korean Peninsula and the South China Sea. For these purposes, close coordination among the P5 members of the United Nations and members of various regional security arrangements are important. There are no ready-made answers to security in Asia other than flexible and creative combinations of contributions by the United Nations, regionalism, and individual states.

Notes

1. On the examination of this tendency, see Louise Fawcett, "Regionalism in Historical Perspective," in Fawcett and Hurrell (eds.), *Regionalism in World Politics: Regional Organization and International Order* (Oxford: Oxford University Press, 1995), chapter 2.
2. *United States Security Strategy for the East Asia-Pacific* (Department of Defense, Office of International Security Affairs, February 1995).
3. Here we use the words "regional arrangement" and "regionalism" interchangeably. On various meanings of "regionalism," see Andrew Hurrell, "Regionalism in Theoretical Perspective," in Fawcett and Hurrell, op. cit., chapter 3.
4. *Ajia doko nenpo 1996 (Yearbook of Asian Affairs 1996)* (Ajia keizai Kenkyujo, Tokyo, 1996), p. 241.
5. Research Institute for Peace and Security, *Ajia no anzenhosho 1996–1997 (Asian Security 1996–1997)* (Tokyo: Asagumo shimbunsha, 1996), pp. 206–7.
6. *Strategic Survey 1991–1992* (The International Institute for Strategic Studies, London: Brassey's 1992), p. 164.
7. Statement by Robin Raphel, Assistant Secretary of State for South Asian Affairs, before the Senate Foreign Relations Committee on Near Eastern and South Asian Affairs (Department of State, 7 March 1995).
8. Ibid.
9. *Ajia doko nenpo 1996*, pp. 486–7.
10. Terry L. Deibel, "Alliances and Security Relationships: A Dialogue with Kennan and His Critics," in Terry L. Deibel and John Lewis Gaddis (eds.), *Containment: Concept and Policy* (Washington, D. C.: National Defense University Press, 1986), p. 199.
11. Susumu Yamakage, *ASEAN: Shinboru kara shisutemu he (ASEAN: From Symbol to System)* (Tokyo: Tokyo daigaku shuppankai, 1991); Michael Leifer, *ASEAN and the Security of South-East Asia* (London: Routledge, 1989). Documents available in *ASEAN Document Series 1967–1988*, 3rd edition (Jakarta: The ASEAN Secretariat, 1988); Leifer, pp. 160–94; http://www.asean.or.id/.
12. *ASEAN Document Series 1967–1988*, pp. 27–8.
13. Ibid., pp. 34–5.
14. Ibid., pp. 36–8.
15. Ibid., pp. 39–42.
16. ASEAN Declaration on the Arab–Israel Conflict (Jakarta, 28 November 1973) in ibid., p. 606.

17. Verinder Grover (ed.), *UNO, NAM, NIEO, SAARC, and India's Foreign Policy* (New Delhi: Deep & Deep Publications, 1992), Part V. Documents available in ibid., pp. 699–750; http://www.south-asia.com/saarc/.

18. *ASEAN Document Series 1967–1988*, pp. 39–42; http://www.asean.or.id/POLITICS/POL_AGR2.HTM.

19. Protocol Amending the Treaty of Amity and Cooperation in South-East Asia (Manila, 15 December 1987) in *ASEAN Document Series 1967–1988*, pp. 43–4.

20. Documents available at http://www.asean.or.id/amm/prog_arf.htm.

21. On this argument, see Alan K. Henrikson, "The Growth of Regional Organizations and the Role of the United Nations," in Fawcett and Hurrell, op. cit., chapter 5.

22. According to Harada's preliminary research, the numbers of wars in other regions are: 27 in Africa, 25 in the Middle East, 17 in Latin America, and 8 in the former USSR and East Europe. The figures are all based on the same preliminary research.

23. But the first four among the listed wars seem to be waning and nearing termination.

24. As for the basis of the typology of war termination used here, see Paul R. Pillar, *Negotiating Peace: War Termination as a Bargaining Process* (Princeton: Princeton University Press, 1983), pp. 13–16. Our concept of "termination by mutual explicit agreement" is a combination of his "termination by international organizations" and "termination by negotiation."

25. The rate of mutually agreed termination in other regions are: 10 out of 22 (45.5 per cent) in Africa, 13 out of 22 (59.1 per cent) in the Middle East, 5 out of 15 (33.3 per cent) in Latin America, and 4 out of 7 (57.1 per cent) in the former USSR and Europe. The total rate is 39 out of 89 (43.8 per cent).

26. The rate of mutually agreed termination is 27 out of 65 (41.5 per cent) in intra-state wars, while it is 13 out of 23 (56.5 per cent) in inter-state wars. The numbers of inter-state wars, all terminated, are eight in Asia, two in Africa, nine in the Middle East, two in Latin America, and two in the former USSR and Europe.

27. The rate of mutually agreed termination is 3 out of 8 (37.5 per cent) in Asia, while it is 10 out of 15 (66.7 per cent) in the other regions combined.

28. General sources for this case study are as follows: Yasushi Tomiyama, *Kanbojia senki Minzoku wakai heno michi* (*A Record of Cambodian War: A Road to National Reconciliation*) (Tokyo: Chuo koron sha, 1992); Leifer, op. cit., chapters 4 and 5; *Strategic Survey* (International Institute for Strategic Studies, London, 1979–1992). A more theoretical framework-oriented analysis is given by Muthiah Alagappa in "Regionalism and the Quest for Security: ASEAN and the Cambodian Conflict," *Journal of International Affairs*, vol. 46 (1993), pp. 448–67. The UN commitment is centred by Berdal and Leifer, "Cambodia," in James Mayall (ed.), *The New Interventionism 1991–1994: United Nations Experience in Cambodia, Former Yugoslavia, and Somalia* (Cambridge: Cambridge University Press, 1996), pp. 25–58.

29. *Strategic Survey 1979* (International Institute for Strategic Studies, London, 1980), p. 62.

30. *Strategic Survey 1981–1982* (International Institute for Strategic Studies, London, 1982), p. 100.

31. Berdal and Leifer, op. cit., pp. 30–1.

32. *Strategic Survey 1982–1983* (London: International Institute for Strategic Studies, 1983), p. 96.

33. Leifer, op. cit., pp. 130–2.

34. *Strategic Survey 1987–1988* (London: International Institute for Strategic Studies, 1988), p. 180.

35. "The non-return to the universally condemned policies and practices of a recent past" in A/RES/43/19.

36. *Asian Security 1989–90* (RIPS, Tokyo: Asagumo shimbunsha, 1989), p. 162.

37. Ibid.
38. Tomiyama, op. cit., pp. 162–5.
39. Ibid., pp. 165–9.
40. Muthiah Alagappa, "Regionalism and Conflict Management: A Framework for Analysis," *Review of International Studies*, vol. 21 (1995), pp. 361–71.
41. As for the Muslim rebellion in Mindanao, Indonesia is playing a mediator role, but not through ASEAN.

15

Regional arrangements, the United Nations, and security in Latin America

Cristina Eguizábal

Introduction

Many factors are combining to demand that regional security arrangements should be strengthened and updated: the end the Cold War and the global security dynamics which characterized it; the proliferation of domestic, ethnic, and local armed conflicts; the emergence of regional powers; and the formation of regional free trade and economic cooperation zones. However, regions as well as nations are "imagined communities," often with profound historical roots – many pre-dating the Cold War – but nonetheless susceptible to change and liable to disappear while new ones emerge.

From the Latin American perspective, it is important that we ask ourselves of which region are we a part? Is the western hemisphere the region we relate to, or is it Latin America? Is the Caribbean a distinct region by itself? Is it a subregion of the Americas? Could Latin America be considered a subregion of the western hemisphere? These questions merit some attention, but for the purpose of this chapter we shall consider Latin American regionalism as the frame of reference and the Inter American system as the institutional space in which the Latin American region interacts with the superpower.

The Organization of American States (OAS), the regional organization recognized by the United Nations as having responsibility for the settlement of threats to peace in the western hemisphere, is no doubt – along with the Inter American Development Bank – the strongest regional bureaucracy. However, after the Second World War most conflict situations in the "new world" have opposed Washington to one or more Latin American governments. Understandably, in Latin America hemispheric security arrangements have been mostly perceived as one of Washington's favourite instruments to secure US pre-eminence in its traditional sphere of influence.

During most of the Cold War years, the Latin Americans relentlessly invoked the principles of non-intervention and self-determination, and unsuccessfully attempted to use the Inter American system to their advantage. By the mid 1970s, confronted with a dangerously escalating Central American crisis, four newly elected Latin American civilian governments opted to forgo the use of the established hemispheric security arrangements and instead forged informal regional mechanisms which excluded the United States. As long as the goal of the Latin American coalitions was to counterbalance US policy objectives, Washington adamantly opposed them. However, after the fall of the Berlin Wall the US government's opposition began to fade, which allowed existing complementary interests between the United States and Latin American countries to become evident.

Despite the end of the Cold War, the western hemisphere security arrangements established to fight communism have remained in place, and their replacement has not been a priority for the Clinton Administration. Interestingly, however, we are witnessing the emergence of a dense web of Latin American regional organizations with varied missions, ranging from political consultations – including those on security issues – and economic integration to all kinds of sectorial cooperation. The entire web of regional organizations has been thought of as a means for cooperation, indeed, but fostering dialogue and transparency as a set of confidence-building mechanisms as well, and is seen by civilian leaders as the best bulwark against possible interventions by their respective military establishments.

In the following pages, we shall firstly attempt to give a brief description of the formal arrangements and agencies forming the Inter American system, followed by a section describing Latin American regional identity as a source of foreign policy. Then we shall review, as an illustration of this, Latin American mediation and conflict containment efforts in Central America and the role played by the broader international community. Finally, we shall attempt a brief assessment of the current evolving situation and the relationship between the United Nations, the Inter American system, and Latin American regionalism.

The Inter American system

The Inter American system is the oldest and one of the most institution-
ally complex Cold War regional security arrangements. It includes the
Inter American Treaty of Reciprocal Assistance, or Rio Treaty, signed in
Rio de Janeiro in September 1947; the Inter American Treaty on Pacific
Settlements, or Pact of Bogota, signed in March 1948; the Organization of
American States, also established in Bogota in 1948; and the Inter-
American Defense Board.

The OAS is a regional organization under Chapter VII of the UN
Charter. Over the years it has become increasingly complex and multi-
faceted. It covers a number of issues and issue areas, including trade, the
environment, human rights, women, indigenous populations, education,
and many others.

The Rio Treaty – still in force although not really operational any longer – has had two main functions: that of a regional alliance in the face of
external threats; and in the case of intra-hemispheric disputes, that of a
collective security system, legally empowered to impose sanctions –
including the use of force – against the aggressor. Additionally it has
provided for consultations between the region's foreign ministers to consider measures to maintain peace and establish security for a broad range
of other circumstances affecting peace.

The Pact of Bogota was thought of as a second pillar of the security
regime. However, it has rarely been invoked. While it set out a method
for peaceful dispute resolution among members involving collective
arbitration, a series of rigid and precise settlement procedures – which
few states could accept without losing a large measure of sovereignty –
and its failure to provide for any third-party peace-keeping or peace-
observing mechanisms have discouraged its use.

The Inter-American Defense Board (IADB), created in 1942, never
really developed into a full-fledged multilateral institution such as
NATO and has always functioned independently from the political-
diplomatic hemispheric institutions. The military assistance programmes
established in response to the "Cuban threat" created strong bilateral
links between the United States and most Latin American nations, and
these have in fact served as the military infrastructure which was lacking
in the collective security arrangements created by the Rio and Bogota
Pacts.[1]

In 1954, at Caracas, a plurality of western hemispheric countries agreed
– under intense US pressure – to incorporate in the OAS Charter
"communist ideology" and associated instruments of "subversion"
among those aggressive acts which would be considered as threats to the

security of the entire hemisphere. Influenced by US military thinking, Latin American armed forces injected the notion of the East–West conflict into their assessment of social and political internal instability.[2] Subsequently they would expand this definition of threats systematically to include nationalist and reformist policies, until it covered all expressions of dissent against the established order and was labelled the "national security doctrine."

Although interpreted by each US Administration according to its specific circumstances, the definition of hemispheric security agreed upon at the Caracas meeting led to a pattern of systematic US intervention in Latin America, exemplified by direct intrusions – as into the Dominican Republic in 1967, in Grenada in 1982, and Panama in 1989 – and a series of more or less indirect ones: the 1954 CIA-sponsored invasion against Jacobo Arbenz in Guatemala, condoned by the Caracas meeting; the unsuccessful Bay of Pigs invasion against Fidel Castro in 1961; the ITT-sponsored coup against Salvador Allende in Chile in 1973; the Contra war against the Sandinistas in Nicaragua from 1979 to 1991, and, in alliance with the regular armed forces, against the FMLN (Farabundo Marti National Liberation Front) in El Salvador.

The Latin American countries continued to demand that the principles of equality of states and the legal recognition of non-intervention in the internal affairs of others should be respected and enforced. They also advocated a comprehensive definition of security which would link security issues to development. The United States maintained its vision of a Cold War alliance under its leadership, created with the purpose of eliciting Latin American support for its policies and objectives – including, when needed, support for armed intervention in one of the Central American or Caribbean countries! For Washington, the consolidation of a regional security order was after all the most important element of the hegemonic regionalism of the period.

Confronted with the hegemon's natural mistrust of true multilateralism, and the acute asymmetry of power and lack of common interests among the different countries of the Americas, the prospect of building a genuine region in the western hemisphere has been anything but a realistic possibility.

North–south contradictions in the western hemisphere

Washington's insistence on viewing all developments south of its borders through East–West conflict lenses was the source of recurrent tensions between the north and the south of the continent. The years following the Alliance for Progress, launched by President Kennedy as his Administration's response to the Cuban revolution, inaugurated a short period of close alliance between the United States and the Latin American governments menaced by Castro's policy of "exporting revolution." Furthermore, the Alliance, a comprehensive package of aid and reforms, was seen by Latin Americans as Washington's acknowledgment of the need to integrate security and development – the definition of hemispheric security that the Latins had been advancing since the end of the Second World War. Unfortunately, Washington's more traditional security concerns soon surfaced, and the economic and political aspects of the Alliance were gradually abandoned. New contradictions emerged around Latin American economic nationalism and state interventionism, which Washington opposed as contrary to free enterprise.

Concomitantly, with the surge of new countries following the dismemberment of the European colonial powers, Latin America was discovering that in the international arena it had more common interests with Africa and Asia than with its traditional diplomatic counterparts, Western Europe and the United States.

The OAS became the forum in which the recently acquired Latin American third world identity manifested itself. It was particularly clear at the Latin American Economic Commission – better known as CECLA, its Spanish acronym. CECLA had been created as an alternative to the hemispheric OAS's Economic and Social Inter American Committee. The purpose was to establish a forum where Latin Americans could develop a common position in economic and social matters to be discussed with the United States and other industrialized countries at the UN Conference for Trade and Development (UNCTAD).[3]

The only inter-state conflict which took place in the region during this period opposed Honduras to El Salvador in what became to be known as the "Soccer War," because hostilities began after a soccer game between the two national teams vying for World Cup status. The conflict was actually the product of undefined borders, illegal Salvadoran migration into Honduras, and the later policy of massive forceful repatriations which was perceived by the Salvadoran élites as a threat to the high rates of economic growth prevailing at the time.

By the mid-1970s Latin American countries such as Mexico, Brazil, Chile, Peru, Venezuela, and to a certain extent Colombia were developing proactive foreign policy profiles seeking more independence from Washington. The Mexican government championed the idea of a "New International Economic Order," and a former Venezuelan Foreign Minister, Alfonso Pérez Guerrero – one of OPEC's founding fathers – was the third world co-chair at the Conference on Economic Cooperation or North-South Dialogue. For the Latin American governments at the time, two factors had become the symbols of adhering to the third world credo: participation in the Non-Aligned Movement – preferably membership, although observer status would also suffice – and resuming diplomatic ties with Havana.

Latin America's regionalism: A defensive strategy?

In June 1979 the OAS General Assembly became once more the theatre of US and Latin American divergent views, this time concerning the Somoza dictatorship's imminent overthrow. The Sandinista Liberation Front had been the leading force of the struggle against 40 years of Nicaraguan dictatorship. Despite the Sandinistas' well-documented ties with Cuban revolutionaries, the Latin American countries led by the civilian governments in power at the time in Mexico, Venezuela, Colombia, and Costa Rica opposed the Carter Administration's effort of creating an inter-American force – which would deny the Sandinistas their victory, avoid total destruction of the National Guard, and allow for a more "controlled" transition – and opened the way for a total Sandinista success.

By trying to use the OAS as an instrument of its foreign policy, from most Latin Americans' perspective, Washington had disqualified the regional organization as a mediation ground in the Nicaraguan–US conflict.

In El Salvador, the powerful insurgent forces had received a moral and material boost after the Sandinista victory. By October 1979 the country was on the verge of outright civil war. The new Republican Administration decided to form a political and military alliance in the isthmus so as to strengthen local counterinsurgency. At the same time that the US involvement in the Salvadoran civil war was growing, Washington's hostility toward the Sandinistas was also increasing. The establishment of military bases in Honduras, the development of a war machine in El Salvador, the military and naval manoeuvres in the zone, the economic blockade and mining of ports in Nicaragua, and the covert and later overt support for National Resistance rebels or Contras, were elements of an undeclared war by the United States against the Sandinista regime. By 1982, violence threatened to engulf the whole Caribbean Basin.[4]

Until that point Latin American regionalism, mainly rhetoric and legalistic, had conspicuously lacked a security dimension. It therefore appeared inherently weak despite its high profile. The Central American crisis would partially change that: by all accounts, the Latin American countries' mediation effort would proved crucial in preventing full-blown war in Central America during the final stages of the Cold War.

Latin American mediation initiatives in Central America

Confronted by Washington's relentless attacks, the Nicaraguan government first sought bilateral negotiations with the United States. The Reagan

Administration refused and, counting on the support of the strong anti-communist sentiments of the Latin American military still in power in most countries, proposed instead the OAS as the mediation ground. As anticipated, the Central American revolutionaries – the Sandinista government as well as the Salvadoran insurgents – refused and, taking advantage of their membership of the International Socialist Movement and their Cuban ally's prestige among the non-aligned countries, and counting on socialist solidarity, succeeded in internationalizing their conflict with the US government. During the autumn of 1982 the debates at the UN General Assembly were dominated by events in Central America. The majority of the governments of the world voiced their concerns over the Reagan Administration's policy towards the isthmus, and one after another called for negotiated settlements.

Responding to the international community's support for negotiations, and in order to avoid the escalation of violence in the region and wary of conflicts spilling over into their territories, the governments of Mexico, Venezuela, Colombia – three Caribbean Basin regional powers – and Panama launched a diplomatic initiative which became known as the Contadora Process.

In their first declaration, the Contadora Group's foreign ministers set the tone of their diplomatic initiative by dismissing the argument which considered that the root causes of the region's instability were the product of East–West tensions as championed by Washington, and instead espoused the thesis that the essence of the conflicts lay in the chronic economic and social injustice prevailing in Central American countries. The document reaffirmed the principles of non-intervention and self-determination – key to Latin American foreign policies – and called for dialogue and negotiations.

Under very strong pressure from the Reagan Administration, the Central American governments ignored Contadora and tried repeatedly to seek international backing within the Inter American system. While the government of Costa Rica repeatedly urged the OAS to invoke the Rio Treaty to assist in defence of its border conflicts with Nicaragua – exacerbated by the presence of anti-Sandinista combatants in Costa Rican territory – Nicaraguan authorities, facing increased US aggression, periodically took the debate to the UN Security Council and General Assembly, where the Sandinistas enjoyed considerable international support.

Despite US – and Central American – opposition, the Contadora Group prevailed for several years. After Costa Rica accused Nicaragua of a troop incursion into its territory in April 1983, a clear majority at the OAS Council rejected Costa Rica's claim and asked the four Latin American governments sponsoring Contadora to send an observer mission to monitor events at the Costa Rican-Nicaraguan border. Nothing concrete seemed to have been achieved and tensions between the countries remained dangerously high, although conflict did not escalate any further. The observer mission formally initiated the process of drafting and discussing proposals through consultation and coordination. This approach would eventually become characteristic of the Contadora mediation process.

The Contadora diplomats were able to produce a comprehensive peace agreement blueprint, and despite the Central American governments refusal to sign it, its provisions became the basis for subsequent peace efforts.

By July 1985, the Contadora mediation efforts seemed exhausted. In order to revamp the Latin American initiative, a support group comprising Peru, Argentina, Brazil, and Uruguay was organized in Lima. The cooperation of these South American countries increased Contadora's life for a few more months, but neither Latin American support nor the subsequent participation in the collective mediation effort by the Secretary-Generals of the OAS and the United Nations would be enough to neutralize the United States and pressure the Central American states to sign the proposed peace agreement.

Taking advantage of the void left by Contadora's failure to bring peace to the region, Oscar Arias, Costa Rica's newly elected President, presented a new peace initiative in February 1987. His proposal called for the demilitarization and democratization of the region under specific rules. The plan implicitly but clearly recognized the legality of the Sandinista government and the validity of the Nicaraguan constitution. Moreover, like the Contadora proposal, it did not demand far-reaching internal changes in Nicaragua, but explored the demilitarization of the Sandinista regime in exchange for a cease-fire formula – which also applied to other countries fighting internal wars – called for dismantling the armed insurgencies, and specified disarmament plans for all the nations in the region. However, unlike Contadora it called for an outstanding involvement of the international community in the peace process.

By signing the Esquipulas II agreement six months later, the five Central American heads of state voluntarily agreed to relinquish important segments of their countries' sovereignty. They committed themselves and their governments to hold internationally supervised elections and to allow the international community to organize the repatriation of refugees and relocation of displaced persons, and also invited the international community to verify compliance with their pledge not to engage in hostilities or support aggression against neighbouring countries. They had also committed themselves (although their armed forces had not, which would become a problem) to establish cease-fire negotiations where necessary, and political dialogues in all the countries. Finally, the

Central Americans invoked other major players in the region to abstain from supporting insurgencies.

In an effort to build on Contadora's mediation efforts, and with the purpose of eliciting international support, the Central American heads of state called upon their regional allies – foreign ministers as well as the Secretaries-General of the United Nations and the OAS – to form the International Commission of Verification and Follow-up (CIVS). This commission would be responsible for verifying overall compliance. Their report, made public in January 1988 – five months after the peace agreement was signed and 11 months after the Central American initiative was launched – described a dire situation: nobody was complying.

Developments outside the region would allow the process to begin bearing fruits.

The international community and Esquipulas II

Weakened by the Iran-Contra scandal, the Reagan Administration announced in October 1988 that it would not seek Congressional approval to renew military aid to the Contra rebels. The Bush Administration, its successor, soon after its inauguration subscribed to a bipartisan Nicaraguan policy – thus abandoning Reagan's strategy of seeking a military victory over the Sandinistas – and decided to support, albeit critically, the Central American peace initiative. Instead of asking Congress for military assistance to support the Contra war, President Bush solicited humanitarian aid for the Contras' eventual demobilization. Congress approved the request and asked the OAS to administer the aid package.

Facing withering support from its socialist patrons and increasingly criticized by its Nordic supporters, in February 1989, at the fourth Esquipulas II presidential summit, Daniel Ortega agreed to hold internationally supervised elections no later than February 1990, two years before the end of his legal term. UN and OAS observers were both specifically invited to monitor the elections, but no systematic cooperation between the two organizations was envisioned or achieved.

Concerning the demobilization process, despite the Joint Plan for the Demobilization of the Nicaraguan Resistance and their Families, brokered by Esquipulas and signed by early 1989, the disarmament and demobilization of the anti-Sandinista warriors did not really begin until after Ortega's electoral defeat.

Unlike the electoral observation, the demobilization was conceived from the start as an inter-agency collaborative endeavour between the OAS and the United Nations. The OAS component of the International Support and Verification Mission (CIAV-OAS) would be responsible for disarming, feeding, and protecting the former Contras as they left camps in Honduras, while the UN High Commissioner for Refugees (UNHCR) would oversee the repatriation of Nicaraguan refugees and the United Nations Mission in Nicaragua (ONUCA) – originally deployed to survey the region's borders as the international community's response to Esquipulas II's request – would be in charge of disarming and demobilizing Contras in Nicaraguan territory. Once the former resistance combatants were back on Nicaraguan soil, they would be the sole eligible recipients of US humanitarian aid administered by CIAV-OAS.[5] Congress had earmarked US humanitarian aid specifically for ex-Contra combatants, which led to significant problems on the ground between them and other refugees, returnees, and former Sandinista soldiers, all coming back to their places of origin deeply scarred by the war and as poor as ever. Funds from the European Community destined for all parties helped alleviate tensions on the ground. Although not conceived as a conflict resolution device, the CIAV-OAS mission was increasingly called to mediate local conflicts between all the aforementioned groups.

In El Salvador, the peace settlement was more directly linked to an international process led by the United Nations. Direct negotiations between the warring parties had begun under the auspices of the Esquipulas process, but had not advanced much. It was only after the 1989 November offensive which clearly demonstrated a military stalemate on the ground that the warring parties – urged by their external supporters – formally requested the UN Secretary-General to mediate the peace negotiations. Pérez de Cuellar named his fellow Peruvian and close adviser Alvaro de Soto as his personal representative at the negotiations. He also called upon the governments of Colombia, Venezuela, Mexico, and Spain to act as "friends" of the peace process. Because of its privileged access to the Salvadoran armed forces, the US government would also be called to participate. The group became known as the group of "four friends plus one."

The United Nations and the OAS had taken fundamentally different approaches to Latin America over the years. Washington had tried to use the OAS to forestall revolution in Nicaragua via OAS-mediated talks aimed at salvaging at least part of the Somoza regime. Later the United States put forward the OAS as a better alternative to Contadora and Esquipulas II. On the other hand, the Sandinista – the only Central American members of the Non-Aligned Movement – had built a sizeable constituency of third world countries at the UN General Assembly which had unequivocally supported the Contadora Process and the Esquipulas II agreement. The International Court of Justice had even ruled in favour of the Nicaraguan government's demand for war damage compensation from the United States. Understandably, this historical baggage would hamper cooperation between the two organizations in the process of settling peace in the isthmus.

It is interesting to note how the informal mechanisms which the Latin American governments had put in place at the height of the crisis were – to a certain extent – formalized by the UN Secretary-General with the formation of the "group of friends," a mediation mechanism which was subsequently invoked to foster the negotiations leading to President Aristide's restoration in Haiti and to end civil war in Guatemala.

Latin American regionalism: The Rio Group and beyond

The Rio Group was founded by Mexico, Colombia, Venezuela, Peru, Argentina, Brazil, and Uruguay as a means of maintaining the "diplomatic momentum" achieved in seeking peace in Central America. Although not all the heads of state usually attend the presidential summits – the group's governing body – Caribbean and Central American countries participate on a rota system, and today all Latin American and Caribbean countries are represented at the Rio Group.

The group has become the region's highest-level consultation mechanism, addressing at each meeting a broad range of questions from trade issues to drug trafficking, border disputes, and domestic political unrest. The summits provide a very useful forum for informal negotiations between heads of state – for example between Presidents Fujimori of Peru and Bucaram of Ecuador at the meeting in Santa Cruz, where they were able to iron out some of the problems lingering from the last armed confrontation between their two countries. It has also become a useful mechanism of "preventive diplomacy":[6] the group is playing, as is the OAS, an important role as a guarantor of democratic stability. Guatemala, Panama, Peru, and Paraguay have all seen their Rio Group membership suspended while their internal democratic order seemed under attack. Finally, the regional group has played a very important role as a high-level interlocutor for other important multilateral actors in the international system: the European Union, Japan, China, and ASEAN. Only Washington – following its traditional mistrust of multilateralism – remains reluctant to accept the group as a legitimate regional partner.[7]

For years, high tariffs and an extensive public sector were perceived in Latin America as the best path towards development. In most countries, democracy was seen as a luxury at best and a danger to political stability at worse. Today, all the countries of the region have accepted democratic rights as a prerequisite to economic development, and the defence of human rights and of representative democracy have become legitimate security issues closely associated with the maintenance of peace. International obligations and responsibilities contracted through the integration and cooperation process are increasingly seen as means of promoting pluralism and strengthening the rule of law. The Rio Group is only one grouping in the midst of a dense intergovernmental web which nowadays includes – albeit partially – the non-Spanish-speaking Caribbean as well. The Latin American Integration Association (LAIA), the Caribbean Community (CARICOM), the Central American Common Market (CACM), the Andean Group, the Group of Three – Mexico, Colombia, and Venezuela – the Southern Cone Common Market (MERCOSUR), and the Association of Caribbean States (ACS) are other good examples of intergovernmental forums which are bound to have a decisive influence on the development of a future Inter American cooperation and regional security regime.

Lingering traditional conflicts

The foundations of the traditional balance-of-power configurations in South America have been significantly altered during recent years. Differing rates of economic and demographic growth among the participants account for this transformation, but there is no doubt that the cooperation dynamic triggered by the regional economic integration effort has played an important role. Despite these welcome developments, the traditional system of rivalries, power balances, and historical alliances originating in the nineteenth century remains an important variable to consider when analyzing potential sources of armed conflict. Argentina fighting for influence over Bolivia, Paraguay, and Uruguay has traditionally confronted Brazil; Chile has also been a traditional Argentine foe competing for hegemony in the South Atlantic and Antarctica, and has historically confronted Peru and Bolivia. These traditional enmities gave birth to mostly informal alliances between Brazil and Chile on one hand, and Argentina and Peru on the other. The Peru–Ecuador conflict, in turn, led to ties between Ecuador and Chile. The Amazon Basin, an immense empty space, served to separate this South American alliance system from territorial disputes in the South American north between Venezuela and the United Kingdom, the colonial power in Guyana, and between Venezuela and Colombia.

Historically, most inter-state armed conflicts among Latin Americans have been territorial conflicts arisen from border disputes, in many cases going as far back as the colonial period. Very often they have been compounded by conflicts over raw materials, energy, and sea resources – and accompanied by displacements of populations across borders, giving rise to migratory conflicts. Attempts by one power to impose its supremacy in a particular region and conflicts over hegemony have been relatively rare, although present – however, the danger of hegemonic rivalries escalating into armed conflicts disappeared altogether during the Cold War. With the exception of Central America and the Caribbean, ideological differences between two states – systemic conflicts – have also, albeit rarely, been a source of armed conflict and when they have occurred, the differences have usually pitched a Latin American country against the neighbouring superpower and its regional allies, as was the case in Central America. The conflict between Argentina and the United Kingdom over the Falkland/Malvinas Islands (one of the rare armed conflicts between a Latin American country and an extraregional power) can be classified as both hegemonic – a colonial dispute – and territorial. So can conflicts opposing Venezuela and Guyana, and Guatemala and Belize. Disputes between Chile and Argentina and between Colombia and Venezuela combine territorial, resource, and migratory elements, and the conflicts between Chile and Bolivia (over Bolivian access to the sea), Venezuela and Colombia (over the Gulf of Venezuela), and Ecuador and Peru (over the Amazonian headwaters) are of territorial and resource origin.[8]

In 1980 border incidents occurred in the Cordillera del Condor, a sector where there is no boundary line between Peru and Ecuador, and led the two governments to seek different conflict settlement paths. Ecuador sought an OAS settlement of the conflict, while Peru favoured the mechanism of the 1942 Rio de Janeiro Protocol, which established that the governments of Argentina, Brazil, Chile, and the United States were to be guarantors of peace and commit themselves to continue to be involved in the negotiation process until the borders between the two countries were definitively determined. The diplomatic solution which was worked out on this occasion was to use the OAS as the international mediating instrument, with "friendly country" members – the four Protocol guarantors – as its agents. The Protocol guarantors succeeded in restoring the peace within the organizational rubric of the OAS, but they were not successful in securing any firm resolution of the underlying bases of the dispute itself. The conflict erupted once more at the end of January 1995. Rapid recourse to the Rio de Janeiro Protocol and the mediation of the guarantors was quite unexpected, given Ecuador's position since 1960. Guarantor country representatives met in Brasilia and invited Peru and Ecuador to participate. Even though the peace agreement, the "Itamaraty Declaration," was signed by both parties and by representatives of the guarantors on 17 February, armed confrontation continued along the disputed border section. The parties reaffirmed their commitment to a peaceful settlement of their dispute in Montevideo on 28 February, when representatives of all the affected parties gathered for the inauguration of the President of Uruguay. Only after this declaration did the hostilities cease, which then permitted the guarantors' observer mission, Military Observer Mission, Ecuador-Peru (MOMEP), to be organized and carry out its duties: separation of forces, their withdrawal from the disputed area, and establishment of a demilitarized zone. The Rio Protocol and its guarantors have been able to oversee the successful delineation of over 95 per cent of the border. Thus, many argue that in a very real sense the Rio de Janeiro Protocol has served over the years as a conflict prevention mechanism in the region. The dispute is not yet settled and the guarantors continue to sponsor negotiations. The most recent chapter was a meeting between President Fujimori of Peru and the then newly elected Ecuadorian President Bucaram at the occasion of the Cochabamba Latin American summit convened by the Rio Group, the other regional arrangement for conflict prevention and containment to which we have alluded.

Concerning the other outstanding unsettled conflict in the region, Argentina maintains its claim to what the United Kingdom calls the Falkland Islands. Britain maintains its garrison there and, until very recently, an arms embargo against the invaders, but the two governments have also turned to practical cooperation – over oil first, with a fisheries agreement to come – on the basis that nothing so agreed affects their rival claims to sovereignty.

In recent years, following the European example of French-German cooperation as a main axis of the European Community, an intense cooperation dynamic is being developed between Brazil and Argentina as the main axis of MERCOSUR, the subregional economic integration scheme originally formed by those countries along with Uruguay and Paraguay. In 1990 both governments committed themselves at Foz de Iguazú not to build atomic weapons. Subsequently, economic austerity measures implemented by their civilian governments have obliged both countries to downgrade their nuclear programmes. More recently, Argentine and Brazilian armed forces have been conducting unprecedented joint military exercises, and their governments have publicized their plans to operate in the near future under a unified military command to confront common problems such as drug trafficking and to participate together in peace-building missions abroad.

Chile has become MERCOSUR's first associated member, and negotiations with Venezuela and Bolivia, both members of the Andean Group, are advancing rapidly. Although not all border agreements between Chile and Argentina have been duly ratified, the growing economic interdependence between the two countries has structurally changed their threat perceptions.[9] Moreover, during the last iteration of the Peru and Ecuador border dispute, Argentina reversed its traditional alliance with Peru when the Menem government decided to sell arms to Ecuador.

Undefined borders in different parts of the continent will continue to be sources of conflict easily exploited for political purposes by civilian and military alike, but the risks of these conflicts escalating and getting out of control seem to be remoter than ever.

The prospects for a new OAS

Hegemonic powers have sought to avoid coercive force. They have done this firstly through the creation and maintenance of regimes and institutions that both set the agenda and decide which issues should be accorded importance and how they are to be treated; second, through the provision of benefits to weaker partners; and third, through the conscious cultivation of common values designed to legitimize authority. Hegemony involves a sharing of benefits and a degree of active consensus on the part of the weaker states, which has indeed been present in the Inter American system. Furthermore, in the western hemisphere today the asymmetry of the overall relationship is at least partially balanced by the need for the United States to find solutions to such non-traditional security concerns as drugs, migration, and the environment.

Additionally, the gradual implementation of liberal market policies throughout the region has removed many of the sources of friction that have traditionally set the United States in opposition to Latin America. The changed character of Latin American foreign economic policy goals and the importance of the United States as a market as well as source of capital have created strong incentives to prevent friction on non-economic issues from disrupting economic relations between the Americas.

Last but not least, Canadian and British Caribbean countries taking an increasingly active role in the hemispheric organization has profoundly changed its dynamics. The former British colonies have become a virtual third bloc of countries with important voting power. While sharing common problems with the rest of the region – particularly with the small Central American and Spanish- and French-speaking Caribbean countries – their relationship with the United States is devoid of historical animosities.

The desire to modernize the Inter American security system has been manifested in recent debates at the OAS on cooperative security and non-traditional threats. However, with communism defeated and the common enemy gone, a definition of regional security has been as hard to come by in the Americas as elsewhere. Furthermore, each subregion in the hemisphere faces its own particular security challenges, which explains the difficulties of establishing a new hemispheric security regime.

Various kinds of regional disarmament measures are already in place, including the arms-reduction process in Central America, the OAS's demining initiative in that region, the strengthening of the non-proliferation regime, and the establishment a UN conventional arms register. Most Latin American countries have signed and ratified the

Treaty of Tlatelolco, declaring the region a denuclearized zone. Brazil and Argentina, the two countries which have developed their own nuclear capacity, have signed the treaty on the understanding that it does not prohibit nuclear tests for peaceful purposes.

A resolution on cooperation for security in the hemisphere was introduced by Canada at the 1991 OAS annual meeting in Santiago. A year later a Special Commission on Hemispheric Security, whose mandate is to rethink regional security arrangements and institutions in accordance with the changing international context, was established and has been working on the implementation of confidence-building measures, particularly among countries with long-standing border disputes still unresolved or among traditional rivals such as Argentina and Chile.

Although all governments agree on the importance of defending democracy, needless to say perspectives differ markedly on how to do it. The key issue is of course the use of force. While some argue that the OAS should not engage in any enforcement action, and conceive of the organization as a political institution designed to build coalitions and act by way of diplomatic influence, others think that it has an important role to play in "enforcing democracy" via political pressure, economic sanctions, and (why not?) collective military intervention if necessary.

Efforts to restore democracy in Haiti, Peru, and Guatemala, as well as the contributions made by the OAS in the observation of electoral processes in Nicaragua, El Salvador, the Dominican Republic, Haiti, Surinam, Paraguay, and elsewhere, bear witness of the heightened organizational commitment to democracy. However, as the Haitian case clearly demonstrates, in spite of the strong reaction to the September 1991 coup that ousted President Aristide, the OAS's actions were not decisive in restoring the constitutional government – the UN Security Council had to come into play, and ultimately the United States had to provide the bulk of the troops deployed.

The OAS has begun playing an important diplomatic role in the process of hemispheric consultation launched by President Bush with the Initiative of the Americas following the North American Free Trade Agreement's signature. Inter-American ministerial gatherings have been taking place periodically, notably among trade and finance ministers, and defence ministers as well. In the trade and financial realms the organization has assumed a constructive function, providing technical support for small countries, and has formed in collaboration with the Inter American Development Bank and the UN Economic Commission for Latin America and the Caribbean (ECLAC) a trade unit for the benefit of all countries.

Concerning the defence of human rights, 26 of the 35 member states of the OAS have ratified the American Convention, and 15 countries have recognized the binding jurisdiction of the Inter-American court. The effectiveness of the system has increased substantially, a fact that has been widely acknowledged by human rights advocates.[10]

With regard to the drug problem and the environment, the OAS has been increasingly collaborating with the United Nations, particularly the UN Drug Control Programme and the UN Commission on Sustainable Development. The Inter-American Drug Abuse Control Commission, created in 1986, is responsible for harmonization of national legislation and promotion of judiciary cooperation, in addition to the functions of training and information.

In March 1996, in Caracas, the OAS's 35 member states – including the United States and Canada – signed a cooperation agreement to fight corruption. The aim is to encourage development of national anti-graft laws in countries which do not have them, and to provide cross-border cooperation to track down wrongdoers and bring them to justice. Under the 28 articles of the convention, countries agree to forgo banking secrecy, although extradition remains dependent on the laws of individual countries.

The Inter-American Action Programme for Environmental Protection was adopted a few months before the Rio Summit, signalling the OAS's environmental concerns. A permanent Commission on the Environment has been designed to facilitate the coordination and assessment of national environmental policies.

The OAS's expanding agenda, covering an increased number of common problems which can only be solved through diplomatic means – as well as the recent admittance of Guyana and Belize – clearly confirms the organization's status as a key political forum in the hemisphere. It has begun playing a very constructive norm-setting function and encouraged the adoption of confidence-building security measures among its Latin American members. It has also become an important instrument for community building across cultural and linguistic traditions, bringing the English-speaking Caribbean and the Latin American nations closer together. Although undoubtedly the best-placed agency to build bridges between the United States and its southern neighbours, this continues to be an elusive goal, as tensions over Washington's policy towards Cuba attest.

Final remarks

Some international regimes are deeply rooted in history even though, ironically, they might appear spontaneous occurrences to the modern observer. Other might be the product of arduous and elaborated negotiations or imposed by a more powerful partner. While Latin American

regional practice stems from the first and partially the second, hemispheric arrangements have clearly been the product of the third, although
evolving towards the second.

In recent experience, the emerging hemispheric security arrangement
seems to have at its core the UN Security Council representing the international community (with Latin American representation in an expanded
Security Council as a goal), the Rio Group as the Latin American
regional interlocutor, and the OAS as the privileged space for hemispheric consultation and cooperation. Subregional integration schemes
would provide "political space" for negotiations, but when necessary
could become leverages of political pressure.[11]

Unresolved border disputes are likely to remain important sources of
conflict, and unfortunately might escalate dangerously as long as the
military and unscrupulous political demagogues are willing to play with
the nationalistic sentiments of their people. However, as in the past, in
the foreseeable future the main threat for Latin American countries will
probably come from domestic social and political instability. As important would be Washington's definition of the situation, and the extent to
which it would consider the turmoil south of its borders as seriously
affecting the superpower's interests. If recent history offers any clue, from
the US perspective the most important threat perception comes from a
scenario where waves of immigrants flee violence in their countries of
origin, seeking political and economic asylum in the United States.
Unfortunately, this continues to be a possible future scenario for Mexico,
Haiti, and Cuba. The three countries in question are going through difficult processes of political and economic change that seem reasonably on
track but which could derail at any moment and degenerate into widespread violence.

The perceived threat coming from drug trafficking will probably continue to be very serious. It involves mainly the Caribbean – including
Puerto Rico – and Colombia. In the 1970s and early 1980s much of the
cocaine and marijuana bound for the United States was shipped through
the Caribbean. In the mid-1980s, however, the flow began shifting
towards Mexico as law enforcement officials targeted the Caribbean for
interdiction efforts. While law enforcement efforts and public attention
were focused on Mexico, Colombian cartels reactivated their Caribbean
drug-smuggling routes, now moving not only cocaine but heroin as well.
Regional cooperation is progressing. Nine Caribbean nations have signed
"hot pursuit" agreements with the United States to allow US Coast
Guard vessels to intercept suspected drug traffickers in their territorial
waters. A regional effort is under way to set up a witness protection
programme, and for the nations to exchange judges and prosecutors in

sensitive narcotics cases so it would be more difficult to intimidate and corrupt the judiciary.

Washington is unlikely to act unilaterally. If in the past it sought the OAS imprimatur, in the future it is likely to reach out for the legitimacy mantle of the UN Security Council – preferably before the fact, but a posteriori if necessary. From the Latin American perspective it is worth noting that the Rio Group countries have been linking their preventive diplomacy efforts more often to the UN Secretary-General's Agenda for Peace than to any of the OAS's provisions for conflict resolution in the region.

From a longer-term perspective the gravest threat to the region's security would come from the failure of the state as a viable social institution. This prospect would seem only the purview of the most fragile among them – in Central America and the Caribbean – but unfortunately it is also as a possible scenario for bigger and more powerful actors: Mexico, Colombia, and Venezuela come to mind. The drug trade has become an incredibly powerful disruptive element, threatening the social fabric and the integrity of the political systems in most countries of the region, particularly in the Greater Caribbean Basin but also in Peru and Bolivia. Ethnic strife may also become a source of internal conflict in countries with large indigenous populations, such as Mexico, Guatemala, Bolivia, Peru, and Ecuador.

The region seems relatively well equipped politically as well as institutionally to prevent the escalation of traditional inter-state conflicts and settle them when they get out of hand. The eradication of internal sources of conflict which loom dangerously on the horizon will depend not so much on the effectiveness of conflict resolution mechanisms, but on the ability of governments in the region to achieve prosperity for the majority of their citizens and not just for the few. Never before has conflict prevention in the Americas been so inextricably intertwined with economic development.

Notes

1. Carlos Portales, "South American Regional Security," in Augusto Varas (ed.), *Hemispheric Security and US Policy in Latin America*, Boulder: Westview Press, 1989.
2. Ibid.
3. Peter H. Smith, *Talons of the Eagle. Dynamics of US-Latin American Relations*, New York: Oxford University Press, 1966, pp. 205–11.
4. Howard J. Wiarda, "At the Root of the Problem: Conceptual Failures in US–Central American Relations," in Robert S. Leiken, *Central America. Anatomy of Conflict*, New York: Pergamon Press, 1984, pp. 259–79.

5. Jack Child, *The Central American Peace Process, 1983–1991: Sheathing Swords, Building Confidence*, Boulder: Lynne Rienner, 1992, p. 159.

6. Franciso Rojas Aravena, "El Grupo de Río y la seguridad regional en América Latina," in Olga Pellicer (ed.), *La seguridad internacional en América Latina y el Caribe. El debate contemporáneo*, UNU/Instituto Matías Romero de Estudios Diplomáticos, Mexico D.F., 1995 pp. 173–202.

7. Jean Philippe Thérien, Michel Fortmann, and Guy Gosselin, "The Organization of American States: Restructuring Inter American Multilateralism," *Global Governance*, vol. 2 (1996), p. 223.

8. See Wolf Grabendorff, "Interstate Conflict Behavior and Regional Potential for Conflict in Latin America," *Journal of Inter American Studies and World Affairs*, vol. 24, 3, August 1982, pp. 267–94 for more details on this conflict typology.

9. Area de Relaciones Internacionales y Militares FALCSO-Chile, "La agenda de seguridad chileno-argentina," *Informe*, No. 4, March 1995, p. 1.

10. José Miguel Vivanco, "International Human Rights Litigation in Latin America," in Carl Kaysen, Robert Pastor, and Laura Reed (eds.), *Collective Response to Regional Problems: The Case of Latin America and the Caribbean*, Cambridge: CIIS/American Academy of Arts and Sciences, 1994, p. 80.

11. For another approach towards the integration of both dynamics see Viron Vaki, "Obstacles and Dilemmas Confronting the OAS," in Viron Vaki and Heraldo Muñoz, *The Future of the Organization of American States*, New York: The Twentieth Century Fund Press, 1993, p. 34.

International organizations in peace and security

16

Introduction

Michael W. Doyle

A central focus and concern of the UN21 project is how effectively international organizations have coped with the new security challenges of the post-Cold War international system. Stymied by Cold War deadlock for much of the past 50 years, the United Nations finally became what is was designed by its founders to be when a working consensus emerged on the Security Council in the late 1980s. For the first time in its history, the Security Council adopted the central role in international peace and security that the United Nations' founders had written into the UN Charter in 1945. But together with remarkable semi-successes in collective security in the Gulf and complex, multidimensional peace-keeping in Namibia, El Salvador, Cambodia, and Mozambique, crises that revealed the limits of UN action overtook the organization in Somalia and Bosnia and Herzegovina. Some of these difficulties led to a renewed interest in preventive action as a means to address crises before they became destructive and costly. The International Atomic Energy Agency and UNSCOM (set up to disarm Iraq's nuclear, chemical, and biological weapons capability following the Gulf War) also motivated a revival that led states and NGOs to begin to outline an ambitious programme of comprehensive nuclear arms control.

As the United Nations reached its fiftieth anniversary, retrenchment became the watchword of the day in peace operations. Unfulfilled expectations and escalating violence in Somalia, Rwanda, and Bosnia and Herzegovina, rising costs for even the more successful peace-keeping

369

operations – such as those that took place in Cambodia, El Salvador, and Mozambique – and a growing awareness of the complexity of intervening in ethnic and civil wars gave rise to a compelling impetus to rethink and restructure. But rethinking and restructuring, it was soon realized, are not the same as abandonment. Rational retrenchment requires the international community to assess which UN activities are successful and which are not, consider ways in which UN peace operations might be strengthened, and investigate ways to employ scarce resources more effectively. There is therefore an urgent need to examine those aspects of UN peace activities that will continue to be necessary to assure international order and justice, and to explore what resources the international community should devote to international order, given the likelihood of continuing demands in the years ahead.

The next section discusses the future in the light of the mixed record of UN activity in peace and security. A striking growth in UN peace operations, especially since 1988, reflected the new credibility the organization had come to enjoy since the end of the Cold War. But the growing costs, the escalating violence of Somalia and Bosnia and Herzegovina, the vociferous criticism coming from some UN members states, and the financial crisis that soon ensued: all questioned whether the United Nations could or should continue to take on the active role it had come to play.

In this chapter I consider whether and, if so, how much the UN role in peace and security has changed. In chapter 21 I examine the demonstrated difficulties the United Nations has experienced as a "manager" of global peace and security. I also explore the sources of demand for a continuing UN role – as a "tool" for peace and security. I conclude with the challenges that are likely to arise if the UN role is limited to the global "arena," farming out security operations to great powers which may or may not be willing to undertake them.

This chapter thus builds upon a growing concern for the future of peace-keeping which reflects the expanding and innovative role the United Nations undertook, the crisis in peace enforcement that ensued, and the new search for a role in a world of diminished resources and expectations.

The United Nations' expanding agenda for peace

In the early 1990s, with the end of the Cold War, the United Nations' agenda for peace and security rapidly expanded. At the request of the UN Security Council summit of January 1992, Secretary-General Boutros Boutros-Ghali prepared the conceptual foundations for an ambitious UN role in peace and security in his seminal report, An Agenda for Peace (1992). The Secretary-General outlined five interconnected roles that he hoped the United Nations would play in the fast-changing context of post-Cold War international politics.

- Preventive diplomacy. Action undertaken in order "to prevent disputes from arising between parties, to prevent existing disputes from escalating into conflicts, and to limit the spread of the latter when they occur." Involving confidence-building measures, fact-finding, early warning, and possibly "preventive deployment" of UN-authorized forces, preventive diplomacy seeks to reduce the danger of violence and increase the prospect of peaceful settlement.
- Peace enforcement. Action with or without the consent of the parties in order to ensure compliance with a cease-fire mandated by the Security Council acting under the authority of Chapter VII of the UN Charter. These military forces are composed of heavily armed national forces operating under the direction of the Secretary-General.
- Peace-making. Mediation and negotiations designed "to bring hostile parties to agreement" through peaceful means, such as those found in Chapter VI of the UN Charter. Drawing upon judicial settlement, mediation, and other forms of negotiation, UN peace-making initiatives would seek to persuade parties to arrive at a peaceful settlement of their differences.
- Peace-keeping. Military and civilian deployments for the sake of establishing a "United Nations presence in the field, hitherto with the consent of all the parties concerned," as a confidence-building measure to monitor a truce between the parties while diplomats strive to negotiate a comprehensive peace or officials to implement an agreed peace.
- Post-conflict peace building. Measures organized to foster economic and social cooperation, with the purpose of building confidence among previously warring parties; developing the social, political, and economic infrastructure to prevent future violence; and laying the foundations for a durable peace.

Between 1987 and 1994, the Security Council quadrupled the number of resolutions it issued, tripled the peace-keeping operations it authorized, and increased from one to seven per year the number of economic sanctions it imposed. Military forces deployed in peace-keeping operations increased in number from fewer than 10,000 to more than 70,000. The annual peace-keeping budget accordingly skyrocketed from US$230 million to US$3.6 billion in the same period, thus reaching about three times the regular UN operating budget of US$1.2 billion.[1] The activities of the Security Council in preventive diplomacy and sanctions, the Secretariat's role in election monitoring, and above all the massive growth in peace-keeping and peace enforcement: all these factors testified to the new expanded role that the international community wanted the United Nations to perform.

These initiatives, peace enforcement most striking among them, also reflected significant shifts in the international legal and political environment in which the United Nations operated. Member states of the United Nations subtly extended the acceptable scope of UN activity by altering the definition of what was once considered to be essentially sovereign, national activity. Matters once legally preserved from UN intervention, such as civil conflicts and humanitarian emergencies within sovereign states, now became legitimate issues of UN concern. Gross violations of global standards of human rights were seen to override domestic sovereignty, becoming a defining issue for what was a legitimate matter of international attention. Human rights were then increasingly claimed to be inherently global, a proposition endorsed by the Vienna Conference on Human Rights (June 1993).[2]

The Security Council also expanded the operational meaning of the UN Charter Article 2(7) authority to override domestic sovereignty: "threats to peace, breaches of the peace, acts of aggression." The new interpretation of UN jurisdiction soon appeared to include a wide range of what were once seen as infringements of traditional sovereignty. Indeed, "threats to peace, etc." came to mean protracted civil wars which resisted international efforts at settlement, armed interference with humanitarian assistance in emergencies, and, almost, whatever nine members of the Security Council (in the absence of a Permanent Member veto) said it meant.[3]

These two developments had roots in the striking changes in the international system that emerged at the end of the Cold War. A new spirit of multilateral cooperation from the USSR, beginning with President Gorbachev's reforms, met a new spirit of tolerance from the United States. Together the two former adversaries broke the 40-year gridlock in the UN Security Council. Post-Cold War cooperation meant that the Security Council was now functioning as the global guardian of peace and security. The Security Council had now become what it was supposed to have been since 1945 – the continuation, incorporated in the design of the UN Charter, of the Second World War Grand Alliance reestablished on a genuinely multilateral, collective basis. At the same time there also emerged an ideological community of human rights values that gave specific content to the cooperative initiatives of these years. The Vienna Conference on Human Rights and President Gorbachev's plea before the General Assembly for "global human values" (A/43/PV72) signified that human rights were no longer merely a Western but rather a global principle of good governance.

Those two changes coincided with a temporary conjunction of power and will. Following the collapse of the USSR, the United Sations experienced a "unipolar moment" when its power eclipsed that of all other states. At the same time the Security Council, building on the initiatives of the United Kingdom, began to evolve toward what the United States would later call a strategy of "assertive multilateralism," a strategy which flourished from the Gulf War in January 1991 until the 3 October 1993 disaster in Mogadishu, Somalia. The five Permanent Members of the Security Council, led by the United States, provided a degree of commitment and resourceful leadership that the United Nations had rarely seen before. Eschewing the international role of "Globocop" in order to address a pressing domestic agenda, the Clinton Administration encouraged UN Secretary-General Boutros Boutros-Ghali to take an ever more assertive role in international crises. The small dissenting minority in the Security Council – which included China on some occasions – was not prepared to resist the United States on issues which did not affect their paramount national interests.

For the enthusiasts of the moment, multilateral action seemed to be the politically available solution to a difficult dilemma. It reconciled an advocacy of collective security, universal human rights, and humanitarian solidarity overseas with the need to refocus Cold War spending on domestic reform at home. Multilateral action under the UN Charter was not only the prescribed legal route to world order; it also appeared to be a practical solution to global community, when each nation caring a little seemed sufficient to ensure that all together cared enough. Although far from universal in its reach, the spirit of collective security was sufficient to mobilize a successful multilateral effort to reverse Saddam Hussein's aggression in the Gulf, and the December 1992 US-led rescue of segments of the Somali population from starvation heralded what appeared to be a remarkable partnership. The Security Council decreed, the United States led, and – conveniently, for the while – many other states paid and supported.

Together these developments made the new globalism feasible and legitimate. Collective intervention by the United Nations was morally, politically, and legally acceptable where unilateral intervention was not. Because it appeared more impartial and not self-serving, the UN community was perceived to be acting as a whole, speaking for the whole community of nations. The traditional suspicion of intervention was thus allayed and the traditional moral, legal, and political restraints were lifted – perhaps, in retrospect, too readily.

In a survey of UN military operations in the 1990s, Professor Thomas Weiss of Brown University argues that the United Nations must rethink its role in military operations in order to avoid continuing overextension. By focusing on its core capabilities in peace and security, and delegating where feasible, Weiss suggests the United Nations may be able to improve its performance all round. Ambassador David Malone of the

Canadian Ministry of Foreign Affairs, in "The Security Council in the Post-Cold War Era," draws our attention to the central role which that key organ of the UN system – once an arena of vituperative Cold War debate – has recently come to play as a manager of international peace and security. Malone proceeds to point out the significant failings of the Security Council, and the weaknesses stemming from poor information and slow procedures that continue to plague the UN's key repository of the responsibility to preserve future generations from the scourge of war. Dr. Connie Peck of UNITAR assesses one widely proclaimed solution to the United Nations' current overextension in "UN Preventive Action." She argues that by merging security and development into a comprehensive conception of preventive action – both focused at the regional level – the international community can make a significant contribution to reducing the chances of war (and relieving the burden now placed on the United Nations). Dr. Brahma Chellaney of the Centre for Policy Research (New Delhi) examines "Arms Control: The Role of the IAEA and UNSCOM." Chellaney notes serious dangers in the emerging strength of the non-proliferation regime as evident in the disarmament of Iraq: a strong global security regime, albeit desirable in some aspects of international security, can have serious distributional consequences. While serving the short-term interests of status quo powers (the current nuclear states), these regimes can dangerously neglect the developing world's long-term interests in nuclear security and sustainable energy.

The chapters together suggest that while the UN community has responded to the unprecedented opportunities for international action presented by the end of the Cold War, it has yet to solve the challenging problems of how to manage international action in a manner that is effective, forward-looking, and that respects the deepest principles of human security and sovereign equality. I return to these challenges in chapter 21.

Notes

1. *Supplement to "An Agenda for Peace": Position Paper of the Secretary-General on the Occasion of the Fiftieth Anniversary of the United Nations*, A/50/60;S/1995/1, 3 January 1995, p. 4.
2. *Vienna Declaration and Program of Action* (draft reference number: A/CONF. 157/23).
3. For a discussion of the traditional Cold War interpretations of "threats to the peace etc." see Leland M. Goodrich, E. Hambro, and Anne Simons, *Charter of the United Nations* (New York: Columbia University Press, 1969), pp. 293–300. But it should be recalled that post-Cold War expansiveness is not unprecedented. Even during the Cold War, the severe and prolonged violations of human rights associated with racial apartheid led to Chapter VII-mandated sanctions against the Republic of South Africa.

17

Arms control: The role of the IAEA and UNSCOM

Brahma Chellaney

Introduction

The end of the Cold War has not reduced the importance of arms control. The incentives for the proliferation of conventional and non-conventional arms remain fairly strong. The cessation of the East–West conflict and the collapse of the Warsaw Pact and Soviet Union marked the end of the post-Second World War security order. A new security order has yet to emerge. The present global political-military situation seems in a state of transition, with no clear indications of what a future world order will look like. The uncertainties have made it more difficult to rid the world of all weapons of mass destruction (WMD).

In the years ahead, nuclear disarmament will remain problematic despite the process of quantitative reductions in US and Russian Federation nuclear armouries. In the new global power equilibrium that will emerge, the security of a number of nations will remain inextricably linked with nuclear weapons. It is no accident that virtually all important economies of the world today are sheltered by a nuclear arsenal or nuclear umbrella. Much of Western Europe, North America, Australia, Japan, China, the Russian Federation, and the Republic of Korea rely, directly or indirectly, on nuclear weapons to feel secure in order to advance their political and economic interests. The continuing utility of nuclear weapons is reflected not only in the determination of India, Israel, and Pakistan to retain their nuclear options but also in the scramble among Eastern European states to enter the 16-member NATO and come under its nuclear and collective security umbrella, as enshrined in Article 5 of the Washington Treaty. Today, about two dozen states in the world have their security tied to nuclear weapons through independent nuclear armouries or through nuclear-umbrella protection provided by the United States.

Nuclear weapons are a technology from the 1940s and within the reach of many nations. As US President Harry Truman said after the first hydrogen bomb test: "We must realize that no advantage we make is unattainable by others, that no advantage ... can be more than temporary." By wresting an indefinite extension of the Nuclear Non-proliferation Treaty (NPT) without legally binding reciprocal commitments, the nuclear weapons states (NWSs) have sought to build a base for retaining their nuclear monopoly in perpetuity. However, unless the role of nuclear weapons diminishes markedly in national strategies, the focus of proliferation could shift in the early part of the twenty-first century from the developing to the developed world, especially if there is a radical change in the present structure of security alliances and umbrellas.

If the bulk of the countries with the technological capability and economic resources have not sought to build their own nuclear weapons so far, it is because they see the possible advantages of nuclear arms as outweighed by political costs or alternatively available from an alliance with a nuclear power. However, their perception of the value of an independent arsenal could change in a different geostrategic setting. If the momentous developments since the 1989 fall of the Berlin Wall indicate any trend, it is that perceptions and interests of nations and alliances can shift rapidly.

Having got what they wanted – a permanent extension of their political instrument, the NPT, and a new technical non-proliferation tool in the form of the Comprehensive Test Ban Treaty (CTBT) – the nuclear powers will be hard put to justify their continued refusal to accept even the idea of international negotiations on nuclear disarmament. Recent developments are already beginning to challenge the right of the nuclear powers to employ indefinitely weapons of mass annihilation as lawful instruments of national security.

First came a landmark International Court of Justice (ICJ) ruling which declared the threat or use of nuclear weapons to be "generally contrary to international law" and expounded a legal obligation to achieve the complete dismantlement of nuclear arsenals. The 14 judges ruled unanimously in July 1996 that the nuclear powers are legally obliged not only to negotiate in good faith, but "to achieve a precise result – nuclear disarmament in all its aspects."

Then in August 1996 a commission appointed by a close US ally which had already midwifed the back-room delivery of the CTBT released a report calling for "immediate and determined efforts" to eliminate nuclear weapons. The Canberra Commission said, "Nuclear weapons are held by a handful of states which insist that these weapons provide unique security benefits, and yet reserve uniquely to themselves the right to own them. This situation is highly discriminatory and thus unstable; it cannot be sustained." The Commission held that nuclear weapons have no military utility against a comparably equipped opponent, and that their use against a non-nuclear state is politically and morally indefensible. This view has also been backed by a growing number of retired military generals in the West who have called for steps toward non-nuclear security.

This chapter will analyze the role of international organizations, such as the United Nations, the International Atomic Energy Agency (IAEA), and UNSCOM, in arms control. It is important to draw a clear distinction between "arms control" and "disarmament." "Disarmament" is not a term in favour with US policy makers. For example, there is no mention of the term in the latest White House report on national security strategy.[1] The term "arms control" is the popular term in American expression. The reason for that is not hard to find. The United States is essentially a status quo power which wishes to preserve and reinforce its economic, political, and military supremacy in the world. The focus of its national security strategy, therefore, is on projecting and sustaining US power. The term "disarmament" suggests a material change in the status quo – or at least the willingness to accept change in the status quo. Arms control, on the other hand, is designed to stabilize the prevailing balance of power – to quote from the White House report, to "contribute to a more stable and calculable balance of power."[2]

The theory and practice of arms control involved the "notion that adversaries could cooperate in creating force postures that would place less pressure on political leaders to use their forces or lose them."[3] This included deterring a first strike. In the period after the end of the Cold War the theory and practice of arms control has not changed much, except that international organizations are being asked to play a bigger role and the focus has shifted to non-proliferation.

Fundamentally, non-proliferation seeks to achieve two objectives: to preserve and reinforce the military and technological superiority of the great powers; and to deny to potential adversaries and other states weapons or technologies that could blunt or neutralize the capacity of a great power to wreak devastating and overwhelming punishment. The greatest danger perceived by the great powers to their strategic interests comes from the proliferation of NBC (nuclear, biological, and chemical) technologies. "Non-proliferation," a classical status quoist term, involves a strategy to create international norms and traditions that make the spread of NBC capabilities to new countries look morally bad and unacceptable in international law or in the framework of international political institutions, such as the United Nations. Of course, this approach to defence and arms control cannot but be pockmarked with contradictions. For instance, the United States, despite emerging as the world's unchallenged conventional military power in the 1990s, sees nuclear weapons as essential for its security but demands that other nations not build such weapons in the interest of international security.

Arms control is today perceived as an important instrument of national security strategy by all the leading powers. This is because regional and global arms-control agreements can serve their interests by reducing a potential adversary's incentives to initiate aggression or develop/procure sensitive technologies; they could help determine and enhance predictability regarding the size and structure of another country's force; impose significant technological constraints on another country or group of countries which are technologically less advanced by accepting parallel restrictions on one's own national defence industry, thereby preserving the technological edge; employ verification to ensure compliance; and, most importantly, contribute to a more stable power structure.

International organizations have a key role to play in arms control and disarmament. Multilaterally sponsored arms control cannot be negotiated or implemented without the assistance of existing or specially established international organizations. In the immediate aftermath of the Cold War, expectations were high that international organizations, particularly the United Nations, its specialized agencies, and regional organizations, would play a much bigger role in arms control and regional security. At a January 1992 UN summit meeting, the Security Council president issued a consensus statement on behalf of the Council members branding the proliferation of weapons of mass destruction "a threat to international peace and security." But that statement was never turned into a resolution to empower the Security Council to treat proliferation as a global threat.

The initial euphoria over the post-Cold War potential of the United Nations and other international organizations has given way to the realization that their structures and approaches would have to be radically altered for them to meet the new expectations. Slowly, it has also emerged that at least some of the great powers are not willing to back fully and fund international organizations to enable them to carry out their mandates. For instance, the United States alone owes more than half of the UN's current US$2.8 billion debt, a delinquency that has greatly impaired even the UN's peace-keeping missions. Alliances, groupings such as the G-7, and unilateral strategies are again playing the lead role on arms control and security issues. This chapter analyzes the arms-control role of two important international organizations, the International Atomic Energy Agency (IAEA), and the UN Special Commission (UNSCOM) which was set up to disarm Iraq of its nuclear, chemical, and biological weapons capabilities.

The International Atomic Energy Agency

The IAEA, established in 1957, was a corollary to the US "Atoms for Peace" policy unveiled by President Dwight Eisenhower in a 1953 address to the UN General Assembly.[4] The policy called for sale of US commercial nuclear power technology under "safeguards," or international inspections. The Atoms for Peace programme was conceived in the aftermath of a Soviet hydrogen test, Britain's first nuclear detonation, and the launch of national nuclear programmes in Canada, France, Belgium, and Italy. These developments occurred despite the US policy of nuclear secrecy and technology denial, and a domestic law that imposed the death penalty for leakage of nuclear technology. The events led to major changes in American policy, with the US Congress in 1954 extensively rewriting the 1946 Atomic Energy Act to give effect to Eisenhower's Atoms for Peace proposals. The proposals spurred the creation of the institutional base of the Atoms for Peace programme, the IAEA. It was hoped that this would discourage the spread of nuclear weapons to more states.[5]

The establishment of the IAEA's safeguards system was clearly intended to be part of a bargain with non-nuclear weapon states (NNWSs) – accept safeguards in return for access to peaceful nuclear technology. Cooperation on non-proliferation and peaceful applications of nuclear energy was also the centrepiece of the bargain that was struck in 1968 between nuclear weapons states and non-nuclear states with regard to the NPT, designed as a political and legal instrument to prevent the rise of new nuclear powers. Safeguards were devised to ensure that the goals of non-proliferation were not undermined by cooperation in peaceful uses of nuclear energy.

The IAEA was given two key responsibilities. First, as its statute says, it is to ensure "so far as it is able" that nuclear programmes under its inspections regime in the NNWSs are not misused for military purposes. Second, it is to encourage worldwide research and development of peaceful uses of atomic energy by facilitating exchange of scientific and technical information and transfer of nuclear materials. Article II of the IAEA statute requires that "the Agency shall seek to accelerate and

enlarge the contribution of atomic energy for peace, health, and prosperity throughout the world." As part of its obligation to promote
peaceful nuclear cooperation, the IAEA has maintained substantial
technical cooperation programmes in the areas of commercial nuclear
power, nuclear safety, and nuclear medicine.

IAEA safeguards – a system of record-keeping, audits, and inspections
– have been designed fundamentally to detect diversion of "significant
quantities" of nuclear material for possible nuclear explosive or other
military use, and to provide timely warning of such diversions. The safeguards have been progressively expanded and tightened, but even the
original, more limited safeguards fashioned in the 1950s were viewed by a
number of developing countries as an interference in the internal affairs
of states. The broadening of the safeguards regime, including the fash-
ioning of new tools and techniques, has not come without fierce criticism.
What we have today is a safeguards system that bears little resemblance
to the regime devised in the 1950s. The latest reform of the safeguards
regime "implies a further derogation of sovereignty by the NPT's NNWS
parties, and an increased burden on industrial operators in those states."[6]

IAEA safeguards have broadened in three main evolutionary stages in
response to the growing importance of non-proliferation for great-power
interests. The first stage involved safeguards on the specific nuclear technology and nuclear material transferred to a recipient country. This
arrangement, which was covered by what was labelled INFCIRC 66,
applied to individual nuclear installations and supplies of nuclear fuel. In
the period after the NPT came into force in 1970, comprehensive or "full-
scope" safeguards were developed and implemented under INFCIRC
153-type agreements that covered the entire nuclear programme of a
NNWS party to the NPT or to a regional nuclear-weapons-free zone
(NWFZ). Non-signatories to the NPT or a regional NWFZ treaty, of
course, were not covered by INFCIRC 153. The revised system mandated
that all nuclear facilities be declared and that the safeguards apply to all
such declared installations. In the period since the 1991 Gulf War, the
IAEA has been given verification assignments and responsibilities that go
"far beyond its safeguards responsibilities," as illustrated by the examples of Iraq and the Democratic People's Republic of Korea (DPRK).[7]

The great powers today view the IAEA as an important tool to deter
nuclear proliferation. They perceive further proliferation threats to
come not from declared, safeguarded nuclear installations but from small
weapons-dedicated clandestine facilities, as was revealed by the Iraq
experience. Therefore, a highly intrusive safeguards regime is now being
implemented. The 93 + 2 programme provides for expanded safeguards
and monitoring capabilities, and intrusive inspections by the IAEA. In
essence, the new safeguards approach turns the orginal verification prin-

ciple on its head: instead of the Agency confirming good behaviour, the subscribing state will be obligated to show it is not engaged in bad behaviour. The requirement is not that there has been no diversion of safeguarded material, but that no undeclared facilities are in existence and no weapons-related activity is taking place with clandestinely procured nuclear materials.

To facilitate such verification, a NNWS party to the NPT has to allow unhindered access to the IAEA inspectors at all times and accept new technical measures, such as environmental monitoring. A key feature of the 93 + 2 programme is that the IAEA will increase its access to information through expanded declarations from subscribing states and data collected by national technical means (NTM) and supplied to the Agency. Critics charge that the new safeguards proposals go beyond the IAEA statute and the NPT by redefining the purposes of inspections and turning safeguards into police-like measures. In effect, IAEA inspectors would have the right to roam around in a NNWS like supercops, and demand immediate access to places, persons, and data.

The NNWSs are being asked to accept additional commitments without any new reciprocal obligations by the nuclear powers. This is unsettling the original bargain, tilting it in favor of the NWSs. International cooperation on non-proliferation and peaceful nuclear cooperation has also been complicated by extra-legal instruments, such as the nuclear suppliers' cartel, the London Club, and national embargoes on all civil nuclear technology sales even under full-scope safeguards, such as the US policy to deny any peaceful nuclear assistance to Iran, an NPT signatory under full-scope safeguards. Non-proliferation concerns have risen to such an extent that an interest in commercial nuclear power is seen as potential interest in acquiring nuclear weapons capability. The Arab League, for instance, has complained that supplier nations have imposed a "selective embargo" on export of nuclear components and technology to its member states. Western non-proliferation zealots also have expressed concerns over the civil plutonium economy in Japan, a linchpin of the international non-proliferation regime. There has to be a proper balance between non-proliferation concerns and the rights of nations to meet their energy requirements through commercial nuclear power programmes.

In recent years, the IAEA has through various devices strengthened its oversight capabilities, including better knowledge of the nuclear activities of nations under full-scope safeguards. In February 1993 it set up the Universal Reporting System, which by mandating both exporters and importers to notify nuclear-related transfers can help detect clandestine activity. Since it will be difficult for most nations to build all the nuclear equipment and components needed for a clandestine project, the Universal Reporting System should aid the IAEA's detection efforts. Moreover, a year earlier the IAEA Board of Governors endorsed the Agency's right to carry out "challenge" inspections. However, the Agency's very first attempt in its history to carry out a special inspection triggered a political crisis, with a defiant DPRK notifying its withdrawal from the NPT and the United States eventually signing an agreement with the DPRK (called the "Agreed Framework") that in essence helped defuse the crisis but undercut the IAEA's role.

An expanded safeguards regime providing, among other things, unlimited access for field inspectors will pose important challenges with regard to national sovereignty, constitutional rights protecting the sanctity of the individual and of private property, and financial costs. A major issue of concern relates to the use of national technical means in IAEA safeguards and monitoring. IAEA Director-General Hans Blix argued way back in 1991 that the Agency should have access to national intelligence data, including high-resolution imagery and signals intelligence. Subsequently, information provided by the US CIA and other sources was used by IAEA in work relating to Iraq and the DPRK. The Agency "is now routinely receiving national technical means (NTM) and other intelligence information from the United States and several other countries."[8]

The assimilation of national intelligence information in the IAEA safeguards and monitoring system risks the long-term viability and credibility of the Agency for short-term benefits. The sort of intelligence data that the IAEA may find useful in its verification activities, including high-quality satellite imagery, is available not commercially but from national intelligence. As an international organization, the IAEA cannot allow itself to be used to serve the narrow security interests of the great powers. "The fact that intelligence assets are concentrated in the hands of the current nuclear weapons states may be particularly troubling."[9] The IAEA has no means of verifying the intelligence data it receives for its own verification activities except through "challenge" inspections. Not only can the provider of NTM data twist information to suit its strategic interests, it could also release intelligence data to the IAEA at a time of its choosing to help orchestrate an international uproar or crisis. Verification work employing unverified data, even if only at the initial stage, could seriously undermine the IAEA's credibility.

The IAEA faces a number of major challenges as the volume of its safeguards and monitoring responsibilities continues to expand. The United States, for example, has placed under IAEA safeguards a small portion of its fissile material from dismantled warheads, and plans to safeguard more material. The Agency has had to confront a zero-growth budget for nearly a decade and depend on extra-budgetary support for fulfilling some its additional safeguards responsibilities. The focus on safeguards and safeguards reforms has helped dilute, in the public perception, the Agency's original aims and objectives. The Agency has become an arm of the NPT, and fights shy of promoting commercial nuclear power at a time when energy demands in the developing world are spiralling and there is growing concern over the environmental effects of fossil-fuelled plants. In fact, many people in the US government view the IAEA's technical cooperation and technology-transfer programmes as conflicting with its non-proliferation responsibilities. However, it should not be forgotten that safeguards are a *quid pro quo* for access to peaceful technology.

The IAEA's technical cooperation budget has not grown with its safeguards budget, with the result that the original balance between the two has been unsettled. The developing world's access to the peaceful applications of nuclear energy has shrunk in the face of national and multilateral export control barriers erected by the advanced industrial states. The technology controls have continued to grow, first focusing on controlling the spread of plutonium – viewing plutonium as the root of the problem, as reflected in India's 1974 detonation of a nuclear device. Then the controls were expanded to prohibit the transfer of all technologies and components related to uranium enrichment and separation of plutonium from irradiated fuel. Later came even more sweeping restrictions in the form of controls on dual-use items and technologies. Last came lists of "countries of proliferation concern" with whom all nuclear cooperation, including safety-related assistance, is proscribed, irrespective of whether they are or not under full-scope safeguards.

The Agency could better secure its future by broadening the base of its decision-making structure and drawing more personnel from the developing world, where the bulk of the global population lives. Western states and the Russian Federation have resisted third world demands, articulated through IAEA general conference resolutions, to broaden the membership of the Agency's policy-making body, the Board of Governors, which is dominated by the developed world, with virtually permanent seats for 13 advanced nuclear states. Nearly two-thirds of the Agency's senior staff and three-quarters of the total professional staff are from the developed world. The pace of recruiting third world nationals to senior and other professional positions needs to be accelerated.

The IAEA is affiliated to the United Nations without being under its control. However, in recent years the Agency has, in its own words, emerged as a "nuclear verification arm" of the Security Council, while it views the Security Council as the "political organ" to deal with violations of its safeguards agreements. This avowed institutional linkage, underscored by the cases of Iraq and the DPRK, is rooted in the 1992 Security Council summit statement (not resolution) that Council members would "take appropriate measures in the case of any violation notified to them by the IAEA." The legal basis of this linkage is tenuous, and the relationship between the Security Council and the IAEA calls for serious discussion, especially since the Council, by its very design, is an instrument of great-power muscle and IAEA safeguards are primarily intended to safeguard the nuclear hegemony of the great powers.

While few would dispute the right of the IAEA to verify that subscribing nations are not diverting safeguarded nuclear material and building bombs in the basement, the Agency's long-term viability cannot be sustained if it were turned into a foreign policy and security instrument of the nuclear powers through a greatly expanded safeguards system seeking to employ police-like measures and encroach on the national sovereignty of states. No safeguards regime can be foolproof in the face of a determined proliferator. Anti-proliferation technical measures, such as on-site inspections and export controls, can lengthen the proliferation fuse, provide timely warning of illicit activity, and help raise unacceptable risks of punitive sanctions against potential violators. But they will work in the medium to long term only if they are supplemented by political disincentives to nuclearization, such as technical cooperation on peaceful technology and steps toward disarmament.

The United Nations Special Commission

The United Nations Special Commission (UNSCOM) on disarming Iraq has been in operation since 1991. Iraq has grudgingly cooperated with UNSCOM, gradually revealing the extent of its nuclear, chemical, and biological weapons programmes and its missile development. Although Iraq has been stripped of much of its national sovereignty and is reeling under unremitting international sanctions, UNSCOM after over six years of extensive operations has still to give Iraq a clean bill of health. This has prevented the lifting of sanctions, which have hit the ordinary Iraqis very hard. Although a deal to allow Iraq to export a limited quantity of oil and import much-needed food has finally been worked out, before it became operational UNICEF reported that about 4,500 children under the age of five were dying every month in Iraq.[10] The UN World Food Programme has said that a 30 per cent fall in food production in 1996 exacerbated Iraqi shortages, leaving 180,000 malnourished children and 900,000 war widows "highly vulnerable."[11] The experience with UNSCOM raises important issues relating to the role of international organizations in arms control.

When the 1991 Gulf War ended, the United States, in agreement with its allies, decided to seek Iraq's disarmament through an international organization. This marked a rare occasion in history when the United States used an international organization to disarm its opponent. Since the United States had waged its battle against Iraq and its occupation of Kuwait with the support of two separate Security Council resolutions, it made sense to disarm Iraq through the United Nations and enhance the international sanctity of the allied operation against Baghdad.

The United Nations and the IAEA were given responsibility through Security Council resolutions to dismantle Iraq's weapons of mass destruction (WMD) infrastructure and put in place long-term monitoring and verification. Resolution 687 in April 1991 established UNSCOM to eliminate Iraq's chemical and biological weapons capabilities and specified missiles. UNSCOM was also tasked to assist the IAEA in destroying or removing from Iraq all materials, equipment, and facilities related to nuclear weapons. Resolution 707, passed in August 1991, established the right of UNSCOM and IAEA inspection teams to conduct "both fixed-wing and helicopter flights throughout Iraq for all relevant purposes," and demanded that Iraq provide UNSCOM with "a full, final, and complete disclosure" of all aspects of its programmes to develop WMD and ballistic missiles. Resolution 715 in October 1991 called for a programme of ongoing monitoring and verification to ensure that Iraq did not resume its WMD and missile programmes.

These three resolutions together require the following measures.

- Iraq's "unconditional acceptance of the destruction, removal, or rendering harmless, under international supervision," of all chemical and biological weapons, agents, and components, and all R&D, support, and production facilities; and all ballistic missiles with ranges greater than 150 kilometres (93 miles), along with their spare parts and repair and manufacturing facilities.
- UNSCOM's conduct of on-site inspections of Iraq's facilities disclosed by Baghdad and identified by the Commission itself.
- The Commission is to supervise the "destruction, removal, or rendering harmless" of all items it specifies.
- UNSCOM is to develop a plan for future monitoring and verification to deter Iraq from using, developing, constructing, or acquiring any of the above items.
- Iraq's unconditional pledge not to research, develop, or acquire nuclear weapons or their subsystems or components; its declaration of all locations, amounts, and types of nuclear materials; its placement of all materials under IAEA control for destruction; and its agreement to on-site inspection and monitoring to ensure future compliance.

The key point is that Iraq will remain under long-term rigorous monitoring. Baghdad accepted Resolution 715 on long-term monitoring only in November 1993, opening the way for UNSCOM to set up the Ongoing

Monitoring and Verification (OMV) regime. The Baghdad Centre houses OMV operations, including human monitors.

When sanctions are lifted, Iraq will – on a long-term basis – also be subjected to a specially established export-import control regime. Pursuant to Resolution 715, an export-import monitoring mechanism is being developed to control any trade in items relevant to Resolution 687. Indicative of UNSCOM's own long term, the mechanism will detail procedures for notification to the Commission and the IAEA of exports of dual-use items to Iraq. Both Iraq and the exporter will have to provide notifications.

The degree of intrusiveness and liberty allowed to UNSCOM in Iraq is unprecedented in the history of arms control. UNSCOM inspectors have complete, unrestricted access in Iraq, "anytime, anywhere." On-site inspections have been supplemented with aerial overflights, access to huge quantities of very revealing Iraqi documents, the application of national intelligence information, and the use of ground-installed sensors. Hundreds of aerial inspections using a US U-2 reconnaissance aircraft and German and other helicopters have been carried out since mid-1991. Quite often, on-site inspections have been conducted in tandem with aerial inspection of the same area, making it difficult for Iraqi authorities to conceal any clandestine activity. And when Iraq has balked at allowing unhindered UNSCOM operations, it has faced US-led air strikes to force it to comply with the UN resolutions.

The experience with UNSCOM has shown that such an intrusive, all-embracing inspections regime is an expensive one. However, the costs have not been an issue because "frozen" Iraqi funds have mainly been employed to achieve Iraq's disarmament. This funding pattern is also the reason why the likely long-term continuance of UNSCOM is not much of a financial issue. An escrow account established by the UN Secretary-General to finance UNSCOM and other UN activities related to Iraq has attracted contributions from states drawing largely on frozen Iraqi assets. For example, the United States, according to its official statements, has provided US$200 million to this account from Iraqi assets frozen by it before the Gulf War. The United States has also made available for UNSCOM operations its U-2 aircraft, sensors, analysts, and inspectors.

UNSCOM-type monitoring and verification cannot be replicated for general arms-control purposes, not only because of its prohibitive cost, but because the stripping of national sovereignty that it demands can be applied solely to a defeated country. However, there are a number of lessons from the UNSCOM experience that could be applied to the monitoring and verification of international or bilateral arms-control agreements. These include the benefits of the coordinated use of on-site inspections and aerial reconnaissance, and the use of new techniques to detect clandestine activity.

There are also a number of disturbing lessons from the UNSCOM experience that need to be examined in the context of the future role of international organizations in international arms control and disarmament. The biggest one relates to the failure of UNSCOM even after over six years of extensive operations to give Iraq a clean bill of health with regard to dangerous arms. UNSCOM has sent more than 375 inspection teams to Iraq, undertaken hundreds of U-2 missions, and supervised the destruction of many WMD facilities and equipment, chemical munitions, and Scud missiles. In the chemical weapons area, UNSCOM has destroyed 28,000 chemical munitions, 480,000 litres of chemical agents, and 1.8 million litres and 1 million kilograms of 45 different precursor chemicals. Besides destroying assorted biological weapons production equipment, the entire Al-Hakam biological complex has been dismantled. In the nuclear weapons area, the entire fissile material production infrastructure has been flattened and all quantities of enriched uranium and plutonium found in Iraq have been removed. Yet, in its latest half-yearly report to the Security Council, UNSCOM has said Iraq may still be hiding small but highly significant quantities of missiles and chemical and biological warfare agents.

Iraq has been guilty of repeatedly attempting to prevaricate and dupe UNSCOM. Iraq's duplicity and falsification came out starkly when in the aftermath of the August 1995 defection to Jordan of two of Iraqi President Saddam Hussein's sons-in-law, Baghdad admitted particulars of its biological and other weapons programmes which it had consistently denied, handing over more than 700,000 pages of documents to UNSCOM. However, the deception of a defenceless country already divested of its national sovereignty and unable to feed its citizens properly in the face of harsh international sanctions should not act as a rationale for prolonging the suffering of its people. When the Iraq sanctions resolution was moved in the Security Council in 1990, its sponsors sought to assure other member states that it would not come in the way of food supplies and other humanitarian assistance. In practice, though, the sanctions have been all-embracing. An important lesson of history is that when a defeated state has been punished too severely it can come back to haunt its subjugators. UNSCOM should pursue its mission in such a way that it is judged by historians as an international organization which carried out its mandate justly.

A complicating factor is the role of the country which led the victorious forces against Iraq. The United States, which has a very close relationship with UNSCOM, has publicly opposed the Commission giving a "nodiscrepancies" report on Iraq and has imposed additional conditionalities for the lifting of sanctions. In addition to Iraq's full disclosure of its WMD programmes, the United States has insisted on the following conditions being met by Baghdad before sanctions could be lifted: return of Kuwaiti property and accounting for the 600 or so Kuwaitis still missing; ending its "export" of terrorism; and suspending the suppression of Kurds and improving its human rights record. According to US Secretary of State Madeleine Albright, "the sanctions regime has been in fact been quite successful and needs to remain in place ... But, as I said, we are prepared to deal with a successor" government in Baghdad.[12]

UNSCOM's reliance on national intelligence information is also a troubling fact. It has been openly acknowledged that the CIA guided the initial UNSCOM inspection teams to Iraqi facilities, and to the Agriculture Ministry building where thousands of very compromising documents were seized after a standoff lasting several days. The funnelling of national intelligence information to international organizations, informally or institutionally, and the use of such data for inspections or reporting would seriously erode the credibility and legitimacy of international organizations. International organizations have to ensure that they do not become, wittingly or unwittingly, tools to serve great-power interests. UNSCOM has set in motion a dangerous trend that should be reversed.

UNSCOM also needs to mirror its international character more truly. The Commission has drawn professional assistance largely from the Western bloc and the Russion Federation.

Unlike its WMD physical infrastructure, Iraq's intellectual infrastructure cannot be dismantled by UNSCOM. However, UNSCOM's long-term monitoring regime is intended to prevent Iraq's "brain power" from rebuilding the dismantled physical infrastructure. This regime should provide sufficient assurance against Iraq resuming production of proscribed weapons after the lifting of sanctions.

Conclusion

Power and force remain at the heart of international relations. With the pursuit of military power and economic power intended to reinforce each other, international organizations are increasingly being employed to serve the interests of the wealthy and powerful states. The World Trade Organization has come in handy to the rich nations to push their commercial interests, centred on greater access to foreign markets for their goods and services. In the political realm, a selective use of international organizations to promote great-power interests is taking place, as the wealthy states seek to hold on to their traditional advantages in the face of rising competition from Asian and other nations.

With most Western economies sheltered by a nuclear arsenal or a nuclear umbrella, and the developing world no longer a consolidated bloc with common interests, the UN Security Council, the IAEA and UNSCOM have emerged in recent years as the favourite organizations of the strong. These organizations supplement the great powers' unilateral strategies, pivoted on the readiness to employ force to defend vital interests. Credibly conveying the threat to use force to defend national interests is for these states as important as actually employing force. Meanwhile, the original balance between non-proliferation and disarmament that helped create the NPT and the IAEA safeguards regime has been visibly eroded.

Since the end of the Cold War, the great powers and their allies are claiming that WMD proliferation has replaced the Cold War as the main threat to international peace and security. The ghost of Iraq is being seen everywhere. Strenuous efforts are being made to strengthen non-proliferation norms, erect new technical barriers to proliferation, and involve international organizations in arms control and non-proliferation in a big way.

Arms control is sought to be pursued mainly to reinforce the present status quo in the global power structure. One of the tools of arms control is technology control and denial. The major powers and their allies have been engaged in recent years in tightening and expanding domestic and international export-control mechanisms. Security-linked technology controls have ominously changed from an East–West to a North–South perspective after the Cold War. Today, the major states harp on about the dangers of the spread of dual-use technologies and run ad hoc, non-transparent regimes without the UN's sanction. History, however, bears testimony to the long-term ineffectiveness of technology-control strategies.

The main arms-control efforts have been concentrated on two objectives: making "non-proliferation" a respectable and lawful enterprise through international agreements, treaties, and norms; and stabilizing deterrence. Multilateral arms-control agreements are tied by one common theme: when they were signed, they did not clash with the vital interests of the great powers. The great powers, eager to boost their disarmament credentials, have always been ready to accept a treaty so long as it does not significantly constrain the control, movement, and deployment of nuclear weapons. This has spawned treaties bordering on the ridiculous that declare nuclear-free the seabed as well as the moon and all other celestial bodies within the solar system – except the Earth!

No international arms-control agreement has yet been concluded that seeks materially to alter the status quo. The NPT and CTBT are clearly intended to preserve the status quo. The CTBT is the first treaty in history which seeks not merely to compel its signatories to comply with its provisions, but demands that certain states be its signatories or face unspecified "measures consistent with international law." The 1993 Chemical Weapons Convention was concluded after two decades of negotiations only when such weapons came to be widely viewed as a "poor nation's deterrent."

Against this background, what role can international organizations play in arms control? Today, the United Nations is in crisis and there are growing demands for major reforms to broaden its decision-making structure and allow it to play an independent role. Its present structure, fashioned by the Second World War victors, is such that it has very little independent power and its effective functioning rests on unity among the great powers. UN reforms would also impact on other international organizations. The United Nations and other international organizations have to promote a truly collective form of security rather than serve the partisan interests of some or all of the great powers.

International organizations should be careful not to lend legitimacy to the orchestration of any threat. The claim that the proliferation problem has dramatically worsened after the end of the Cold War is one example. The Democratic People's Republic of Korea, Libya, Iran, and Iraq have became the archetypical justifications for stepped-up non-proliferation efforts. The use of these examples serves to exaggerate deliberately the gravity of potential threats from the third world. There are few new pro-liferant candidates in the developing world. Most such candidates are in the advanced industrial world – but under a US nuclear umbrella. The so-called "rogue" states in the third world serve as useful bugbears for some of the major powers to gain domestic support for retaining Cold War military postures and doctrines, finding new strategic goals and mis-sions, and employing coalitions and cartels to reinforce their interests. The rogue-states doctrine has also come in handy to launch the US counter-proliferation initiative, which includes the threat of military action.

With strength respecting strength in international relations, the stepped-up use of national intelligence assets to promote national interests asser-tively can only be expected, even against allies. The recent controversies regarding American intelligence activities in Germany, France, and Japan underscore the escalating technological and commercial rivalries in the advanced industrial world. Little attention, however, has been paid to the furtive use of national intelligence assets by the wealthy and powerful states to influence the agendas of international organizations individually and collectively. Information gathered by national technical means is worming its way to select organizations without any international sanction. The NTM-aided "discoveries" by one organization can be used to shape the agenda of another international organization. For example, UNSCOM's periodic Western-intelligence-assisted disclosures on Iraq help lend support to demands for arming the IAEA with police-style search powers to prevent clandestine proliferation activity. They are also used to support claims that WMD proliferation has replaced the Cold War as the main threat to international security. The funnelling of national intelligence information to, and its use by, the IAEA and UNSCOM are bound to generate international concern and controversy.

Certain international organizations today are playing a larger role in arms control and non-proliferation. But not the UN General Assembly, the most representative international organization. The General Assembly has passed many nuclear disarmament resolutions with overwhelming support from its member states, but has been unsuccessful in implementing them because of opposition by the nuclear powers and their allies. The very first resolution passed in early 1946 mandated "the elimination from national armaments of atomic weapons." Since then, the General Assembly has repeatedly called for negotiations on a phased, time-bound disarmament programme, and every year the world is reminded that nuclear weapons' use would be "a crime against humanity." But as the real power in international relations is with the five nuclear powers, who are also the Permanent Members of the Security Council, the General Assembly has remained toothless.

The selective use of international organizations for arms control is best illustrated by the disdain with which the 1996 ICJ advisory opinion has been treated by the great powers. The Court said the nuclear powers are legally obliged not only to negotiate in good faith, but to achieve the dismantlement of all weapons of mass extermination. "The obligation involved here is an obligation to achieve a precise result – nuclear disarmament in all its aspects – by adopting a particular course of conduct, namely, the pursuit of negotiations on the matter in good faith."[13] With unanimous weight thrown behind it, that twofold obligation, according to ICJ President Mohammed Bedjaoui, has now assumed customary force in international law.

The new legal principles – a major boost to global efforts to strip nuclear weapons of their halo as lawful instruments of security for the great powers and their allies – should be viewed as making it criminal to unleash a Hiroshima- or Nagasaki-style nuclear holocaust. The advisory opinion removes any claim of legitimacy from offensive first-use nuclear doctrines, maintained by four of the five nuclear powers. The fifth power, China, added conditionality to its no-first-use posture in 1995 to exclude its rival India.

Since the only grey area in law now relates to a self-defence situation where the state's very existence is at stake, extended deterrence pivoted on the constant threat to use nuclear arms first should be seen as contrary to international law. The legality of tactical or battlefield "nukes" is also open to challenge, since they cannot and are not intended to safeguard the survival of a nation. China is known to have such weapons, while the US-Russian bilateral accord on elimination of tactical arms specifically excludes air-launched "nukes." The United States has recently added a new tactical nuclear warhead to its armoury, the bunker-busting "B-61 mod-11."

In addition to the ICJ opinion that the nuclear powers are legally obliged to begin and conclude disarmament negotiations, there is a General Assembly resolution requiring the setting up of an ad hoc negotiating committee on disarmament at the Geneva-based Conference on Disarmament. But the great powers have contemptuously refused to begin negotiations, and have questioned the very appropriateness of the Conference on Disarmament as a forum for negotiating deep cuts in existing nuclear arsenals.

The future success of non-proliferation will essentially depend on the incentives for nuclear weapons' acquisition being eroded or eliminated. This demands that the military and political value of nuclear weapons be de-emphasized. As long as nuclear weapons remain instruments of power, influence, and intimidation in international politics and serve as the "strategic equalizer" to the conventional military superiority of an adversary or adversaries, nations outside security alliances will be attracted to them.

Lastly, it is well to remember that proliferation is a political problem. Technical fixes by themselves cannot help resolve, or even deal with, a political problem. A political problem needs international cooperation and support for settlement.

Notes

1. The White House, *A National Security Strategy of Engagement and Enlargement* (Washington, DC: February 1996).
2. Ibid., p. 21.
3. Institute for National Strategic Studies, *Strategic Assessment 1996* (Washington, DC: National Defense University, 1996), p. 85.
4. See Lawrence Scheinman, *The International Atomic Energy Agency and World Nuclear Order* (Washington, DC: Resources for the Future, 1987); Joseph F. Pilat, Robert F. Pemdley, and Charles K. Ebinger (eds.), *Atoms for Peace: An Analysis After Thirty Years* (Boulder: Westview, 1985); Paul Szasz, *The Law and Practices of the International Atomic Energy Agency* (Vienna: IAEA, 1970); Office of Technology Assessment, *Nuclear Safeguards and the International Atomic Energy Agency* (Washington, DC: US Government Printing Office, June 1995); and Bertrand Goldchmidt, *The Atomic Com-*

plex: A Worldwide Political History of Nuclear Energy (La Grange Parl, Illinois: American Nuclear Society, 1982).

5. Michael Mandelbaum, *The Nuclear Question* (Cambridge, UK: Cambridge University Press, 1979), p. 35.

6. David Albright, Frans Berkhout, and William Walker, *Plutonium and Highly Enriched Uranium 1996*, SIPRI (New York: Oxford University Press, 1997), p. 426.

7. Statement of Berhan Andemicael of the IAEA, *Disarmament*, volume on "Ending Reliance on Nuclear and Conventional Arms" (United Nations, 1995), p. 55.

8. David A. V. Fischer, "Viewpoint: New Directions and Tools For Strengthening IAEA Safeguards," *The Non-proliferation Review* (Winter 1996), p. 71.

9. Steve Fetter, "Verifying Nuclear Disarmament," Occasional Paper 29 (Washington, DC: Henry L. Stimson Center, October 1996), p. 28.

10. Barbara Crossette, "Iraqi Children Are Main Victims of Sanctions, UNICEF Says," *International Herald Tribune*, 26–27 October 1996, p. 2.

11. Ibid.

12. Secretary of State Madeleine Albright, Question-and-Answer Session at Georgetown University, 26 March 1997, *Official Text*, p. 2.

13. International Court of Justice, Legality of the Threat or Use of Nuclear Weapons, Advisory Opinion (The Hague: ICJ, 8 July 1996).

18

The Security Council in the post-Cold War era

David Malone[1]

Introduction

Practically from the launch of the United Nations in 1945 until the mid-1980s, its Security Council's potential to contribute to international peace and security was hobbled by Cold War rivalries. The Council did play a useful role in brokering cease-fires and mediating certain disputes, but as long as the United Sates and USSR (with their respective allies) duelled for global supremacy, often through regional proxies, use of the veto ensured that the Council's margin for manoeuvre remained narrow. However, the ascension to power of Mikhail Gorbachev in Moscow yielded early signs at the United Nations of a thaw in the Cold War when the Permanent Five (P-5) members of the Council consulted closely on the selection of a UN Secretary-General in 1986. In late 1986, Sir John Thomson (United Kingdom) took the initiative to call together the P-5 Ambassadors at his residence for an informal discussion on how they could hasten the end of the murderous Iran–Iraq war.[2] Although China remained somewhat leery of active P-5 coordination for some time, a system of regular P-5 informal meetings soon took hold. These meetings helped anticipate and defuse friction among the five and allowed them to exchange notes respecting various crises, if not formally to coordinate their positions.

In spite of Gorbachev's celebrated *Pravda* and *Izvestia* article of 17

September 1987 seeking "wider use of ... the institution of UN military observers and UN peace-keeping forces in disengaging the troops of warring sides, observing cease-fires and armistice agreements," and calling for the P-5 to become "guarantors" of international security, some representatives on the Council during the years from 1988 to 1990 report that the Soviet delegation, on issues such as Namibia, was prone to revert to "type," in other words declaratory diplomacy and the threat of stonewalling. Former Soviet diplomats remember matters differently, stressing that they were merely defending legitimate Soviet perspectives on the substantive questions before the Council. However, converging perspectives among the P-5 allowed the Council to initiate action towards settlement of several international crises. It thus launched the missions to address crises affecting Iran and Iraq, Afghanistan, Angola, Namibia, and Central America, all prior to the outbreak of the Iraq–Kuwait hostilities in August 1990.

The Iraqi invasion and subsequent annexation of Kuwait in August 1990 led the Council to adopt assertive mandates to reverse these Iraqi steps. Robust Council decisions during the entire Iraq–Kuwait crisis, including measures adopted following the March 1991 cease-fire by members of the anti-Iraq coalition to establish no-fly zones within Iraq and to provide humanitarian assistance to the Kurdish population, proved important not only in their own right but also because they proved precedential in many respects.[3]

The success of the anti-Iraq coalition, under its Security Council mandate, induced an era of euphoria in the Council which could not have arisen under the balance-of-power politics of the Cold War. It lasted roughly from March 1991 (the end of hostilities in the Gulf region) to October 1993 (with the deaths of 18 US Rangers in Mogadishu and the withdrawal from Port-au-Prince harbour, in the face of a small demonstration, of the US troop transporter *Harlan County* carrying Canadian and US peacekeepers to Haiti). During these 31 months, the Security Council accelerated its activities, launching 14 new peace-keeping and observer missions as compared to 17 in the previous 46 years, and adopting 187 resolutions (compared to 685).

The Security Council summit and "An Agenda for Peace"

Building on an emerging consensus in much of the world that the Security Council was at last coming into its own, the first-ever Security Council summit was convened on 31 January 1992 to discuss new orientations and activities for the Council. In his remarks on this occasion, the new

Secretary-General, Boutros Boutros-Ghali, emphasized "democratization at the national and international levels," noting that state sovereignty was taking on a new meaning:

Added to its dimension of right is the dimension of responsibility, both internal and external.... Civil wars are no longer civil, and the carnage they inflict will not let the world remain indifferent. The narrow nationalism that would oppose or disregard the norms of a stable international order and the micro-nationalism that resists healthy economic or political integration can disrupt a peaceful global existence.[4]

The representatives of China and Zimbabwe echoed President Bush's 1991 talk of a "new world order" (a phrase Bush avoided at this summit), but China pointed to the importance of mutual respect for sovereignty and "non-interference in each other's affairs."[5]

At its conclusion, the summit invited the Secretary-General to prepare a report on "ways of strengthening ... the capacity of the United Nations for preventive diplomacy, for peace-making, and for peace-keeping."[6] In June 1992, the Secretary-General responded with a wide-ranging and ambitious document, "An Agenda for Peace." It advocated, *inter alia*, consideration of a "preventive deployment" of UN peacekeepers to forestall hostilities known to be looming;[7] the widespread negotiation of standby agreements between the United Nations and member states allowing for more rapid identification of potential peace-keeping units and their deployment to theatres of operation;[8] and, when warranted, the use of force by the United Nations itself rather than by coalitions of member states.[9] Much of the document's substance was gutted by an open-ended working group of the General Assembly active in 1992 and 1993, which could agree only on lowest-common-denominator bromides. Interventionist provisions were combated by many non-aligned countries, while the P-5 seemed eager to protect their Council prerogatives, particularly by opposing Boutros-Ghali's calls for a greater International Court of Justice (ICJ) role in the UN's work on peace and security and his suggestion that the Secretary-General be authorized to seek advisory opinions from the Court.[10]

By 1995, in his supplement to an Agenda for Peace (more of a reassessment than an addendum), Boutros-Ghali sounded a more sombre note:

Neither the Security Council nor the Secretary-General at present has the capacity to deploy, direct, command, or control [enforcement] operations except perhaps on a very limited scale... It would be folly to attempt to do so at the present time when the Organization is resource-starved and hard pressed to handle the less demanding peace-making and peace-keeping responsibilities entrusted to it.[11]

Nevertheless, the Secretary-General did advance the need for a UN "rapid reaction force" composed of battalion-sized units trained to similar standards, stationed in their home countries but maintained in a high state of readiness.[12] This suggestion built on research and planning work undertaken earlier by Canada, Denmark, and the Netherlands.[13] As of March 1997, plans for a UN rapid-deployment mission headquarters were well in hand at the United Nations.

Cooperation among the P-5

Since 1990, relations among the P-5 have fluctuated. The Soviet Union (later the Russian Federation) has generally cooperated closely with its Western partners. Whatever the reservations of some of its foreign policy experts may have been, the USSR yielded to strong American leadership during the 1990–1991 Gulf crisis – a pattern that would continue to prevail in the Council, albeit along a bumpier course, particularly with respect to the former Yugoslavia. However, since 1994 there have been growing complaints from the Russian delegation that "double standards" have arisen under which the United States gets pretty much what it wants, for example on Haiti and in securing Council acquiescence to the Dayton Accords, while Western support for a UN mission in Georgia to observe the CIS (Confederation of Independent States) peace-keeping operation in Abkhazia was grudging at best. Tensions also developed between the United States and its Western European partners over the former Yugoslavia. Disagreement prevailed among the P-3 (France, the United Kingdom, and the United States) over Bosnia and Herzegovina throughout 1993 and 1994, when France and the United Kingdom were bearing the brunt of risk and casualties within UNPROFOR (UN Protection Force in Former Yugoslavia) while the United States cavilled from the side-lines, advocating approaches it soon abandoned when it took the lead in forging a peace settlement at Dayton. The Russian Federation, for its part, disagreed with Western policies on the former Yugoslavia but did participate in UNPROFOR alongside France and the United Kingdom.

Tensions over the former Yugoslavia were effectively quarantined, with France, the United Kingdom, and the United States cooperating closely on other issues, often with active Russian support. Indeed, accommodations between France, the Russian Federation, and the United States in mid-1994 allowed France tenuously to secure Council authorization to lead Opération Turquoise to stabilize south-western Rwanda (a proposal which had aroused deep suspicion in New York, given France's close ties to Hutu politicians), Moscow to extract the reluctant consent of its Western P-5 partners for an expansion of UNOMIG (United Nations Observer Mission in Georgia), and the United States to obtain Council authorization to undertake military action against the de facto régime in Haiti. These developments, taken together, raised concern over the possible emergence of "spheres of influence" brokered in the Security Council. Nevertheless, accommodations among the P-5 have limits, particularly where perceptions of unilateralism on the part of one of the five undermine consensus. In September 1996 the United Kingdom signally failed to rally the support of France, the Russian Federation, or China for a Council resolution essentially supporting US bombing raids in Iraq in retaliation for Iraqi involvement in internecine Kurdish fighting some days earlier.

China swung into action only when its national interests were at stake, as it did in February 1996 when it insisted on the down-sizing of UNOMIH (United Nations Observer Mission in Haiti) to punish the Haitian government for an ill-advised high-level dalliance with Taiwan, and again in January 1997 when it initially refused to consent to the deployment of UN military observers in Guatemala on similar grounds. It is remarkable how little China dissented actively from P-4 initiatives, although it often sought to distance itself from the decisions involved through explanations of vote. Overall, the much-improved climate among the P-5, directly attributable to the end of the Cold War, can be gauged by the sharp decline in the use of the veto: only five have been invoked since May 1990, relative to 193 during the first 45 years of the UN's history.[14]

The P-5's dominant position is reflected in the Council's relations with the UN Secretariat, which is sometimes perceived as excessively compliant to the wishes of the Permanent Members. The *modus operandi* in drafting a report from the Secretary-General to stimulate Council decisions on a given problem is often to take the pulse of the P-5 and establish the parameters of action they would favour. The report is then generally tailored accordingly.[15] Military advice, particularly from the field, is often the first casualty.[16]

The P-5 and the Non-Aligned Movement

While the Security Council's action on Iraq was broadly supported by the UN membership, several non-aligned states within the Council (notably Cuba, Yemen, Ecuador, India, and Zimbabwe), along with China, at different times dissented from or abstained on some of the Council's decisions on Iraq, signalling some tension between the P-4 (France, the United Kingdom, the United States, and the former Soviet Union) and strands of Non-Aligned Movement (NAM) opinion at a time when the initiative of drafting Security Council resolutions was sliding inexorably from the NAM (and its traditional issues such as apartheid and the Arab–Israeli dispute) to the P-4 (and its emerging concerns). With the end of the Cold War, the ability of NAM members in the Council to play the superpowers off against each other has vanished, while at the same time differences in perspective and interests among the NAM countries have come to the fore. The NAM caucus of the Council has been able to assert itself only when divisions among the P-5 present it with opportunities, as was the case with the Council's approach to Bosnia and Herzegovina from 1993 to 1995. Even here, an attempt on 28 June 1993 by the five-country NAM caucus, joined by the United States, to have the UN arms embargo against Bosnia and Herzegovina lifted failed when the Council's other members abstained *en masse*, depriving the NAM of the nine positive votes it required to carry the day.[17] It is only through the influence of individual dynamic, highly-regarded representatives such as Pakistan's Jamshid Marker, Malaysia's Razali Ismail, Venezuela's Diego Arria, Egypt's Nabil Elarabi, and Chile's Juan Somavia that the NAM has recently helped shape Council decisions.[18]

Tensions between Security Council and General Assembly

With the new-found activism of the Security Council came apprehensions among General Assembly members, particularly those belonging to the NAM, that the Council could venture into territory hitherto within the Assembly's ambit. Fears over the expansion of the Council's powers came to a head in 1989 over the deployment of a UN mission to Nicaragua to observe elections. Once the Secretary-General had reached agreement with Nicaragua to dispatch this mission (ONUVEN), the Council's NAM members insisted that the General Assembly and not the Council endorse it. When the Secretary-General in 1990 raised the prospect with the Council of sending a second such electoral observation mission to Haiti, Colombia, and Cuba, the then Latin American members on the Council argued strongly that the mission should be authorized by the General Assembly. Manoeuvring on this issue lasted several months, eventually resulting in General Assembly authorization of the mission in October 1990.[19] Similar tensions arose over the creation of a UN human rights verification mission in Guatemala in 1994. The Secretary-General had initially anticipated that it would constitute the first component of a broader mission, including military staff, called upon to monitor a nego-tiated settlement to the civil strife in Guatemala. Accordingly, he had planned to approach the Security Council to authorize the mission as a whole, with advance deployment of its human rights component. However, following sharp protests from within the NAM, he redirected the request for authorization of the human rights mission to the General Assembly.[20] As P-5 members pay a higher proportion of peace-keeping costs incurred through Security Council decisions than they do of items approved under the UN's "regular" scale of assessments, several P-5 members were happy to see the General Assembly saddled with responsibility for financing such missions.[21]

The Security Council and internal conflicts

Following the conclusion of Operation Desert Storm, the Security Council was increasingly inclined to tackle other conflicts. In apparent disregard of UN Charter Article 2 (7), inveighing against UN intervention in "matters which are essentially within the domestic jurisdiction of any state," the Council, with or without the consent of the governments involved, addressed internal crises in Haiti, Cambodia, El Salvador, Georgia, Liberia, Mozambique, Rwanda, Somalia, and Tajikistan, and built on earlier Council activity on Angola.[22] However much these conflicts may have had international implications, several of them could not credibly be construed as constituting a threat to international peace and security. The concept of sovereignty has been eroded, with consequences we can only guess at today. Ultimately, this aspect of the Council's activities in the 1990s may prove the most important.

The United Nations' involvement in civil conflict was not new: the UN operations in Congo, 1960–1964, and in Cyprus since 1964, aimed to stabilize volatile domestic situations portrayed as threatening regional peace and security. However, these operations were never regarded as precedential within the United Nations. After the Cold War ended, the Security Council waded into internal conflicts because these were the wars on offer (the "CNN effect" ensuring that several – but by no means all – of them received saturation coverage, particularly in their impact on civilians) and because, with P-5 cooperation now taking hold, it became possible to address them actively. A belief took hold within the Council that it had not only the capacity but the duty to act.[23]

The Council, under pressure of rapidly unfolding events, displayed a high degree of creativity, developing hybrid forms of operation new to the United Nations, starting with UNTAG (United Nations Transitional Assistance Group) in Namibia in 1989–1990. These hybrids involved more frequent resort to civilian components responsible, *inter alia*, for humanitarian assistance, human rights, electoral assistance, and economic rehabilitation. Growing UN promotion of democratic processes (and respect for human rights) to overcome civil strife would never have been possible in the Cold War era. Countries such as China have accepted and even supported these activities on a case-by-case basis in "exceptional" circumstances. A significant body of precedent has now built up.

The use of force

Perhaps the most striking development in Council decision-making since 1990 has been its disposition to authorize the use of force. Sometimes the use of force, under Chapter VII of the Charter, was planned virtually from the outset, and sometimes it was not. Resistance on the ground to aspects of UN peace-keeping activities sometimes led to a process of "mission creep," in which the Council moved beyond impartiality and the consent for UN activities by parties to a conflict to enforcement measures against one or several of them. The piecemeal addition of enforcement duties to peace-keeping operations ill-equipped to handle them was a major source of difficulties in Bosnia and Herzegovina, and the proximate cause of the UN's inability to continue functioning in Somalia. In retrospect, the Council was not sufficiently sensitive to the operational difficulties experienced or anticipated by UN field personnel and headquarters peace-keeping staff. Indeed, at times it mandated action in the knowledge that its decisions could not be fully implemented, for example in creating safe areas in Bosnia and Herzegovina in 1993. The eventual result was disastrous for the civilians overrun in 1995 in Srebrenica, and the UN's credibility was seriously undermined.[24] In Somalia, the Council does not appear to have appreciated the extent to which national concerns over the safety of personnel deployed under the UN flag could undermine the chain of command of UNOSOM (UN Operation in Somalia) II, which began to unravel in June 1993.

This does not mean that enforcement is always the wrong approach for the international community.[25] President Aristide would never have been restored in Haiti without the threat of force in mid-September 1994. Equally, the hostilities in Bosnia and Herzegovina might have continued indefinitely without massive bombing by NATO in 1995, which, together with a shift in military advantage on the ground, brought Serbia to the negotiating table at Dayton. The authorization and capacity to use force of IFOR (Implementation Force in Croatia and Bosnia and Herzegovina) doubtless contributed to the successful implementation of the Dayton military provisions in 1996. However, the Council is unlikely soon again to seek to enforce its decisions through a UN peace-keeping operation. Rather, it will continue to turn to coalitions of member states to implement enforcement mandates agreed within the Council.

Even bearing in mind the special difficulties militating against forcible international involvement in internal conflicts, public opinion will continue to demand action in cases of widely reported suffering among civilians. An inclination within the Council to involve the United Nations on the ground only in ideal circumstances may again yield to such pressure in the future.[26]

New legal ground is broken

A notable feature of the Council's new activism was the creation of international criminal tribunals to try breaches of humanitarian law in the former Yugoslavia (1993) and Rwanda (1994).[27] By creating tribunals, the Council significantly raised the stakes in efforts to punish war crimes without having settled (for example, in the resolution authorizing IFOR) the priority to be given to these tasks relative to others discharged by the international community. The risks to the Council's credibility should not be underestimated: experience to date suggests that the tribunals may find it impossible to convict many indictees, given a lack of resolve by the international community in seeking their arrest.

Institutional development

The Council's institutional life also evolved in the 1990s. Because of its increased activism and growing importance in the early 1990s, pressure grew for reform of both its composition and its working methods. The NAM pressed for greater representation on the Security Council, with many of its members advocating new permanent seats for developing countries, while Germany and Japan advanced claims for a permanent seat each. As of early 1997, General Assembly negotiations on this question were deadlocked, in part because of the inability of several regional groups, notably Asia and Africa, to develop a consensus on which of their members might qualify. National positions have been predictably self-interested. Countries tend to support schemes which would maximize their own representation in the Council. They prefer the status quo to proposals which do not achieve this narrow end. However, the log-jam could be broken, if only because, in these fiscally-straitened times, Germany and Japan's ability to help finance the United Nations may force attention to their claims.

Less publicized has been the evolution in the Council's working methods brought about by pressure from the membership at large, particularly by troop-contributing nations (TCNs), for more openness and consultation by the Council.[28] As early as 1992, TCNs such as the Scandinavians, Malaysia, Argentina, and Canada hinted broadly that their participation in peace-keeping operations should not be taken for granted by a Council apparently indifferent to their views. The arrival of Madeleine Albright as US Permanent Representative in early 1993 accelerated change: she was openly sympathetic to demands for greater Council transparency. In mid-1993 the Council decided that the provisional agenda for each Council meeting should be included in the daily *Journal of the United Nations*, a useful innovation for those delegations wishing to lobby Council members on given questions. A month later, the Council decided that its monthly forecast of work should be made available to all member states.[29] Under pressure from within (notably from Argentina and New Zealand) as well as from TCNs at large, the Council in May 1994 recognized the need for greater consultation with TCNs in a variety of formats.[30] The Council also came to recognize that its habit of conducting most business during closed informal consultations was grating, and decided that there should be greater recourse to open meetings.[31] Other decisions made more transparent the workings of the various committees established by the Council to monitor and implement sanctions regimes.[32]

Further suggestions have been made in the General Assembly, including the participation of potential TCNs as well as countries already contributing troops in consultations with the Secretariat and Council on given peace-keeping operations; the launch of "orientation debates" when the Council takes up a new question (allowing the remaining member states to become conversant with the particulars of the issue); the opening of Sanctions Committee meetings to all member states; the creation of a body subsidiary to the Council to monitor important peace-keeping operations with the participation of TCNs; a closer relationship between the Council and the International Court of Justice, including the option for the Council to seek the opinion of the Court on controversial matters with legal implications; and consultation with third parties affected by sanctions imposed on a country, paying greater attention to Article 50 of the UN Charter.[33] Some of these measures will probably be adopted in the future.

Groups of friends

An important development has been the emergence of informal groupings of countries, some members of the Council, others not, to steer given issues at the United Nations. The phenomenon is not entirely new – for example, the "Contact Group" for Namibia from 1978 to 1990. However, such groups have proliferated in the 1990s, generally under the rubric of "Friends of the Secretary-General," who nominally invites these countries to advise him on a given problem (in fact, the groups are largely self-selecting). They have played a leading role in the design and implementation of UN strategies in, for example, Cambodia, El Salvador, and Haiti.[34]

However, the emergence of such groups, while useful to the Secretary-General and welcomed by most Security Council members as preparing the ground effectively for Council action, was greeted with dismay by others, such as New Zealand. They complained that these "self-appointed" groups were undermining the sovereign equality of all Council members, as recommendations from a "group of friends" were not easily challenged within the Council. These groups have also not always been viewed as impartial: for example, the group of friends for the Western Sahara is perceived by many as frankly sympathetic to Morocco's position in the dispute. They have equally not always been effective: for instance, the group of friends for Georgia, in spite of Russian membership, has succeeded principally in stymieing the Russian desire for greater UN involvement in Abkhazia and a clear UN endorsement of the CIS peace-keeping role there. It has not, to date, greatly assisted in resolution of the conflict within Georgia.

Nevertheless, groups of friends seem to be here to stay. One important by-product of their emergence is that they have often taken over the crucial drafting role earlier monopolized by the P-5 in preparing Council resolutions, thus somewhat diffusing the power of the P-5 to lead above all other member states. The involvement of non-permanent, and indeed non-Council, members in the drafting process may prove salutary in tempering P-5 idiosyncracies, although P-5 members largely dominate within groups of friends.

Future orientations for the Council

An important lesson learned in the period 1992–1995, particularly in Somalia, has been that the Council should not attempt to enforce its resolutions unless both the political will and the necessary resources are available to do so – the latter now unlikely with the UN's financial crisis ever deepening. The Security Council must define clearly both objectives and strategy prior to the launch of a peace-keeping operation. It must also develop staying power, combating the obvious attractions of "early exit" scenarios and unrealistic "sunset" clauses (driven in large measure by the United States), if its action is to succeed lastingly. The Council must learn to be more sensitive to military advice from the Secretariat, and may need to consider more carefully the legal implications of its decisions. There are growing calls for legal review of Council decisions (by the ICJ), with Council decisions on Libya and Serbia already under challenge in The Hague.[35]

Conclusions

During the era of euphoria, 1991–1993, when a particular approach mandated by the Council was perceived to be failing or inadequate, another was often instituted, sometimes quite abruptly. In retrospect, this era of the Council's life seems one of optimistic experimentation, often on a heroic scale, grounded in the belief that under a new world order the Security Council's will could be imposed, by means of arms if necessary.

The Security Council today is a cautious body, heavily weighed down by financial constraints, arising in part from recent "overstretch." Its mood seems set mostly by that of the United States. Until late 1995, US power in the Council, although vastly greater than that of any other country, was circumscribed to some extent by disagreements with France and the United Kingdom over the former Yugoslavia. However, since Dayton, American power has been overwhelming: according to one Council ambassador, the United States is no longer the last remaining superpower, but rather "the supreme power." As long as Congressional sentiment remains negative towards the United Nations, a dramatic revival of the Council's leadership on distant crises such as that in Burundi is unlikely unless public pressure becomes overwhelming.[36] Presidential leadership could make a difference. It was George Bush who put the United Nations on the map again in 1990 by channelling international reaction to the Iraqi invasion of Kuwait through the Security Council. The manner of the US Administration's announcement, in the mid-1996 presidential election campaign, that it wished to see Boutros Boutros-Ghali replaced and its later use of the veto to this end seemed crass, but the election of Kofi Annan, with whom Washington is more comfortable, may provide the opportunity for new departures. Close cooperation between Washington and the Secretary-General is vital to the UN's capacity to function and to the Security Council's effectiveness. Whether the new Secretary-General will be more successful in securing payment of US financial obligations to the United Nations remains an open question. And whether a sounder financial foundation for the United Nations will encourage greater Security Council activism is also open to debate.

There is evidence that the Council has been absorbing the lessons of the recent past. The greatest risk today is not that the Council will again overextend itself but rather that, in years ahead, budgetary constraints and risk-aversion will lead it to underutilize its powers.[37] We should not turn our backs on the United Nations because it stumbled on occasion, sometimes spectacularly, in addressing the Security Council's ambitious agenda of the early 1990s. Nor should the Council be condemned for testing the limits of its authority and power in a new era of international cooperation. Rather, as Marrack Goulding argues,[38] the Council must develop a view of what it realistically can and should achieve over time. The UN's finances also need to be set on a more solid footing. If these modest conditions are met, the United Nations will continue to be a vital instrument in the promotion of international peace and security. It is hard to identify any promising alternative.

Notes

1. The author is grateful for a generous grant for research and writing from the John D. and Catherine T. MacArthur Foundation supporting his research on the Security Council. The views in this chapter are his alone and do not necessarily reflect those of the Canadian government.
2. For a fascinating account of how evolving dynamics among the P-5 allowed the Council to play a key role in ending the Iran–Iraq war, see Cameron Hume, *The United Nations, Iran and Iraq: How Peace-making Changed*, Bloomington: University of Indiana Press, 1994.
3. Several measures adopted by coalition members following the cease-fire, particularly in northern Iraq to protect and provide assistance to the Kurds, were initiated without explicit Council authorization. These measures were, however, never meaningfully challenged within the Council. A number of them were eventually taken over by the United Nations.
4. UN Document S/PV.3046 of 31 January 1992, pp. 8–9.
5. Ibid., pp. 91–2, remarks of Prime Minister Li Peng. Concerns over selectivity in the Council's work, the impact of sanctions on third parties, and interpretation of UN human rights agreements were voiced by Prime Minister Rao (India), pp. 95–102.
6. UN Document S/23500 of 31 January 1992, p. 3.
7. The first, and so far only, such preventive deployment, a modest but useful operation, was launched in Macedonia in 1992.
8. Standby agreements have now been negotiated with many member states. While useful as planning tools, they have proved unreliable: when asked to provide troops for risky operations, governments frequently decline. Thus, in some instances standby arrangements have simply allowed the United Nations to be turned down more rapidly by potential troop contributors.
9. Boutros-Ghali advocated the activation of the UN Charter's Article 43, whereby member states undertake to make armed forces, assistance, and facilities available to the Security Council for enforcement purposes. (The offering state relinquishes control over these assets to the Security Council under Article 43.) No such offers of personnel or equipment have ever, to date, been made to the United Nations.
10. For a revealing account of the follow-up within the United Nations to An Agenda for Peace, see David Cox, *Exploring An Agenda for Peace: Issues Arising from the Report of the Secretary-General*, Ottawa: Canadian Centre for Global Security, 1993.

11. UN Document A/50/60 of 3 January 1995, p. 18.
12. Ibid., p. 11.
13. For a useful discussion of the issues involved in providing the United Nations with a rapid-deployment force, see David Cox and Albert Legault (eds.), *UN Rapid Reaction Capabilities: Requirements and Prospects*, Clementsport: The Canadian Peacekeeping Press, 1995.
14. The five vetoes have been two by the Russian Federation (one in May 1993 over the financing of UNFICYP in Cyprus and another in December 1994 over sanctions against Serbia); two by the United States (in May 1995 over Israeli expropriation of land in East Jerusalem and another in April 1996 over Israeli military action against Lebanon); and one by China (in January 1997 in opposition to a UN military observer mission in Guatemala).
15. Boutros-Ghali did on several occasions confront the P-5 with unwelcome advice, for example opposing the creation of safe areas in Bosnia and Herzegovina in 1993 unless vastly increased military resources were offered to back up UN commitments to protect these communities. In July 1994, he also opposed a UN enforcement mission to Haiti (an option then preferred by the United States), in effect recommending a coalition effort to restore President Aristide to power.
16. To address this problem some suggest energizing the Military Staff Committee, but few member states are keen to enhance further the influence of the P-5, which control this body. Others advocate creating a Security Council subsidiary body composed of military advisers of Council members. However, cumbersome new machinery could inhibit the Council's flexibility and speed, which are among its key assets.
17. See UN Documents S/25997 for the text of the draft resolution and S/PV.3247 for the bitter Council debate on this text.
18. NAM members cite their efforts early in 1996 to prevent the United Nations from shutting down its stalled operation in Western Sahara as an example of their ability to overcome P-5 bloc positions. However, it is not clear that all of the P-5 strongly backed the Secretary-General's inclination to shut down MINURSO (United Nations Mission for the Referendum in Western Sahara).
19. The NAM argument in favour of General Assembly action was that election monitoring was not an international peace and security issue, and that ONUVEH (the UN electoral observation mission in Haiti) was not a peace-keeping operation. In fact, ONUVEH did include several dozen military "security staff," but was never defined in the Council as a peace-keeping operation.
20. UN Document A/48/985 of 18 August 1994.
21. For more detail, see Sally Morphet, "The influence of States and Groups of States in the Security Council and General Assembly, 1980–1994," *The Review of International Studies*, vol. 21, 1995, pp. 435–62.
22. Security Council action in internal crises, decided with the consent of the parties to a conflict, is considered by many not to conflict with Article 2(7).
23. A lively debate arose within the United Nations and beyond, particularly in the period 1992–1994, on the international community's "right to intervene" in civil conflicts in pursuit of humanitarian objectives. The debate was spearheaded by French Humanitarian Affairs Minister Bernard Kouchner, a founder of the NGO Médécins Sans Frontières. Some commentators, although few states, argued that there also exists a duty to intervene when civilians in large numbers are threatened. This debate subsided to some extent in 1995, with the complexities of many civil wars and the risks involved in outside intervention becoming more clearly understood.
24. For an interesting account of the improvisatory nature of much Security Council decision-making on Bosnia and Herzegovina, including on the "safe areas" concept, see

Sir David Hannay, "The UN's Role in Bosnia," *Oxford International Review*, Spring 1996, pp. 4–11.

25. For a useful discussion of this issue, see Adam Roberts, "From San Francisco to Sarajevo: The UN and the Use of Force," *Survival*, vol. 37, 4, Winter 1995–96, pp. 7–28.

26. It was public opinion through its pressure on governments which forced the Council on 16 May 1994 to reverse its decision some weeks earlier to scale back UNAMIR (United Nations Assistance Mission for Rwanda) following the upsurge of violence and the death of 10 Belgian peacekeepers there. However, by the time the additional UN units were able to deploy, most of the genocide was over.

27. The tribunal approach contrasts with the creation of a non-judicial Truth Commission in El Salvador under the terms agreed in the April 1991 Mexico Agreements. Implementation of its 1993 report has not always been smooth, but its acceptance in principle by the parties to the conflict helped to exorcise some of the demons released by the fighting. For an account of some difficulties encountered, see Alvaro de Soto and Graciana del Castillo, "Implementation of Comprehensive Peace Agreements: Staying the Course in El Salvador," *Global Governance*, 1 (1995), pp. 189–203. (Variations on the Truth Commission concept have been launched in both Haiti and South Africa, with disappointing results in the former case.)

28. See Michael Wood, "Security Council Working Methods and Procedure: Recent Developments," *The International and Comparative Law Quarterly*, vol. 45, January 1996, pp. 150–61.

29. UN Documents S/260 15 of 30 June 1993 and S/PRST/1994/62 of 4 November 1994.

30. UN Document S/PRST/1994/22 of 3 May 1994. Until this date, the Council held the view that TCN interests were confined to the implementation of mandates by the Secretariat rather than also including their formulation by the Council. In March 1996 the Council elaborated on the usefulness of consultations with TCNs and established a more structured approach to their organization (see UN Document S/PRST/1996/13 of 28 March 1996).

31. See UN Document S/PRST/1994/81 of 16 December 1996.

32. UN Documents S/1995/234 of 29 March 1995; S/1995/438 of 31 May 1995; and S/1996/54 of 24 January 1996.

33. UN Document A/AC.247/1996/CRP.4 of 16 April 1996, pp. 7–11. In the view of many member states, Article 50 by implication foresees compensation for or exemption from enforcement measures for a country "which finds itself confronted with special economic problems arising from the carrying out of those measures," although formally it provides only for "consultation" with the Council on a "solution of those problems." In practice, Article 50 has remained a dead letter throughout the 1990s.

34. For a first-hand account of a group of friends at work, see Diego Arria, "Diplomacy and the Four Friends of Haiti," in *Haitian Frustrations, Dilemmas for US Policy*, Center for Strategic and International Studies: Washington, DC, 1995, pp. 96–7.

35. Arguments for and against judicial review of Council decisions are outlined in Mohammed Bedjaoui, *The New World Order and the Security Council: Testing the Legality of its Acts*, Dordrecht: M. Neijhoff, 1994. See also Societé francaise pour le droit international, *Le Chapitre VII des la Charte des Nations unies*, Paris: A. Pédone, 1995.

36. Nevertheless, a small new observer mission in Guatemala was agreed on 20 January 1997 and another is likely in Sierra Leone.

37. See David M. Malone and John G. Cockell, *The Security Council in the 1990s: Lessons and Priorities*, Jules Léger Seminar Report, Ottawa: Department of Foreign Affairs and International Trade, 1996.

38. Marrack Goulding, "The Use of Force by the United Nations," Mountbatten-Tata Memorial Lecture at the University of Southampton, 23 November 1993.

19

UN military operations in the 1990s: "Lessons" from the recent past and directions for the near future

Thomas G. Weiss

Introduction

Euphoria at the end of the Cold War was short-lived. George Bush's "new world order" and Bill Clinton's "assertive multilateralism" ceded quickly to more sombre views, if not yet a more sober slogan.[1] Optimism about the possibilities for human security, democratization, and conflict resolution spread, along with the plague of micro-nationalism, fragmentation, and massive human displacement. The demise of East–West tensions did not mark what Francis Fukuyama and others hoped would be the peaceful triumph of Western liberalism and capitalism in "the end of history," but rather unleashed a more painful epoch of intense fragmentation of identities and societies.[2]

The onset of the post-Cold War era initially witnessed a reinvigorated United Nations dealing with threats to international peace and security. For a brief moment a new collegiality among the Permanent Members of the Security Council moved the world organization towards what its founders had imagined. However, Gulf War bullishness became multilateral doom and gloom following well-publicized, if not always accurate, depictions of UN shortcomings or outright failures. Observers usually point to 1993 and developments in the Horn of Africa as the turning point. Pollyannaish notions about intervening militarily to thwart aggression or thugs, and to help sustain civilians trapped in war zones or fleeing from them, were replaced by more realistic estimates about the limits of such undertakings – what has become known as the "Somalia syndrome." But former US Assistant Secretary of State Richard Holbrooke, who is generally credited with engineering the Dayton Accords, suggests that "The damage that Bosnia did to the United Nations was incalculable."[3] Whichever debacle wins first prize, the conventional wisdom in policy circles now is to refrain from UN military operations and to disdain UN involvement in crises. Nonetheless, at the dawn of the twenty-first century, is it too much to hope for enhanced global governance – better-ordered and more reliable responses to problems that go beyond the individual and even collective capacities of powerful states – in the field of international peace and security?

The working assumption behind this chapter is a partially affirmative response to this not-so-rhetorical question. The focus is on international groping and coping in the 1990–1996 period with "military operations" – a term selected to include both the traditional peace-keeping ilk and more muscular varieties, up to and including enforcement. Aware of the incomparabilities of many of the cases, of the significant geopolitical changes that have occurred since the collapse of the bipolar system, and of debates about whether the present disorder is new or old,[4] I will nonetheless with some trepidation draw key general policy lessons across disparate cases in the post-Cold War era.

Lessons for the United Nations as dependent variable ("arena" and "tool")

International organizations are arenas in which member states lay out their ambitions and pursue their foreign policy interests. The Security Council is often the centre stage, and states have taken their roles on it seriously in the post-Cold War era, which undoubtedly explains the diplomatic push in the middle of the decade to reform it.[5] The Charter shapes the terms of the contest in which nations seek to enhance their power and prestige. In the same period, UN military operations and those mounted by others but approved by the Council have also been tools for states pursuing their foreign policy goals. In the light of current geopolitical trends and UN overextension, states using the world organization as an arena or a tool should keep the following four lessons in mind.

Lesson 1: Establish without compromise a secure physical environment during a coercive military intervention

The first lesson about coercive military intervention necessitates a revision of conventional wisdom regarding the lack of consent for Chapter

VII operations.[6] Intervention does not require "consent" from the warring parties, but it does from the domestic constituencies of troop-contributing countries and from affected local populations. There is a progression of three steps underlying the first lesson. First, intervention must be preceded by establishing and maintaining support from the publics who send their sons and daughters into hostile environments. For example, Americans were prepared for possible casualties prior to Washington's involvement on the ground in Kuwait and Iraq; but the Administration did not prepare them in the Somalia case. Second, although consent by definition is not forthcoming from local belligerents for Chapter VII operations, widespread approval from local populations must be sought and nurtured. Again, Somalia illustrates the neglect by third-party interveners of local populations manipulated easily by belligerents into believing that those who came to assist them were contributing to their pain. Third and finally, with legitimacy established for possible deaths in action of soldiers and for the presence of "outsiders," there should be no compromises in robustly taking all requisite military efforts to establish a secure environment quickly.

If there is no commitment to satisfying all three of these steps, then there should be no intervention. The "messiness" of intervention comes from both lack of legitimacy and lack of efficiency. A well-planned, systematic response is required, but only after steps have been taken to garner consent from local populations in both troop-contributing states and the area of conflict. It is necessary for outsiders to re-establish security quickly and credibly in part of a disputed territory, even if subsequently additional reinforcements are sent or another strategy evolves. This is the opposite of a "slowly-turning-the-screws" approach, in the hopes that either political will or a meaningful strategy will somehow appear.

There are numerous pressures in other directions. While Western citizens, legislatures, and governments seek to avoid commitments, poignant media coverage sometimes elicits halfway measures. When massive and egregious abuses of civilians as well as widespread violence and starvation become unpalatable, the "CNN factor" often provokes action. But it also encourages much wishful thinking, underestimates long-term realities, and overlooks crises where journalists do not find convincing copy or footage for their editors.[7] Contributing countries must ask their citizenry if they are prepared to accrue casualties in order to succeed; if not, the emotions stirred by the media must find some outlet for expression other than half-hearted intervention.

Although the longer-term political prospects are uncertain – both for the Hussein regime and for the Kurds – the military efforts in northern Iraq were sufficient to maintain access. The determination to stay the course was and, as the events of late 1996 suggest, still is present. The initial deployment of troops from the United States, Britain, France, and Holland was backed by NATO air cover. When the soldiers withdrew, aircraft based in Turkey continually remained an effective threat because bombing sorties were authorized along with sanctions and other coercive measures. The same could be said for the initial US-led efforts in 1994 and the subsequent UN ones to restore the elected government of Jean-Bertrand Aristide in Haiti. In the case of Haiti, the Clinton Administration had to make the case to the American people in September 1994 after having failed to do so a year earlier, when a rowdy crowd on the docks in Port au Prince had led to an order for the retreat of the USS *Harlan County*. Similarly, no case was made for involvement in Bosnia and Herzegovina until the Dayton Accords, and then the initial sales pitch of deploying troops only for a year was far more closely linked to American domestic electoral concerns than to the reality on the ground in the Balkans.

The Iraqi Kurds and the Haitian people thus fared better than their Somali or Bosnian counterparts. The ineptitude of the first UN Operation in Somalia (UNOSOM I) was followed by the narrowness of the mandate for the Unified Task Force (UNITAF), or Operation Restore Hope. The American unwillingness to remove heavy arms from warring factions reflected a fear of casualties, and thereby compromised the goal of establishing a secure environment. Moreover, US soldiers failed to remain firmly in place until a semblance of a government was functioning, which reflected a basic design failure that ignored the crying need for an overall political strategy and for firmly establishing the consent of and communication with the Somali people.

The second UN Operation in Somalia (UNOSOM II) was doomed to fail. Chapter VII was invoked. For the first time the Secretary-General was in charge of such an operation. And for the first time the United Nations intervened in the domestic affairs of a member state even though Somalia did not present a military threat to its neighbours. But the initial US-led intervention was not early enough, long enough, or ambitious enough to ensure the preconditions for a successful UN take-over.

For Bosnia and Herzegovina, governments switched their rhetoric from the peaceful settlement tone of Chapter VI to the shrill enforcement decibel levels of Chapter VII, albeit initially to protect personnel. However, this rhetoric lacked both a political and a military commitment to implement the mandate for the UN Protection Force in the former Yugoslavia (UNPROFOR). The member states of the United Nations condemned its Bluehelmets to "wandering in the void" between peace-keeping and enforcement.[8]

What I have called "collective spinelessness"[9] is the antithesis of the timeliness and robustness of this first lesson about intervention. One of the explanations for proceeding otherwise within the United Nations is that states have failed to prepare UN operations. The result is that major powers are "particularly prone to crisis-induced reactions chosen for their symbolic value and ease of execution rather than their decisive effect."[10] The visceral reaction is to seek magical "quick fixes" and respond incrementally, hoping that warring parties will somehow come to their senses.

Options, for outsiders and local authorities, diminish with increasing violence and atrocities. It may be wiser to wait if robust intervention does not occur early in a crisis. Peace-keeping, traditional or muscular, can more easily take place after belligerents occupy relatively homogeneous and contiguous areas. Although many observers look upon partition as unstable and immoral, there is evidence of the potentially positive impact of ethnic homogeneity on conflict resolution. One scholar has written about the Balkans, for example, that "As the progress of the war has left fewer and fewer unmoved people still to move, more realistic proposals have gradually emerged."[11] If intervention is not timely, uniform swaths of territory rather than a multi-ethnic fabric then make UN peace-keeping viable and feasible. We should not overlook history in this context; the UN's efforts after 1974 in Cyprus could be interpreted as the first UN-assisted ethnic cleansing.

Lesson 2: Emphasize prevention, but without illusions

This repugnant reality lends yet another reason to pursue prevention – which, in fact, is an early form of external intrusion into domestic affairs. A "stitch in time" resonates nicely in multilateral ears. But such a desirable framework usually also provides the least plausible rationale for states to use UN military operations. Stephen Stedman has compared prevention to "alchemy"; I have compared it to a "pipe-dream."[12] Preventive diplomacy is the latest conceptual fashion – according to an honest formulation, "an idea in search of a strategy."[13]

Such preventive actions as the expanded use of fact-finding missions and human rights' monitors are being discussed and attempted. Economic and social development are generally viewed as essential to help prevent armed conflicts, even if the results of substantial aid and investment in the former Yugoslavia and Rwanda are hardly encouraging for those like the former UN Secretary-General wishing to make a case for "preventive development" as a "necessary complement to preventive diplomacy."[14] Such efforts have in fact been UN emphases for half a century.

But what is new in terms of forestalling massive displacement and suffering is information and a military capacity to respond. The former, consisting of various aspects of early warning, occurs in peacetime, is feasible, and could be improved, although no independent intelligence-gathering capacity is possible. But the second and essential preventive capacity for times of crisis – and the one of direct concern for this chapter – is non-existent. Although it has been heralded by many as a success, the symbolic deployment of a detachment of UN Bluehelmets to Macedonia has worked only because the international bluff has not yet been called.

To be a successful deterrent, preventive soldiers must be backed by contingency plans and reserve fire-power for immediate retaliation against aggressors. This amounts to advance authorization for Chapter VII operations in the event that a preventive force is challenged. Otherwise there is no basis for deterrence other than hope. Acknowledging, for example, that the combined forces of the Yugoslav People's Army (JNA) and the Bosnian Serbs would have been very hard to intimidate, nonetheless automatic back-up is essential. Although one is tempted always to argue that something is better than nothing, UN credibility can ill afford additional and inevitable black eyes. If there is no response when the UN's bluff is called, the currency of preventive UN military action will be devalued to such an extent that preventive action should not have been attempted in the first place. The rub is, of course, obvious: prevention is cost-effective in the long run but cost-intensive in the short term. The growing preoccupation with saving public resources could alter such myopia, although the political risks in sustaining fatalities or getting bogged down in a quagmire are usually high enough to outweigh any purported economic benefits. As pundits and professors are fond of indicating, democratically elected governments can rarely imagine action whose time-horizon extends beyond the next public opinion poll, and certainly not beyond the next electoral campaign. Dithering in late 1996 in the Great Lakes – to Burundi's seething ethnic cauldron and to lawlessness in eastern former Zaire – indicated that the terms of international discourse have indeed changed; but the willingness to deploy troops preventively lags substantially behind the rhetoric.

Lesson 3: Use regional organizations, without naivete and with accountability

Advocates for regional institutions find them an attractive alternative to an overextended United Nations. As member states of these institutions suffer most from the destabilizing consequences of war in their locales, they have the greatest stake in the management and resolution of regional conflicts. Regional actors also understand the dynamics of strife and cultures more intimately than outsiders, and thus they are in a better position to mediate. Issues relating to local conflict are also more likely to be given full and urgent consideration in regional forums than in global ones, where there are broader agendas, competing priorities, and distractions.[15]

Theory contrasts starkly with practice. The list of failures by regional organizations is familiar to students of international conflict management. Most such organizations in the third world have virtually no military experience or resources. Even in the "best case" of industrialized Europe, the density of well-endowed and seemingly powerful institutions was at most of limited utility – and at worst counter-productive – for the first four years of the former Yugoslavia's wars.

Nonetheless, if coercion occurs at all, interventions in the near future will have to compensate for the military inadequacies of the United Nations. As such, experience suggests that UN decisions should trigger interventions to be subcontracted to coalitions of major states. Regional powers (for instance, Nigeria within West Africa and the Russian Federation within the erstwhile Soviet republics) could take the lead combined with larger regional bodies (in these cases, the Economic Community of West African States and the Commonwealth of Independent States) or global coalitions. Perhaps only when regional powers cannot or will not take such a lead should more global powers (for example, France in Rwanda or the United States in Somalia) be expected to do so. However, blocking humanitarian intervention, which some powers are willing to conduct when other are reluctant to get involved (for example, the United States *vis-à-vis* Rwanda between early April and late June 1994), should be ruled out.

The multilateral capacity for coercion will no doubt depend in the future upon ad hoc coalitions, regional powers, and even hegemons. Bill Maynes dubbed this "benign *realpolitik*," which amounts to a revival of spheres of influence with UN overviews.[16] The Security Council is experimenting with a type of great-power manipulation of decision-making and enforcement, which the United Nations had originally been founded to end but which is increasingly pertinent in the light of some of the inherent difficulties of multilateral mobilization and management of military force.[17] Boutros-Ghali recognized this reality when he called for "a new division of labour between the United Nations and regional organizations, under which the regional organization carries the main burden but a small United Nations operation supports it and verifies that it is functioning in a manner consistent with positions adopted by the Security Council."[18]

An observer might well ask what is new about rationalization? Was the former Secretary-General not grasping at straws in justifying gunboat diplomacy for the 1990s? Is this not simply *realpolitik*? The difference could be that major powers or their coalitions act on their own behalf as well as on behalf of the Security Council – thus they should be held accountable for their actions by the wider community of states authorizing outside interventions.[19] While major powers inevitably flex their military muscles when it is in their perceived interests to do so, they do not necessarily agree in advance to subject themselves to international law and outside monitoring of their behaviour. The political and economic advantages attached to an imprimatur from the Security Council provide some leverage for the community of states to foster accountability from would-be subcontractors. The third lesson is clear: there is frankly no alternative to making better use of regional organizations, without naivete and with accountability. As UN Under-Secretary-General Marrack Goulding has written: "It is likely to become the standard approach when the Security Council decides that enforcement action is required."[20]

Lesson 4: Control the humanitarian impulse

In spite of a widespread tendency among both analysts and practitioners to lump them into a single category, military-civilian humanitarianism (or the coming together of military forces and civilian aid agencies to deal with suffering from complex humanitarian emergencies) has actually taken a variety of forms.[21] Without going into the variations in success and failure, it should suffice to point out that the humanitarian impulse cannot replace hard-headed calculations of *raisons d'état* if humanitarian intervention is to be sustained. The unceremonious US departure from Somalia and their ignominious retreat from Haiti (in October 1993), as well as the French and British threats to do the same with their own hostage-cum-human-shields peacekeepers in the former Yugoslavia, indicated the extent to which even discussions about body-bags can suffice to cut short a coercive intervention. Without serious leadership by important governments and honesty about the goals and durations of operations, a zero-casualty foreign policy emerges. This is not the foundation for a serious humanitarian intervention.

The visible and growing international concern with rescue is a remarkable historical development. What makes this issue stand out so vividly is the "impulse" – some, for example the International Committee of the Red Cross, would say "imperative" – to respond viscerally to relieve suffering, and recently even to seek access in cases where sovereignty presents a legal prohibition. Whether we actually are in Raimo Vayrenen's "age of humanitarian emergencies,"[22] humanitarian impulses by themselves are inadequate. Moreover, there is a growing rumbling about counter-productive humanitarianism.[23] In the prescient prose of Alain Destexhe, the former Secretary-General of the International Office of Médécins Sans Frontières: "Humanitarian action is noble when coupled with political action and justice. Without them, it is doomed to failure and, especially in the emergencies covered by the media, becomes little more than a play-thing of international politics, a conscience-solving gimmick."[24]

Good will is not a substitute for political will. *Mediapolitik* can not replace *realpolitik*. As Richard Betts noted, "An intervention that can be stopped in its tracks by a few dozen casualties, like the US operation in Somalia, is one that should never have begun."[25] The proverbial bottom line is that the humanitarian impulse by itself is insufficient and should be controlled.

Lessons for the United Nations as independent variable ("actor")

The United Nations is also an independent variable whose member states have endowed its military operations with a semi-independent identity and staffed them with a semi-autonomous civil service. In the vocabulary of this volume, the UN's image as an actor falls on a spectrum between a minimalist "global counsel" and a more activist "global manager." Most of the time the former image is far more apt than the latter. In fact, wishful thinking about UN managerial capacities for military operations has led to operational problems. Accordingly, I suggest three lessons for the United Nations as an actor.

Lesson 5: Avoid enforcement

Without putting too fine a point on it, the United Nations is incapable of exercising command and control over combat operations. The capacity to plan, support, and command peace-keeping, let alone peace-enforcement, missions is scarcely greater now than during the Cold War. And this situation will not change in the foreseeable future.

There are two reasons for arguing that the United Nations as actor should distance itself from forcible coercion. First, states are unwilling to provide the Secretary-General with the necessary military tools for Chapter VII operations. Standby troops and funds, independent intelligence, and appropriate systems for command and control along with professional personnel are simply not forthcoming. There is simply no question of independent action.

Second, and perhaps more important, the strength of the office of the Secretary-General lies in its impartiality, which is derived from the lack of vested interests. Adam Roberts has suggested "that there is a UN culture which, while not being explicitly pacifist, is opposed to associating the UN with the management of force."[26] Former UN Assistant Secretary-General Giandomenico Picco has argued that this culture is the world organization's strong suit and that "Transforming the institution of the Secretary-General into a pale imitation of a state to manage the use of force may well be a suicidal embrace."[27] Inis Claude has taken a similar view in recommending that the UN member states take charge of coercion and leave the non-coercive consensual and neutral actions to the UN Secretariat.[28] When the security situation has somewhat stabilized, the Secretary-General must be prepared to facilitate mediation, and perhaps even the administration of weak states, but only after the warring parties themselves are exhausted or cleansed from a territory, or following a humanitarian intervention. In order to maintain credibility as a third party, the United Nations should refrain from taking sides. Fen Hampson concludes his comprehensive study about the United Nations negotiating the end to five ethnic conflicts with the suggestion that "Enforcement is therefore best left to others."[29]

The failure to distinguish between the military operations that the UN Secretariat can manage (traditional and even slightly muscular peace-keeping), and those that it cannot and should not (enforcement), has led to obfuscation. Dangerous humanitarian interventions are problematic under any circumstances, but they have given governments which are unable and unwilling to act decisively the opportunity to treat the United Nations as a scapegoat. The decision to deploy peacekeepers both in UNOSOM II and in UNPROFOR, rather than the soldiers of coalition forces with sufficient military wherewithal for effective intervention, called into question the viability of peace-keeping and indeed the credibility of the world organization.

In spite of differences in emphases, virtually everyone agrees about the professional inadequacy of the UN Secretariat to handle combat operations. Deficiencies in United Nations command and control traditionally reflect three shortcomings. On the purely technical side, communications are notoriously difficult because of multiple languages, procedures, and equipment – problems which are exacerbated by the lack of common training for individual contingents. Operations also suffer from multiple chains of command within a theatre, and between the military and the civilian sides of the Secretariat. Lastly, and most importantly for our discussion here, the normal tendency for contingents to seek guidance from their own capitals is intensified according to the complexity and danger of situations; and humanitarian interventions are not only complex and dangerous, but soldiers also often become specific targets and even hostages.

States have made modest improvements to the UN Secretariat, but the actual or pending modifications are insufficient to make the militaries of major or middle powers at ease about placing the United Nations in charge of combat missions. With the world organization and its member states increasingly bogged down in multifaceted operations in civil wars – hardly imagined by the framers of the UN Charter and certainly not where successes have been commonplace – there are increasing political, economic, and military pressures in Washington and other Western capitals to avoid engagement. The May 1994 Presidential Decision Directive (PDD 25), for instance, was a spectacular example of an official and embarrassing 180-degree public reversal in policy and acknowledgment that the United Nations is out of its depth with enforcement operations. To countervail ever-growing public and state disenchantment with its activities, the United Nations as actor would be well advised to avoid enforcement.

Lesson 6: Provide multi-functional services, particularly human rights

Michael Doyle has argued that "the United Nations has proven itself to be a very ineffective war maker." At the same time, he wisely suggested that "we should avoid throwing the 'baby' out with the bathwater."[30] The advent of multi-functional operations in civil wars,[31] or what were earlier called "second generation operations,"[32] means that several types of inputs – from election and human rights' monitoring to disarmament and civil administration – are now not only possible but in the future will also be undoubtedly the most desirable tasks for UN military operations. Given the proper sets of circumstances and support, the United Nations has acquitted itself well in many such assignments in the post-Cold War world. Mistakes have been made and considerable additional research is required to improve such sensitive efforts as disarmament.[33] But carrying them out in a cost-effective manner has highlighted a UN comparative advantage in situations as diverse as Cambodia and El Salvador.[34] The decision to expand these functions seems straightforward, provided that a host country consents to UN soldiers and civilians as part of such efforts, and that there are sufficient international resources to conduct such assignments professionally.

In spite of the general consensus surrounding the expansion of such tasks in future UN military operations, human rights' protection is a far more controversial multi-functional task that has divided analysts who examine its feasibility. The evidence suggests that the United Nations – member states for obvious reasons, but less justifiably the political, humanitarian, and military professionals in its employ who also concern us here – has been too timid in confronting the perpetrators of human rights' abuses and war crimes. Former Secretary-General Boutros-Ghali has retreated from his earlier bullishness almost continually since An Agenda for Peace was published in 1992; and the reluctance to confront political authorities became official policy in his 1995 Supplement to An Agenda for Peace.

Operational implications arise from sustaining the shibboleth of domestic jurisdiction. With the exception of El Salvador, the United Nations receives mediocre and sometimes failing grades for its human rights record in multi-functional operations. The need to reinforce the neutrality of the United Nations provides the most sanguine explanation. The world organization's leadership routinely wishes to sidestep confrontations with states, move ahead with negotiations, and be seen as an impartial partner once cease-fires are in effect. The promotion of human rights is a victim, however, of such misplaced evenhandedness.

Treating human rights more as non-essential luxuries than as central elements in UN military operations – in Cambodia, Somalia, and Iraq as well as the former Yugoslavia – caused Human Rights Watch to lament this "lost agenda" that has "led to a squandering of the UN's unique capacity on the global stage to articulate fundamental human rights values and to legitimize their enforcement."[35] The UN's limits as an actor are painfully encapsulated in these experiences, as well as more recently in Rwanda. The lack of political will and leadership – more understandable for states than for international secretariats – undermines the utility of these initiatives, with repercussions not only for today's but also for tomorrow's war victims. The potential value of precedents of tribunals for the former Yugoslavia and Rwanda, not simply as moral statements but also as effective deterrents, should not be minimized. UN officials are well placed to use the bully pulpit for human rights. The UN's stature as an actor in multi-functional operations would benefit from taking fuller advantage of this potential.

Lesson 7: Make better use of NGOs

Rather than lamenting, as a world federalist might, the inability of the UN system to meet human needs across an ever-widening front, it is more pragmatic and sensible to ask who does what best, or at least better – to foster multilateralism through a better division of labour. As a semi-autonomous actor, the United Nations should take maximum advantage of subcontracting possibilities, not only for regional organizations but also for non-governmental organizations.[36] In recent civil wars, NGOs have made significant contributions.[37] Indeed, the total transferred through NGOs outweighs that disbursed by the UN system (excluding the Washington-based financial institutions).[38]

What commends NGOs is their working relations with community groups. These contacts are further strengthened by their commitment to staying on and their relatively low costs (on average and except for the senior managers of the largest ones, their salaries and benefits are considerably less than those of international civil servants). NGOs have earned a reputation for being more flexible, forthcoming, and responsive than other members of the international humanitarian system. Whether an international NGO is small or large, focused or far-flung, its activities tend to concentrate on the practical needs of ordinary people. NGOs endeavour to customize their activities for the grass-roots, which can be legitimately distinguished for the most part from the "wholesale" assistance provided by donor governments and the UN system. These explain why the United Nations, in addition to governmental and individual donors, should continue expanding resources made available directly to private agencies.

External NGOs also bring weaknesses to the scene of disasters. Their energy may lend frenzy and confusion. Careful planning and evaluation are rarer than they should be. The desire to get on with the next emergency contributes to a lack of reflectiveness and an inattention to institutional learning. Fund-raising imperatives make NGOs "crisis junkies" that are not any less subject than other bureaucracies to concerns about organizational expansion and turf. Well-known impatience with bureaucratic constraints often reflects naivete about the highly political contexts in which NGOs increasingly operate, and about the ramifications of activities. Some NGOs guard their independence so closely that they miss evident opportunities to expand the impact of their actions by combining forces with like-minded institutions. How much of rising expenditure is due to inefficiencies and increasing administrative costs is, for example, not clear. Having literally hundreds of subcontractors delivering similar goods and services in a disjointed and competitive market-place during the tumult of wars means that part of the dramatic growth in expenditure must be driven by NGOs themselves.[39]

As a *quid pro quo* for channelling more resources through NGOs and providing them with better access to decision-making, donors should insist upon more formal cooperation between NGOs and the United Nations on the one hand, and more self-regulation among NGOs themselves on the other. Perhaps the thorniest decisions for international NGOs will revolve around the need for enhanced coordination, almost certain to be under UN auspices within comprehensive responses to internal armed conflicts. Andrew Natsios has summarized what may be the best-case scenario: "The marriage of convenience between NGOs and the UN system in relief responses over time may become comfortable enough that ad hoc arrangements will work, even if a passionate love affair never occurs." His rationale is clear: "Organizational autonomy and complexity are enemies of speed and strategic coherence."[40]

Another advantage of involving more NGOs with the United Nations is that the world organization's legitimacy could be enhanced by its association with what are widely viewed as popular, effective, and representative organizations. Making better use of NGOs in tandem with UN military operations could only help build a wider basis of support for the United Nations as an independent actor, and for multilateralism more generally.

Conclusion

The increase in the number of UN military missions has been dramatic – twice as many operations in the last eight years as in the previous 40 years – but the proliferation of analyses about multilateral military operations has been no less remarkable.[41] Within this context, too little has been "learned" from both successes and failures of UN military operations in this decade. Learning lessons is different from adapting, with the latter being more reactive, less comprehensive, and represented by incremental and often ambiguous institutional change.

The United Nations still has to make a substantial effort to digest the seven lessons outlined here, and formulate a workable strategy for future military operations. The mere establishment of the "Lessons-Learned Unit" in the Department of Peace-keeping Operations (DPKO), along with similarly labelled units in the Departments of Political Affairs (DPA) and Humanitarian Affairs (DHA), is not necessarily evidence of progress. Jan Pronk, the Dutch Minister for Development Cooperation, commented that: "Learning from mistakes, however, requires more than a compilation of experiences. A condition for learning lessons and improving our performance is an environment that is favourable for frank criticism, both from inside the organization and from outside researchers."[42]

The increasing violence and displacement in civil wars are being mixed with shrinking resources and widespread public dissatisfaction, a fairly lethal combination for multilateralism. Yet analysts should be wary of being tied too closely to contemporary events. For instance, in April 1991 the dominant mood in policy and analytical circles after the Gulf War and Operation Provide Comfort was "we can do anything." And barely three years later, almost day to day in April 1994, the mood was distinct: "we can do nothing" to halt the genocide in Rwanda.

We should thus be careful not to extrapolate only from the most recent experiences with UN military operations. The present moment strikes me as somewhat akin to the early and mid-1980s, when the subject of UN military operations was exotic and of interest to only a small group of cognescenti. This had followed other periods of enthusiasm about peace-keeping (after 1956 and again in the mid-1970s concerning an expansion in the Middle East) and despair (in the mid-1960s after the Congo). Alan James commented that "Peace-keeping is ad hoc in every way, including its frequency and popularity."

There are bound to be instances in which traditional peace-keeping, peace enforcement, and everything messy in between will be options in the next decade. Modesty, both analytical and political, may be the most crucial orientation to help prevent the eclipse of the United Nations and its military operations in the post-post-Cold War era.

Notes

1. For a bipartisan overview, see George Soros, chairman of an independent task force, *American National Interest and the United Nations* (New York: Council on Foreign Relations, 1996). For a more academic analysis, see John Gerard Ruggie, *Winning the Peace: America and World Order in the New Era* (New York: Columbia University Press, 1996).

2. Francis Fukuyama, *The End of History and the Last Man* (New York: Free Press, 1992). For the phenomenon of fragmentation, see Lori Fisler Damrosch (ed.), *Enforcing Restraint: Collective Intervention in Internal Conflicts* (New York: Council on Foreign Relations Press, 1993); Michael E. Brown (ed.), *International Dimensions of Internal Conflicts* (Cambridge, Massachusetts: MIT Press, 1996); Ted Robert Gurr and Barbara Harff, *Ethnic Conflict in World Politics* (Boulder: Westview, 1994); and "Reconstructing Nations and States," special issue of *Dædalus*, vol. 22, 3 (Summer 1993).

3. Quoted by Alison Mitchell, "Clinton's About-Face," *New York Times*, 24 September 1996, p. A8. For a discussion of the impact of Somalia, see Tom J. Farer, "Intervention in Unnatural Humanitarian Emergencies: Lessons of the First Phase," *Human Rights Quarterly,* vol. 18, 1 (February 1996), pp. 1–22; and Thomas G. Weiss, "Overcoming the Somalia Syndrome – 'Operation Rekindle Hope'?" *Global Governance* vol. 1, 2 (May–August 1995), pp. 171–87.

4. See Mohammed Ayoob, "The New-Old Disorder in the Third World," in Thomas G. Weiss (ed.), *Collective Security in a Changing World* (Boulder: Lynne Rienner, 1993), pp. 13–30; Mohammed Ayoob, *The Third World Security Predicament: State Making, Regional Conflict, and the International System* (Boulder. Lynne Rienner, 1995); Kalevi J. Holsti, *The State, War, and the State of War* (Cambridge, UK: Cambridge University Press, 1996); and Robert Jackson, *Quasi States: Sovereignty, International Relations, and the Third World* (Cambridge, UK: Cambridge University Press, 1990).

5. See Bruce Russett, James S. Sutterlin, and Barry O'Neill, "Breaking the Security Council Restructuring Logjam," *Global Governance*, vol. 2, 1 (January–April 1996), pp. 65–80.

6. I am grateful to Cindy Collins for this insight and to Jarat Chopra for comments on earlier drafts.

7. For discussions of this phenomenon, see Robert I. Rotberg and Thomas G. Weiss (eds.), *From Massacres to Genocide: The Media, Public Policy, and Humanitarian Crises*

(Washington, DC: Brookings Institution, 1996); Larry Minear, Colin Scott, and Thomas G. Weiss, *The News Media, Civil War, and Humanitarian Action* (Boulder: Lynne Rienner, 1996); Charles C. Moskos and Thomas E. Ricks, *Reporting War When There Is No War* (Chicago: McCormick Tribune Foundation, 1996); Edward Girardet (ed.), *Somalia, Rwanda, and Beyond: The Role of the International Media in Wars and Humanitarian Criss* (Dublin: Crosslines Communications, 1995), Crosslines Special Report 1; Johanna Neuman, *Lights, Camera, War* (New York: St. Martin's, 1996); and Nik Gowing, *Real-Time Television Coverage of Armed Conflicts and Diplomatic Crises* (Cambridge, Massachusetts: Harvard University Shorenstein Center, 1994).

8. John Gerard Ruggie, "Wandering in the Void," *Foreign Affairs*, vol. 72, 5 (November–December 1993), pp. 26–31.

9. See Thomas G. Weiss, "Collective Spinelessness: UN Actions in the Former Yugoslavia," in Richard H. Ullman (ed.), *The World and Yugoslavia's Wars* (New York: Council on Foreign Relations, 1996), pp. 59–96.

10. John Steinbruner, "Memorandum: Civil Violence as an International Security Problem," reproduced as Annex C in Francis M. Deng, *Protecting the Dispossessed: A Challenge for the International Community* (Washington, DC: Brookings Institution, 1993), p. 155.

11. Chaim Kaufmann, "Possible and Impossible Solutions to Ethnic Civil Wars," *International Security*, vol. 20, 4 (Spring 1996), p. 167. For an opposite view, see Radha Kumar, "The Troubled History of Partition," *Foreign Affairs*, vol. 76, 1 (January–February 1997), pp. 22–34.

12. Stephen John Stedman, "Alchemy for a New World Order: Overselling 'Preventive Diplomacy,'" *Foreign Affairs*, vol. 74, 3 (May–June 1995), pp. 14–20; and Thomas G. Weiss, "The UN's Prevention Pipe-dream," *Berkeley Journal of International Law*, vol. 14, 2 (March 1997), pp. 501–15.

13. Michael S. Lund, *Preventive Diplomacy and American Foreign Policy* (Washington, DC: US Institute of Peace Press, 1994), p. 27. See also his *Preventing Violent Conflicts: A Strategy for Preventive Diplomacy* (Washington, DC: US Institute of Peace Press, 1996).

14. Boutros Boutros-Ghali, *An Agenda for Development 1995* (New York: United Nations, 1995), under "Recommendatons," p. 99.

15. See S. Neil MacFarlane and Thomas G. Weiss, "The United Nations, Regional Organizations, and Human Security," *Third World Quarterly*, vol. 15, 2 (April 1994), pp. 277–95.

16. Charles W. Maynes, "A Workable Clinton Doctrine," *Foreign Policy*, vol. 93 (Winter 1993–1994), pp. 3–20.

17. For an outspoken realist statement of the supposedly insuperable problems associated with such efforts, see John J. Mearsheimer, "The False Promise of International Institutions," *International Security*, vol. 19, 3 (Winter 1994–1995), pp. 5–49.

18. Boutros-Ghali, "Supplement to An Agenda for Peace," para. 86, reproduced along with the original "An Agenda for Peace" in *An Agenda for Peace 1995* (New York: United Nations, 1995). For a sceptical view, see Benjamin Rivlin, "Prospects for a Division of Labour Between the United Nations and Regional Bodies in Peace-keeping," in Klaus Hüfner (ed.), *Agenda for Change* (Opladen: Leske and Budrich, 1995), pp. 137–49. For a discussion of a "partnership," see Alan K. Henrikson, "The Growth of Regionalism and the Role of the United Nations," in Louise Fawcett and Andrew Hurrell (eds.), *Regionalism in World Politics: Regional Organizations and World Order* (Oxford: Oxford University Press, 1996), pp. 122–68.

19. For a discussion with reference to the former Soviet bloc, see Jarat Chopra and Thomas G. Weiss, "Containing Conflict in the former Second World," *Security Studies*, vol. 4, 3 (Spring 1995), pp. 552–83.

20. Marrack Goulding, "The Use of Force by the United Nations," *International Peace-keeping*, vol. 3, 1 (Spring 1996), p. 5.
21. See Thomas G. Weiss, "Military-Civilian Humanitarianism: The 'Age of Innocence' Is Over," *International Peacekeeping* vol. 2, 2 (Summer 1995), pp. 157–74.
22. Raimo Väyrenen, *The Age of Humanitarian Emergencies* (Helsinki: World Institute for Development Economics Research, June 1996), Research for Action 25. For an exhaustive review of the literature, see Oliver Famsbotham and Tom Woodhouse, *Humanitarian Intervention in Contemporary Conflict* (Oxford: Polity Press, 1996). See also John Harriss (ed.), *The Politics of Humanitarian Intervention* (London: Pinter, 1995); James Mayall (ed.), *The New Interventionism: United Nations Experience in Cambodia, Former Yugoslavia, and Somalia* (New York: Cambridge University Press, 1996); Jan Neederveen Pieterse (ed.), *World Orders in the Making: The Case of Humanitarian Intervention* (London: Macmillan, forthcoming); and Nigel Rodney (ed.), *To Loose the Bonds of Wickedness: International Intervention in Defence of Human Rights* (London: Brassey's, 1992).
23. The debate on the politics of humanitarianism is inspiring a vital and growing literature. The most controversial analysis is Rakiya Omaar and Alex de Waal, *Humanitarianism Unbound? Current Dilemmas Facing Multi-Mandate Relief Operations in Political Emergencies* (London: African Rights, 1994), Discussion Paper No. 5. See also a special issue on "Rescue – The Paradoxes of Virtue," *Social Research*, vol. 62, 1 (Spring 1995), especially Michael Walzer's "The Politics of Rescue," pp. 53–66; and David Rieff, "The Humanitarian Trap," *World Policy Journal*, XII, no. 4 (Winter 1994–1995), pp. 1–11. With particular reference to the Balkans, see Amir Pasic and Thomas G. Weiss, "The Politics of Rescue: Yugoslavia's Wars and the Humanitarian Impulse, 1991–1995," *Ethics and International Affairs*, XI (1997), pp. 105–31.
24. Alain Destexhe, "Foreword," in François Jean (ed.), *Populations in Danger 1995* (London: Médécins Sans Frontières), pp. 13–14.
25. Richard K. Betts, "The Delusion of Impartial Intervention," *Foreign Affairs*, vol. 73, 6 (November–December 1994), p. 31.
26. Roberts, "From San Francisco to Sarajevo," p. 15.
27. Giandomenico Picco, "The UN and the Use of Force," *Foreign Affairs*, vol. 73, 5 (September–October 1994), p. 15.
28. Inis I. Claude, Jr., "Peace and Security: Prospective Roles for the Two United Nations," *Global Governance* vol. 2, 3 (September–December 1996), pp. 289–98.
29. Fen Osler Hampson, *Nurturing Peace: Why Peace Settlements Succeed or Fail* (Washington, DC: US Institute of Peace Press, 1996), p. 226.
30. Michael W. Doyle, "Making Global Security: The United Nations Not a War Maker, a Peace Maker, " in Charles William Maynes and Richard S. Williamson (eds.), *US Foreign Policy and the United Nations System* (New York: Norton, 1996), pp. 55–86, quote at p. 87.
31. See Thomas G. Weiss (ed.), *The United Nations and Civil Wars* (Boulder: Lynne Rienner, 1995).
32. See John Mackinlay and Jarat Chopra, "Second Generationn Multinational Forces," *Washington Quarterly*, vol. 15, 3 (Summer 1992), pp. 113–31; John Mackinlay and Jarat Chopra, *A Draft Concept of Second Generation Multinational Operations 1993* (Providence: Watson Institute, 1993); and John Mackinlay (ed.), *A Guide to Peace Support Operations* (Providence: Watson Institute, 1996).
33. See Mats Berdal, *Disarmanment and Demobilization after Civil Wars* (Oxford: Oxford University Press, 1996), Adelphi Paper 303.
34. See, for example, Stephen R. Ratner, *The New UN Peace-keeping: Building Peace in Lands of War After the Cold War* (New York: St. Martin's, 1993); Michael Doyle, *UN*

Peace-keeping in Cambodia: UNTAC's Civil Mandate (Boulder: Lynne Rienner, 1995); Ian Johnstone, *Rights and Reconciliation: UN Strategies in El Salvador* (Boulder: Lynne Rienner, 1995); and Cristina Eguizábal, David Lewis, Larry Minear, Peter Sollis, and Thomas G. Weiss, *Humanitarian Challenges in Central America: Learning the Lessons of Recent Armed Conflicts* (Providence: Watson Institute, 1993), Occasional Paper 14.

35. See *The Lost Agenda: Human Rights and UN Field Operations* (New York: Human Rights Watch, 1993); and *Human Rights Watch World Report 1995* (New York: Human Rights Watch, 1994), p. xiv. See also Paul LaRose-Edwards, *Human Rights Principles and Practice in United Nations Field Operations* (Ottawa: Department of Foreign Affairs, September 1995); and Alice H. Henkin (ed.), *Honoring Human Rights and Keeping the Peace: Lessons from El Salvador, Cambodia, and Haiti* (Washington, DC: Aspen Institute, 1995).

36. See Thomas G. Weiss (ed.), *Beyond UN Subcontracting: Task-sharing with Regional Security Arrangements and Service-providing NGOs*, a special issue of *Third World Quarterly*, vol. 18, 3 (1997), to be published afterwards by Macmillan in London.

37. The argument about NGOs draws upon Thomas G. Weiss, "Non-governmental Organizations and Internal Conflicts," in Michael E. Brown (ed.), *International Dimensions of Internal Conflicts*, pp. 435–59. The emphasis here is on external NGOs, although local NGOs are experiencing similar growth. See also Thomas G. Weiss and Leon Gordenker (eds.), *NGOs, the UN, and Global Governance* (Boulder: Lynne Rienner, 1996).

38. See Ian Smillie, *The Alms Bazaar: Altruism under Fire – Non-profit Organizations and International Development* (West Hartford, Connecticut: Kumarian Press, 1995); and Judith Randell and Tony German (eds.), *The Reality of Aid, 1996* (London: Earthscan, 1996).

39. See Jon Bennett, *Meeting Needs: NGO Coordination in Practice* (London: Earthscan, 1995); and A. Fowler, *Non-governmental Organizations in Africa: Achieving Comparative Advantage in Relief and Micro-development* (Sussex: Institute of Development Studies, 1988), Discussion Paper 249.

40. Andrew Natsios, "NGOs and the UN in Complex Emergencies: Contlict or Cooperation," *Third World Quarterly*, vol. 16, 3 (September 1995), p. 418; and "Humanitarian Relief Interventions in Somalia: The Economics of Chaos," *International Peacekeeping*, vol. 3, 1 (Spring 1996), p. 88.

41. See Thomas G. Weiss and Cindy Collins, *Review of the Peace-keeping Literature, 1990–1996* (Providence: Watson Institute, 1997), Occasional Paper 28. The author would like to express his gratitude to the Ford Foundation for support that was also useful in writing this chapter.

42. Jan Pronk, "Statement in the General Debate in the Second Committee," New York, 14 October 1996, Permanent Mission of the Kingdom of the Netherlands to the United Nations, p. 2.

20

UN preventive action

Connie Peck

The end of the Cold War led to optimism that the United Nations would finally be able to prevent conflict more effectively, but the hoped-for outcome has not materialized. The organization has continued to focus its actions downstream on conflict management rather than upstream on conflict prevention. And in spite of the fact that 91 of the 95 armed conflicts since the end of the Cold War have occurred within states,[1] the United Nations has not developed a new methodology which could address intra-state conflict, but instead has tried to recast and remould a power-based collective security approach which was developed for inter-state disputes.

This chapter will briefly consider the UN's attempts to develop a capacity for preventive action, and the obstacles which have blocked its realization. It will suggest that a more appropriate and widely accepted methodology is needed to match the new strategic environment.

The response by member states

The 1992 Security Council summit and An Agenda for Peace attempted to outline a set of approaches to peace and security which *inter alia* included "preventive diplomacy." Paradoxically, however, in the ensuing debate the more preventive diplomacy was discussed, the more resistance to the concept grew. Since it was not clearly defined or operationalized, the idea began to face opposition.

The greatest problem was created by the sudden emergence of the Security Council's ability to exert its power once the log-jam of the Cold War was broken. The Council's new capacity to reach consensus and take powerful actions, as exemplified by the Gulf War, created considerable hope in some parts of the organization that finally the United Nations would be able to develop its long-dormant collective security system, with peace-keeping and peace enforcement as its principal *modus operandi*. The enthusiasm was not, however, universal. Many in the developing world responded with apprehension. For those who had experienced colonial domination, the renewed eagerness which they detected for strengthening the Council's peace and security agenda stimulated old fears about interventionism and great-power hegemony. Now that the Security Council could actually wield power, the great-power privileges of Permanent Membership and the veto, along with the Council's lack of adequate representation and consultation, were increasingly called into question. The perception grew that the Council was applying different standards to different cases and that, in some situations, its actions were taken to pursue the geopolitical aims of its Permanent Members, rather than the organization as a whole. These fears quickly affected perceptions of preventive diplomacy, which became a lightning rod for fear of interventionist intent. Concern grew that preventive diplomacy could become the thin end of another neo-colonialist wedge. Arguments about non-intervention, sovereignty, and the dangers of "internationalizing" a problem were mounted in response. Since preventive diplomacy was not yet developed, it became a line which could be drawn in the sand.

Member states of the South were also disappointed by the lack of interest by many in the North to their social development needs and concerns, and they worried that the UN's new preoccupation with peace and security (and the huge peace-keeping bill which was accumulating) would drain resources and energy from efforts to resolve what they saw as the root causes of conflict. As the financial crisis within the system deepened, their concerns intensified. Thus, in the debate between the peace and security agenda and the social development agenda, preventive diplomacy became linked to the peace and security side of the debate, and its linkage to the social and development side remained largely unexplored.

In spite of this, some support for the concept of prevention was forthcoming from middle-level developed countries, which wanted to see both the peace and security agenda and a social development agenda advanced in a way that would truly address the root causes of conflict and create institutions and norms which could lay down the foundation for lasting social justice. Gareth Evans, in his book *Cooperating for Peace: The Global Agenda for the 1990s and Beyond*, outlined such a vision of "cooperative security."[2] Unfortunately, this conceptualization of prevention had difficulty competing with the fears, paralysis, and general scepticism which accompanied the growing malaise within the system.

The response from the UN Secretariat

The first formal mechanism for prevention was introduced into the UN system in 1987 with the establishment of the Office for Research and the Collection of Information (ORCI). Six professional staff were assigned to tackle "early warning" by collecting and analyzing information and providing recommendations for action to the Secretary-General, but no comparable system was created for early action. Hence, when political officers sent their early-warning notes about deteriorating situations to the Secretary-General, his office was so overwhelmed with the many full-blown crises already on its agenda that little was done. Moreover, the main purpose was to predict where crises would erupt at the late prevention stage, rather than analyze why a given problem was occurring so that preventive action could be undertaken at an earlier stage.

In 1992, when Secretary-General Boutros Boutros-Ghali reorganized the Secretariat, ORCI was dismantled and its early-warning functions were taken over by the creation of six regional divisions in the new Department of Political Affairs (DPA). But many of the problems inherent in ORCI remained. Although early warning was located in the DPA, early action still resided largely in the executive office of the Secretary-General, thus creating a schism between those who gathered and analyzed information and those who decided whether action should be taken. Despite the fact that the number of staff collecting information grew, there were still no permanent staff for implementing preventive action. In those few instances where preventive action was taken, the practice of appointing ad hoc personal representatives or special envoys – the modality which has been traditionally used in peace-making, but which is not very well suited to systematic preventive diplomacy – was adopted.

Further, the difficulty of obtaining an in-depth understanding of a complex situation from UN headquarters in New York remained. Since information collected directly from the field is more easily interpreted in its cultural, historical, and political context, talking to relevant actors, visiting an area where tensions are high, or observing the problem first-hand provides a greater understanding of the situation than reading a newspaper report or talking to the parties when they visit New York. Moreover, developing relationships with the parties, understanding their interests, gaining their trust, and nudging them in the direction of negotiation are difficult to carry out by telephone or fax from New York. But the DPA's woefully inadequate travel budget has meant that some political officers have never even been to the region which they are supposed to track.

In short, without a consensus from members it has been difficult for the Secretariat to develop appropriate mechanisms for carrying out preventive diplomacy. The UN Secretariat still lacks the capacity to undertake conflict prevention at an early stage in a systematic and structured way. What is needed, therefore, is a more widely accepted approach to prevention which can receive support from member states, and a mechanism which can implement that approach.

Beginning with the root causes of conflict

In developing a new methodology for preventing conflict within states, a better understanding of the root causes of this type of conflict is essential. It is now widely recognized that the systematic frustration of basic human needs is a major causal factor.[3] When needs for physical safety and well-being, access to political and economic participation, and cultural or religious expression are threatened or frustrated over long periods of time, grievances and feelings of injustice grow – especially when one's self or one's identity group is perceived to be unfairly disadvantaged in relation to other groups. When groups believe that their physical safety or cultural identity is threatened, they may mobilize to express their collective concern and seek redress.[4]

Since it is the state which provides physical and cultural safety and regulates political and economic access, the prime objective of mobilization is usually to gain political access to decision-making. Where governments recognize, listen to, and accommodate dissatisfied groups, grievances may be lessened or resolved. Problems arise, however, when governments ignore or repress these concerns.

Recently, the concept of "human security" has been advanced as a prescription for addressing human needs and as the best foundation upon which "state security" can be built. Those states which are most secure tend to be those which provide the greatest human security to their populations. Weak states are those which do not, or cannot, provide human security. Often this very weakness leads political élites into a vicious cycle which further weakens their security. In an attempt to increase security, they amass the trappings of strength, investing heavily in military hardware or employing repressive tactics. But diversion of money away from their people's needs or massive repression (although it may seem effective in the short term) typically leads to greater discontent among the populace and increased vulnerability for the élite.

An agenda for prevention: Good governance

Recently, the linkage between development, democracy, human rights, and peace has been more widely recognized and articulated than ever before.[5] This synthesis is useful because it introduces a new element into the old development versus security debate. That new element is the need for a fairer process – a process capable of reducing grievances before they can grow into problems. It suggests that what is needed to create the opportunity for both development and peace is good governance, which will allow people to determine their own priorities; safeguard and promote their civil, political, economic, social, and cultural rights; and provide a pluralist environment within which they can live with one another in peace – with the freedom to develop in all ways. To be effective, good governance must be instituted at all levels of society – local, national, regional, and international. Moreover, all levels have to endeavour to develop the protection of individual human rights, as well as the procedures and mechanisms necessary to protect and balance adequately the many contending demands from various groups.

Thus, one goal of prevention should be to provide assistance in building human security through the development of an international architecture made up of the building blocks of good governance structures. This means helping local and national governments to build good governance, with special assistance for weak states. It also means strengthening the governance structures and mechanisms available through subregional, regional, and international organizations – to create a "voice" for all peoples and a fairer distribution of resources within and between regions. The task is to create a set of mutually reinforcing, self-correcting dispute settlement systems, through the development of interlocking good governance structures, which operate effectively to prevent and resolve disputes in a constructive manner.

Following the lead of the Brundtland Commission, which blended environmental responsibility and development into the new and more dynamic concept of sustainable development, it will be argued that the pairing of good governance and conflict prevention offers the best path to what will be called "sustainable peace."[6] Together, the twin concepts of sustainable development and sustainable peace could provide a full and more focused agenda for the United Nations.

To accompany this new agenda for prevention, a new methodology is also needed. At the early prevention stage, coercive power-based methods of influence are not as likely to be effective as more cooperative approaches, such as socialization, assistance, and problem solving, which if developed properly could provide powerful incentives for gradual and constructive change. The UN's power-based collective security approach, of course, always remains available as a back-up for cases which do not yield to a cooperative security approach.

Promoting agreed-upon standards and norms for good governance

The first steps toward promoting good governance have already been taken through the development of agreed-upon standards for satisfying human needs – in the more than 70 human rights instruments which the United Nations has endorsed over the past 50 years. The Universal Declaration of Human Rights, the International Covenant on Civil and Political Rights, the International Covenant on Economic, Social, and Cultural Rights, and the declarations which have followed in their wake, provide an excellent blueprint for good governance which specifies exactly how "human security" can be provided. The key demands of communal groups – the desire for political access to decision-making, for access to economic opportunity, and for cultural rights – are all pre-scribed as the duty of states in these documents. The connection between human needs and conflict prevention was clearly recognized in the pre-amble to the Universal Declaration, which states: "Whereas it is essential, if man is not to be compelled to have recourse, as a last resort, to rebellion against tyranny and oppression, that human rights should be protected by the rule of law."[7]

But if "human security" and good governance are to be developed, the establishment of widely agreed-upon norms is only the first step. What will be crucial in translating these norms into reality is the provision of assistance and the development of positive incentives to encourage governance structures at all levels to move in this direction. Thus, a major focal point for prevention might involve using socialization, assistance, and problem solving to strengthen the capacity of states to provide human security.

Providing assistance for good governance

In the last few years, a new preventive methodology has gradually been developing, within both the United Nations and regional organizations, and although it has not attracted much attention, it has been received with enthusiasm by the consumers. This is the methodology of offering technical assistance to member states. Within the United Nations, for example, the Centre for Human Rights, which has been unpopular with some states because of its involvement in monitoring human rights' abuses, has received praise and support from these same states for the development of its advisory services and technical assistance, offering governments help in drafting constitutions, legislation, or bills of rights, and in bringing national laws into conformity with international standards.

A similar development can be seen in the UN Electoral Assistance Division, which upon request provides a range of electoral assistance. As evidenced in the numerous requests for electoral assistance in a short period of time, the response has been enthusiastic. Electoral assistance is now also offered by the Council of Europe (COE), the Organization for Security and Cooperation in Europe (OSCE), the Organization of American States, and the Organization of African Unity. In addition, the COE, OSCE, and OAS have moved a step further by offering assistance in building democratic institutions.

Another variation of assistance can be seen in the work of the OSCE High Commissioner on National Minorities, who offers assistance to OSCE participating states in finding solutions to minority problems. Through discussion with the those concerned, he seeks to understand the basis for minority grievances and then to offer specific recommendations for change to legislation, regulation, or practice. His informal, quiet approach, which does not involve either "early warning" or formal mediation, overcomes the traditional opposition of governments to preventive diplomacy within states, since it avoids "internationalizing" the problem and bypasses government concern over recognizing or legitimizing leaders of disaffected minority movements. Since the government is never required to sit down at the table with the leaders of these groups, it does not have to recognize them formally. It is simply asked to listen to and consider the suggestions of the High Commissioner.

The OSCE's long-term preventive diplomacy missions offer a similar kind of assistance. They are typically small (8 to 20 personnel), are deployed at the invitation of participating states, and provide an "on-the-ground" presence which assists the national government in devising means of reducing tension within the country.

What all effective assistance programmes share is the availability of advice and options which governments are free to choose or refuse – but which they have usually accepted. Indeed, this type of assistance has been enthusiastically embraced by states with a wide range of types of governance. Such assistance is attractive to governments – precisely because it is low-key, subject to their consent, and builds "local capacity." Most importantly, this approach provides an acceptable basis for international organizations to become involved in conflict prevention within states. It ensures that when a government is ready to take even halting steps toward reform, there is international support to help it move in that direction.

It will be essential, however, that the new methodologies for sustainable peace through the promotion of good governance should not be viewed as a neo-colonial imposition of "Western democracy" or the "Western system" on the rest of the world. Rather, they should be viewed as means of empowerment for local peoples and ideas, and tailored to local cultural norms and practices, as well as to local issues. What is transferable in terms of assistance is information about how to establish a fair process (for example, a fair electoral or judicial process), but the agenda which that process addresses and the way it will evolve in a given context must be decided by the local and regional community. Ultimately, the greatest success will be achieved by demonstrating to governments how they will be advantaged by the provision of human security and good governance to their people.

Providing incentives for good governance

One of the most important incentives for change is group socialization. One form of socialization occurs when a critical mass of states, with a common agenda for promoting good governance, coalesces. This exerts a pull on the other members of the community, who want to be accepted into the "club." When accompanied by an expectation of related advantages, socialization can be particularly strong. For example, Eastern European and CIS (Commonwealth of Independent States) countries have been eager to join the Council of Europe and to meet its requirements for democratization and conformity with the principles of human rights, in order to have the option of joining other parts of the European architecture, such as the European Union, with its consequent economic advantages, or NATO, with its security umbrella. Thus political forums which meet regularly to discuss problems and provide feedback and recommendations socialize governments to conform to group norms.

A related form of socialization can be seen in Latin America and Africa over the last 10 years, where there has been a trend toward rapid democratization. In what is essentially a "demonstration effect," observation by citizens and governments of models of governance which appear to be more successful than their own causes them to want to reform their own structures, in the hope that reform will bring the same advantages.

If good governance were to be recognized as a key to prevention, a more explicit approach could be adopted wherein financial organizations (such as the Bretton Woods institutions or bilateral aid organizations) could provide financial assistance to help a government fight corruption, strengthen an independent judiciary, restructure and retrain their police force, develop an electoral commission, set up a parliament, create a commission for minorities, or develop an ombudsman's office.

Developing regional assistance programmes

This chapter will propose that the locus of UN preventive action should be moved to the regional level through the creation of UN Regional Centres for Sustainable Peace.[8] Regional centres could draw upon a strategic coalition of actors to offer a more integrative and acceptable approach to conflict prevention, through a programme for assistance in developing good governance and a programme for assistance in dispute settlement. Each would have one or more teams of well-trained professional staff, headed by full-time special advisers who would be similar to permanent special representatives for each region.

Such centres could be established under the auspices of the Department of Political Affairs, and draw upon the entire UN system to assist in promoting good governance and dispute settlement. It would also be important for centres to work closely with regional organizations, so they could pool expertise, use their comparative advantages, and be better informed. A joint approach would also provide the opportunity to share responsibility and truly coordinate activities – thus fulfilling the spirit of Chapter VIII of the UN Charter.

Centres could also liaise closely with appropriate NGOs, as well as with regional research institutions and think-tanks, to extend their knowledge base and "reach" into all levels of civil society. This would ensure that constructive ideas at all levels are heard and incorporated into solutions which are well tailored to local concerns, culture, and circumstances. Moreover, the concept of horizontal transfer of knowledge and experience within each region would be a cornerstone of this approach. Those within the region who have found solutions to their problems or developed successful models could be tapped to assist others in this endeavour.

Regional centres would need to maintain an exclusive focus on prevention in order to overcome past problems, when attention to full-blown conflicts left little time for prevention. They would also need to concentrate effort at the early prevention stage. When the assistance methodology was not effective and when a dispute was escalating rapidly, the situation could be referred to the Secretary-General or, if he deemed it appropriate, to the Security Council.

Overall, programmes would need to adopt a quiet, proactive assistance approach, offering help and support and relying on regional and international socialization to provide positive incentives for cooperation. Historically, the United Nations and regional organizations have tended to wait to be asked before offering assistance. But while parties are often reluctant to request help (fearing that it might be viewed as a sign of weakness), they may be willing to accept assistance which is quietly offered. Even if disputing parties were at first disinterested, they could be urged (through repeated contacts) to take advantage of assistance. To be effective, it would be essential for regional programmes to maintain a clear "assistance" identity and not become involved in coercive action. Where deemed necessary, such action can be more effectively carried out by the political and legal structures which have been established to persuade states to meet their obligations.

Expert knowledge and skill would be fundamental to the work of regional centres. Senior staff with expertise in governance structures, as well as those with expert knowledge and experience in dispute settlement, would be required, along with regional or area experts who are well-versed in the cultural, historical, and political perspectives of states and actors in the region. This would mean recruiting staff (to supplement existing personnel) from the upper echelons of the diplomatic corps, from the senior levels of academia, and from among experienced professionals who have been working in similar settings.

Regional programmes for assistance in developing good governance

In an attempt to sketch how a programme for good governance could contribute to conflict prevention, some of the types of assistance which might be offered will be outlined briefly below.

Providing assistance for transition to democracy

Over the past decade there has been a marked increase in the number of countries making the transition to democracy. While this may eventually lead to a reduced incidence of violent conflict, the transition process can be fraught with potential danger – unless carefully managed.

In multi-ethnic states, one of the most important factors in avoiding ethnic conflict during periods of transition has been the willingness to address ethnic issues early in the process, through the writing of an appropriate constitution and the inclusion of ethnic groups in a satisfactory power-sharing arrangement.[9] In such situations, regional centre staff could assist by providing information about the need to ensure representation from all significant groups in central and local governments, as well as knowledge about how this can be achieved.

Assistance in the development of fair rules, law, and practice

Assistance could also be provided in studying a state's constitution, laws, regulations, and practices, and specific changes could be recommended to bring these into line with regional or international standards. Reference to similar laws in other countries could be provided, and advice offered in the drafting of constitutions or legislation. A few of the kinds of issues about which advice might be offered are the separation of government powers; freedom of expression, association, or assembly; independence of the judiciary; the role of the judiciary in overseeing the police and prison systems; protection of national minorities; electoral laws; and citizenship and asylum laws.

Assistance in the development of institutions to administer laws and regulate conflict

Since certain institutions within a society have a fundamental role to play in good governance through the administration of law and the regulation of conflict, it is crucial that these institutions are encouraged to function in a manner which upholds individual freedoms and the due process of law, and safeguards human rights. Technical and financial assistance could be provided for special training programmes for judges, magistrates, lawyers, prosecutors, police officers, prison personnel, and mediators. Seminars and workshops with experienced professionals could be scheduled to discuss issues related to fair and independent systems for administering justice; professional ethics; independence of judges and lawyers; fair trial procedures; human rights during investigations; use of force; torture; legal means of crowd control; issues of police command, management, and control; standards for the treatment of prisoners; prison administration and discipline; or community policing. Other key institutions, such as the media, could also benefit from workshops on topics such as freedom of information and expression; access to information; professional codes of ethics; censorship; and the importance of the press in developing multicultural understanding. Exposure to systems where these institutions function effectively is another means of introducing such concepts, and study visits to observe how things are done elsewhere could be useful.

The separation of military institutions from civilian administration

When states are in transition to civilian rule from a military regime, or where the military has been actively involved in governing a state in the recent past, providing assistance to the military in finding a new role for itself may be vital. This is, of course, a delicate task which must be handled sensitively. Exchanges with other military establishments which enjoy a good relationship with civilian government might be one approach. Carefully structured workshops could provide another means to explore this topic. Finally, appropriate norms could be introduced into existing training programmes for military personnel and new recruits.

Assistance in mechanisms to encourage more honest governance

Both financial and technical assistance could be provided to governments in the establishment of anti-corruption legislation, monitoring, and enforcement. Successful experience from other countries could be shared with local and national officials, and special training in anti-corruption investigation and prosecution offered. Assistance with campaigns to change public attitudes and behaviour could also be provided.

Assistance in promoting greater economic opportunity and access

In the same way that democracy is sometimes inappropriately considered a panacea, development has often been considered the key to minority groups' economic concerns. But just as a more nuanced approach is usually needed in the structuring of democracy in multi-ethnic societies, so a more sophisticated approach is needed to development policy – since, if not properly managed, development can actually exacerbate rather than ameliorate ethnic problems. For example, unmanaged, rapid, growth-oriented development strategies can lead to the deepening of a dual economy in which the modern sector becomes prosperous while the urban and rural poor are further marginalized, sowing the seeds for discontent.[10]

Thus, assistance in how to minimize such problems may be helpful. Advice could be offered to governments in how to achieve sectoral, regional, or communal balance in development. Assistance might also be provided in initiating and implementing programmes of land reform, where expert assistance can point to successful programmes elsewhere and help governments develop programmes for compensation and distribution. As well, advice and assistance might be given in devising more individualistic policies for overcoming past discrimination and providing economic opportunity, such as quotas for members of minority groups in government hiring or military recruitment, special loans, or special arrangements for entry to university.[11] Good governance teams may also be able gradually to help governments realize that reallocating some of their military budgets to social policy initiatives aimed at increasing human security can be an effective means of creating real security.

Assistance in promoting pluralism, cultural understanding, and tolerance

Encouragement could be also given in the adoption of policies more conducive to tolerance and cross-cultural understanding. Models for multiculturalism could be introduced through seminars for government ministries, the media, local authorities, and minority groups, so that they could consider how such models might be adapted locally. In societies where the mass media are pervasive, encouragement (including financial incentives) could be provided for multicultural programming.

Schools offer an excellent venue for programmes which foster tolerance in and appreciation of other cultures. In mixed communities, education in and appreciation of different groups' languages and cultures could be promoted. Teachers and curriculum planners could be urged to introduce programmes to inoculate against racial or ethnic discrimination. Where appropriate, assistance could be provided for the introduction of laws and judicial practices which prohibit incitement to ethnic or racial hatred, discrimination, or violence.

Regional programmes for assistance in dispute settlement

This section will outline the kinds of expert assistance that could be offered by a programme in dispute settlement to help in reducing tension between groups, whether between or within states.

Listening to and understanding concerns

A special adviser and staff could make regular and routine visits throughout the region to discuss problems with relevant actors. Such visits would allow them to become well-acquainted with local and regional problems, and would help to develop relationships, trust, and a reputation for fairness. Quiet assistance could thus progress in a manner which did not call attention to itself and did not "internationalize" the dispute.

Providing new ideas and recommendations

The special adviser and his or her team could approach problems within states much as the OSCE High Commissioner on National Minorities has done. After obtaining a thorough understanding of the problem, the High Commissioner offers non-binding recommendations to the government in a low-key manner by writing a letter to the foreign minister, thanking him for the government's helpfulness, defining the problems as he sees them, and offering suggestions for change. Such letters often legitimize a minority group's most important concerns, but may also express an understanding of the difficulties from the government's perspective. Most importantly, these letters typically offer sets of specific non-binding recommendations, citing international or regional obligations and standards and expressing the High Commissioner's belief that the government will, naturally, wish to live up to these. This approach, developed with a high level of diplomatic and problem-solving skill by the OSCE High Commissioner, has been called "one-way mediation," since the government in question is the only interlocutor with whom the international organization has any formal status.[12] Within the OSCE this approach has been widely accepted by participating states, with no state refusing the High Commissioner's visit and most adopting his recommendations.

At the same time, on an informal basis, the High Commissioner and his advisers usually have considerable influence with minority groups, and often remind them of their obligations to use constructive means in pursuing their interests. Indeed, the mere presence of a high-level representative of the international community who is offering his or her services in problem solving can calm a situation. It makes minority groups feel less desperate, and more willing and empowered to pursue legal or politically constructive means of redress.

Encouraging the establishment of forums for ongoing dialogue

Although forums for dialogue between groups exist in inter-state disputes, they are often lacking in intra-state situations. Thus, assistance in creating new institutional mechanisms for ongoing dialogue and problem solving may help to establish much-needed "habits of dialogue." This may be required not only at the national level, but also at the community level. Assistance may involve round-table discussions, ombudsmen's offices, or special commissions for minority issues.

Providing good offices

In crises, the special adviser and his or her team could offer their good offices to avert violence, either through formal or informal meetings with both sides or through shuttle diplomacy.

Accessing expert assistance

Sometimes problems, especially when they are highly technical, may be so complex that outside experts are needed to study a situation and make recommendations. In this case, special advisers should be able to call upon the full range of regional or UN agencies as well as member states to provide economic or technical assistance. The OSCE High Commissioner has stressed the importance of even modest amounts of funds in alleviating ethnic tension. Hence, it might be useful to establish a central fund which could be tapped by regional centres for such projects.

Offering assistance in inter-state disputes

Of course, regular and routine visits throughout the region would also allow special advisers and their teams to become familiar with inter-state disputes and offer timely assistance by encouraging parties to de-escalate tensions through confidence-building measures; facilitating multi-track diplomacy; encouraging and supporting negotiation; offering to provide good offices or mediation; helping parties seek conciliation, arbitration, or adjudication; monitoring compliance with agreements; or acting as a "trip wire" when a situation was escalating.

Making use of all available resources

Using small assistance missions

In some situations, it might be advantageous to deploy small expert assistance missions as a further extension of both programmes. In giving assistance with good governance, such missions could provide a greater degree of ongoing support for good governance reforms. Small assistance missions might also be helpful in dispute settlement by providing an "on-the-ground" presence, which could serve as a calming influence by showing that the international community was aware of the problems and interested in helping to resolve them. Of course, this would not rule out the use of large-scale preventive deployment missions when needed, but they would not be part of a regional centre's mandate.

Using the expertise of regional and international scholars

To tailor skills to local conditions, regional research institutes, universities, and think-tanks could support both programmes. A network of regional and international scholars and other experts could be established to assist each programme and act as consultants. They could help programme staff sharpen their analysis of specific problems and broaden their consideration of potential solutions, as well as assist in developing a deeper understanding of the root causes of conflict and a more effective long-term agenda for tackling these.

Using the expertise of NGOs and civil society

NGOs working in the area of conflict resolution, democracy, human rights, and development could also be utilized to extend the work of both programmes. NGOs with expertise in human rights and democracy could work with local governments and communities to make them aware of the need to incorporate human rights' safeguards into local laws and practice, and to highlight the advantages of widespread participation in decision-making. They could encourage a communal consensus on what is required for good governance. NGOs with appropriate expertise in conflict resolution could train local actors in problem solving, disseminate information on problem-solving methods, and contribute to the development of an active civil society.

Using the experience of regional leaders

High-level councils, composed of former prime ministers, presidents, judges, Nobel Laureates, prominent intellectuals, and other high-profile persons could also be formed to work alongside programme staff in order to extend the programme's work upward into the highest levels of government. A regional council on good governance could meet regularly with programme staff, scholars, and NGO representatives to ascertain which areas might be in most need of the programme's assistance and to analyze priority issues. Council members could work quietly with government leaders to urge them to move in the direction of good governance and to make good governance issues salient in the region, for example by hosting high-level conferences within and between states on specific governance issues.

A second council on dispute settlement could be convened on a regular basis for off-the-record meetings with programme staff and selected scholars to identify and analyze emerging or existing disputes. This council could also host high-level meetings of leaders or officials to analyze regional or subregional problems and consider a range of possible structural solutions. In some instances, council members might be asked to provide good offices or mediation (with back-up from programme staff).

Benefits of a strategic coalition of actors

Drawing together these different actors into a strategic alliance would help to overcome the obstacle which NGOs typically face – that of having to gain a government's consent before its staff can do anything. Although the activities of regional centres themselves would be subject to the direct consent of governments, the other three sets of actors (NGOs, scholars, and regional councils) would be able to promote the programme's agenda even in cases where a country has not been formally involved with the regional centre. Thus, such an alliance would not only extend the reach in terms of finding ways to tackle a problem at all levels of society, but it would also find a way around the common barriers to NGO influence.

Conclusion

The development of UN Regional Centres for Sustainable Peace could bring together the United Nations, regional organizations, NGOs, and scholars in a new alliance to promote good governance and conflict prevention within and between states. Centres could be proactive in offering assistance and support, relying on a cooperative assistance approach backed up by the positive incentives of regional and international socialization. If properly resourced, regional centres could help to reorient the United Nations to a more preventive approach and establish a more solid international foundation upon which, step by step, sustainable peace could be built.[13]

Notes

1. P. Wallensteen and M. Sollenberg, "The End of International War? Armed Conflict, 1989–1995," *Journal of Peace Research*, No. 33, 1996, pp. 335–70.
2. Gareth Evans, *Cooperating for Peace: The Global Agenda for the 1990s and Beyond.* Sydney, Australia: Allen and Unwin, 1993.
3. Edward Azar, *The Management of Protracted Social Conflict: Theory and Cases.* Hampshire, England: Dartmouth Publishing, 1990.
4. Ted Robert Gurr, *Minorities at Risk.* Washington, DC: US Institute of Peace, 1993.
5. Boutros Boutros-Ghali, *An Agenda for Democratization.* New York: United Nations, 1996.
6. Connie Peck, *Sustainable Peace: The Role of the UN and Regional Organizations.* New York: Rowman and Littlefield (forthcoming).
7. Azar, op. cit.
8. Peck, op. cit.
9. Timothy Sisk, *Power Sharing and International Mediation in Ethnic Conflicts.* Washington, DC: US Institute of Peace, 1996.
10. Azar, op. cit.

11. Donald L. Horowitz, "Making Moderation Pay: The Comparative Politics of Ethnic Conflict Management," in Joseph Montville (ed.), *Conflict and Peace-making in Multi-ethnic Society*. Lexington, Massachusetts: Lexington Books, 1990.
12. D. Chigas, E. McClintock, and C. Kamp, "Preventive Diplomacy and the Organization for Security and Cooperation in Europe: Creating Incentives for Dialogue and Cooperation," in Abraham and Antonia Chayes (eds.), *Preventing Conflict in the Post-Communist World*, Washington, DC: The Brookings Institution, 1995.
13. This work draws heavily on a study carried out by the author for the Carnegie Commission on Preventing Deadly Conflict. For a fuller version of this study, see *Sustainable Peace: The Role of the UN and Regional Organizations* by Connie Peck. Opinions expressed in this paper are those of the author and do not necessarily reflect the views of the United Nations or UNITAR.

21

Conclusion: International organizations, peace, and security

Michael W. Doyle

International organizations have long been seen as classic solutions to cooperation in international security. Well aware that security tends to be both relative and competitive, states have sometimes sought multilateral organization as an escape from spiralling and counter-productive competition.[1] As a rejection of bilateralism and all the coercive possibilities it entails, multilateralism expresses a preference for cooperation on an equal basis, open to the participation of all states (which meet certain minimal criteria, such as being "peace loving") on a non-discriminatory and equal basis.[2]

That does not mean that the United Nations is free from political competition. The new agenda for international organization in security has made the United Nations a more important arena for competition, and cooperation has emerged that goes beyond the role of arena and regime to that of being a key tool of political competition and, sometimes, a manager of common purposes. With the outbreak of internal wars, a role for the United Nations and regional organizations as conflict managers has come to the fore. What are the prospects?

From security arena to power tool

For a multilateral institution to become an arena of power and then an effective tool of state interest, it must meet certain basic conditions of consensus and effectiveness, otherwise it will simply be neglected. During the Cold War, the United Nations served as an arena of East-West and North-South debate. Occasionally, the common interests of the super-powers permitted a limited role for the United Nations, as happened when the powers sought to keep an issue away from the Cold War divide. But only with the end of the Cold War did the full potential of the United Nations as a tool of state interest emerge. Brahma Chellaney, in his sceptical interpretation of the non-proliferation regime, illustrates the ironies of this potential in his discussion of the IAEA and UNSCOM.

Only when the great powers had a vital interest did the United Nations become a powerful tool. As Chellaney notes, because "arms control is today perceived as an important instrument of national security strategy," particularly by the United States in its campaign to halt the spread of nuclear and chemical arms to non-nuclear powers, the IAEA in general and UNSCOM in the particular case of Iraq emerged as international organizations with real clout. Drawing on an expanded safeguards regime and nationally (US) provided intelligence, the IAEA has become "the nuclear verification arm" of the empowered Security Council. UNSCOM demonstrates unprecedented UN intrusiveness in the defeated sovereignty of Iraq. The success of each, however, raises questions about how multilateral and equitable the regime being enforced truly is. Will international organizations also succeed in the complementary effort of reducing the salience of weapons of mass destruction in world politics, as has been made obligatory by the recent advisory opinion of the International Court of Justice? Doubters therefore question whether the strengthening of the nuclear non-proliferation tool is a strengthening of multilateralism.

The problematic role of the United Nations as a security manager

Although the UN's record in peace operations by no means exhibits the crude power of the new anti-proliferation regime, the managerial record in peace operations – before, during, and after the assertive period we have just experienced – is long, various, and distinguished by accomplishments and failures. Most importantly, it is innovative. Indeed, it is that record of evolutionary flexibility which suggests that the United Nations can weather the overextension and strife it is currently experiencing.

Peace-keeping operations have come to encompass three distinct activities which have evolved as "generations" of UN peace operations.[3] They include not only the early activities of "first-generation" peace-keeping, which requires the interposition of a force after a truce has been reached, but also a far more ambitious group of "second-generation" operations which rely on the consent of parties, and an even more ambitious group of "third-generation" operations which operate with Chapter VII mandates and without a comprehensive agreement reflecting the acquiescence of the parties. In today's circumstances, these operations involve less inter-state conflict and more factions in domestic civil wars, not all of whom are clearly identifiable and few of whom are stable negotiating parties. Current peace operations thus intrude into aspects of domestic sovereignty once thought to be beyond the purview of UN activity.

As Thomas Weiss has noted, in traditional peace-keeping – sometimes called "first-generation" peace-keeping – unarmed or lightly armed UN forces were stationed between hostile parties to monitor a truce, troop withdrawal, or buffer zone while political negotiations went forward.[4] They provided transparency – an impartial assurance that the other party was not violating the truce – and raised the costs of defecting from and the benefits of abiding with the agreement by the threat of exposure, the potential resistance of the peace-keeping force, and the legitimacy of UN mandates. The benefits were obvious: armed conflict was held at bay. Their price, as in the long Cyprus operation, was sometimes paid in conflicts delayed rather than resolved. Today these monitoring activities continue to play an important role in Tajikistan, Georgia, and on the border between Kuwait and Iraq.

The second category, called "second-generation" operations by the Secretary-General, involves the implementation of complex multidimensional peace agreements. In addition to the traditional military functions, the peacekeepers are often engaged in various police and civilian tasks, the goal of which is a long-term settlement of the underlying conflict. Taking a substantial step beyond "first-generation" operations, "second-generation" multidimensional operations are based on consent of the parties. But the nature of and purposes for which consent is granted are qualitatively different from traditional peace-keeping.

In these operations, the United Nations is typically involved in implementing peace agreements that go to the roots of the conflict and helping to build long-term foundations for stable, legitimate government. As Secretary-General Boutros-Ghali observed in An Agenda for Peace, "peace-making and peace-keeping operations, to be truly successful, must come to include comprehensive efforts to identify and support structures which will tend to consolidate peace... [They] may include disarming the previously warring parties and the restoration of order, the custody and possible destruction of weapons, repatriating refugees, advisory and training support for security personnel, monitoring elections, advancing efforts to protect human rights, reforming or strengthening governmental institutions, and promoting formal and informal processes of political participation."

The United Nations has a commendable record of success in second-generation multidimensional peace-keeping operations as diverse as those in Namibia (UNTAG), El Salvador (ONUSAL), and Cambodia (UNTAC).[5] The UN's role in helping settle those conflicts has been threefold. It served as a peacemaker, facilitating a peace treaty among the parties; as a peacekeeper monitoring the cantonment and demobilization of military forces, resettling refugees, and supervising transitional civilian authorities; and as a peace builder monitoring, and in some cases organizing, the implementation of human rights, national democratic elections, and economic rehabilitation.

In the Secretary-General's lexicon "peace-enforcing" missions – which in effect are war-making missions – are "third-generation" operations, which extend from low-level military operations to protect the delivery of humanitarian assistance to the enforcement of cease-fires and when necessary assistance in the rebuilding of so-called "failed states." Like Chapter VII UN enforcement action to roll back aggression, as in Korea in 1950 and against Iraq in the Gulf War, the defining characteristic of "third-generation" operations is the lack of consent by one or more of the parties to some or all of the UN mandate.[6] Unlike traditional Chapter VII collective security, these operations focus on internal strife.

Neither Somalia nor Bosnia and Herzegovina reflected a coherent plan to restore peace by force. Instead, both were composites of coercive restraints (no-fly zones, arms embargoes, humanitarian protection, safe areas) with broad-brush or piecemeal local endorsements (such as the signing by many factions of the Addis Ababa Accords of February 1993 concerning Somalia).

Insightful doctrine for peace-enforcing operations appeared just as Somalia and Bosnia and Herzegovina exposed their limitations. Recent studies have thoughtfully mapped out the logic of what it might take to succeed in this political terrain. In order to preclude an outcome based on the use of force by the parties, the United Nations instead uses collective force (if necessary) to persuade the parties to settle the conflict by negotiation. This strategic terrain, however, is murky. Forcing a peace depends on achieving a complicated preponderance in which the forces (both United Nations and local) supporting a settlement acceptable to the international community acquire both a superiority of military might and a predominance of popular support, which together permit them to impose a peace on the recalcitrant local military forces and their popular supporters.

The result of these three "generations" operating together in the post-

Table 21.1 The Changing UN Role in Peace and Security: 1988–1996[7]

	31 January 1988	31 January 1992	16 December 1994	30 November 1996
Security Council resolutions in previous 12 months	15	53	78	57
Sanctions imposed by Security Council	1	2	7	1
Preventive diplomacy and peace-making	11	13	28	13
Electoral activities	–	6	21	11
Peace-keeping operations	5	11	17	16
Deployed, total: military personnel	9,570	11,495	73,390	20,833
civilian police	35	155	2,130	2,721
civilian personnel	1,516	1,206	2,260	2,739
Countries contributing personnel	26	56	76	71
UN budget for peace-keeping, US$ million	230.4	1,689.6	3,610	1,400–1,600

Cold War world was an unprecedented expansion of the UN's role in the protection of world order and the promotion of basic human rights in countries until recently torn by costly civil wars. Self-determination and sovereignty were enhanced and a modicum of peace and rehabilitation was introduced in Namibia, Cambodia, El Salvador, Haiti, and Mozambique. Tens – perhaps even hundreds – of thousands of lives were saved in Somalia and the former Yugoslavia.

But in 1993 and 1994, the more ambitious elements of "third-generation" peace enforcement encountered many of the problems interventionist and imperial strategies have faced in the past, and discovered fresh problems peculiar to the UN's global character. The United Nations proved itself ineffective in imposing order by force, whether to disarm factions in Somalia or provide humanitarian protection in Bosnia and Herzegovina. Instead it became complicit in a record of inadequate protection, seemingly unnecessary casualties, and Viet Nam-like escalation on the one hand with 1930s'-style appeasement on the other. The result was a reduction in the number operations assigned to direct UN management.

As David Malone has noted, the Security Council's "war-making" suffers from severe disabilities, ranging from those that are a product of the organization's incapacity to others that are a product of the kind of wars which the United Nations has tried to address:

Although the United Nations seemed to have the advantage of global impartiality, which should (and often did) win it more local acceptance when it intervened, this was not universally the case. Israel maintained a suspicion of UN involvement dating back to the General Assembly's notorious anti-Zionism resolutions of the 1970s. In Somalia, Egypt's support for the former dictator, Siad Barre, seemed to taint the role that Secretary-General Boutros-Ghali, a former Egyptian Minister of State for Foreign Affairs, sought to play as an impartial Secretary-General. And there was lingering distrust of the United Nations in other parts of Africa due to its role in the Congo.[8] Many smaller non-Western states, moreover, distrusted the use of the Security Council by the great powers, and particularly the Western "P-3" (France, the United Kingdom, and the United States), which sometimes appeared to be trying to impose a selective vision of world order on weaker states.[9]

The United Nations was particularly poorly suited to interventionist strategies involving the strategic employment of coercive force. The political roots of the UN's "command and control" problems were threefold.

First, countries with battalions in UN peace operations were reluctant to see their (often lightly armed) troops engaged in combat under UN direction, fearing that a UN force commander of any nationality other than their own would fail to take due care to minimize risks.

Second, countries with seats on the Security Council, pressured to achieve a response to humanitarian crises and unwilling to confront the UN's ongoing resource crisis, assigned missions to UN peace operations without providing adequate means to achieve them.

And third, the UN's traditional ideology, despite recent practice, was highly protective of national sovereignty. To its credit, the United Nations lacked the callousness or psychological distance required to inflict coercive punishment on political movements with even the smallest of popular support.[10] To its cost, the United Nations rarely planned the peace-building process as a comprehensive effort to re-establish (or establish) a legitimate, effective political order.

"Peace-enforcing fatigue," moreover, is afflicting the UN's contributing countries, whether new or old. States are rarely willing to invest their resources or the lives of their soldiers in war other than for a vital interest, such as oil in the Persian Gulf. But if states have a vital national interest in a dispute, they are not likely to exercise the impartiality that a UN peace operation requires. Nor are they likely to cede decision-making control over or command of their forces to the United Nations. As a result, the United Nations is finding it increasingly difficult to acquire troops for the dangerous operations, such as Rwanda, and to supervise the delegated operations, such as the Russian Federation operation in Georgia.

Lastly, the very act of intervention, even by the United Nations, can mobilize nationalist opposition against the foreign forces. In Somalia, according to some observers, it contributed to a significant growth of support for Aideed's Somali National Alliance. Aideed's supporters soon roundly condemned UN "colonialism."[11] The strategic balance is not static. Military intervention tilts two local balances, improving the military correlation of forces but often at the cost of undermining the more important political balance.

Coercively intervening for eventual self-determination, as John Stuart Mill noted over a century ago, is very often a self-contradictory enterprise.[12] If the local forces of freedom, self-determination, and human rights cannot achieve sovereignty without a foreign military intervention, then they are very unlikely to be able to hold on to power after the intervention force leaves. Either the installed forces of freedom will collapse, or they themselves will employ those very coercive methods that provoked and justified the initial intervention. The Kurds, for example, won widespread sympathy for their resistance to Saddam Hussein and benefited from a UN-endorsed US-French-British intervention in the aftermath of the war against Iraq. Now the Kurdish factions are so divided that they appear incapable of establishing law and order in their territory. Instead, three factions have divided the region. None appears capable of sustaining itself against whatever attempts to reincorporate Kurdistan Saddam Hussein may make. The international community has thus placed itself in the awkward position of either adopting Kurdistan as a long-term ward or returning it to the not-so-tender mercies of the Iraqi ruler.[13]

The United Nations, in the role of assertively multilateral peace enforcer, thus presented an almost textbook case of multiple strategic incapacity. But encountering strategic problems while intervening in ethnic and civil wars is not unique to the United Nations. The multinational force in Lebanon created even larger catastrophes of misdirected, overly violent, and intrusive intervention in 1983. Even with national-quality command and control, the United States failed to impose peace in Viet Nam in the 1960s, just as the Soviets failed in Afghanistan in the 1970s and 1980s. The United Nations, moreover, is essentially the collective agent of its member states. Many of the UN's organizational incapacities could be corrected by additional resources from its members states, which devote but a tiny fraction of the resources they spend on national security to collective action under the umbrella of the United Nations.

An inescapable role for the United Nations?

The crises in Somalia and Bosnia and Herzegovina, together with the wider limitations those crises exposed, constituted a challenge to the international community. The United Nations must now develop a combination of initiatives which enhances capacities, retrenches responsibilities, reviews strategies, and redefines roles.

The importance of reforming the United Nations is widely recognized. Abandonment is thus not an option. Indeed, for many there is no alternative to the United Nations in the roles it should be playing in peace and security. Emilio Cardenas, former Permanent Representative of Argentina to the United Nations, expressed this well when he noted:

The United Nations, notwithstanding its apparent decline in terms of ability to forward and maintain international security, remains the central institution in the security realm. And, in my view, it should be so. Otherwise, we will all be confronted with the "return of the strong" to the centre of the world's scenario. And this is certainly not what we agreed upon in 1945.[14]

Reflecting both legal legitimacy and practical support, the United Nations holds a unique claim on legitimate authority in international peace and war.[15]

- The United Nations is the only international organization formally entrusted with the legal authority to preserve peace in cases other than national or collective self-defence. At the same time, as the only multipurpose universal organization, it has the authority to promote those wider political, social, and economic conditions that are conducive to preventing violent conflict and redressing its causes once it has occurred.
- The United Nations is again the only institution which is truly global in scope, where the states of the world can explore their common interests and aspirations as equal members of the international community. It allows for, indeed requires, dialogue across cultures, races, and economic systems.
- The United Nations is the delegatee of last resort (often the "scapegoat") for global conflict and hard-to-resolve disputes. For the vast majority of nations preferring to focus on domestic welfare and wishing to avoid having to become global policemen themselves, the United

Nations has stood ready to be the international emergency service. Even in the United States, 73 per cent of the respondents in a national poll favoured strengthening the United Nations, as the alternative to the United States having to go it alone as a world policeman.[16] Although the United Nations does need to learn when to say "No," it is rightly assumed to be the place where such a decision will be made based upon the principles of collective security, self-determination, and fundamental human freedoms.

- As described earlier, the United Nations has effectively delivered both first-generation truce supervision and second-generation multidimensional peace-building operations. The United Nations has proven ineffectual at third-generation enforcement and weak at operations in the "grey zone" where violence disrupts peace building, but these failings should not lead us to neglect the vital and effective role the United Nations has played in those other crucial operations. Its involvement has prevented disputes from spreading across borders and begun to address the root causes of long-lingering conflicts, such as those in El Salvador and Cambodia.
- The United Nations, moreover, is the institution which promotes and reformulates the rules that govern the growing interdependence of nations. Ranging from choosing a common language of communication for air traffic controllers (a useful convention) to protecting the 45 million refugees around the world (a moral commitment), the organization provides the institutional foundation for the emergence of an increasingly interdependent world.

No one initiative alone could bear the entire burden of revising the international organization's role in peace-making and peace-keeping in the years to come. We need instead a combination of initiatives in order to avoid a retreat from the responsibilities towards peace and security for which the international community relies on the United Nations. We also need, on the other hand, areas for restraint and reconsideration, seeking – where one can – measures that would allow the United Nations to economize on scarce resources while continuing, perhaps even expanding, the role it could play in effectively furthering international peace and security.

Supplements to the United Nations?

When the United Nations cannot negotiate a peace, should the international community abandon the cause? What responses should have been made to acts of overt aggression, such as Iraq's invasion of Kuwait, or to the looming humanitarian disasters in Bosnia and Herzegovina and

Somalia in 1992 or Rwanda in the spring of 1994? And when the international community cannot advance on an equitable basis the security of its member states, should national action, as Brahma Chellaney notes, be the preferred solution?

Delegation to national action has become, as it was in Korea in 1950, the UN's answer to extreme emergencies – international aggression and humanitarian catastrophe. It offers a traditional national solution to the UN's typical command-and-control problems. Now it is becoming so widespread that it is being designated "fourth-generation" peace-keeping. Stimulated by the temporary success of UNITAF and by the delegations to the Russian Federation in Georgia, to France in Rwanda, and to the United States in Haiti, the United Nations is surmounting contributors' fatigue by assigning mandates to the national states willing to accept and perhaps enforce them. This, indeed, may be the best compromise available in difficult circumstances.[17] In itself, however, it does little to address the longer-term problems of leaving behind a stable form of locally legitimate government. Here there remains an important "hand-off" role for the United Nations. Imposing a scheme of public order should be avoided in favour of mobilizing the peace-making, peace-keeping, and peace-building strategies of enhanced consent that the United Nations exercises well. The UNITAF to UNOSOM II hand-off failed because peace-making stopped short of negotiating a comprehensive, implementable agreement which included both the warlords and civil society. Instead, the United Nations attempted to impose law and order from New York and Washington, with all the consequences. In these cases, the United Nations should try to recruit the beginnings of a "Friends" coalition of interested states to assist and help monitor the intervenor. These "Friends" will also be needed to help negotiate, fund, and manage a peace on a multilateral basis.

Delegation raises difficult issues of UN responsibility. Can the Security Council be confident that the mandate it assigns will be implemented in ways that fulfil multilateral principles and serve the interests of the United Nations as a whole? Security Council "licences" to intervene with pre-ordained but renewable expiration clauses should address some of these concerns. But, in our dangerous times, will states volunteer in reliably large enough numbers for international public service?

As Connie Peck has suggested, another alternative centres around new attention to the possibilities of regional prevention, peace-making, and peace-keeping – a multilateral burden-sharing strategy recommended in the Secretary-General's Agenda for Peace. A regional approach appears designed to elicit a more locally sensitive approach to political disputes. But the lack of institutional, military, and financial capacity in the regional organizations (with the exception perhaps of NATO) remains a considerable hurdle.

As yet another alternative, Sir Brian Urquhart has issued an eloquent manifesto in favour of a UN rapid-reaction force of 5,000–10,000 personnel. Small and centrally controlled, it would be suited for overcoming delays occasioned by the recruiting of peace-keeping forces, enabling the United Nations to engage in rapid interventions that can sometimes prevent an escalating crisis. Had they been available, these forces might have been decisive in Somalia in early 1992 or Rwanda in the spring of 1994.[18] Very few countries, however, have expressed a willingness to establish such a force. Current discussions centre on a less global but still valuable ready-reaction force consisting of designated national units, trained in peace-keeping and available at short notice.

When no state, group of states, or organization will volunteer to intervene, then sometimes the best that can be done is to try to mitigate the consequences of natural disaster or war. Humanitarian assistance from "above" – state efforts to establish "humanitarian corridors" as has been done in the Sudan, or protected convoys, and even, at the minimum, airdrops as were essayed in Bosnia and Herzegovina – can make a valuable difference. Assistance from "below" by non-governmental organizations taking all the considerable risks of independent action can also provide relief, as the voluntary agencies did in Somalia until they were overwhelmed in late 1992.[19] In these circumstances, the United Nations should continue to attempt to recruit coalitions of states – "Friends" – which will dedicate their energies to negotiating and managing a peace. UNPROFOR, to its credit, has remained committed to negotiating, rather than imposing, a peace. But the Security Council should avoid making promises – such as the Bosnian "safe havens" or the Croatian disarmed and protected "protected areas" – unless it either has the consent of all the parties and plans to provide adequate forces to implement the agreement against likely slippage or, irrespective of consent, is prepared to enforce the pledges against opposition. As the Secretary-General recently noted, there are often other areas of the world where – if the UN's resources are fixed – those UN resources can sometimes be put to better use, saving more people in situations closer to a negotiable solution.[20]

When states experience competitive security concerns, as they do in nuclear deterrence and nuclear energy, international organizations will need to discover new bases for common action unless they are going to be become simple arenas for conflict. As Chellaney has argued, the IAEA regime raises perceived distributional consequences, reinforcing the pre-eminence of the nuclear powers. Are there common purposes that can mitigate the distributional conflict, if not on a global level, then regionally? Worth further investigation are regimes of nuclear control that constitute multilateral guarantees – arms restraints in return for progress on regional disputes, as may be occurring in the Middle East, where progress in peace is regarded as the alternative to increasing pressures for proliferation.

Neither UN peace-making nor these alternative strategies will eliminate the formidable challenges of making, keeping, and building peace in the midst of protracted civil wars. Some crises will not find their solution. But today, as the United Nations is under attack in the United States and elsewhere, we should not neglect its authentic peace-making potential. Employing strategies of enhanced consent, the United Nations can play a constructive role in the forging of peace and reconstruction in those areas of the world in need of assistance. Avoiding the dangerous and often counter-productive effects of armed imposition, whether unilateral or multilateral, the United Nations can be the legitimating broker in the making, keeping, and building of a stable peace that takes the first steps toward the opening of political space for human rights and participatory communal self-expression.

Notes

1. See Robert Jervis, "Cooperation Under the Security Dilemma," *World Politics* (1978); and John Ruggie (ed.), *Multilateralism Matters* (New York: Columbia University Press, 1993).
2. Miles Kahler, "Multilateralism with Small and Large Numbers," in Ruggie (ed.), *Multilateralism Matters*, pp. 295–326.
3. It is worth recalling that the time-line of evolution has by no means been chronologically straightforward. The most extensive "third-generation" operation undertaken by the United Nations was ONUC (United Nations Force in the Congo) in the then Congo between 1960 and 1964, which preceded the spate of "second-generation" operations which began with UNTAG in Namibia in 1989.
4. Traditional peace-keeping is a shorthand term that describes many but by no means all Cold War peace-keeping missions (the most notable exception being the Congo operation). For a cogent analysis of different types of peace-keeping, see Marrack Goulding, "The Evolution of United Nations Peace-keeping," *International Affairs*, vol. 69, 3 (July 1993).
5. Before the United Nations became involved, during the Cold War when action by the Security Council was stymied by the lack of consensus among its five Permanent Members, the international community allowed Cambodia to suffer an auto-genocide and El Salvador a brutal civil war. Indeed, the great powers were involved in arming, funding, and training the factions who inflicted some of the worst aspects of the violence the two countries suffered. We should keep this is mind when we consider the international community's more recent difficulties in Somalia and Bosnia and Herzegovina.
6. Other recent categories include "preventive deployments" deployed with the intention of deterring a possible attack, as in the former Yugoslav Republic of Macedonia today. The credibility of the deterring force must ensure that the potential aggressor knows that there will be no easy victory. In the event of an armed challenge, the result will be an international war that involves costs so grave as to outweigh the temptations of conquest. Enforcement action against aggression (Korea or the Gulf), conversely, is a matter of achieving victory – "the decisive, comprehensive, and synchronized application of

preponderant military force to shock, disrupt, demoralize, and defeat opponents" – the traditional zero-sum terrain of military strategy. See John Mackinlay and Jarat Chopra, *A Draft Concept of Second-Generation Operations* (Brown University: Watson Institute, 1993); and John Ruggie, "The United Nations Stuck in a Fog Between Peace-keeping and Peace Enforcement," *McNair Paper 25* (Washington: National Defense University, 1993).

7. Boutros Boutros-Ghali, *Supplement to An Agenda for Peace: Position Paper of the Secretary-General on the Occasion of the Fiftieth Anniversary of the United Nations*, A/50/60;S/1995/1, 3 January 1995, p. 4; *The Military Balance* (London: Oxford University Press, 1996) p. 293; and UN Department of Public Information, *Year in Review 1996: United Nations Peace Missions* (United Nations: DPI, December 1996). I am grateful for the assistance of Ms Elise Oliver in the assembling of these figures.

8. Recently this distrust has given way to a sense of urgency about Africa's conflicts, in which UN involvement is seen as necessary. See *The OAU and Conflict Management in Africa*, report of a joint OAU/IPA consultation, Addis Ababa, May 1993.

9. See the panel discussion among UN permanent representatives at the UNHCR/IPA Conference on Conflict and Humanitarian, reported in *Conflict and Humanitarian Action* (UNHCR/IPA, 1994) by Michael Doyle and Ian Johnstone, rapporteurs.

10. An added problem is that the use of force in civil wars frequently causes casualties among civilians, opening the United Nations and its members to accusations of neo-colonialism and brutality. Adam Roberts, *The Crisis in Peace-keeping*, (Institutt for Forsvarsstudier, 2/1994) p. 24.

11. Abdi Hassan Awale, an Aidid adviser in Mogadishu, complains, "... the United Nations wants to rule this country. They do not want a Somali government to be established. The United Nations wants to stay and colonize us." *New York Times*, 2 March 1994.

12. For a classic discussion of these problems see John Stuart Mill, "A Few Words on Non-intervention," (1859) in Gertrude Himmelfarb (ed.), *Essays on Politics and Culture* (Gloucester: P. Smith, 1973).

13. Chris Hedges, "Quarrels of Kurdish Leaders Sour Dreams of a Homeland," *New York Times*, 18 June 1994, p. A1.

14. As quoted in Dr. Tommie Sue Montgomery, rapporteur, *Multilateral Approaches to Peace-making and Democratization in the Hemisphere*, a report of the North-South Center (University of Miami, 1996) p. 19.

15. For a penetrating discussion of the value of the United Nations to US foreign policy, see Edward Luck, "The United Nations, Multilateralism, and US Interests," in C. William Maynes and Richard S. Williamson (eds.), *US Foreign Policy and the United Nations System* (New York: W. W. Norton, 1996), pp. 27–53.

16. Steven Kull, *Americans on Defense Spending* (Program on International Policy Attitudes, 19 January 1996) p. 23.

17. For a case for an option similar to this, called "benign spheres of influence," see Charles William Maynes, "A Workable Clinton Doctrine," *Foreign Policy*, vol. 93, Winter 1993–1994.

18. Sir Brian Urquhart, "For a UN Volunteer Military Force," *New York Review of Books*, 10 June 1993. See also "Four Views," *New York Review of Books*, 24 June 1993.

19. For a valuable discussion see Stephen Jackson, "Survival of the Cutest," *The Irish Reporter*, no. 12, 4th quarter, 1993. pp. 5–7.

20. Barbara Crossette, "UN Chief Ponders Future of Peacekeepers," *New York Times*, 3 March 1995. The Secretary-General referred specifically to transferring resources from UNPROFOR to possible operations in Afghanistan or Tajikistan.

Conclusion

Three frameworks of peace and security in the next millennium

Takashi Inoguchi

We have posed at the outset the two key questions whereby we can organize our thoughts on the nature of peace and security in global politics and the possible roles the United Nations could play therein. In the preceding chapters we have done our best to answer these two questions. Recapitulating them would be more tedious than necessary. Therefore, I would like to bring back a possibly more fundamental question and try to give answers in a slightly different fashion. The question is: what kinds of frameworks of global politics will compete and possibly prevail in the next millenium as global politics start to take a clearer shape from the current state of flux?

Let me start with three books of major importance which have been published in the last few years. They are Henry Kissinger's *Diplomacy*, Bruce Russett's *Grasping the Democratic Peace*, and Samuel Huntington's *The Clash of Civilizations and the Remaking of World Order*. I take them as representative articulators of three totally different streams of thought which according to them govern, ought to govern, and will govern global politics in the next millennium. Kissinger's *Diplomacy* is Westphalian; Russett's *Grasping the Democratic Peace* is Philadelphian; and Huntington's *Clash of Civilizations* is anti-utopian. By Westphalian I mean a framework in which state sovereignty reigns supreme. By Philadelphian I mean a framework in which popular sovereignty stands firm. By anti-utopian I mean a framework in which the loss of sovereignty is the key feature. The presumption is that these three frameworks of global politics are competing, and that it is not quite clear which one will prevail. I will briefly spell out the key features of these three frameworks in terms of key concept, systemic features, and behavioural modalities, and the key role of the United Nations in these frameworks.

The Westphalian framework has been predominant over the past three centuries, and especially over the past century and a half. The territorially-based nation-states and their competition in Europe and beyond intermittently created havoc globally and regionally. State sovereignty means order within and anarchy without. Systemic features are thus anarchy, and anarchy without can only be restrained by competition itself. Behavioural modalities are characterized by balancing and bandwagonning By balancing I mean the propensity of actors to defend the system by moving to counteract those actors who show their ambition to prevail. By bandwagonning I mean the propensity of actors to join the likely-to-prevail actors in the interest of maximizing their gains with minimum costs.

The Philadelphian framework has existed since the colonial period as a result of the American Civil War. It was a system in which legal procedures and amicable agreement prevailed when conflicts of interests needed to be resolved. There was order, but not necessarily hierarchy amongst different interests. Behavioural modalities are characterized by binding and hiding. By binding I mean the propensity of actors to shape agreements whereby actors are constrained. By hiding I mean the propensity of actors to move away from agreements whereby actors are constrained.

The anti-utopian framework has existed since the West started to colonize the rest of the world. It was a colonial framework. The key components of colonialism are civilizing missions and territorial aggrandizement. The latter disappeared in the mid-twentieth century, largely because of the diffusion of the Westphalian framework. When the United Nations was established in 1945, the number of member states was far fewer than 50. The headquarters building in New York was designed with the estimated number of member states reaching some 100. But the fact was that by the end of the 1960s the number reached more than 100, and by the end of this century it will reach 185.

The Westphalian framework has been on the steady rise for the last half-century, judging by the number of states of the United Nations. It is a clear departure, however, from the nineteenth century Westphalian framework, in which about five major European powers were engaged in balance-of-power politics. There are far too many states in which state sovereignty is not firmly exercised. Some of them are visibly failed states or failing states. Furthermore, in tandem with globalization and market liberalization comes the loosening of the Westphalian framework. State sovereignty itself has become more difficult to claim with effectiveness as the state's legitimate space has become more easily encroached by businesses and non-governmental organizations which act across borders.

The Philadelphian framework has been resuscitated, with some of the Westphalian framework being incorporated. The extraordinary growth of economic interdependence, international organizations, and democratization for the last half-century is the driving force of the renaissance of the Philadelphian framework at the turn of the millennium. Relentless globalization makes it more difficult for states to pursue balance-of-power games, since the national interest has become more complicated to define. Binding networks of international agreements and organizations have become truly formidable. And the third wave of democratization has created an atmosphere in which resort to violence has become less frequent as the instrument of resolution of international disputes.

The anti-utopian framework has been revised, with some of the Philadelphian components incorporated. The Philadelphian framework stresses civilizing missions without territorial aggrandizement. Different vocabularies, such as humanitarian assistance, global governance, and human security, are used to motivate action on the part of major and minor states and international organizations which intervene in peacekeeping, building, and enforcing operations, disaster relief operations, and preventive diplomacy. As long as globalization rewards some and punishes others, those actors which are understood better with the anti-utopian framework go up in number. Some of them are failed states and failing states which have not been sufficiently agile and able to adapt to the global market.

Having spelled out, if briefly, the three competing framework of global politics, I now turn to the role of the United Nations. The United Nations is the product of the Westphalian framework. Nothing is clearer than the fact that member states reign supreme in the United Nations. The United Nations is one of the measures of war settlement. The five Permanent Members of the Security Council are a victors' alliance. It is there that the basic understanding of world situations is shared more or less among the five, and that the United Nations' military action is legitimated with the five's approval.

Yet the Philadelphian situation has become increasingly more common. Even if member states reign supreme, non-governmental organizations can move mountains, i.e. member states. The latest agreement on anti-personnel mines has been brought to success due in large part to the NGOs' success in persuading a number of key member states, including the host state, Canada, to acquiesce. In the first half of the 1990s three UN agencies stood out in terms of their vigour in getting donations, expanding the size of personnel, and enlarging their activities. They are the UNHCR, UNICEF, and the World Food Programme. They were most skilful and successful in mobilizing world mass media, like CNN and the *Herald Tribune*, and getting money collected for their just causes. These three agencies happen to be headed by women: Sadako Ogata, Carol Bellami, and Catherine Bertini respectively. In other words, the United Nations is not strictly Westphalian but is also Philadelphian.

Another important point not to be overlooked with respect to the United Nations is the fact that the United Nations itself exists largely for those actors which cannot exercise influence in other arenas and markets, i.e. weak actors. Major powers in the Westphalian framework can assert themselves in ways normal to Westphalian actors, such as arms build-up, economic sanctions, and alliance. Major actors in the Philadelphian framework can shape norms and rules in ways normal to Philadelphian actors, such as a multilateral free trade regime, IMF regime, human rights regime, and global environmental regime. Yet those actors whose framework is more anti-utopian than other kinds are forced to rely on certain international forums such as the United Nations to voice their grievances and to oppose stronger and richer actors whose reliance on the United Nations is far smaller.

Looked at from these three angles, the United Nations is an instrument, an actor, and an arena at the same time. First, the United Nations is an instrument of major Westphalian actors. It lends to them the banner of legitimacy for actions which presumably serve the interests of major powers, especially the world leader, the United States. Second, the United Nations is an actor on its own when it can mobilize support and build power bases somewhat independent of member states. Its appeal to just causes and to correct banners often enables the United Nations to surmount the logic and power of Westphalian actors. Although the United Nations can enjoy neither the authority to tax nor the authority to conscript, it can sway. Third, the United Nations is an arena in which many weak actors express their complaints and submit their demands. It is a widely utilized space where words do matter, rather than might or money. Just like the frameworks of global politics, the United Nations does work under the three frameworks: Westphalian, Philadelphian, and anti-utopian. Accordingly it has three faces: instrument, actor, and arena.

The question then is which framework is going to prevail in the next millennium. It is hard to answer the question in a straightforward fashion. But it is possible to identify two major parameters that give certain directions to global politics. One is globalization, while the other is state protection. Globalization weakens Westphalian actors, since it tends to reduce the relative scope and authority of state sovereignty. Globalization increases the number of those actors which are more than ever before at the mercy of market forces and security dynamics shaped outside the borders. In other words, globalization marginalizes many actors and creates many drop-outs and hollow-outs. Those weak actors then seek state protection and the umbrella of international organizations such as the United Nations. Yet globalization creates more resilient Philadelphian actors. And the force of globalization hinges in part on the presence of the global economy and the global hegemony. The excessive pursuit of globalization is bound to undermine the Philadelphian framework via the weakening of Westphalian actors and via the increase in the number of failed/failing states, since under the Philadelphian framework there will be no powerful federal world government and therefore many of the burdens of the Philadelphian framework fall on the shoulders of the United States. That could easily become too much for the United States in the longer term, especially because the force of the global market is too often beyond the power of the United States federal government to control, even in the short term.

Thinking along this line, I am somewhat agnostic as to which framework will prevail. What I can do is echo Deng Xiaoping, who declared that Hong Kong, after its return to the fold of Chinese sovereignty in 1997, will experience a "one-country, two-systems" scheme for half a century. Global politics in the next millennium will experience the three frameworks for at least the first half-century.

Glossary of Acronyms

ABM	anti-ballistic missile
ACS	Association of Caribbean States
ANZUS	Australia, New Zealand, and the United States Security Treaty, 1951
APDOVE	Association of Protestant Development Organizations in Europe
APEC	Asia-Pacific Economic Cooperation Forum
ARF	ASEAN Regional Forum
ASEAN	Association of South-East Asian Nations
ASPAC	Asian and Pacific Council
BCC	Boni County Council
BJP	Bharatiya Janata Party
BKA	Bundeskriminalamt
CACM	Central American Common Market
CARE	Cooperative for American Remittances to Europe
CARICOM	Caribbean Community
CCIC	Canadian Council for International Cooperation
CD	Conference on Disarmament
CECLA	Latin American Economic Commission
CENTO	Central Treaty Organization
CGDK	Coalition Government of Democratic Kampuchea
CIA	Central Intelligence Agency
CIAV-OAS	International Support and Verification Mission
CIDSE	Coopération Internationale pour le Développement et la Solidarité
CIS	Commonwealth of Independent States
CISS	Canadian Institute of Strategic Studies

CIVS	International Commission of Verification and Follow-up
CMOC	civilian military operation centre
CNN	Cable News Network
COE	Council of Europe
CPVA	Canadian Peacekeeping Veterans Association
CRC-NPFL	Central Revolutionary Council of the National Patriotic Front of Liberia
CSCE	Conference on Security and Cooperation in Europe
CTB	comprehensive test ban
CTBT	Comprehensive Test Ban Treaty
DC	developed country
DHA	Department of Humanitarian Affairs
DPA	Department of Political Affairs
DPKO	Department of Peace-keeping Operations
EC	European Community
ECHO	European Community Humanitarian Organization
ECLAC	United Nations Economic Commision for Latin America and the Caribbean
ECO	Economic Cooperation Organization
ECOMOG	Economic Community Monitoring Group
ECOSOC	United Nations Economic and Social Council
ECOWAS	Economic Community of West African States
EU	European Union
FAO	Food and Agricultural Organization
FAS	Federation of American Scientists
FBI	Federal Bureau of Investigation
FMLN	Farabundo Marti National Liberation Front
GATT	General Agreement on Tariffs and Trade
GCC	Gulf Cooperation Council
GUNT	Interim Government of Chad
HIOC	humanitarian integrated operations centre
IADB	Inter-American Defense Board
IAEA	International Atomic Energy Agency
IAPTC	International Association of Peacekeeping Training Centres
IASC	United Nations Interagency Standing Committee
ICJ	International Court of Justice
ICRC	International Committee of the Red Cross
ICVA	International Council of Volunteer Agencies
IFOR	Implementation Force in Croatia and Bosnia and Herzegovina
IFRC	International Federation of Red Cross and Red Crescent Societies
IIRSEM	informal information and resource sharing/exchange mechanism
IMF	International Monetary Fund
INF	intermediate-range nuclear forces
INGO	international non-governmental organization
IOM	International Organization for Migration
IPA	International Peace Academy

IPPNW	International Physicians for the Prevention of Nuclear War
ISG	Inter-sessional Support Group
ISM	Inter-sessional Meeting
JCC	Joint Consultative Commission
JIM	Jakarta Informal Meeting
JNA	Yugoslav People's Army
KGB	Komitet Gosudarstvennoi Bezopasnosti (USSR State Security Committee)
KPNLF	Khmer People's National Liberation Front
LAIA	Latin American Integration Association
LAS	League of Arab States
LDC	less developed country
LDF	Lofa Defence Force
LLDC	least less developed country
LNC	Liberian National Congress
LPC	Liberian Peace Council
MERCOSUR	Southern Cone Common Market
MICIVIH	International Civilian Mission in Haiti
MINUGUA	United Nations Verification Mission in Guatemala
MINURSO	United Nations Mission for the Referendum in Western Sahara
MOMEP	Military Observer Mission, Ecuador-Peru
MSF	Médécins Sans Frontières
NAM	Non-Aligned Movement
NATO	North Atlantic Treaty Organization
NBC	nuclear, biological, and chemical
NCAI	National Committee on Atomic Information
NGO	non-governmental organization
NNWS	non-nuclear weapons state
NPFL	National Patriotic Front of Liberia
NPP	New Peace-keeping Partnership
NPT	Non-Proliferation Treaty
NRDC	National Resources Defense Council
NTM	national technical means
NWFZ	nuclear-weapons-free zone
NWS	nuclear weapons state
OAS	Organization of American States
OAU	Organization of African Unity
ODI	Overseas Development Institute
OECD	Organization for Economic Cooperation and Development
OMV	Ongoing Monitoring and Verification (Iraq)
ONUC	United Nations Force in the Congo
ONUCA	United Nations Mission in Nicaragua
ONUSAL	United Nations Observer Mission in El Salvador
ONUVEH	United Nations Electoral Observer Mission to Haiti
ONUVEN	United Nations Electoral Observer Mission to Nicaragua
OPEC	Organization of Petroleum Exporting Countries
ORCI	Office for Research and the Collection of Information

OSCE	Organization for Security and Cooperation in Europe
PPC	Pearson Peacekeeping Centre
PRK	People's Republic of Kampuchea
PSAC	Presidential Science Advisory Committee
PTBT	Partial Test Ban Treaty
RENAMO	Resistencia Nacional Mocambicana
RPF	Rwandan Patriotic Front
RUF	Revolutionary United Front (Sierra Leone)
SAARC	South Asian Association for Regional Cooperation
SADC	Southern African Development Community
SAP	Structural Adjustment Policy
SAS	Soviet Academy of Sciences
SC	Supreme Council (Cambodia)
SEANWFZ	South-East Asia Nuclear Weapon-Free Zone
SEATO	South-East Asia Treaty Organization
SMO	social movement organization
SNC	Supreme National Council (Cambodia)
TAC	Treaty of Amity and Cooperation in South-East Asia
TCN	troop-contributing nation
TCO	transnational criminal organization
TNC	transnational corporation
TSMO	transnational social movement organization
ULIMO	United Liberian Movement for Democracy
ULIMO J	United Liberian Movement for Democracy Johnson
ULIMO K	United Liberian Movement for Democracy Kromah
UN	United Nations
UNAMIR	United Nations Assistance Mission in Rwanda
UNCTAD	United Nations Conference for Trade and Development
UNDCP	United Nations Drug Control Programme
UNDP	United Nations Development Programme
UNEF	United Nations Emergency Force
UNESCO	United Nations Educational, Scientific, and Cultural Organization
UNFICYP	United Nations Force in Cyprus
UNHCR	United Nations High Commissioner for Refugees
UNICEF	United Nations International Children's Emergency Fund
UNIDIR	United Nations Institute for Disarmament Research
UNITA	National Union for the Total Independence of Angola
UNITAF	United Nations International Task Force in Somalia
UNITAR	United Nations Institute for Training and Research
UNOMIG	United Nations Observer Mission in Georgia
UNOMIH	United Nations Observer Mission in Haiti
UNOMIL	United Nations Operations to Liberia
UNOMSA	United Nations Observer Mission in South Africa
UNOSOM	United Nations Operation in Somalia
UNPROFOR	United Nations Protection Force in the Former Yugoslavia
UNSCOM	United Nations Special Commission (Iraq)
UNTAC	United Nations Transitional Authority in Cambodia

UNTAG	United Nations Transitional Assistance Group
UNU	United Nations University
WFP	World Food Programme
WHO	World Health Organization
WMD	weapons of mass destruction
WTO	World Trade Organization
ZOPFAN	zone of peace, freedom, and neutrality

Contributors

Dr Muthiah Alagappa
East West Center

Professor Charles Abiodun Alao
Department of War Studies, King's
  College, University of London

Ms Stephanie A. Blair
Lester B. Pearson International
  Peacekeeping Training Centre

Dr Brahma Chellaney
Centre for Policy Research

Professor Michael W. Doyle
Center of International Studies,
  Princeton University

Dr Cristina Eguizábal
The Ford Foundation

Dr Shiro Harada
University of Tokyo

Professor Takashi Inoguchi
Institute of Oriental Culture,
  University of Tokyo

Dr Roland Koch
Institute of Social Sciences, Technical
  University of Munich

Professor Atul Kohli
Woodrow Wilson School of Public and
  International Affairs, Princeton
  University

Dr David Malone
International Peace Academy, New
  York

Professor Alex Morrison
Lester B. Pearson International
  Peacekeeping Training Centre

Dr Connie Peck
United Nations Institute for Training
  and Research

Professor Volker Rittberger
Institute of Political Science,
  Eberhard-Karls-University
  Tuebingen

Dr Amin Saikal
Center for Middle Eastern and Central

469

Asian Studies, Australian National
University, Canberra

Ms Christina Schrade
Institute of Political Science,
Eberhard-Karls-University
Tuebingen

Ms Daniela Schwarzer
Institute of Political Science,
Eberhard-Karls-University
Tuebingen

Dr Sherle R. Schwenninger
World Policy Institute, New School for
Social Research, New York

Dr Jackie Smith
Joan B. Kroc Institute for International
Peace Studies

Professor Georg Sørensen
Department of Political Science,
University of Aarhrus, Denmark

Professor Akihiko Tanaka
Institute of Oriental Culture,
University of Tokyo

Ms Margaret A. Vogt
International Peace Academy

Professor Thomas G. Weiss
Thomas J. Watson Jr. Institute for
International Studies, Brown
University

Professor Phil Williams
Ridgway Center for International
Security Studies, University of
Pittsburgh

Index

United Nations (*cont.*)
  lessons from military operations 410–423
    avoidance of enforcement 417–419
    establishment of secure physical
      environment 410–413
    humanitarian interventions 416–417
    multi-functional operations 419–420
    preventive actions 413–414
    use of NGOs 420–422
    use of regional organizations 414–416
  NGO recognition by 227–228
  peace enforcement action 311–312, 401–
    402
    avoidance 417–419
  reform 80, 369–370, 452–453
    proposals 316–317
  role 3–18, 63, 104–105, 445–453, 461–463
    crime prevention 127
  standing army 46–47
  supplements to 453–456
    delegation 454
    rapid reaction 455
  UN21 project 1–3, 110–111, 369
  see also Security Council; UN General
    Assembly
United States 1, 6, 7, 104, 462
  as superpower 7, 25, 43–60, 63, 405
  ASEAN 13–14, 15
  decline of internationalism 44–51
    American culture 55–56
    domestic constraints on inter-
      nationalism 52–56
    financial obligations 9, 47–49, 52, 57,
      378
    military power and world order 45–47
    unilateralist tendencies 49–51
  Gulf War 7, 45–46, 50–51, 386, 387–388
  international role 56–60
  intervention in Latin America 350
  Italian Mafia 183, 184–185
  nuclear weapons 392
  policy towards Asia 47, 56, 58–59, 324
    bilateral defence arrangements 325
    China 51, 58–59, 71
    multilateral defence arrangements
      327
  policy towards Europe 47, 56–59
  policy towards former Yugoslavia 397
  post-modern statehood 33, 36
  relations within Security Council 397–398
  relationship with Israel 78–79

Universal Declaration of Human Rights
  432
Universal Reporting System 381
unsubstantial states 22, 23, 28–30, 104
  conflict patterns 33–34, 36
  cooperation patterns 34–35
  external relations 34–35
  future development 37–38
  see also failed states; weak states
Urquhart, Sir Brian 455
Uruguay 30, 354, 358, 360
USSR *see* Soviet Union

Venezuela 351, 352, 353, 360
  inter-state conflicts 358, 359
Vienna Conference on Human Rights 372
Viet Nam 285, 325–326, 327, 451
  invasion of Cambodia 325–326, 333, 334–
    339
  relations with Soviet Union 325–326, 335
Viet Nam War 46, 333
von Hippel, Frank 148, 166

Waddeyi, Goukouni 298, 307
war crime tribunals 402
weak states 7–8, 9–10, 29–30, 34–35, 64
  human security 430
  organized crime 176–178
  see also failed states; unsubstantial states
weapons control *see* arms control
Western Sahara 98, 282, 304
  group of friends 404
Westphalian framework 459–461, 462
Westphalian states 22, 26–28, 39, 64
  conflict patterns 33, 37
  cooperation patterns 33, 37
  future development 37
Winer, Jonathan 197
without borders approach 229–230
  see also complex humanitarian emer-
    gencies; humanitarian assistance
Wo group, China 191, 193
World Bank 8, 47–49
  Africa 86–87
World Council of Churches 143
World Food Programme (WFP) 213, 232,
  258, 384, 462
World Health Organization (WHO) 213,
  258
world order 63, 80, 103, 396, 405, 409
  American military power 45–47